PILGRIMAGE
IN
LATIN AMERICA

**Recent Titles in
Contributions to the Study of Anthropology**

A Nilotic World: The Atuot-Speaking Peoples of the Southern Sudan
John W. Burton

Culture and Christianity: The Dialectics of Transformation
George R. Saunders, editor

The Psychodynamics of Culture: Abram Kardiner and Neo-Freudian
Anthropology
William C. Manson

PILGRIMAGE IN LATIN AMERICA

Edited by
N. Ross Crumrine
and Alan Morinis

Contributions to the Study of Anthropology, Number 4

GREENWOOD PRESS
NEW YORK • WESTPORT, CONNECTICUT • LONDON

Library of Congress Cataloging-in-Publication Data

Pilgrimage in Latin America / edited by N. Ross Crumrine and Alan Morinis.

    p. cm.—(Contributions to the study of anthropology, ISSN 0890-9377 ; no. 4)

    Bibliography: p.

    Includes index.

    ISBN 0-313-26110-5 (lib. bdg. : alk. paper)

    1. Pilgrims and pilgrimages—Latin America. 2. Rites and ceremonies—Latin America. 3. Latin America—Religious life and customs. I. Crumrine, N. Ross. II. Morinis, Alan. III. Series.

BL619.P5P52   1991

291.4′ 46—dc20   89-11845

British Library Cataloguing in Publication Data is available.

Library of Congress Catalog Card Number: 89-11845

ISBN: 0-313-26110-5

ISSN: 0890-9377

First published in 1991

Greenwood Press, 88 Post Road West, Westport, CT 06881
An imprint of Greenwood Publishing Group, Inc.

Printed in the United States of America

The paper used in this book complies with the Permanent Paper Standard issued by the National Information Standards Organization (Z39.48-1984).

10 9 8 7 6 5 4 3 2 1

Figure Credits

Figures 4.1-4.3 are courtesy N. Ross Crumrine

Figures 5.1-5.5 are courtesy H. R. Harvey

Figures 6.1-6.5 are courtesy Walter Randolph Adams

Figures 9.1-9.3 are courtesy Leslie Ellen Straub, O.P.

Figures 12.1-12.11 are courtesy Helaine Silverman

Figure 13.1 is courtesy James M. Vreeland, Jr. and Foto Servicio Aero-fotográfico Nacional

Figures 13.2-13.8 are courtesy James M. Vreeland, Jr.

Figure 13.9 is by H. Brüning, 1907, and is courtesy of James M. Vreeland, Jr. and Richard P. Schaedel

Figures 14.1-14.7 are courtesy Richard P. Schaedel

Figures 15.1-15.4 are courtesy N. Ross Crumrine

Figures 17.1-17.14 are courtesy Deborah A. Poole

Contents

Tables   ix

Figures   x

Foreword   xiii
Luis Millones

I. INTRODUCTION

1. *La Peregrinación:* The Latin American Pilgrimage   1
   Alan Morinis and N. Ross Crumrine

2. The European Roots of Latin American Pilgrimage   19
   Mary Lee Nolan

II. MIDDLE AMERICA

3. *Do-It-Yourself* Religion: The Diffusion of Folk Catholicism
   on Mexico's Northern Frontier 1821-46   53
   Henry F. Dobyns

4. Fiestas and Exchange Pilgrimages: The Yorem Pahko and
   Mayo Identity, Northwest Mexico   71
   N. Ross Crumrine

5. Pilgrimage and Shrine: Religious Practices among the
   Otomi of Huixquilucan, Mexico   91
   H. R. Harvey

6. Social Structure in Pilgrimage and Prayer: Tzeltales as
   Lords and Servants   109
   Walter Randolph Adams

7. Pilgrimage as Cyclical Process: The Unending Pilgrimage
   of the Holy Cross of the Quintana Roo Maya   123
   Herman W. Konrad

8. The Politics of Pilgrimage: The Black Christ of Esquipulas   139
   Carl Kendall

9. Through the Fields to Amatitlán   157
   Leslie Ellen Straub, O.P.

III. SOUTH AMERICA

10. The Literature of Pilgrimage: Present-day Miracle Stories
from Northeast Brazil   175
Candace Slater

11. Pilgrimages to Sorte in the Cult of María Lionza in
Venezuela   205
Angelina Pollak-Eltz

12. The Ethnography and Archaeology of Two Andean
Pilgrimage Centers   215
Helaine Silverman

13. Pilgrim's Progress: The Emergence of Secular Authority
in a Traditional Andean Pilgrimage   229
James M. Vreeland, Jr.

14. Locational Symbolism: The Fiesta de los Reyes o del Niño
in Northern Peru   257
Richard P. Schaedel

15. A Pilgrimage Fiesta: Easter Week Ritual at Catacaos,
Piura, Peru   269
N. Ross Crumrine

16. Dual Cosmology and Ethnic Division in an Andean
Pilgrimage Cult   281
Michael J. Sallnow

17. Rituals of Movement, Rites of Transformation: Pilgrimage
and Dance in the Highlands of Cuzco, Peru   307
Deborah A. Poole

18. Mythic Andean Discourse and Pilgrimages   339
Henrique Urbano

IV. CONCLUSION

19. Discussion and Conclusions: Agrarian Conflict and
Pilgrimage   357
Frans J. Schryer

References   369

Index   413

Contributors   427

Tables

2.1 Number and Location of Inventoried Shrines — 22
2.2 Periods of Shrine Establishment — 23
2.3 Primary Subjects of Devotion Regional Percentages — 27
2.4 Subjects of Devotion at Catholic Reformation Period Shrines — 31
2.5 Specific Features at Shrines with Sacred Environmental Aspects of Site Regional Percentages — 34
2.6 Shrine Origin Stories Regional Percentages — 37
2.7 Selected traits Associated with European Pilgrimage — 39
8.1 Ethnic Self-Identification — 149
8.2 Means of Transportation of Pilgrimage Population — 150
8.3 Participation in the Pilgrimage by Nationality—January 1973 — 151
8.4 Origin Point of Pilgrim — 152
10.1 Orally Transmitted Stories and their Features in Relation to the *Literatura de Cordel* — 195
13.1 Population series for Motupe district and principal settlements which mark the route of the Cruz de Chalpón in its ceremonial procession from Guayaquil to Zapote, Salitral, and finally to Motupe accompanied by thousands of pilgrims each year — 235
13.2 Preliminary calendar of Hispano-Catholic traditonal north coast festivals — 236
13.3 Official receipts recorded by concejo for six-year period, during annual and semi-annual festivals, indicating number of lots leased to *tolderos*, receipts from the lots, and receipts from itinerant merchants (*ambulantes*) — 237
13.4 Rate of flow of pilgrims past the Cross of Chalpón during its adoration in chapels listed by place, date, and time of day — 241
13.5 Number of pilgrims from different towns, listed by departments — 242
13.6 Official records of receipts and expenditures for year 1980 of Comisión Multisectorial. Receipts include cash offerings plus sale of spent wax and *ex votos* in months marked with *. Offerings comprise those made in the cave shrine, various chapels, and town church — 243
13.7 Annual balance sheet listing major sources of receipts and expenditures, the official records, Comisión Multisectorial "Cruz de Chalpón", since its formation in November 1972 — 244
16.1 Principal Processions of Titular Fiesta of Señor de Qoyllur Rit'i — 283

Figures

4.1 Espíritu Santo of Etchojoa   72
4.2 Santísima Tiniran of Júpare   73
4.3 Some Pahkome with the Mo'oro on the left   75
4.4 Komchepte for Guadelupe with Pahkome and Matachinim   70
4.5 Guadalupe at the foot of the Altar after the Komchepte   70
5.1 Map of the Huixquilucan Region   92
5.2 Chapel, Sta Cruz Ayotusco   96
5.3 El Rostro Divino, the "pilgrim," Sta Cruz Ayotusco   97
5.4 Sacred ahuehuete tree, road to Chalma   102
5.5 The sanctuary of Chalma with the town of Chalma in the
    foreground   103
6.1 Map of the Pilgrimage Paths, Southeastern Mexico   110
6.2 A *ramiete* as made by the Tzeltal priostes   112
6.3 Pilgrims carrying their belongings   113
6.4 Offerings left by the pilgrims   114
6.5 Social structural organization, Southeastern Chiapas   119
9.1 El Niño de Atocha between Saint Joseph and the Virgin Mary   157
9.2 Parish church in San Juan de Amatitlán housing the shrine
    of el Niño de Atocha with the weekend market in front
    of the church   160
9.3 La Silla del Niño, where El Niño de Atocha rests on May 3rd.,
    Lake Amatitlán, Guatemala, 1982   165
9.4 The type of Launch which carries the Image of El Niño de
    Atocha, May 3rd.   69
9.5 El Castillo, northern shore, Lake Amatitlán   69
12.1 Archaeological Ruins of Cahuachi, Nazca River   216
12.2 Map of the South Coast of Peru   217
12.3 Dessication in the Region   218
12.4 The Shrine of Yauca, Ica   219
12.5 The Plaza in Yauca during the Festival   220
12.6 The Plaza in Yauca after the Festival   221
12.7 Round Depressions in the main plaza, Cahuachi   224
12.8 Cooking in Temporary Facilities at Yauca   224
12.9 The Construction of a Simple Cane Wall   225
12.10 Broken Plates Remain at Yauca after the Festival   225
12.11 Reconstructed from Remains of a Fine Goblet, Cahuachi   226
13.1 Motupe with central road connecting to Cerro Chalpón   230
13.2 Santísima Cruz del Cerro Chalpón in processional
     embroidered raiments festooned with silver
     adornments and filigree arc   231
13.3 Grotto shrine clings to the rocky flanks of Cerro Chalpón   234
13.4 Vendors of traditional medicines to sell in Motupe   238
13.5 Hundreds of thousands of miniature replicas of the Cruz de
     Chalpón are made by local artisans and sold   239

13.6 On the steps of the church, members of the secular Comision
      Multisectorial count pilgrims' offerings, which amounted
      to over 11,000,000 Peruvian soles in 1980   240
13.7 Adoration of the Cross in an open chapel-like tent outside
      the church on Motupe's central plaza, filled with
      pilgrims and vendors' stalls. As of this writing church
      policy prohibits giving mass here   246
13.8 Bishop and curate of Motupe surrounded by Catholic clergy
      invited to celebrate the annual festival of the Cross
      in the mid 1960s   247
13.9 Adoration of The Cruz de Chalpon on the steps of the
      Motupe church altar, August 1907   252
14.1 The chapel (*huaca*), also called "cathedral" by Narigualeños   258
14.2 Positioning of el Niño before the ascent to the chapel   259
14.3 The Mayordomos bring el Niño from the shrine (residence)
      up to the chapel (Huaca)   260
14.4 Procession of *pastorcitas* descending from the chapel after
      "baptism" with el Niño in canopy, going through the
      community graveyard   261
14.5 *Mayordomos* with standards lead the *pastorcitas*,
      accompanying el Niño toward his shrine (residence),
      where he will receive adoration   262
14.6 The three kings and ambassador arriving in Narigualá from
      Catacaos with the Vaca Loca between two of the kings   263
14.7 The three kings just before they ascend the *huaca*, prior
      to being received by Herod   263
15.1 The "Last Supper", Catacaos   274
15.2 The "Last Supper" with The Monument of Angels   275
15.3 The Crucifixion, Good Friday, Catacaos   276
15.4 Virigin of Transito, Returning to the Church, Easter
      Sunday, Catacaos   277
16.1 Map of the Qoyllur Rit'i Shrine Complex   282
17.1 *Kanchis Comparsa* with *Ukukus* Kneeling in Front Row
      and the *Capitán Kanchis* Standing to the Left Rear
      Holding up the *Vara*   312
17.2 *Kanchis* Movement, A-1, Salutation Formation   314
17.3 *Kanchis* Movement, A-2, Parallel *Vara* Formation with
      vara and leather whips   314
17.4 *Kanchis* Movement, B-1, Linked Whip Formation   315
17.5 *Kanchis* Movement, B-2, Weaving Formation   315
17.6 *Kanchis* Movement, B-3, Concentric Formation with
      Whips   316
17.7 *Awqa Chilenos*; *Ukuku* and *Sanitario*, Pampak'ucho, 1981   317
17.8 *Awqa Chileno*; *Diablo* and *Maqt'acha*, Pampak'ucho, 1981   318
17.9 *Awqa Chileno*, *Chingana* Movement   319

17.10 *Awqa Chileno, Pasapuentes* Movement   319
17.11 *Awqa Chileno, Rueda* Movement   320
17.12 *Awqa Chileno, Pasapuentes* Movement, Pampak'ucho, 1981 320
17.13 Wall Mural in Popular Cuzco Picanteria Depicting *Doctor*
         Dancer as Repressor of Indigenous Culture and Language
         as He Reads a Law Condeming the Quechua Language
         and Those Who Speak It to Death   321
17.14 *Alzados*, Sankha, 1981   324
17.15 *Alzados'* Choreography   325

Foreword

LUIS MILLONES

Since pilgrimage represents a universal experience, its meaning has been enriched by the history and culture of all the peoples who compose the human family. Even though Latin America has been closely associated with the West since the sixteenth century it also has contributed its own surviving autochthonous components. These elements not only have been incorporated into developed Christian traditions, but also have been interwoven in diverse ways throughout the continent.

In some pilgrimage centers, the traditional pre-Christian power of the sanctuary prevails over the European gods and languages and maintains the flow of pilgrims who repeat with little modification the rituals observed by their ancient ancestors. In other centers, the evangelizing passion of the missionaries seems to have been divinely justified by miraculous apparitions of saints and virgins. Their presence weakens the continued traditional functioning of ancient shrines. However, each pilgrim will construct his or her specific ideological synthesis, which will lie between these two poles, that then provides the basis for their decision to visit the divinity. Thus to some degree the traditions that are found between these extremes will almost always reflect the orientation of the individual believers.

One of the difficulties faced in editing a book based on this theme lies in the absence of a satisfactory method for the controlled comparison of

Latin American societies. Although highly divergent before the time of contact, these societies developed in a similar fashion as a result of their common experience in the colonial system. It is important to observe that the questionable theoretical models for the understanding of these societies were developed from African and Asian data. Thus, in light of these divergences, any attempt to compile such a volume would prove difficult. Nevertheless, this research is essential to fill a widely felt vacuum. This organizing of indispensable factual materials by Ross Crumrine and Alan Morinis is enriched by the proposals of novel theoretical perspectives. In the future and based upon these data, the interpretative propositions which will emerge, will illuminate this dialogue initiated here by the present authors.

The chapters which comprise this book focus on discussions about each case in relation to the Hispanic and pre-Columbian traditions. Concerning this relationship, the chapter by Mary Lee Nolan provides a glimpse at European pilgrimage. She reviews the apparent flow of modern European influences upon the patterns of Latin American pilgrimage. From another vantage point, Henrique Urbano endeavors to recover from the Andean mythology the still prevailing pre-Hispanic models.

Taking into account these two poles, it is appropriate at this point to present some of my own reflections. The Christian tradition reproduces in its pilgrimages an expiatory perspective which customarily derives from the following passage:

> In my Father's house are many mansions: if it were not so, would I have told you. I go to prepare a place for you. And if I go and prepare a place for you, I will come again, and receive you unto myself; that where I am, there ye may be also. And whither I go ye know, and the way ye know. Thomas said unto him, Lord, we know not whither thou goest; and how can we know the way? Jesus said unto him, I am the way the truth, and the life. (St. John 14, 2-6)

This message is repeated and made explicit in Hebrews 9, 24 and 10, 19-21, which states that access to the sanctuary, that is to say, to heaven is by means of the blood of Jesus, "a new and living way," which He "consecrated for us." This perspective served as a basis for the historical lineality of the Christian concept as first formulated by Saint Augustine. He established an origin, development, and end to human actions. As is well known, "The City of God" represents his answer to the classic concept of time. In contrast to the Christian lineal image, he considers the classic notion of time to be without faith or hope, rather as phases of a cycle which did not have a beginning nor would it have an end.

This observation about the faith of the pilgrim explains in a certain way the preference for intermediary divinities such as saints and virgins and also contributes to an understanding of the transient character of the faithful participant. The passage through the valley of tears is a cleansing which becomes even more explicit if the pilgrims carry crosses or rocks in order to make it more painful. They also may whip or wound themselves to emphasize even more powerfully the necessity to clearly assert the arduous passage through this world. In chapter 7, Herman Konrad points out that the Maya term *u ximbal ek'ob*, which signifies "the pilgrim," literally means "passage and course of the stars." This double meaning suggests a parallel in their perception of the cyclical character, of both the course of the stars and the ritual process of the pilgrimage in American civilizations. Although this inference might be questioned, it reveals a series of perspectives that provide the means for a comparison of the superimposed traditions, that began with the evangelization of the New World. It further implies that the difficulties in understanding aboriginal culture are also derived from the polymorphous integration of differing conceptions of time and space.

If the ethnographic reference is sound, it would be difficult to equate the motivation that characterized the pilgrim of the Andean area with the Christian concept of expiating original or worldly sin. Perhaps his or her motivation could be better perceived of as an attendance at a festive reunion. The solidarity of such a gathering is expressed in the exchange of material goods, in intense feelings, and in the relationship with the deities from whom the pilgrims request miracles or to whom they give thanks for those already received.

In Quechua one does not say *richkani risakuq* (I am going to pray, I alone am going to pray), when one is going to visit a sanctuary. The correct expression is *richkani risapakuq* (I am going to pray, I am going with them to pray, I am going to help them to pray). Or even better, one says *richkani watapakuq* (I am going to help "fasten," that is to say, to attach flowers or adornments to the litters of the saint).

It is not that there did not exist ceremonies to purge sins. In a certain way the Capacocha of the Incas fulfilled this function. An important part of this ceremony involved the movement of its participants in straight lines over considerable distances without making use of roads. Clearly this ritual influenced the sixteenth-century translation of *quimray* (to cross the road), which was "to make a pilgrimage." In contemporary Quechua the translation would be "on one side, on one flank." Even in this ceremony, families and future victims of human sacrifices were obligated to express happiness. *Tumay* represents the other term for denoting the pilgrimage that the quechua scholars of the sixteenth century and their informants discovered. It seems to be associated with the ritualized conduct that was observed at the sanctuary. In *tumay*, victims carrying offerings wove circles around the "statues" of the gods before the sacrifice. If we summarize this ideology of pilgrimage in their terms, we should note that Quechua and bilingual speakers refer to the trip as "to go to the fiesta."

In the analysis of the phenomena, all these divergences can be better understood in terms of the material presented in this book. Other sources of data, for example those drawn from African populations that enriched

Latin American religiosity, will provide additional insight. Studies developing this theme, such as those of Angelina Pollak-Eltz and Candace Slater, will supply the appropriate basis for investigations that critically observe the ideological syntheses that have formed in the New World. This process may also be analyzed from perspectives that will facilitate the understanding of the phenomena in relation to more ample categories. The studies of Carl Kendall and Walter Adams deal with political and social systems while that of Michael Sallnow, for the Andean case set within the Indian-mestizo environment, discusses ethnic themes. Thus a global examination of the social processes that accompany pilgrimage reveals other important interpretive avenues. The cult of el Señor de los Milagros (our Lord of Miracles) in Lima would be an appropriate example. In this modern religious group, black cofradías maintain the Christian deity who, in part, has his origin in the most ancient cult of the coast, el Señor de Pachacamac (Lord of Pachacamac).

The materials, orientations, and directions of the present anthology imply the necessity to control the critical variables that permit generalization beyond more than one Latin American region. From this perspective, Ross Crumrine seems to be the likely individual to lead the way, and we eagerly await his future publications.

The results of all academic investigation are transitory. My desire, regarding this important beginning, is not only that it continues but also stimulates the exploration of all the possibilities that these chapters contain.

I
INTRODUCTION

La Peregrinación:
The Latin American Pilgrimage

ALAN MORINIS and N. ROSS CRUMRINE

In every region of Latin America, there are sacred shrines which draw tens of thousands of pilgrims for the performance of rites, the making of vows, the celebration of festivals, the honoring of saints, and a myriad of other purposes. At present, most of these pilgrimages are overtly Catholic, but the roots of the contemporary practice are in fact multiple: European Christian, indigenous pre-Columbian, African slave, and other religious traditions have all contributed to Latin American pilgrimage as we find it today. This volume is dedicated to exploring the historical development, range of diversity, and the structure and impacts of this widespread religious practice.

The idea for this volume originated in a session on pilgrimage in Latin America held as part of the conference, "Pilgrimage: the Human Quest."[1] The meetings generated numerous spirited discussions, which are reflected in those articles in this book written by the participants of this symposia. Additional scholars also were invited to contribute original articles to the volume. The collection therefore represents an up-to-date consideration of this subject. We hope that it will be read as a statement of contemporary thought, and that it will in turn spur further research in this rich vein of the Latin American tradition. With this goal in mind, we will use this introductory essay to summarize what seem to us to be the main theoretical trends embodied in the articles that follow. This will not only guide the reader through the volume, but will also open a theoretical dialogue which will lead to greater insights into the impressive tradition of pilgrimage in Latin America.

This is not the first work to focus on pilgrimage in Latin America but the treatment given to the subject thus far has been particularistic.[2] We seek here to create a general framework for understanding this regional religious practice which will subsume the previous research. While our focus is predominantly anthropological, the contributors are drawn from numerous disciplines such as archaeology, geography, and religious and literary history. This diversity reflects the fact that pilgrimage is a multifaceted institution which incorporates geographical, social, cultural, religious, historical, literary, architectural, artistic, and other dimensions. This complexity has contributed to the previous general neglect of the study of pilgrimage by scholars. But now, with collaboration across disciplinary boundaries, we are in a good position to investigate those revered *places* which cultures have often erected in the most awe-inspiring locations, honored with the highest manifestations of their arts and crafts, revered as the earthly seat of God, and given much of blood, sweat, tears, and money to visit. In this vein, it is interesting to note that research on pilgrimage tends to require a scholar to raid the cupboard of other disciplines in order to obtain analytical tools. For example, the chapter by Candace Slater in this volume is concerned with the analysis of literary materials. To gather these materials and in order to understand the context in which they are created and delivered, Slater had to take up residence, anthropologist-like, on the main street of the Brazilian pilgrimage town itself. Anthropologists return the compliment by referring to published historical and literary documents. It is the complex nature of the pilgrimage that forces this breach of disciplinary lines. Future research should see more use of the research methods of many disciplines for studying single centers and pilgrimages. Interdisciplinary collaboration in team research is one of the most sensible ways to investigate such complex institutions as pilgrimages.

THE INSTITUTION OF PILGRIMAGE

The pilgrimage, as we use the term, has several meanings. At the individual level, it involves the journey undertaken to the sacred shrine for religious purposes.[3] Certain places are generally recognized and known as pilgrimage shrines, and it is this category of site that draws people to leave their homes and journey beyond the range of their usual travels.

But the pilgrimage is also an institution which comprises a wide variety of actors, places, behaviors, times, and specialists. In this usage, the pilgrimage refers to the full set of human and material aspects which feature in individuals' journeys to shrines. Thus to speak of the pilgrimage to Guadalupe, Mexico or to Bom Jesus de Lapa, Brazil, for example, is to invoke the many-faceted sociocultural complex which focuses on those sites. In this latter sense, the pilgrimage is seen as a complex and interrelated feature of the social and cultural life of a community. It is important in looking at any facet of pilgrimage practice and belief to remember that each aspect is integrated into the whole of the pilgrimage. Each draws its meaning, form, and functions in its full integration into the whole.

The chapters of this volume are quite varied both in data and analysis yet each documents one or more of these facets which make up the whole of the pilgrimage. All of the articles treat pilgrims, the pilgrimage center, the ritual performances, and the audience as major components, and examine the interrelationships among these dimensions. To our minds, a theory of pilgrimage should focus on the sets of relationships among all these factors in any particular pilgrimage or group of pilgrimages. In this holistic sense pilgrimages are conceptualized as sociocultural institutions and more generally as human systems. As systems, they embody charters or explanatory myths, personnel occupying differing social positions or status, and norms or sets of rules which structure the roles and performances of the personnel. These systems are oriented toward activities and work to generate cooperation in the interests of achieving certain goals. This model is drawn from Malinowski's (1944:52-54) discussion of the "institution" or "concrete isolate." We add it to another dimension, that of symbols and meaning. A pilgrimage institution always incorporates elaborate patterns of ritual and symbolism. Those of any pilgrimage are clustered, in terms of a limited set of root metaphors or meta-ritual symbols. Retaining Malinowski's holistic orientation we restate the concrete isolate for our purposes: rationalized in charter-myths, groups of personnel organized through accepted norms utilize material apparatus in the actualization of activities, which are structured in terms of clusters of symbols unified in root metaphors.

But although we emphasize the importance of this holistic perspective in approaching each pilgrimage, it is crucial to stress as well that the pilgrimage does not exist in real isolation. As a popular institution and an institution of popular culture, the pilgrimage is woven securely into its regional cultural field (see Chapter 3). Although its geographical location may be remote (as in Chapter 12), socially and culturally it draws critical elements from wider patterns of belief and practice of the region. These complex linkages to other aspects of society force the pilgrimage institution to be dynamic even more so than the inner principle of dynamism it contains simply by virtue of being a human system. In fact, since the geographical component of place figures so importantly in pilgrimages, we find that ecological, demographic, and certain other factors in addition to the sociocultural ones exert influence over the form and content of a pilgrimage.

This model of a dynamic concrete isolate in constant feedback with wider physical and human systems of which it is part provides a unifying principle for approaching the chapters of this volume, each of which focuses on an aspect or aspects of the whole. In general, each analysis can be read as a case study of a facet of pilgrimage which is to be found in every instance of the practice in Latin America. Each chapter in this book therefore provides data and insight into a specific pilgrimage, but also reflection on an important variable in the institution of pilgrimage in all cases.

Latin American pilgrimage is to a great extent typical of religious pilgrimage wherever it occurs. The foregoing model can as easily be applied to pilgrimage to Jerusalem or Mecca as Esquipulas or Guadalupe. However, the distinctiveness of the Latin American pilgrimage tradition emerges when we address the content of each of these components of the model system. Latin American pilgrimage is unique because it tends to combine sources rooted in a diversity of religious traditions. The merging of European Catholicism and indigenous pre-Columbian religious thought and practice is the typical case (see Chapters 5 and 9). In other instances, the influence of African religious systems (see Chapter 11), Hinduism, and Protestantism is to be observed. Furthermore, as dynamic systems, the pilgrimages of Latin America themselves have evolved in the centuries since the Catholic and indigenous religious traditions first confronted each other (see especially Chapter 18). Some pilgrimages show the influence of distinctly Latin American cults that have emerged autochthonously from the fertile religious consciousness of the continent. To our minds, the Latin American pilgrimage tradition is the only major instance of such practice which draws upon such multi-stranded origins. When we look at any particular facet of any Latin American pilgrimage, such as ritual, belief, or personnel, we are immediately struck by the multiple influences that have shaped the ideas, roles, structures, and performances of these ceremonials.

It is religion in Latin America in general, not just pilgrimage, which is forged from multiple sources. Thus the pilgrimage tends to conform to the cultural patterns of its field of patrons. In other words, it "images" the culture of its time and place (Sumption 1975). The ritual, iconography, myth, and meaning of a pilgrimage are usually wholly representative of patterns within the area from which pilgrims are drawn. The pilgrimage shrine achieves this fit in order to win patronge. It *belongs* to the culture. This familiarity makes it possible for pilgrims to negotiate the cultural pathways of the sacred center far from their home parish. But ironically perhaps, achieving fit is only half of the establishment of a sacred shrine. The center must also differentiate itself enough to gain acceptance as an exceptionally holy shrine. It must be able to assert claim to power which will gain it patronage over and against the competing pulls of the local church and other pilgrimage shrines. This it accomplishes by claiming to be the repository of the typical ideals of the religious culture, but in their highest, most concentrated, and most potent form. These opposed tendencies to cultural linkage and differentiation are clearly to be seen in the objects which are the central focus of the shrines and their pilgrimages, the shrine icons.

It is typical of Latin American pilgrimage that contemporary sacred places are held to be sites where apparitions have appeared or images of wood or stone have come to life. The shrines and pilgrimages that have developed as a result of these miracles tend to focus on a single exceptional fact, the vital, breathing, living reality of the divine in that place. The divinities of the centers are none other than the same saints, Mary, and Jesus who appear as peeling, painted images in the local church or in plastic or printed forms on the walls or altars of homes. Thus the connection exists between shrine and cultural field. But in the sacred pilgrimage center these familiar figures take on a magnified, intensified form; hence the differentiation of the center from its field. The image of the shrine is no abstract symbol. It is a vital reality, for example in the way the Mayo images (see Chapter 4) are bowed to one another, are brought close for an *embrace*, and *visit* one another in their home church centers. In most of the centers, the images have appeared, living, are worshipped as alive, and are of concern to devotees as such. The pilgrimage shrine thus lays claim to an especially potent form of universally revered divinity and is itself held to be especially invested with sacred power as a result.

The belief system that is focused on the pilgrimage shrine and deity is influenced by the ideological formulations that are dominant within the cultural field. Konrad's excellent chapter on the Maya illustrates this point. He explores the features of Mayan cosmology that inform the concept of pilgrimage in both the historical and contemporary eras. He identifies homologies in Mayan thought between the concept of pilgrimage as a circular movement and other patterns of cosmic motion, notably the circulation of the stars. Patterns of human movement in pilgrimage are seen to take on cosmological significance, as journeys to shrines are identified with macrocosmic cycles of movement among the astral bodies. Konrad supports his argument by exploring the recurrence of astral symbolism in pilgrimage art and performance.

These beliefs are the source of inspiration for the corpus of tales and legends that weave a web of wonder and awe around every pilgrimage shrine and its divinity. Often these involve miracles, but always they concern the extraordinary, superhuman exalted nature of the earthly home of God. The spoken and written word has many important functions in the pilgrimage, but of concern to us here is the fact that the tales, poems, songs, and folk dramas that circulate in the region and tell of the wonders that have happened and continue to take place at sacred shrines are an especially important link between the sacred center and its population. In Chapter 18, Urbano discusses the Wiracocha, important legendary heroes of Andean pilgrimage, and concludes that there has been thematic continuity from the preconquest period into the contemporary era. The symbolic preoccupations of these traditional pre-Columbian heroes have been maintained in contemporary mythic discourse. In Chapter 14 Schaedel discusses a theatrical performance or folk drama that both depicts themes of pilgrimage and is staged, embedded, within a pilgrimage fiesta. In this case the drama is shown to be a development on the European strand that has been woven into the contemporary Latin American pilgrimage tradition, namely the *performance* of a *pageant*, although here cross-fertilization also has taken place and many of the cosmological themes of the drama can be traced to pre-Columbian ancestry.

The communicated word is the vehicle through which the potential pilgrims learn that the pilgrimage shrine is of his or her culture and is open to their approach, but also at the same time that it is a place set apart from their culture because it is exalted above it. Through formal performances, the written word, and informal legends and conversation, the pilgrims are initiated into the pilgrimage and its belief system long before any journeying is begun. This oral or written literature often occupies an important place in the regional culture as an aspect of its literary and artistic traditions. In this volume Slater analyzes the blending of belief and literary composition that is so integral a part of the pilgrimage institution as a mainstay of its public facade and a link to its social field. Adams analyzes another sort of literary source concerning pilgrimage, the text of a pilgrims' prayer. He uses this piece of contemporary data as a key to the reconstruction of the social and cultural history of the people of Chiapas, Mexico, again demonstrating the important link between the communicated word and the human field within which a pilgrimage place is situated.

The essays by Schaedel and Poole concerning dance and drama in the context of pilgrimage both document another sort of linkage between the expressive cultural performance, both verbal and nonverbal, and pilgrimage. In both the drama and the dance we find that the pilgrimage itself is a central motif of the performance. This artistic presentation of themes of pilgrimage in the context of pilgrimage performance serves to impress upon the audience of pilgrims the meaning of the activity in which they are participating, as conceived within the tradition. At the same time, these performances tend to be used to express and, as Poole indicates, transform and renew important social relationships, forces, and hierarchies that exist within the field of the pilgrimage. These cases demonstrate that pilgrimage occupies an important place within the consciousness of the cultural group and also illustrate how expressive performances in the context of pilgrimage can play an effective role in the social affairs of the community that patronizes the shrine. The conclusion is clear that the pilgrimage place is enmeshed in social and cultural networks at a regional level.

In general, a sacred shrine draws participants from a restricted population, the boundaries of which delimit the social field of the pilgrimage. The patterns of participation in pilgrimage within this group are usually a fairly true reflection of, or a reaction to, dominant social structures and forces within the social field. The social field focused on a pilgrimage shrine is seldom homogeneous socially, and so it is more correct to speak of plural social fields of the pilgrimage as discussed by Sallnow. Insofar as a society is differentiated by class, race, political affiliation, or other groupings, this tends to appear in the social formation of the pilgrimage field. Sometimes separate groups in society have their own preferred pilgrimage centers. At major pilgrimage places, we see socially intersecting communities, each with their own relationship to the shrine center (see Chapters 8 and 13).

It is often the case that socially differentiated groups carry out their observances at the pilgrimage shrine in such a way as to maintain boundaries between themselves and other social groups. In fact, this behavioral separation based on differential social fields is but one dimension of the polymorphic quality of the shrine and pilgrimage. Beyond ritual behavior, we find different groups maintaining their own sets of beliefs about shrine centers, so that it is not an exaggeration to say that in some cases different groups visit "different" pilgrimage shrines located in the same building and at the same site. The difference lies in the varying composition of the shrine reality constructed by different groups. Images, symbols, actions, and history, when interpreted differently and integrated into a unique whole by a social group, compose a unique pilgrimage. This is true even where the raw data, such as statues, objects, movements, and events, or even interpreted perceptions are shared with other social groupings. Each separate group interprets these data differently and integrates them into a different pilgrimage focused on the same site and shrine.

The chapters by Kendall on contemporary pilgrimage in Guatemala, Konrad on Mexico, Urbano on the prehistoric pilgrim heroes of Peru, Vreeland concerning Motupe in Peru, and Crumrine on the pilgrimages of the Mayo in Mexico, all document important linkages between the temporal order and the pilgrimage. Urbano concludes that pre-Columbian pilgrimage in the Andes was a celebration of the social identity of a people, or *nation*. However, this function was largely supplanted with the introduction of the Catholic model of pilgrimage to the region. In the case of the contemporary Mayo, the ritual of the pilgrimage incorporates the local social hierarchies, so that various representatives of the secular order take part and the pilgrimage serves as an expressive representation of the existing social order. This study shows how pilgrimage can work to reinforce the social image and identity of a group within a diversified ethnic population. Kendall and Vreeland provide examples of political groups which try to validate the social system they advocate, and solidify their position within it, by capturing the sacred power of the pilgrimage center, either by associating themselves with it or by quite directly taking over the control and operation of the shrine itself. Schaedel provides a case from Peru which reveals how the symbolism involved in the dramatic performances of a pilgrimage festival expresses the anti-authoritarian social concerns of the local people. Dobyns analyzes the ability of the *folk* in developing their own pilgrimage, or "do-it-yourself" power. Crumrine, in discussing Easter week in Peru, provides an example of another mode of interaction of social order and pilgrimage which is common throughout Latin America. In this case local groups constituted to manage the complex rituals of the pilgrimage become corporate groups with local political influence as social bodies.

All of these cases represent the various ways in which the sacred center and the observances carried out within it are linked to the temporal order of the social field of the pilgrimage. In theory, the sacred place is a place apart, preserved above and beyond the vicissitudes of sociopolitical reality as illustrated for example in Silverman's study. She shows behavioral and ritual parallels between archaeological sites and an isolated modern pilgrimage center on the central coast of Peru. In point of fact, as a center of great social importance by virtue of the reverence in which it is held, the numbers of people that frequent it, and the amounts of wealth it generates, the pilgrimage center is too valuable a political resource to be ignored by combatant groups within the social order. Both sociologically and theologically, the sacred place has a power which secular groups seek to tap and channel for their own temporal purposes. It is an irony of being a place apart that this otherworldliness is the source of the power which ultimately leads pilgrimage centers to become embroiled in political rivalries, in which any kind of power is a potential resource.

This structuring of social performances in pilgrimage assumes greater significance when we note that the sacred place by definition embodies the collective ideals of the group. What more important public stage is there on which to enact and work out social processes, relationships, and conflicts? Furthermore, since the pilgrimage site is geographically and socially separate from the home community, performances which embody social content are displayed in this "place apart" as if purely in the abstract. The ceremonies attain a meaningful coherence and strength from display outside the complex and complicated realities of the everyday home community. They also draw strength from the sacred potency of the stage of their enactment. Social forces lay claim to a timeless, divine sanction by association with the sacred shrine and its divinity. This trait is highlighted in several chapters and especially by Poole in her study of the place of dance in Andean pilgrimages. She shows how the structure and symbolism of dance performed in conjunction with shrine visits serves to express important social themes. In the context of pilgrimage, dance, she argues, works a transformation and renewal of social forms in the participating community.

One must also not neglect the fact that a pilgrimage exists within an historical context and takes shape in a dynamic relationship to forces playing within and outside the institution itself, as discussed by Dobyns for the Northwest Mexican frontier and the Magdalena pilgrimage. New pilgrimages arise and old ones fade in importance, like the development of new forms of worship or celebration and the transformation of old patterns to serve new ends. It is because the pilgrimage is so complexly linked to its social and cultural environment that in its structure and performance it absorbs the changing patterns of the wider context. Especially important for the study of pilgrimage in Latin America is the question of continuity and change in preconquest and postconquest religions. Thus it is not surprising to find this issue arising in almost every chapter. The roots of contemporary Latin America pilgrimage are clearly traced in the overview chapter by Nolan. In the studies of the Otomi in Mexico by Harvey and of Amatitlán, Guatemala, by Straub we see cases in which ritual, belief, and symbolism, or cultural content, display continuity with precontact society as well as the strong transformative influence of Catholicism. Urbano shows that despite the strong thrust of the Church to do away with pagan ritual content, the Incas were able to continue using pilgrimage sites as resources in political contests. Whereas in preconquest society, pilgrimage shrines established the dominance of Inca cults in subject regions, following the conquest, the descendants of the Incas adapted this deep-level politico-religious strategy in order to align themselves with the dominant subjugating Spanish power. It was the Incas, not the Spanish, who worked these transformations of the shrines. Here we see historical continuities of social process, as opposed to cultural content, focused on pilgrimage.

As dynamic institutions, pilgrimages are constantly changing, yet one of the more constant elements is the sacred location itself. We can trace this socio-cultural development in a pilgrimage by investigating changes in the association of the site and the religious complex of the pilgrimage. But because pilgrimage at its core is structured interaction of human belief and behavior with particular geographical locations, it is also possible to trace the development of a pilgrimage in the changes wrought to landscape over time. Shrines are raised, steps are cut, topography is altered, and settlement patterns change, all as a result of the historical development of the pilgrimage. Here we trace the swells and recessions of flows of people, and the impacts which these tides register on sites elevated to the status of divine abodes on earth.

All of these perspectives point to the complexity of the pilgrimage institution. As an institutional whole in its own right, it is a rich tapestry of geographical features, social processes, cultural artifacts, belief, ritual, spirituality, psychology, literature, art, architecture and other factors. Then too, the threads woven into this cloth are drawn from wider patterns of thought, behavior, communication, history, transport, administration, and conflict in the broader expanses of the social field. The pilgrimage is a rather unique, and remarkable, human creation.

THE STRUCTURE OF PILGRIMAGE

That every pilgrimage is in and of itself an institution and yet exists in dynamic interrelations with the forces of the wider society are factors which give rise to the underlying structural patterns of the institution. We can identify structural relations which pattern the pilgrimage institution internally and other sets of relations which dominate the patterning of the relationship between the pilgrimage and its sociocultural environment.

Internally, the pilgrimage is structured to reflect the dichotomy of the sacred and profane. While these categories have been shown to be more fuzzy than Durkheim would have liked (see Stanner 1967) in the context of pilgrimage, they are dominant themes. The pilgrimage place is by definition a sacred place, most often sacralized by the reputed direct presence at that spot of some manifestation of the divine, such as a saint or apparition. It is this magnified presence of the holy which sets the pilgrimage place apart.

At one level, the sacred place participates in the sacred-versus-profane opposition by representing the sacred within the profane sphere. The shrine is usually remote from the homes of pilgrims and is bounded by ecclesiastical architecture. Within the shrine, the sacredness of the place is defined by God's presence.

But at another level, the pilgrimage shrine does not occupy a pole in the opposition between sacred and profane but rather plays an important role in mediating the two poles. The profane pole is located in the mundane, everyday home life of the believer, with all its entanglements, confusion, and sorrows. The sacred pole is located in the heart of Jesus or Mary, in heaven, beyond any perceptible form. The pilgrimage place plays a key role as the privileged site where the otherworldly sacred pole is made accessible, in a sense, where heaven issues forth onto earth.

The sacred place is revered because it represents the sacred and mediation with the sacred. This deep-level structural form gives rise to many other themes involved with the pilgrimage. In the everyday world-view of the believer, a number of oppositions relevant to the pilgrimage can be noted. These oppositions represent the concerns of people navigating a course through the difficult passage of life. Sickness and health, powerlessness and power, and fruitfulness and barrenness are examples of such concerns. The positive pole in the pairings is associated directly with the sacred, which embodies within itself all virtue. When uncertainty or misfortune motivates a desire to tap the grace of the sacred, then the pilgrimage shrine looms as the obvious mediating channel for the approach and appeal.

These structural relations can be represented schematically in models which suggest possible relations at a much deeper and more general level than the model of the pilgrimage as an institution. However, at this point in our discussion, as in the case of the concrete isolate model, they should be conceived of as handy means of perceiving pilgrimage structure rather than reality itself.

At its simplest, the pilgrimage represents an opposition between the sacred and the profane such that the pilgrimage is situated as a mediating intermediary between the wholly profane and wholly sacred realms. This relationship can be represented structurally as:

profane	is to	*pilgrimage*	as	*pilgrimage*	is to	*sacred*
1	:	2	::	2	:	3

This scheme represents the static, ideological oppositions paired in the structure of the pilgrimage. When we attempt to represent as well the dynamic, human aspect of the process of pilgrimage, we must add a new dimension to this model. Guidance here is provided by Arnold van Gennep (1960), who in his study of rites of passage identifies a process of separation, transition, and reincorporation which underlies all of these types of rituals. While pilgrimages are not rites of passage in the strict sense of birth, initiation, marriage, or death, all share important features. Like the latter, pilgrimages are meant to be transformative processes, from which the individual emerges altered from his or her previous situation. While in rites of passage this change is focused on alterations in social status, in pilgrimage the transformation is more commonly concerned with changing personal matters such as health, mental state, and spiritual life. Thus to represent the pilgrimage process schematically, the following considerations are incorporated into our model: 1) separation from home or from the profane, 2) transition within the profane to the sacred, 3) transition within the sacred to the profane, 4) reincorporation within the profane

Numbers 1 and 4 are clearly distinct processes, while 2 and 3 are actually two phases of one process. Numbers 1 and 4 represent passages to and from the pilgrimage core process, while 2 and 3 involve the pilgrimage core itself. We can therefore recast these four considertions schematically as *a*, *b*, and *c*. To encode the relationships among these three, we draw on Lévi-Strauss's (1966) triangular model of the dual set of oppositions: nature *versus* culture and elaborated *versus* unelaborated:

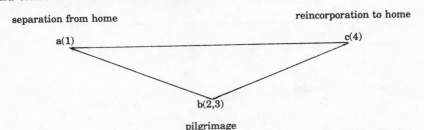

separation from home   reincorporation to home

a(1)   c(4)

b(2,3)

pilgrimage

This model sets up a number of key oppositions:

> *a* is clearly opposed to *c* because separation and reincorporation are oppositional (a ≠ c); this axis (a ≠ c) stands in opposition to *b*, as home to pilgrimage but more importantly as opposed processes. Separation and incorporation are linked because both are processes that breach the boundaries of home. In contrast, *b* is a transitional process in its own right. It is itself bounded by *a* and *c*.

Therefore, we find the opposition (a ≠ c) ≠ *b*, or:

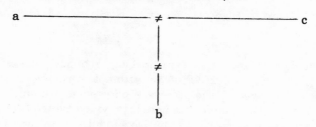

When we add notation to mark the categorical differences between the top and bottom of the original triangle, we get:

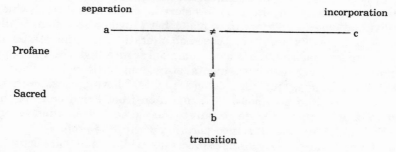

To translate this model back into the terms suggested by Lévi-Strauss, we add the oppositions of nature vs. culture and elaborated vs. unelaborated:

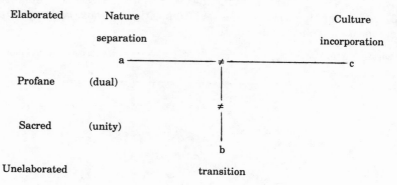

This model suggests that the profane is elaborated and consists of individuals who have not had the pilgrimage experience and so remain natural and unmodified, and individuals who have incorporated the sacred through the pilgrimage and are culturally designated modified. The transition or experience of the sacred is unelaborated and represents the supernatural unity, the Sacred.

This model captures some of the transformative aspect of the pilgrimage but still fails to represent the full power of the pilgrimage which is inherent in the structure of the performance. The power of the pilgrimage derives from its ability to mediate the profane vs. sacred opposition. Can we show this more clearly than we have already done? Lévi-Strauss suggests another more powerful permutational transformational structural model (1963:228):

$$F_x(a) \quad : \quad F_y(b) \quad :: \quad F_x(b) \quad : \quad F_{a-1}(y)$$

Additional variables and relations appear in this transformational permutational model, the term (a) is transformed into its opposite (a^{-1}) while the function of (y) is permutated to the term (y) and the term (a) to the function (F_{a-1}). This model represents a logical elaboration of the triangle of double oppositions however with the additions of the x and y functions, the replacement of c by a^{-1}, and the permutation of a term and a function. In the case of pilgrimage the model reveals the following relations:

$$F_{profane}(\text{separation}) : F_{sacred}(\text{transition}) :: F_{incorporation}(\text{transition}) : F_{profane}(\text{health})$$
$$(\text{illness}) \qquad (\text{health}) \qquad (\text{death}) \qquad (\text{life,sacred})$$

Placing the pilgrim in the role of term a and the pilgrimage as b, it generates the final victory or outcome of the pilgrimage experience. The pilgrim, a, specified by a negative function, F_x, such as illness or lack of spiritual power or salvation, undergoes the permutational transformation by means of the pilgrimage process which both leads him or her to and through the sacred, $F_y(b)$ and back to the profane, $F_x(b)$. Yet the pilgrim's final victory, $F_{a-1}(y)$, involves both a transformation and a permutation. While returning to the profane he or she is imbued with the sacred, gaining health and power, becoming a function of the later $F_{a-1}(y)$.

Thus these three structural models increase in complexity from the first to the last. The permutational transformational model provides the most complex and abstract account of the power produced by means of the pilgrimage process and its productive mediation of the sacred versus profane opposition. It suggests one type of explanation of the popularity of pilgrimage.

THE ROLES OF THE PILGRIMAGE

It is obvious from the foregoing that the pilgrimage is conceived of as an important means by which individuals can gain access to the sources of power believed to control their destiny. The pilgrimage in Latin America is, at this level, predominantly an instrumental practice. One approaches the earthly divine abode in the hopes of acquiring or achieving the boons of divine intercession in this life.

At the individual level, the role of the pilgrimage is to provide a means of influencing one's fate or future, where more obvious means of doing so are not available. It is for this reason that the purposes for which pilgrimage is undertaken are so frequently concerned with the cure of a medically untreatable disorder, the relief from barrenness, the retrieval of a lost person or object, and other such goals which do not appear to be attainable without the direct blessing of the grace of God.

It is the instrumental nature of the pilgrimage that has influenced the patterns of pilgrim practices and even the nature of the objects of their veneration. Pilgrims commonly undertake pilgrimage with a vow in mind. The vow is a promise to the divine that the pilgrim will undertake specified acts, such as to go on the same pilgrimage annually for ten years, to make a significant offering to the Church, or to give a charitable donation, if and only if the favor requested is granted. When a vow is involved, the pilgrimage is centered on the communication mediated through the channel of the pilgrimage center. The intention is to establish a reciprocal relationship with the divine which the believer hopes will prove pleasing to both parties.

Because the pilgrimage shrine is so frequently a mediator for instrumental communication between heaven and earth, it is not surprising to note that in the majority of cases the central figures of veneration in the shrines are the saints and Mother Mary. These figures are appropriate intercessors between mortal people and God and His Son, and so share in the intermediary quality of the divine abode on earth. But even though instrumentality is so important a factor in the pilgrimage we should not neglect other roles of the institution and practice, even at the individual level.

Although the pilgrim frequently has a practical goal in mind and hopes to establish an equitable exchange relationship with the divine power-sources, it would be wrong to cast this as a calculated, hard headed business deal. The regional culture stresses that the pilgrim must approach the divine on earth with a certain quality of genuine openheartedness. The pilgrimage is an exercise in humble supplication, surrender, and prayer in which the ideal qualities of the Christian heart are cultivated. The goal of the performance might be business success or a successful court case, but the stipulated means includes the practice of personal spiritual virtue.

We can speculate at this point that the access to power which is cast in a divine mold in the pilgrimage has something to do with the accessing of inner personal power through the ritual experience. One means of effecting change in one's future is to transform oneself, and so from this perspective the instrumentality and spirituality of the pilgrimage are not separate. The spiritual cultivation of the heart which is stressed in the pilgrimage may have psychological and somatic effects that do indeed work changes in health, fertility, and aspects of life where attitude is relevant.

This power of the pilgrimage is set loose by the direct experiences of the pilgrim. The sacred journey often involves prescribed actions which induce peaks of sensory experience, with resultant predictable psycho-physical effects. One common means to stimulate a self-transformative perceptual peak on pilgrimage is through pain induction, as in the well-reported practice of pilgrims performing penance by crossing stone courtyards or mounting long stone stairways on their bare knees (Chapters 8 and 16). The expected behavior of pilgrims often involves displays of extraordinary emotion, especially of devotion or sorrow. The intoxication, feasting, music, and dance of the fiestas which frequently accompany pilgrimages serve the same purpose by providing the pilgrim with extraordinary peaks of sensation. From a sociological point of view, all of these intense experiences serve to mark off the pilgrim's behavior as exceptional and so make it appropriate for the extraordinary time and place of the pilgrimage. They designate to pilgrim and to witnessing community that an extraordinary event is in progress, one appropriate to the special sacredness of the pilgrimage shrines and practices.

Beyond their marking function, which is performed as well by special dress, codes of conduct, and food, the peak experiences of the pilgrimage have a physiological role in inducing altered states of consciousness. In many cases, these experiences are deliberately structured into the pilgrimage to occur as the very climax of the individual's journey. This structuring, which has developed over centuries of cultural experimentation, is based on a recognition of basic human characteristics and the possibilities that exist for manipulating these. Whether the individual is motivated by instrumental or spiritual goals, the reaching out to God on the pilgrimage has implicit within it the reaching inward to the depths of one's own being. The extraordinary communication and communion sought in the home of heaven on earth must come forward from the inner core of the devotee. Extreme experiences such as self-inflicted pain open the pathways through ego to the inner sanctums where the roots of being are anchored. Access to these ordinarily closed levels of self is a precondition to the spiritually transformative experience of the pilgrimage and also to the accomplishment of instrumental goals reached by prayer to God.

That this access to inner power takes place in a ritual context socializes it and renders it manageable. The individual is destructured by the extreme experiences, but does not simply dissolve, because he or she is surrounded by a supportive environment which carries him or her along through the experience and back into reintegration, hopefully in a new form with problem cured. The pilgrimage is often about individual improvement and transformation, but it is a mass popular practice. Thus it is given the form of a conventional cultural structure with built-in mechanisms which manipulate the mind and body of the average participant. In this aspect, the pilgrimage is a pathway to change founded in a recognition of essential human psycho-physical structure and process.

The pathway of pilgrimage experience is open to all, but not all walk that way. In reality, few pilgrims cross the harsh stone courtyards on their knees, or drink to ecstasy. Earlier we commented on the polymorphism of pilgrimage in its social dimension. The same can be said at the level of individual conception and involvement in the pilgrimage. Without denying the role of culturally derived perception, it is nevertheless the case that each individual beholds a sacred shrine and image that corresponds to his or her own beliefs, personality, need, and experience. The culturally prescribed characteristics of the pilgrimage are always interpreted by the individual, and the result is always unique. Recognizing this polymorphic quality of pilgrimage at the individual level permits us to understand that a single shrine and image can be the focus for many different sorts of behavior and belief. There is no single pilgrimage reality — there are many, each composed by a pilgrim according to his or her knowledge, need, and nature. The pilgrimage shrine and its meaning are always open to individual interpretation within limits. These limits are set more by the human imagination than by the cultural prescriptions of the shrine supporters. This open reality of the pilgrimage fits with the cultural tradition that pilgrimage is a voluntary act undertaken by individuals who set out to meet their God for their own personal purposes. In its individual polymorphic aspect, the pilgrimage provides individuals with a culturally approved means of approaching God in a way appropriate to their unique character and situation.

Beyond the individual level, the roles of the pilgrimage are many. Social groups which are especially affected by pilgrimages include: pilgrims, home community, host community, and ritual specialists. Several chapters in this volume document the economic, political, and social impact the pilgrimage has on these categories of social groups in different cases.

CONCLUSION

The pilgrimage is important in Latin America for several reasons. Religiously, the sites to which pilgrimages are made are the most revered centers of Catholicism in the region. Socially, pilgrimages can reinforce group identity and the important relationship between the community of believers and the protective power of divinity. It is not an inconsequential fact that millions of people annually undertake pilgrimages, with all of the social, economic, and cultural effects such large-scale movements of people entail. When pilgrimage shrines are identified with the nation-state they can play an important role as national symbols, linking the celestial and terrestrial power sources. When pilgrimage shrines are identified against the social order, gatherings and ritual practices can be subversive to state and power structures. And at the individual level, the pilgrimage offers a means of engaging in spiritual practices which embody the human ideals of the culture. The practice also holds out hope of achieving desired ends for those who have tried other means and are now left no recourse but a humble entreaty at God's door.

The place of pilgrimage in the regional culture, in personal, national, and even international dimensions, gives the study of pilgrimage its importance. With this present volume, we begin systematizing the analytical study of this important institution, initiate the exercise of comparison which is so vital to understanding the diversity and order that exists within the regional tradition, and also offer the first steps toward a theoretical framework for studying the pilgrimage in Latin America. We express our thanks to those who have contributed to what knowledge we have now achieved concerning this practice and welcome the future efforts of those who will enhance our understanding by further studies and deeper reflection on the theory and practice of pilgrimage.

NOTES

1. Held at Pittsburgh in May, 1981, under the co-sponsorship of Simon Fraser University and University of Pittsburgh.
2. We draw the reader's attention to the extensive References section at the end of this volume.
3. The sacred goal is a feature of all Latin American pilgrimage. However, in some pilgrimage traditions of other cultural regions, the pilgrimage may have no goal, and is best defined as a sacred journey.

REFERENCES

Lévi-Strauss 1963, 1966
Malinowski 1944
Stanner 1967

Sumption 1975
van Gennep 1960

2

The European Roots of Latin American Pilgrimage

MARY LEE NOLAN

Christian pilgrimage in Latin America is intimately tied to the continuing evolution of pilgrimage in Western Europe. Traditions that developed in the Old World hearth lands of Western Christendom displayed a remarkable capacity for adjustment to changing times. Although pilgrimage has undergone periods of greater and lesser popularity, the institution has never been seriously threatened in predominately Roman Catholic countries. At present, there are Catholic pilgrimage shrines in every Western European country, and formal pilgrimages have been reestablished by High Church Anglican and Lutheran congregations in the United Kingdom, Sweden, and West Germany. In combination, Western Europe's more than 6,000 active shrines receive an estimated 70 million religiously motivated visits each year. Many shrines of historical or artistic importance draw large numbers of tourists as well as pilgrims. Total visits to Europe's holy places probably exceed 100 million annually by a considerable margin (Nolan and Nolan 1989).

The transmission of this dynamic Western European tradition to the New World began in the late fifteenth century and has continued to the present. There has been some flow of American ideas about pilgrimage to Europe since the sixteenth century, but the predominant direction of diffusion continues to be from Western Europe to the Americas.

Some Latin American pilgrimages have evolved from a syncretism of Christian and non-Christian traditions. In regions where the slave trade introduced large numbers of blacks, a strong African influence affected the development of New World cults. Where new Afro-American religions emerged, the Christian input into the development of pilgrimage may be relatively minor. In most parts of Latin America, however, the European contribution to syncretic traditions appears to be of major importance and it seems likely that indigenous American elements of pilgrimage with the highest survival potential were those sufficiently familiar to European missionaries as to be encouraged or tolerated. At least three aspects of European pilgrimage merit serious consideration for the interpretation of Latin American pilgrimages. First, it is important to examine the variation in belief and behavior within Europe and the frequencies with which certain traits are found on both sides of the Atlantic. This kind of information is particularly important to scholars who are interested in unraveling the threads of syncretism or in tracing continuance of pre-Columbian themes. Second, the Latin Americanist particularly needs information on pilgrimage expressions and the nature of cult formation in sixteenth, seventeenth, and eighteenth-century Europe. This period marks the initial transatlantic transfer of Christianity and was also a time of extensive cult-formative activity in Western Europe. A third area of concern relates to the impact of nineteenth and twentieth-century European shrine formations on New World pilgrimage. Several of these have given rise to subsidiary shrines in the Americas.

LITERATURE REVIEW AND PROCEDURES

This chapter summarizes changes in cult-formative trends in Western Europe and compares selected characteristics of active European and Latin American pilgrimage shrines. The analysis is based on information accumulated between 1964 and 1984. During the 1960s and early 1970s my research focused on Mexico (Nolan 1967, 1972, 1973). In 1975, I began collecting information on contemporary Western European shrines. Sources included materials sent by diocese offices and shrine administrators in response to mail queries, books and pamphlets collected at shrines, listings of pilgrimage events provided by national and regional tourism agencies, and published compendia describing shrines in particular countries or regions.[1] These materials were supplemented with observations at 848 shrines visited during a total of 26 months of field research in Europe between 1976 and 1984. Field work undertaken in Mexico during the late 1960s and early 1970s was supplemented with visits to shrines in Ecuador, Peru, and Bolivia during the summer of 1984.

I also collected data on 937 Hispanic Latin American pilgrimage centers through correspondence with Latin American bishops and shrine administrators. Two hundred and seventy diocese offices responded to letters of inquiry with letters, brochures, church bulletins, advertisements announcing pilgrimage events, postcards, typed or mimeographed shrine lists, and publications or references to publications. Materials on specific shrines were received by mail from 140 individual shrine administrators. Additional information was obtained by surveying travel, ethnographic, and religious literature.[2] Published shrine-specific works on Latin American shrines include a number of booklets, books, and articles, most of which were obtained at shrines or sent by diocese or shrine offices.[3]

Although Hispanic American shrines inventoried to date probably reflect only a portion of places visited by pilgrims, it seems probable that most of the larger, better known pilgrimage centers are included. In addition, the number is large enough to suggest some of the aggregate characteristics of pilgrimage in the region for comparative purposes. Table 2.1 indicates the number of shrines identified in the various European and Latin American countries. Several of the other tables accompanying this article compare selected attributes of active shrines in Latin America with active shrines in Western Europe. It is assumed that the characteristics of shrines surviving from particular periods can be considered a surrogate indicator of tendencies in various regions during past time periods. Therefore, the tables also include data on currently visited shrines established in Iberia between 700 and 1530 and those founded between 1500 and 1799 in regions that were under Spanish or Austrian Hapsburg rule. The Germanic Hapsburg regions are included because missionary efforts in Latin America were apparently influenced by cult-formative activities in Germany from the late sixteenth through the eighteenth centuries.

TIME PERIODS OF CULT FORMATION

Contemporary Western European pilgrimage evolved from a syncretism of pagan and Christian belief systems that took place largely between the fourth and eleventh centuries. Since then, there have been several periods of decline and resurgence in enthusiasm for pilgrimage. These appear to be related to periods of major social change, particularly in the cases of low points in cult formations that occurred during the early sixteenth and late eighteenth centuries. Clusters of decades producing few surviving shrines were also characterized by the weakening of many existing cults. Some shrines became dormant or extinct as places of pilgrimage. After each low point in shrine formations, however, there was a resurgence of pilgrimage activity, including new cult formations and increased numbers of visitors to those older shrines that survived the transition. Cycles of pilgrimage florescence seem to begin with a series of reinterpretations of belief and practice that apparently improve the fit between pilgrimage and other dimensions of a changing social order. Innovations often appear first at

Table 2.1 Number and Location of Inventoried Shrines

Western Europe	Number	Latin America	Number
Italy	1,194	Mexico	223
France	1,034	Brazil	121
Spain	1,014	Peru	106
West Germany	938	Argentina	93
Austria	925	Ecuador	91
Portugal	332	Chile	74
Switzerland	283	Colombia	68
Benelux	199	Bolivia	41
Ireland	135	Venezuela	41
England & Scotland	86	Uruguay	16
Scandinavia	10	El Salvador	14
		Guatemala	12
		Honduras	9
		Puerto Rico	7
		Dominican Republic	5
		Nacaragua	5
		Panama	5
		Cuba	3
		Paraguay	2
		Costa Rica	1
Totals:	6,150		937

newly established shrines although some changes may be adopted at surviving older shrines. As a result of this continuing process, the aggregate nature of shrine characteristics changes through time.

Six percent of Europe's active shrines date from before the eighth century and nearly one-third were established between the eighth and fourteenth centuries (Table 2.2). Many of Europe's shrines, however, are of fairly recent vintage. Sixty-two percent of the 4,049 shrines which could be dated were founded after the turn of the fifteenth century and nearly half were established after the initial years of the Protestant Reformation.

Table 2.2 Periods of Shrine Establishment

Western	Europe		Latin	America
Period	% of dated shrines n=4049	Period		% of dated shrines n=479
Early Christian (To 699) n=248	6			
Early Medieval (700-1099) n=407	10			
High Medieval (1100-1399) n=893	22			
Renaissance (1400-1529) n=623	15			
Post Reformation (1530-1779) n=1308	32	Colonial (1492-1799) n=299		62
Modern (1780-1980) n=570	14	Modern (1800-1980) n=180		38

	Modern	Period	Subdivided
Dates	% of exactly dated modern shrines n=551	Dates	% of exactly dated modern shrines n=157
1780-1899 n=330	60	1800-99 n=51	32
1900-1980 n=221	40	1900-80 n=106	68

Several changes in shrine origin stories and in pilgrim behaviors occurred during the fifteenth century, apparently as part of the cultural reorientation of the Renaissance. Some of these changes are reflected by a substantial increase in the proportion of shrines established as thanks offerings by individuals and an apparent increase in emphasis on personal relationships between holy persons in heaven and ordinary individuals on earth (see Cousin 1981). Perhaps more significantly, a previously unrecorded type of apparition was experienced by visionaries at several places in Italy and Spain during the fifteenth century. These apparitions were not characterized by the discovery of an image. Mary appeared alone, without the Christ Child, and delivered a message calling for repentance to avoid divine wrath. This is precisely the type of Marian apparition interpreted by Victor and Edith Turner (1978) as a response to "post-industrial" conditions in nineteenth-century Europe. The Turners' discussion of the social-symbolic implications of this vision type seems plausible. It is, therefore, important to note that this new type of cult-formative apparition, along with several other characteristics that distinguish contemporary pilgrimages from their medieval precursors, date from the fifteenth century rather than the nineteenth century as the Turners' supposed.

During the initial period of the American discoveries and colonizations, European pilgrimage was flourishing. At least 137 of Europe's active shrines were established between 1492 and 1529. During the 1530s, the number of new cult formations with survival value declined precipitously as Europeans were caught up in the intellectual and political ferment of the Protestant Reformation. Then, shortly after the First Council of Trent (1545-47) launched the Catholic Reformation (or Counter Reformation), shrine establishment increased. The greatest amount of new activity was initially in Italy and France, but the wave of post-Reformation cult formation soon spread to Germany where it reached its fullest expression in the seventeenth century. The post-Reformation period, between 1530 and 1779, accounts for the creation of 1,308 active shrines, or nearly one-third of Europe's datable places of contemporary pilgrimage. During the seventeenth century, an average of six new shrines came into being each year, counting only those which have survived and can be dated. After a peak decade in the 1650s, which accounts for 80 of today's pilgrimage centers, cult-formative activity began a gradual decline toward a low point in the 1770s.

In spite of its importance for the interpretation of both European and American pilgrimage traditions, pilgrimage in Catholic Reformation Europe has received little scholarly attention until recently. Christian's (1981a, 1981b) studies of apparitions and popular religion in sixteenth-century Spain and a steadily increasing body of work in German (see Kolb 1976, 1980; Hartinger 1984a, 1984b; Pötzl 1984) were not available when the Turners were developing their pioneering study of symbolism in Christian pilgrimage. Their lack of information on pilgrimages in Catholic Reformation Europe apparently led them into perpetuating a misleading model that interprets Latin American pilgrimage as a New World continuation of medieval European themes (Turner and Turner 1978:49, 162-63).

Given the power of old, frequently repeated assumptions, it is important to stress that the missionaries who took Christianity to the New World were not medieval men and did not carry medieval models of pilgrimage cult formation. Pilgrimage and ideas about place sanctification had undergone important reinterpretations before the Americas were discovered. The earliest missionaries to the Americas were men of the Renaissance. A second wave was composed of people who had matured during the low period of shrine formations, which seems to have occurred on a virtually pan-European basis in the 1530s and 1540s. Most missionaries born after about 1535 grew up in a Catholic Reformation milieu of weeping Madonnas, bleeding crucifixes, sudden cures by wayside votive images, and joyous celebrations of the acquisition of wondrous objects from far places. Each of these phenomena led to the creation of new pilgrimage shrines. Although Spaniards were strongly discouraged from reporting visionary experiences after the second decade of the sixteenth century (Christian 1981b:150-87), apparitions remained important as cult-formative events in Italy, France, and the Catholic Germanic lands throughout the post-Reformation period.

During the colonial period in Hispanic America influences from Iberia combined with a considerable input from Italy and Germany. In South America, Italian missionary priests promoted the Loreto cults and other Italian devotions (Vargas Ugarte 1956), and at least one shrine, at Laguna de los Padres, Argentina, was established by an eighteenth-century Jesuit of English origin. Father Kino, and other conveyors of Christianity in northwestern New Spain, provide examples of missionaries from Germanic regions (Kay 1977). The German connection is particularly interesting because the Catholic Reformation pilgrimage florescence reached its greatest levels of expression in Hapsburg Austria and other Germanic lands. In those regions, new cult formations remained at high levels well into the eighteenth century, decades after the intellectual inroads of the Enlightenment or other factors resulted in a general decline in pilgrimage activity in other parts of Catholic Europe.

Although the frequency of cult formation in Europe never again reached its seventeenth-century peak, several of the shrines established since 1780 are among the most important religious centers in Christendom. France, Italy, and the Germanic regions have the highest proportions of shrines dating from the nineteenth century. In contrast, very few Spanish shrines survive from the period between 1800 and 1899. From the turn of the twentieth century through the 1950s, the greatest numbers of new shrines emerged in Italy and Germany, although the most famous early twentieth-century pilgrimage centers are in Portugal and Belgium. Many shrines in the United Kingdom and all in Scandinavia were established or revitalized after the turn of the twentieth century. New pilgrimage centers are still being formed and administrators at established shrines in many parts of Europe have reported a marked increase in visitation during the past two decades.

Periods of Shrine Formation in Latin America

Sixty-two percent of the Latin American shrines for which dates were obtained became Christian pilgrimage centers before the turn of the nineteenth century (Table 2.2). Of the 240 colonial period shrines which can be assigned to specific centuries, 30 percent were established by 1599, 33 percent date from the seventeenth century, and 37 percent were founded between 1700 and 1799. Relatively few Latin American shrines date from the nineteenth century, but the twentieth century has been a time of substantial shrine-formative activity. Regional variations tend to reflect the course of settlement and/or periods of extensive increase in populations through immigration. More than half of the dated shrines in Argentina,

Brazil, Chile, and Uruguay, for example, were established after the turn of the nineteenth century as compared with countries such as Mexico and Peru that have larger proportions of colonial period shrines.

SUBJECTS AND OBJECTS OF VENERATION

The vast majority of pilgrimage shrines in Western Europe and Latin America are focused on the veneration of a specific holy person. These persons are the Virgin Mary, Christ, or one of the saints, including folk saints, venerated persons not yet canonized, and officially canonized saints. Some shrines are characterized by cults related to two or more persons, but in these cases one holy individual nearly always supersedes the other in the pilgrims' view. In continental Europe as in the Americas, the subject of pilgrim devotion is usually symbolized by a movable object, such as a relic or an image, that is thought to have very special or miraculous qualities.

Marian Shrines

The proportion of pilgrimage centers devoted to the Virgin Mary is somewhat lower in the Americas than in Europe, but on both sides of the Atlantic she is the principal subject of veneration at a majority of shrines (Table 2.3). This was not always the case in Western Europe. Early Christian cults were initially centered on the physical remains of saints, most of whom were males (Brown 1981; Rothkrug 1979, 1980). Although ideas of Mother-Goddess shrines and image veneration had foundations in pagan Western European traditions (Sharbrough 1977), Marian cults developed much more slowly in the West than in Eastern Mediterranean lands. Some historians (Sumption 1975; Rothkrug 1979) dismiss claims of very early, image-focused Marian pilgrimage cults in the West, although such stories may not be entirely without foundation. Images of Mary were painted in Roman catacombs as early as the third century and some in Roman churches date to the late fifth and early sixth centuries. Oral traditions along with some iconographic evidence suggest that refugees from Islamic expansion and Byzantine iconoclasm were arriving in Italy with venerated Marian icons, or the ideas of creating them, by the eighth century (Vinciotti 1960). Early Marian shrines in France developed around relics such as the "Virgin's Milk" from the Milk Grotto in Bethlehem. Others, as at Orleans, France, seem to have developed around images venerated by enclaves of merchant-immigrants from Eastern Mediterranean lands, perhaps as early as the fifth century (Leroy 1984). Nevertheless, most shrines established in the West prior to the eleventh century were based

Table 2.3 Primary Subjects of Devotion Regional Percentages

Subject	Latin America 1500-1980 n=903	Western Europe 40-1980 n=6051	Medieval Iberia 700-1530 n=360	Hapsburg Regions 1531-1799 n=556
Mary	58	66	83	75
Christ	25	8	5	12
Saints*	17	27	13	13
Totals**	100	101	101	100
Percentage of Male and Female Subjects				
Christ and Male Saints	39	27	14	22
Mary and Female Saints	61	73	86	78
Totals	100	100	100	100

* Saints include folk saints, angels, holy persons not yet canonized, and canonized saints.
** Percentages do not always total 100 due to rounding.

on the relics of saints.

Image veneration, important for the full development of Marian cults, probably received impetus from a custom of encasing saints' relics in effigies that was practiced as early as the tenth century in southern France (Mâle 1978:4; Sumption 1975:51). During the eleventh century, the medieval interpretation of the cult of the Virgin rapidly gained importance in Western Europe. Stimulated by vigorous Cistercian promotion, the popularity of Marian devotions had become a revolutionary force for change in the pilgrimage patterns of Western Europe by the early twelfth century. From that time to the present, a substantial majority of new shrines were created in honor of the Virgin Mary. Several of the saints' shrines founded prior to 1100 eventually became Marian pilgrimage centers with devotions primarily focused on statues or paintings of Mary and only to a lesser extent directed toward the relics of the saint who was the original pilgrim-attracting person.

Marian shrines were established in the Americas soon after Europeans arrived. According to tradition, the oldest Christian pilgrimage center in the New World is at Santo Cerro in the Dominican Republic where Christopher Columbus erected a cross to celebrate victory over a group of Indians in 1495. If the traditional date of 1531 is accepted, the great shrine of the Virgin of Guadalupe on the outskirts of Mexico City is also one of the oldest in the Americas. This Marian apparitional shrine has spawned numerous subsidiary pilgrimage centers in Mexico, elsewhere in Latin America, in the United States, and even in Europe. Although named for the famous medieval pilgrimage center at Guadalupe, Spain, the Mexican Virgin of Guadalupe, in the guise of an Indian maiden, is quintessentially American. The sixteenth-century cults of the Virgin of Guadalupe at Guadalupe, Peru (ca. 1560), and Guapulo, Ecuador (ca. 1581), are directly derived from the Spanish shrine of Guadalupe. Other well-known Marian shrines, which were probably established before the midpoint of the sixteenth century, are found at Ocotlán, Pátzcuaro, San Bartolo Naucalpan, and Zapopan in Mexico and at Arequipa, Peru. The most important Marian shrines in other Latin American countries came into being during the late sixteenth through eighteenth centuries.

Several very important European pilgrimage centers have been generated by reports of Marian apparitions since 1800. At Lourdes, France, a young girl, now canonized as Saint Bernadette, saw visions of the Virgin Mary in 1858. This apparitional site is visited by four to five million pilgrims each year and has generated at least twelve subsidiary shrines in Latin America. Marian apparitions at Fátima, Portugal, in 1917 resulted in a pilgrimage center that draws at least a million devotees per year and Latin America has at least eight well-visited ones dedicated to Our Lady of Fátima. Other Latin American shrines celebrate nineteenth-century Marian apparitions at the Rue de Bac Convent in Paris and at La Salette in the French Alps. Four shrines in Argentina and Chile focus on a cult that developed in the late nineteenth century at Pompeii, Italy, after a devout man found a painting of the Madonna and Child in an antique shop and at least fourteen shrines promote the German-based Schönstatt movement that has attained worldwide importance during the past few decades.

On both sides of the Atlantic, pilgrims currently flock to locations where recent reports of Marian apparitions have not received ecclesiastical acknowledgment. San Damiano, Italy, and San Sebastian Garabandal, Spain, both places where apparitional reports began in the 1960s, are among the better known examples of such unofficial pilgrimage centers in Europe. Both sites are visited by Latin American pilgrims as is the much-publicized village of Medjugorje, Yugoslavia, where reports of apparitions began in 1981 (Laurentin and Rupcic 1984). Recent reports of Marian apparitions have also generated new pilgrimages in Latin America. Incidents described in letters from diocese offices include the appearance of an image of the Virgin of Guadalupe on the window pane of a school in Limón, Tamaulipas, Mexico,[4] visions beheld by up to 600 people in the diocese of Los Teques, Venezuela, and the important Marian apparitional shrine at Caupa, Nicaragua, where visions began in 1980.

Saints' Shrines

During the first ten centuries of Christendom, most European shrines were dedicated to saints. The survival of many old saint-oriented shrines helps explain the higher proportion of this type of cult in Europe than in Latin America (Table 2.3). The twentieth century has witnessed a proportional increase in pilgrimages related to European saints. Many of these shrines are dedicated to historical individuals who have recently been canonized, as, for example, Saint Rita of Cassia, Italy. This fifteenth-century holy woman has long been revered in Italy, but was not officially canonized until 1900. An abused wife and mother, Saint Rita found release from the difficulties of her life by escaping to a convent after her cruel husband died and the children were grown. She became quite popular in Latin America after her canonization and is the primary subject of veneration at several shrines in Chile and Argentina. Other recently canonized Italian saints honored at pilgrimage centers in the Americas are the eighteenth-century Redemptorist mystic Saint Geraldo Majella and the nineteenth-century visionary Saint Gemma Galagni.

Large numbers of devotees also visit the European burial places of not-yet-canonized holy persons. The Granada tomb of a Capuchin monk, Fray Leopoldo, draws more than a million pilgrims each year, mostly from Spain and Latin America. Pilgrims from all over the world are found at the birthplace of Pope John XXIII in Sotto il Monte near Milan, Italy, and at the tomb of Padre Pio, a Capuchin priest who died in 1967 at San Giovanni Rotondo in southern Italy.

An increased emphasis on saints also seems to be characteristic of modern-era cult formations in Latin America. Only seven percent of the shrines which could definitely be attributed to the colonial period are dedicated to saints as compared with 24 percent of the shrines established during the past 180 years. A considerable number of these shrines have developed around regionally important Old World saints whose cults were brought to Latin America by nineteenth and twentieth-century immigrants from various parts of Europe. In addition, recent canonizations have helped spread the reputation of American saints such as Martin de Porres, a mulatto lay brother at the Rosary Convent in Lima, Peru, who died in 1639 and was canonized in 1962. Shrines dedicated to this saint are found in Peru, Colombia, and Mexico. His images are displayed in many Latin American churches and are occasionally found in European churches.

Other Latin American saints' cults are centered on persons who have not been canonized. Some are laypersons who gained a reputation for healing during their lifetimes, as, for example, Melchorita Saravia Tasayco, whose tomb at San Pedro de Grocio Prado, Peru, has been visited since her death in 1951 (Crumrine 1977b:81). More widely known is the Venezuelan physician and third-order Franciscan José Hernandez, who died in 1919. Large numbers of pilgrims visit his birthplace in Isnotu, Venezuela, and many others pay respects at the Church of Jesus del Gran Poder in Guayaquil, Ecuador, where some relics of this kindly "doctor to the poor" are kept in the crypt. Other uncanonized holy persons who inspire pilgrim journeys are Padre Julio Matovelle, venerated in Cuenca, Ecuador, Madre Mercedes Molina, whose tomb attracts pilgrims to Riobamba, Ecuador, and Fray Pedro Urraca, venerated in Lima, Peru. Several places in Argentina are dedicated to the Indian Ceferino Namuncura, whose case for beatification is pending.

Christ-centered Shrines

The proportion of Christ-centered pilgrimages in Europe is only eight percent as compared with 25 percent for the shrines inventoried in Hispanic America. Christ-centered shrines are of considerable antiquity in Europe, but most of those established during medieval times focus on a relic of the Passion, such as a splinter of the cross or earth from the Holy Land thought to have been touched with drops of blood from His wounds. The majority of these relics are found at shrines in Germanic countries. During the sixteenth through eighteenth centuries there was a definite increase in the number of new shrines focused on miraculous images of Christ in Germany and Iberia.

William Christian (1981a) has documented the rise of Christ-centered pilgrimage in New Castile between 1580 and 1780 (Table 2.4). My figures, based on surviving Iberian shrines, reveal a similar pattern. Slightly fewer than five percent of the Iberian shrines dating from 700 to 1529 are focused on Christ as compared with 19 percent of those found in the same region dating from 1530 to 1779. A major Spanish pilgrimage center developed at Limpias in Santander Province when an image of Christ reportedly moved its eyes in 1919, and a devotion to the Sacred Heart of Christ near Madrid grew into a major cult after an enormous statue was "executed" by firing squad during the Spanish Civil War. In general, however, the Hispanic emphasis on Christ, which characterized the post-Reformation period, diminished after the turn of the nineteenth century.

Christ-centered devotions showed a similar rise and decline in Germanic regions during the same period, but do not appear to have had much impact in France or Italy. Naturally, the Catholic Reformation focus on miraculous images of Christ did not emerge in Protestant regions where pilgrimages were banned, nor in the underground Catholicism of Protestant-dominated Ireland. Thus, the Baroque period enthusiasm for miraculous images of the Saviour was an essentially Ibero-Germanic phenomenon and suggests a particularly important exchange of ideas about the creation of pilgrimage shrines between these regions.

The orientations of colonizing countries are still reflected in New World shrines. In contrast with the 25 percent of Hispanic American shrines

Table 2.4 Subjects of Devotion at Catholic Reformation Period Shrines

Regions	Christ	Mary	Saints
New Castilian shrines active in 1580. n=133 [a]	5%	67%	29%
New Castilian shrines active in 1780. n=67 [b]	31%	55%	14%
Currently-active Iberian shrines established between 1530 and 1779. n=140	19%	68%	13%
Currently-active German and Austrian shrines established between 1530 and 1779. n=546	14%	71%	15%
Currently-active Italian shrines established between 1530 and 1779. n=285	3%	89%	8%
Currently-active French and Belgian shrines established between 1530 and 1779. n=162	1%	87%	12%

(a) Data from Christian (1981a:74)
(b) Data from Christian (1981a:183)

dedicated to Christ, only six percent of the 85 shrines identified in Quebec and the French Caribbean have Christ as a devotional subject. All but one of these shrines is dedicated to the Sacred Heart of Christ, a devotion based on the visions of a seventeenth-century French nun that led to the development of an important cult after the turn of the nineteenth century.

Clearly, the Hispanic American focus on Christ reflects Ibero-Germanic ideas of the Catholic Reformation. These may have fortuitously melded with indigenous predilections. Countries with more than 28 percent of their identified shrines oriented toward Christ extend from Mexico through Central America and Panama to the Andean countries of Colombia, Ecuador, and Peru.

Other lines of evidence more directly suggest a connection between Christ cults and pre-Columbian survivals. Some of the most important American Christ shrines are found at places that were sacred to pre-Columbian male deities. The Black Christ of Esquipulas, Guatemala, and the miraculous images at Chalma, Amecameca, and Tlacotepec in Mexico are well-known examples. In addition, 52 percent of the 73 shrines referred to in available literature as traditional Indian pilgrimage centers are dedicated to Christ. There is also a Latin American propensity to venerate black or dark images of Christ. Nearly 10 percent of the Christ-centered shrines I have found in Latin America focus on dark images and two-thirds of these figures are found at the shrines described as traditionally Indian.

Dark Images

Miraculous dark Christ images are probably not an American innovation. A crucifix called the "Volto Santo" has been venerated in Lucca, Italy, since at least the eleventh century, and tradition dates its acquisition to 782 (Lazzarini 1980). The image is currently represented as dark in skin tone, although how long this has been the case is uncertain. A dark crucifix has been venerated at a Dutch shrine since the early nineteenth century, and a few Spanish crucifixes are fairly dark. Dark images of Christ, however, are proportionately much less common in Europe than in the Americas.

If the statue venerated at Lucca has been portrayed as dark since the fifteenth century or earlier, this famous image could have lent the New World emergence of dark Christ images an aura of respectability, thus leading to their ecclesiastical acceptance as appropriate cult objects. Similarly, acceptance of dark Madonnas in the New World was probably related to the previous existence of such images in Europe. Black representations of especially powerful mother goddess figures were venerated in Europe during Greco-Roman times, or even earlier, and many of the "Black Virgins" of Christian Europe are quite literally black in skin tone (see Neumann 1972; Durand-Lefebvre 1937; Moss and Cappannari 1982). There is some question, however, as to when image darkness came to be valued in the Christian tradition. Most of the older dark images seem to have acquired their coloration sometime after their creation, suggesting that the association of darkness with special Christian sanctity may have been a post-medieval innovation (see Forsyth 1972; Christian 1985). Curiously, except for numerous copies of the slightly tan-skinned image of the Mexican Virgin of Guadalupe, dark Madonnas seem to be fairly rare in Latin America. The Ecuadorian Virgin of Quiche and the famous Bolivian image at Copacabana are often described as dark in shrine-related literature, but both were light in skin tone when I saw them in 1984.

Cults Based on Movable Objects

The continental European emphasis on cults related to movable objects such as relics and images helps explain the relative ease with which Western Christian pilgrimage traditions were transplanted to the Iberian New World. The separation of holy objects from holy places, which characterizes the Western European Christian tradition outside of Ireland (Nolan 1983), began by the late fourth century when pieces of saints' remains were sent as gifts from their shrine tombs to other parts of Christendom. A saint was believed to be present in any place which had a small fragment of his or her body, or even a piece of cloth or other object that had touched that body (Brown 1981). The ancient connection between shrines and sacred features of the site was reduced in significance as focus shifted toward such movable objects, although the pull of the old sacred site features never completely disappeared. A number of cult-formative legends developed in Europe explaining how a relic or a miraculous image chose a particular place characterized by height, water, grotto, or other attributes. This idea that images could, perhaps even should, choose the places where they were to be venerated was deeply embedded in the European tradition long before the American discoveries.

The frequent transfer of sacred objects from one place to another gave rise to legends creating an aura of mystery and miraculousness around the transfer events. For example, the Volto Santo, said to have been brought to Italian shores by refugees from iconoclasm in eighth-century Byzantium, became the icon of Lucca when the oxen pulling the cart bearing the crucifix stopped there and refused to move. Nearly a thousand years after the traditional date of this event, an ox cart carrying an image of the Virgin Mary supposedly got stuck in the mud at a place called Lujan in Argentina. When human efforts failed to dislodge the cart, it was taken as a sign that the Virgin had determined where she should be venerated. From the small chapel built at this site, both the town of Lujan and the most powerful pilgrimage of Argentina were born. Thus, ancient European themes were replayed in the New World as the American pilgrimage shrines came into being.

Sacred Site Features

Certain attributes of landscape seem to have special potential for sacredness in nearly all cultural traditions. In pagan Europe and pre-Columbian America, holy places were often associated with heights, water, sacred trees and groves, natural caverns, and sacred stones. Many Christian shrines in both regions also have such associations. The proportion of Latin American shrines described as having special site features is lower than for Western Europe, but this may reflect a lack of sufficiently detailed information on many Latin American cases.

European shrines surviving from the early Christian period are more likely to have sacred site features than those established later. Some shrines, especially among those that were pagan holy places, have several natural features. The shrine of Saint Mary Magdalene at La-Ste-Baume in southern France provides an example. The sanctuary is located in a cave part way up a cliff face and water dripping from the cavern walls is considered to have special powers. The grove below the cave-church was sacred to the pagans, and a chapel at the top of the cliff draws modern pilgrims to the heights.

Shrines established after 1400 are somewhat less likely to have sacred water features, caves, or stones than those from earlier ages. Shrines with sanctity attributed to trees or groves reached their greatest proportional importance during the post-Reformation period and are more common in Germanic areas than elsewhere in Europe. Because so many shrines were founded during the sixteenth through eighteenth centuries, a considerable number of modern Europe's holy hills, springs, and other sacred landscape features were incorporated into pilgrimage traditions during that period. Obviously, establishment of colonial period Latin American shrines at places marked by the same kinds of natural site features was well within the scope of the evolving European tradition.

Frequencies of different types of site features at those shrines which have such associations are similar on both sides of the Atlantic (Table 2.5).

Table 2.5 Specific Features at Shrines with Sacred Environmental Aspects of the Site, in Regional Percentages

Site Fea-ture	Latin America 1500-1980 n*=158	Western Europe 40-198 n*=2022	Medieval Lberia 700-1530 n*=138	Hapsburg Regions 1531-1799 n*=197
Height	54	48	54	48
Water	32	35	29	39
Trees	20	21	23	39
Stones	14	10	9	6
Caves	13	10	22	9

n* represents the number of shrines that are described as having one or more environmental site features. Percentages do not total 100 because some shrines have two to five such features.

There is a stronger American emphasis on sacred caves and grottos than is the case for Europe in general, but such site features are proportionally even more pervasive among shrines surviving from medieval Iberia. A possible explanation relates to the frequency with which early Iberian shrines initially developed around grottos that sheltered holy hermits. According to Christian (1981a), the period of hermits was largely over in Spain by the late Middle Ages, but accounts of American cult formations suggest that Spaniards of later generations with a predilection for living as hermits in caves found their personal utopias in the Americas. Other reasons are undoubtedly involved, but the data on medieval Iberia tend to undermine any argument that sacred caves are more common in the Americas because of indigenous tendencies.

Sacred stones are also proportionately more common in the Americas than in Europe. European stone cults, however, reach back thousands of years before the advent of Christianity, and are especially important at shrines established before the end of the eighth century. On both continents there are frequent associations between stone-related cults and pre-Christian traditions of place sanctity. Shrines established because paintings supposedly appeared on stones are especially common in southern Italy (Nolan and Nolan 1989).

Cults related to trees and groves often involve stories of pilgrimages developing after images were found in trees, or in the wake of apparitions in wooded areas or near a tree. In Europe, manifestations of the Virgin Mary are far more likely to involve oaks than any other tree species. It seems possible that the connection between Mary and oak trees is related to an ancient European veneration focused on oaks (see Taylor 1979). Sacred plants of American cults, when mentioned by name, are most likely to be ciebas, ahuehuetes, or magueys, all of which probably had sacred associations in pre-Columbian times. Images of Mary are also said to have been found in American oak trees, as, for example, at Monterrey, Mexico, in about 1650 (Cassidy 1958). It can be concluded that emphasis on the same kinds of sacred site features was common to both Amerindian and European traditions. There does not appear to be anything peculiarly American about cults related to landscape features except for a possible differential emphasis on certain plant species.

SHRINE ORIGIN STORIES

Recurrent themes in shrine origin accounts suggest seven basic types of formation stories, as indicated in Table 2.6. The most common story in Latin America derives cults from a newly acquired object, usually an image. This type of origin story is obviously related to the ancient movable object focus of continental European traditions and to the historical circumstances of mission work in the New World. Numerous images were shipped across the Atlantic, and by the mid-sixteenth century, images from the workshops of Hispanic colonial cities were being taken to frontier zones where proof of their miraculous qualities aided the effort of conversion.

Images proving to be miraculous on, or shortly after, arrival in their present places of veneration were brought or sent in numerous ways by people representing a wide range of occupations and social classes. Popular tales often involve mules, missionaries, or mysterious strangers. Mysterious strangers are found on both sides of the Atlantic, but with a difference in emphasis. In Latin America, the stranger leaves an image as he passes through a community, whereas in Europe he more typically dies in the place which becomes the shrine town and his physical remains become the object of pilgrim veneration. Stories of shrines established because animals transporting images or relics refuse to move are common in both Europe and the Americas. In Europe, however, recalcitrant animals are usually oxen, whereas in Latin America the role is more often played by mules. Missionaries and holy hermits as bearers of miraculous images are also found on both sides of the Atlantic. In Europe, shrines founded because of object acquisition are proportionately less common than in the Americas, with a somewhat higher percentage found among shrines from the post-Reformation period than from Iberia during medieval times.

The second most important type of story in Latin America involves the *miraculous finding* of a holy object. Proportions of Latin American shrines with this origin story are similar to those at shrines founded in Hapsburg-influenced regions during the post-Reformation period. The story type is less prevalent for Europe as a whole, but far more common for Iberian shrines established between 700 and 1530. As at Santiago de Compostela, Spain, where bones believed to be those of Saint James the Greater were discovered in the ninth century, the discovered object is usually a relic at shrines established before the eleventh century. At shrines established later in Europe and at those in Latin America, the object is most often an image. The classic medieval Iberian version of the story, which is also told somewhat less frequently in other parts of Europe, involves the discovery of a long-lost statue of the Virgin Mary by a shepherd. The scenarios differ from shrine to shrine, but often include proofs of the miraculous nature of the image and an explanation as to why the shrine church or chapel was built in a given place. There is an overlap between cult-formative stories involving found objects and accounts of apparitions. As observed by Christian (1981a:76), "There is a gray area between images that were found and images that 'appeared' which in some cases ought to read as 'turned up'." In Table 2.6 I categorized "appearing" images with found images, although there is sometimes a problem of interpretation. Stories from several parts of Europe describe images which "appeared" and initially behaved as if they were alive by moving and speaking to the visionary.

Sometimes an account of image discovery begins with an apparition. The image may be given to the visionary, or the seer may be told to look for it in a particular place. Accounts of this kind are well-documented after about 1400 in several parts of Europe, by which time shrines were also being established as a result of apparition reports that did not include image discoveries. Several Latin American accounts, including the famous origin story from Guadalupe, Mexico, involve the appearance or discovery of an image, which according to tradition, is taken as "proof" of the apparition's validity. In Europe apparitions account for the greatest proportion of formation stories among those shrines established during the Renaissance period, and apparitional shrines continued to be established through the eighteenth century, mostly outside of Iberia after 1530. Beginning in the

Table 2.6 Shrine Origin Stories, in Regional Percentages

Site Feature	Latin America 1500-1980 n*=387	Western Europe 40-198 n*=3131	Medieval Lberia 700-1530 n*=296	Hapsburg Regions 1531-1799 n*=471
Acquired Object: Cult develops after an object is brought from another place.	26	15	13	15
Found Object: Cult develops when image or relic is discovered; typically under unusual circumstances.	22	18	44	21
Spontaneous Miracle: Cult develops when a site or object located there proves to be miraculous.	17	15	5	20
Ex voto: Created as a thanks offering for group or personal salvation from catastrophe.	13	19	12	25
Apparition: Cult develops because of an apparition or simlar type of vision report.	8	11	17	12
Devotional: Shrine established as a result of human action unrelated to miracles and/or unusual events.	8	5	1	3
Significant Site: Places related to events in a saint's life or in the historical development of Christanity in the region.	6	17	8	5

n* represents number of shrines of which origin stories were recorded and classified.

early nineteenth century a series of widely publicized apparitions in France, Ireland, Portugal, and Belgium laid the foundation for extremely important modern shrines.

Hundreds of apparitions have been reported in the twentieth century (see Billet 1976). Few recent vision reports, however, have received ecclesiastical approval or even toleration. It seems probable that apparitions and other unusual manifestations of the kind potentially leading to creation of pilgrimage shrines occur with some frequency in both Europe and Latin America. Most are not publicized beyond a limited area and the incipient cult withers due to lack of encouragement. Apparitional accounts are somewhat more common as shrine formation stories in Europe than in Latin America, possibly reflecting the Spanish Inquisition's lack of tolerance for apparitions that affected shrine formations in Spain after the early sixteenth century.

During early Christian times, visionaries were usually churchmen or nobles. At shrines from the Middle Ages, however, the majority of European visionaries were described as poor lay persons. Shrines established because of visions beheld by persons representing the middle sectors of society increased during the Renaissance and later periods. Adult males monopolized socially accepted visionary experiences through the eighteenth century. During the nineteenth and twentieth centuries there has been a marked increase in the proportion of shrines established because of reports by female and child visionaries on both sides of the Atlantic.

Stories of spontaneous miracles such as weeping Madonnas, bleeding Christs, and sudden cures by roadside images are the third most common story found in Latin America. Miracles associated with images already in place were most frequent in Europe during Renaissance and post-Reformation times. This type of origin story is not commonly told at shrines established during medieval times in Iberia or elsewhere in Europe. It is, however, one of the more frequently told types of origin stories at shrines created during the sixteenth through eighteenth centuries in the Hapsburg-influenced parts of Europe.

The *ex voto*, or thanks offering, shrine is common throughout Europe and was the most frequent type in Hapsburg-influenced areas during the post-Reformation period. It appears to be somewhat less common as a type in Latin America. Proportions of shrines created as votives show a steady increase through time in Europe. This may reflect relatively short life spans for these types of shrines rather than any real temporal trend. If, as seems likely, many ex voto and devotional shrines die out as pilgrimage centers after a few centuries and are replaced by new shrines of a similar type in the same regions, this origin type inevitably becomes proportionally more numerous among recently established shrines than among surviving shrines of earlier periods. Christian's (1972) study of religion in a northern Spanish valley provides insights into this process. Stories of shrines established for purely devotional reasons are somewhat more frequently found in Latin America than in Europe. In both regions, most shrines with such stories were established fairly recently, perhaps reflecting a modern tendency to encourage pilgrimages not associated with miracles or other unusual events.

Shrines classified as "significant sites" are considerably less common in Latin America than in Europe. These shrines are defined as places related to sites of events in the lives of saints or some episode in the development of the history of the religion. A sizable proportion of such shrines in Europe were established before the end of the eleventh century. There has been a proportional rise in shrines of this type during the past century as a result of an increased European emphasis on saints of the past few centuries and the establishment or recreation of pilgrimages at many old churches and monastic centers in areas which were long exclusively

Protestant. The fact that Latin America has relatively few canonized saints, perhaps combined with a lack of information on the whereabouts of the probably numerous folk shrines devoted to famous healers of the past century, could explain the low frequency of this origin type in the New World.

It is beyond the scope of this paper to suggest all the parallels between Latin American and European pilgrimage practices and traditions. Table 2.7 outlines some of the behaviors, legends, offerings, and beliefs associated with pilgrimages in twentieth-century Western Europe. My research over the past decade has indicated that several pilgrimage-related beliefs and behaviors which I once supposed to be peculiarly Hispanic American, are common in contemporary Europe. The information presented in Table 2.7 is far from comprehensive, and it should not be assumed that a trait unlisted in the table is not found in Europe. It is also possible, of course, that similar behaviors have quite different meanings to the participants.

Table 2.7 Selected Traits Associated with European Pilgrimage

Actions	Present Concentration
Climbing sacred mountains barefoot and/or at night	Ireland and Austria
Crawling to or around the shrine on one's knees	Southern and Alpine Europe
Processions with images and relics	Pan-European
Processions in total silence	Spain and Portugal
Placing stones in piles along the pilgrimage route	Ireland, France, and Austria
Ritual use of stones, often man-placed or modified in pre-Christian times Includes lying on or sitting in stone hollows	Primarily Ireland and Austria
Use of sacred water for internal and external cures	Pan-European
Dipping cult objects in flowing water to prevent or end drought	Spain and Italy
Collecting and consuming dirt from holy graves, plaster from religious structures, paint or splinters from images, etc.	Scattered throughout Europe, but especially in Ireland and Austria
Stripping trees for talismans	Continental Western Europe
Special pilgrimages for animals	Pan-European
Sacred meaning attached to right-hand turns	Ireland (possibly elsewhere)

Actions (continued)	*Present Concentration*
Image transhumance (carried to country chapel for summer and returned to community church for winter)	Southern and Alpine Europe
Image sharing (cult object periodically taken from shrine to visit or spend time in churches on one or more other communities)	Southern Europe
Combining pilgrimage with festivals, fairs, pageants, and other secular events	General, but especially in Southern Europe
Animal sacrifice as part of pilgrimage ritual	Southern Austria as recently as the mid-20th century
Different communities make pilgrimage to the same shrine on different, specified days	Pan-European
Images dressed in elaborate costumes which are changed periodically during the year	Continental Western Europe
Images and relics kissed, rubbed, or otherwise touched	Continental Western Europe

Legends	*Present Concentration*
Object determines its place of veneration by returning to the site, usually three times	Continental Western Europe
Image is chained to the altar, or otherwise "imprisoned," but still manages to escape and return to its preferred site	Especially Austria
Image "agrees" to stay in place provided that the people perform certain rituals	Especially Austria
Object bleeds, oozes, cries, opens eyes, moves and/or changes color	Continental Western Europe
Object becomes too heavy to lift	Primarily Southern Europe
Object is brought to site by animals that refuse to go farther	Primarily Southern Europe
Animal kneels or otherwise expresses devotion to an object, usually one that was hidden at that time	Primarily Southern Europe
Deer, birds, or other wild animals indicate the holy place	Scattered throughout Western Europe
Ship carrying object cannot leave a harbor	Primarily Southern Europe
Plants bloom at the wrong time of the year or do other unusual things in association with the cult object	Pan-European
Image found in tree or an apparition occurs in a tree or forest	Continental Western Europe, especially France and Germany

Strange lights or fire mark the site where object is found	Scattered throughout Continental Western Europe
Music or voices from heaven are heard at the site	Pan-European
Water springs forth from the ground	Pan-European
Image is washed up by the sea, floats ashore on a lake, or is carried by a river	Continental Western Europe
Object does not burn in a fire	Continental Western Europe
Heavy object floats on water	Continental Western Europe
Object avenges a desecration of itself	Primarily Germanic
Object is brought by a mysterious stranger or a holy persons, such as a hermit	Continental Western Europe
Church to enshrine object is started in a settlement, but when workmen are injured, birds carry blood-stained shingles to a remote site	Primarily Austria
Footprints of a holy person are left on stone	Especially Austria, and Ireland
Image takes nocturnal walks	Southern Europe

Offerings	*Present Concentration*
Rags draped on trees, especially thorn trees, and on barbed-wire fences adjacent to a holy place	Ireland and Scotland
Flowers and other plant materials	Pan-European
Live snakes	Cocullo in the Italian Abruzzi
Devotional dances	Spain
Metal reproductions of body parts	Primarily Southern Europe
Wood reproductions of body parts	Switzerland
Wax reproductions of body parts	Primarily Portugal
Narrow candles as long as the combined height and girth of a person	Portugal
Hair	Spain, Portugal, & Italy
Jewelry, often hung on image	Southern Europe
Special garments such as wedding gowns, christening dresses, and uniforms	Primarily Southern Europe

Offerings (continued)	*Present Concentration*
Crutches, bandages, or other items no longer needed due to a cure	Pan-European
Paintings, depicting miraculous events	Scattered throughout Continental Western Europe
Marble feet and footprints of the pilgrim	Southern Europe
Marble or wooden plaques expressing thanks	France & adjacent areas
Elaborate silver hearts	Italy & Southern France
Eggs, wax, and salt	Portugal
Notes, newspaper clippings, and photos	Pan-European
Devotional prints, needlework, etc.	Scattered throughout Western Europe
Money thrown on floor of tomb or pinned to image's vestments	Iberia and Italy
Pins, nails, or coins driven into trees	Ireland and Scotland
Coins thrown into wells	Ireland and Scotland
Nails driven into wooden crosses	Germanic Alpine areas
Twigs shaped into crosses and nailed to structures, or crosses carved into the wood of structures	Germanic Alpine areas
Crosses scratched into stone of churches, or on rocks associated with a holy place	Especially common in Ireland at present
Hand prints outlined on structures	Southern Italy

A Few Popular Beliefs	*Occurrence*
Floral offering left at a shrine can be dried and used to make a curative tea.	San Damiano, near Piacenza, Italy
Anything touched by a saint, his or her bones or an image has curative powers. This may apply to water into which image or relic has been dipped.	Originally all Western European, but surviving mostly in Southern Europe
If a person does not make pilgrimage during the human lifetime, then he or she will make the journey as an insect or slug in the afterlife.	San Andres de Teixido, Spain
A holy person is visited by an image which "comes to life" and carries on conversations.	Especially Germany, Italy, & Switzerland
Waters of certain holy springs or wells have miraculous properties only at one time during the year.	Mostly Ireland, but also in Wales and Scotland
If an especially arduous pilgrimage circuit is not completed within 24 hours, the world will end.	Four Mountain Pilgrimage, Southern Austria

A Few Popular Beliefs (continued)	Occurrence
The Virgin Mary is especially manifest in the sun so that one may experience unusual things by looking at or photographing the sun.	San Damiano, Italy[1]
Black or dark images are especially miraculous.	Continental Western Europe
Stillborn infants brought to the shrine return to life long enough to receive baptism.	Primarily Alpine regions
Holy persons, while alive, could be in two places at once.	Frequently claimed for Padre Pio[2]
Different shrines and/or saints specialize in dealing with specific problems.	Pan-European

1 Possibly influenced by the miracle of the sun at Fatima in 1917.
2 An Italian Capuchin priest who died in 1967 after having the stigmata of the Crucifixion for 50 years.

SUMMARY AND CONCLUSIONS

The European roots of Latin American pilgrimage are evident in the strong similarities of the two traditions. Cult-formative types and legends are much the same on both sides of the Atlantic. Proportions of visionaries representing different ages, sex, and socio-economic groups are similar. In both areas, a tendency to focus pilgrimage cults primarily on movable objects such as relics, and especially images, combines with a lingering veneration of natural site features and a feeling for the sacred power of certain places, some of which were holy before the advent of Christianity. Stories of images, visions, and apparitions which indicated the sites where a shrine should be established were common in Europe centuries before the American discoveries, and were repeated as Christian pilgrimage developed in the New World.

The Virgin Mary is the primary subject of devotion at a majority of shrines in both regions. However, Latin America does differ from Europe in having a higher percentage of shrines dedicated to Christ. Comparatively high proportions of dark Christ images, and concentration of Christ cults at shrines traditionally visited by Amerindians support case study claims of relationships between some Christ cults and pre-Columbian survivals. On the other hand, there is ample evidence that development of pilgrimages around miraculous Christ images reached higher than usual levels in Iberia and Germany during the colonial contact period. Therefore, the Latin American emphasis on Christ can also be explained as the overseas transplantation of a European pilgrimage fashion of the times.

I have not found much evidence for large-scale continuity of pre-Columbian pilgrimage expressions that are alien to the European tradition. This suggests a model based on the concept of *permissibility of the familiar*. The model assumes acceptance, if not encouragement, of whatever practices Christian missionaries and/or subsequent authorities found to be sufficiently familiar as to be tolerated, combined with efforts to suppress or eradicate patterns which were unfamiliar, or in a few cases, such as human sacrifice, unacceptable although known from the European pagan past. For example, pilgrimage rituals in Mesoamerica included human sacrifice, drawing blood from body parts, especially the tongue, offering dances as acts of devotion, processing up sacred hills, and attributing special powers to *black* deities. So far as I know, neither human sacrifice nor tongue piercing are practiced as pilgrim rituals in modern Mexico, nor are such practices found in Europe. In contrast, the dance as a shrine offering, pilgrimage processions up holy mountains, and special powers attributed to black images remain quite common in Mexico and are still found in Europe, where such things were part of the pilgrimage system long before the discovery of the Americas.

The *permissibility of the familiar* model makes ample allowance for a policy of Christianizing indigenous pilgrimage sites, sanctifying site features in the introduced tradition, and assigning tasks of specialized deities to saints. These were time-honored strategies for the conversion of pagan Europe and, as suggested by Christian (1981a:91), were still going on in a modified form during the Middle Ages. In fact, the use of cult establishment and pilgrimage as a means of conversion or reorientation of popular religious practices never ceased. New cults were created or fostered by Counter-Reformation strategists to stem the tide of Protestantism in France and Germany even as other European clerics were sponsoring the formation of Christian pilgrimages in the Americas. Official encouragement of nineteenth-century French apparitional cults, as at La Salette and Lourdes, has been interpreted as a response to the perceived threats of secularism and socialism (Kselman 1978). Today, shrine administrators ponder the problem of how to use the artistic or historical drawing power of great shrine churches to transform tourists into pilgrims, and modern transportation and communications technologies are incorporated into constantly changing pilgrimage traditions.

Modern technology and ancient legends sometimes combine in curious ways as new pilgrimage centers emerge. During the late 1950s a Spanish nun wandering about with a statue of the infant Christ was inspired to end her peregrinations on a hill near the hamlet of Collevalenza in central Italy. As pilgrims sometimes tell the story, the Christ Child image often "came to life" at night and visited with the nun in the kitchen where she stayed up late preparing food for the few other nuns with her. The other nuns could always tell when the image had paid a nocturnal visit because it took off its bootees in order to tiptoe barefoot to the meetings. One night, at

Collevalenza, the Christ Child told the nun to order the drilling of a well from the top of the hill. With the aid of a few contributions and a modern drilling rig and crew, the well was sunk deep into the bowels of the hill. As in the most ancient cult formative legends, water poured forth, crystalline, pure, and curative. As befits a twentieth-century tale, its rich mineral content was soon pronounced "therapeutic" in the modern scientific-medical sense of the term. A hospital complex developed around the growing shrine. Because the cancer remission rate is said to be unusually high at this shrine-treatment center, even nonbelievers come, and some are converted or reawakened in their traditional religious faith. Collevalenza, with its publications in six languages, does not advertise its more mystic traditions centered upon its founder's visions or the miraculous Christ Child image. It also has impeccable credentials as a new, but proper, place of pilgrimage and was the first place visited by Pope John Paul II after the 1981 attempt on his life.

At Collevalenza, we find one case of a growing syncretism between pilgrimage as an ancient tradition and pilgrimage on the cutting edge of the conflict between our modern trust in scientifically spawned technology and our need for faith when technology fails to solve our problems. The Western European pilgrimage tradition evolved and continues to develop by means of its flexibility and power continually to create new syncretisms.

In this context, Latin America provided another non-Christian base on which to erect the Catholic pilgrimage structure. That many aspects of the pre-Columbian root stock remained relatively unchanged is not surprising. It reflects implementation of a policy that had worked for over 1,000 years in Western Europe. In a sense, Catholic encouragement or at least toleration of indigenous beliefs sufficiently familiar to be acceptable, placed New World pilgrimage expression more fully in the European mainstream than might otherwise have been the case.

Throughout the development of Christian pilgrimage, what was acceptable from a root tradition was preempted. Thus, ancient holy places and acceptable behaviors associated with them have become part of the Christian tradition. Indeed, the more completely pagan origins are acknowledged, the more Christian the ancient phenomena become because they symbolize the triumph of the new religion in a special way. In addition, when much continuity of belief and practice is allowed, the development of underground traditions is, perhaps, less likely.

The relative importance of pre-Columbian influences on contemporary Latin American pilgrimages undoubtedly varies from region to region and from shrine to shrine within given areas. I would expect to find the greatest perseverance of uniquely or preponderantly pre-Columbian beliefs and practices in those parts of Latin America where, due to difficulty of access, lack of European interest in local resources, or other factors, the introduction of Christianity was relegated to a smashing of idols without adequate substitution of new shrines in or near the old holy places. Regions with substantial indigenous populations left for long periods of time without clerical guidance might also be areas where old, possibly reinterpreted, traditions might have resurfaced in spite of intensive early mission efforts. In the European context, Ireland provides a case of reversion to an extremely archaic pilgrimage system as the result of several centuries of Protestant British repression and consequent lack of input from the evolving tradition of continental Europe (Nolan 1983).

In regions where dense pre-Columbian populations subscribed to the sophisticated theologies of their urban-based civilizations, and which attracted European settlers, I would expect to find shrines, such as Guadalupe in Mexico, with pre-Columbian sanctity built into the pilgrimage mystique. Acclamation of pre-Christian origins for pilgrimage places probably reflects an ideological propensity with a very uneven history. It is certainly in an ascendant phase in contemporary Europe, where an emphasis on folk traditions is in vogue. I would suspect that emphasis on pre-Christian origins is also fashionable in the Americas, where many people are seeking to define their indigenous national identities.

In places such as Argentina, southern Brazil, and parts of Chile, where the population is not only predominantly of European origin but largely reflects nineteenth and twentieth century immigration from Europe, I would expect little, if any, input of pre-Columbian traits into the contemporary pilgrimage system. Interestingly, much contemporary pilgrimage in the Brazilian diocese of Eparquia, in Parana, reflects the Byzantine Rite traditions of the large Ukrainian population.

My general conclusion is that Latin American pilgrimages surviving from the colonial period are best viewed as an overseas extension of the great Catholic-Reformation pilgrimage cult florescence of Western Europe. As such, they do not reflect a simple transfer of medieval Iberian traditions to the Americas, nor can they be interpreted purely in terms of diffusion from sixteenth through eighteenth-century Iberia. The Catholic-Reformation cult-formative period was most fully expressed in Germanic lands, where apparently certain kinds of folk cults were less subjected to repression than was the case in Spain during the period in question. There is evidence for direct Germanic and Italian contacts in the American mission fields, as well as for interchange of ideas about pilgrimages and cult formations along an Ibero-Germanic-Italian axis. Indeed, Christian (1981b:221) presents evidence indicating that some of the devotional styles which became manifest in late medieval and Renaissance Spain were common much earlier in Italian and Germanic regions. Obviously, a Latin American pilgrimage trait that does not seem to be typical of medieval Iberia is not necessarily American in origin. It could be characteristic of Baroque era Germanic traditions.

A more substantial body of information on Latin American pilgrimage is needed to develop more extensive quantitative comparisons with the European tradition. Identification of regional variations within Latin

America will also become more feasible with the collection of additional data. Interpretation of specific Latin American pilgrimages or pilgrimage regions calls for investigation of any pre-Columbian traditions that may be relevant to the site or region in question. It also requires knowledge about the ethnic backgrounds of Europeans involved in the cult-formative process, and later promotion of cults. Examination of concurrent events in appropriate parts of Europe is important. This approach should lead toward better understanding of colonial period syncretism. As this is accomplished, more scholarly attention should be turned toward the fascinating problem of a new syncretism of older religious traditions and modernism which is now occurring on both sides of the Atlantic. Detailed examination of pilgrimages currently being created would be useful for gaining insight into cult-formative processes. Other important themes for future research include examination of ways in which pilgrimage cults adapt to changing socioeconomic and political conditions, processes whereby innovations diffuse from shrine to shrine, and regional variations in the functions of pilgrimage as a means of coping with environmental stress and uncertainty. Exploration of the latter theme has already provided insights into the perception of environmental threats in Europe (Nolan 1978, 1989). Climatic differences between Europe and Latin America, including reversal of temperate zone seasons in southern South America, offer excellent possibilities for testing the hypothesis that the pilgrimage cycle is related to the agricultural year (Nolan 1979).

Finally, a more comprehensive understanding of Latin American pilgrimage would be useful for scholars primarily concerned with the contemporary European tradition. Diffusion routes typically carry innovations in both directions. Although I have not found much evidence for an extensive pilgrimage-related transfer of ideas from the Americas to Europe, diffusion from the Americas may be more pervasive than it appears to be on the surface. Careful studies of American shrines, such as by Straub in Chapter 9, may eventually reveal traits present on both sides of the Atlantic, but of essentially American origin.

NOTES

Acknowledgements. This study was made possible by grants from the Oregon State University College of Liberal Arts Research Program and the Oregon State University Foundation, contracts from Educational Filmstrips Company of Huntsville, Texas, and a research grant from the National Endowment for the Humanities (Grant #1081-80). Sidney D. Nolan Jr., co-investigator on the N.E.H. grant, has shared all field investigations and has provided substantial assistance in the preparation of this article.

1. Representative works include those by Adair (1978), Antier (1979), Couturier de Chefdubois (1953), Christian (1976), Colangeli (1977), Consejo Superior de Investigaciones Científicas (1978), Dorn (1975), Fischer and Stoll (1977-79), Gabrielli (1949), Gugitz (1956-58), Henggeler (1968), Hole (1954), Ladame (1980), Lustenberger (1978), Manfredi (1954), Mould (1955), Rosenegger and Bartl (1980), Schaffer and Peda (1978), Staercke (1954), and Vinciotti

(1960).

2. See Argentina (n.d.), Brooks (1980), Cassidy (1958), Comision National Corrdinadora de Santuarios de Chile (1977-79), Crumrine (1977b, 1978), García Huidobro (1978), Gonzalez and van Ronzelen (1983), Gross (1971), Hoyt (1963), Manfredi (1954), Marzal (1983), Mexican Government Tourism Department (1968), Paredes Candia (1974), Smith (1963), Toor (1947), and Vargas Ugarte (1956).

3. See Barragán (1985), Besen (1977), Brustoloni (1982), Casillas (1974), Carrillo Dueñas (1975), Coordenação Diocesana de Pastoral de Turismo do São Paula (1976), Demarest and Taylor (1956), Demonte de Torres (1980), Elias (1981), Enriquez (1984), Fontenelle (1970), Fuentes Aguirre (1978), Kocik (1982), Machado (1981), Meza (1973), Medina Villegas (1971), Nava Rodriguez (1975), Ochoa (1961), Ojeda Sanchez (1973), Paz Soldan (1985), Pélach y Feliu (1972), Polaco Brito (1979, 1984), Presas (1961), Ramirez (1968), Ribeiro Filho (1977), Serracino Calamata (n.d.), Smith (1979), Palacios (1980), Tonna (1983), Toranzos (n.d.), Vargas (1976), Zambrano Palacios (1978), Zavala (1972), and Zavala Paz (1965).

4. Editor's note. Recently, Crumrine accompanied some of his Mayo friends in a visit to a new shelter chapel just north of the Mayo valley, which covers an "image of Guadalupe." When one stands with the light just right the figure can be seen in a window pane apparently similar to this appearance of Guadalupe at Limon, Tamaulipas. See also Crumrine (1975).

REFERENCES

Adair 1978
Antier 1979
Argentina n.d.
Barragán 1985
Besen 1977
Billet 1976
Brooks 1980
Brown 1981
Brustoloni 1982
Carrillo Duenas 1975
Casillas 1974
Cassidy 1958
Christian 1972, 1976,
   1981a, 1981b, 1985
Colangeli 1977
Comision National Coordinadora
   de Santuarios 1977
Consejo Superior de
   Invest. Cientificas 1978
Coordenacao Diocesana de
   Pastoral de Turismo 1979
Costa Clavell 1980
Cousin 1981
Couturier de Chefdubois 1953
Crumrine 1975, 1977b, 1978
Demarest-eds. 1956
Demonte de Torres 1980
Dorn 1975
Durand-Lefebvre 1937
Elias 1981

Enriquez 1984
Fischer-Stoll 1977
Fontenelle 1970
Forsyth 1972
Fuentes Aguirre 1978
Gabrielli 1949
Garcia Huidobro 1978
Gillet 1949
Gonzalez-Ronzelen 1983
Gross 1971
Gugitz 1956
Hartinger 1984, 1984
Henggeler 1968
Hole 1954
Hoyt 1963
Kay 1977
Kocik 1982
Kolb 1976, 1980
Kselman 1978
Ladame 1980
Lazzarini 1980
Laurentin and Rupcic 1984
Lefeuvre 1980
Leroy 1984
Lustenberger 1978
Machado 1981
Male 1978
Manfredi 1954
Marzal 1983
Medina Villegas 1971

Mexican Government Tourism
  Department 1968
Meza 1973
Moss-Cappannari 1982
Mould 1955
Nava 1975
Neumann 1972
Nolan 1967, 1972, 1973,
  1978, 1979, 1983, 1989
Ochoa 1961
Ojeda Sanchez 1973
Palacios 1980
Paredes Candia 1974
Paz 1985
Pelach y Feliu 1972
Perez Martin del Campo 1969
Polaco Brito 1979, 1984
Pötzl 1984
Presas 1961
Ramirez 1968

Ribeiro Filho 1977
Rossenegger-Bartl 1980
Rothkrug 1979, 1980
Schaffer-Peda 1978
Serracino Calamata n.d.
Sharbrough 1977
Smith 1979
Staercke 1954
Sumption 1975
Taylor 1979
Tonna 1983
Toor 1947
Toranzo n.d.
Turner-Turner 1978
Vargas 1976
Vargas Ugarte 1956
Vinciotti 1960
Zambrano Palacios 1978
Zavala 1972
Zavala Paz 1965

II
MIDDLE AMERICA

3

Do-It-Yourself Religion:
The Diffusion of Folk Catholicism
on Mexico's Northern Frontier 1821-46

HENRY F. DOBYNS

Historians, anthropologists, and sociologists all may on occasion consult historical documents in order to examine the dynamics of cultural stability or change. Scholars trained in these disciplines can analyze more or less the same series of events, yet arrive at rather different conclusions as to their causes because their analytical concepts differ.[1] Scholars in these disciplines also may identify different causes of change because their diverse orientations prompt them to consult different sources of information. Different sources can not only describe the same events distinctly, but also refer to other events pertinent to an accurate analysis.

These methodological considerations arise in the interpretation of the situation of the Roman Catholic Church in Mexico's frontier provinces during the period from national independence in 1821 until United States forces invaded in 1846. Many missions that the Spanish government had subsidized were secularized, thus shifting responsibility for ministering to members of their congregations and making new converts. "Secular" or parish-supported curates under the full authority of diocesan bishops assumed the responsibility for people formerly ministered to by *regular* priests. The latter belonged to religious orders, such as the Order of Friars Minor, living according to rules and answering to their own provincials as well as to bishops. Describing the secularized church in the north Mexican states up until the United States went to war with Mexico in 1846, historian David J. Weber discussed the "Failure of a Frontier Institution" (Weber 1981:125). The present essay takes Weber's exposition as representative of analyses by professional historians in order to explore the methodological issues mentioned above. Weber asserted that when the United States "swept to the Pacific," its citizens "found the Catholic Church on the Mexican frontier in shambles." Weber's analysis falls into a well-established historical genre of Spanish borderlands studies. He consulted sources with which he and other historians are familiar.

The present disquisition argues that the Church as a religious institution changed during the 1821-46 period on the Mexican northern frontier. In fact, more persons belonging to more ethnic groups considered themselves practicing Christians in 1846 than in 1821. Thus the failure that Weber perceived was not real in demographic terms. This conclusion can be reached by employing different perspectives and consulting sources other than those Weber used.

Weber's essay constitutes a good example of an historian's concentration on a series of events that occur in a limited period of time and a restricted geographic area. Social scientists often employ a comparative analytical model. That is, they identify change by comparing like events that happen in various areas at more or less the same time. Alternatively, they compare like events occurring in an ethnic group at different times (Eggan 1954:743-63). By illustrating this comparative approach, one throws a different light upon facts Weber cited to support his thesis.

Weber took a real shortage of secular priests and long delays in appointing bishops as part of the proof of institutional failure. One familiar with contemporary and recent problems of *deficient* vocations to the clergy throughout Latin America perceives the desirability for illuminating comparison. The dearth of vocations to the clergy during the 1821-46 period compares with a relative dearth in recent decades throughout Spanish-speaking America. There is in the twentieth century a widespread shortage of priests.[2] The very first sentence in one sociological study of this "priestly problem" in Latin America clearly poses the issue. "It is an enigma for anyone who assumes that Latin America is a Catholic continent, that the Latin Americans are not giving priests in numbers proportional to their population" (Laballa 1964:9).[3]

Were an anticlerical government to take power in Peru tomorrow and expel foreign-born clergymen, the Church there would be plunged into much the same desperate straits as the Mexican Church was after the republican expulsion of Spanish priests in 1828. Expelling regular clerics would leave scores of urban and many rural parishes without priests. There simply are not enough secular clergy to staff all extant parishes.[4] Comparison reveals that Weber's thesis is regionalist and cannot be sustained.

The north Mexican frontier is too small an area to reveal without comparative analysis that ecclesiastical behavior there followed a general pattern of postcolonial Church social structure in former Ibero-America. Weber interpreted as a special temporal-geographic case what is actually only a regional manifestation of a continent-wide postcolonial process. The shortage of priests that Weber described in north Mexican states was a local expression of the crisis that independence and subsequent departure of Iberian clerics precipitated all over Ibero-America.[5] What was not restricted to the frontier zone neither explains nor can be explained by that small geographic zone.

A scarcity of cities in northern Mexico may have misled Weber with regard to another basic characteristic of the Church crucial to his thesis. The colonial Church in New Spain had been precisely what it was in colonial Peru and continued to be in nineteenth and twentieth-century Peru and Mexico. The Church is first and foremost an urban institution. Cardinals, archbishops, bishops, and diocesan clerics live and work in cities.[6] Weber almost recognized this inherent characteristic of the secular Church. He contrasted the over 1,000 priests who served the single city of Puebla at the beginning of the nineteenth century with the fewer than 80 in the northernmost provinces of California, New Mexico, and Texas.[7] Falling just short of explicit recognition of the fundamentally urban nature of the secular church, Weber considered the reluctance of several bishops of Sonora to reside in Arizpe as part of institutional failure. Urban residence was not an episcopal behavior restricted to the north Mexican frontier as a limited geographic perspective implies. Episcopal preference for more urban settlements expressed a fundamental cultural pattern of Iberian and derivative Latin American Catholic-ism.[8] The problem with Arizpe was less that it lay near a frontier than that it was essentially rural.[9] The cultural urbanism of the secular Church's personnel compounded the problem of lack of vocations by keeping small the number of priests and bishops living near the national frontier.[10]

Pointing out that the secular Roman Catholic Church was basically an urban institution that was never designed to function as a proselytizing frontier institution raises a question about Weberian interpretation. Comparative analysis only allows one to question Weber's claim that the secular Church was a "shambles" on the north Mexican frontier by 1846. Dramatic evidence of thoroughgoing penetration of Christianity among residents of northern Mexico between 1821 and 1846 is to be found in information that Weber did not utilize. During that period, a significant expansion in the number of Native American Christians and a northward extension of the true rim of Christendom occurred.

Liberal or at least anticlerical national governments curtailed Church power during the nineteenth century. The revolutionary 1917 constitution of Mexico contains distinctly anticlerical clauses. What is extraordinary about northern Mexico is, therefore, not that the institution lacks manpower and appears structurally weak, but that the populace is predominately Roman Catholic![11] The Catholic form of Christianity is part and parcel of the culture of modern Mexicans. It is so fundamental that a sociologist can utilize behaviors such as choice of ritual kinsmen to measure changes among rural villagers toward national urban norms (Kunkel 1961:51-63).

The cultural Catholicism of northern Mexicans is no less than that of central Mexicans. The descriptions of New Mexico and other northern states that Protestants published on the basis of their Mexican War experiences indicate that Catholicism had been firmly established throughout the frontier zone by 1846.[12] Despite an obvious shortage of personnel, the secular Church achieved its goal of converting pagans between 1821 and 1846.

What really happened in the northern states can be clarified by distinguishing between "formal" and "folk" Catholics. This is not simply a difference between urban and rural residents. The anthropologist Allen Spitzer drew this distinction after studying different behaviors among two ethnic groups in Mérida, capital city of the Mexican state of Yucatán. The formal Catholics are Spanish-speaking urbanites who attend Mass regularly, belong to Church-sponsored sodalities, and interact frequently with the parish priests. The folk Catholics in Mérida are as often as not Mayan-speakers who hear Mass infrequently but merrily celebrate family festivals at their homes (Spitzer 1958:1-20).

Both types of Catholics live in the north Mexican states today, and did in 1846. To resort to the vernacular, folk Catholics are *do-it-yourself* religionists. The New Mexican Penitentes represent this type of Catholic. The scarcity of ordained secular clerics in New Mexico allowed devout folk Catholics to seize a degree of initiative in religious affairs that was not possible where elitist, authoritarian ecclesiastics abounded. The result was not any failure of faith, but an intensification of both public and private devotion within the broad cultural norms of the denomination (Chavez 1954:97-123).

Because of its very *do-it-yourself* characteristics, and the diversity of ethnic groups inhabiting the north Mexican states, folk Catholicism is not uniform throughout the region. The New Mexican Penitente movement was but one local devotee solution to the scarcity of priests. So Weber's comments on the Penitentes illustrate the necessity for analyzing local historical events in an appropriate comparative perspective in order to interpret them correctly.[13] There is good evidence outside New Mexico that the handful of secular priests and their Church did not fail to further their faith between 1821 and 1846.

I will not attempt to describe all of the local folk Catholic movements in the north Mexican states, but for the sake of brevity and clarity will select illustrative ethnic groups and religious movements in the western frontier state of Sonora. In this area, Christianity spread far among northern Piman-speaking Native Americans between 1821 and 1846, for another half-century without missionaries after 1841, and at times with only two parish priests at the southern edge of Piman aboriginal territory.

The northern Pimans are the peoples among whom the Jesuit pioneer missionary Eusebio F. Kino initiated his missionary activity (Kino 1919:1-19). After Kino died in 1711, the effective rim of Christendom stalled almost where he left it. That was on the Concepción-Altar, Magdalena, San Miguel, and Sonora rivers flowing south and west into the Gulf of California. Later Jesuits advanced northward to the upper Santa Cruz and San Pedro Rivers flowing north into the Gila River. Franciscans who replaced the expelled Jesuits in 1768 did not move the mission frontier north beyond Jesuit-founded San Francisco Xavier del Bac on the Santa Cruz River. About 1810, Friar Juan Bautista Llorens did found one visitation station farther northwest called Santa Ana de Cuiquiburitac (Fontana 1987:133-59). The limit of Christendom remained in 1821 only at the southern and eastern edges of northern Piman country.

One major reason why the frontier stalled was both cultural and environmental. Most northern Piman territory is arid Sonoran desert lacking surface-flowing streams. The colonial Spaniards differentiated the desert as the Papaguería and its native inhabitants became known as Papagos. In their own Piman language, they term themselves the "desert people" (Joseph, Spicer, and Chesky 1949). Spaniards and Jesuit missionaries from elsewhere in Europe never changed their woodlands culture to cope effectively with the desert. Thus the Spanish colonial missionary program could and did operate only in riverine oases where irrigation could produce crop surpluses. All of the so-called "Kino Missions" were located within a ribbon-shaped riverine oasis in the valley of one of the permanent surface-flowing streams along the southern or eastern margin of the Papaguería (Fontana 1983:137).

Exploratory journeys across the Papaguería by Kino and Friar Francisco Garcés did not accomplish significant conversion. Yet, when United States Protestant and later Roman Catholic missionaries began to proselytize among Desert People in the late nineteenth and early twentieth centuries, they discovered that the natives were devout folk Catholics. Small family religious chapels stood in many Papaguerían hamlets. Although people were poor, devout families managed to furnish their hand-made chapels and household altars with a few cheap religious prints from Europe and statues of favorite saints (Joseph, Spicer, and Chesky 1949:80-81). Devout women ritual leaders recited the rosary in Spanish and led hymns sung in that foreign language. Some did so from memory while others followed their notes written in cheap ruled notebooks (Dobyns 1960). Folk Catholicism spread to the Desert People after the collapse of the Franciscan missions in the wake of Mexico's 1828 expulsion of Spanish clerics and prior to the initiation of modern missionary efforts by United States clergymen. That diffusion of Christianity throughout the Papago population and even to the Gila River Pimas refutes the Weberian thesis that the Roman Catholic Church failed on Mexico's entire northern frontier.

The socioreligious mechanism that spread folk Catholicism among unmissionized northern Piman-speakers was a pilgrimage festival. Many shrines attract Christian pilgrims in the Old and New Worlds. The image of St. Francis Xavier in the parish church in Magdalena de Kino, Sonora, Mexico, draws pilgrims from as far south as Guadalajara, as far west as Los Angeles, and as far east as the Sierra Madre Occidental. This pilgrimage provided an elitist secular clergy with an effective means for bridging the gap between urbanites and rural folk by maximizing the impact of a single parish priest ministering to scattered thousands of parishioners, particularly unmissionized Piman-speakers. Since World War II, thousands of Papago pilgrims have participated in every annual festival of St. Francis Xavier. Paradoxically, this festival is observed on the day of St. Francisco of Assisi, October 4th (Dobyns 1950:28).[14] The scale and style of the pilgrimage have changed dramatically since it began.

During the 1821-46 period, only men made the long pilgrimage from Papaguerían home villages to Magdalena. After 1825, Apache raiders posed a threat to pilgrims, although most Desert People traveled along interior trails little exposed to hostile Apaches. The social structure of pilgrimage from Kaka, a village near the northern edge of the contemporary Papago Indian Reservation, reflects the transition from indigenous to Great Religious Tradition. A hunt leader known as *taupatam* organized communal jackrabbit hunts on foot or horseback. During the earliest period of pilgrimage from Kaka to Magdalena, a leader just like a *taupatam* organized and led the pilgrimage. People called him *ooks chukam*, a new term for a new social role. He sent word to the River People on the middle Gila, who responded by specifying how many horses the Kaka people were to reserve for them to ride to Magdalena. The *ooks chukam* could "talk" to the pilgrims when they encamped for the night en route.

Later, women joined the pilgrimage, riding horseback like the men. This horseback pilgrimage from Kaka required three days of riding and four overnight encampments. Like all devout pilgrims, the Kaka Papagos visited the image of St. Francis immediately upon arriving in Magdalena. Then they made such purchases as their slender purses permitted. When they had bought what they wanted and could afford, they returned to the parish church to see the image "and tell him they're going home." Timing their arrival for the morning, Kaka pilgrims would be in the saddle again northbound by late afternoon.[15] Thus, they spent one week on pilgrimage.

Papaguerían pilgrims began riding four-wheeled wagons during the 1880s, soon after the Southern Pacific Railroad laid tracks across the northern portion of their territory. Gradually, the Desert People cleared and "built" dirt wagon roads (Bliss 1952:23-32; Cosulich, 1939:1, 7). The United States negotiated peace with Western Apaches in 1871 and 1872 after the Pima-Maricopa Confederation army joined United States troops in numerous effective campaigns (Dobyns 1986). The *Pax Americana* and the acquisition of numerous wagons helped to transform the pilgrimage to

Magdalena into more of a family affair than it had been. Children traveled with their parents on the lumbering white canvas-covered wagons rolling into Magdalena early every October. Wagon-borne pilgrims also began staying overnight in Magdalena, affording greater opportunities for them to learn additional details of folk Catholicism.

Horse-drawn wagons survived World War II by only a few years. During that conflict, cotton growers in southern Arizona desperately needed pickers after aircraft factories hired former migrant workers. Growers recruited interned Japanese and Japanese-Americans and Native Americans (Spicer 1952:41-54). The Magdalena pilgrimage period falls in the midst of cotton harvest. In 1942, 1943, and 1944, growers discovered that the best way to shorten the pilgrimage was to furnish workers with motorized transportation. Many farmers took their pickers to Magdalena on their flatbed trucks, in spite of thin tires and gasoline rationing (Dobyns 1951b:86-95). Even though mechanical cotton pickers soon displaced nearly all hand harvesters, hundreds of Desert People left their reservations more or less permanently to work on riverine oasis farms in such positions as irrigators, and tractor drivers. In the wake of this and other changes in the Desert People's economy, today most of them drive their own pickup trucks or automobiles over paved highways from all parts of the Papaguería to Magdalena (Dobyns 1950).

The details of the origin and development of the regional cult of St. Francis at Magdalena are not all known. Enough information is available, however, to make clear that the period 1821-46 was the crucial time span in its emergence. Comparative microhistory reveals the chronology of key events. Franciscan missionaries built the so-called "Kino Mission" church buildings late in Spanish colonial times. Friar Juan Bautista Llorens supervised completion of the Va:k mission church, except for a missing dome over one tower, in 1797 (Dobyns 1976:41). Ramon Liberós saw the Tumacacori church nearly finished, lacking bell tower and mortuary chapel roof, before his 1828 expulsion (Kessell 1976:271). Cash from the sale of hundreds of mission cattle financed the Tumacacori construction. Va:k and Tumacacori were the only missions in the Santa Cruz River Valley east of the Papaguería.

The other "Kino" missions were located in riverine oasis south of the Papaguería. The western flank of the chain, the Caborca mission church, was completed in 1809 (Roca 1967:120). Up the Río Altar to the east, the Pitiquito chapel was completed prior to 1786, although it has been remodeled several times (Roca 1967:117). Farther upstream, Franciscans finished their church of Saints Peter and Paul at Tubutama certainly by 1786 and possibly a decade earlier (Roca 1967:106). Near the headwaters, the Franciscans built a new brick church at Saric prior to 1788 (Roca 1967:97).

On the Río Magdalena, Friar Francisco Zúñiga built a vaulted-roof brick church at Mission San Ignacio de Caburica between 1772 and 1780 (Roca 1967:61). At that time, Magdalena was still only a visitation station of San

Ignacio Mission. The latter had become the residence of the friar elected Father President of the Pimería Alta missions. Juan Vaño moved there from Va:k when elected to the post in 1824 (Kessell 1976:259). Captain Pedro Villaescusa delivered the Mexican government's expulsion order to Vaño at San Ignacio during Holy Week in 1828 (Kessell 1976:270). Then Friar José María Pérez Llera became Father President, headquartered at San Ignacio but spending much of his time in the saddle visiting other settlements. The people at Caborca did not allow government officials to expel their gruff, ailing Spanish priest, Friar Faustino Gonzalez. Rafael Díaz ministered to the Santa Cruz River Valley military posts from Cocospera Mission. Juan Maldonado served at Tubutama (Kessell 1976:280).

A few such Creole Franciscans continued ministering to the peoples of Pimería Alta until 1841, as Weber recognized (Weber 1981:125). What he did not mention is Pérez Llera's brick-and-mortar triumph at St. Mary Magdalene. In stark refutation of Weber's thesis of institutional failure, Pérez Llera financed the erection of a new and relatively capacious church in the Magdalena visitation station. He dedicated the new temple in 1832, only four years after Mexico expelled most of its Spanish priests (Dobyns 1960:390). Then Pérez Llera built three additional rooms at Magdalena hoping to start a school if he could obtain more missionaries. In 1833, Pérez Llera traveled to the Franciscan order's College of the Holy Cross in Querétaro seeking reinforcements and obtained two missionaries (Kessell 1976:292). Pérez Llera's church at Magdalena is all the more noteworthy because the Mexican government had for years not paid missionaries the stipends they had received from the Spanish crown. The gifts pilgrims dropped into the metal strongbox at the head of the image of St. Francis lying on its catafalque were almost the only source of funds that Pérez Llera could have used to pay the contractor and his construction crews. Some wealthy and devout Creole or Mestizo cattle ranchers may have contributed to the church construction fund, but such people were not noted for their philanthropy at that time and in that place.

The date when Pérez Llera's Magdalena church was completed is rather conclusive proof that the pilgrimage of St. Francis Xavier had already grown financially to very significant proportions. There are other clues that the pilgrimage steadily gained folk Catholic adherents during the years between Mexican independence and the U.S.-Mexican war. In 1801, the San Ignacio Mission reported only 502 inhabitants, with "citizens" outnumbering Native Americans nearly four to one (Dobyns 1960:95). Immigration into the Magdalena River Valley during the peaceful late colonial years increased the population of San Ignacio, Magdalena, and five other settlements to just over 1,500 persons on the eve of independence. Magdalena alone reached that size shortly after the Mexican War (Dobyns 1960:94). Consequently, government officials in 1843 reclassified the growing settlement as a town, and in 1862 upgraded it to a *villa*. Magdalena achieved official status as a city in 1923 (Dobyns 1960:93).

At least some Magdalena immigrants perceived economic opportunities in the religious pilgrimage and organized a complex commercial fair running concurrently with the religious festival. By mid-nineteenth century, the fair was a fully developed ten-day enterprise of no small magnitude. United States Boundary Commissioner John R. Bartlett reported that "thousands" of pilgrims flocked to Magdalena in 1851 (Bartlett 1854:425). A significant pattern of comparison appears in foreigners' descriptions of the fair and festival in which these visitors compared the apogee of Magdalena's annual economic round to the most urban and urbane cities in their own countries! No doubt the ultimate accolade was bestowed by a Frenchman:

> Over all these food-dishes fluttered a multitude of little paper banners painted with all tints, which enhanced their air of display, and the pyramids of flowers cut with the vegetables, which would not have dishonored the Parisian taste, enhanced the symmetry of the women vendors. (de Lambertie 1955:57)

A Yankee wrote that the booths "on every side of the plaza, and along the principal streets" seemed to him "much like those which it was customary to erect in New York on the Fourth of July" (Bartlett 1854:428). If the bustling annual fair at Magdalena reminded sophisticated Americans and Frenchmen of their major cities, it must have indelibly impressed the Desert People riding in from scores of desert hamlets such as Kaka.

This is not the place to attempt to describe in detail the total impact of the St. Francis pilgrimage on either Magdalena or the various ethnic groups participating in it. Enough has been said to indicate that the vitality of this regional pilgrimage and its contribution to the conversion of northern Piman-speaking peoples between 1821 and 1846 refutes Weber's thesis of secular Church failure. To say no more would be to fall into the same methodological error as Weber, that is, failing to perceive the multi-institutional and indeed multicultural context of what really did occur in the north Mexican states between 1821 and 1846. To comprehend correctly the weakness or strength of the Roman Catholic Church in that region during that period, one must recognize that it fared little better or worse than other institutions in the same region at that time.

Pioneer historian Herbert E. Bolton noted that the mission system in Spanish Florida and from Texas to California developed in close conjunction with royal military posts (Bolton 1917:51-54). The latter, however, did not fare well under postcolonial Creole management. To be sure, Mexican troops engaged in a burst of active campaigning on the northern frontier immediately after independence. At the western end of the frontier, a Lower Californian missionary arrived in 1823 at the Sonoran frontier post of Tucson. With Native American guides, he had found a Lower Colorado River crossing not interdicted by the Quechan after their 1781 destruction of Spanish settlements. Tucson commandant José Romero then blundered about southern California for almost three years before he followed a Cocomaricopa guide back across the Colorado River toward Tucson (Bean and Mason 1962). Meanwhile, General José S. Figueroa y Parra became Commanding Inspector General of the new state of Occidente. Figueroa arrived in Arizpe early in the summer of 1825. He set out that October with a force of 400 men to investigate reports of gold mines near the Gila and Colorado Rivers. Messengers with news of a Yaqui revolt reached Figueroa when he was near the confluence of the rivers, so he turned back to negotiate with Yaqui and Mayo leaders in southern Sonora (Hutchinson 1973:285-88).

Mexican interest in reopening overland communication between Sonora and Alta California stimulated Cocomaricopas to act as couriers between the two states (Ezell 1968). Figueroa's probe constituted the high-water mark of Mexican military activity on the Pimería Alta frontier of western Sonora. The military posts survived, but garrison efficiency declined. In 1830, Captain Antonio Comaduran at Tucson could lead an effective cavalry-infantry-peaceful Apache scouting foray into the heart of Apachería (Dobyns 1981:15-26). By 1842, Comaduran suffered the acute embarrassment of having a "large number" of rebel Desert People boldly enter his post through holes in its sun-dried brick walls led by the government-recognized governors of Santa Ana, Santa Rosa, and Lofia. Arms in hand, these desert warriors caught Comaduran at his home. When the Mexican post commander refused to attack the local peaceful Apaches, the Desert People did so, knocking over the intrepid Mexican officer when he stood unarmed between the two ethnic groups and tried to avoid a battle.[16] A few weeks later, Comaduran pleaded with his superiors for new saddles because the garrison's old ones caused so many saddlesores that horses quickly became unrideable. Comaduran was also reduced to borrowing firearms from the Tubac post.[17]

During the 1840s, foreign travelers took the same sort of derogatory view of Mexican military posts and their garrisons as of priests and the Roman Catholic Church. In October 1848, a United States Dragoon subaltern wrote in his journal that none of the troops at Santa Cruz, not even the officers, "would be taken for soldiers" (Couts 1961:54). The Tubac post could be mistaken for an Indian village, according to the same United States Army officer, because peaceful Apaches there outnumbered Mexicans two to one (Couts 1961:59). At Santa Cruz, Forty-Niners forced some local women to dance with them, drawing their pistols on a garrison detachment that started to interfere. These Southerners also threw entrails from slaughtered beef into the mayor's house in a material expression of disdain (Harris 1960:76). When Apache raiders killed or kidnapped pilgrims from Santa Cruz going to the 1850 Magdalena festival, its inhabitants reportedly abandoned the place (Bartlett 1854:409).

The devastation that Apache economic raiders wrought on the north Mexican states combined with the concentration of resources in the central areas of the republic reduced the frontier military posts, churches, and other institutions to the dire straits in which they existed in the 1840s. Colonial conditions had been quite different. Royal forces conquered most Apaches during the 1780s. By the end of the eighteenth century, nearly all Apaches lived on Spanish rations in the shadow of royal military posts (Moorhead 1968:182-269; Dobyns 1976:97-105). The final colonial years were peaceful and prosperous in the north Mexican provinces (Bancroft 1962:378-79, 401-02).

Beginning about 1825, Apache bands began drifting away from military posts because their rations did not arrive. They returned to economic raiding, irrigation gardening, and cattle and horse husbandry (Spicer 1962:240-41; Dobyns 1981:24-25). By 1833, Western Apaches had resumed intensive economic raiding as far south as Ures in central Sonora. In 1846, Lipan Apaches raided as far south as San Luís Potosí on the central plateau (Edwards 1966:139-40) and Comanches annually raided the area between Durango and Chihuahua City during what they called "Mexico month" (Ruxton 1847:101). Frontier military posts collapsed so often that Mexican officials devised a new type of military "colony" (Faulk 1968:39-47) to reclaim abandoned settlements and stabilize the frontier. On the Sonoran frontier, Mexicans relied on the Pima-Maricopa Confederation's standing army to stem the Apache tide. The Tucson military post provided a ready market for Apache children that the Native American army captured. Either the post commandant or sutler rewarded the commanding general of the Confederation's army for ears representing slain Apaches with firearms, gunsmithing, munitions, clothing, food, and alcoholic beverages (Dobyns 1986). In midsummer 1855, United States Boundary Commissioner William H. Emory conferred with a Pima-Maricopa Confederation delegation at Los Nogales on the new international boundary marking the southern limit of the Gadsden Purchase. Emory formally requested that the Pima-Maricopa Confederation continue military campaigning against hostile Apaches, sealing the requested agreement with "all the blankets and cloths which could be spared from our camp" in addition to "some silver dollars."[18]

A comparative perspective on Mexico's frontier institutions between 1821 and 1846 would be incomplete without consideration of another Native American ethnic group intermittently hostile to Mexico yet participating in the regional pilgrimage to Magdalena. During the period under examination, a populous ethnic minority opened what was in effect a second front for Mexicans in southwest Sonora. I have already mentioned General Figueroa's abrupt abandonment of his Colorado River expedition to deal with hostile Yaquis. Yaqui warriors had halted the Spanish advance north from Sinaloa at the beginning of the seventeenth century (Johnson 1945:208-10). Then Yaqui leaders suddenly requested missionaries and welcomed them in 1617. The Jesuits quickly altered Yaqui settlement patterns, much Yaqui technology, and some core beliefs (Spicer 1961:14-15; de Ribas 1944:76-83). Caught up in a power struggle between a provincial governor and missionaries, Yaquis rebelled in a "strange" series of actions in 1740. Thereafter they remained peaceful and loyal to the crown until the end of the colonial period (Spicer 1980:15-32), providing most of the labor on Sonoran farms, ranches, and mines. In 1825, Mexican officials entered Yaqui territory to identify land for non-native settlement, while Yaquis resisted. A Rahum Pueblo leader had visions that prompted him to raise an ethnic army of 2,000 men that fended off the Mexicans until 1827. Not until 100 years later did Yaqui-Mexican hostilities end (Spicer 1980:36-57, 119-30). Provincial *caudillos* fought each other for the Sonoran governorship off and on from 1821 until the Mexican War. They often involved Yaqui forces in their internecine struggles.

Yaquis consistently pursued their goal of political autonomy and territorial integrity and defended their lands against incursions by the provincial landed elite. Although Yaquis did not seek conflict, they contributed as much if not more than Apaches to Sonoran institutional debility. Intermittent conflicts did not win the Yaquis political independence, but did sever their long connection with the Roman Catholic Church. Racist warfare between Mexicans and Yaquis meant that non-Native American secular priests who had replaced the Jesuits expelled in 1767 did not dare remain in Yaqui towns. No ordained priest set foot in Yaqui country to celebrate any ritual for Yaquis until after World War II (Spicer 1980:130-61, 224-35).

Under these circumstances, Yaquis did not abandon their Catholicism. Instead, they became *do-it-yourself* folk Catholics. Unlike the Desert-People, among whom individuals had to volunteer to organize pilgrimages or lead rituals, Yaquis possessed a cadre of trained religious leaders. From the beginning of their Yaqui ministry, Jesuit missionaries trained native assistants. Such men became literate in Yaqui as well as Spanish, read prayers, sermons, and even portions of the Mass, and led female choirs in hymn singing. A dozen or so such *malehto* clustered at each ethnic church. A senior *malehto* shared decision-making for the town with a few other elders (Spicer 1954:109). Thus, Yaqui *malehto* and members of ethnic ceremonial sodalities rather closely resembled the Penitente leaders and organizations that emerged in New Mexico at approximately the same time. Yaquis also forged devotional links between themselves and members of the dominant Sonoran ethnic group during the very period of strife. Yaquis joined the pilgrimage to Magdalena. Perhaps Yaqui pilgrims came more from the labor force of Euroamerican farms, ranches, towns, and mine camps rather than from the conservative, militant Yaqui river pueblos.

Yaqui pilgrimage participation is very visible. Deer dance groups are pilgrims. Theirs is a gripping representation of a hunted deer performed to a musical accompaniment. The national Ballet Folklórico has adapted it for performances in the capital city and outside Mexico. Instead of joining the line of pilgrims filing past the image of St. Francis Xavier, Yaqui deer dancers perform in front of the church as soon as they arrive in Magdalena. The musicians kneel on the paved square, and the dancer performs his best dance. They fulfill earnest vows not to St. Francis Xavier, but to the Virgin of Guadalupe. Secular behaviors are incorporated into this initial vow-fulfilling dance before the parish church. Musicians spread a piece of cloth in front of their drum as a visual signal to entranced spectators that the group accepts cash donations. Once the first dance ends, the members of the group repeat the performance many times. They circulate through the crowd of pilgrims, and halt at a temporary *cantina* or food booth where there appears to be an interested crowd likely to donate to the financial well-being or to lubricate the throats of the dancers and musicians. One of the musicians is not backward about passing an inverted *sombrero* after a dance if spectators are not generous in tossing coins and bills onto the ground cloth. Hundreds of other Yaqui pilgrims are colorful if less conspicuous. Buses and trucks transport them from Yaqui river towns to Magdalena and back.

Thus, the regional pilgrimage to Magdalena de Kino and its accompanying fair draw thousands of pilgrims and tourists to rub elbows and eye one another during the early days of each October. Every fall, the Magdalena pilgrimage provides colorful disproof of the idea that the frontier Roman Catholic Church "failed" between 1821 and 1846.

A final point may be made about the relationship between narrative history and social science analysis. Among several ethnic groups on the northwestern frontier of Mexico, what have been labeled above as *do-it-yourself* religious leaders succeeded in maintaining or spreading folk Catholicism where priests did not venture. Indeed, the *do-it-yourselfers* spread folk Catholicism well beyond the high-water mark of European missionary conversions of Native Americans. The Weberian interpretation of events on Mexico's northern frontier overlooks the *do-it-yourselfers'* achievements and does not even recognize the question of *how* they accomplished more than the missionaries who were professional, full-time proselytizers.

The answer to the analytical question is that formal conversion to Christianity was a European program of planned cultural change imposed on Native Americans (Spicer 1980:184-85), but folk Catholicism developed from within native populations with freedom of choice. The analysis of numerous case studies of planned cultural change points to a theoretical statement. A planned program succeeds to the extent that the people are brought into its planning and then execute the plans (Spicer 1962:288-98). As long as professional proselytizers sought converts, Native Americans could not become involved either in planning or carrying out the mission program. Conversion was consequently impeded (Dobyns 1951a:32). The moment missionaries and other priests were expelled from the frontier, interested Desert People, Yaquis, Creoles, Mestizos, and others were freed to plan and carry out their own conversions. Obtaining their basic doctrinal and ritual information on pilgrimages, they did so! Such *do-it-yourselfers* can easily confound any unwary historian who relies upon elitist written records without checking on what the typically nonliterate folk were up to.

NOTES

1. Often scholars do not venture across traditional disciplinary boundaries. In *The Use and Abuse of History*, classical historian M. I. Finley (1975:87) acknowledged that "archaeological evidence received no more than lip service from historians." The present essay clearly does utilize data of classes typically analyzed by historians and anthropologists, constituting an exercise in ethnohistory.

This essay to some degree follows the wisdom that Margaret Hodgen displayed in *Change and History* (1952). Analyzing 900 years of technological change in England, Hodgen submitted data from numerous detailed *Victoria Histories of the Countries of England* "to geographical and distributional analysis"(21). Hodgen also pointed out that scientific analysis of a temporal phenomenon such as technological change in England or religious change in Sonora, makes "inadmissable" the sort of sampling in which the narrative historian typically engages (36).

To the extent that the "history" of pilgrimage and north Mexican Native American conversion to Roman Catholicism remains unwritten, this essay is based on the author's field research. As in Jerome R. Mintz's *The Anarchists of Casas Viejas* (1982:9-10), this essay illuminates past behavioral changes by presenting "new data" obtained from relatively uneducated and not always literate individuals who belong to a socioeconomically subordinate ethnic enclave of "a despised station" composed of those who "made the pottery, sowed the fields and cut the stones" (Dobyns and Doughty 1976:4).

The method that guides this essay resembles closely, therefore, that which Victoria R. Bricker used in *The Indian Christ, the Indian King: The Historical Substrate of Maya Myth and Ritual* (1981). The present case study gains scientific value because historical Papago conversion to Catholicism parallels yet in key ways contrasts with the repeated Mayan quests for local ritual control over local ethnic congregations. Both the Mayan and the Papago cases are analyzable in terms of the basic assumption "that there is an intelligent unity behind all the diversity of human historical experience" (McNeill 1986:145).

2. A century after 1846, the Maryknoll priest John J. Considine issued a *Call for Forty Thousand* (1946). The book's title stated its theme:40,000 additional priests were wanted to minister to 80,000,000 nominal Catholics at a rate of one cleric per 2,000 people. Each priest in the United States served only 650 Catholics (9). In 1960, the Argentine Church, for example, averaged but one priest for each 8,857 inhabitants (Amato 1965:189). Secular clergy constituted only 66.4 percent of the priests serving urban parishes, and 79.4 percent of those in rural parishes (Amato 1965:182-83).

3. Author's translation.

4. About 1960, Peru had 10,000 inhabitants per resident parish priest. No less than 58.5 percent of those engaged in parish labors belonged to orders (Alonso et al., 1962:102-03). Some 207 of 833 parishes lacked a priest (34, 101). Regular clergy served in 191 parishes, or 23 percent. While over 90 percent of secular priests were native-born, no less than 92.3 percent of regular clergymen serving parishes were foreigners (111, 113). Paradoxically, Mexico had more priests per inhabitant than either Peru or Argentina, at 5,037 persons per priest (Ramos and Alonso 1962:61).

5. Pérez R. y Labella (1964:17, explicitly traced the twentieth century shortage back to postindependence expulsions. The dearth of vocations has not been limited to Spanish-speaking America. Brazil had a parallel shortage of priests and dependence on foreign-born

clerics. In 1960, Brazil had one priest per 6,349 inhabitants or 5,714 Catholics . At the time, 40.5 percent of Brazil's priests were foreign-born (Pérez et al. 1965:15, 24).

6. Urban Spaniards and Creoles long monopolized churches and priests in Peru, excluding Native Americans and slaves who could enter main churches only on special occasions (Dobyns and Doughty 1976:82). In 1966, 31 percent of all priests in Peru still lived in the Lima archdiocese (Doughty 1976:102).

7. Weber (1981:130). "Priests tended to avoid isolation, hardship, danger, and low salaries and began to gravitate toward more comfortable urban parishes." Weber erred in inferring a change. Secular clerics consistently preferred urban life. That longstanding trait led to the mission manned by regular priests becoming a colonial frontier institution.

8. In Guatemala, for example, 45 percent of the clergy worked in the archdiocese of the capital city about 1960. Thus, people had a priest per 4,970 inhabitants. In largely Mayan dioceses such as Sololá, there was but one priest for 17,064 people with Jalapa at the extreme of 20,556 inhabitants per priest (Pérez R. y Labella 1964:18). Its large contemporary Native American populace makes Guatemala comparable to northern Mexico of 1821-46.

9. When Sonora's first bishop elected in 1783 to reside in Alamos, that mining centre boasted 5,000 inhabitants with another 3,000 in nearby mines. Wealthy families with marriageable daughters also provided opportunity for the bishop's lay nephew who accompanied him from Spain (Stagg 1976:74; Miles 1962:10-11).

10. About 1960, the north Mexican states still had proportionately fewer priests than central Mexico. The ecclesiastical province of Chihuahua had a priest per 8,582 inhabitants; that of Monterrey had one per 7,996 compared to one per 2,957 in Morelia, 4,270 in Puebla, and 5,989 in Mexico province (Ramos and Garre 1962:61-62).

11. From 90 to 95 percent of the population of Northern Baja California and Chihuahua is Catholic. The proportion is 95 to 97 percent in Sonora, Coahuila, Nuevo Leon, and Tamaulipas (Ramos and Garre 1962:93).

12. Among many examples are Frank S. Edwards, *A Campaign in New Mexico with Colonel Doniphan* (1847:46, 61-62, 64, 69, 72-74), and Susan S. Magoffin, *Down the Santa Fé Trail and into Mexico* (1926:38, 119, 126, 129-30, 137-38, 165).

13. Weber (1981:139) realized that: "Penitentes developed their own liturgy and ceremonies." He even noted that "the brotherhood grew rapidly in the early nineteenth century as a result of neglect by the priests." Yet Weber accepted the elitist conception of Penitentes as notorious, aberrant, and unique.

14. In 1950 there were an estimated 1,600 to 2,000 Papago pilgrims.

15. Unpublished interview, transcribed by the author, with Jose Enos, Kaka village, Papago Indian Reservation, 31 December 1957, pp. 33, 37-38.

16. Ant.o Comaduran. Diciembre 3 de 1842. Tucson. Al S.or Comandante Militar Segundo Gefe de la Comandancia General D. Jose Maria Elias Gonzales, Rayon. (MS 38 for Vol. 3, Documentos para la Historia de Sonora, The Bancroft Library, University of California-Berkeley).

17. Ant.o Comaduran. Tucson, Enero 15 de 1843 al S.or Comand.te Militar y 2o Gefe de la Comand.a Gral. D. José María Elias Gonzales, Rayon. (No 41, Pinart Collection, Documentos para la Historia de Sonora, Vol. 3, Bancroft Library, University of California-Berkeley).

18. William H. Emory, *Report on the United States and Mexican Boundary Survey, Made under the Direction of the Secretary of the Interior* (1857:96). The commissioner's reliance on the Pima-Maricopa Confederation reemphasizes that in mid-1855 the United States could no more deliver effective military power to the Gadsden Purchase than could Mexico. This reality throws additional comparative perspective on the idea that Mexican frontier institutions "failed."

REFERENCES

Alonso-Bellido 1962
Amato 1965
Bancroft 1962
Bartlett 1854
Bean-eds. 1962
Bliss 1952
Bolton 1917
Bricker 1981
Chavez 1954
Considine 1946
Cosulich 1939
Couts 1961
de Lambertie 1955
de Ribas 1944
Dobyns 1950, 1951a, 1951b,
    1960, 1976, 1981, 1986
Dobyns-Doughty 1976
Doughty 1976
Edwards 1847, 1966
Eggan 1954
Emory 1857
Ezell 1968
Faulk 1968
Finley 1975

Fontana 1983, 1987
Hodgen 1952
Harris 1960
Hutchinson 1973
Johnson 1945
Joseph-Chesky 1949
Kessell 1976
Kino 1919
Kunkel 1961
Magoffin 1926
McNeill 1986
Miles 1962
Mintz 1982
Moorhead 1968
Labella 1965
Pérez Ramírez 1964
Ramos-Garre 1962
Roca 1967
Ruxton 1847
Spicer 1952, 1954, 1961,
    1962, 1980
Spitzer 1958
Stagg 1976
Weber 1981

Figure 9.4 The Type of Launch which carries the Image of El Niño de Atocha, May 3rd.

Figure 9.5 El Castillo, northern shore, Lake Amatitlán

Figure 4.4 Komchepte for Guadelupe with Pahkome and Matachin Dancers

Figure 4.5 Guadalupe at the foot of the Altar after the Komchepte

4

Fiestas and Exchange Pilgrimages: The Yorem Pahko and Mayo Identity, Northwest Mexico

N. ROSS CRUMRINE

Yearly, Mayo Indians of the lower Mayo River valley, Sonora, Northwest Mexico, engage in two large exchange pilgrimages (*pasom*) which involve ritual visiting (*bisitam*) of church-based sodalities, their patron saints, and church center membership. Although numerous smaller visits link church centers into an integrated network, the major exchange pilgrimages focus upon the Sundays of the Espíritu Santo (Holy Spirit, Figure 4.1) or Itom Aye (Our Mother) and of the Santísima Tiniran (Holy Trinity, Figure 4.2) or Itom Achai (Our Father), which are moveable and usually fall toward the end of the month of May. The smaller church centers and their exchange *bisitam* usually do not cut across *municipio* (municipal) or "pueblo" boundaries, however, the Holy Spirit-Holy Trinity exchanges unify the two "pueblos" of the lower river valley, Etchojoa (Etchojoa *municipio*) and Santa Cruz (Huatabampo *municipio*). Since Mayos perceive both of these rituals as *yorem paskom* or *yorem kostumbre*, and each center, Etchojoa (Espíritu Santo) and Santa Cruz, now Júpare (Santísima Tiniran), as representing one of the "Eight Mission Pueblos Jurisdictions," this pattern of exchange pilgrimages restates the Mayo Goh Naike Pueblo Hurasionim ideology and reinforces their image of Yoremes (Mayos) as a separate and unique people.

Figure 4.1 Espíritu Santo of Etchojoa

In a very general sense, my research suggests modern Mayos exhibit an intermediary stage in their development from an autonomous tribal society to either a well-defined ethnic enclave or a fully assimilated condition, at which time Mayos as such would cease to exist. Today Mayos are neither completely autonomous nor have they lost that unique set of common understandings and shared system of symbols which we call the enduring identity symbol system or, more generally, the Mayo way of life. They are "betwixt and between," a partial Mayo society characterized by a rather highly integrated symbolic and ritual system supplemented by modern Mexican society. This cultural system is maintained by a rather mobile, heterogeneous group of people whom we call the Mayos. The facts that Mayo peasant farming and their more modern irrigated commercial agriculture must be supplemented by wage labour and that their identity symbol system must be supported by cycles of ceremonials require some mobility within the river valley and even between river valleys. This state of transition and mobility makes it difficult to draw clear boundaries between Mayos and mestizos as many aspects of mestizo culture and society are shared by Mayos. In certain cultural aspects Mayos seem quite assimilated, whereas in others, especially the *pahko* complex, they appear quite different from mestizos.

MAYO CULTURAL ECOLOGY

The ecological limitations in terms of which Mayo ceremonialism must be adapted prove to be extremely complex. Living in a zone of high-production irrigation agriculture on the coastal plain of southern Sonora and northern Sinaloa, the modern Mayos are characterized by almost

complete technico-economic
assimilation (see Crumrine
1977a). Depending upon the
figures which one wishes to
accept, the modern Mayo
population is placed some-
where between 20,000 and
60,000 individuals. The
region receives an average of
40 to 80 centimeters. of rain
per year and is characterized by two principle seasons, a cold time (*sebe tiempo*), with temperatures
which drop almost to zero
degrees Celsius during the
coldest nights of winter, and
a hot season (*tata tiempo*),
with occasional summer
temperatures which reach
45 degrees or more during
the hottest days of summer.

Many Mayos farm small
plots of land, around four to
six hectares, as members of
ejidos (governmentally established landholding societ-
ies) or as small property owners. By far the majority of Mayos identify
themselves as farmers although most must supplement their meager
income through wage labor. However, as farmers, Mayos are little different
from many poor, undereducated mestizo Mexican peasants living in the
river valley. Charles Erasmus (1967) describes this Mayo-mestizo peasant
farming and discusses the problems of reform and rural poverty. In recent
years peasant farming has become more complex, costly, and cash-crop
oriented. Modern technology such as insecticides, fertilizers, hybrid seed,
tractors, and complex leveling equipment, and even small airplanes which
spray insecticides, fertilizers, and even chemical seeding the clouds to
produce rain, is a daily part of the life of all Mayos.

Many Mayos still utilize the rapidly disappearing thorn forest and desert
areas for firewood, construction materials, and cactus fruit. Most families
keep some domestic animals, such as chickens and pigs. Much of the
material culture of the river valley is shared by both Mayos and mestizo
Mexicans. In their sleeping rooms most Mayo families have a small table
altar with pictures and images of selected saints, and perhaps a wooden
cross or metal crucifix, while a wooden cross stands in the *tabat* (patio) of

Figure 4.2 Santísima Tiniran of Júpare

many Mayo families, especially during Lent or at the time of funeral rituals for a death in the family. Thus with the exception of this *tebatpo kuru* (patio cross), Mayo material culture is quite identical to that of the poorer mestizo Mexican farmers of the Mayo River valley.

However, modern Mayo ceremonialism and the use of the Mayo language provides a complete contrast with this pattern of technico-economic assimilation. Mayo identity, insofar as it represents a system apart from that of mestizo Mexico, is crucially linked with the Mayo mythico-ritual system and with the sacred societies or sodalities which produce Mayo ceremonials. Within this Mayo symbolico-ritual system, the ceremonials of Lent and Holy Week, of the Santa Kuru (Holy Cross) on the third of May, of the dead the first and second of November, and of Espíritu Santo and Santísima Tiniran in late May or early June represent the most complex and important ritual events in the Mayo ceremonial cycle of the lower river valley. This present ceremonial system is the result of a number of structural and historical processes: a marginal position combined with early Jesuit missionary activities before their expulsion from the New World, followed by years of relative autonomy leading to recent pacification and present embedding within modern Mexico (see Crumrine 1977a, 1983, 1987). In the production of the cycle of Mayo *pahkom* and *bisitam* or pilgrimages, the Mayo ceremonial sodalities or *cofradias* socially maintain, produce, and adapt this symbolico-ritual system.

Within the modern river valley, Mayo families live in several different settlement patterns (Crumrine 1977a:35-37). In all these settlement patterns Mayos and mestizo Mexicans live as neighbors generally without special regard to Indian or non-Indian identification, although some types provide more privacy and isolation from the outside world than others. Modern Mayo social organization is rather simple, consisting of four levels: the family, the household, the ceremonial kindred, and the ceremonial center consisting of the ritual sodalities, church, and church officials. Most modern households consist of nuclear families although many include additional relatives such as one or several old parents or one or more siblings with their own families. During the typical times of the rites of passage, a traditional extended household will cooperate and new alliances will be established through the selection of godparents for the newborn, the marrying couple, or the initiate into a ritual sodality. When an individual sponsors a ceremonial, his or her household and group of relatives and compadres become an important cooperative unit. Recovery from an illness or escape from a life-threatening situation after making a promise (*manda*) to God or one of the saints means that one must repay the supernatural by helping produce a ceremonial (*pahko*) or a cycle of *pahkom* in the saint's honor. Modern Mayo public ceremonials reveal a fusion of aboriginal and early Jesuit traditions modified by several hundred years of dynamic adjustment with first Spanish and later Mexican society and culture. The highly integrated modern Mayo folk culture as well as the modern church-pueblo ceremonial organization remain intact as a kind of living history of Mayo contact with the world beyond the river valley. The modern church-pueblo organization includes (1) the five church governors and five helpers, generally elected by the pueblo for extended terms, (2) the Maestrom (lay ministers), (3) Matachini dance sodality (church dancers), (4) the Parisero sodality (the Lenten masked society), and (5) the Pahkome (fiesteros, Figure 4.3). The Pahkome pay their promise (*manda*) for a cure by praying each Sunday at the church, producing the saint's day ceremony (*pahko*), and providing the fireworks, food, and entertainment in the form of Pahkola and *Maso* (deer) dancers and musicians during the period of the *pahko*. In the lower river valley ceremonial centers, the

Figure 4.3 Some Pahkome with the Mo'oro on the left

Pahkome must make two major ceremonials for their saint's *pahkom* as well as participate in certain funerals and remembrance rituals. Assisted by the Pahkome, the Pariserom enact the life, death, and resurrection of Christ from the first of the year through Easter week. The *pahkom* for the Holy Cross (Santa Kuru) take place in early May and September, for the Espíritu Santo and Santísima Tiniran late in May or early in June, for San Juan late in June, and for Guadalupe early in December. All of these *pahkom* involve ritual exchange and *bisitam* of neighboring Pahkome, although the *pahkom* of Espíritu Santo and Santísima Tiniran represent the most elaborate examples of this ritual pattern.

Dedicated to their specific patron saint, the Pahkome consist of twelve ranked *personasim* (persons): four Parinam, four Alperesim, and four Alawasim. These individuals generally have made a promise to serve the saint for three years; however, they are usually able to work only a year at a time and rest for several years before taking on the cargo for another year of service. During the major days of the *pahko* the Pahkome must kill a bull for meat and provide the bread, coffee, tortillas, and meat stew to be eaten by the participants. Nevertheless, much of the meat is given to relatives, compadres, and close friends as repayment for their assistance or in order to establish debts to ensure future aid for following *pahkom*. In this sense the Mayo Pahkome distributes food and in doing so reinforces social ties producing a cooperative group which through its return support of the Pahkome makes possible the *pahko*. Thus Mayo social ties and group identity are reinforced by means of the *pahko* institution and an equality among the "poor" is established.

On a more general symbolic level for the Mayo set of exchange *pahkom* in honor of the Espíritu Santo and the Santísima Tiniran, members of each ceremonial center participate in and thus actualize two ritual structures: (1) *paso* (pilgrimage), *pahko* (fiesta), and *paso* (return pilgrimage), and (2) *komchepte* (descent of the saint), *nobena* (nine days of prayers), and *pahko* (fiesta). From one weekend to the next the human visitor-host relationship flips over while Itom Aye (Our Mother, Espíritu Santo) first hosts Itom Achai (Our Father, Santísima Tiniran) and then is hosted by Him as the supernatural roles also reverse. In the *pahko* context the unity of visitor and host also creates a mediation of the human-deity opposition as the saints also participate in and enjoy the ritual. In this chapter both the Mayo status as an embedded, enduring people and the unifying and mediating powers of the exchange *pahko* will be described and analyzed.

THE SANTISIMA TINIRAN KOMCHEPTE

The first important rituals associated with the Santísima Tiniran role in the exchange pilgrimage actualize the *komchepte*, the coming down of the power of the Santísima Tiniran, and initiate the nine days of prayer (*nobena*) preceding the Santísima Tiniran *pahko*. The *komchepte* takes place during the noon hours nine days before the Holy Trinity Sunday; in 1983 the *komchepte* occurred on Thursday, May 19th, and Holy Trinity on Sunday, May 29th.

When I arrived in Júpare on the morning of May 19th and entered the church, I immediately noticed that the main altar was different. The Santísima Tiniran was gone and placed on the top of the altar were two crucifixes. There were primarily a number of big vases full of flowers on the altar, a few yellow ones, but mainly white lilies. The donation box was in the lower center of the altar and the large Santísima Tiniran in the anteroom to the left of the altar. It was practically impossible to get inside the little anteroom as it was jammed with worshipers. The Santísima Tiniran was resting on a table just as you went in to your right, against that right-hand wall.

As I left the church through the side door I discovered the Pahkome *kontiing* (encircling) the church carrying the *bera castillom* (fireworks). These were not the large *castillom* (fireworks displays), but a smaller single flat type of *castillo* which they stuck in the ground and shot off during the *komchepte*.

Led by a Mo'oro (ritual advisor) all the *Alawasim* (lowest-ranking Pahkome) moved around the church in a counter-clockwise direction, while appearing from the other direction I saw the Parinam and the Alparesim (higher ranking Pahkome). The Parinam and Alparesim were followed by eleven men carrying these *bera castillom* and the Alawasim were followed by seven men also carrying *bera castillom*. The lines kontied (circled) around the church three times. They formed two lines in front of the church and then carried these *bera castillom* up one by one and dipped them in front of the church. Then they carried them out to an area just beyond the church bells and cross to set them up in the ground.

I returned to the church which was beginning to fill up. They had put down mats directly in front of the altar and in front of the two side altars to the worshipers' left where the other two images of the Santísima Tiniran rested, and then threw flower petals and a lot of lilies down on the mats. The *Matachinim* (church dancers) had danced earlier and the *Pahkolas* and *maso* dancers (professional *pahko* dancer-entertainers) were dancing in their ramada out beyond the church at this time. As the Pahkome returned to the church, I noticed the four flags of the four different sets of Pahkome, from Navowaxia, Pozo Dulce, Pueblo'ora, and Júpare.

The Mo'oro lit several candles that stood by a kneeling rail in front of the altar. Someone else brought a chair for the old *Cantora* (church singer) and she sat down as the *Maestrom* (lay ministers) knelt and began to chant and pray. As this happened inside, outside the church *kamaram* (large fire crackers) and the little *bera castillom* began going off and I assumed the *maso* and *pahkola* dancers and the Matachins began dancing in front of the church. Then assisted by the Mo'oro and a couple of the Pahkome wearing the kerchiefs over their heads, they carried the Santísima Tiniran into the church, emerging from the door of the little anteroom. They held it way up high and lowered it clear down to the floor of the church. Then they held it up again and lowered it down again, however when they had it part way down, they turned it, first to the right hand side of the church and then to the left hand side of the church. Thus in its descent the Santísima Tiniran swung in front of the worshipers as they brought it to the center and dropped it clear down to the floor. Then they lifted it up again, drew it down part way, did these turns and lowered it to the floor again. Afterwards, the Mo'oro told me that it should descend 12 times, although in the excitement I lost count as they were doing it reasonably fast. At the same time, other individuals did the *komchepte* with the side altar images of the Santísima Tiniran.

When they finished lowering them, and as the Maestros went into another set of prayers, they rested the three images on the mats at the foot of the altars. Then individually the Pahkome began to come up, were given a cloth, crossed themselves, and wiped and dusted the main image as they knelt in front of it, which took quite awhile. During this time the Mo'oro was constantly ringing a small hand bell, the Maestros and the Cantora were singing and praying, and many people were holding candles which they lit just before the descent. Outside there was a great din as the fireworks were set off, the large church bells were rung, and the dancers were dancing. Inside, the church was completely filled with people who seemed very excited even though it was extremely hot and many were sweating, complaining, and fanning themselves.

As the Pahkome finished greeting the Santísima Tiniran other individuals in the church went up to cross themselves, kneel, and pray. Soon the Pahkome returned with the *maso* and *pahkola* dancers and musicians who also greeted the image. Then the dancers did the *hinangkiwa* (a procession form in which the dancers move to and fro as the procession advances) with all these different Pahkome and their flags escorting the Pahkolas and Maso back to the *pahkola* ramada. The Matachins were dancing in two long lines also accompanying the *hinangkiwa*.

After the *hinangkiwa* was over, the Maestros, Cantora, and head Pahkola prayed at the ramada cross and the *maso* and *pahkola* dancers danced for three songs. The Fiesteros did their *ehersisio* (ritual) at the ramada cross, which took quite a long while as there were four different groups of Pahkome taking part.

As they finished the ritual and the Júpare Pahkome tied their flag to the cross, I returned to the church. Most people had left the church, although the images were still resting on their mats and had not been replaced on the altars. The visiting Pahkome then entered the church, rolled up their flags and placed them to the left of the main altar, and left the church going in the direction of the Júpare cooking ramadas for their lunch. By this time it was around 1:30 P.M., since the *komchepte* had taken place at noon. After more *pahkola* and *maso* dancing and additional feasting the visiting Pahkome bid goodbye in a brief ritual and left, although by this time most people were already on their way home and the Santísima Tiniran *komchepte* was concluded for another year. Nine days of rather brief prayers and chants, the *nobena*, would follow, leading to the *pahko* which would take place the next Saturday-Sunday in slightly over a week.

THE SANTISIMA TINIRAN BISITA AND ESPIRITU SANTO PAHKO

A week earlier the Espíritu Santo *komchepte* had taken place and now Her Pahkome were organizing the *pahko* in Her honor in Etchojoa. On Saturday, May 21st, slightly before 3:00 A.M. I arrived at the church in Júpare. The Matachins were dancing in front of the church and there were quite a few people standing around. I was a bit surprised since it was very early. I went directly into the church. Just a little while after I had arrived the Pahkome lined up with the visitors from Pozo Dulce, Pueblo'ora, and Navowaxia, as well as the locals from Júpare. The Maestro knelt on the kneeling bench and he gave the *nobena* prayers for the second Santísima Tiniran *nobena*, which did not last very long.

As the *nobena* concluded, they removed the image from the altar and brought up a *heeka* (small canopy to shade an image). The Matachins, who had been dancing since I arrived, preceded the main body of the procession as they would for the entire *bisita* and return. The Pahkome left the church first with the image, the Maestros and Cantora singing and the people following. The procession moved around the west side of the church out to the main highway, across a drainage canal, and along that canal to the Mayo River banks. Many people had large candles which they were burning. Also a few people had flashlights, so there was enough light to see what was taking place.

We went down and crossed the Mayo River, stopping just along its bank. There was a little prayer service there and they wrapped the image, carefully, for the road. The Matachins had gone on ahead. We followed them with the Pahkome and then finally came the image and the Maestros. We left the river bank about 4:00 A.M., went on in the road that goes past the penitentiary, and arrived at the edge of Huatabampo about 5:00 A.M. as it was beginning to get light. Just before we crossed the canal bridge as you enter Huatabampo, the Pahkome unrolled their flags and we enjoyed two short rest stops as they set the image on a little table. After we crossed the canal, they made another rest stop. During all the rest stops, the Pahkome stood in their typical formal pattern, out in the street facing the image. In this pattern, the Parinam and the Alperesim stand in a line across and directly facing the image, and the line of Alawasim are directly to their right and perpendicular to the image with the Mo'oro at their head. Then at the third rest stop just as we entered town, they unwrapped the image. As we moved through Huatabampo toward the church, the procession continued making several more rest stops as it was joined by many townspeople. Finally there was a fifth rest stop, before we turned and went down the road that goes into the square of Huatabampo. Hurrying ahead of the procession I went in the side door of the Huatabampo church. There was a brass band in front of the church that was playing as the image approached and entered the main church door.

Our Pahkome entered while I observed that the Pahkome and their Santísima Tiniran image from Etchoropo, a neighboring village, had already arrived. The Parinam and the Alperesim sat on the left-hand side of the church while the Alawasim sat on the worshipers' right-hand side. They simply sat down in the center of the church where they could find room among the other non-Mayo people that had begun to gather. The image was carried directly down the main aisle. When they approached the front rail, they dipped the image a number of times to the big Santísima Tiniran above the altar that is the patron saint of the Huatabampo church. Then they dipped it to their left side and to their right side. Finally they carried it over to the side altar on the far right. They put the Júpare image on the worshipers' far left where it joined the Etchoropo image and an image of Guadalupe which was positioned in the center. As they had at all of the rest stops, townspeople also went up now and *muhtied* (crossed themselves, knelt, prayed, touched the image, touched themselves, and crossed themselves again). At 6:30 A.M. the lights were turned on and the local priest came out, recited the Mass, and talked a little about the fiesta. Very few people and none of the Pahkome or Mayos went up to the rail to receive communion. Most of the Matachins stayed outside and there appeared to be rather few Mayos inside the church, although it was very crowded. The few Mayos I saw were just sitting among everyone else on the benches or standing along the walls beyond the seating area. After the Mass was over and the priest left the altar area, the Pahkome with their flags and regalia moved out of the church and the two images were picked up. There was no greeting at all between the Etchoropo and the Júpare Pahkome.

The procession came out of the front door of the church, turned left and went on around the park where we had entered, and continued to the Etchojoa edge of town, making three brief stops in route. By about 7:30 A.M., having reached the corner of Huatabampo, they rested the images up against a wall and wrapped them and rolled the flags for travelling. Approximately halfway down the highway to Etchojoa the procession made a rest stop at La Liña. I noted that there were several ambulances following along behind the procession, which had become very large as we were picking up people standing along the highway as well as a large number of individuals who had joined in Huatabampo.

On this procession to Etchojoa a woman approached with several doves that she released in front of the covered images, many people came with donations which they placed in money boxes carried just in front of the images, and at least two people began walking on their knees as the procession neared them. The procession would open and the images would move up to these people and then stop as they prayed and made their contributions. Thus as we approached Etchojoa, the procession proceeded much more slowly. The weather was cool and clear early this morning, a nice temperature for a fast walk, although it would have been cold just in shirt sleeves, had one not been walking hard. After dawn it remained cool, although from La Liña on it began to warm up and by the time we got to Etchojoa it was extremely warm. People were perspiring and were very hot.

A number of people asked me if I was tired, which was a major topic of conversation on the pilgrimage. Clearly the value here involves a fast, tiring walk as part of the repayment to the Santísima Tiniran for His intervention in a previous cure. The Matachins also dance in compensation for a cure, good health, or a favor. As we reached the edge of Huatabampo, I counted around 50 girls directly in front of the Pahkome and then two long lines of boys with perhaps 100 in each line. Certainly the Matachins surpassed 200 individuals and there may have been more than 300 including those not dancing and scattered in the crowd.

Around 10:00 A.M. we arrived at the outskirts of Etchojoa, were met by masses of people everywhere, and proceeded directly to an open area in a relatively new children's park where one line of Alawasim and a second one of Alperesim and Parinam from Etchojoa, Seaba'a, and Wichaka ritual centers awaited the formal greeting of Pahkome. This greeting would link the ritual centers of Júpare, Etchoropo, Pozo Dulce, Pueblo'ora, and Nabowaxia all from Santa Kuru Pueblo, Huatabampo Municipio, with Etchojoa, Seaba'a, and Wichaka from Etchojoa Pueblo, Etchojoa Municipio. As we approached, our Alawasim and Alperesim-Parinam filled the two remaining open sides of a square. The visitors' Mo'oro, that is our Mo'oro, followed by all our Pahkome, began shaking hands and greeting the host Pahkome moving from right to left down the Alperesim-Parinam line and then from left to right down the Alawasim line. After this greeting when everyone had returned to their places, our head Mo'oro stepped out from his line and called out "dios emchania" (Mayo greeting like "good day" or "hello") and their Mo'oro responded. The two groups of Pahkome came together and led the images and procession over to two covered niches which are on top of a round flat brick platform. The images were carried up onto the platform, turned around, placed underneath those arch niches and uncovered. The masked *pahkola* dancers, who arrived with the Etchojoa personnel, began to perform down in front of the Pahkome who were lined up on the ground in front of this little platform. Beyond the crowd at the platform a brass band also was playing. The Pahkolas moved up on the platform, crossed themselves, prayed, and danced directly in front of the images. Preceded by the Matachins, with the Pahkolas dancing the *hinangkiwa* between the images and the Pahkome, and followed by the Maestros and the brass band, the images were carried into Etchojoa and to a private home where they rested. There the Maestros prayed, the visiting Pahkome did their ritual *ehersisio* (exercise), the Matachins danced, and everyone also rested and ate. This ritual resting is called the *kopana* or *kopanake*, and also gives people in the host community a chance to greet and pray to the visiting images.

Around 4:00 P.M. the procession left the resting home and moved through town to the area in front of the Etchojoa church. The Matachins were dancing at the front followed by the Pahkome, the images, and the band playing a processional tune. The procession made several brief stops for worshipers who came up to donate money and pray before the images. As the line of Alperesim-Parinam moved to the far side of the street, we stopped on the street corner nearest the church and watched as the Holy Spirit procession and the Holy Spirit came up rapidly to meet the Holy Trinities. As the images moved closer together and when they were a meter or so apart, they bowed them, going first to the Júpare Santísima Tiniran and bowing both images. They pushed the images right up close together as though they were embracing and bowed both up and down a number of times. Then they backed off the Holy Spirit and moved Her over and bowed Her also to the Etchoropo Santísima Tiniran, again bringing the Holy Spirit right up close so it was practically, if not actually, touching the Santísima Tiniran. Finally, they turned Her around and walked behind the image of Etchoropo. Thus the three images did not walk abreast, but the Holy Spirit walked behind the other two. Again the Pahkome fell into their proper formation and the procession moved on past the church and down to the area where the church bells and cross are located, where we turned to our left twice and entered the side church door, the front door being rather high and a more difficult access. As we entered the door there was a great crush of people with this large crowd all jamming inside. However, they were able to return the Espíritu Santo to Her place rather high above the center altar. On a table in the back-right hand corner of the altar area they placed the Etchoropo Santísima Tiniran and in the back left-hand corner they put the Holy Trinity from Júpare. As they were arranging the images the Pahkome left the church and set up in the area between the cross and bells and the church. They were preparing to exchange the bread rosaries, the *panim kokam*, which consisted of tied strings of buns and oranges instead of beads.

The Pahkome lined up, the Etchojoa Pueblo Alperesim-Parinam with their backs to the cross and bells and the Santa Kuru Pueblo Alperesim-Parinam directly across from them and facing them with their backs to the church and the Alawasim on both remaining sides, forming a square with an open center. They put down mats which they covered with their bread rosaries. Standing in the center area, the Mo'orom from the different church centers organized and directed the exchange. First the Alawasim exchanged their *bastons*, little wooden sticks with ribbons attached to one end, and then the Alperesim-Parinam exchanged their flags. The Mo'orom called a pair of individuals from different church centers into the open center of the square. They crossed themselves while they were standing up, knelt and crossed themselves, then circled each other's head with the baston or flag and exchanged them, crossed themselves, stood up again, crossed themselves and then walked back to the lines.

It was after 5:00 P.M. when they began to exchange the bread rosaries. The Mo'orom pointed to two Pahkome from different *pueblos* who picked up a bread rosary which they held first in their left hand because they had their usual rosary in their right hand. They carried the bread rosaries into the center, stood up first facing each other, crossed themselves, and then they knelt and crossed themselves. They were holding the bread rosary in their left hand. Some switched it over to their right hand and put it on the shoulder of the person directly across from their right hand. Others continued to use their left hand and put it on the other shoulder of the person across from them. After they had both exchanged, and the other person held it on his or her shoulder, they stood up, crossed themselves again, and went back to their positions behind the mats. A few Pahkome did try and throw the *panim kokam* over the other person's head. There was some laughter in the crowd, especially when this was successful. Toward the end there were a few *panim kokam* left and the Pahkome gave these to their Mo'oro, and the Mo'oro took them then and simply gave them without any ritual to some of the other Mo'oro. Our head Mo'oro was able to throw one or two over the heads of some of the other Mo'orom, which produced laughter among the Pahkome and in the crowd. Thus the Mo'orom finalized the exchanges of the bread rosaries while people put them in boxes to carry away. The Pahkome returned to the church, rolled up their flags, put some in the upper left-hand corner and others in the upper right-hand corner of the church, and disappeared out the side door of the church. *Pahkola* and *maso* dancing and entertainment, eating, drinking, social dancing, and a large fireworks (*kastiom*) display followed during the night and early Sunday morning.

Sunday morning the Matachins danced in the church and a white wooden table with an altar cloth and a chalice, etc., was placed in the front altar area of the church. The local Etchojoa priest arrived, heard about two dozen confessions at the table-altar from individuals who did not appear to be Mayos, passed out a little newspaper with a responsive reading, read from that responsive reading, and went into the sermon. During the sermon the Pahkome began to drift into the church and to go up to the altar area to obtain their flags, etc. While they passed out a dish for a collection and most of the Pahkome had entered the church, the priest said Mass and offered the host to a few apparently non-Mayo people who moved through the crowd up to the altar area. When the Mass was over he came right down immediately and started changing the Etchojoa Pahkomes' rosaries from the present Pahkome to those entering the position for the coming year. He began with the high ranking Pahkome, the Parinam and the Alperesim, and changed them going right down the line in the same order as the greeting handshake which had characterized our initial entry into Etchojoa yesterday. Then he moved to the head of the Alawasim and back down that line exchanging their rosaries. This all happened very quickly. When it was completed the Pahkome went up to the altar area, wrapped up their flags again, put them up by their images, and then disappeared out the side door of the church.

The Matachin dancing, confessions, Mass, and changing of the rosaries took place around 10 A.M. to 11 A.M. Afterwards I wandered by the *pahkola* ramada where there was very little dancing and more drinking, chatting, and sleeping. Then a lot of *kamaram* bombs were set off at the Pahkome kitchen ramadas indicating the *mabedwa* was in progress. In the *mabedwa*, the Etchojoa Pahkome, old and new, were giving out large baskets of food, bread, and small rockets to selected families. These gifts represented either repayment for assistance or obligated the recipient to return the food two-fold to the Pahkome at the time of the next *pahko*, thus establishing a debt. After the *mabedwa*, around 2:30 P.M. the Pahkome drifted back into the church as the visitors were getting anxious to go. Some visitors started out the side door of the church, but then they came quickly back in. The Pahkolas, Maso, and their musicians were being brought into the church by the local Pahkome. They danced in front of the altar, in front of the Holy Spirit. The Mo'oro climbed up on the altar and took the wire down that holds up the Espíritu Santo. He dropped Her down, and set Her on the altar while the Pahkolas danced up to Her a number of times, dancing right in front of the altar for a short while. Then they began the *konti* (procession around the church) doing the *hinangkiwa*. We went out the side church door. The Matachins were already dancing outside. They were followed by the Pahkome with the Maso and Pahkolas and their musicians playing and dancing back and forth, *hinangkiwa*, between them and the images, with the two Holy Trinities first and the Holy Spirit following. The procession moved counter-clockwise in a decorated aisle, which ran toward the *pahkola* ramada and around to the front of the church. But when we reached the front of the church, instead of going back in, the procession stopped in the street and Itom Aye said goodbye to Itom Achai. They dipped both sets of images and brought the Espíritu Santo right up close to both the Santísima Tinirans of Júpare and of Etchoropo. As the Espíritu Santo turned back toward the church, we moved down this street clear to the end of town, turned left and crossed the Huatabampo highway. Just across the highway they rested the Santísima Tiniran images up against a tree and wrapped them for the road. The Pahkome formed their square, and returned their paraphernalia. The visitors, the Santa Kuru Pueblo Pahkome, shook hands with the Etchojoa Pueblo Pahkome and the head Mo'oro of the visitors made a little speech saying that they would welcome them next week in Júpare for the Santísima Tiniran Pahko and goodbye for now. The visitors then took to the road.

We walked directly down the highway making only a short stop at La Liña and directly on until we hit the outskirts of Huatabampo. As we entered Huatabampo the procession stopped to uncover the images. Then there were four additional stops before reaching the Huatabampo church.

Overall, the time required to return to the church in Huatabampo was not as long as the procession to Etchojoa the preceding day. The *konti* around the church in Etchojoa took place before 3:00 P.M. By about 3:15

the visitors were on the road back to Huatabampo. We arrived in Huatabampo around 4:30 and a little after 5:00 P.M. were in the Huatabampo
church ready for the evening Mass. This return walk seemed much faster
and considerably more tiring than the preceding day since there were not
so many stops this afternoon.

The images were carried into the church, bowed, and placed on the side
altar. After a series of prayers the priest explained that this was the
Sunday for the Holy Spirit and next Sunday it would be the Holy Trinity
celebration in Júpare. The Mass was somewhat more formal than the one
the preceding day. After 6:00 P.M. we were on the road again to Júpare.

After leaving the church and starting around the central plaza of
Huatabampo, the Pahkome from Etchoropo continued straight ahead down
the street that parallels the side of the church, whereas the Pahkome from
the Júpare area turned and went on around the park. Some of them waved
to each other as they split, however there was no handshaking ritual. They
turned the two Santísima Tiniran images so they faced each other and
brought the Etchoropo image up to the Júpare one. The images were bowed
in front of each other, moved very close together as though they were
embracing, bowed again, backed off, turned, and as the Júpare Santísima
Tiniran went on around the plaza, the Etchoropo Santísima Tiniran moved
straight on down the road leading to Etchoropo. Accompanied by a huge
mass of townspeople, our procession observed the same brief stops which
we had made entering town the preceding day. At the fifth stop the image
was covered while the last stop took place across the little drainage canal.
During the fast march to the Mayo River bank it was getting dark, as the
procession left Huatabampo a little before 7:00 P.M.

Several *cohetes* (small rockets) were shot when the procession reached
the river and the image was uncovered. Then we marched directly into
Júpare arriving around 8:00 P.M. They brought the Santísima Tiniran right
on into the church and rested Him in front of the altar. There were a lot
of people in Júpare, some candles were set out on the far side of the canal
to greet the image and many Matachins were dancing in front of the
church. Everyone seemed to be waiting for the procession to arrive. The
Pahkome quickly rolled up their flags and left them all up in the front
corner and disappeared out of the church door. As local people drifted into
the church crossing themselves and praying to the image and the Matachins continued dancing out front, worshipers placed a large cluster of lit
candles just in front of the church cross. Thus the *bisita* to the *pahko* of
the Espíritu Santo in Etchojoa was complete for another year. As we
returned to Huatabampo an older Mayo who had walked from Huatabampo
to Júpare with me said "we will all certainly sleep very well tonight, and
in a day or two the sores of the *bisita* will be gone."

THE SANTISIMA TINIRAN *PAHKO*

For the next *pahko* the Júpare visitors now became hosts. Each day the *nobena* prayers continued in the Júpare church as small commercial stands and numerous games and carnival rides were set up in the open area in front of the church. Although larger numbers of persons attended the Santísima Tiniran pahko as it is believed to be more miraculous, the visiting Pahkome are fewer because a competing *pahko* in honor of the Santísima Tiniran was taking place in Etchoropo. The events which we have described for the *bisita* and *pahko* in Etchojoa in honor of the Espíritu Santo are repeated for the Santísima Tiniran. Thursday evening and Friday night the Maso and Pahkolas danced and entertained the worshipers. Saturday morning the arriving Espíritu Santo and Her Pahkome were met at the river bank and escorted to a home in Júpare where the image was rested until late afternoon. Saturday afternoon the two images, Santísima Tiniran and Espíritu Santo met and the Espíritu Santo was accompanied into the Júpare church where She remained until the *konti* procession and Her leave-taking late Sunday afternoon. The Pahkolas and Maso and Matachinis danced, several *castillom* (fireworks displays) were shot off Saturday night, a Mass and the exchange of the rosaries took place within the church, the bread rosaries and flags were exchanged and returned in front of the church by the Pahkome, the *mabedwa* took place Sunday afternoon, and the Espíritu Santo was sent on Her way back to Etchojoa after saying goodbye Sunday afternoon. During the *bisita* the church was jammed with people entering to cross themselves and pray to the image. Thus a very similar pattern was enacted during the second half of this set of exchange *pahkom*.

THE HISTORY OF THE PAHKO AND OF *SANTA KURU PUEBLO*

Before the Spanish conquest, the Mayos likely lived as small scale farmers, hunters, and fishermen in rancherias of less than 300 inhabitants. In 1533 the Spaniard Diego de Guzman made the first contacts with the Mayos and in 1609 Captain Diego de Hurdaide established a peace treaty with the Mayos, who requested missionaries. By 1614 several Jesuits had appeared in the Mayo region. They were welcomed by large groups of Mayos and initiated their conversion activities. The Jesuits concentrated the Mayos into a chain of mission pueblos extending from the coast into the foothills of the Sierra Madre mountains. Although it depends upon how far one considers Jesuit settlements into the foothills of the mountains as actually Mayo and what one counts as a *pueblo*, modern Mayo ideology claims eight original mission-pueblos, Goh Naiki Pueblo Huracionim. In addition to initiating a program of concentration, the Jesuits taught in the Mayo language, cooperated with and worked through the Mayo leadership, and lived among the Mayos without the support or overt threat of the Spanish military. Their program produced far-reaching changes in the Mayo sociocultural system, both in the technico-economic and social system as well as in Mayo ritual and ceremonialism. They most likely modified Mayo war societies, founding sacred sodalities or *cofradias* such as the Pariserom and the Pahkome. In 1767 the Jesuits were expelled from the New World and thereafter the Mayos took more or less complete control of their ceremonies, churches, and chapels.

The 1800s were years of autonomy and turmoil, with gradual increase of mestizo Mexican military and political power, or encroaching colonization, and of land loss to mestizo colonists. Years of both peace and rebellion characterized this autonomous period, which closed with the final pacification of the Mayos in the 1880s.

Although the town of Etchojoa has remained the ceremonial center of the original Mayo Etchojoa Pueblo, the history of Santa Kuru Pueblo appears more complex yet more integrally Mayo. One comes to realize that the Mayo concept of *pueblo* includes not only the village itself but also the general region under the control of the ceremonial center. Thus the modern Santa Kuru Pueblo as a region of Mayo identity is essentially identical to the Huatabampo Municipio and Etchojoa Pueblo to Etchojoa Municipio. Until the 1880s the Santa Kuru mission-village (the modern Pueblo'ora) remained the ceremonial center of Santa Kuru Pueblo, after which time it was gradually depopulated and the church-ceremonial center shifted to Huatabampo. In the early twentieth century, as Mayos gradually lost control of Huatabampo, they established a new church-ceremonial center in Júpare. Gradually tensions grew in Júpare and during a flood an unfriendly split took place. The dissenting group formed the Etchoropo church center, also with the Santísima Tiniran as their patron saint, thus competing with Júpare. Closer to Huatabampo a church dedicated to the Santa Kuru was constructed at Nabowaxia, a friendly church center which for years has supported a full set of Pahkome, very recently has established its own Easter ceremonial, and maintains a pattern of *bisitam* with the Júpare Pahkome.

Through a process of incorporation of and adaptation to recent historical events, traditional Mayo symbolism, mythology, and ceremonialism has provided a dynamic basis for ceremonial revitalization and new cult development (see Crumrine 1977a and Macklin & Crumrine 1973). In 1926, President Calles enforced both established and new anti-Church legislation, which resulted in the burning of Mayo churches in the river valley, including the Júpare church. Although such church burnings took place in other areas of Mexico, Mayos believe that the local mestizo power structure took this occasion as a chance for revenge against Mayos. These events and especially the burning of the Júpare church images at Crusacitas, still marked with several decorated crosses by which the procession to Etchojoa passes, are clearly remembered by Santa Kuru Pueblo Mayos.

In the late 1920s and early 1930s lands were redistributed in the form of
ejido society memberships and by the late 1930s the Júpare church had
been rebuilt and Mayo ceremonialism revived. Since that time Mayos have
been rebuilding their churches and reviving and adjusting their traditional
way of life (see Crumrine 1977a).

In the late 1950s and early 1960s a very powerful new religious cult
developed in the area and many Mayo families made home *pahkom* as gifts
to God. A young man had seen and talked with God and proceeded to make
speeches informing Mayos that God was very angry and He would destroy
mankind if ceremonials were not made. For several years his message was
generally accepted by traditional Mayos. Even though the cult eventually
died out, the Santa Kuru church in Pozo Dulce resulted from the excitement
and home rituals which the cult generated in this predominantly Mayo *ejido*
community. Thus the Pozo Dulce church with its Pahkome organization
was established as recently as the mid-1960s.

Pueblo'ora, with a small home chapel housing an image of the Santa
Kuru, customarily hosted a social dance for the May celebration of the
Santa Kuru. However, only some very few years ago a formal group of
Pahkome was established and now a full *pahko* is offered to the Santa
Kuru. In fact, by 1986 a brick church was under construction and gradually
nearing completion in 1988.

CONCLUSION

I have argued that modern Mayos are in an intermediary stage at some
point between a precontact tribal society and a modern ethnic or fully
assimilated status (see Crumrine 1964, 1977a, 1981). Today I would
hesitate to predict whether Mayos will become a more deeply entrenched
ethnic enclave, embedded in modern mestizo Mexico, or move toward more
assimilated status. Clearly, at this point in time, Mayos are maintaining
and reviving their traditional way of life and dynamically adapting their
key symbols, values, and rituals to the cultural ecology of the modern Mayo
River valley. In an important sociopolitical sense the exchange *pahkom* in
honor of the Espíritu Santo and the Santísima Tiniran unify Mayos at the
Pueblo or intermunicipio level and contribute to the maintenance of their
social group and cultural traditions as separate from those of non-Mayos.
For example, at the Espíritu Santo pahko, numerous Mayos pointed out
to me that these were the Goh Naiki Pueblo Hurasionim as well as
discussing this ceremonial and political unit among other attending Mayos.
Calling my attention to the eight flags of the Pahkome groups, they argued
that each flag represented a *pueblo*, which symbolically is very powerful,
although in reality each flag is from a church center, all within only two
of the eight original Pueblo Hurasionim. It would seem to be a fortunate
accident that the flags total eight, an increase over the five church centers

that we observed participating in the *bisita* of 1959 (Crumrine 1969). Thus the *bisita* and *pahko* ritual pattern is extremely dynamic and capable of reflecting and adapting to recent historical and cultural ecological processes. In addition a number of Mayos participating in or attending the Espíritu Santo pahko argued that this was a Mayo ceremony, the people attending were all Mayos, all Yoremes, and that the land was Mayo *bwiya* (land). Clearly all this discourse carries messianic implications and messianic symbolism, which characterizes other levels of Mayo ritual as well as the exchange *pahkom*. In summary, the exchange *bisitam* represent and symbolize Mayo unity and their shared historical experiences and also contribute to continued Mayo existence as an enduring people.

At a more general symbolic level, these exchange *pahkom* provide two structural patterns, the *bisita* and the *pakho*, in which the roles of the participants and the ritual patterns are reversed from one weekend to the next. The visiting *pueblo* moves across the *pueblo* boundary, passing through space, in order to meet the hosting Pahkome at their sacred church center and to celebrate the special feast day of the patron saint. In doing so they not only unify the *pueblos* but also establish contact with the saint through the *nobena* and *pahko* rituals. As *pueblo* oppositions are unified into the Goh Naiki Pueblo Hurasionim, the human-deity oppositions are also mediated and Mayos communicate not only among themselves but also with their shared past and with God and the saints.

REFERENCES

Crumrine 1964, 1969, 1971,
   1977a, 1981, 1983, 1987

Erasmus 1967
Macklin-Crumrine 1973

5

Pilgrimage and Shrine:
Religious Practices among the Otomi
of Huixquilucan, Mexico

H. R. HARVEY

In contemporary Mexico, pilgrimage to a sacred shrine is an important component of religious practice for a broad segment of society, urban and rural, Indian and peasant. It was also an important practice in pre-Hispanic Mexico and many of the most prominent Christian shrines have their roots in pagan antiquity. Martínez Marín's (1972) survey of colonial documents reveals the widespread occurrence of pilgrimage from the Central Mexican highlands to the Yucatán peninsula. The indigenous sacred landscape included mountains, caves, springs, and other natural features, an environment with religious significance far more ample than specific documentation records. Part of the early missionary strategy involved converting a selected portion of this landscape to serve Christian ends. Thus, the miraculous Christian apparition of the Virgin of Guadalupe occurred at Tepeyac, the sacred hill of Tonantzin. Christ on the Cross miraculously appeared in a cave at Chalma, replacing the shattered stone idol of the old, Ocuiltec Lord of the Cave. Many sites were not converted, however, such as Mount Tlaloc near Texcoco, possibly the most prominent rain god shrine of all. Their use persisted well into this century, and for some, may still continue. The incomplete conversion of the native sacred landscape was probably an important factor contributing to the persistence of paganism. It fostered visitation to selected ancient sanctuaries, perhaps enhancing rather than diminishing their supernatural power. Had all the shrines been converted or had worship at local shrines been prohibited, paganism might have succumbed to suppression or subversion and the spiritual conquest of Mesoamerica would have been more perfectly achieved.

The municipality of Huixquilucan in the state of Mexico is one of the many Otomí communities where pilgrimage continues to be a major part of public life. Embedded within the pilgrimage practices described here are survivals of indigenous Otomí religious concepts. Symbolic linkages and transformations between paganism and popular Catholicism become evident through examination of the religious sanctuaries, the timing and activities associated with pilgrimage events, and the oral tradition.

MUNICIPIO OF HUIXQUILUCAN

The *municipio* of Huixquilucan is situated in the Sierra de las Cruces between the valley of Mexico and the valley of Toluca (Figure 5.1). Modern

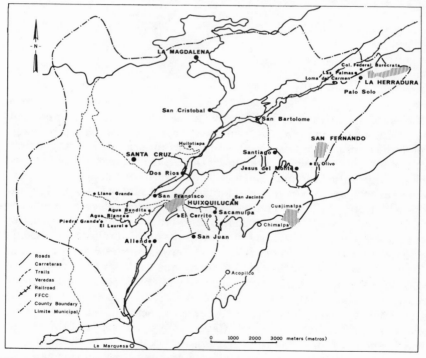

Figure 5.1 Map of the Huixquilucan Region

highways pass immediately to the north and south, although prior to their construction, the *municipio* was directly on the main route between the two valleys. A few fading vestiges of this former traffic still persist, especially around the *cabecera*, San Antonio Huixquilucan de Degollado, which traditionally served as broker to the outside world. In the 1960s, when many of the present data were collected, Huixquilucan was only beginning to stir from its traditional ways, which time and geographic isolation had imposed.[1]

At the time of Spanish conquest, Huixquilucan belonged to the imperial tribute province of Cuahuacan, one of seven administered by the Tepanecs, whose seat of power was the city of Tlacopan, now Tacuba (Zantwijk 1969:123-55). Local tradition acknowledges this historic connection with Tacuba and a colonial period overthrow of Tepanec hegemony (Harvey n.d.). Shortly after the conquest, Huixquilucan was among the towns given as dowry to Moctezuma's daughter, Doña Isabel, in her marriage to the conqueror Alonso de Grado. This act cemented the relationship which had prevailed pre-Hispanically between the predominantly Otomí-speaking *municipio* and the Nahuatl-speaking nobility of Tacuba. It also assured missionary support in converting the population of the *municipio* to Christianity, because Doña Isabel early on became a devout Catholic and was famous for her zeal in promoting the work of the Church. In 1579, the Jesuits established themselves at Jesús del Monte on the southeast end of the *municipio* and for a few years, while studying the Otomí language, their order ministered to the locals. Huixquilucan, therefore, has been under direct persuasion of the Church for more than four centuries. Notwithstanding, a significant number of its people retain vestiges of their traditional native religion, and a few may retain more than vestiges. Particularly appropriate, when applied to the religious status of Huixquilucan and similar localities with a surviving Indian population, is Gibson's comment that: "Although it cannot really be demonstrated, it may be assumed that the pagan components of modern Indian religions have survived in an unbroken tradition to the present day" (1964:134).

There are probably very few, if any, adults in Huixquilucan who have not visited a religious sanctuary either as a participant in an organized pilgrimage or as a personal visit. Pilgrimage is very important in the ceremonial calendar and most communities sponsor or participate in one or more pilgrimages to a sacred shrine each year. The pilgrimage calendar is common knowledge and devotion at a sacred shrine is part of a common religious expression. Most local fiestas terminate with a pilgrimage, but there is considerable variation within the *municipio* as to which shrines pilgrimages are directed. There is also variation in their manner of organization and mode of sponsorship. The principal sanctuaries routinely visited by organized group pilgrimages are: the regional shrine of Santa Cruz Ayotusco in the heart of the *municipio*; Chalma, some 90 kilometers to the southeast; Guadalupe on the northern edge of Mexico City; and los

Remedios on the western edge near Tacuba, Naucalpan. The latter three are shrines of national reputation. The shrine at Santa Cruz is an extremely important regional shrine which has not been described previously. Other shrines also attract people from Huixquilucan who may join pilgrimages organized outside the *municipio*. Among the less-frequented are San Juan de los Lagos and the Sacromonte. Just as the treatment of illness requires preliminary diagnosis to enable selection of the proper practitioner, a native curer for certain maladies or a physician trained in Western medicine for others, sacred shrines also have their particular specialties. The felt need to visit a shrine may direct a person to a sanctuary that is not customarily visited by people from Huixquilucan. In addition, 11 percent of the population in 1974 were immigrants to the *municipio*, meaning that some of them must fulfill their vows at shrines other than those traditionally favored by natives of Huixquilucan (Harvey and Williams 1975:28).

OTOMI PANTHEON

The most conspicuous and powerful survivors in the Otomí pantheon in the Huixquilucan region are Makatá and Makamé, Old Father and Old Mother. Both Indians and non-Indians are acquainted with these supernatural personages. They are not only realities in the belief system of many Indians, but also ceremonies and songs shared by the non-Indian population still allude to them. Conceptually, they appear analogous to the Nahua creator pair, Ometeotl and Omecihuatl, or Tonacatecuhtli and Tonacacihuatl.

Makatá is worshipped on mountain tops and is the Lord of the Mountain, the God of Fire. In addition he exercises control over rain, although the Otomí also distinguish a Lord of the Rain as a separate supernatural personage. The cross symbolizes both Makatá and Tlaloc: a cross painted green possibly represents Makatá, one painted blue, Tlaloc. Makatá's main ceremonies, which help to ensure a good crop, take place in the spring, at the end of April, the third of May and the 25th of May. Makamé is the Earth Mother, called "the spirit of the grain field" by Garibay (1957:13). She is the goddess of flowers, of fecundity, and also of the moon, especially revered by the Otomí. Her abode is natural caves and springs, and her ceremonies mark the first fruits of harvest.

It is somewhat curious that only the primordial couple has clearly survived until the present, while the footprints of other possible deities in the Otomí pantheon are now so faint. Animistic beliefs described for the Otomí in the historical chronicles and in other geographic areas are also held by Huixquilucan's Otomí. Every tree, plant, spring, rock, and even every seed has a spirit. Perhaps it was the personification of these that provided equivalents to the Nahua pantheon. The Spirit or Lord of the Tree probably equates with the fire god, the Nahua Ocotecuhtli, Xiuhtecuhtli, or Huehueteotl, but the identification is by no means certain. Carrasco (1950:138-46) concluded that Otonteuctli or Ocotecutli, the fire god, was prominent in the Otomí pantheon, but in Huixquilucan, the fire god seems to have been subsumed under Makatá. Because Makatá is associated with fire, he also is associated with the sun. Thus, the major ceremony of Makatá on the 25th of May coincides with the fiesta of Huitzilopochtli.

Most scholars who have addressed the question of Otomí religion, such as Carrasco (1950) and Nicholson (1971), believe that the Nahua pantheon was shared by the Otomí. That may be exactly what the Huixquilucan data reflect, an imposed or borrowed Nahua pantheon synthesized into the Otomí primordial couple. What survived in Huixquilucan is what was Otomí. Another possibility, of course, might have been the existence of substantial variation between Otomí groups. More fieldwork might resolve such questions, but modern practitioners of indigenous religion often will not admit, much less discuss, their beliefs and rituals. Those who leave offerings at pagan shrines are always "other" people. Native religion in part has survived because it went underground, practiced clandestinely probably since the 16th century during those decades dedicated to stamping out idolatry or the idolaters. Many people in the *municipio* who distance themselves from paganism nevertheless believe that the old gods did perform miracles and may have been effective for the people then. In other words, they are tolerant of non-Christian religion as carried on by others, and in the remote past.

Although we do not know the identity of strictly Otomí deities in Huixquilucan other than the primordial couple, and almost nothing of how they viewed the universe, we do know that pilgrimage to sacred shrines was a religious practice that predated the conquest, and was and is associated with the worship of the primordial couple.

THE SANCTUARY OF SANTA CRUZ AYOTUSCO

Group pilgrimages in Huixquilucan take place during the spring and at harvest time. Those linked with Makatá occur in the spring, those with Makamé in the fall. The *municipio* has or had several mountaintop and cave shrines. The most sacred locality within the *municipio* is the sanctuary of Santa Cruz Ayotusco. This mountaintop shrine commands a breathtaking view of the core area of the *municipio*, the *cabecera* and its environs. The ascent to the shrine (elevation 3,050 meters) from the "center" of Santa Cruz (2,850 meters) is marked by a series of small chapels (Figure 5.2) representing the stations of the cross. Most of these are of stone, large enough to hold no more than three people, and dedicated to a Catholic personage. Devotional activity is evidenced by the remains of offerings such as flowers, copal, paper, etc., reverently placed by pilgrims as they ascend to the shrine.

Figure 5.2 Chapel, Sta Cruz Ayotusco

A broad, level, open plaza commands the top of the sacred mountain, dominated on its southern end by a late-nineteenth-century church. Above the altar in this church is the sacred image, a cross with the "Divine Face" (*el Rostro Divino* (Figure 5.3) that people have come to adore. The cross is draped with cloth which obscures the face of Christ worked in silver. Both ends of the cross arms are also silver and exposed to view. Oral tradition relates that the cross first appeared on September 14th, year unspecified. In remote times, the mountain was densely forested. Shepherds had to be on guard so that their animals would not wander into the forest and become lost. One day a shepherd was whistling for his animals which had strayed and the whistle was returned. Hearing it again, the shepherd became curious and went to look for the source of the whistling, whereupon he found the cross with two burned candles by its side. Thus, the appearance of the cross was miraculous, and everyone agrees that the Rostro Divino of Santa Cruz can perform miracles. But people disagree about which classes of miracles it best performs. It can both cure miraculously or become angry and cause illness if vows are not kept.

Besides the church at the Santa Cruz sanctuary with the Divine Face and an array of saints, there is a long, single-story building on the western exposure of the plaza which serves both as a dormitory for encamped pilgrims and as a dining area providing protection from the vagaries of weather. Since many of the festive events celebrated at the shrine occur in the rainy season and at an altitude of over 3000 meters, the rains can

Figure 5.3 El Rostro Divino, the "pilgrim," Sta Cruz Ayotusco

often be torrential. Also in the plaza are two wooden crosses, free-standing at the point of greatest elevation and commanding attention with their usual fresh coat of light green paint.

Behind the church, which obscures it from view, is a small stone chapel. This structure appears to have been constructed in the latter decades of the sixteenth century. It is a place of offerings, flowers, and incense, and contains a copy of the Divine Face. The face is more Indian in appearance and the cross is supported on a marble base but in other respects the cross in the church and the one in the chapel are similar. The copy in the chapel is referred to as the "pilgrim," because this is the image carried to the town's fiesta on the third of May and taken to the fiesta of San Antonio Huixquilucan in June, along with the other patron saints of Huixquilucan's subject communities. The chapel also houses an image of Señor de la Caña (Lord of the Cane), interesting from the point of view that the local tradition in Lerma, where the Lord of the Cane is patron, credits Huixquilucan with originally supplying its image (Henning 1911). This small, colonial period chapel is distinctive in that it sits atop a pre-Hispanic stone pyramid. There is no question, therefore, that this sanctuary precedes the Spanish conquest as a sacred locality attracting pilgrims.

Apparently there are no extant colonial period records of the sanctuary, nor are there any archaeological data as with most shrine sites. The only sources of records are oral tradition and inference from behavioral practice. Clearly, Santa Cruz is a prominent place of devotion today, even though its constituency of clients has been dwindling in the past two to three decades. It must have been very prominent in the nineteenth century, when a local landholder donated the land and constructed the church in 1879. At that time, it was perhaps in shambles from the devastation of the reform in the 1850s, when churches, cemeteries, and sanctuaries were laid waste and the sacred relics of the past widely destroyed. Local people say that in addition to the small chapel which still stands, there had been an old, small church on the site, perhaps from the colonial era, that the present structure replaced.

When Father Garibay (1957:14) was parish priest in Huixquilucan in the 1920s, groups of over 5,000 Mazahuas and Otomís from the Ixtlahuaca district in the valley of Toluca visited and camped at the shrine. Today, there are still regular pilgrimages from nearby towns such as Atarasquillo, Xochicuautla, San Miguel Ameyalco, and others. Except for universal religious holidays such as Easter week, the itinerary at the shrine is governed by the staggered calendar of patron saint festivities in the various towns, since pilgrimage to a sacred shrine terminates such an event. Within a relatively restricted geographic area there may well be a fiesta in progress nearly every week of the year, especially taking into account that most towns celebrate their patron's day twice a year. Pilgrims come to Santa Cruz several times during the year. Atarasquillo, for example, has a pilgrimage on the first of January, another on a moveable date in June for the Holy Trinity, and still another in August. On some fiesta occasions pilgrims from several localities converge on Santa Cruz. On the eighth of September, for example, a pilgrimage from Xochicuautla, San Lorenzo Huitzizilapan, Chimalpa el Grande, La Magdalena Chichicaspa and nearby San Cristobal Texcalucan arrives. In another instance, on the 15th of August a pilgrimage leaves the village of San Miguel Ameyalco at 5:00 A.M. It passes through Santa María Atarasquillo where Mass is heard, and then proceeds to San Mateo Atarasquillo and Santiaguito Analco, at which point the pilgrimage is joined by people from Xochicuautla. The pilgrims stop for lunch at Sabanilla, after which they head directly to Santa Cruz, arriving about 5:30 P.M. When they reach the final climb to the shrine, they stop at each station of the cross to pray and make offerings. At the tenth station, the procession stops and waits for the rest of the group to catch up. Then the standards are unfurled, one or more for each town in the pilgrimage. They continue toward the sanctuary praying with their rosaries as they walk along. The melodious sounds of two primitive violins provide the musical background for the solemn procession. When they arrive, they go directly to the church, although a few go first to the old chapel behind the church.

Arriving too late for a Mass, the pilgrims offer prayers to the Divine Face before eating and bedding down for the night in the *portal*. Usually, families are separated, with women sleeping apart from the men. Because of the hardship of the long walk in the rainy season, few children or elderly people make the pilgrimage. Early the next morning, at 4:00 or 5:00 A.M., they sing the *mañanitas*, and later attend Mass. They prepare the food brought with them for the day's meal. The next morning, Mass is again heard, after which the group begins the return home.

The sanctuary of Santa Cruz Ayotusco is blessed with a miraculous image, the Divine Face. Except for the legend of his miraculous or mysterious appearance, however, he is not unique. Many variants of this cross in stone and wood are found in the region that date to the colonial period, such as the one nearby on the Cerro de la Campana, which contains a group of stone crosses. The tallest has a face of Christ crowned in thorns while a second has a face of the Virgin. Smaller crosses display star motifs, which Henning (1911) identified as *tlaloque* (rain) symbols. Even though, for the third of May ceremony, pilgrims destined for Santa Cruz sometimes stop first at the Cerro de la Campana sanctuary, the Cerro de la Campana is also a pilgrimage destination in its own right. To the Otomí both are shrines of Makatá, sacred mountaintops on which he resides. The coming of the Christians did not dislodge Old Father. He is still there. Both pagans and Christians identify with his shrine.

RAIN

In Indian Mexico the cross is very often a symbol of the rain god, and such an interpretation cuts across linguistic and ethnic borders. In Huixquilucan and probably elsewhere in the Otomían world, the cross more directly symbolized the fire god, and rain is simply an aspect of this deity's jurisdiction. For example, on the third of May, people come from various towns in the *municipio* to the small church of San Francisco Ayotusco bearing their household crosses to have them blessed. These will protect the household from strikes by bolts of lightning. Thus, here as elsewhere, lightning, a manifestation of Makatá, provides the conceptual linkage between the binary opposites of fire and water. Notwithstanding, the Huixquilucan Otomís appear also to have recognized a distinct rain deity. Some mountaintops, such as the Cerro de San Francisco and that of San Bartolomé Coatepec, appear from the ceramic offerings to have been largely rain god shrines. That of San Francisco has a large wooden cross, where oblations of food, pulque, copal, and the like are regularly placed. If the Cerro de San Bartolomé ever had a cross, it no longer does. Local people insist that it was devastated during the Revolution of 1910 when Carranza's troops supposedly camped there and also destroyed two large pottery *ollas* that once graced the top of the hill. Similar tales, told with conviction, are not uncommon in the region to account for the destruction of old rain deity shrines. The Cerro de Coatepec was also enchanted, although the story of its enchantment is recounted more in the realm of myth than historical reality. Once, a man and his wife were cutting wood on the hill. When the wife wandered off and did not return, her husband went to find her. He found her at the spring where she had been transformed into a half woman, half serpent, the Nahua Cihuacoatl and probably the Otomí counterpart, Makamé. Such legends, other oral traditions, and occasional continuing devotions serve to identify the cult of the rain gods. The offerings perhaps also preserve a trace of an old rain-fertility related Xipe cult. Many of the little pottery jars left as offerings are better labeled Xipe jars rather than Tlaloc jars. Soustelle (1937) felt that Sahagún's Yocippa was Xipe, and we know from other sources that Xipe was an important deity in the Tepanec area. For the local Otomí, the expression of a Xipe-like supernatural may well have been Makamé, the earth mother and moon goddess. Modern informants of San Bartolomé also question the ancient affiliation of their sacred mountain. They ask if their mountain could once have been the abode of the Lord of Chalma. They sense some connection because pilgrims from the Tula area en route to Chalma used to visit the Cerro de Coatepec until, people say, the late 1930s or early 1940s.

A link between the Lord of Chalma and the Lord of Rain is made by people from Chimalpa el Grande. Their Tlaloc sanctuary atop the Cerro de la Malinche is said to be the birthplace of the Lord of Chalma, who once fought the Devil before moving on to the caves at Chalma (Harvey 1980).

PILGRIMAGE TO CHALMA

The Lord of Chalma is deeply revered in Huixquilucan. His picture is adored in most household shrines and many people from the towns and rancherias of Huixquilucan have made pilgrimages to the sanctuary of Chalma, or else have gone there on personal *visitas*. There is a substantial number of organized pilgrimages to Chalma throughout the year, by foot or by bus. The third and the 25th of May are especially popular dates for traditional pilgrimages originating from the *cabecera* Ayotusco region.

There is an expanding anthropological literature on pilgrimage to Chalma based on first-hand participation and observation, such as Hobgood's 1958 trek from Huixquilocan (1970a), Benuzzi's from San Pedro Tultepec (1980), and Gilberto Giménez's study of Atlapulco (1978). They attest to the fundamental role that pilgrimage, traditional and modern, plays in the religious life of families and communities. For example, San Pedro Tultepec jealously guards its prestigious role in providing entertainment at the shrine at Christmas. In Huixquilucan, the May pilgrimages from San Francisco and Santa Cruz Ayotusco stream south in small groups of two or three families. From Huixquilucan, Chalma is an exhausting two-day walk, even for people accustomed to the altitude and precipitous terrain of the *municipio*. The physical hardship, however, is not a deterrent but a challenge, and the pilgrim knows that he or she will be renewed, exhilarated by the experience. In fact, many people in Huixquilucan have gone to Chalma by foot a number of times.

The groups start early in the morning passing through La Marquesa to San Pedro Atlapulco, where breakfast is eaten. They then trudge on to Santiago Tianguistengo, which is often teeming with other pilgrims also heading toward Chalma. The Huixquilucan group, which Hobgood joined, spent the night at the little town of San Mateo Texcalyacac, where the leaders had friends with whom they exchanged hospitality when the latter passed through Huixquilucan bound for the villa of Guadalupe or Los Remedios. The second morning, the aching group again started off early. Their route was by no means direct. Rather, it favored archaeological sites rather than minimizing distance. In the valley of Tenancingo, the group stopped at a broken stone cross where they picked nettles and flogged themselves before proceeding onward. The stated purpose of the self-flagellation was not only to relieve fatigue but also to "do penance" (Hobgood 1970a:14). They next stopped at a pyramid near Malinalco, which supported three stone crosses. It was here that the cloth bags containing umbilical cords of a nephew and a niece of one of the female pilgrims were deposited. Not to leave umbilical cords would be to break a vow to the Lord of Chalma, and also, by doing this, the children's health would be protected and the male children would be virile. When the group arrived in the Chalma vicinity it went to a cave, one of a cluster of four, in the hills above the sanctuary. The group would stay in that cave while attending the festivities of the Holy Cross and share it with others from Huixquilucan.

Had the group gone via Ocuila, they would have passed the ahuehuete tree (Figure 5.4) and deposited the umbilical cords there. At this ancient tree, those going to Chalma for the first time should dance and place crowns of flowers on their heads. Women might leave an article of clothing at the tree, or perhaps a braid as a personal offering to the Lord of Chalma. To offer one's hair is to give a part of one's self. The ahuehuete is very sacred because it grows over a spring thought to be the origin of water. To assure fecundity, women who have not previously done so should bathe in its waters, as well as in the nearby river.

Who is the Lord of Chalma? Many in Huixquilucan believe that the image of the crucifix in the church of Chalma is a copy. The real Lord of Chalma is locked in a crypt below the church, opened only on the Days of the Dead. Many feel that were he not locked up by the friars, he would spend most of his time near the ahuehuete tree. Notwithstanding, he does get out and goes places. The people of Tecozpa in Milpa Alta think that the Lord of Chalma visits his brother there in June at the time of their patron's fiesta (Madsen 1960). For some, the Lord of Chalma is Jesus, the son of God; for others, he is God. For still others, he may be the Lord of the Cave,

Figure 5.4 Sacred ahuehuete tree, road to Chalma

the Lord of the Mountain, or the Lord of Rain.

Although there is only slight mention in ethnohistorical sources of the sanctuary at Chalma, there is no question that it was an important shrine, at least to the Ocuiltec. The sacred landscape of the Chalma vicinity possesses a rich combination of natural features associated with the ancient Mesoamerican supernatural realm: huge caves, springs, and high mountain peaks (Figure 5.5). To the Ocuiltec, it was the abode of Oztoteotl, Lord of the Cave. Scholarly opinion is divided on the questions of the identification of Oztoteotl in the Nahua pantheon and his relation to the deities of the Ocuiltec linguistic kin, the Otomí. Most feel that the Nahua took over this important sanctuary, installing their own god(s), and that the Christian Lord of Chalma, Christ on the cross, replaced it. Hobgood argues convincingly that the Lord of Chalma was Huitzilopochtli and that the conceptual linkage was the Virgin birth. Perhaps not coincidently, a pilgrimage from Huixquilucan reaches Chalma to celebrate the 25th of May, Huitzilopochtli's fiesta day. Aspects of this sun god do associate him with the water deities and with earth. For example, he shared the Templo Mayor of Tenochtitlan with Tlaloc. On the other hand, Horcasitas (1979) identifies Chalma as a Tlaloc shrine, and Romero Quiroz (1957) sees an identification with Tezcatlipoca, the heart of the mountain. To the Otomí of Huixquilucan, the Lord of Chalma is probably their own Makatá, there with his wife, Makamé.

Whether the Otomí of Huixquilucan made pilgrimages to the sanctuary at Chalma prior to the Spanish conquest is another question. Kubler (1981)

Figure 5.5 The sanctuary of Chalma with the town of Chalma in the foreground

does not believe that long-distance pilgrimage was a common religious practice in precontact times for the majority of the population. Instead, he feels that pilgrimage was practiced by the elites and merchants only, that *macehuals* did not venture from their home territories. On the other hand, Chalma and many other towns in the old Tepanec domain, such as San Pedro Atlapulco, Tenancingo, Tenango, and Calimaya, were added to the empire of the Triple Alliance under Axayacatl and at least from that time, if not earlier, the Otomí of Huixquilucan would have had safe passage. Pilgrimage to Chalma is so deeply embedded in the pagan fabric of these many communities that it probably was pre-Hispanic. The miraculous appearance of the Christian Lord of Chalma in a cave which had housed a broken idol was hardly coincidence (Mendizabal 1925; Turner and Turner 1978). Whether its patronage gained momentum after the conquest or simply continued is a question that needs further study. Today, it is a national shrine and its patrons come long distances, frequently on foot even from places as remote as the Isthmus of Tehuantepec.

HARVEST-TIME PILGRIMAGES

Major pilgrimage activity to Santa Cruz and Chalma clusters in May, the beginning of the new crop season. Also, as harvests begin a series of pilgrimages take place. The people in Huixquilucan strongly revere both the Virgin of Los Remedios and the Virgin of Guadalupe, who are identified with their indigenous creator deity Makamé. Makamé represents the Virgin, who especially understands them because she speaks their language, Otomí.

A colorful pilgrimage is organized each year in the town of San Francisco Ayotusco and its parent community Santa Cruz Ayotusco. It has a moveable date, the first Thursday of August. Its destination is the sanctuary of the Virgin of Los Remedios in Naucalpan, a seven-hour trek from the little church in San Francisco. The Virgin of los Remedios gained fame in the 16th century for relieving drought and her image was carried many times in the colonial era to Mexico City (Gibson 1964: 315). Oral tradition in the Ayotusco area also associates drought with the origin of their pilgrimage. In the seventeenth century, or perhaps earlier, the crops were drying up and the people went to seek help from the bishop. He told them to make an annual pilgrimage, taking children to dance at the sanctuary of Los Remedios both to relieve the drought and to assure that it would not reoccur. The people of San Francisco vowed to make the annual pilgrimage. Not to honor their vow would anger the Virgin and result in her seeking revenge.

San Francisco and Santa Cruz Ayotusco have separate pilgrimage *mayordomos* and separate ceremonial groups, but they travel together. The pilgrimage begins Thursday morning with a walk to the sanctuary of Santa Cruz where they spend the night in the *portal* before returning Friday morning to hear Mass in the San Francisco church. After Mass, the combined group departs for Los Remedios. At the shrine the pilgrims stay for four nights and enjoy festal food cooked at the site. Sunday is the main day for the fiesta, for music and dancing. Many people from Huixquilucan join the group for the day. The dancers, children from four to eight years old, in costumes, new clothes, and carrying rattles, have been instructed in the dance since May by teachers, who as children had once been lead dancers in this ceremonial group. San Francisco's group will usually be composed of six boys and six girls, although more children can be accommodated, whereas Santa Cruz's group is restricted to boys. Such local variation on common themes is typical in Mexican folk religion. Interestingly, the lead roles in San Francisco's group are Hernán Cortés and the daughter of the "Reina Xochitl." In local legend, it was Cortés who first directed the Indians to the miraculous powers of the Virgin of Los Remedios in relieving drought and other calamities. Xochiquetzal in the Nahua pantheon is Tlaloc's first wife, the goddess of flowers, a deity whose attributes are thoroughly consistent with Makamé. On Tuesday, the group returns to San Francisco, to the house of the *mayordomo*, where a ceremonial dinner is served and where the group spends the last night of the pilgrimage. On Wednesday it disperses. It has fulfilled the town's obligations to the Virgin for having relieved their crop destroying drought and protected their communities over the long centuries. The *mayordomo* and his assistants have been rewarded with prestige, respect, and the esteem of neighbors and relatives.

The sanctuary of the Virgin of Los Remedios is a supra-local shrine with links to Makamé. One local place of worship of Makamé is the shrine of Santa Cruz. Some older informants insist that six or seven decades ago when they were children, there were caves underlying the sanctuary which were guarded by Indian vigilantes. Later the entrances were blocked or filled in. The story may not be apocryphal, since the cave entrances on Cerro San Francisco and Cerro San Martín were closed by Garibay's time, which could have been a recent event. Similarly, the upper entrance to the cave on nearby Cerro la Malinche was filled with debris. Such filling was a common practice at pagan shrines that possessed caves. Although the caves of Santa Cruz are no longer known, at the base of the Cerro of Santa Cruz is a very visible natural shrine, the Moon Rock (Piedra de la Luna), recalling the lunar association of Makamé, perhaps an element contributing to the widespread fame of Santa Cruz mountain.

The early August timing of the San Francisco Ayotusco pilgrimage first to Santa Cruz, then to Los Remedios, and its dances by a group of young children recalls the pre-Hispanic ceremonial during the month of Xocothuetzin. Although Huixquilucan's activities are a few days earlier than similar ceremonies in other localities, such syncretism is indeed plausible. The first fruits of harvest, the tender *elotes* (ears of green or roasting corn) in this case, tend to be universally celebrated. Another feature of this particular pilgrimage, which links two very sacred sanctuaries and primarily attracts Indian participants, places emphasis on the traditional customs. For example, the adult women wear typical dress and carry embroidered *ayates*.

Makamé is also widely celebrated on the eighth of September, when household altars are decorated with flowers, both wild and made of paper, and candles are burned. Many put *elotes* and beans on their altars and *elotes*, beans, and potatoes are taken to the Cerro of Santa cruz for the blessing of God. In addition to these activities at home and in the local sanctuary, people also participate in a pilgrimage to Los Remedios. A few still go on foot, but for this occasion, the majority take public transportation.

Many people in Huixquilucan also identify Makamé with the Virgin of Guadalupe. In the *municipio*, numerous pilgrimages to the villa are organized each year. For example, an organized pilgrimage leaves the *cabecera* December 30th. Another terminates the fiesta of San Martín, a barrio of the *cabecera*, in late January. Sacamulpa terminates its fiesta likewise with a pilgrimage to Guadalupe. If locally organized pilgrimages are not frequent enough, people may visit the Basilica on a personal *visita*. Clearly, the shrine of the Virgin of Guadalupe is the most popular and widely venerated in Mexico. The people of Huixquilucan share in this adoration, not only in frequent attendance at Her shrine, but in their private, family worship. Her picture or image adorns every household shrine in the villages and towns of the *municipio*.

Most organized pilgrimages to Her shrine are by bus. Those who prefer traditional pilgrimage, however, may join any one of a number of groups who walk to the shrine. A great spectacle is the church-organized pilgrimage from the state of Mexico in January. One hundred thousand or more pilgrims thread their way along the highway connecting the Valley of Toluca with the Valley of Mexico with persons from each locality grouped behind its banners and standards. A group from Huixquilucan, of course, joins this great procession.

Since the adoration of the Virgin of Guadalupe is so profound, Cámara and Reyes (1975) suggest that perhaps the presence of the Virgin serves to attract rural migrants to Mexico City. She would provide security and protection in an otherwise unfamiliar and insecure urban environment. Huixquilucan with its flow of migrants to the city would be an appropriate test case for the hypothesis, but we have no data to evaluate the impact of the miraculous apparition on an individual or family's decision to migrate.

CONCLUSION

Pilgrimage to a sacred shrine provides a major religious activity in the *municipio* of Huixquilucan. A pre-Hispanic practice, it has survived to the present and would appear to be responsible, in no small measure, for the persistence of the core concepts and rituals of basic Otomí religion. But, as elsewhere in Indian Mexico, it partially exists within the framework of Catholicism. As Henning concluded at the turn of the century, the Otomí "are Catholic only in those points in which the rite and dogma of the church is in agreement with their ancient beliefs" (1911:69) and like the Maya, their response did not bring about the rejection of the basic tenets of their own religion (Madsen 1967; Thompson 1954). They can still worship in those localities where their gods are present even if those sites are shared with a Christian personage.

Economic modernization, as Mexico has shifted from a preindustrial society, has taken a greater toll on paganism than four centuries of proselytizing friars and priests. However, the same forces of modernization have not diminished the importance of religious pilgrimage. Attendance at national shrines appears to have increased proportionate to the general demographic explosion. What has changed is the mode of transport. Indeed, mechanized transport is edging out foot power, and personal *visitas* appear to be on the increase in the less traditional components of the population.

The dominant motive for participating in a pilgrimage, whether personal or corporate, is religious. Pilgrimage is a vehicle which transports a person to the presence of the divine. In that charged atmosphere, both pagans and Christians petition for favors. They make their offerings, perform their rituals, fulfill their vows. The sacred presence does not discriminate.

NOTES

1. I wish to thank Barbara J. Williams for her helpful discussion and review of the manuscript. Also, some information included is based on field notes of B. J. Williams, D. Ryesky, and N. Quezada, taken during the 1965 and 1966 summer field seasons.

REFERENCES

Benuzzi 1980
Carrasco Pizana 1950
Cámara Barbachano-
  Couturier 1975
Garibay K. 1957
Gibson 1964
Giménez 1978
Harvey n.d., 1980
Harvey-Williams 1975
Henning 1911
Hobgood 1970a, 1970b

Horcasitas 1979
Kubler 1981
Madsen 1960, 1967
Martínez Marín 1972
Mendizabal 1925
Nicholson 1971
Romero Quiroz 1957
Soustelle 1937
Thompson 1954
Turner-Turner 1978
Zantwijk 1969

6

Social Structure
in Pilgrimage and Prayer:
Tzeltales as Lords and Servants

WALTER RANDOLPH ADAMS

Although the southern Mexican state of Chiapas has been the subject of many anthropological and historical studies, the southeastern portion of the state is little-known.[1] The New World Archeological Foundation initiated scientific studies by conducting ethnohistoric and linguistic research in that region. As part of that project I acquired, transcribed, and translated a prayer, the *Rezo Tzeltal*, which Tzeltal religious authorities (*rezadores*) recite during pilgrimages. By describing the system and presenting an analysis of associated ritual and prayer, I will show that pilgrimages and their related institutions contain data that permit a historical, regional reconstruction that rests on actual events rather than legends. Thus the pilgrimages and associated prayers conducted in Chiapas by the Tojolabales and Tzeltales furnish a case study, a framework on which to place other social structures, and a historical reconstruction of the area.[2]

THE PILGRIMAGES

The Tzeltales and Tojolabales conducted four pilgrimages each year to San Mateo Ixtatan, Guatemala (second Friday of Lent), Oxchuc (April 11),

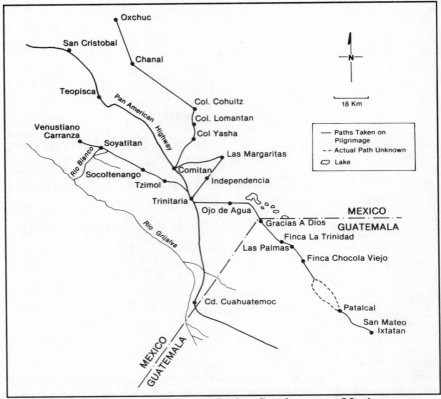

Figure 6.1 Map of the Pilgrimage Paths, Southeastern Mexico

Venustiano Carranza (April 26, now discontinued), and Las Margaritas (July 11) (Figure 6.1).[3] They were intended as petitions for bountiful harvests and plentiful, though not damaging, rains. These dates correspond to critical stages in the growing season for maize, the primary subsistence crop. The second Friday of Lent correlates closely with the beginning of the agricultural cycle (Cancian 1965:67). The two pilgrimages which take place in April harmonize with the collection of stalks left over from the previous year's crop and the burning of the fields later that month (Cancian 1965:67). The pilgrimage occurring in July coincides with the clearing of weeds from the new fields (Cancian 1965:68). This correspondence between these rites and the agricultural growing cycle is consistent with Wallace's (1966:111) observation for rituals of intensification.

Consultants stated that the pilgrimages (*romerias*) were gatherings of "all the Tojolabal brothers and sisters [sic], some Tzeltales, and a few Ladinos." This suggests the pilgrimages were primarily Tojolabal events, and individuals from other groups could participate if they desired.

However, the Tzeltal religious leaders were crucial to the pilgrimage, which could not occur without the particular skills they provided. Thus Tojolabales were ritually dependent upon the Tzeltales, who led the Tojolabales on the pilgrimages and performed curing rituals for the latter. The Tojolabales could not engage in these rites alone.[4] When asked why, the Tzeltales responded, "*somos los fiadores de dios*" (literally, we are God's trustees). The Tojolabales said they did not know Tzeltal. These statements suggest the Tojolabales were linguistically and ritualistically subservient to the Tzeltales.[5]

This relative position of the Tzeltales and the Tojolabales is also mirrored in the political economy. The Tzeltales' agricultural fields were characterized by fertile soil in contrast to those belonging to the Tojolabales, at lower elevations, which were visibly less fertile. As a result, the Tzeltales rarely worked on the coffee plantations while many of the Tojolabal informants indicated that they had worked on these plantations.

The specific pilgrimage to San Mateo Ixtatan exemplifies these sacred journeys in general terms. The event began when the Catholic priest at San Mateo informed the Tzeltal religious leader (*encargado*) when the second Friday of Lent would fall. Then, on September 21, the day of San Mateo, the Tzeltal *encargado* provided this information to the Tojolabal *encargado*. The latter then notified the appropriate village and hamlet officials in the Tojolabal area.[6]

About two weeks before the second Friday of Lent, one of the two *alfereces* (the lowest-level position in the cargo system) in these villages collected money from fellow villagers. Traditionally, each person contributed one peso, but such uniformity is not common today. In 1976 people donated what they could afford. These funds were carried to the Tojolabal *encargado*, who presented them to the Tzeltal *encargado* on the first Friday of Lent. The Tzeltal *encargado* recorded the names of the villages represented and the priest at San Mateo mentioned them during the Mass. Informants stated the deities would be benevolent to those communities making contributions.

The amount of money required for these pilgrimages depended on the cost of the Mass, the fireworks (*cohetes*), candles, and other materials used on the pilgrimage. In case of a deficit, the Tojolabal *encargado* had to make up the difference and sometimes, had to ask the villages for additional donations. By 1976, the Tzeltal *encargado* also contributed money as a result of increased costs, lower contributions, and decreased participation.

A few Tzeltales prepared for the pilgrimage to San Mateo. The Tzeltal *encargado* used a portion of the funds he received from the Tojolabal leader earlier to purchase *cohetes* and candles. Another portion was reserved for the priest at San Mateo. He also had to secure a border pass allowing the pilgrims to enter Guatemala. About two days before the pilgrimage, the Tzeltal *priostes* (the equivalent to the Tojolabal *alfereces*) collected a certain flower and lemon leaves and fashioned them into *ramietes* (a bouquet,

Figure 6.2 A *ramiete* as made by the Tzeltal priostes

Figure 6.2). These were left along with candles, *cohetes* and a recitation of the *Rezo Tzeltal* at the crosses, caves, and wells along the way to San Mateo. It is important to observe that these offerings, unlike those given by the Tojolabales, did not arrive at the pilgrimage center.

The Tojolabales completed the majority of their preparation for the pilgrimages in time to arrive in Trinitaria on the Thursday before the first Friday of Lent. The day before they left their village, they collected flowers from around the village which they would leave as offerings at the church in San Mateo Ixtatan. That evening the pilgrims went to Confession. The Tojolabales set off for Trinitaria early the next morning in specific formations. The only aspect of this formation that is important for the present study is the position of the red and white church flags carried by the *alfereces*. The red flag was carried on the left side of the procession and the white one on the right. These flags, as described below, provided clues to the relational status of the Tzeltales and the Tojolabales.

In addition to the flowers the pilgrims carried their own food, water dish (*tecomate*), and a bedroll (Figure 6.3). The pilgrims also sometimes carried candles and icons for the priest in San Mateo to bless. Also some pilgrims took offerings of livestock or chickens to give to the priest. In addition, some individuals reported participating in public works projects at the hosting center. These acts and the collection of money suggest the obvious economic aspects of pilgrimages, and the role of central figures in them.

The Tojolabal pilgrims arrived at the outskirts of Trinitaria on the Thursday preceding the second Friday of Lent. There they waited at a place called *cruz del milagro*, (*soposuk* in Tzeltal). The Tzeltal *encargado* then escorted the pilgrims into Trinitaria. They attended Mass at Trinitaria the evening of their arrival. At 3 A.M. the next morning they met at the house of the *encargado*, where the Rezo Tzeltal was recited. The pilgrims then travelled to San Mateo (Figure 6.1).

When they left Trinitaria the pilgrims traveled in a particular formation with the Tojolabal musicians leading them. The Tojolabal and Tzeltal *encargados* followed, with the Tojolabal walking on the left side of his counterpart and with the village icons carried behind these two leaders. The flags were lined up in two parallel lines with the church flags preceding the paired hamlet flags and the Tzeltal flagbearers going before their Tojolabal counterparts.

The pilgrims arrived at San Mateo Ixtatan after four days of traveling where they were met at the outskirts of the town by masked dancers, who ushered them into town. They circled the central plaza counter-clockwise and entered the church. Before doing so, however, they put their offerings beside the door of the church (Figure 6.4). The icons and the flags were left in the church while the pilgrims were at the center. The *Rezo Tzeltal* was recited every evening following the Catholic services. Three days after their arrival the pilgrims returned to their homes carrying the blessed icons and candles they had brought with them. They left alone or in groups consisting of family or village members.

Figure 6.3 Pilgrims carrying their belongings

A market was held concurrently which included products from throughout the catchment area, as well as products from Taiwan and other foreign countries. This market, its co-occurrence with the pilgrimage, and the range of products offered for sale again point to the economic functions of pilgrimages.

This description characterizes the general events associated with the pilgrimages. In each pilgrimage center there were some minor variations and/or ancillary rites which are not important here.[7] The degree of importance of the differing practices is suggested by the following events. The traditional pilgrimage route to Las Margaritas from Trinitaria via Independencia (Figure 6.1) was bisected in 1975 when the Mexican government constructed an airfield. The pilgrims were prohibited from

Figure 6.4 Offerings left by the pilgrims

using the traditional path. Consequently, they traveled by foot or by bus, individually or in small groups, to Comitan and then to Las Margaritas, gathering at the traditional spot. Thus, neither the route traveled nor the manner of traveling were crucial to the proper conduct of the pilgrimage.

By contrast, the Tzeltal *encargado* abolished the pilgrimage to Venustiano Carranza in 1977. The villagers there had prohibited the carrying of flowers by the pilgrims because they wanted the pilgrims to buy the flowers at the pilgrimage center. The Tzeltal *encargado*, who planned the pilgrimages, objected to this on the grounds that they were making money on a pilgrim's ritual obligations.

In summary, pilgrimages were primarily a Tojolabal event, yet they required the leadership of the Tzeltales to whom the Tojolabales were linguistically and religiously subservient. This subservience is symbolized in the pilgrimage formations in which the red church flags were to the left of the white ones. The Tojolabal *encargado* walked on the left of his Tzeltal counterpart; and the Tojolabal flagbearers follow the Tzeltal flagbearers. In Tojolabal, the word for the red flag is *uinal* (son, minor); the white flag is *alagualal* (father, major). Right, as opposed to left, and leading, as opposed to following, are marks of authority (Vogt 1976). Thus, positioning reflects social status on these pilgrimages, despite lip-service to equality (e.g., "all the Tojolabal brothers and sisters...").

From the Tojolabal perspective, the Tzeltales also determined when the pilgrimages took place and whether they would be made. This observation was true for all of the pilgrimages except that to San Mateo Ixtatan, in which the decision was made by the Catholic priest at San Mateo. In other aspects, however, the Tzeltales directed the pilgrimages.

The Tojolabales bore the brunt of the cost of the pilgrimages. They paid for the Mass, the *cohetes*, and the candles. In case of deficit, it was primarily the Tojolabal *encargado* who made up the difference. The Tojolabales devoted more time and energies for the continuation of these rites and collected flowers for, carried offerings to, and performed labour at the pilgrimage center. This behavior was not mirrored among the Tzeltales. Only a few and selected Tzeltales collected the flowers to be used while on the pilgrimage and the *ramietes* did not reach the pilgrimage center. The Tojolabal political, economic, social, and linguistic subservience contains elements whose meaning are not clear from the tenets of contemporary Catholicism or traditional religion. An understanding of the larger cultural history of the region, particularly with reference to the area's politico-religious system and the *Rezo Tzeltal*, help make these elements more understandable.

THE PILGRIMAGE IN CULTURAL-HISTORICAL CONTEXT

The Tzeltal language had a superior status which was recognized by Tzeltales and Tojolabales alike. It is possible this differential status of the languages reflects a pre-Columbian contrast in political status (Adams 1981a, 1983). Lyle Campbell (personal communication) has indicated that Tzeltal is glottochronologically separated from Chuj by about 800 years. This suggests the Tzeltales migrated from the Chuj area of Guatemala at about A.D. 1200 to their present homeland. This region was then populated by the Tojolabales, whom the Tzeltales subjugated to create a Tzeltal conquest state which included the Tojolabales as a lower social stratum. This differential status was manifested in many aspects of the area's ritual life.

This interpretation would account for the difference in language status, but not for the pilgrimage itself. To understand the role of the pilgrimage in this reconstruction, we must look at the relationship of the Tzeltales to the Chuj, which also requires a knowledge of the politico-religious hierarchy (cargo system). In 1975, the Tzeltales had a three-tiered religio-political hierarchy, consisting of the *encargados*, the *priostes*, and the *mayordomos*, which served only religious purposes. The *encargados* led the pilgrimages and recited the *Rezo Tzeltal*. The *priostes* were low-level officials who were responsible for collecting flowers and taking care of the icons and the church. The *mayordomos*, also low-level functionaries, performed secular functions and were messengers for the *encargados*.

This structure had only been present since 1933, and reveals little about the historical social structure. Information on the earlier social structure was obtained from older consultants. Since the Spaniards did not bring about any major changes in the existing structure (MacLeod 1973:136) and there were no other major influxes of populations after the conquest that would effect the local social structure (Thomas Lee, personal communication 1977), it is assumed the earlier (before 1933) structure was very similar to that which had functioned in the contact period.

According to consultants, the earlier system had five hierarchical levels: the *alcalde, regidores, mayor, priostes,* and *mayordomos.* The *alcalde* was responsible for the well-being of the community. He oversaw public works projects and functioned much as would a city mayor. The *alcalde* had five counselors, the *regidores.* They advised him, served as local justices, and recited the *Rezo Tzeltal* and performed other religious functions. The *mayor* functioned as a tax or tribute collector.[8] The functions of the *prioste* and *mayordomo* were described above.

The *alcalde* and *regidores* functioned as a group and were collectively known as the *calpul.* Data collected in the field suggest that the *calpul* were members of the upper class and that membership was hereditary. Each year this body nominated those who would hold lower-level positions. This description suggesting hereditary membership in the *calpul* is consistent with views presented by Ruz Lhuillier (1964) and for other Mesoamerican groups (see Spores 1967, 1973; Soustelle 1970).

The structural organizational change from a five-tiered to a three-tiered system in 1933 apparently did not affect the Tojolabales. Consultants indicated there were no *regidores* nor *alcaldes* in the Tojolabal system before 1933. When asked why this was so, the Tojolabales responded it was because they did not know how to speak Tzeltal ("God's language"). The presence of functionaries in a position suggesting their knowledge of Tzeltal would be internally inconsistent. The absence of these positions in the hierarchy would place the Tojolabales in a position politically and religiously subservient to the Tzeltales.

These data point to the suggestion that the Tzeltales were perceived as closely related to the deities. In theocratic societies, such as the pre-Hispanic Maya, politics and religion are intricately connected (Webster 1976). By using the "wrath of the gods" as a political weapon, the dominant group could maintain control over its subjects (Webster 1976).

The uppermost level of the Tojolabal politico-religious hierarchy was held by two individuals, called *encargados.* Appointed by the priest at Las Margaritas, their position was analogous to the Tzeltal *mayor.* The *encargado,* like the *mayor,* carried a two-meter staff of quince wood as a symbol of his position. As indicated earlier, the *encargados* received the money from the various communities and carried it to the Tzeltal official. These two individuals divided the Tojolabal region between them.

There were only two hierarchical ranks at the village level, the *alfereces* and *mayordomos*. Elections of these officials occurred on a yearly basis, overseen by a representative of the Mexican government or the Catholic Church. The *alfereces* carried the community flags while the *mayordomos* carried those of the church on the pilgrimages. This inversion of duties with respect to the Tzeltal *prioste* and *mayordomo* is intriguing and not well-understood. I have suggested elsewhere that this may have been a mechanism to defuse rebellion (Adams 1981b). This interpretation, however, needs further study and corroborating evidence.[9]

Although many authors have discussed the Maya cargo system, only Nash's (1970) report of Tzo'ontahal parallels the structure found among the Tojolabales. Although there are major differences in the Tzeltal and Tojolabal organizations, at least one aspect is similar. The elections at the Tojolabal hamlets and the nominations of the Tojolabal *encargados* involved the participation of outside functionaries. These individuals, while not a formal part of the indigenous organization, were integral to it. In a similar fashion, the members of the Tzeltal *calpul* were also overseen by an external agent, the *fiscal*. This individual's role is not clear until the Tzeltales are placed in their social and political context.

In societies with a political structure analogous to that described here, the functionary in the *fiscal*'s position was very powerful. He was often a member of the ruler's own family or close associates and ultimately decided whether the people selected by the local political body would hold that position. He also coordinated the payment of tribute to the ruler at the beginning of the agricultural cycle (Adams 1981a, 1983). This is precisely the pattern observed in the pilgrimage to San Mateo which occurs at the beginning of the agricultural year.

The *Rezo Tzeltal* provides another indication of the *fiscal*'s position in the political structure of southeastern Chiapas. Prayers have not been intensively used as vehicles for understanding social structure in the Maya area. I argue that prayer, as a genre of oral literature, can be studied using methods already established for myth and other oral traditions. While oral traditions may not reveal the entirety of a social structure (Lessa 1966:3), they may offer definite clues. These clues may be corroborated by analyses of behavioral patterns from other institutions.

Gomme (1892:5-6) suggests that "the genealogy of each custom ... goes back for its commencing point to some fact in the history of a people which has escaped the notice of the historian." Much more recently, Rappaport (1979:192-93) observed that the performance of a liturgy indicates that the performer "accepts whatever is encoded in the canons of the liturgical order in which he is participating."

The *Rezo Tzeltal* consists of four sections (Adams n.d.). The first is an introduction, in which reciter addresses the cross, the earth, and the place where the recitation occurs. The second section, by far the longest portion, is a blessing of the world and of the cargo system. The next requests that damaging rains and insects will not plague the agricultural fields. The final section asks forgiveness for the quality of the recitation.

Of special interest, the second section contains many references to the cargo system. The prayer specifically mentions not only the wives of the cargo holders but also the following functionaries in this system; the *alcalde*, *calpul*, *mayor*, *priostes*, and *mayordomos*. The women are very frequently referred to in the same passage as their spouses.[10] Far more important for our purposes is the reference to the *fiscal*.

The *Rezo Tzeltal* moves the participant through a ceremony for the changing of occupants of official positions. Seven men and their retinue are going into the woods to perform this ceremony. They are followed by the *mayores*, *priostes*, *mayordomos*, and their wives. The functionaries lay down the symbols of their office, the *baras* (the symbol of the *calpul*) and the staffs of quince wood (symbol of the *mayordomo*). These signs of office are then picked up by the six incoming year's officials.

The ceremony occurs in a forest at the beginning of the year. The Tzotziles, a linguistic group living just north of the area under study, and who were allied with the Tzeltales until late in the colonial era (Klein 1966), consider the forest a place in which gods and mortals come together and the past and present merge (Gossen 1974:87). It is conceivable that the Tzeltales held a similar reverence for the forests. The occurrence of the event at the beginning of a new year is also significant when placed in the context of the pilgrimage to San Mateo, which also takes place at this time.

There is an obvious discrepancy between the outgoing seven men and the incoming six. I suggest that the seventh man (who has no female counterpart) is the overseer, the *fiscal*. Even though the title itself is of Spanish origin, the prayer is given in Tzeltal, with only the functionaries' positions and the names of the saints in Spanish. This suggests that the institution of *fiscal* predates the Spanish Conquest.

This argument is also supported by Roys' (1957:94) discussion of the *holpop* in pre-Hispanic Maya society. He refers to the *holpop* in various Yucatán provinces; in Sotuta they "were like *mandones* ('overseers') ... [who] consulted with the lord about matters and embassies from outside, others [did] not." The *holpop* conferred with an overlord, external to the local system, in this case, Cocom. The Maya apparently used indirect rule whenever possible (Roys 1957). Roys (1957:7) states that the individual in this position was a member of the most important lineage in the town.[11] This does not mean that the *fiscal* (or *holpop*) did not have influence in the local community. As a case in point, Klein (1966) reports that the Tzeltal rebellion of 1712 was instigated by the *fiscales*. The colonial *fiscal* may have been the pre-Hispanic *holpop*, and, in this case, was a representative of the Chuj empire. As such, he directed the election of Tzeltal officials and approved the Tzeltal nominees. He or a Tzeltal oversaw the election of the

Tojolabal officials. The Tzeltales made a pilgrimage to San Mateo Ixtatan at the beginning of the agricultural cycle to demonstrate their fealty to the Chuj. However, the Tzeltales, as local overlords, passed the brunt of the economic burden onto the Tojolabales.

Further evidence of the Chuj's power is suggested in prayers recited by the Tzotziles, who allied with the Tzeltales pre-Hispanically, during ceremonies for the change of officials. San Juan, the patron saint of San Juan Chamula, is addressed by the phrase, *muk'ul san huan, muk'ul patron* (great San Juan, great patron") (Gossen 1974:203-07), while San Mateo, the patron saint of San Mateo Ixtatan, is invoked by *htot san machyo, kahval* (our father Saint Matthew, our lord) (Gossen 1974:207; see also Paz 1961:07). In brief, although San Juan may have been the local deity, San Mateo was lord. The passages suggest that the Tzotziles, too, were subordinate to the Chuj.

The social structure and the relative positions of the Chuj, Tzeltal, and Tojolabal are portrayed in Figure 6.5. It also depicts the placement of overseers at all political levels, thus linking the Chuj leadership with the entire political hierarchy.

Thus, although the Tzeltales may have been *superordinate* to the Tojolabal, they were *subordinate* to the Chuj. Their superordinate position relative to the Tojolabal is manifested by many features. These include (1) the complete complement of the cargo system, (2) the religious and political leadership of the Tzeltales, and (3) the Tojolabal payment for the pilgrimages. Historically, the Tzeltal were subordinate to the Chuj as is suggested by (1) the pilgrimage to San Mateo which occurred at the

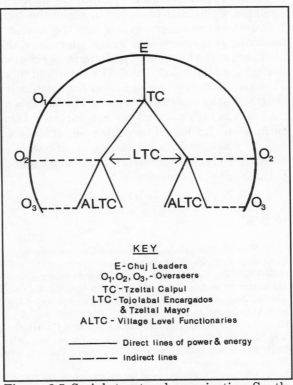

Figure 6.5 Social structural organization, Southeastern Chiapas

beginning of he agricultural cycle, (2) the priest at San Mateo, who set the date for the pilgrimage, and (3) their elections, which were overseen by the *fiscal*. This functionary is mentioned the *Rezo Tzeltal*, a prayer that provides the guidelines for the ceremonial change of officials. Therefore, pre-Hispanically, the *fiscal* may have been a representative of the Chuj.

CONCLUSION

I have developed a social and political history of southeastern Chiapas and southwestern Guatemala using social institutions as purveyors of social truths. Politics and religion, especially in theocratic societies, are intricately connected (Webster 1976). Thus religious institutions provide information about secular matters. Here, I consider pilgrimages as providing political and economic statements about the social structure in southeastern Chiapas, Mexico. An institution does not stand alone, but rather is a part of other social institutions. Additional information was drawn from the analyses of the institutions upon which the pilgrimages rest. Specifically, I examined the cargo system and the ancillary personnel, the market occurring at the same time as the pilgrimage, the rites associated with the pilgrimage, the location of the pilgrimage centers, and the prayers recited during the pilgrimage itself. The results of this analysis suggest that the Tzeltales, although the lords over the Tojolabales, were subordinate to the Chuj of southwestern Guatemala. This assertion rests on the anthropological concept that pilgrimages are part of a larger web made up of other cultural institutions. From this point of view, a pilgrimage and its performance make political, social, and economic statements which can be decoded to provide historical information about the cultures involved in the performance of pilgrimages.[12]

NOTES

1. This chapter is based on fieldwork made possible through a grant from the Phillips Fund of the American Philosophical Society, a grant (No. 020-962A) from the State University of New York Research Foundation, and support from the New World Archeological Foundation. The author expresses his gratitude to these institutions, the individuals who made it possible, and the Tojolabal and Tzeltal consultants who provided the data for the study. Additionally, he acknowledges his debt to Dr. Lyle Campbell and Dr. William N. Fenton of the State University of New York, Albany, and Dr. Joseph Chartkoff of Michigan State University. My wife, Marilyn Adams, made helpful comments leading to the final form of this paper, as did Dr. E. A. Morinis and an anonymous reviewer. The errors found herein, naturally, are made by the author alone.

2. While the Tzeltales have been extensively studied, in part as a result of the Harvard Chiapas Project, Tzeltal was not thought to be spoken in the area which is covered in this study. The Tojolabales, on the other hand, are poorly represented in the ethnographic literature, and only recently have anthropologists initiated field research among them.

3. I use the past tense in this paper because the pilgrimage system in southeastern Chiapas had been subject to many recent changes prior to the investigation. The arrival of about 260,000 Guatemalan and El Salvadoran refugees in this area in the early 1980s (*The Guardian*, June 9, 1982, p. 16, citing the U.N. High Commission for Refugees) has undoubtedly also had an impact on the traditional pilgrimage system.

4. Whether the Tojolabales conducted other rituals which did not require Tzeltal leadership, thus paralleling Tambiah's (1978) observation of spirit cults in Thailand, was not ascertained.

5. Tzeltal was considered to be "God's language" by both linguistic groups. One Tzeltal consultant, an elder religious leader, refused to translate the *Rezo Tzeltal* on the grounds that, as God's language, it could not be translated. A younger Tzeltal speaker (also a religious leader), who did not share this view, agreed to translate the prayer.

6. The other pilgrimages did not involve the priest, but were initiated by the Tzeltales.

7. For example, at San Mateo, pilgrims would go to the sacred salt mines located near the town. The salt they collected would be placed in the vicinity of the home altar (one consultant, for example, had a plastic bag of the salt under his altar). It was said the salt had curative powers. Details about this and other ancillary rites are in Adams 1988).

8. See Adams (1983) for an in-depth discussion of this position.

9. I have also suggested that the flutist and the drummers many have been *alcaldes* and *regidores*, who were, for the same reason, ritually and politically demoted (Adams 1981b).

10. Reina (1966) is one of the few who has reported on the parallel women's religious organization. Many authors, however, have mentioned that a male had to be married before being considered for a position in the civil-religious hierarchy.

11. Alternatively, this individual could have been a member of the overall leader's group. This was usually the case when the subjugated polity resisted political subordination (Adams 1981a).

12. It is acknowledged that not all pilgrimages lend themselves to this sort of analysis. It seems, however, that many of the traditional pilgrimages whose origins lay with theocratic societies can be used to provide historical information.

REFERENCES

Adams n.d., 1981a, 1981b, 1983, 1988
Campbell 1988
Cancian 1965
Gomme 1892
Gossen 1974
Guardian 1982
Klein 1966
Lessa 1966
MacLeod 1973
Malinowski 1922
Nash 1970
Paz 1961
Radcliffe-Brown 1933

Rappaport 1979
Reina 1966
Remesal 1964
Roys 1957
Ruz Lhuillier 1964
Solorzano 1970
Soustelle 1961, 1970
Spicer 1962
Spores 1967, 1973
Tambiah 1978
Vogt 1969a, 1976
Wallace 1966
Webster 1976

7

Pilgrimage as Cyclical Process: The Unending Pilgrimage of the Holy Cross of the Quintana Roo Maya

HERMAN W. KONRAD

Reduced to its essence, pilgrimage signifies a passage or journey. And the pilgrim, regardless of time, place, or circumstances, is someone on a journey. One of the Yucatec Maya terms for pilgrim is *u ximbal ek'ob*, which literally means the "passage and course of the stars" (Barrera Vásquez 1980:944). The Maya association of the word *ximbal* with both pilgrimage and the passage of the stars provides a convenient point of departure for my treatment of pilgrimage as cyclical process; pilgrims, like stars, pass through their cycles in perpetual journeys through space and time. This perspective contrasts with Victor Turner's emphasis upon pilgrimage as liminal phenomena, and a break or interruption associated with rites of passage (1974a, 1974b, 1978). It is not my aim to dispute Turner's insightful and creative investigation which, in essence, appears to have a linear dimension behind its structural analysis. Rather, the intention is to look at the interaction of cyclical and lineal processes evident in pilgrimage activities found among the tropical forest Maya villages in Quintana Roo, Mexico.

The cyclical conception of disappearance and reappearance, of death and rebirth, whether referring to humanity, individuals, or civilizations, has been widespread in both oriental and occidental civilizations. Prior to the emergence of Christianity, which as Mircea Eliade (1959:143) points out, postulates a linear conception — "a straight line traces the course of humanity from the initial Fall to the final Redemption" — cyclical systems dominated cosmological constructions. And among the great civilizations of the New World, such as the Nahuatl, Maya, and Quechua speakers, as well as among those of lesser achievements, the cyclical concepts, although altered and transformed by Christianity, were never eliminated (Lafaye 1976; J. E. Thompson 1934, 1970; Earls 1973). Contemporary pilgrimage practice in Latin America has also retained the conception of cyclical time and events. The overlay of Catholicism is very evident both in actual activities and also as they have been described throughout this volume. On the surface, it appears to dominate much of the pilgrimage ritual. This holds true also for the Maya village of Chumpon during the annual festivities of the Holy Cross in May, but closer observation and participation in such events quickly dispels the notion that merely Christian Catholic ritual is taking place. At a very basic structural level, as well as within actual ritual events, it is possible to identify much more ancient Maya concepts which are being retained. For these Maya, at least, such retentions provide a link between past, present and future, in an unbroken cycle.

The sacred, cyclical aspect of pilgrimage is the other face of the "sequence of social dramas and social enterprises," or "anti-structure" identified by Turner (1974a). Like its more secular side it is grounded upon observable phenomena and experience. In this case they are cosmological, the movement of astral bodies which produce day and night and the seasons and their fluctuations. The sun, the moon, and the stars were, in the first instance, the source of inspiration for the rituals we refer to as pilgrimages. The Maya, in the meanings they ascribe to *ximbal*, have retained this linkage. Eliade, in his classic essay *Cosmos and History: The Myth of the Eternal Return*, has noted the worldwide distribution of the idea of the existence of "an extraterrestrial archetype" or "double"; that for many societies "reality is a function of the imitation of a celestial archetype" (1959:9); and that "rituals and significant profane gestures which acquire meaning attributed to them, materialize that meaning, only because they deliberately repeat such and such acts posited *ab origine* by gods, heroes, or ancestors" (1959:5-6). Both outside and within Christian practice, and particularly within the highly syncretic Latin American contexts, I maintain that pilgrimage ritual offers demonstrable evidence of the covert retention of repetitive, cyclical notions while overtly manifesting a linear progression, which we can associate with such things as "pilgrim's progress" or journeys to sacred shrines for religious purposes.

THE CELESTIAL DIMENSION

The editors of this volume have stressed the "root metaphor" aspect of pilgrimage for understanding society. In Latin America the projection of this idea onto the celestial dimension arises easily due to the antecedents in indigenous cosmological concepts and resultant belief and practice. In pre-Christian Europe and elsewhere the association of gods with observable astral bodies was also widespread (Eliade 1959; Blacker and Loewe 1975). And the Christianization of Europe did not result in the abandonment of such linkages. The tombs of the popes buried in Avignon (1305-78), the sepulchers of the Catholic monarchs of Spain (Ferdinand and Isabella) interred in Granada, and those of countless ecclesiastical and royal personages elsewhere in Europe graphically display the reclining figures with their feet resting firmly upon feline and canine backs. This is clearly visible for any visitor but what is not as generally known is that these animals, aside from representing domesticated species which accompanied the personages in life, were also symbols of astrological significance, associated with the sun and the moon (David Kelley, personal comment 1984). The royal figures, in death, cast in stone and en route to their eternal pilgrimage, are shown firmly planted on symbols of the astral bodies which occupy the heavens.

Though the tombs of such personages have become the object of pilgrimage attention in Europe, the Holy Virgin plays a more dominant role. And she and the Christ Child frequently appear with astral symbols, as in the case of Our Lady of Montserrat, where both the Virgin and Child hold astral spheres in their hands. The Virgin of Rocio, in southern Spain, stands on the crescent moon which has a star at each point. Whether the creators of the Virgin figures consciously added astral symbols or associated the Holy Virgin with them is less important than that they appear. And despite the Christian interpretation of such symbols, their continuing presence provides a visible link to pre-Christian associations of holy sites and personages with celestial bodies.

In New World indigenous religions the conscious and direct linkages of deities and astral bodies was commonplace. This was the case among all of the major civilizations in the Andean and Mesoamerican regions. Their main gods, both male and female, were associated with the sun and the moon. Among the Maya it was held that this celestial pair began to exist first on the earth, after which they took up residence in the sky (J. E. Thompson 1970). And it was only after their pilgrimage to the sky, where they maintain a perpetual journey, that earthly temples and holy sites were constructed in their honor. Such sites, which became the object of human pilgrimage, veneration, sacrifice, and other ritual, linked the individual, at least symbolically, to both the deities and the celestial domain of their habitation. Izamal and Chichen Itza, on the Yucatan peninsula, were only two of the more well-known locations of pre-conquest pilgrimage veneration.

Conversion to Christianity, despite the intentions of the European clerics, did not eliminate the indigenous associations. The emergence of the Virgin of Guadalupe, patron saint of the Americas within the Catholic tradition, can be taken as a case in point. This image of the Virgin Mary miraculously imprinted on the shirt of the Indian Juan Diego hard on the heels of the Spanish conquest of the Aztec Empire in the sixteenth century, shows her standing on the crescent moon. The site of her shrine, on the hillock of Tepeyac, was the location of the Aztec shrine to Coatlicue, terrestrial goddess who had given birth to Huitzilopochtli, the Aztec personification of the blazing sun at noon (Soustelle 1961:102). The widespread Mesoamerican association of the Virgin Mary with the moon goddess (J. E. Thompson 1934), particularly among the Maya, rests on more than the Spanish tradition of painting the Virgin standing on a crescent. Or as J. Eric Thompson (1970) suggests, the moon was confused with the Virgin because of the crescent image. Rather, it rests on a shared association of religious symbols which are linked to celestial objects. And the conquest tradition of building Christian shrines upon the destroyed bases of previous indigenous temples or the use of the same building materials for constructing Christian structures merely provided another structural base for the continuity of previous associations.

The widespread occurrence of pilgrimage cult shrines in Latin America at locations where pre-Columbian deities had been worshipped (see Chapter 2) provided a firm basis for continuity and syncretism. Even today, when indigenous pilgrims fulfill vows by visiting such shrines, it is not possible to clearly separate what is Christian and what is indigenous in the ritual being performed. Christian ritual may be practiced even at clearly indigenous sacred sites, as was observed at the Guatemalan site of Zacaleu in 1976. Here a busload of Maya in ethnic dress and using the Maya language were performing what would normally be interpreted as Christian acts of devotion upon both human and material remains of the ancient Maya temple.

The Christian depiction of Virgins and saints associated with the symbols of astral significance no doubt inadvertently aided in the process of the indigenous synthesis of pre- and postconquest tradition and belief. The Franciscan church in Oxkutzcab, Yucatán, provides an example of the retention of Maya astral symbols within the formal Christian context. This church, completed in 1591, depicts on its frontal facade above the main entrance, the figures of the sun and moon, both represented in the Maya tradition (Fernández 1945). In observing the indigenous pilgrims visiting the shrine of the Virgin of Guadalupe one can also note countless astral symbols on clothing, head-dresses, and other ornaments of the faithful. In the pre-European past, during the conquest and colonial tradition, and at present the visible symbols of celestial association were, and continue to be, in evidence.

My interrelation of symbols representing celestial bodies with the meaning of pilgrimage itself suggests that the individual pilgrim imitates or re-enacts the archetypical phenomena from which pilgrimage derives. This takes place in more than one way, involving both the ritual activity and the structures created to provide the pilgrimage context. My utilization of the ritual activities of a specific Maya village within the context of its annual Holy Cross ceremony serves to illustrate such phenomena. Before turning to analogous contemporary pilgrimage actions, however, I must provide additional information about the Maya context in terms of their concepts of time and space and their relationship with Maya cosmology.

MAYA COSMOLOGY

Maya cosmology indicated that the abode of humans was surrounded by thirteen upper layers and nine lower layers. J. Eric Thompson's (1970:195) description is one of the best:

> Although the Maya spoke of the thirteen *taz* (layers) of the heaven, the *taz* covering such things as blankets spread out one above the other, in fact the thirteen celestial layers were arranged as six steps ascending from the eastern horizon to the seventh, the zenith, whence six more steps led down from the western horizon. Similarly, four more steps led down from the western horizon to the nadir of the underworld, whence four more steps ascended to the eastern horizon. Thus there were really only seven celestial and five infernal layers. The sun followed this sort of stepped rhomboid on his daily journey across the sky and his nightly traverse of the underworld to return to the point of departure each dawn.

The antagonism between the sky and the underworld was understood in terms of the sky's powers of goodness and light and as the source of life and sustenance, while the underworld signified darkness, death, and the power of evil. The thirteen sky gods, like the astral bodies, however, traveled through both spheres and could take on either positive or negative characteristics. For the ancient as well as contemporary Maya the numbers thirteen and nine have been closely associated in ritual behavior with the properties of cosmological areas representing good and evil.

Complementing the geometric structures was a giant tree (the *ceiba*) which stood at the exact center of the earth; its roots penetrated into the underworld, and its trunk and branches the various layers of the sky. This first or 'green' (the *yaaxche*) tree, considered sacred for the Maya, linked the terrestial with the celestial domains. Its color (green) and location (the center) signified the fifth of the cardinal directions, it being the reference point for the other directions, each with its own color association (east = red, west = black, south = yellow, north = white). These primary world directions and colors were frequently applied to the deities themselves, who had a multiplicity of characteristics. The all important rain gods, the *chaacs*, had both directional and color associations yet, at the same time, were conceived of as single entities, a concept similar to the Christian view of the Holy Trinity. For the Maya the sacred green center also became the terrestial center of a cross linking the four cardinal directions, and the *ceiba* tree, the cross that linked the celestial and terrestial domains. That the

Holy Cross of Chumpon is green, as are the roadside crosses that mark the death of unfortunate travelers in the area, seems more than coincidental.

This idea of the cross, with both vertical and horizontal dimensions, was central to Maya cosmological concepts. Portrayals of such concepts are numerous in the remaining structural and pictorial evidence at lowland Maya archaeological sites. That the Maya would retain these earlier concepts even after having been officially converted to Christianity became an ongoing problem for the Catholic cleric and theologian attempting to transform the Maya into orthodox practicing Christians. They never quite succeeded in diminishing the importance the ancient Maya ascribed to numbers such as thirteen, nine, and four; to the sacredness of color associations and the divine importance of the cardinal directions (J. E. Thompson 1934, 1970; D. E. Thompson 1960).

The Maya concept of the meaning of time itself, and how humans relate to it, was also of critical importance. Time was abstract in the sense that it was endless, yet concrete in its association to 52-year repeating cycles (past ages), the sacred year (the 260-day *tzolkin*), and the secular year (the 365-day *haab*). The Maya were rather obsessed with the measurement of time. The basic, concrete, unit was the *kin* (sun or single day) and nine units removed we find the *kinchiltun* (23 billion days), more likely an abstract unit of measurement. The *tzolkin* was made up of 20 days, each with its own deity, repeated thirteen times. The days of this calendar determined individual identity, ceremonial life, and the activities of the community. And although the Maya had very sophisticated systems of chronological reckoning, the particular day of an event seemed to take precedence over its chronological placement within the larger repeating cycles. Even today, when local Maya forest villagers discuss past events, such as the Spanish conquest, Mexican independence, and their own military conflicts in the nineteenth and twentieth centuries, they are treated as simultaneous events. This indicates a greater emphasis upon the event than its actual chronological position in time. Such telescoping of time and its temporal distortion is characteristic in the Maya oral tradition and quite consistent with Maya cyclical notions of time. Victoria Reifler Bricker (1981:8), in making a careful study of Maya myth and ritual, identifies the structural significance of this phenomena:

> Whatever the origin of their cyclical notion of time and history, the modern Maya emphasize structure at the expense of personality in their folklore . . . In the timelessness of oral tradition and ritual there is no place for individuality. The hero of one cycle or century or millennium is the hero of all time. He may be referred to by the names of all the heroes or any one of them. The villain who opposes him can be called by the name of any villain from any time period. What is important is the structural message.

This structural message, I would argue, is also evident in the association of symbols linked to astral bodies. When applied to pilgrimage it indicates a celestial dimension which is always linked to the earthly practice of the participating pilgrim. The pilgrim replicates the heavenly pilgrimage of astral bodies. In the case of the Quintana Roo Maya the crosses themselves also become involved in the process, although the ritual activities are conducted visibly by individuals and communities. Both the deities and the ritual specialists who honor them are bearers or carriers of time (LaFarge and Byers 1931). Within the context of cyclical notions of time and past events, if this was the case in the ancient past, it holds equally true for the present.

CHUMPON AND THE CULT OF THE CROSS

The roughly 200 residents of Chumpon form part of a group of survivors of a nineteenth-century conflict usually referred to as the "War of the Castes" (Reed 1964; Bartholomé and Barabas 1977). After three centuries of submission to Spanish and Mexican conquest the Maya peasants of eastern and southern Yucatán, who were unable to get redress from the oppressive demands of civil and ecclesiastical authorities, attempted a violent solution. The outbreak of hostilities began in 1847 and after significant initial military successes they suffered a series of reversals. The remnant of this peasant uprising, or those who would not be reintegrated again into the regional Mexican society, retreated into the largely uninhabited tropical forests in what is now the state of Quintana Roo. Here they recreated tribal forms of societal organization and livelihood patterns which had many similarities to pre-Hispanic times.

Yet the long period of tutelage under the paternalism of Franciscan priests and the Catholic Church left a legacy of ritual and religious consciousness. These Maya consider themselves as practicing Christians and their devoted adherence to the official rites of the Church in terms of prayers, masses, worship of the saints, and celebration of the events of the Christian calendar substantiates their claim. Yet scholars are divided over the issue of whether or not they are really Christians. The general consensus (Bartholomé and Barabas 1977; Villa Rojas 1945, 1978) is that their religious practice represents a synthesis of Christian and Mayan elements, although one investigator of the region insists that as of 1850 these Maya created a new religion, "the outbreak of the pre-Christian archaic or cosmological mentality under Christian forms, neither Christian or hoax, but a new Cosmological religion born in 1850 and which still gives meaning and continuity to the Maya Indians who practice its cult" (Zimmerman 1963:71).

The cult mentioned by Zimmerman is that of the Holy Cross, which emerged as the most important religious symbol in the area. This cross was in many ways a localized and personalized version of the Catholic crucifix. Villa Rojas has described the Holy Cross as "an intermediary between God and man, for wherever stands a cross, there are the eyes of God" (1945:97).

For the residents of Chumpon, representations of the cross, like the eyes of God, are omnipresent, to be found in the constellation of the Southern Cross, the intersections of the beams and poles of the residential buildings, or in the actual crosses at the four corners of the village, as well as in the family crosses kept in special oratories and those in the church. Most crosses are made of the *kuché* (tree of the gods) or cedar.

The genesis of the Holy Cross of Chumpon goes back to 1850 after the insurrectionary Maya had suffered severe military setbacks. At this point the energy to continue their struggle was renewed when:

> a small cross, carved on the trunk of a mahogany tree appeared at a site later known as Chan Santa Cruz (literally, little holy cross). Miraculously endowed with speech, the cross soon became famous among the Indians for its wonderful powers. It claimed to be the Trinity itself, sent to earth by God the Father to help the Indians in their struggle against the Whites and to protect them from the bullets of their enemies. (Villa Rojas 1945:20)

Chan Santa Cruz quickly became the shrine village of the struggling Maya, their center of worship and political resistance against Mexican authority. Even though government troops successfully assaulted the shrine village and captured the original holy cross, the importance of Chan Santa Cruz grew. Three new crosses appeared and claimed to be the daughters of the original cross which descended from heaven to replace it. They were of cedar and had equal powers of the mother cross. From these crosses descended others, equally powerful, which became the focal point of worship in subtribal regional centers such as Chumpon. Not only did they have the power of speech and reproduction, they were also the source of written instructions which governed the social, political, and religious life of the entire region until well into the twentieth century. Eventually, federal military forces occupied Chan Santa Cruz, commercial forestry industries penetrated the area, and gradually the region became reintegrated into the national life (Konrad 1987). But the local Maya never have readily accepted governmental or official Church institutions.

In the village of Chumpon, even though the practice of having the cross issue spoken and written instructions has fallen into disuse, it still dominates much of the ritual religious activity and it continues as a bridge between the Christian and Maya cosmological concepts. The cross has become the means, as Eliade has indicated, of materializing and repeating "acts posited *ab origine*" (1959:6) by the founder of the regional religious tradition. Not only is it an archetype of the original Holy Cross from 1850 but also of the Christian cross, and of others of ancient Maya tradition.

THE HOLY CROSS CELEBRATIONS

The pilgrimage rituals take place during the first ten days of May in Chumpon, although actually a lapsed time of nine days is involved between opening and closing ceremonies. There are a multiplicity of functions and meanings taking place simultaneously. On the one hand, the residents of Chumpon and its half a dozen dependent, small, forest communities fulfill individual *promesas* (promises). Even persons who have moved to the larger towns and become integrated into national life and formal Catholic Church traditions return to attend. As explained by a lady from Felipe Carrillo Puerto (the area's largest town), she came to "seek the assistance of the very miraculous cross (*la cruz muy milagrosa)*" in her domestic affairs. Even foreigners, such as the author coming from distant Canada and who has attended on five separate occasions, are accepted without comment and assumed to be fulfilling an individual *promesa*. Such attendance practice has much in common with reported pilgrimage activity described by most of the authors in this volume.

On the other hand, for the local and regional Maya believers, attendance becomes a rite of identification with the shared values and experiences of resistance to the encroachment of the larger Mexican world. Attendance, as an overt, formal demonstration of conformity to values directly associated with tropical forest subsistence livelihood patterns and cultural autonomy, includes obedience to the Holy Cross. Within this tradition the Holy Cross plays an active participatory role. That role governs all of life and the cross's "wishes and demands are directly communicated by certain signs. If an individual has committed a fault, the cross signifies its displeasure by causing his candle to go out when it is placed on the altar" (Villa Rojas 1945:98). Villa Rojas' findings, of over 40 years ago, also indicated a procedure for determining the individual's omission and the nature of the required atonement. If it still exists, it is not easily detectable. But community omissions are still considered as operational and, as Villa Rojas found earlier, "the most Holy may express its wrath by inflicting punishment on the entire community, in the form of epizootic plagues, droughts or serious epidemics" (1945:99). The manner in which the actual messages are delivered by the Holy Cross, whether through speech, letters, or signs, remains secondary to the fact that it functions as in the past.

Throughout most of the year the Holy Cross remains in the sacred area of the village church known as *la gloria* (the glory), which is located at the east end of the structure and partitioned off from the main assembly area. The cross faces west, as is the custom in the Franciscan churches throughout Yucatán, stands on its own altar, and is shrouded by a special cloth. Except for the actual religious activities, masses, novenas, rosaries, and other rituals common to Catholics, the church remains locked and is guarded by male members of the village and its adherent communities who rotate in fulfilling their duty of *guardia*. During the Holy Cross festivities, however, the church remains open 24 hours a day and the curtain closing the doorway leading to *la gloria* remains open. This allows any individual to enter the church at any time to offer prayers and to place lighted candles on a candle rack in front of the altar of the cross. An armed sentinel, nevertheless, remains stationed at the side of the entrance to *la gloria* to ensure that no improper conduct takes place and that the Holy Cross is protected. There is always the apprehension that someone, a nonadherent to the true faith, may wish to capture or destroy the cross.

Many events take place during the festivities, including dances, bullfights, special meals, and a great deal of drinking, visiting, and consumption of a rich variety of foodstuffs normally not available throughout the year. All events are considered sacred and involve voluntary contribution of goods and services on the part of community members. During the past decade an element of commercialism has become evident with popular dances including paid musicians and entry fees which take place on the first days. Since the population during the Holy Cross period may exceed by five times the normal village numbers, increased opportunities for commercial gain via the selling of commodities such as liquor, food, goods, and supplies have increased. In time, the Chumpon activities will take on many of the features common to other pilgrimage sites throughout Mexico and Latin America.

The replication of Maya cosmological configurations, visible also throughout the year, are intensified during the special days. Structurally, the village consists of a cluster of thatched houses scattered around a central open area dominated by the church and an enormous tree beside the village well. In terms of structural symbolism, the church represents the center of the world and the four small, open, thatched chapels located at the cardinal direction entry points to the village represent the four corners of the world. Thus the five Maya directional concepts, the center and the four cardinal directions, become replicated on the ground, as it were, by the very structure of the village. Another version of this same principle is evident within the central, sacred area of the village. This includes the location of the Holy Cross, within the church as center, and four small concrete platforms with small wooden crosses located outside of the church. In this configuration the location of the interior cross, not the church itself, becomes the center of the world. Another replication of this same form is the bullring, which they construct for the festivities. Actually a wooden pole fence enclosing a square area, it is located within the central village area but just north of the church. Each side of the "bullring" coincides with a cardinal direction. The center of this area is a ritually planted *ceiba* (*yaaxche*, the same as the tree that links cosmological terrestial and celestial domains). The structural shape of the bullring and of the bullfights that follow are sacred, although the actual fights have secular entertainment characteristics, like bullfights elsewhere. Here the bullfight is seen as an enactment of a religious ritual, since the fight involves role playing rather than actual bulls. The bull is only a wooden and sack frame with a carved bullhead of cedar, *kuché* (tree of the gods), which is strapped onto an individual who takes on the characteristics of a real bull. Half a dozen young men enact the bullfighting as would the conventional bullfighter using capes. Four cowboys with ropes stationed at the cardinal directions capture the bull at given signals from the *patron* (sponsor) of the event. All the individuals involved are, in fact, fulfilling *promesas* and demonstrating their adherence to the community's cultural values (see Konrad 1983 for a more detailed description of this type of bullfight).

While the structural patterns exhibit identifiable Maya symbolism they also express characteristics seen in Christian ecclesiastical structures, which offer countless examples of the use of the cross in architectural design. But whereas the Christian structures were designed to indicate permanence and stability through time, the Chumpon Maya versions allow for continual recreation and repetition. Village locations, church structures, and bullrings are established according to the ongoing necessities. Their removal to other sites within the tropical forest subsistence pattern of shifting cultivation and the relocation of populations takes place easily. What is permanent and endlessly repetitive is the structure or pattern, in Eliade's terms, the celestial archetype.

Even the manner in which the numerous pigs are killed for the preparation of the daily distribution of free food exhibits a replication of the symbol of the cross. The squealing animal is thrown on its back, its four legs are firmly grasped by four individuals at the four corners while the fifth plunges the knife into its heart. The animal is firmly held in place until its death struggle subsides.

These four examples, the village pattern with Maya cosmology, the cross positions with Christian churchyard patterns, the bullfight with Mexican and Spanish rituals, and the pig killing with human sacrifice rituals of earlier times also have reference to past ideas and rituals incorporated through time into Chumpon society. Yet their structural significance also cannot be overlooked. Or, to paraphrase Lévi-Strauss' analogy of myth and the meaning of the French Revolution for the French politician, these configurations represent for the Chumpon Maya both the events and the ideas of the past:

> a timeless pattern that can be detected in the contemporary French [in this case Maya] social structure and which provides a clue for its interpretation, a lead from which to infer future documents . . . The specific pattern described is timeless; it explains the present and the past as well as the future (1963:209).

Structural configurations and movement are complemented by the transit of the Holy Cross. Although the actual cross is not taken from its altar and paraded in ritual procession, as are patron crosses and saints in the Catholic tradition, it has surrogates which do become part of all the ritual processions. Such processions originate within the church and move to the house of the religious leader of Chumpon, the *nohoch tata* (literally, big father), the houses of the sponsors of important corporate events, the *diputados* (deputies), and the four chapels at the village corners. For such activities a small surrogate cross, about eight inches high and stationed on its own little wooden altar platform, is carried by the procession leader. When not on such holy journeys or pilgrimages the little cross rests on the altar in front of the Holy Cross itself. This surrogate Holy Cross initiates and leads human pilgrims attending village ritual activity.

The daily gift of *matan* (food) may be taken to illustrate this role of the cross. After one of the *diputados* and his collaborating associates have spent an afternoon, night, and morning preparing enormous quantities of food such as hogs, chickens, turkeys, maize, and rice, he is responsible for its distribution to all the assembled pilgrims, including residents and guests. Samples of all the foods prepared are placed in special dishes and arranged in distinctive patterns, with combinations of thirteen, nine, seven, and four dominating, on a table in the house of the *diputado*. The dishes have been decorated with flowers and herbs gathered specifically for the occasion. And candles of black wild bee wax have been prepared. When all is ready the officiating ritual specialist and his assistants go to *la gloria* to get the surrogate cross. Before it is taken from the table altar prayers are offered to the Holy Cross. The surrogate then leads the procession, accompanied by musicians playing and the firing of rockets, to the door of the *diputado*. The party of the *diputado* receives the cross on their knees, facing the cross. They recite the *doctrina* (doctrine) and then a much larger procession, with each participant carrying one of the items from the table, makes its way back to the Holy Cross shrine, again accompanied by music and rockets. They follow the little cross into *la gloria*, where additional prayers are offered to the Holy Cross, after which each procession member offers a lighted candle to the officiating ritualist who places it on the Holy Cross altar along with the other food items. It is only after the Holy Cross has received and blessed the food and candles, signifying a personal commitment to the cross, that the distribution of the food in the house of the *diputado* can begin. The items brought to the altar in the church are later distributed to the ranking members within the society and consumed as is the other food. The preparation, distribution, and consumption of the daily feast has many overtones of a communion meal.

During all of the festivities the Holy Cross, via its surrogate, makes a great number of sacred journeys. Musicians, ritual specialists, and village functionaries take turns in participating in the continuous repetition of such processions or localized pilgrimages. The daily *matan* represents only one activity in which the little cross is actively involved. By means of these journeys it links both the ritual events and the participating pilgrims through a series of cyclical repetitive acts which demonstrate adherence to societal values. Although the individual participation and experience may be temporal, sequential, and of short duration, that of the Holy Cross is transcendent, cyclical, and without temporal restraints.

The Holy Cross itself may also make actual journeys to the location of other patron crosses in the region. The cross of Chumpon used to be taken to Tulum (roughly 50 kilometers from Chumpon), which served in the past as a regional subtribal center. Now that tourism has made significant inroads in this community and it has become secularized, this journey is no longer undertaken. When such events occurred in the past it was carried by the men of Chumpon and always accompanied by the *nohoch tata*. The route they took on this sacred journey was the Maya road or trail through the bush rather than along the road built by the federal government. Since 1901, when Mexican military forces invaded the shrine village of Chan Santa Cruz, the Holy Cross has migrated, on numerous occasions, to new shrine sites uncontaminated by outside secular influences.

During a visit to Chumpon in June 1983 I noticed that there were no males older than ten years of age in the village. They were all engaged in sacred work, I was informed by one of the local women, which turned out to be the smoothing and clearing of a bush route linking Chumpon with X-cacal Guardia (located roughly 40 kilometers to the west of Chumpon), where the cross is still venerated. The sacred cross of X-cacal Guardia was about to make a visit to its sister cross in Chumpon. Despite the fact that paved roads would permit a much easier transit between the two communities, and are normally used for intervillage movement of goods and persons, the sacred cross would not be taken on secular roads. This suggests to me that the Holy Cross only moves along the contemporary Maya equivalent of the ancient Maya *sacbe*, an elevated roadway that led to sacred Maya temples and provided connections between some of the important Maya urban centers. Although archaeologists are not in agreement concerning the functional significance of these *sacbeob,* there is considerable consensus that they were used for religious purposes. The Maya still refer to the milky way as a celestial *sacbe*, which is a route over which celestial and terrestrially located deities could move with great rapidity. The Holy Cross' usage of Maya roads, despite slower and more difficult movement between communities today, suggests an incorporation and retention of such past sacred routes. The deities of the past, as do the Holy Crosses of the present, have their preferred mode of travel, the latter replicating the celestial archetype of the former.

CONCLUSION

The treatment of Maya crosses as active participants in the pilgrimage process, both in a structural and functional sense, may be helpful for an understanding of the common factors that transcend both the Christian-European and indigenous elements which combined to produce much of the ritual phenomena visible in Latin America today. At the beginning of this chapter I suggested that Turner's emphasis upon the liminal phenomena placed the stress upon the sequential, linear, aspects of pilgrimage. In contrast to that position my intention is to show that repetitive and cyclical aspects have played a central role in the origin of the phenomena we identify as pilgrimage and that this holds true equally for Christian practice as well as for pre- and postconquest practice in Latin America. Within the Christian tradition we can still find countless reminders of symbols suggesting associations with astral bodies whether they be feline and canine figures resting under the feet of images of important Christians such as kings and popes on their final pilgrimage, or astral objects visible under the feet or in the hands of depictions of the Holy Virgin. Among the New World societies such linkages were always an integral part of cosmological thought. In a village such as Chumpon we see the retention of the common tradition despite, and because of, the synthesis of the two traditions.

In the lowland Maya area (300-900 A.D.) the science of astronomy achieved great advances, which are evident in the development of precise calendar systems to measure linear, secular time and to guide sacred, cyclical ritual activities. Both the secular and sacred calendars were interwoven, inseparably, to form the basis of the 52-year Maya century. But for Maya there was no separation between secular and sacred dimensions of either the passage of time or the activities of humans engaged in everyday or specialized ritual activities. Like the unending cyclical appearance of astral objects, time and humans were destined to repetitive manifestations of both the cosmic and terrestrial universal drama. The arrival of European Christianity, a physical conquest and a cosmology dominated by sequential conceptions, required adaptations. In terms of the new political economy of survival, and within the new ideological order, the Maya were forced to fit into new linear historical sequences. In this sense the pilgrimage process, as manifested by newly acquired saints, shrines, and annual visits by individual devotees, reflects the traditions of Western civilization. At the same time, however, the Maya retained their own cosmological concepts within which they incorporated the new terrestrial arrangements. In this context the pilgrimage process, now as in the ancient past, remains firmly linked to cyclical, astral, and cosmic forces. Thus the movement of the symbols such as crosses, saints, and shrine centers, like that of their "extraterrestrial archetype," takes precedence over the activities of temporal mortals. Clearly contrasted in the case of the Chumpon experience, the unending pilgrimage of the Holy Cross reflects the cosmic drama while the visiting participants to the annual May festivities enact the derivative, less important human drama.

REFERENCES

Barabas 1974
Barrera Vásquez 1980
Bartholomé-Barabas 1977
Bartolomé 1974
Blacker-eds. 1975
Bricker 1981
Earls 1973
Edmonson 1960
Eliade 1959
Fernández 1945
Konrad 1983, 1987
Lévi-Strauss 1963
LaFarge-Byers 1931

Lafaye 1976
Morely-Brainerd 1956
Oakes 1951
Reed 1964
Roys 1967
Soustelle 1961
Thompson, D.E. 1960,
Thompson, J. Eric S.
   1934, 1939, 1970
Turner 1974a, 1974b, 1974c
Turner-Turner 1978
Villa Rojas 1945, 1978
Zimmerman 1963

8

The Politics of Pilgrimage:
The Black Christ of Esquipulas

CARL KENDALL

This chapter discusses the pilgrimage to the Black Christ of Esquipulas, Guatemala (also referred to as *Cristo Negro*, *Milagroso*, and *El Señor de Esquipulas*), an important religious and political shrine. The symposium to which the initial version of this essay was addressed—a symposium on festivals honoring the work of Abner Cohen (1974)—seemed an especially appropriate opportunity to present my research, for Cohen places emphasis on the importance of the political domain in ritual analysis. The political significance of the pilgrimage to El Señor Esquipulas is great.

The study of pilgrimage as symbolic action in modern society owes much to the work of Turner (1974b: 60-97, 166-230; Turner and Turner 1978:218). Turner views pilgrimage in major world religions as analogous to rites of passage and rituals of affliction in "preliterate, small-scale societies" (1974c:65). This analogy allows Turner to apply to religious events concepts such as normative communitas, social drama, and root paradigm which were developed in his earlier work on the Ndembu. His interest seems to have evolved from a concern for liminal and "liminoid" phenomena, which are apparent, for example, in his Morgan lectures, and reflects his endeavor to apply the tools of social anthropological analysis to a broader range of issues and societies than was current at the time.

In transferring his attention to large-scale societies, Turner rightly eschewed the wholesale adoption of the traditional morphological elements of "tribal" analysis—clan, lineage, and kindred, for example—and focused on "principles" of social organization. These principles, often complementary and opposed, are found in the work of many British anthropologists of his generation. They are similar to Fortes' descent and complementary filiation, which are transformed in Turner's analysis into structure and antistructure. The contrasting premises upon which descent and matrilineal filiation are built among the Tallensi, and the different domains—one political, the other domestic—that are linked through these premises, have been documented by Fortes (1945, 1949, 1969). Fortes also demonstrates the contrast between earth shrines and ancestor shrines which manifests the conflict between domestic and political affiliation in the religious domain. These issues find parallels in the schismogenesis of structure and anti-structure within Turner's analysis.

An overly sharp bifurcation into political and religious domains might produce unusual reports of pilgrimage: e.g., on the one hand symbological analyses of images and the objects of pilgrimage, and on the other sociological accounts of the composition of the pilgrimage population (the geography of pilgrimage). For example, the "liminoid" phenomenon of peregrination is essentially the only focus of Turner's pilgrimage study (Turner and Turner 1978). Turner realizes the difficulty of this approach, however, and admonishes sociologists of religion to continue to study the economic and political basis for pilgrimage behavior. For example, he states that "in order fully to understand pilgrimage in Mexico it would be necessary to take into account the contemporaneous structure of Mexican society and culture and to examine its historical vicissitudes and changes" (1974c:208).

An emphasis on iconic analysis seems to follow from the special nature of contemporary religious phenomena at the level of the nation-state. For example, an historical body of material exists for shrine centers that does not exist for most "tribal" societies. The abundance of these materials may also influence the researcher to search for the enduring, "timeless" aspects of social structure in the analysis of icons. The timeless aspects of the "foci" of synchronic structuralist research find a ready counterpart in the goals of pilgrimage in the historical societies that Turner discusses. The visit to the shrine is this counterpart. The identification of the goal as the enduring component may stem from the fact that so many of the other elements of the pilgrimage change so readily.

This emphasis on iconic analysis may also arise because of the difficulty of identifying delimited social fields that manifest "culture" or "cultures" as individual units of analysis. For example, regional, supranational, or interethnic political and economic factors, which may contribute a great deal to the importance of an icon, are not often separated from "local" factors. Corbett and Whiteford (1983) offer an interesting review of the failure of North American anthropologists to deal with regional and national factors.

This chapter will demonstrate the importance of realizing that the pilgrimage to Esquipulas has a significance that must be analyzed in both symbological and political terms. This is due, in part, to the difficulty of identifying delimited social fields for analysis.

ESQUIPULAS

Esquipulas is a small agricultural municipality of 9,000 permanent residents located in the mountains of eastern Guatemala (950 m. elevation, 14° 33'48" N., 89° 21'06" W.), bordering Honduras and close to the Salvadoran border. The municipal headquarters (*cabecera*) is the site of the largest pilgrimage in Central America. Each year 1,000,000 pilgrims descend on the town, primarily between the second week in January and Holy Week.

The icon which is the object of the pilgrimage is a black crucifix carved by the Peruvian sculptor Quirio Cataño in 1594. According to the documents that commissioned the carving, the image was awarded to the town to commemorate the peaceful conquest of the valley. Because the area has sulfur springs and edible clays, both the area and the image became famous for their cures. After the recovery of Archbishop Fray Pedro Pardo de Figueroa in Esquipulas a large Spanish baroque basilica was constructed to commemorate the healing powers of the shrine. Completed in 1758, the temple still houses the Black Christ and the remains of Fray Pedro.

Historical Analogies

J. Thompson (1964) and Borhegyi (1953, 1954) contend that the pilgrimage to Esquipulas reflects the ongoing worship of deities and the performance of rites that predate the conquest. Both Borhegyi and Thompson associate El Señor de Esquipulas with *ek-chuah*, "a Yucatec deity of merchants and cacao, normally painted black and often shown traveling with a staff and back pack" (Weaver 1972:233, 307). The association of the shrine with trade and geography is still current in Esquipulas. Thompson, for example, draws attention to the regular and ongoing trade of tobacco between the Copan Valley and the Motagua Valley and notes that "the holding of a great market to coincide with a religious festival or the situation of markets at important religious shrines, such as Esquipulas, probably reflect pre-Columbian practice, as well as European custom (1964:25)."

Other evidence, including Hammond's (1972) study of trade in obsidian could also be cited to validate this argument. Furthermore, Esquipulas' geographical propinquity to the great Classic Maya sites of Copan and Quirigua and to the area occupied by the Chortí, presumed to be builders of these sites, suggests an historical continuity. A number of historical and ethnographic analogies can be found in the pilgrimage to Esquipulas, some of which are outlined below.

THE PILGRIMAGE

Before the 1968 completion of the highway linking Esquipulas, Guatemala City, and the Pan American Highway, pilgrims to Esquipulas travelled the route taken by Stephens (1969) in 1847:

> Mounted on my new purchase (a mule), we commenced ascending the great Sierra, which divides the streams of the Atlantic from those that empty into the Pacific Ocean. The ascent was rugged and toilsome, but in two hours we reached the top. The scenery was wild and grand, I have no doubt; but the fact is, it rained very hard all the time;... Mr. Catherwood, who crossed on a clear day, says that the view from the top, both ways, was the most magnificent he saw in the country. Descending, the clouds were lifted, and I looked down upon an almost boundless plain, running from the foot of the Sierra, and afar off saw, standing alone in the wilderness, the great church of Esquipulas, like the Church of the Holy Sepulchre in Jerusalem, and the Caaba in Mecca, the holiest of Temples... The plain reminded me of the great wasteplaces of Turkey and Asia Minor, but was more beautiful, being bounded by immense mountains. For three hours the church was our guide. As we approached, it stood out more clearly defined against mountains whose tops were buried in the clouds. (Stephens 1969:165-66, volume I)

Stephens entered the Esquipulas valley from the east, traveling from Copan.

> We...set out to visit the only object of interest, the great church of the pilgrimage, the Holy place of Central America. Every year, on the fifteenth of January, pilgrims visit it, even from Peru and Mexico; the latter being a journey not exceeded in hardship by the pilgrimage to Mecca. As in the East, "it is not forbidden to trade during the pilgrimage"; and when there are no wars to make the roads unsafe, eighty thousand people have assembled among the mountains to barter and pay homage to our "Lord of Esquipulas."
>
> The town contains a population of about fifteen hundred Indians. There was one street nearly a mile long, with mud houses on each side; but most of the houses were shut, being occupied only during the time of the fair. At the head of the street, on elevated ground, stood the great church. About halfway to it we crossed a bridge over a small stream, one of the sources of the great Lempa. It was the first stream I had seen that emptied into the Pacific Ocean, and I saluted it with reverence. Ascending by a flight of massive stone steps in front of the church, we reached a noble platform a hundred and fifty feet broad, and paved with bricks a foot square. The view from this platform of the great plain and the high mountains around was magnificent; and the church, rising in solitary grandeur in a region of wildness and desolation, seemed almost the work of enchantment. (Stephens 1969:168-69, volume I)

The first part of the pilgrimage, a part still significant for Indians and some other rural participants, consists of an offering made at the Rock of the Compadres, two overlapping stones along the old trail two miles from town. The rocks are said to be the petrified remains of a *compadre* and a *comadre*, or male and female ritual kinsmen (co-parents) who, despite the ban on sexual contact between co-parents, indulged themselves. Pilgrims stop to burn *copal* or throw a few stones at this milestone. In addition, during the latter part of the *feria* season, miniature towns, complete with churches and central squares, fields signified by leaves pushed into the loose dirt, and orchards made of twigs with berries, may be constructed at the site of the Rock of the Compadres.

This old highway approach to Esquipulas presents the pilgrim with a view of the basilica at the end of a kilometre-long road that stretches from the old local center located north of the basilica to the church proper at its southern end. The former is the focus of most local and civic events and contains the town hall, police station, and offices, as well as the original home of the *Cristo Negro*, a church (*la parroquia*) which now serves the *municipio* (municipality) of Esquipulas.

Pilgrims will occasionally visit this church on entering town; however, most proceed to the basilica to embark on the activities which constitute the goal of the pilgrimage. Some participants travel the final distance on hands and knees or on elbows and knees, blindfolded because of a "promise" (*promesa*, typically *acción de gracias* or act of thankfulness) made to El Señor. These supplicants are accompanied by their families, but local children produce blankets and sheets which are laid in front of them to cushion their passage. This participation of local representatives reflects the responsibility of the local community in the pilgrimage: to provide for the physical well-being of the participants. Local adults involved in businesses are not usually as altruistic, but families will take in total strangers to house and feed if the necessity arises. The procession, down the long axis of the main street, moves from the civic center through an area of residences and occasional shops to the gaudy hotels, restaurants, and trinket stands that immediately surround the basilica.

Originally, the basilica was built on a large mound in the middle of otherwise unused land, rising dramatically out of a no-man's land of scrub and grass and framed by mountains to its rear. The construction of the new highway, which enters from the west and intersects the old original avenue at its head, near the basilica, has changed the relationship of the basilica to the town and radically altered the value of property surrounding the church. That property, now considered among the most valuable in Esquipulas, poised at the intersection of the old and new highways, was bought in this century for a glass bottle. This property is now valued at close to $100,000. Most new building, including the construction of a new ward (*barrio*), is taking place near the new western focus of the town created by the recently completed highway, in the old transition zone between the town and the basilica.

Although the original architectural effect of the long axis leading to the basilica may have been damaged by the highway, pragmatic and architectural interests prompted the construction of a park and low fence around the church. The fence serves to separate church grounds from local grounds and guides the long line of pilgrims (*cola*) who wish to pass by the image and touch or kiss it. This contact with the image is considered one of the most important elements of pilgrimage activity and during the peak of the pilgrimage season, in January and April, a family may wait eight hours in the church park to see the figure.

From this flat, planted area, a series of gradins rise to the foot of the large plaza on which the church sits. The fence, gradins, and plaza serve to draw the eye along a series of horizontal planes perpendicular to the vertical thrust of the towers that frame the church, and enhance the feeling of massiveness and height of the building. Climbing this series of gradins also lifts one above the level of the town and enables one to see the stretch of the valley within which Esquipulas sits. The new highway has therefore been incorporated as one of a number of architectural elements that create a more complicated visual entity and attempt to enhance the experience of the basilica. In addition, the new elements, constituting as they do assistance from the Guatemalan national government and foreign priests, mark new boundaries for local authority.

The transition at the end of the procession from street to church is marked not only by the fence and the absence of vendors but also by the appearance of employees of the basilica, both religious and otherwise. Policemen are used for crowd control and the maintenance of the *cola* inside the church grounds, and they are clearly marked by basilica uniforms that differentiate them from civil and military authorities. The pilgrims themselves wear specially decorated hats, the manufacture of which is an important cottage industry in Esquipulas. The majority of participants, Indian and Ladino, rural and urban, wear these hats.

Often pilgrims will form a dense cluster of worshippers and, following closely behind a prayer leader (*rezador*), will make an entrance into the church. These are village groups, usually Indian, dressed in *tipica* (Indian-produced clothes) or Western clothes. The litany of pilgrimage songs seems limited and universally known, although songs and dances of local communities may be performed in the plaza as well. Once in the park, pilgrims have two choices; they may approach the image from the rear, by waiting in the *cola*, or they may approach the image through the church. Another stop, external to the temple but within the temple grounds, is the faucet of holy water maintained by the basilica. Drinking the water is an essential element of the pilgrimage.

During the height of the *feria* season, both in January and in April, family and community images of saints are brought to the church for a recharging of spiritual energy (*recarger*). These saints are crowded into the side altars around the images in the walls of the interior of the church. Men from each village are assigned the responsibility of guarding them day and night. Each community puts its saints under an image of their patron saint or a saint they select. The saints from various towns and their human guardians are in close proximity in side altars, but the likely significance of this juxtaposition was not explored.

Many supplicants approach El Señor in the main nave on their knees and chanting. Some individuals approach boldly, to address the image about a personal problem, or to complain about mistreatment by fate or other deities. This behavior, which is acceptable in the church, would be considered mad or drunken and possibly dangerous on the street, especially because the speakers are often members of classes considered to be humble (*humilde*), i.e., rural Ladinos or Indians. The theme of most prayers and oral addresses within the basilica, however, concerns thanksgiving for favors already granted, and it is to this end that most pilgrimages are said to be aimed.

Once a position has been found on the floor of the church or in a pew, pilgrims burn candles, purchased from the vendors lining the streets near the basilica, for all the participants of a pilgrimage and for many who are not present but who participate by virtue of a contribution to the pilgrims. I interviewed several men from highland Guatemala who had purchased more than 50 dollars worth of candles. A further ritual obligation concerns the purchase and ingestion of small cakes of white earth, called *pan del Señor* or Lord's Bread. Pilgrims not only consume them, but take additional cakes home to their families. The cakes are embossed with religious motifs but serve a quite profane purpose, to be discussed below. At regular intervals, benedictions of participants and objects such as memorabilia, saints, or cars are performed by the priests with the same holy water used for drinking. These benedictions are performed on the plaza immediately surrounding the church and within the sacred confines of the walls at the base of the church steps.

The sequence of activities— procession, prayer, passage by the statue, and benediction—may be repeated many times by a pilgrim. The remaining time in town is spent shopping, gaming, drinking, and socializing. These more secular activities begin with a choice of apartment. Pilgrims may choose to rent a room in either of the three classes of hostel: *hotel, pension*, or *hospedaje*. These differing classes of accommodation are municipally recognized entities and offer the gamut of conveniences ranging from private bathroom, in the case of certain hotels, to simple roofed rooms in the hospedaje. Occupancy varies from several adults to a room in the hotel, to as many as ten or fifteen to a room in a hospedaje.

Alternatively, pilgrims may choose to sleep in patios of local residents' houses or in the field. Many buses, especially those from Indian communities, come equipped with large tarpaulins which are stretched out from the bus and provide shelter. Urban Ladinos make an effort to obtain a room, but Indian pilgrims are more likely to sleep outdoors. The buses, which now bring the bulk of pilgrims, park in one selected area of town, and the field which they surround serves as a sleeping and cooking commons. A census conducted in the *cola* line demonstrated that roughly 80 percent (n=630) of all pilgrims at the height of the *feria* sleep in the fields; the *hoteles*, pensiones, and hospedajes, however, are filled.

The large number of pilgrims places a strain on the city water and sewage facilities. Even though many of the pilgrims sleep in the fields to the east of the basilica, which is the lowest part of town, water may not be available by late in the afternoon. Several taps are placed in the field for water, but participants often must carry water from one of the ritual bathing places south of the basilica.

Sewage and other wastes constitute a more difficult problem, but pilgrims are careful to remove trash and other wastes to the city limits. Some pilgrims, especially those travelling on foot, collect firewood along their march, and carry their trash home with them again (see Fought 1972). The city itself has an ordinance to fine littering, but it has proven unnecessary. The potential health hazard is still large, especially for the spread of infectious diseases, including the diarrhea that plagues rural populations. Pharmacies and geophagy, the latter attested to by Borhegyi (1953, 1954), serve to ameliorate the effects of disease. The two large pharmacies in town serve a large number of patent remedies and antibiotics to the pilgrims, aided by the numerous herbalists found in the streets. The *pan del Señor* mentioned above provides another effective remedy. Borhegyi, who first commented on the earth cakes, had one of them analyzed. The major medicinal ingredient, kaolin, is an absorbent frequently used to control diarrhea.

An additional factor in the control of disease is the limited time most pilgrims stay in Esquipulas. The survey of pilgrims, described below, showed that 80 percent (n=634) remained in Esquipulas for four days or less, and many preferred to bring their food for that period. The majority of pilgrims who do not arrive for the January and April ceremonies remain a shorter time. Additional activities such as the processions of Holy Week or the fireworks display produced by El Salvador, encourage pilgrims to remain for longer periods. More than one-third of all pilgrims arrive in the month of January or in the Holy Week.

Pilgrims flock, as well, to the more than 2,000 stalls and amusements on the grounds east of the basilica, or visit nearby springs and rivers or a curious tunnel in one of the mountains near Esquipulas (*la cueva*). The tunnel, part of an old iron mine 100 feet long, is shaped like a cross, and *copal* (pitch pine) may be burned at the entrance. One version of the origin myth of the icon is that it was generated from the metal and dirt removed from this tunnel.

If the pilgrimage activities themselves do not appear striking, it is because we have yet to consider the incongruities represented by the pilgrimage population. Ladinos and Indians, rural and urban participants, rich and poor, Honduran, Salvadoran, Guatemalan, and Mexican pilgrims co-participate. It is this co-participation in the face of these ethnic, economic, and national cleavages that makes the pilgrimage such a distinctive event.

DESCRIPTIVE CATEGORIES OF THE PILGRIMAGE

Generalizations about one to two million tourists need be suspect. A non-ego-centered nongroup (Boissevain 1968) as transitory as this pilgrimage population constitutes an unusual ethnographic entity (see Fortes 1971:5). The pilgrimage population is a "heterogeneous urban aggregate," to borrow Fortes' phrase, with a very narrow temporal depth. Furthermore, the participants are not necessarily bound to Esquipulas either by the traditional sorts of relationships characteristic of *municipio* community members in their ethnographic context, or by relations generated by occupation, residence, and ethnicity in urban environments (although some pilgrims do come to trade).

The aggregate is only connected, in fact, by common participation in the cult of El Señor and the communion that this participation entails (see Schmalenbach 1965:331). This common purpose characterizes a population that transcends many of the traditional ethnographic boundaries but nonetheless constitutes a significant social entity. Central Americans recognize the short-lived communion generated by participation in the pilgrimage and greet with respect and friendship the wearer of the pilgrim's hat. The affective bonds that constitute this communion are short-lived, however, and the pilgrims remove their hats when they return home and take up their daily routine. Furthermore, the pilgrimage stay is invariably short. Pilgrims who come between the feast of El Señor and *Semana Santa* (Easter Week) usually stay four days, while the majority of pilgrims who come for the feast days stay only two days. Yet pilgrims return, year after year. Ninety-three percent (733) of all pilgrims sampled claimed they visited every year.

The size and the urban nature of the population necessitated a questionnaire and some efforts at sampling. However, the categorization of the population into ethnic, economic, and geographic categories suffers from the artificial nature of their proximity in Esquipulas. The accouterments of these categories are sometimes evident and sometimes not. The pilgrimage population's expression of wealth, urban arrogance, and national chauvinism—descriptive as they may be of the original urban or rural social contexts of the pilgrims—fail to describe this new and momentary social entity. Nonetheless, certain categorizations pertinent to the anthropological literature of Central America will be attempted.

Ethnic Distinctions

The first distinction, central to a discussion of Mesoamerica, is that of Ladino, or mestizo, and Indian. The dichotomy of Western clothes and handwoven Indian clothes, distinctive styles of walking and presentation, hairdressing, and facial and body types, seemingly marking the difference between folk and urban societies, strike the observer. But as Pitt-Rivers (1967:71) has noted for Chiapas, the distinction between Indian and Ladino, or between Indian and Hispanic culture, cannot be made easily. Many Indians wear Ladino clothes; some the baggy pants and bright shirts of the *campesino*, and some, such as the astute traders of Momostenango, tailored clothes and hats with narrow snap brims. Many wear the native costumes that symbolize the syncretism of Spanish and native customs and serve to segregate Indians by community.

The cleavage of Indian and Ladino encompasses much more, of course, than styles of dress and somatyping. Although the division between Ladino and Indian is apparent everywhere in Guatemala, exclusive and distinctive attributes of these two groups are hard to determine. The persistent ethnic difference has been discussed in a number of frameworks. Colby and van den Berghe (1969) have applied M. G. Smith's and Furnivall's notion of plural society to these two groups; Wagley (1968:179) developed the notion of social race to account for the nonbiological nature of the distinction; one recent work lays the division on an economic doorstep (W. Smith 1975:226); Wolf and Hansen (1972:71-100) feel that the difference reflects distinctive forms of rural social organization: "closed" and "open." Although this is only a short list of treatments of Indian-Ladino relations (see also Tax 1953:231-39; Mendez-Domínguez 1975:542 ff.), the approach is not unusual. Each of the researchers touches on part of the difference, discussing economic, rural-urban, ethnic, and sociohistorical phenomena. Most analyses fail, however, to separate the social *persona*, Indian or Ladino, from the various statuses which individuals may conjoin. It must be remembered that ethnic membership and identity are not generated by the above-mentioned effects. They derive from a self-identification that may be part of a polythetic arrangement (Needham 1975) of statuses in which family membership, village membership, tribal and linguistic affinities, and vocational, class, and political affiliations all play a part. As Tax (1953:95) has noted, "the chief trouble is that the characteristics of the people who are known as Indians in some places are the same as the characteristics of people who are not known as Indians in other places." Furthermore, the validity of this major distinction has been questioned (Mendez-Domínguez 1975:542). At the local level, the inhabitants of Santiago Atítlan differentiate not only between Indian and Ladino, but also between Indians of San Lucas and Panajachel on the one hand and Ladinos and Gringos on the other (see Tax and Hinshaw 1970:192 ff.). It is this need and desire, in so many contexts, to differentiate these social categories that makes co-participation in Esquipulas unusual.

Given the field situation in Esquipulas and the state of the Indian-Ladino distinction in ethnography, eliciting self-identifications from pilgrims seemed the only way to measure ethnic dentity. Yet this identification is hampered by several difficulties. Esquipulas, situated as it is in the Ladino crescent of Guatemala, may serve for many Indians as a test or short trial of their skills for participation in a non-Indian world. In this sense, the pilgrimage to Esquipulas is a manifestation of a national internal "exo-migration." Although the stay in Esquipulas is brief, individuals may "pass," or break, rules on premarital dating or wandering alone at night with little fear of sanction. Secondly, the researcher of pilgrimage populations does not have the information on the economic, political, and sociohistorical circumstances and personal life-history of the individual and group that are used by so many anthropologists to determine ethnic membership. Thirdly, Ladinos constitute the dominant political and economic population in most of Guatemala. As rulers, Ladinos often see Indians as "problems": for example, in daily interaction, Indians may be abused both verbally and physically. Therefore, some not inconsiderable pressure might be felt in the interview situation. Finally, inadequacy in Spanish is characteristic of some members of Indian communities. This undoubtedly created problems in communication.

With these caveats the data is presented. A stratified sample was selected of every fifth person standing in the *cola* to see the shrine. Only heads of family groups were surveyed. They answered both for themselves and for their groups. A tabulation of the survey (n=788) produced the following results (Table 8.1).

Table 8.1   Ethnic Self-Identification

No Answer	Indian	Ladino
1.3% (59)	33.5% (264)	59.0% (465)

Ethnic identity comprises one set of statuses, here incompletely explored, of the pilgrimage population. Actors who participate in this ethnic dichotomy are not independent of the economic and rural-urban distinctions discussed in the following sections. Treatment of these conjoined statuses, however, must be left to some larger work, as the categorization is not clear-cut. Not all Indians are rural and poor, but these ethnic, economic, and geographic categories constitute important elements of sociological description and contribute to the impact of the pilgrimage ceremonies on the participants.

Economic Distinctions

Economic differentiation is clearly manifest in the pilgrimage population. Differences in wealth of the participants are reflected not only in choices of rooms, but also in the modes of transportation used to reach Esquipulas. Buses transport 62.8 percent of the pilgrimage population to Esquipulas;

11.1 percent arrive by horse, mule, or on foot; and 26.1 percent utilize private or rented cars. The cost of bus transportation from Guatemala City to Esquipulas was three dollars (U.S.). Thus, generally, the rural and urban poor will be found on buses, while wealthy Ladinos and Indians will bring their cars (Table 8.2).

Table 8.2 Means of Transportation of Pilgrimage Population

Transport	Number	Percent
Bus	494	62.8
Private Car	205	26.1
Horse, Foot	87	11.1
Total	788	100.0

Accommodations vary as well, as previously indicated. Seventy-six percent (n=599) of the pilgrims sleep in the fields adjacent to the church grounds, either in a chartered bus or under a tarpaulin attached to the bus. Many pilgrims ask for space on a porch or in a courtyard of a house, often returning year after year or creating ritual kin ties with families who offer hospitality. The wealthier find space in one of the crowded hotels. Many families choose to eat in the *campo* or field as well. Of all respondents 80.8 percent cooked or bought cooked food in this open field. Other pilgrims eat at one of the hotel restaurants.

Although the data are suspect, the questionnaire did show that pilgrimage costs varied greatly; adults spent between nine and 40 U.S. dollars, with a mean of 25 dollars. This money, however, did not necessarily represent individual assets, for many rural and Indian participants spent money contributed by family and friends. One Quiché man bought and burned 85 dollars worth of candles for a sizable group of relatives and co-workers.

These economic differences however, do not produce a differentiation in the observance of ceremonial activities. Wagley's (1953) study of the cult of St. Benedict in Ita, Brazil, illustrates how economic cleavages within the pilgrimage population are reflected in the worship of St. Benedict and the worship of St. Anthony, patron saint of Ita. St. Benedict is associated with the poor and St. Anthony with the rich. Religious observance, including participation in the religious fraternities or *hermandades*, is organized by class. In Esquipulas, although economic differentiation of participants can be found, differences of wealth have little real meaning in the shops and stalls surrounding the temple and are not reflected in the waiting time in the *cola* or participation in the Mass or benediction.

International Distinctions

A status of some significance in Central America, at least for Ladinos, is national citizenship. Representative national groups do co-participate throughout the *feria* season. Countries and *hermandades* from shrines within these countries set their pilgrimage schedules on a consistent but informal basis. Most Mexicans, for example, choose the month of January to complete their pilgrimages, although Mexicans may be found in Esquipulas throughout the year. The breakdown by nationality in January according to our sample is as follows (Table 8.3).

Table 8.3 Participation in the Pilgrimage by Nationality – January 1973

Guatemala	469	59.5%
Honduras	65	8.2%
El Salvador	239	30.3%
[Mexico, Nicaragua, Costa Rica]	15	2.0%
Total	788	100.0%

A potential for violence given, for example, the 1969 Honduran-Salvadoran conflict, is an ever-present reality in this context. Esquipulas was home for more than 4,000 refugees following this war and more than half of them stayed in Esquipulas after the settlement. Nonetheless, examples of conflict based on national identity are rare in Esquipulas, and the town was chosen for several international conventions on the basis of this. Esquipulas views itself as the capital of the faithful in Central America, and this religious sincerity would seem to generate a communion (see Schmalenbach 1965) even within quite secular realms.

Urban-Rural Distinctions

Urban or rural status was elicited through the questionnaire. Table 8.4 lists the origin of pilgrims. "Rural" means that pilgrims and their group originated in an *aldea* (hamlet) or *caserio* (village). Esquipulas was traditionally a pilgrimage goal for predominantly rural participants, but the increasing migration of rural homesteaders to urban centers such as Guatemala City and Quetzaltenango, or to the major cities in El Salvador and Honduras, has produced an urban and rural pilgrimage population. Although it may be argued that the migrating populations maintain rural social customs and are therefore "rural," politicians and foreigners present in Esquipulas belie this interpretation.

When the national cathedral of El Salvador was gutted by fire, a pilgrimage was started to Esquipulas. On January 11 of each year, wealthy urban Ladinos of El Salvador provide a display of fireworks. The display, although more elaborate, mirrors the use of fireworks by many small rural communities in Esquipulas. The growth of a significant demand for luxury hotel accommodations in Esquipulas on the one hand, and the development, since 1968, of regular and frequent bus service to Guatemala City on the other, are indicative of increasing urban participation in the pilgrimage.

Male-Female Distinctions

Although the differences in behaviors of men and women are noted in most ethnographic contexts, most surveys of ethnic, economic, and political distinctions fail to include this important category. While male or female participation in religious events within local communities may vary from community to community, the Esquipulas pilgrimage population is roughly half male and half female.

Table 8.4 Origins of Pilgrims

Rural	533	67.6%
Urban	255	32.4%
Total	788	100.0%

Women co-participate in religious ceremonies, although women do not guard the saints in the side altar. As the lesson of the Rock of the Compadres might indicate, traveling companions are on the best of terms, and in one sense, all pilgrims are traveling companions. Freedom of expression for women in Esquipulas seems relatively untrammelled. Many shopkeepers, store owners, and restaurant owners are women, and, for their part, the pilgrims' behavior in Esquipulas is not subject to local censure. The pilgrimage population is surprisingly adult. Seventy-two percent of the population were over 18. This may reflect concern for illness, the trepidations of the journey, or nonparticipation of new householders with unweaned children. Whatever its origin, it does allow women a freedom to join in the *feria* celebrations with an unusual abandon. In addition to providing a carnival packed with strangers within which to lose oneself, the *feria* time provides a release from home cares, especially for Indian women, even though they still must cook and take care of children and other attendant problems.

It should not be assumed, of course, that outside of the church yard, women share identical behaviors, or that the coitus proscribed within Esquipulas between compadre and comadre extends to the prostitutes of Esquipulas. Still, women may walk freely through the stalls and *cantinas* at all hours, smile and flirt with whom they please, and become part of the rowdy *feria* crowd. Women participate in a public sense in the ceremonies and celebrations in Esquipulas. Although this behavior is not unique to the pilgrimage, the social context of the pilgrimage is not reproduced in the daily rounds of events, nor in the local fiestas in which the pilgrims participate.

The year in Esquipulas is divided into *feria* and non*feria* seasons. *Feria* season is bracketed by January 15, the feast day of Esquipulas, and Holy Week. In the last decade, however, it has been extended to accommodate more pilgrims. The *feria* season now starts several days prior to January 11, when Salvadorans hold a national festival in Esquipulas, and extends to April. The date of January 15 is traditionally justified as a feast day because it is the ninth day or *novena* following January 6, the epiphany. This season coincides with the dry cycle in Guatemala, a period of relatively little agricultural activity. This timing facilitates the participation of a more rural and agricultural pilgrimage population.

The *feria* season for the town of Esquipulas is a time given over to the pilgrimage. The commemoration of the arrival of the image in Esquipulas is celebrated by a procession sponsored by a brotherhood based in the capital city of Guatemala and accompanied by Indian ritual sponsors from a hamlet of Esquipulas. The cycle of *feria* ceremonies incorporates the diverse population that participates in the pilgrimage, while separating the distinct contributions of each type of participant. For example, the town's festival for its patron saint, Santiago, takes place June 25, during the non*feria* season, and is, by contrast, a wholly local undertaking.

Chortí and Other Mayan Pilgrims

Studying the Chortí in the 1930s, Wisdom devoted almost no attention to Esquipulas in his 1940 monograph on the Chortí. Reina (1969), following Wisdom, states that the Chortí, who now occupy the municipalities of Jocotán and Comotán immediately to the north of Esquipulas, did not even include the feast day of Esquipulas in their calendar. Not until Fought's (1972) transcription of the Chortí texts of Isidro Gonzalez, a Protestant, do we have proof of local indigenous participation. Fought notes, "it is clear that the pilgrimage to Esquipulas is a preliminary part of the cycle of New Year Ceremonies" (1972:524). Pilgrimages to Esquipulas by the Chortí occur in January and April. My own research in Tunocó, a hamlet of Jocotán, shows that January 15 is one of four major feast days in that community, and that El Señor de Esquipulas, or Milagroso, is intimately associated with household shrines and ritual geography. The Chortí description of the pilgrimage, according to Isidro Gonzalez, is as follows: the basilica is built over a lake that contains a pair of tethered chicchanes—bisexual, bimorphous deities; Milagroso controls the serpents via nooses; men are buried in the walls of the basilica; and Milagroso is married to the Marian image of La Pastora in Chortí Olopa (Fought 1972:455). A successful pilgrimage to Esquipulas for the Chortí is initiated with the announcement of the proposed trip. Many hamlet residents contribute money to be donated to Milagroso. The pilgrims are escorted to the limits of the hamlet by neighbors who fire rockets. Many penitents carry stones to Esquipulas, as well as their food and firewood. Switches are cut to beat the legs of the penitents. Pilgrims are welcomed upon return, and their families are responsible for preparation of a party.

This pattern is reported in many Mesoamerican towns fitting van Gennep's and Turner's pattern of pre-liminal, liminal, and postliminal processes that mark *les rites de passage*. The difficulty in analysis is that the "passage" refers to the crossing of magico-territorial boundaries, as discussed in van Gennep (1960), and not to the transition across status and role boundaries in the community which ethnographic data isolate. The community formed by all the pilgrims forms a strange congery, indeed. Other western highland communities may send large delegations. Even in the nineteenth century, Maudsley (1899) reported the entrance of a large group of pilgrims returning to Santiago Atitlán from Esquipulas. This pattern persists today.

THE POLITICAL TRADITION OF ESQUIPULAS

These few data and brief sketches, while they do not exhaust the diversity of pilgrimage performance, set the stage for the social drama of the pilgrimage. It would be a mistake, however, to terminate an analysis with an encyclopedic delimitation of national, linguistic, and ethnic groups and of the diverse socioeconomic categories involved in the pilgrimage, and mark these as social fields for analysis. The result would be an incomplete characterization of the pilgrimage. The difficulty involves the characterization of the relations between these groups—for the communion and tension of the pilgrimage, the "miracle" of the pilgrimage, is dependent on the nature of the sodality under which these diverse statuses can be grouped. Political and economic relationships would have to play an extensive role in this analysis. This approach, parallel to the symbological analysis of the icon but in secular contradistinction, identifies the common element for the pilgrims: what they do, in fact, share besides devotion to the image. This is the secular identification of the meaning of the pilgrimage—the context of regional, national, and international issues: in short, the politics of the pilgrimage.

The icon of Esquipulas, from the time of the conquest, has stood as a symbol of political, as well as ethnic, accommodation. This is well-accepted for the conquest, but a measure of this accommodation is revealed as well in the 1873 conservative revolt of Rafael Carrera called the War of La Montaña. Although Esquipulas was not directly implicated in this revolt, issues that relate to the contemporary political significance of Esquipulas are evident.

The liberal reforms of the nineteenth century attempted to transform Guatemala from a traditional colony of Spain to a government that embodied the ideals of the Enlightenment (see Woodward 1972, 1976). For example, Spanish law, the *fueros*, and administrative practice, supported by the Church, had protected the Indian and Indian lands from the Ladino population by enforcing communal tenure and denying all civil rights to Indians. At the same time, the government maintained guilds and trade monopolies to control the major export industries, primarily cochineal and textiles. The liberal government of 1829-39 attempted to impose radical anticlerical and economic programs to change this pattern. The resulting conflict was not, as Woodward (1972) points out, just another liberal-conservative dispute among the urban elite in Guatemala City, but a genuine social revolution, centered in the mountains of Eastern Guatemala and organized by Rafael Carrera, former swineherd and arch-example of the Latin American political leader, the *caudillo*. Time and again, institutional reforms inspired by liberal rhetoric encountered resistance from special interests on the one hand, and produced unexpected consequences on the other. For Indians, private ownership meant the loss of their lands. Free trade meant competition with cheap English textiles. The expulsion of clerics meant that small communities lost not only ritual specialists, but judges and arbitrators as well. Trial by jury meant that issues were decided on the basis of local standards of evidence and points of law, and competition with immigrant foreigners meant increased pressure on land.

These factors, coupled with a widespread cholera epidemic, led to open revolt. Enlightenment, self-fulfillment, and individuation were rejected in favor of a paternalistic and hierarchical system of political and economic organization that offered stability and that characterized the *caudillo* form of government. The revolt affected all of Central America, dealt a death blow to regional political unity, and established conservative Carrera as president until his death in 1865.

The issues embodied in the Carrera revolt are explicit in the politics of Esquipulas in this century. The icon has served as an important political symbol for the present national government since Monseñor Mariano Rosell Arellano, Archbishop of Guatemala, removed the image from the basilica and toured the country with it to organize opposition to the liberal Arbenz government. That tour and his pastoral letter of April 4, 1954, are said to have been significant factors in the 1954 CIA-sponsored coup. Esquipulas was the first major town entered by Castillo Armas and his army. After the battle (or more properly skirmish) of Chiquimula was fought and won by Castillo Armas, the Black Christ of Esquipulas was closely associated with the political party he founded, the National Liberation Movement (MLN). To this day, the MLN and other right-wing parties often initiate electoral campaigns in Esquipulas, and their leaders frequently participate in the pilgrimage to Esquipulas. Furthermore, the political parties they represent find much support in non-urban Guatemala, especially the rural eastern section. In fact, the pilgrimage to Esquipulas can be seen as semi-officially endorsed by the governments of Guatemala, El Salvador, and Honduras, who share conservative governments, and the site is sometimes used to negotiate disputes between these and other countries. In recent years, the Central American peace accords were signed in Esquipulas.

The central theme of sacrifice embodied in the crucifix, the hierarchy of penitent, priest, saint, and god, and the temporary pluralistic democracy found in the pilgrimage "communitas" are politically valorized events. The current popularity of the pilgrimage in Esquipulas is linked to the political events cited above and the ideology of conflict and power embodied in *caudillismo*, as it is to the felicity of symbol and meaning in a liturgical and ethnohistorical sense. To ignore these aspects of the symbol is to misinterpret the popular response to them.

REFERENCES

Boissevain 1968
Borhegyi 1953, 1954
Cohen 1974
Colby-Berghe 1969
Corbett and Whiteford 1983
Fortes 1945, 1949, 1969, 1971
Fought 1972
Grimes 1976
Hammond 1972
Méndez-Domínguez 1975
Maudsley-Maudsley 1899
Needham 1975
Pitt-Rivers 1967
Reina 1969
Rosaldo 1968
Schmalenbach 1965
Smith, Waldemar 1975
Stephens 1969
Tax 1953
Tax-Hinshaw 1970
Thompson, J.Eric S. 1964
Turner 1974
Turner-Turner 1978
van Gennep 1960
Wagley 1953, 1968
Weaver 1972
Wisdom 1940
Wolf 1966
Wolf-Hansen 1972
Woodward 1972, 1976

9

Through the
Fields to Amatitlán

LESLIE ELLEN STRAUB, O.P.

Figure 9.1 El Niño de Atocha between Saint Joseph and the Virgin Mary

Pilgrims come to the town of San Juan de Amatitlán in the eastern Central Highlands of Guatemala to visit El Niño de Atocha (the Child of Atocha, Figure 9.1, the Image of El Niño de Atocha between the images of Saint Joseph and the Virgin Mary; the shrine and parish church of Amatitlán, San Juan de Amititlán, Guatemala 1982). They come through the fields, literally as well as metaphorically, bearing an identity, background, beliefs, hopes, and expectations regarding their sojourn at this pilgrimage center. The town, too, has an identity and a history, located as it is on the southern shore of Lake Amatitlán, a resort area which offers attractions for a variety of visitors, only some of whom are pilgrims.

People, beliefs, practices, and place are constituent elements of any pilgrimage. It is my intention to ask two related questions about them as they pertain to the pilgrimage (romería) to Amatitlán.[1] First, what continuity can be traced in the development of the pilgrimage from preconquest times to the present? Second, what have been the conceptions of the identity, personal characteristics, and special province of concern of the Niño which have drawn pilgrims to him? Data from archaeological, ethnographic, and ethnohistoric research provide some of the answers to these questions.

THE LAKE, THE TOWN, AND EARLY PILGRIMAGES

As a journey through the fields to Amatitlán nears its end, the route followed may allow the pilgrim a view of a large, volcanic lake shaped like a figure-eight, 28 kilometers by highway south-southwest of Guatemala City. The Pacaya volcano rises above it to the south. Geysers appear on the south shore and there are springs of sulfurous water in the lake and on the land around it. A species of fig tree from the bark of which paper was made, the Amate (Gage 1958:301, n.1), grows along the shore. The lake takes its name from these trees, Lago de Amatitlán (Lake at the Place of the Paper Trees).

A short distance from the lake-front is the town of San Juan de Amatitlán, which takes its full name partly from the trees and partly from the saint, John the Baptist, on whose feast day, June 24, it might have been founded in 1549 (Chinchilla Aguilar 1961:29, 32). Amatitlán, as it is commonly known, was constituted a reducción formed by the merger of five Indian pueblos named Pampichí, Tzacualpa, El Salitre, El Llano de Animas, and Panquejechó (Chinchilla Aguilar 1961:28). Today it is a municipal capital in the Department of Guatemala; it is predominantly, perhaps totally, Ladino in population.[2]

On the basis of archaeological evidence, we can trace human occupancy of sites on the shore of the lake back to approximately 1,000 B.C. (Borhegyi 1958:123). A complex of four small mounds at a site called "Mejicanos" suggests that pilgrimage activity was underway by 200 A.D., for the complex seems to mark a shrine built especially for pilgrims who were coming "in droves" (Borhegyi 1959:105, 108). Residents of the lake sites and pilgrims as well were apparently Pokom-speaking Maya or Nahuatl-speakers called Pipil who were intermixed in southeastern Guatemala and El Salvador in preconquest times (Miles 1957:742). The Maya presence is known both from mounds built on the shore and from artifacts recovered from the lake which depict Maya gods such as those of the sun, water, and wind, the jaguar, and death, as well as everyday items like cacao fruit, which was used as currency (Borhegyi 1959:105-06; 1958:122). Pipil motifs, including representations of speech scrolls, jaguars, spider monkeys, human skulls, and intricately designed flowers and vines appear on objects recovered from the floor of the lake (Borhegyi 1959:110). The objects and their locations suggest that pilgrims came to the lake to make offerings to their gods and that those offerings of beautiful and precious goods, and human bodies as well, were associated with their concern about life, fertility, rain, health, and growth.

Pilgrimages in the region around Lake Amatitlán continued after the Spanish Conquest in 1524 and judging from the manuscript town record book of San Juan de Amatitlán, 1559-1562, probably involved the Pokomam and Pipil populations until the latter group disappeared from the area (Miles 1957:742).[3] Thomas Gage, the Dominican priest in charge at Amatitlán in 1635, described a wooden figure set up in a cave between the towns of Mixco and San Juan Sacatepéquez which was worshipped by people from both locales (1958:278-85). Possibly at that same time, a pilgrimage to the shrine of a deity, Christian in name and form, took root in a village called Pampichí, the first location of Amatitlán and the present-day hamlet of Belén.[4] The first explicit reference to this pilgrimage was written in 1690:

> The pueblo of Pampichí, situated on the southern shore of the lake where Amatitlán was located before its two transfers, and which later was like a country place to the pueblo of Amatitlán, has a population of 30 very poor people. Thus its church constructed of thatch is dilapidated and poor as well, even though it is frequented by pilgrims by reason of the miraculous image of the Holy Child of Bethlehem [El Santo Niño de Belén] which they have there and which is the patron of that little place. (Fuentes y Guzmán 1969:I, 381, my translation)

The pilgrimage which the Indians and perhaps some Ladinos and Spaniards were making to the Niño in Pampichí grew until a major change in location had to be made. We read in the next explicit reference to the pilgrimage written by Juarros, that in Amatitlán,

> there is . . . a large respectable church which contains an image of the infant Saviour, that is held in such high esteem by the devout, as to attract a great concourse of visitants from the neighboring, and even from distant villages, particularly on the first Sunday of May, when the principal festival is celebrated. The sacred effigy was originally placed in a little hermitage, about 3 [sic] leagues distant, at a place called

Bethlehem [Belén — formerly, Pampichí(n)]; but to prevent the mischiefs occasioned by large meetings in retired places, the archbishop of Guatemala ordered it to be transferred to the parish church in 1789. (1823:99)

Juarros seems to have been mistaken in thinking that the building in Amatitlán was the parish church. Another text dated 1883 states: "In this year, precisely on May 3, the image of the Niño Dios de Belén was transferred in solemn religious procession from the chapel of the Dominicans [that is] the chapel in the *convento* of Amatitlán, to the parish church" (Chinchilla Aguilar 1961:65, my translation). It is helpful to note that Chinchilla Aguilar (1965:203) identifies that image of the Niño Dios de Belén with the image, Niño de Belén, found at the present time in the

Figure 9.2 Parish church in San Juan de Amatitlán housing the shrine of el Niño de Atocha with the weekend market in front of the church

parish church of Amatitlán (Figure 9.2). In the contemporary period, "Niño de Atocha" and "Niño Dios de Amatitlán" are other titles given to the same image (Chinchilla Aguilar 1961:63,67).

THE NIÑO AND POKOMAM CULTURE

There is no written record of the actual installation of the image in the shrine at Pampichí; nor is there a description of the image or of the kind of worship given the Niño in those early days of the pilgrimage. We do know that Indians of the area were active as "owners" of the saints' images in the churches. The Indians cared for the saints (*santos*), carried them in procession, celebrated their feast day, presented them with white wax candles, cocoa, or fruit, and, on Christmas Day, brought them to offer gifts to a child made of wood, painted and gilded, who represented the newborn Christ. The child was placed between Mary and Joseph in a little thatched house resembling a stall set up in a corner of the church. There were wise men, shepherds with their country gifts, animals, angels, and a star. The stall was called Bethlehem (Gage 1958:239).

Specific characteristics of the Pokomam culture in the sixteenth century prepared the Indians to participate comfortably in this kind of religious practice, although the people were often confused about the concepts of formal Catholicism which were involved. Among the Pokomam, there was a pronounced emphasis upon classification and rank order in the political, religious, and social realms. A lesser ruler paid tribute to a higher one and sent representatives to important functions at his residence. Religious functionaries and duties were finely subdivided, as was the pantheon of deities worshipped (Miles 1957:750). These elements also entered into the Pokomam's formulation of the identity or identities, functions, and spheres of influence of the holy personages whose names and images they so readily adopted from Catholicism.

Other cultural traits were also important in this regard. First, within the family, rank according to age and sex was expressed in the kinship terminology. For example, in Pokom-Mayan, there were terms for "older brother" and "younger brother" but not simply for "brother". Patterns of behavior were connoted by the terms: the older sibling had authority over the younger one of the same sex. By extension of meaning, the political ruler had authority over all free men, all of whom he called his "younger brother" (Miles 1957: 755-58, 777). Second, the Pokomam culture was closely related to the Lowland Maya civilization rather than that of the Highland Maya. In religion this affiliation was expressed in the high degree of stratification of religious offices, the great development of religious duties and practices, and the arrangement of the ritual calendar. It was also evident in the roster of deities, which included the prominent Lowland Maya names of Itzam(ná), the sky god, and Ixchel, the moon goddess, which do not appear in the important Highland sources, namely, the *Popul Vuh*, the *Annals of the Cakchiquel*, and the *Title of the Lords of Totonicapán*. It excluded the name of Xbalanque, one of the hero-twins of the *Popul Vuh* (Miles 1957:748; Carmack 1981:208, 318, 384).

Likely as early as the seventeenth century, the Niño visited at Pampichí had acquired an identity, function, and sphere of influence all his own, and these individual characteristics had become even more sharply defined when the association of the child with the Feast of the Holy Cross, May 3, was clearly established. Certainly, the Niño was separated by Indians from other Niños in the chapel, or church, at Amatitlán. We know at least two of these Niños, namely, the child representing the newborn Christ in the stall called Bethlehem and the child in the arms of Our Lady of the Rosary as she was portrayed in the statue commissioned for the church in 1696 (Chinchilla Aguilar 1961:69). By the late nineteenth century, the Niño was perceived to be quite human. It was profoundly believed that he would not permit the construction of an embankment carrying railroad tracks over the narrow neck of the lake; he wanted to return to his poor little church in the hamlet of fishermen called Pampichí at one time; he was seen by fishermen on the water of the lake, at a place along the north shore named Los Organos by the archaeologists, and La Silla de los Organos by local people (Chinchilla Aguilar 1961:65; Mata Amado 1964:64); and most recently, he swam in the lake at night, returning to church in the morning with wet, sandy skin (Osborne 1959:479).

The precise origin of these ideas about the Niño is unknown. However, they bear a striking resemblance to ideas held by Pokomam Indians of Santa Cruz de Chinauta, a pueblo once subordinate to the Dominican priory in Amatitlán, who were making pilgrimages (romerías) annually to Amatitlán at least until 1962 and possibly until the present (Reina 1966:178).[5] The patron of the pueblo is El Niño de Otocha (sic), who appeared first at a sacred spring on the feast of the Exaltation of the Holy Cross, September 15, year unknown. The image represents the Niño holding a staff with a star on it in one hand, and the world in the other.

The Chinautlecos did not identify the Niño with any other of several Niños in their pueblo, including the Christmas Niño. Like their seventeenth-century ancestors and other contemporary Indians in Guatemala, members of the community who were following its sacred traditions understood each santo, that is, each "holy person", and "the image of the person" as well, to be a separate individual (Reina 1966:152, 152 note 17, 175). There were Chinautlecos who treated images as living beings and believed that some of them had the power to intervene in human affairs, to be rather unpredictable because they were sacred, and to have very human emotions (Reina 1966:172-73, 175). They believed that the Niño de Atocha could not be moved from the altar. Thus the Virgin of the Conception represented him in the procession of the fiesta in his honor (Reina 1966:145). He did wander of his own free will and when he was absent the sacristan could not open the church doors. The sacristan knew when the Niño had gone to his sacred hill at night because he found sand in the child's sandals (Reina 1966:172-73). One of the Niño's trips was particularly interesting: he visited his younger brother in Amatitlán during the titular feast. At those times, the church doors could not be opened either (Reina 1966:173). On May 2-3, the Chinautlecos celebrated the feast of the finding of the Holy Cross with music and a procession. They visited all of the crosses in the community, including the ones at the boundaries of the pueblo, and families built crosses in their front yards. Because of this ritual activity one would not expect to find Chinautlecos at Amatitlán on this feast. However, when it was deemed necessary, they were busy at the end of April and during the first week of May making pilgrimages (romerías) to different locales, such as Santa María de Jesús Sacatepéquez, at the foot of the Agua volcano, to request rain (Reina 1966:321).

EL NIÑO DE ATOCHA: SHRINE, IMAGE, RITUAL

In 1954 there were, in addition to Chinautlecos, other Indians and Ladinos from neighboring departments going in pilgrimage to Amatitlán (Adams 1957:362).[6] Either these people went on May 2-3 or they went, ordinarily in small groups, to visit El Niño de Atocha in his shrine sometime during the rest of the year.

The shrine is housed in the parish church, which is built on the plaza (see Figure 9.2). The building was badly damaged by the 1976 earthquake and was still under repair when I first went to Amatitlán in January 1980. The newly built shrine was located in an area at the rear of the church perpendicular to the main body. It was a stone structure reminiscent of a truncated Maya pyramid. Cut into the lower, wider portion of the shrine was a tabernacle which, on the day of my visit, was covered with a sheer green veil. In the upper, slightly more narrow portion of the shrine, was an open space containing the images of the Niño and, on either side of him, of Mary and Joseph. The image of the child looked to me to be that of a small boy seated on a little wooden chair, and garbed in a blue dress the front of which was almost completely covered by what appeared to be a large white bib. A gold-colored chain hung from around his neck. He held the world, a globe, in his left hand. A vase of flowers and a vase holding a sheaf of wheat stood to either side of the upper portion of the shrine. A wooden staircase allowed one to climb up behind the statues and an offering box placed in the shrine beneath the level of the chair was accessible from those steps. A garland of pine needles and fruit, which though artificial was traditionally Maya, hung from the ceiling above the shrine.

We might wonder what contribution the title, El Niño de Atocha, made to pilgrims' understanding of the identity and role of the child, and hence to their expectations regarding him. The devotion to the Niño de Atocha originated in the community of Plateros in the silver-mining area of Fresnillo, Mexico. A statue of the Virgin of Atocha, whose history goes back to the twelfth century (Sánchez Pérez 1943:62-64), had been brought to the community from Spain in 1789.[7] It is a standing image of Mary holding the Christ Child in one of her hands. At some point in the nineteenth century when the child was removed from the main statue and venerated independently, the personalized title, "Niño de Atocha," came into use. From Fresnillo, the devotion spread throughout Spanish America and was taken at last to Spain in the 1920s. There the image of El Niño de Atocha was especially venerated in the basilica attached to the Dominican priory in Madrid (Lange 1978:3-4).

The image now at Fresnillo is dark in color. The Christ Child is seated in a chair and wears a pilgrim garb of long robe and cape with cockle-shell trim, a wide-brimmed hat, and sandals. In his right hand he holds a traveler's staff from which a water-gourd is suspended, and in his left an empty basket. Other representations of the Niño de Atocha found in Mexico illustrate variations. The basket may be missing. The child may hold, in addition to the staff, a sheaf of wheat or flowers (Lange 1978:4-5).

The attributes of the Fresnillo image reflect the legend about the Niño de Atocha. The legend relates that Christ appeared as the Holy Child dressed in pilgrim garb. Thus attired, he managed to slip into a Spanish prison closed by the Moors to all free adults in order to take food, water, and spiritual consolation to the prisoners (Boyd 1946:126). Since then, other persons in need have sought relief from him for all kinds of trouble. One wonders whether the legend is known among pilgrims coming to Amatitlán, since there is very little about the image of the Niño there to remind them of its content.

There is no indication that devotion to the Niño in Fresnillo was linked with the celebration of the Feast of the Holy Cross on May 2-3, in Amatitlán. This linkage makes the problem of the identity and functions of the Niño more complex, as is indicated by the brief account of the fiesta ceremony which I gleaned in 1980 from the literature and from several informants. The celebration of the titular feast of the Holy Cross extends from May 1 to May 7. During this period there is special veneration of the Niño de Atocha or de Belén, who once a year at this time goes out of the church (Diccionario Geográfico 1961-62(I):20). One version of the event is that on May 3, the Niño is carried in a boat decorated with cross-shaped ornaments to the Silla del Niño (his seat or bench, Figure 9.3), after which he is brought back to the church (Osborne 1959:479). A different version relates that the Niño is placed on the large stone Silla the night of May 2, a vigil is kept by him during the night, and on May 3 he is carried back to the church (Sapia Martino 1963:79). The procession on the lake involves many boats, flowers, music, and singing. Water sports, a fair, and the sale of candy in decorated boxes are a part of the town's celebration (Kelsey and Osborne 1978:215) and would add excitement and color to the pilgrims' sojourn at this combination resort-pilgrimage center.

There is a legend attached to the two accounts given thus far which describes the Niño's trip to and from his seat at Los Organos. In the story, the Niño who is kept in the church always wants to go back to the Silla del Niño on the shore of the lake. He always wants to return to this stone seat because before God sent the religion of Jesus Christ, evil people met there at the time of the summer solstice to carry out pagan rites before a stone idol found there. People gave the idol great offerings which they brought with them from far away, offerings which they threw into the lake (Osborne 1959:479).

A third version of the procession was given to me by a visitor to Amatitlán who heard it from a friend there. Another Niño whose chapel is called La Silla del Niño comes by boat from a place called El Castillo near Los Organos (pp. 69) to assist at Mass in the church at Amatitlán on May 3. This version was supported by two women of the town, while the elderly

Figure 9.3 La Silla del Niño, where El Niño de Atocha rests on May 3rd.,
Lake Amatitlán, Guatemala, 1982

woman who takes care of the Niño de Atocha confirmed the statements of
the others that the Niño de Atocha never leaves the church. If this is so,
who would the other Niño be? Is he a junior in rank perhaps? Or is he El
Niño de Otocha from Chinautla coming to visit his younger brother?

Information gathered during my 1982 field trip to Guatemala bears
directly upon problems emerging from these three versions of the procession
which takes place on the Feast of the Holy Cross.[8] On the first of several
visits to Amatitlán in January 1982, I was surprised to see an image of a
child, enclosed in a case made of glass with a wooden frame, placed just
inside the church facing the main entrance. The child was clothed in
priestly garb, which included a chasuble over his gown, stole, and biretta,
and he sat in a small, ornate chair. His visage was a smiling one. The case

was so placed that the image was on the eye-level of all but the smaller children, and many finger-marks on the glass bore witness to the ease with which people of all ages approached the child. The elderly lady selling candles at a table nearby identified the image as also El Niño. This Niño is the "representative" of El Niño de Atocha, that is, the "representative" of the first-ranking image of the Niño de Atocha.

The latter, more solemn in countenance, was seated, in state now, between the statues of the Virgin Mary and St. Joseph in the shrine in the side chapel where I had first seen him two years earlier. The conversation with the seller of candles continued and the question as to whether or not the Niño de Atocha ever leaves the church was answered. The first-ranking Niño de Atocha never goes out of the church. It is the smiling little child, the representative, who is carried in procession through the town and over the lake in the May celebration of the finding of the Holy Cross.

The pilot of a launch similar to the one in which the image of El Niño is borne on Lake Amatitlán outlined the itinerary of the procession. The procession leaves the church in Amatitlán at 8:00 A.M.and reaches what I call the public beach on the lake at 9:00 A.M. Then the image is transported in a richly decorated launch in a southeasterly direction along the shore of the lake, around to a point on the northern shore where the Silla del Niño stands out in relief against a wall of rock directly on the water. The Niño is placed on his bench, or seat, where he remains during most of the day. Then he is taken in procession by boat in a westerly direction along the northern shore of the lake and arrives at the same beach once more at approximately 6:00 P.M. The hours cited by the pilot may change from year to year. However, the answer which that gentleman provided to the question of whether or not the Niño de Atocha rests at the Silla overnight is clear. At the present time, the representative Niño occupies his bench on the north shore only during the daylight hours of the Feast of the Holy Cross, May 3.

Ofelia De León, of the University of San Carlos of Guatemala, wrote about the procession of the "Niño de Amatitlán o de Belén" which took place on May 3, 1980. Her account (1980:6-7) substantiates the major points in the data which I gathered in 1982. In addition, she mentions the presence of two "visiting Niños:" one from the village of Tacatón on the southern shore of the lake near Belén, and the other from Llano de Animas, a village located inland from the southern shore near Amatitlán. De León's informants told her that there were more "visiting Niños" in years past, but no details about these images are recorded in her account.

IDENTITY OF THE NIÑO AND CONTINUITY OF FAITH

Four elements are common to the multiple versions of the ritual involving El Niño de Atocha on May 2-3, namely, the Child, the bench, the procession to and from Los Organos (which is aligned with Amatitlán approximately along an east-west axis), and the Feast of the Holy Cross. By examining this combination of elements, we might come closer to the basic identity and role that the Child had for Indians and some Ladinos regardless of the title used for him in almost three hundred years of pilgrimage under the aegis of the Catholic Church and discern some continuity in the faith and hope which have motivated pilgrimage to the Lake Amatitlán region for about 1,785 years.

Recall that the region of Lake Amatitlán was in Pokomam territory, Amatitlán was a Pokomam pueblo, and there were still Pokomam Indians making pilgrimages there in the middle of the 20th century. Remember too, that these Indians had close religious and cultural ties with the Lowland Maya culture which is expressed most faithfully in the contemporary period by the Chortí people (Girard 1966:2), who are grouped with the Pokomam in the EasternHighland category of Maya Indians on the basis of similar environmental, cultural, and linguistic features (Vogt 1969b:14). Rich data are available from ethnographic studies of the Chortí by Charles Wisdom (1940) and, especially, Rafael Girard (1966) which describe the meaning of the specific forms of elements in the Amatitlán ritual when these forms are embedded in an exclusively Indian matrix. In such context, the elements must be viewed in relation to the traditional agricultural year of the Maya, which consists of precisely demarcated cycles calculated according to mathematical laws expressed in the calendars. Within these cycles, Indians have combined their own work in the fields with cosmic movements of various deities, expectations about those activities which the deities must fulfill in order to provide sustenance and nourishment, and religious practices appropriate to each phase of the cycle.

The most important part of the agricultural year for the Chortí is the time immediately preceding the rainy season (*el invierno*), when the greatest ceremony in the ritual calendar takes place during the anticipatory cycle to inaugurate the coming of the rain. The "great ceremony" opens on the Feast of St. Mark (April 25) and closes on the Feast of the Holy Cross (May 3). During these days, all aspirations revolve around the rains to come, for without this divine gift of moisture there would be no growth of the seeds planted in the next cycle. Prayers of petition, acts of reverence and care for the deities, and magical acts intended to insure the coming of the first rains at the right time, for example, May 4, in Jocotán, Chiquimula, are integrated in a complex ritual which reaches its climax on the night of May 2-3 (Girard 1966:198).

The cross had a prominent place in the "great ceremony" of the Chortí and, in some way, appears everywhere in the religious culture of the descendants of the ancient Maya. It is difficult to ascertain the meaning, or meanings, of this extremely complex symbol. Oliver La Farge summed up the matter nicely: "I am unsure whether to regard the whole complex built around the cross as predominantly Mayan or Christian in origin... it stands today as a specific cult partway between Christian and non-Christian ceremonial" (1947:109). Among the Chortí, who linked crosses inseparably with the agricultural cycle, the cross was not a Christian symbol in the context of their own Indian rituals. Rather, it was part of the symbolism of fertility. The spiritual leaders of the Chortí community insisted to Rafael Girard that there were two types of crosses: one belonging to them, that is to the Indians, and the Catholic one. The leaders further insisted that only their cross, made of special wood, ritually prepared, and re-adorned with fresh, green leaves of a specific shape for the May 3 festival, had the virtue to attend to their petitions for rain and nourishment (Girard 1966:188-89).

Another symbol which figured prominently in the Chortí rituals was a small wooden image of a child, beautifully carved in the colonial epoch, which was the objectification of the young god of the maize. This image, El Dios-Niño, was kept in a wooden tabernacle or niche in the Indian ceremonial house. The Niño was the young god of the maize enclosed in the womb of mother earth, that is the seed struggling to burst forth into the light of the sun, when functioning in the agricultural rituals carried out by the Indians at night in their own temples and sacred places in the countryside around them. He was also the solar god when functioning in the rituals centering on the patron saint of the community which were carried out during the day in the churches. In the agricultural ceremony, the Dios-Niño was referred to as the *hijo* or "child" of the Cross (Girard 1966:142). On the Feast of the Holy Cross, the image was bathed in fragrant water as a magical act designed to bring rain, and was reclothed. Except for the performance of this rite, the Niño was never removed from his niche (Girard 1966:155). During rituals focused on the patron saint, the Dios-Niño, as solar god, still in his niche, wore the little round sombrero symbolizing the solar disc, which at other times hung from a small wooden cross resting against the side of the niche or tabernacle, while the image of the saint provided for the solar god his anthropomorphic form (Girard 1966:142, 243).

Symbolism expressing the notion that the sun god rests on a seat or bench (Silla) at the positions which he occupies at the solstitial points of the world, was also present in the "great ceremony." However, the ritual imitation of the cosmic movement of the deities from one seat to another is more highly emphasized in the solstice rites carried out in December and June, when the chair on which rests the image of the principal deity representing the solar god in his function of fertility god was carried in procession from one ceremonial house to another. In each of the two houses there was a *silla*, one which the god occupied and the other which was left vacant. The movement of the god was to the east in June and back again to the west in December (Girard 1966:198-201). The stone seat itself is a very old cultural element represented in preconquest, monolithic sculpture found throughout much of Indian America. Among the Maya, the stone bench was reserved in religious usage for the gods of fertility and for the priests who represented them (Girard 1966:374).

Unwarranted comparison between the outward form of the four common elements in the versions of the Amatitlán ritual and that of the Chortí "great ceremony," must be avoided. We note, for example, that the agricultural rites of the Chortí Indian Catholics have been celebrated in the Indian temples and sacred places. While we do not have information about specific ceremonies, or lack of them, associated with the shrine at Pampichí, we do know that in Amatitlán, at least some part of the veneration of El Niño de Atocha on the Feast of the Holy Cross takes place within the parish church where the shrine is ordinarily located.

Nevertheless, we cannot help but be struck by parallels in form. These suggest that at some time in the history of the pilgrimage to the Niño in Amatitlán, Indians, and perhaps some Ladinos have conceived the identity and functions of the Child to be those of the young god of the maize. If this be so, probably only the forms of the image of the divine person, the position in a ritual calendar, and the procession to and from a seat in a fixed place in the east remain. The forms may now be devoid of their traditional Maya meaning for the pilgrims, a meaning which simply becomes one of many interpretations accruing to their complex symbolism. Among these interpretations, the Christian may be the predominant and prevailing one. In this respect, the forms of the Amatitlán ritual reflect, in the layering of their meanings, which extend outward from the core of indigenous interpretation to the surface of Christian exegesis, the chronological stratification of the pilgrimage "vertical shaft" (Turner and Turner 1978:106). The pilgrimage itself developed in successive contexts of pre-Columbian religion, colonial syncretistic blend of Spanish Catholicism with Mayan belief and practice, and contemporary amalgam of formal and folk levels of Catholicism.

CONCLUSIONS

Archaeological, ethnographic, and ethnohistorical research in the Lake Amatitlán region has charted the course for further work on the pilgrimage to El Niño de Atocha. Some old questions and some new ones remain to be answered. For example, when and how was the devotion introduced into Guatemala and into Amatitlán? Is the title, "Niño de Atocha," giving place to the titles "Niño de Belén" or "Niño Dios de Amatitlán?" If this substitution is a fact, what does the change signify? The presence of the image which represents the primary one of El Niño de Atocha raises questions. When and how was the representative "Niño" with the smiling face brought to Amatitlán? What are the history and characteristics of the representative? What are his functions in addition to being carried to La Silla de Los Organos on May 3?

In the context of Pokomam traditions and the custom of saints' visiting found in the wider Maya and Latin American cultures, inquiry regarding the "visiting Niños" acquires considerable importance. How many Niños have visited Amatitlán down through the years and on what occasions? What are the titles and roles of the visiting images? What is the relationship of these Niños, and that of the communities to which they belong, to El Niño de Atocha and to Amatitlán? Is the visiting among various Niños and communities reciprocal? Do Chinautlecos and El Niño de Otocha still come to Amatitlán?

Detailed description of the symbols and ritual activity involved in the pilgrimage awaits further field research. Is there modification in the complex of symbols and rites surrounding the image, the shrine, and the celebration of the Feast of the Holy Cross? Are there symbols and rituals which are no longer in use? What would such reduction in these constituents of devotion reveal about the content of belief and related practice?

Answers to these questions and to others which are corollary to them will aid in understanding more fully the concepts held by pilgrims regarding the Child of Atocha, his shrine, and the Feast of the Holy Cross. Those answers will eliminate some of the lacunae in the history of pilgrimage to Amatitlán, delineate more clearly the place of the devotion to El Niño de Atocha in the lives of contemporary Guatemalans, and contribute to formation of a baseline according to which future change in the pilgrimage center and patterns can be identified.

Both change and continuity are evident in the veneration of El Niño de Atocha. There have been various perceptions and nuanced understandings held by people making the pilgrimage to Amatitlán. There have also been one sure line of continuity in its development and one common denominator of experience of the pilgrims. The preconquest Indians who travelled to the lake to offer their precious gifts to the gods were anxious about very basic needs and values in their lives: life, health, fertility, and nourishment. The Pokomam took these same concerns with them to Pampichí and to the chapel in San Juan de Amatitlán. Indians and Ladinos now visiting the Niño de Atocha may bring to him the same kinds of desires and aspirations translated into individual cases as well as communal ones. For centuries now, all have come walking or riding through the fields in faith (Turner and Turner 1978:241), to a sacred place and a sacred person. His power and province is to listen attentively and act efficaciously in their behalf.

NOTES

1. This translation of "pilgrimage" as *romería* rather than *peregrinación* follows Guatemalan usage. For a study of the problem inherent in the English translation of Spanish terminology regarding pilgrimage, the relationship between *romería* and *peregrinación* as forms of pilgrimage, and the influence of Spanish models of pilgrimage upon Guatamalan patterns, see Straub (1985).

2. A Ladino population is one belonging to the sociocultural group which combines Indian and Spanish traits and which may have some historical racial parallels as well (Adams 1957:267).

3. Of the 72 folios which comprise the record book, eighteen folio pages are written in Pokom, fourteen are in Pipil, and 21 are in Spanish (Miles 1957:742).

4. According to Fuentes y Guzmán, the second location of what is now called Amatitlán was Tzacualpa (1969:I, 247).

5. The rank of the Dominican house in San Juan de Amatitlán was raised from that of a small residence called a doctrina, recognized by the provincial chapter in 1553, to that of priory in 1638 (Gage 1958:296, n. 14). Within the hierarchical, ecclesiastical structure of the region, Chinautla (Chignactán), Pampichín, San Pedro Martyr, Petapa, Santa Inés, Mixco, Pinula, and San Cristobal Amatitlán, which is now known as Palín, were subject to the Dominican authority in Amatitlán (Fuentes y Guzmán 1969:I, 247). For the history of Dominican foundations in Guatemala, consult also Julian Fuente, *Los heraldos de la civilización centro-americana, reseña histórica de la provincia dominicana de San Vicente de Chiapa y Guatemala* (Vergara: Tip. de "El Santísimo Rosario," 1929).

6. On the basis of data gathered in a survey of 30 Guatemalan towns in 1954, Richard Adams classified Amatitlán, Rio Hondo (Department of Zacapa), Taxisco, Muluá, Masagua, Tactic, and Jumaitepeque as tertiary pilgrimage centers in Guatemala. Secondary centers included Ayutla, Chiantla, and Chajul. Esquipulas (Chiquimula), Antigua, and San Felipe (Sacatepéquez) were primary centers (1957:361-62).

7. There is a suburb of Madrid, Spain, called Atocha, where a hermitage was built in 1162 in honor of the Virgin Mary, whose image was believed to have first been brought to Spain by one of the Apostles and then, after a succession of events, to have come to rest in Atocha. A church to which a Dominican priory became attached in 1523 was built to replace the hermitage (Sánchez Pérez 1943:62-64).

8. This work was supported, in part, by a grant from the Penrose Fund of the American Philosophical Society and by the Providence College Fund to Aid Faculty Research. This support is gratefully acknowledged.

REFERENCES

Adams 1957
Borhegyi 1958, 1959
Boyd 1946
Carmack 1981
Chinchilla Aguilar 1961, 1965
De León Meléndez 1980
Diccionario Geográfico de Guatemala 1961
Fuente 1929
Fuentes y Guzmán 1969
Gage 1958
Girard 1966
Juarros 1823

Kelsey-Osborne 1978
La Farge 1947
Lange 1978
Mata Amado 1964
Miles 1957
Osborne 1959
Reina 1966
Sánchez Pérez 1943
Sapia Martino 1963
Straub 1985
Turner-Turner 1978
Vogt 1969b
Wisdom 1940

III
SOUTH AMERICA

10

The Literature of Pilgrimage: Present-day Miracle Stories from Northeast Brazil

CANDACE SLATER

Tales of powerful "saints" and supernatural exploits are an important part of the spiritual life of northeast Brazil. The best-known of these figures in the vast and arid backlands is undoubtedly a priest, Padre Cícero Romão Batista, who died in 1934.[1] Convinced of this leader's continued wonder-working abilities, close to a million persons come to visit his adopted city, Juazeiro do Norte, every year. Because hearing, reading, and telling stories about Padre Cícero is central to the pilgrimage experience, I shall concentrate upon these narratives in the following discussion.

Like similar miracle texts from other times and places, the Padre Cícero stories perform a variety of functions.[2] They assert linkages between Padre Cícero and a long line of other Christian holy figures. At the same time, they provide validation for his followers' claims regarding the priest's powers and thus serve as a charter for their own actions and beliefs. For the individual pilgrim who makes the long and often difficult journey to "holy Juazeiro," the stories are an affirmation of both hope and faith.

The tales in question here are told by ordinary people and by folk poets who sell printed tales, called *folhetos* or *literatura de cordel*, in open-air markets and along the pilgrimage route. Because they depend on their verses for a livelihood and public acceptance is essential to their sense of artistic worth, *cordel* authors set out to write a tale which will find favor with their audience. Oral storytellers, for their part, seek to "tell things as they really happened" and are therefore more apt to introduce extraneous or contradictory material. Both sets of narrators, however, draw on a larger folk tradition. Just as *cordel* poets look to oral material for inspiration, so oral storytellers incorporate bits and pieces of written tales.

This chapter's chief concern is the relationship between oral and written stories. Unlike some scholars who have insisted upon inherent differences in the mental processes underlying literate versus nonliterate modes of composition, I shall argue that the critical division between these narratives lies in individual storytellers' conceptions of their role.[3] Because both kinds of tales grow out of a common pilgrimage experience, both are necessarily expressions of a particular vision of the world.

Before looking at the historical background of the stories and then their oral and written versions, the reader will want to have some idea of their narrative content. Almost all of the tales deal with Padre Cícero's ability either to protect or cure his followers, or to punish his detractors. The following list of 20 of the best-known orally transmitted stories should provide a helpful overview. In each case, I have presented in Table 10.1 (pp. 195) additional information regarding the story in question and the *Literatura de Cordel*. A tale classified as "developed" must have at least eight stanzas or a minimum of 48 verse lines. The approximately 1,200 narratives on which this list is based represent the contributions of just over a hundred individuals in Juazeiro do Norte during the spring of 1978 and the summer of 1981.

ORALLY TRANSMITTED MIRACLE STORIES

1. *Padre Cícero's birth*. A beautiful woman (whom some storytellers identify as the Virgin Mary) carrying an infant arrives at the door of Padre Cícero's mother, Dona Quinou, just after the latter has given birth. Because the new mother is sleeping, the mysterious woman is able to exchange the child in her arms (Padre Cícero) for Quinou's baby son. Upon awaking, Quinou perceives that the child's cry is different and suspects that an exchange has occurred. She is unable to confirm these suspicions, however, because of a sudden, permanent loss of sight.

2. *The hat that stuck to the wall*. When he was a child, Padre Cícero had a habit of arriving late to school. (Some informants explain that the future priest always stopped to pray before a small altar which he himself had constructed in the woods.) Because of the late hour, the boy is never able to find a vacant peg on the wall on which to hang his straw hat. He therefore tosses the hat up against the wall where it remains mysteriously suspended.

3. *The man from São Pedro*. A man (usually called Pedro) is working his fields in the municipality of São Pedro. He is bitten by a snake, and sensing that he is about to die, sends for Padre Cícero to administer the last rites. The priest sets out immediately for São Pedro. He is informed along the way that the man has died, but insists on going to the man's house anyway. When he arrives, he calls him by name three times. The man revives and receives the last rites. Padre Cícero then asks him if he would rather go to heaven or remain on earth. Usually he chooses to go to heaven.

4. *Manuel Correia's fall*. A carpenter named Manuel Correia falls from the scaffolding during construction of the Horto church. Padre Cícero is summoned and calls the dead man's name three times. When he responds, the priest asks whether he wants to die and go to

heaven, or whether he prefers to return to life. Most informants say that the man chooses to return to life either "because he had children to raise" or "because he wanted to marry a girl named Manuela."

5. *The enchanted grove*. Workmen constructing the same church on the Horto hilltop find themselves without food one day. They tell Padre Cícero that they are hungry, and the priest sends them into the barren expanse behind the construction site to look for food. Although the men grumbled that the sun must be affecting the patriarch's wits, they find a grove of coconut palms/mango trees/orange trees. They eat their fill, but next day when they return on their own to pick more fruit, they encounter nothing but brambles.

6. *The lost dagger*. A pilgrim sets out for Juazeiro to meet Padre Cícero. On the way, he spends the night beneath a *juá* tree under which he inadvertently leaves the golden dagger which is his prized possession. When he arrives in Juazeiro, he goes to see Padre Cícero, who immediately tells where he can find the lost dagger. When he stops at the *juá* tree on his way home, the dagger is still there.

7. *The girl from Cajazeiras*. A young woman from the city of Cajazeiras in the neighboring state of Paraíba has been tormented by the Devil for many years. She comes to Juazeiro to ask Padre Cícero to drive out the evil spirit. The Devil at first taunts the priest but is eventually forced to flee. The girl and her parents are delighted and become devoted followers of Padre Cícero.

8. *Padre Cícero stops a war in Germany*. Padre Cícero is in the midst of his daily sermon when he suddenly closes his eyes. Those near the priest ask him if he is feeling ill, but he does not respond. Only after what seems like hours does Padre Cícero open his eyes. He then explains that he has been busy stopping a war in a distant country. His followers do not know what to think until some weeks later when two photographers arrive in Juazeiro. The men are looking for a priest who descended from a cloud to stop a terrible war in their homeland, Germany. When the men show the photograph they had taken of this individual to the residents of Juazeiro, everybody recognizes Padre Cícero.

9. *Padre Cícero saves Juazeiro in the War of 1914*. When the state militia marches against the city in 1914, Padre Cícero promises its residents that they will emerge unscathed if they follow his orders. He directs them to dig a trench around the city, and to remain within its walls. All but an old man and a boy follow his orders. These two individuals are killed by enemy bullets, but everyone else is saved.

10. *Dr. Floro challenges Padre Cícero*. Padre Cícero's political advisor, Dr. Floro Bartolomeu, begins to challenge the priest's authority after the War of 1914. He directs his soldiers to celebrate Carnival despite Padre Cícero's orders to the contrary. The priest therefore calls him in and says, "Be careful, Flory, he who made you great can also make you very small." Dr. Floro refuses to listen. While the soldiers are making merry, he falls ill and sets out for Rio to consult the doctors there instead of calling on Padre Cícero. The priest then tells his followers that the doctor is destined to die on the road.

11. *The rancher who asked for rain*. A haughty rancher sends a messenger to Padre Cícero with a mocking request. "Tell Padre Cícero that I want two cents of rain," he says. The messenger is afraid to relay the rancher's request, but Padre Cícero asks this individual if he does not have something to give him. The priest then takes one of the two coins, directing the man to return the second to the rancher with the message that he has overpaid. A tremendous storm ensues in which the unbeliever's ranch, his cattle, and his wife and children are destroyed.

12. *The man who asked for a miracle*. A young pilgrim makes the trip to Juazeiro because he wants to witness a miracle firsthand. When nothing extraordinary occurs, he personally asks Padre Cícero to demonstrate his powers so that he will have something to talk about back home. The priest laughs at the young man, but the latter insists. Padre Cícero then informs him that if he wants to see a miracle, he should first make amends to the neighbor from whom he stole a goat/calf/gold dagger before setting out for Juazeiro. Everybody laughs at the young man's discomfort.

13. *The would-be assassin in the hammock.* An unbeliever decides to test Padre Cícero by having his men bring him before the priest in a hammock. Sick people were traditionally brought to a healer in a hammock when they were too ill to walk. When Padre Cícero appears in his window, the men tell him that they have brought an ailing individual for him to cure. He informs them that he can do nothing because the man has already died. They refuse to believe him but when they part the folds of the hammock, they find the would-be assassin dead, a dagger in his left hand.

14. *The martyrdom of Clara.* A virtuous young woman named Clara is afflicted with an ailment that causes her stomach to swell. Her brothers suspect that she is pregnant and set out to ask Padre Cícero's advice. On the way to his house they meet the priest, who directs them to kill their sister. They therefore return home and crush her to death with a board while she protests her innocence. When Padre Cícero hears what has happened, he declares that Clara has been unjustly martyred and demands an explanation. The brothers realize that they have been misled by the Devil in the priest's guise and leave town. Years later, they reappear in Juazeiro, sure that no one will recognize them. Padre Cícero, however, immediately singles them out in the crowd.

15. *The girl who turned into a dog or snake or horse.* A rebellious daughter tells her mother that she will only believe in Padre Cícero's miraculous powers if he turns her into a dog (or a horse or snake). Ignoring her mother's pleas to mend her ways, the girl continues to speak ill of the priest and is turned into a beast with a woman's head. She is then forced to wander through the world for seven years as a warning to others. Finally, suitably repentant, she is restored to human form.

16. *The young man who turned into a toad.* A young man (or the mother-to-be of the young man) expresses disbelief at the priest's miraculous powers. In punishment, he is turned into a toad and forced to hop about on all fours. He then resolves to go to Juazeiro to seek Padre Cícero's pardon. The priest forces the toad to repent publicly, then turns him back into a young man.

17. *Padre Monteiro denies Padre Cícero's miraculous powers.* After the transformation of the host into the blood of Christ (allegedly in 1889), a priest called Padre Monteiro swears that he will affirm the truth of this miracle no matter what may befall him. "May I lose the light of my eyes if I betray you, Padre Cícero," he says. A few days later, he does indeed deny that the miracle has occurred. The next morning he awakens blind.

18. *The opening of the church door.* The pope calls Padre Cícero to Rome in order to test his power, directing him to open a church door closed by Saint Peter. Padre Cícero initially refuses, but the pope threatens to destroy Juazeiro if he does not comply. Padre Cícero therefore approaches the door and says, "Door, may God who closed you, now open you," three times. The door then swings open. Often, Padre Cícero enters, finds an image of the Sacred Heart of Jesus, and proceeds to take it back with him to Juazeiro.

19. *The mute boy who spoke.* Sometimes when Padre Cícero opens the church door, he finds a mute boy inside. The Pope (sometimes the bishop of Fortaleza) asks him to make the boy speak. Padre Cícero then calls his name three times, asking the boy to tell everyone the identity of his mother and father. The boy then tells the crowd that his father is the bishop of Fortaleza and his mother the mother superior of the convent.

20. *The slipper in the tomb.* After Padre Cícero dies and is buried, the bishop of Crato and his fellow priests return to the church to exhume the body. When they open the coffin at midnight, they find a single slipper amidst a heap of rose petals. There is no other sign of Padre Cícero.

HISTORICAL BACKGROUND

A knowledge of Padre Cícero and of Juazeiro is essential in understanding the preceding stories.[4] I shall therefore summarize the principal events in the life of the priest and his adopted city before going on to analyze crossovers between oral and written versions of the tales.

Cícero Romão Batista was born in 1844 in the backlands city of Crato, Ceará. When the boy showed signs of religious vocation, a wealthy relative agreed to finance his education at the seminary run by Lazarist fathers in Fortaleza, the state capital. After his ordination in 1870, the priest had no intention of resuming life in the interior. Nevertheless, a prophetic dream led him to accept the chaplaincy of Juazeiro, Crato's impoverished neighbor, in 1872.

Precisely in the year that Padre Cícero moved to Juazeiro, a dispute arose between the Brazilian emperor, Pedro II, and leaders of the Roman Catholic Church. This "Imperial Religious Question" threatened the alliance between Church and state which had been in effect ever since Brazil declared its independence from Portugal in 1822.[5]

Religious doubts were not the only problems to plague backlands inhabitants. In the drought of 1877-79, over a third of the population of Ceará, or approximately 300,000 persons, either emigrated or died.[6] Given the magnitude of this disaster, it is not surprising that people throughout the interior should panic when rains failed to fall again in 1889. When the residents of the Cariri Valley began a series of novenas and vigils, Padre Cícero was one of their leaders.

On the first Friday in March, Padre Cícero offered communion to several women who had come to attend the monthly Mass in honor of the Sacred Heart of Jesus. One of these individuals was Maria de Araújo, an unmarried, illiterate, 28-year-old mulatta laundress who lived with her mother and brothers in the hamlet of Juazeiro.

Although Maria de Araújo had no canonical standing, she enjoyed a certain prestige as a *beata*, or one of a number of lay sisters common at that time in the backlands of Brazil. The founding of a number of "Houses of Charity" in the Cariri Valley by Padre José Maria Ibiapina in the 1860s had attracted a number of women from the lower classes, many of mixed blood. These houses or *Casas de Caridade* were meant to serve as schools for the daughters of wealthy landowners and merchants, as orphanages for the poor, as centers for the manufacture of cheap textiles, and as religious sisterhoods. Despite the fact that neither Rome nor any Brazilian bishop had given him the authority to do so, Ibiapina required his *beatas* to wear the habit and to make a profession of vows. Although the cleric himself was forced to leave Ceará by religious officials, the *casas* and the *beatas* continued to function.

Before March of 1889, Maria de Araújo had not stood apart in any way from her sister *beatas*. When, however, Padre Cícero placed the communion wafer upon her tongue on that fateful first Friday of the month, the host allegedly grew red with blood, a fragment falling to the floor. Padre Cícero picked up the bloody wafer with an alter towel, later placing both objects in a glass urn. This receptacle was removed to Crato in 1892 because Crato was the seat of the larger *município*. The initial transformation was followed by a recurrence of the event on every Wednesday and Friday until Easter, and then daily until the Feast of Christ's Ascension.[7] It is worth noting that although Padre Cícero's followers credit him with many miracles, this is the only allegedly supernatural event with which the priest associated himself.

Furthermore, he was initially uncertain about the "miraculous" nature of the transformation. Perhaps because he was aware that the *beata* had been infirm since childhood, he continued to ask Maria de Araújo for a divine sign which would prove the veracity of the transformation. His caution was not shared, however, by individuals such as Monsignor Francisco Monteiro, rector of the Crato seminary and longtime friend and distant relative. On July 7, the liturgical feast day of the Precious Blood, the rector led a pilgrimage of some 3,000 persons from Crato to Juazeiro. He then mounted the pulpit waving a fistful of altar linens which he solemnly declared to bear the stains of Christ's blood,

The evidence suggests that Padre Cícero's early hesitation gradually yielded to the arguments of his friends and peers eager to reaffirm the Catholic faith in the face of growing secularism. Thus a report written by him 10 months after the event, perhaps not coincidentally just after a military coup had overthrown the empire, states that the host received by Maria de Araújo had become the blood of Christ. Not only the poor, but a number of fellow clerics and powerful laymen were quick to echo this assertion. Church officials, for their part, responded with dismay.

The bishop of Fortaleza, Dom Joaquim José Vieira, first received news of the "miracle" in November of 1889 through a newspaper account. He was particularly disturbed by implications of a Second Coming because of the messianic expectations already widespread among lower-class Northeasterners imbued with Portuguese Sebastianism and eager for a less precarious mode of life.[8] The bishop therefore placed the burden of proof entirely upon Padre Cícero. Forbidding the priest to label the events miraculous until the matter had been clarified to the Church's satisfaction, he dispatched an official commission of inquiry to Juazeiro in 1891. When this mission appeared to accept Padre Cícero's account without question, Dom Joaquim sent a second fact find-ing panel. After its arrival in the city a year later, this group failed to find any evidence of divine intervention. It also reported the theft from the Crato altar of the urn containing the hosts and linens. This urn would be discovered among the personal effects of José Joaquim Telles Marrocos, a journalist and cousin of Padre Cícero, at the time of Marrocos' death in 1910. The theft confirmed the bishop's suspicions that Padre Cícero was either an active participant in a hoax or else the pawn of individuals with dubious intentions. He therefore suspended the cleric from preaching, hearing confessions and counseling the faithful.

Dom Joaquim's actions diminished Padre Cícero's support among the upper classes and the clergy, but did nothing to stem the tide of pilgrims to Juazeiro. Although these individuals often had little more than a few pennies to their name, they were able as a group to finance the priest's trip to Rome. There, in 1898, he presented his case to Pope Leo XIII. Despite the fact that the pontiff did not restore his orders, Padre Cícero gained considerable prestige from the trip and received a hero's welcome upon returning to Brazil.

Northeasterners' growing belief in the priest's miraculous powers had profound economic and political ramifications. As new waves of pilgrims chose to settle in Juazeiro, the once tiny city began to dwarf its neighbors. One result of this rapid expansion was Padre Cícero's increasing involvement in practical matters. The arrival in Juazeiro in 1908 of Dr. Floro Bartolomeu, a politically astute physician from the state of Bahia, foreshadowed the priest's official entry into the secular arena. Even though Padre Cícero appears to have accepted his growing power with limited enthusiasm, he nevertheless became the first mayor of Juazeiro in 1911. A year later, politicians eager to insure popular support for their own troubled regime had the priest elected third vice-governor of Ceará. When these same politicians turned against Juazeiro a year later, Padre Cícero mobilized his followers, who soundly defeated the state militia when it attacked the city in 1913-14. After his victory, a new administration assumed power and the priest found himself promoted to first vice-governor of the state.

Padre Cícero's increasing participation in local, state, and then national affairs as a delegate to the Brazilian congress did not dampen his desire for recognition of the events of 1889. On the contrary, he may have hoped that growing secular support would strengthen his case in the eyes of Church authorities. Although this was not to be the case, Padre Cícero's failure to regain his orders had little effect on his reputation as a miracle worker. If anything, opposition to the patriarch of Juazeiro by leaders of the official Church served to confirm his followers' vision of him as a martyr and a saint. His fame as such has grown until today. Some 50 years after his death, about a million pilgrims from all over the vast, dry Northeast travel to Juazeiro every year. The statue of Padre Cícero that stands vigil over the city is second only to that of Rio de Janeiro's famed Corcovado in terms of size. This massive likeness of the priest is a symbol of his importance to many contemporary Brazilians. Given the major role which he still plays in the lives of these people, it is not surprising that stories about him should be so numerous and well-known.

ORALLY TRANSMITTED STORIES

The stories summarized in the preceding pages were told to me by residents of the Rua do Horto. This two-mile stretch of rudimentary houses interspersed with stations of the cross was my home during the summer of 1981. A conscious imitation of Jerusalem's Via Sacra, the Rua do Horto is required passage for the city's hundreds of thousands of pilgrims. Although the street's official name is the Rua Santos Dumont, it is called the Rua do Horto after the hilltop overlooking the city. Padre Cícero referred to this part of the Catole mountain range as the Horto or garden in a conscious attempt to recall the Garden of Gethsemane. It was here that he began work on a cathedral to the Sacred Heart of Jesus which was never completed because of opposition by the bishop. It is also here that the enormous statue of Padre Cícero already mentioned stands today.

The great majority of persons who live on the Rua do Horto originally came to Juazeiro from various parts of the Northeast. Although many of these people are long-time residents of the city, they nevertheless consider themselves *romeiros* or pilgrims. In their eyes, the true mark of a *romeiro* is the rosary which he or she wears around the neck. I shall therefore use the term "pilgrim-resident" for these people in order to distinguish them from inhabitants of the city who are not believers, and those believers whose home is elsewhere.

The Rua do Horto is typical of the poorer neighborhoods of many northeastern Brazilian cities. Of the approximately 500 houses which line the street, some two-thirds are made of stucco over sun-baked brick. Electricity became available in 1976 and almost half of the homes now have indoor lighting. Although the city began supplying water on an intermittent basis in 1978, there is only one indoor bathroom. Most houses consist of three or four small rooms. Hammocks are strung from the walls at night in order to provide sleeping accommodations. Some houses now have gas stoves, but charcoal, wood, or a combination of these fuels is still more common.

Radios are ubiquitous in the Rua do Horto. The most popular programs are religious offerings such as *The Ave Maria Hour*, and shows featuring regional singers called *repentistas* or *cantadores*. There are also some 20 television sets, one of which is mounted in the public plaza at the beginning of the street. Approximately two dozen families now have refrigerators, most of which are used to make the popsicles which are sold to visitors. There is one private and two public telephones. An erratic bus line, called the Good Savior Transport Company, was established in 1979.

Some 2,000 people live along this thoroughfare. The great majority of the men work in fields located further up and over the hill which they rent from private landowners. The small number of male residents who are not farmers work in factories, construction sites, and brickyards. In the summer of 1981, the average daily wage was 200 cruzeiros (around $2.00).

Women customarily help their husbands and fathers in the fields on a part-time basis. They may also work in backyard gardens and care for pigs and chickens. Almost all of the street's female residents engage in some kind of artisanal work such as weaving straw hats or painting plaster figurines of Padre Cícero. During the principle pilgrimage season, which runs from late August through February, men, women, and children supplement the family income by selling food and drink. They also offer a variety of religious articles such as pictures of Padre Cícero or rosaries made of tiny coconuts to the endless visitors who trudge up the Rua do Horto singing at the top of their voices at all hours of the day and night.

Life is clearly not easy for the people who live in the Rua do Horto. Only three persons have had the equivalent of a grade school education. Infant mortality remains a chronic problem and both adults and children are debilitated by parasitic diseases. The standard diet of beans and manioc flour is inadequate for the sustained physical labor required by most jobs available to residents, but few people can afford better food or the monthly payments which would make them eligible for government-sponsored medical assistance. Given both these bleak circumstances and the high rate of unemployment within Juazeiro, it is not surprising that increasing numbers of young people should leave home for the coastal cities or the industrial south.

And yet, despite the fact that people are unhappy about their living conditions, most remain convinced that Padre Cícero's Juazeiro is the new Jerusalem. Given their belief in the priest's continuing powers, it is not surprising that virtually everyone above the age of twelve should have at least one story to tell about the priest.

These tales do not have to deal with supernatural forces. On the contrary, many pilgrim-residents find the most apparently simple occurrences "miraculous." Because their lives are so difficult, they may consider an especially abundant harvest or a cure effected with prescription drugs to be an extraordinary event. "Dig here for a well," "Don't plant before the first rainfall." Thus a good number of the priest's practical suggestions came to be considered miracles by the people who profited by his advice.

Many residents of the Rua do Horto can remember stories which they first learned on the way to Juazeiro. These tales typically animated a long and difficult journey. In talking and hearing about the wonders which the priest had worked for others, individuals came to regard as normal a series of experiences which they would otherwise have considered impossible.

Today, as in the past, miracle stories prepare people in multiple ways for their arrival in Juazeiro. Pilgrims often learn from others that they are expected to set off firecrackers upon entering the city or to fill their pockets with stones from the Rua do Horto in order to brew a special "miracle tea" upon returning home. They arrive prepared to circumambulate the church of Our Lady of Sorrows and to pass over and under a series of boulders at the site known as the Holy Sepulchre. In short, the route which they will follow upon reaching Juazeiro is enriched if not actually traced out by their fellow travelers.

Perhaps most important, orally transmitted miracle stories unite both friends and persons who might otherwise be strangers by affirming a common faith transcending differences in geography or occupation. "A pilgrimage truck is always a family," says one newcomer to Juazeiro. "There can be no secrets when people set out to visit Padre Cícero."[9]Miracle stories, however, do not always reflect the sort of fellow feeling which has been labeled *communitas*.[10] Although persons who dislike each other sometimes forget their differences for the moment, they may also use the occasion to launch verbal attacks in the guise of miracle tales. An individual, for instance, may tell the story of how Padre Cícero hated thieves "and especially those who stole chickens from their neighbors," with a meaningful look in the direction of a person suspected of raiding another's barnyard.

Naturally, tales are not only recounted during the pilgrimage proper, but may be repeated many times after the journey has become a memory. Miracle stories often grow out of ordinary conversation. "I would never dream of wearing a dress like the one which Dona Maria was running about in just yesterday," says one old woman. "After all, Padre Cícero always said that short skirts were the work of the Devil..." She then proceeds to recount the story of the young woman who "turned into the most ferocious beast in all of Brazil" after ignoring the priest's advice to lower her hemline.[11]

Pilgrim-residents treat their favorite stories as they would a treasured possession. Long after other mementos of the original journey have been lost or broken, these tales function as reminders of enduring truths. Then too, stories confer a certain status upon the teller. Accounts passed down from parents to children function as if they were verbal relics, the words taking on new power with each repetition.

For those pilgrims who have chosen to settle in Padre Cícero's adopted city, miracle tales often help to justify a difficult choice. Not only must individuals struggle for survival in Juazeiro, but these persons have often left behind friends and family. As members of a culture which stresses personal ties, they naturally have occasional doubts about their decision. Thus at the same time that they entertain, inform, and celebrate the past, the Padre Cícero stories reinforce these persons' sense of having made the right choice. "Padre Cícero said that everyone who came here should bring three sacks of money and then a sack of patience for when the money ran out," one old man says with obvious pride.[12]

Running again through the list of the narratives at the beginning of this paper, one can see that most events believed to have occurred after Padre Cícero's death are told in the first person. The majority of these stories deal with cures or protective measures taken by the patriarch on a follower's behalf. A smaller percentage of stories are descriptions of punishments meted out to unbelievers. Still others are dreams or visions in which Padre Cícero customarily reveals some aspect of the future or affords the narrator a privileged glimpse of heaven or hell. Although no two of these stories are exactly alike, it is easy to isolate a half-dozen recurring themes. All of these bear a strong resemblance to others dealing with non-Brazilian saints.

More idiosyncratic and for that reason potentially more revealing are those accounts of events believed to have taken place during Padre Cícero's

life. Many of these tales, which are normally told in the third person, deal
with a small number of incidents which are repeated time and again.
Narrators generally take pains to affirm the veracity of these stories, and
many identify their sources as a matter of course. "The women who lived
next door to my mother in São Pedro told her this story," one individual
says. "I didn't see Padre Cícero cure that blind man myself but my uncle
was there and he saw the whole thing," another asserts. Occasionally,
someone may express doubt about one or another incident, but most people
are convinced that they are transmitting facts. "I'm not telling you a *story*,"
one woman exclaimed when I asked her to repeat "the tale" she had just
finished recounting. "I was just explaining what happened to my brother
Pedro two years ago last March."[13]

Several of the miracle tales are little more than affirmations of Padre
Cícero's supernatural identity. The tales of his birth (story 1) and of the
hat that stuck to the wall (story 2), for instance, function as explanations
of the powers illustrated in succeeding stories. The remainder of these
narratives, however, fall into two groups. The first are positive challenges
which take the form of requests for help on the part of believers. These
requests are usually answered with protective or curative measures. The
second group can be seen as negative challenges. These may be subdivided
into cases involving high-placed religious authorities and others involving
clerics of lesser importance and nonclergy.

If the challengers in this second group are important ecclesiastical
authorities (a bishop, the pope), Padre Cícero simply complies with their
clearly unreasonable and often threatening requests. He thus opens a door
which has been locked for centuries (story 18) and makes a previously mute
boy speak (story 19). If, however, the challengers are laymen or simple
clerics, they will be punished by humiliation, physical suffering, or material
loss. Thus the priest who denies Padre Cícero's miraculous powers loses
his eyesight (story 17), the girl who mocks the patriarch is turned into a
dog (story 15), and the rancher who asks for rain loses everything he owns
in a deluge (story 11).

The autocratic or even brutal character of many of the plot summaries
reflects the harsh realities of most pilgrim-residents' lives. As the majority
of narrators face apparently insuperable social, economic, and geographic
barriers, it is understandable that they should vent their own frustrations
in tales concerning unbelievers. Furthermore, as many persons view human
life as a battle between Good and Evil, they feel bound to emphasize Padre
Cícero's virtues by insisting on his enemies' vices.

Looking back over these tales, the reader can see that the outlines of
the *passio*, or medieval martyr saint's tale, remain visible beneath the
surface of these orally transmitted stories.[14] It is important, however, to
note some of the differences between contemporary Brazilian narratives
and their European forebears. The *passio*, for instance, is distinguished by
a climactic moment in which a Christian cries out to God for help against

the pagan authorities demanding that he or she recant or pay homage to an alien deity. Although the Padre Cícero stories frequently place the priest in seemingly impossible situations, he almost never calls for divine aid. Because he himself is already atypically omnipotent, he is free to reward or punish would-be challengers.

Another important difference between medieval European and modern Brazilian saints' lives is the latter's close relationship to a specifically Northeastern folk tradition. The European stories reveal numerous folk elements, many of which reappear within Brazil. Nevertheless, it is worth remembering that the saint's life was originally as much an erudite as a popular form. This is not the case today as both oral storytellers and poets are almost always members of the Northeastern lower classes.

The Padre Cícero stories also rely more directly upon historical events. A number of early saints' lives draw on documentable occurrences, but it is natural that names and places should have become less important over time. This muting process has not had time to happen in the Brazilian narratives. The War of 1914, for instance, is living memory for some of the older residents of Juazeiro. The Dr. Floro and the "Padre" (really "Monsenhor" or "Monsignor") Monteiro of the miracle stories were definitely real people.

It is certain that storytellers suppress some details and change others. Nevertheless, their debts to fact, or apparent fact, are clear. The attempt on Padre Cícero's life in 1896 by five unidentified men who drew knives on the priest while he preached his evening homily may well be the source for the tale of the would-be assassin in the hammock. Similarly, the tale of "Padre" Monteiro's loss of sight after his negation of the transformation's miraculous nature undoubtedly reflects the fact that the rector of the Crato seminary, Monsignor Francisco Monteiro, died blind.

Although the cases of the would-be assassin and of Padre Monteiro are particularly striking, few if any tales are purely imaginary in origin. The tale of how Padre Cícero opened the church door "which was closed by Saint Peter" may grow out of the priest's frequent accounts of his trip to Rome. There, according to various informants, he was particularly impressed by a church customarily opened by the pontiff once every 25 years. The story of the rancher who asks for two pennies' worth of rain may recall an unusually severe flash flood said to have destroyed the ranch of an avowed disbeliever, as well as the property of numerous believers, in a nearby city fittingly called Milagres (Miracles). Tales of Padre Cícero's miraculous cures reflect his knowledge of herbal remedies as well as his ability to distinguish epileptic seizures from genuinely fatal attacks. The priest's success in prevailing upon local pharmacists to prescribe, if not donate, medicines reinforces the images of him as a healer.

Orally transmitted narratives often grow out of firsthand knowledge or secondhand experience. There appears, for instance, to have been a carpenter named Manuel Correia who fell while working on the scaffolding of the Horto church. It is therefore common for individuals to stop the story in midstream in order to point out the Correia house or to note that their second cousin later married the carpenter's youngest son.

Then too, narrators frequently personalize well-known stories by introducing friends, relatives, or even themselves as participants in the action. One individual tells about how his father went running to find Padre Cícero after Manuel Correia's fall. Another describes "the very white fur" of the girl who turned into a dog. At least half a dozen people claim to have been strolling by chance past the church in which Padre Cícero had been buried the night when a group of priests discovered the empty tomb. Still other individuals tell of eating oranges picked by a friend or cousin in the enchanted grove. "Oh, what a delicious flavor! I shall never forget it."

It is even more common for a narrator to individualize a story by introducing material only tangentially related to the event in question. Many narrators, for instance, begin their accounts of Padre Cícero's escape from the tomb with a detailed description of what they themselves were doing at the moment of his death. Similarly, stories about the War of 1914 frequently focus on the activities of family members who happened to be in Juazeiro at the time.

The effects of historical "fact" and individual experience on orally transmitted miracle stories cannot be underestimated. This material is not simply inserted into but often exerts considerable impact upon preexisting literary molds. At times, the narrator's desire "to tell things just the way they happened" may lead to the introduction of material which has nothing to do with, or which actually contradicts, the story's underlying structure.

THE *LITERATURA DE CORDEL*

The Brazilian chapbooks called *folhetos* or *literatura de cordel* grow out of the medieval European ballad and broadside tradition brought to Brazil by the first Portuguese colonists.[15] Stories in prose and verse became particularly popular in the relatively isolated backlands, where other sources of information and entertainment were few and far between. During the nineteenth century a series of land reforms and the introduction of a new kind of drought-resistant cotton fostered a dramatic increase in population. Particularly in the backlands of Pernambuco, Paraíba, Ceará, and Rio Grande do Norte, a series of rotating fairs grew up to meet the needs of subsistence farmers. This network of open-air markets allowed for the distribution of stories in verse. Their authors had these tales printed on second-hand presses, which became increasingly easy to obtain as time went on.

Although chapbooks had been popular in the backlands ever since the sixteenth century, local authors first began to publish their own stories in quantity toward the end of the nineteenth century. Many of these writers, who were always male, were also improvisers (*repentistas, cantadores*). It is therefore no surprise to find Northeastern *folhetos* written in *sextilhas*, the rhyming six-line stanzas typical of improvised verse.[16]

Because so many of their customers were illiterate, *cordel* vendors routinely chanted stories written by themselves or others in the marketplace. Buyers attracted by their reading or by appealing cover illustrations would take the booklets home to a literate friend or relative who could reperform them.

As they were constructed by folding and then re-folding larger sheets of paper, most *folhetos* numbered eight, sixteen or 32 pages. Today, as in the past, stories tend to be one of these fixed lengths. The poet, and for my research *cordel* author, usually prefaces his third-person account with an appeal to the muses or saints for inspiration. He then ends the tale by reiterating its underlying message and calling for his audience's financial as well as moral support. The stories themselves often draw on traditional material such as the Carolingian romances, which enjoyed a renewed popularity in nineteenth-century Brazil, or the folktales called *trancosos*. They may also be accounts of current events, prophecies, love stories, tales of outlaws, or duels in verse (*pelejas*) composed specifically for publication.

In the beginning, *cordel* authors paid others to print their stories. With time, however, the more successful writers were able to acquire their own presses. One of the best-known poets of all time, Leandro Gomes de Barros, purchased a press in the coastal city of Recife which turned out chapbooks by the hundreds of thousands. His successor, João Martins de Ataíde, was to sell the business to José Bernardo da Silva of Juazeiro do Norte.

The *literatura de cordel* peaked in the early 1950s. Today, changes in the traditional market system and increasing competition from radio and television have diminished the number of poets. Rising costs of publication and transportation have also made the *cordel* less attractive to would-be authors. Then too, whereas the *folheto* trade represented one of the few alternatives to subsistence farming, today persons seeking a better life routinely move to São Paulo or Rio de Janeiro. Nevertheless, there are still a half-dozen poets in Juazeiro do Norte. Three of them, João de Cristo Rei, Manoel Caboclo e Silva, and Expedito Sebastião da Silva, knew Padre Cícero.[17]

Aside from these three men, there are a number of improvisers such as Pedro Bandeira, João Alexandre Sobrinho, and Geraldo Amâncio, who write *folhetos* from time to time. There is also a scattering of younger authors, but the majority of stories written today in Juazeiro about Padre Cícero are the work of the first three poets, who are regarded as mainstays of the *folheto* tradition.

To be sure, not all *cordel* stories about Padre Cícero are written in Juazeiro. In fact, it is hard to find a poet who does not have at least one *folheto* about the priest. Because, however, the obvious market for such stories is the pilgrimage, the selection of tales about Padre Cícero is undoubtedly greater in Juazeiro than anywhere else in Brazil.

This is not to say that every *folheto* is available in Juazeiro. Some of the Padre Cícero stories have undoubtedly been lost to time. Even today, when increased scholarly interest in folk traditions has fostered the establishment of numerous *folheto* libraries, a number of tales by local poets still go unnoticed. Other, older stories remain tucked away in dusty collections while still others survive exclusively within the oral tradition. Usually these tales exist as fragments, although occasionally they can be found intact. One blind informant, for instance, is still able to recite a 32-page account of how Padre Cícero restored a woman's eyesight in 1922.[18]

In terms of sales, miracle stories are the most popular group of *folhetos* which can be found today in Juazeiro. Prophecies, however, are actually more numerous. These are usually a series of apocalyptic warnings presented in chronological order: in 1984 the sky will turn black, in 1985 all the fish in the sea will expire, and in 1986 there will be a famine. Although poets may attribute these warnings to the patriarch in order to convince pilgrims to buy their stories, most such prophecies have little or nothing to do with the priest. Padre Cícero did indeed predict that the world would end, but the same sort of general warnings can be found in *folhetos* attributed to a variety of other sources.

Folhetos about the priest may also deal with events of a more or less factual nature. These may be biographies or descriptions of events such as the dedication of a new hospital bearing Padre Cícero's name. There are also a small number of stylized dialogues (*pelejas*) between the priest and opponents such as a *cachaceiro* (rum guzzler) or Protestant. These categories, to be sure, are not necessarily exclusive. Prophecies, for instance, may be inserted into miracle stories, whereas miracles frequently appear within a biographical frame.[19]

During August of 1981, about a month before the beginning of the pilgrimage season, there were just over three dozen full-fledged miracle *folhetos* readily available in Juazeiro. About a third of these were by authors living in or around the city. The remaining two-thirds were the work of individuals from other parts of the Northeast and from Rio de Janeiro. Almost a dozen, or roughly one-third of the miracle tales might be considered *cordel* classics. These are older tales reprinted over many decades such as *O Nascimento Misterioso de Padrinho Cícero* (The Mysterious Birth of Padrinho Cícero), *A Moça que Virou Cobra* (The Girl Who Turned into a Snake) and *A Moça de Cajazeiras* (The Girl from Cajazeiras).[20] Another ten or so of the stories represent reworking and recombinations of well-known themes. These include two more accounts of Padre Cícero's birth, several summaries of miracles told in more detail elsewhere, and an incident illustrating the kind of bilocality found in the story of Padre Cícero's intercession in a distant war. The remaining, about sixteen, stories are generally of topical interest: the blind man whose sight is suddenly restored, the child who falls from the top floor of a skyscraper, the airplane which lands in a tree instead of crashing thanks to Padre Cícero's intervention. I would expect the number of this third group of stories to increase markedly during the pilgrimage season.

ORAL AND WRITTEN STORIES: A COMPARISON

As should be evident from even this brief description, there is considerable interplay between oral and written miracle tales. The seeds of almost every *cordel* story can be found within an oral tradition which itself has been absorbing written influences for many centuries.

Cordel authors are the first to affirm the importance of oral sources to their work. According to them, buyers not only prefer but actually insist that tales be constructed around familiar elements. "If people do not already believe that such-and-such-a-thing has happened, it does no good to write about it," says one poet. "I can enlarge upon an action, I can even change it, but I can never invent something from thin air."[21]

Pilgrim-residents' rejection of that small number of *folhetos* which have no correlates within the oral tradition of Juazeiro supports this poet's assertion. *O Monstro que Raptava Moças* (The Monster Who Kidnapped Young Women) and *O Crente que Profanou do Padre Cícero* (The Protestant Who Mocked Padre Cícero) are two good examples of stories which are not related by oral storytellers. Individuals generally dismiss both of these *folhetos* as "sem fundamento" or without a base in truth. A third *cordel* story, *O Boi que Falava* (The Bull Who Talked) is thought to be closer to reality.[22] Most individuals, however, would agree with the following informant that the author has taken unmerited liberties with the tale:

> I think that the poet who wrote that story of the bull who talks must have been thinking of a bull that belonged to Padre Cícero. Everybody liked that bull very much and some women tied ribbons to his hide for decoration. So the rumor started that people were making *promessas* [saints' vows] to an animal and the soldiers killed the bull and made everybody eat a piece of the carcass. Even today there are people who will not eat beef because of what happened that day. But no one ever said that the bull talked and so you shouldn't believe that story. Poets make ten words out of none. You really cannot trust them.[23]

At first glance then, the differences between oral and written miracle tales would appear obvious. *Folhetos* are verse accounts of fixed length composed by professional poets and performed in public with the hope of financial gain. Orally transmitted narratives are unpublished prose accounts of varying length told by ordinary men and women in diverse circumstances. If, for instance, one compares the following five stanzas from a *folheto* with two orally transmitted versions of Padre Cícero's birth, variations in both style and content are clear.

O Nascimento Misterioso de
Padrinho Cícero

"The Mysterious Birth of Padrinho
Cícero"

E quando a mãe dele teve
o primeiro garotinho
lhe apareceu uma dona
com outro bem bonitinho
e quando em seu lar entrou
seu filho depositou
junto do outro novinho.

And when his mother had
her first child,
a lady appeared before her with
another very pretty little baby and
when that woman entered the house
she lay her own son
beside the other newborn baby.

Então a dona da casa
estava nessa ocasião
de resguardo e no momento
não havia um só cristão
que lá em seu ambiente
lhe desse o suficiente
de sua alimentação.

The woman of the house, Quinou,
was at this time recuperating
from the delivery
and there was not a soul
in that place
who could give her
the food she needed.

A mulher compadecida
cheia de amor e carinho
disse para a dona da casa:
seu lar não está sozinho
fique aí que vou cuidar
tudo que necessitar
a senhora e seu filhinho.

The compassionate woman
full of love and affection,
said to Quinou,
"Your house is not alone.
You stay there and I
will see to everything
that you and your baby need."

Dizendo assim sem demora
para a mulher preparou
tudo que ela precisava
nisso o marido chegou
deu-lhe o agradecimento
e ela nesse momento
o seu menino trocou.

After the woman said this,
she immediately prepared everything
that Quinou needed, and at this point
Quinou's husband arrived.
He thanked the woman
and in a moment, that
woman changed her son for theirs.

Deixando o dela na cama
no outro aplicou um beijo
e disse para o casal:
pronto, já fiz meu desejo
vão criar meu filho lindo;
e retirou-se sorrindo
com seu olhar benfasejo.
(Cristo Rei n.d.:2-3)

Leaving her own son in the bed,
the woman kissed the other baby
and said to the couple,
"Well then, I've done as I wanted.
Bring up my handsome little son."
and she left with a smile
and a benevolent look in her eyes.
[My translation]

The poet, for instance, omits the climactic blinding of Dona Quinou, Padre Cícero's mother, who did indeed go blind, but long after her son became an adult. He does this not because he does not know the story, which he told me in two separate conversations, but because he prefers to go on to other incidents. He also keeps his protagonists at a considerably greater distance than the oral storytellers, who individualize the events by drawing friends and relatives into the story. Moreover, although the nonpoets tend to devote less attention to narrative development, they have a strong dramatic sense which maintains the listener's interest.

ORALLY TRANSMITTED TALES

1. "Padre Cícero was born in Crato. But his father and mother, the late Dona Quinou, were very poor. They built a straw hut and she remained there with that child, so poor that the mother of Manuel Cândido – the friend who told me this story – so poor that his mother made a point of taking milk to the baby. When one day she went to take the milk she found a woman leaving the straw hut with a bundle under her arm but she couldn't make out what it was. She didn't see the woman's face, you understand, because it was covered. Well then, she entered the hut and saw the child playing, but it wasn't Dona Quinou's son because he was dark-skinned and this child was white with very blue eyes. At this point the woman Manuel Cândido's mother said, "Dona Quinou, look at your son!" "Woman," she said, "I can't because I am blind." "Dona Quinou, this child is not yours!" she said and she was right, because Padre Cícero was not like other children" (José Dantas Filho; born 1904, Juazeiro do Norte, Ceará; retired peddlar; interview July 12, 1981).

2. "Because everyone says so, and then too, because Padre Cícero's mother was blind, I believe that Padre Cícero was exchanged for another child. My aunt, she was really the mother-in-law of one of my uncles, always told the story. She said that a woman arrived at Padre Cícero's house to visit. And when she opened her eyes she could no longer see anything. She told her husband that this child was not theirs but he said that she must be crazy. Then Padre Cícero's mother insisted and insisted that the child had been exchanged but she couldn't prove anything because she had lost her sight. She was a very pretty woman, Dona Quinou, but blind in both eyes" (Jósefa André Gonçalves; born 1916, Limoeiro de Anadías, Alagoas; arrived Juazeiro 1923; earns a living ironing and making straw hats; interview July 3, 1981).

The differences between oral and written stories are not, however, so clear-cut as might initially appear. It is true, for example, that *cordel* stories are by definition printed, but it does not necessarily follow that the author must be literate.[24] A small but nevertheless significant number of poets do not know how to read or write and therefore compose their stories in their heads before dictating them to a literate wife or school-age child. Other authors who do know how to write may nevertheless complete an entire 32-page story in their head before committing it to paper.

Furthermore, while it is true that the *folhetos* are printed verse compositions, it would be a mistake to assume that the *literatura de cordel* is simply a collection of texts. Because of their public's high degree of illiteracy, poets have always relied heavily on oral performances. Not only may they modify words or whole stanzas to suit their audience of the moment, but they routinely introduce prose asides called *trancas* or *chaves* which may double or even triple the time required for reading the verses themselves. These interjections are crucial to the success of a given story. "Someone may already have a particular *folheto*," one vendor notes:

> but he will buy a new copy of the same story if he likes the way it is read. Then too, you often run across someone who will complain that the story that he bought the other day isn't the same one he heard in the marketplace. Well of course it isn't because the poet isn't there with him to explain every detail, to tell a joke, or to remind him of what happened earlier in the tale.[25]

Moreover, although the *cordel* text is relatively stable, printing does not guarantee uniformity. Printers, for example, may modify whole stanzas either through design or carelessness. Pirated editions have always been common. Then too, it is not unusual for more than one poet to write about the same subject. Particularly successful stories may be adapted by a new author, and a half-dozen different poets may seize upon an especially promising new theme.

And yet, if the *cordel*'s written identity is open to serious question, its public character cannot be disputed. The poet's reliance upon his stories for a livelihood means that his performance will be geared toward potential customers. Before the advent of transistor radios, *folheto* authors not only sold their verses in weekly open-air markets but were paid to recite their verses at night to audiences in one or another farmhouse. Today, poets must rely on a considerably more limited distribution network.

Cordel authors, however, do not see their verses only as a source of income. On the contrary, they consider themselves moral spokesmen and "artists of the word." This vision of their profession results in a fusion of aesthetic and financial motives. "The best poet is the one who sells the most *folhetos* because he knows how to please the people," one poet explains.[26]

In order "to please the people," a writer must compose his stories in accord with preestablished expectations. This means that he will have definite ideas of what he can and cannot include in a given tale. Thus at the same time that an authority may swear that a particular *folheto* is absolutely true, he will often admit to altering one or another word for the sake of rhyme or to adding a variety of details "in order to make the story clearer."

The poet's vision of himself as a creator is critical in distinguishing oral from written miracle stories. Even though he may not be fully conscious of what he is doing, he nevertheless structures his material in a consistent manner. There is no doubt but that the best-known orally transmitted narratives reveal a limited number of underlying patterns. Nevertheless, the oral storyteller is less aware that he or she is creating a fiction and therefore less adept at winnowing out extraneous or contradictory elements.

In order to illustrate the differences as well as similarities between oral and written miracle stories, it is useful to return to the orally transmitted narratives previously outlined in this paper. At first glance, there is no clear reason why some of these particularly well-known tales should become *folhetos* while others do not. And yet, some sort of funneling process is obviously at work.

The poets currently living in Juazeiro are of little help in articulating why some incidents should be more likely than others to pass into print. In fact, most of these individuals dismiss the question with a shrug. "There are many stories and the author has to choose the one which he likes best," is the most common explanation. "You know, you have given me an idea and one of these days I am going to write a story about the man who turned into a toad," one poet says.[27] "I think that I once saw a *folheto* about Santa Clara," another asserts: "but then again, maybe I didn't. In any case, my mother knew the woman who lived next door to where that chapel to her stands today."[28]

Because luck and temperament play a major role in the creative process, it is possible to accept these poets' suggestion of arbitrary selection. And yet, the more closely one examines both tape recorded and printed stories, the more an underlying logic would appear to emerge.

This logic is linked to more general patterns discernible within the *literatura de cordel*. From past observation of how *folheto* authors adapt or, in their own words, "translate" a wide range of material into verse, one can abstract principles which might be expected to function as well in the passage of oral to written miracle stories. These include the tendency for poets to present a trial situation; their fondness for stereotypical, noncontroversial characters; their desire not to offend powerful persons; and their preference for situations which corroborate existing literary themes.

Although *cordel* authors are not necessarily conscious of a six-step pattern, the overwhelming majority of their stories can be broken down into a half-dozen steps. These include a period of *initial harmony, trial, right* or *wrong response, counter response, punishment* or *reward*, and *restoration of harmony*.[29] *Folhetos* can be further divided depending on the identity of the protagonist who either passes the trial and is rewarded, or who fails and is punished in accord with the seriousness of his or her offense. Naturally, each poet enlarges upon this framework in his own way. In order to make his underlying message clearer, the poet favors stereotypical characters. Heroes should be loyal and courageous and heroines devout and modest. Villains should be stingy, vain, and deceitful and rogues should have big heads, skinny arms, and ludicrous last names. Often, though not always, the poet will present a life-or-death situation which emphasizes the importance of moral choice. The *cordel* author also avoids characters about whom his readers might have opposing opinions or who might otherwise cast doubt upon his story. He will not be eager, for instance, to recount an incident about which various eyewitnesses disagree. He will also avoid the tale of two young sweethearts who fall out love or who refuse to marry.

Because the poet recognizes the vulnerability of his own social position, he will also take care not to offend any powerful person. Thus while he may berate a fictional rancher for greed or cruelty, he will make clear that this individual represents an exception and that he is not attacking ranchers as a group.

Finally, *cordel* authors favor situations which fall into existing literary categories. They will be particularly apt to develop oral prophecies or *pelejas*. They will also lean toward themes already utilized by other *folheto* writers. As metamorphoses of human beings into animals are common in the *literatura de cordel*, for instance, it is not surprising that the poet should choose to develop similar orally transmitted stories.

With these principles in mind, we can turn back to our list of 20 best-known stories. It would be reasonable to assume that poets would favor those oral accounts which can be seen as (1) trials involving (2) noncontroversial protagonists involved in (3) situations which will not offend powerful individuals. Although it is not necessary that a story (4) portray a life-or-death situation, the poet will lean toward these. He will also be attracted to incidents which (5) suggest preexisting literary categories. I would therefore hypothesize that in order for an orally transmitted story to be developed, that is, to merit eight or more stanzas, the incidents would have to rate a "yes" in the first three categories on Table 10.1. A "no" in any of these first three columns would seriously hinder its appeal. A "yes" in either categories 4 or 5 in addition to 1, 2, and 3 would all but assure the story's appearance in *folheto* form. "No's" in both categories 4 and 5 would make it more likely that the story would be mentioned instead of developed.

Table 10.1 Orally Transmitted Stories and their Features in Relation to the *Literatura de Cordel* (* = Exception to Rule; D** = Developed; M** = Mentioned; NM** = Not Mentioned)

Column	1	2	3	4	5	6	7
Orally transmitted story	Trial situation	Workable characters	Inoffensive to powerful people	Life-or-death situations	Precedents within *cordel* tradition	Other considerations	Status within *literaura de cordel*
1.* Padre Cícero's birth	No	Yes	Yes	No	No	Extremely popular story; needed explanation; biblical parallels	D**

Column	1	2	3	4	5	6	7
2. The hat that stuck to the wall	No	Yes	Yes	No	No	Same as above	M**
3. The man from São Pedro	Yes	Yes	Yes	Yes	No		D**
4. Manuel Correia's fall	Yes	No	Yes	Yes	No	Similar to São Pedro story	NM**
5. The enchanted grove	Yes	Yes	Yes	No	No	Group rather than individual protagonist	M**
6. The lost dagger	Yes	Yes	Yes	No	No	Incident somewhat inconsequential in terms of *cordel* stories	M**
7. The girl from Cajazeiras	Yes	Yes	Yes	No	Yes (*Peleja*)		D**
8. Padre Cícero stops a war in Germany	Yes	Yes	Yes	No	No	Group rather than individual protagonist	D**
9. Cícero saves Juazeiro in the War of 1914						concerns salvation of group protagonist *and* punishment of individuals	
10. Dr. Floro challenges Padre Cícero suitable	Yes	Yes, if poet maintains neutrality	Yes (Floro's family in far-away Bahia)	Yes	No	Poet identifies but does not develop character	M**
11. The rancher who asked for rain	Yes	Yes	Yes	Yes	No	Historical basis in real flash flood	D**

196

12. The man who asked for a miracle	Yes	Yes	Yes	No	No	Popular tale involving public humiliation	M**
13.* The would-be assassin in the hammock	Yes	Yes	Yes	Yes	No		NM**
14. The martyrdom of Clara	No	No (real-life Clara not conventional herione)	Yes	Yes	No	Padre Cícero plays peripheral, unappealingly ambiguous role	NM**
15. The girl who turned into dog/horse/snake	Yes	Yes	Yes	No	Yes (metamorphosis)		D**
16. The young man who turned into a toad	Yes	No (Toad-like resident of Juazeiro)	Yes	No	Yes (but protagonists almost always women)	Similar to story of girl who turned into dog/horse/snake	NM**
17. Padre Monteiro denies Padre Cícero's miraculous powers	Yes	Yes	No (Padre Monteiro was rector of Crato seminary)	No	No		NM**
18. The opening of the church door	Yes	Yes	No	Yes	No		NM**
19. The mute boy who spoke	Yes	Yes	No	Yes	No	A typically short *cordel* story avoids mention of religious authorities	M**
20. The slipper in the tomb	Yes	Yes	No	No	No	Heretical overtones more pronounced here than in birth story	NM**

197

In general, this breakdown confirms the presence of larger *cordel* patterns within the miracle corpus. Five of the six oral stories which are developed are clearly trial situations involving characters which are neither contradictory nor offensive to powerful persons. Although the tale of the girl who turned into a dog or snake or horse (story 15) does not involve a life-or-death situation, this incident has numerous literary precedents which would make it attractive to *cordel* authors.

The only exceptions to the rule would appear to be the account of Padre Cícero's birth (story 1) and of the assassin in the hammock (story 13). The birth story, which one would not expect to be developed, appears as a *folheto* while the apparently promising tale of the would-be murderer is completely ignored.

The most obvious reason for the birth story's selection is its overwhelming popularity. Because the incident is probably the single most widely told tale in Juazeiro today, because it does not offend powerful persons, and because it provides a needed explanation for Padre Cícero's deeds, it has become a *folheto* despite its lack of a trial framework. The fact that this tale suggests divine intervention and approval would strike the poet as being another point in its favor.

The case of the would-be assassin is more difficult to understand. I myself do not see why it has not generated a *folheto*. The incident would appear to satisfy all of the prerequisites for a successful *cordel* narrative without posing any of the problems associated with other rejected tales. It is therefore possible that the tale exemplifies the principle of luck on which poets insist. The existence of verse fragments within the oral tradition suggests that a *folheto* version of the incident does or did exist, and that it is simply not available in Juazeiro at this time.

Turning to the remaining stories on our chart we can see that the desire not to offend powerful people assures the elimination of three of the last four tales involving religious figures. The one incident which has been mentioned by a poet, that of the mute boy, appears in the last two pages of an atypically short *folheto* entitled *Padre Cícero em Roma* (Padre Cícero in Rome).[30] Not only has the story been reduced to a mere four pages, but the author has taken pains to modify the plot. In his account, the priest no longer prompts the mute boy to identify his parents as a bishop and the mother superior of a local convent. Instead, the child becomes the son of two nobles, thereby eliminating the suggestion of unorthodox behavior on the part of ecclesiastical authorities.

The three other missing stories are also fairly easy to explain. In two of these three cases, that of Manuel Correia's fall and that of the young man who turned into a toad, the incident is very similar to another which *cordel* authors have developed. There is therefore no need for poets to grapple with the problems which these stories pose.

It is understandable that *cordel* authors should prefer the story of the man from São Pedro to the tale of Manuel Correira's fall. Although both incidents involve resurrections, the first is more dramatic because of the protagonist's decision to go straight to heaven rather that return to a humdrum existence on earth. The fact that the man bitten by a snake chooses to die also means that the poet does not have to worry about what a living protagonist might have to say about his tale. Because the real Manuel Correia lived to a ripe old age beneath his neighbors' eyes, it is more difficult to make him into an ideal *folheto* hero.

The tale of the young man who turned into a toad presents a similar problem in that an apparently misshapen individual is said to have existed in Juazeiro at one time.[31] The presence of such a person within the community would create a potential pull between fact and fiction. It would also suggest that such *cordel* personages are supposed to turn back into human form at the end of a given time span, usually seven years. Then too, as the great majority of *folheto* protagonists are women, it is easy to see why poets would prefer the story of the girl who turned into a dog.

Finally, the martyrdom of Clara poses a particularly large number of problems. First, there are conflicting oral accounts about the real-life heroine. Some residents of Juazeiro, for example, insist that Clara was not the unmarried and virtuous young woman expected by *cordel* readers. According to them, the individual in question was actually the mother of several small children who was forced to sell rice puddings in the streets after finding herself abandoned by her husband. Next, Padre Cícero is peripheral to the story which, although it is well-known in Juazeiro, is seldom heard outside the city. As *folheto* authors are eager to maximize sales, they would be likely to select a better-known topic. Third, and most critical from a poet's viewpoint, Padre Cícero plays an uncharacteristically ambiguous role in the story. Pilgrim-residents of Juazeiro firmly believe that the Devil is capable of disguising himself in any form, including that of a priest. Nevertheless, Satan's unmitigated success in the case of Clara's death is upsetting to readers accustomed to seeing virtue triumph. Even though Padre Cícero finally punishes the cruel brothers, the story is considerably less clear-cut and, for this reason, less appealing than most tales involving martyrs.

The remaining seven stories are mentioned but not developed by *cordel* authors. All of these except for the story of the hat that stuck to the wall satisfy the first three categories; trial, stereotypical characters, and acceptability to powerful persons. They do not, however, rate a "yes" in either category 4 (life-or-death situation) or 5 (literary precedents). The story of the hat is mentioned by poets even though it does not portray a trial because it, like the birth story, provides a necessary affirmation of Padre Cícero's supernatural identity.

The fact that one can predict the fate of a given story on our chart with considerable accuracy confirms the existence of rules governing the interchange between oral and written spheres. Although this interchange occurs in both directions, there are obviously more oral than written stories.

It is therefore useful to isolate the patterns which determine in large part which oral material will appeal to poets. It is once again his conscious or unconscious allegiance to these patterns which separates the *cordel* author from the oral storyteller.

CONCLUSION

Close examination of stories about Padre Cícero of Juazeiro reveals differences as well as similarities between oral and written composition. In this case, however, it is impossible to make the usual cut-and-dried distinctions based on literacy versus illiteracy, poetry versus prose, or written versus oral transmission. It *is* possible to contrast the intentions of oral storytellers, who think that they are simply relaying information, and *cordel* authors who, although they are necessarily caught up at some level in their own stories, nevertheless remain conscious that they are creating a fiction. Because poets depend on their verses for a living, they cannot afford to let their readers frown or yawn. They are therefore unlike the great majority of oral storytellers who set out to describe "something that happened," and who are thus less aware of, or less concerned with, questions of content and narrative form.

In the final analysis, *cordel* stories are not only more structured but more consistent than their oral counterparts. They do, however, retain much in common with tales told by persons who do not have to depend on these for a livelihood. Although poets tend to eliminate considerable amounts of extraneous or contradictory material, they continue to draw on sources common to all members of the larger community. This means that the relationship between oral and written tales should be envisioned less as a division or even a continuum that as a many stranded abacus in which the beads are constantly regrouping.

Furthermore, both kinds of stories are united not only in their reliance upon a larger folk tradition, but in their reflection of a common social reality. If both oral and written tales are fictions, they are also documents of desperation, literary solutions to problems which the secular order is unwilling or unable to address. As such, they are important to the people who find in them the courage to face the difficulties of daily life. "In the past," says one woman:

there were no roads and so pilgrims bound for Juazeiro cut crosses into the bark of trees to mark the way for those to come. Well, to my mind, these stories are a little like those crosses. Together they form a trail that leads to Padre Cícero. Today there are paved roads and getting here is easy. But we still need those stories to tell us "This is the way. Go on."[32]

NOTES

1. Padre Cícero was canonized in 1973 by the Igreja Brasileira Apostólica (Brazilian Apostolic Church). The Igreja Brasileira Apostólica is a breakaway faction of the Roman Catholic Church, which does not recognize Padre Cícero as a saint.

2. For useful background to the Brazilian narratives see Aigrain (1953), Delehaye (1921) and Tubach (1969). A number of more general articles on contemporary Brazilian pilgrimages are listed in Oliveira (1980).

3. There is a sizable literature on the relationship between oral and written communication. For two representative viewpoints see Ong (1975) and Ricoeur (1971).

4. Although there is a large bibliography on Padre Cícero, much of this material is of a highly polemical nature. For a detailed and more objective treatment of this see della Cava (1970). A useful critical summary of book-length studies of the priest is provided by Silveira (1976).

Brazilians are fond of assigning unusual names to children and the choice of "Cícero" by the future priest's parents may or may not have had anything to do with the Roman orator.

5. The "Imperial Religious Question" erupted in 1872 when Emperor Dom Pedro II had two Brazilian bishops arrested and convicted for their failure to obtain royal permission to attack Freemasonry. The dispute, which dragged on for three years, prompted the Church to take a newly militant stand against not only the Freemasons, but positivists, republicans, and Protestants. For a discussion of the affair see Mecham (1934:316-21).

6. The damage occasioned by periodic droughts explains backlands inhabitants' frenzied efforts to ward off potential disaster. Between 1877 and 1915, one minor and four major droughts struck the Northeast, bringing agriculture to a halt and causing hundreds of thousands of deaths. For a discussion of the worst of the catastrophes see Cunniff (1971).

7. Reports of bleeding hosts were common in Europe from the thirteenth century onward. See Browe (1938). These sorts of miracles, however, were generally not associated with a Second Coming, but were taken as definitive proofs of the doctrine of transubstantiation.

The appearance of the alleged divine blood at a time of great social stress has parallels in the rise of Marian apparitions in similar moments of tension. See Christian, Jr. (1981b). It is worth noting that the transformation of the host is the only one of the numerous acts attributed to Padre Cícero which he himself appears to have regarded as miraculous.

8. For an introduction to messianic movements in Brazil see Queiroz (1965). Brazilian messianism related in part to Portuguese Sebastianism. After the death of King Sebastian in the battle of Alcácer-Quibir in Northern Africa, Portugal was annexed by Spain for 60 years. In reaction to this period between 1580 and 1640 known as "The Captivity," people invented stories in which King Sebastian was said to be alive and planning his return. These tales were undoubtedly taken to the Brazilian Northeast by the first colonists.

9. João Martins da Silva (João Romeiro), born 1935, Capela, Alagoas. Arrived Juazeiro 1980; works at odd jobs. Interview July 28, 1981.

The most common means of transportation among contemporary pilgrims is the open truck called a *pau-de-arara* or "parrot perch." The name comes from the overhead bar to which the standing passengers cling. Other pilgrims arrive in Juazeiro on foot, on horseback or donkey, or via bus, car, or train. Informants claim that followers of Padre Cícero also come by airplane and ocean liner, but I have never met anyone who did.

10. See Turner and Turner (1978).

11. Antônia Domingo da Silva (Antônia Fateira), born 1911, Palmeira dos Indios, Alagoas. Arrived Juazeiro 1948; formerly meat seller.

12. Olímpio Praciano de França, born 1901, Palmeira dos Indios, Alagoas. Arrived Juazeiro 1922, still works as farmer. Interview July 30, 1981.

13. Rosalva de Conceição Lima (Rosinha Seriema), born 1920, Palmeira dos Indios, Alagoas. Arrived Juazeiro 1926; makes straw hats. Interview July 7, 1981.

There are two terms for "story," *história* and the invented term "*estória*." An *estória* implies that the account is a fiction. An *história* can be either a fictional or factual account. I had inadvertently used the term *estória*.

14. For useful comments on the structure of early miracle stories see Altman (1975:1-11).

15. There is an extensive bibliography on Brazilian pamphlet literature. For a general introduction see Almeida and Sobrinho (1978), Batista (1977), Câmara Cascudo (1939), Curran (1973), Florentino Duarte et al. (1976), *Literatura popular em Verso* (1962-1977), and Maranhão de Souza (1976).

For an overview of the *folheto* tradition in English see Slater (1981).

16. For a discussion of the relationship between improvised and chapbook poetry see Suassuna (1974:162-90).

17. João de Cristo Rei's first *folheto* was the story of a miraculous cure. After hearing of how Padre Cícero had healed one of his distant relatives in the city of Jataobá, the young man decided to write the story in *cordel* form. The resulting *folheto* was highly successful and when João showed the story to Padre Cícero, the priest counseled him to continue writing. Interview in Juazeiro do Norte, Ceará; July 29, 1981.

Manoel Caboclo and Expedito both worked for the late José Bernardo da Silva. Manoel Caboclo now has his own business. Expedito still works at José Bernardo's press, which is now owned by the state of Ceará.

18. Maria Ignácia Conceição de Jesus (Maria Cega), born 1919, Juazeiro; retired (blind). Interview July 26, 1981.

19. An excellent example of a *folheto* which might be classed as either a prophecy or a miracle story is João de Cristo Rei's *Profecia Misteriosa sobre os 3 Dias Escuros* (Juazeiro do Norte: n.p., n.d.).

20. José Bernardo da Silva, *O Nascimento Misterioso de Padrinho Cícero* (Juazeiro do Norte: Tipografia São Francisco, n.d.); Severino Gonçalves de Oliveira, *A Moça que Virou Cobra* (n.p., n.d.). Antônio Caetano de Souza, *A Moça de Cajazeiras* (Juazeiro do Norte: Tipografia São Francisco, n.d.).

Padrinho means "little father" or "godfather" in Portuguese. Pilgrim-residents generally refer to Padre Cícero as their "padrinho," emphasizing ties of both affection and respect.

21. Expedito Sebastião da Silva, born 1928, Juazeiro do Norte; poet. Interview July 5, 1981.

22. Sebastião Pereira dos Santos, *O Monstro que Raptava Moças e os Milagres do Padre Cícero* (n.p., n.d.); José Pedro Pontual, *O Crente que Profanou do Padre Cícero* (Recife: Edison Pinto, prop., n.d.b). Anon., *O Boi que Falava* (n.d., n.p.).

23. Maria Selvina da Silva, born 1922, Juazeiro; does ironing. Interview July 10, 1981.

24. A good example of a poet who, although illiterate, is still regarded as one of today's best authors is Mocó (Cícero Viera da Silva), a native of Paraíba who is now a resident of Rio de Janeiro.

25. Olegário Fernandes da Silva, born 1932, São Caetano, Pernambuco. Lives in Caruaru, Pernambuco: poet. Interview August 14, 1981, Caruaru.

26. José Francisco Borges, born 1935, Bezerros, Pernambuco. Lives in Bezerros; poet, printmaker. Interview August 14, 1981, Bezerros.

27. Manoel Caboclo e Silva, born 1916, Juazeiro do Norte; poet. Interview July 2, 1981.

28. Expedito Sebastião da Silva, interview July 19, 1981.

29. See Slater 1981:54-79.

30. Manoel Caboclo e Silva, *O Padre Cícero em Roma* (Juazeiro do Norte: Folhetaria Casa dos Horóscopos, n.d.).

31. As noted in the plot summaries, some informants blame the man's plight on his mother, claiming that it was not the son but the pregnant mother who mocked Padre Cícero.

32. Maria Cândida da Conceição, born ca. 1900, Pão de Açucar, Alagoas; still tends vegetables. Interview August 5, 1981.

FOLHETO REFERENCES

Alves dos Santos, Apolônio
  n.d. Nascimento, Vida e Morte do Padre Cícero Romão. Guarabira: Tipografia Pontes.

Anonymous
n.d. A Surra que o Padre Cícero Deu no Diabo ou a Moça de Cajazeira. n.p.
Anonymous
n.d. Milagres de Padre Cícero de Juazeiro. n.p.
Anonymous
n.d. O Boi Milagroso de Padre Cícero. n.p.
Anonymous
n.d. O Boi Que Falava. n.p.
Anonymous
n.d. Padre Cícero e o Romeiro
Anonymous
n.d. Padre Cícero Romão e os seus Feitos Milagrosos. n.p.
Bandeira, Pedro and Joao Bandeira de Caldas
n.d. O Cego de Várzea Alegre que o Padre Cícero Curou. Juazeiro do Norte: n.p.
Cavalcanti e Ferreira Dila, José
n.d. São Pedro e Jesus. Caruaru: São José.
Coelho Cavalcante, Rodolfo
1973 Padre Cícero, O Santo de Juazeiro. Salvador. n.p.
Coelho Cavalcante, Rodolfo
n.d. Padre Cícero.
Costa Leite, José
n.d. O Frei Damião Sonhou com o Padre Cícero Romão. n.p.
Cristo Rei, João de
n.d. A Vida Milagrosa de Padre Cícero. Juazeiro do Norte. n.p.
Cristo Rei, João de
n.d. Os Milagres de Padrinho Cícero. Juazeiro do Norte. n.p.
Cristo Rei, João de
n.d. História da Guerra de Juazeiro em 1914. Juazeiro do Norte: Manoel Caboclo e Silva.
d'Almeida, Manuel Filho
1979 Padre Cícero, o Santo de Juazeiro. São Paulo: Luzeiro.
Fernandes, Olegário
1978 Interview, Caruaru, Pernambuco; March 17, 1978.
José da Silva, João
1961 Palavras do Padre Cícero sobre a Guerra Nuclear. Recife: João José da Silva.
José da Silva, João
n.d. A Mendiga da Estrada e os Milagres do Padre Cícero. Recife: João José da Silva.
José de Maria, Enoque
n.d. A Voz do Padre Cícero. n.p.
Lourenco Filho, M.B.
n.d. Juazeiro do Padre Cícero. 3rd ed. São Paulo: Melhoramentos.
Pontual, José Pedro
n.d. O Crente que Profanou do Padre Cícero. Recife: Edison Pinto, prop., (folheto)
Rodrigues, Estévao
1976 Grande Milagre do Padre Cícero: O Garoto que Caiu do 6 Andar e não Morreu.
Juazeiro do Norte: n.p.
Sales Areda, Francisco
n.d. Jesus e São Pedro. Caruaru: São José.
Santos, Sebastião Pereira
n.d. O Monstro que Raptava Moças e os Milagres do Padre Cícero. n.p. (folheto)
Serafim, Manuel
n.d. O Protestante que Virou num Urubu porque Quis Matar Padre Cícero. Condado: José
Costa Leite.
Sobrinho, João Quinto (João de Cristo Rei).
n.d. Profecia Misteriosa sobre os 3 Dias Escuros. Juazeiro do Norte: n.p. (folheto)

REFERENCES

Aigrain 1953
Almeida-Sobrinho 1978
Altman 1975
Alves dos Santos
Andrade 1963
Anselmo 1908
Apostolic Brazilian
  Catholic Church 1980
Azzi 1978
Bandeira-Caldas
Batista 1977
Benevides 1969
Browe 1938
Cámara Cascudo 1939
Caboclo e Silva 1978
Camilo dos Santos
Campos 1951
Cantel 1972
Cava 1970
Cavalcanti e Ferreira Dila
Christian, Jr. 1981
Coelho Cavalcante n.d, 1973
Comblin 1977
Costa Leite
Crane 1967
Cristo Rei n.d.
Cunniff 1971
Curran 1973
d' Almeida 1979
Daus 1969
Delehaye 1921
Duarte, et al. 1976
Fernandes 1978
Florentino Durate 1976

Forman 1972
Gonçalves n.d.
Hulet 1980
Jose da Silva n.d., 1961
Jose de Maria n.d.
Lessa 1973
Lewin n.d.
Literatura popular em verso:
  Antologia I-IV. 1962
Lourenco Filho n.d.
Maranhao de Souza 1976
Mecham 1934
Nolan-Nolan 1989
Oliveira n.d., 1980
Ong 1975
Pedro Pontual n.d.a, n.d.b
Pereira dos Santos n.d.
Queiros 1965
Ricoeur 1971
Rodrigues 1976
Salres Areda n.d.
Santos n.d.
Serafim n.d.
Silva n.d.
Silveira 1976
Slater 1981
Sobrinho n.d.
Souto Maior 1970
Souza n.d., 1976
Strickton-Greenfield 1972
Suassuna 1974
Tubach 1969
Turner-Turner 1978
Xavier de Oliveira 1969

11

Pilgrimages to Sorte in the Cult of María Lionza in Venezuela

ANGELINA POLLAK-ELTZ

Although Venezuela is a Catholic country, folk Catholicism is very different from the orthodox teachings of the Church. In addition, few priests are available to change the attitudes and concepts of the people, sentiments which have become customary over the centuries. Pilgrimages, an example of traditional behavior, are of great importance for many of the faithful. They are undertaken in order to fulfill a vow or to request a miracle. The utilitarian character of folk religion is obvious. Saints are not worshipped just to pay homage to them; they are invoked in order to solve the problems of the faithful that they cannot cope with by themselves. Catholics go on pilgrimages to the three most important national sanctuaries, where the Virgin Mary supposedly appeared during colonial times: the Virgen del Valle is appealed to by the inhabitants of the eastern states of Venezuela at her shrine on the Island of Margarita; the Virgen de la Chiquinquirá is the patroness of the western states and her sanctuary is found in Maracaibo; while the most important holy site is found in Guanare in central Venezuela for the Virgen de Coromoto, considered to be the true patroness of the country. Pilgrimages are organized to these sites by groups or by parish priests.

There are, however, many other sacred places in the country where individual pilgrims go to ask for help in their afflictions and to give thanks for a miracle. These places are associated with folk saints, who have never been canonized. They are historical or legendary persons who for one reason or another were turned into "saints" in the belief of the people. Also called "Animas," they may have died in an accident, led a saintly life, or been killed in a revolution. The sites where their shrines are found are connected with the death of the person. These pilgrimages are never organized, but are sporadic and individualistic and have mainly a utilitarian aspect.

The most popular folk saint is Dr. José Gregorio Hernanez, who was a well-known medical doctor in Caracas who died in a car accident in 1918. The doctor's popularity is proven by the fact that in the majority of lower-class homes his statue or lithograph is displayed on an altar or placed in the corner of the main room. When people are asked who would be the "saint of their special worship," the answer is usually "José Gregorio." His tomb in a centrally located church in Caracas is visited frequently by the faithful and pilgrimages are organized to his birthplace in Isnotu in the Andes of Trujillo, where a church was built with the money that the pilgrims donated. These pilgrimages are organized not only by independent groups but also by parish priests. The Venezuelan Church started a process in Rome in order to canonize the doctor, but so far the matter is pending. Since pilgrimages to Isnotu are undertaken in order to cure disease, the utilitarian character is apparent. People bathe in a lagoon near the village of Isnotu or drink the water of a "sacred" well. Pilgrimages are an important aspect of orthodox and folk Catholicism in Venezuela, and they also play a part in the cult of María Lionza.

In the following analysis of pilgrimages to the holy mountain of Sorte (Yaracuy) by the followers of the cult of María Lionza, I have used the theoretical framework revealed by Turner and Turner (1978:139), which indicates that pilgrimages contain some of the same attributes of liminality as do other rites of passage: release from mundane structures, homogenization of status, simplicity of dress and behavior, comunitas, ordeal, reflection on the meaning of basic religious and cultural values, ritualized enactment of correspondence between religious paradigms and shared human experiences, movement from a mundane center to a sacred periphery which becomes central for the individual, an aspect of penance, financial sacrifices, ludic and solemn aspects, and leisure activity. Pilgrimages often originate in vows and the pilgrims' motivation involves a cure. Even in Christian pilgrimages, magical aspects abound, such as the belief in the curative power of sacred springs, prayers, and ritual acts (Turner and Turner 1978:13-14). Faith is strengthened and miracles are expected. The Turners (1978:11) compare pilgrimages with "rituals of affliction" that are performed to exorcise supernatural beings or propitiate such forces, believed to be the cause of illness, bad luck, and death. The curative process is conducted by an association of religious specialists or "doctors", often recruited from former patients. It is believed that due to personal experience with illness and/or misfortune, they have special contact with and knowledge of the invisible entities that shape human life. Power is ascribed to all rituals, especially the rituals performed in a sacred place. The curative and charismatic aspects of pilgrimages are stressed (Turner and Turner 1978:14), although in Christian pilgrimages a deeper level of religious participation is reached and the morale of the pilgrim is raised. Most of these aspects described by the Turners can also be found in the case from Venezuela, which I will describe.

THE CULT OF MARIA LIONZA

The cult of María Lionza is a magico-religious movement that has its roots in Amerindian, African, and Christian beliefs and rituals, but in its present form emerged only in the course of the past four decades. The cult is utilitarian and syncretistic and was influenced by Santería, esoterism, and the spiritism of Kardec. Thus it is changing continuously. No codification of beliefs and rites has ever been undertaken and most cult leaders work pretty much on their own and in competition with each other. Nevertheless, the rites are basically similar in that they are geared toward the solution of the problems of the faithful: health, strife in the family, lack of work, envy. The cult is not exclusive, as the majority of the faithful consider themselves to be Catholics at the same time.

The cult originated in the state of Yaracuy, where the sanctuary of Sorte is located, but developed in the urban environment of the large cities of central Venezuela after the rural exodus started about 40 years ago. In the cult, spiritual entities (spirits of nature, divinities, and the souls of important deceased persons) are considered to be intermediaries between humans and the Supreme Being (God the Father). They are summoned to speak through mediums in trance, to listen to the problems of the faithful and to give advice on how to cure an illness, get rid of an evil spell, and protect oneself against black magic. The spirits, supposed to speak from the mouth of the mediums, prescribe the appropriate rites to deal with the problems or the remedies to buy or prepare. The rites are later executed by the leader and his assistants.

The cult absorbed former superstitions, healing practices, and magical rites that existed in Venezuela and has borrowed heavily in recent years from Cuban Santería, which was introduced to the Caribbean area through Miami after the beginning of the Cuban exodus in 1959. Santería is an Afro-American cult based on the religion of the Yoruba in Nigeria, but fused with Christian concepts. Thus, the Catholic saints were identified with African divinities. Numerous magical rites are performed in order to solve the problems of the faithful by means of the aid of supernatural beings, who may speak through mediums in trance or the oracle handled by *babalaos*.

In the cult of María Lionza, the most important spiritual entity is María Lionza herself, a nature spirit and guardian of the flora and fauna in her territory, the mountain range of Sorte. She has aspects of a mother goddess and the Virgin Mary. Female spirits were worshiped by the Jirajara and Caquetío Indians of central Venezuela as early as pre-Columbian times. According to old documents, the devil was implored by Indians and mestizos on the mountain of Sorte during colonial times, which means that the sanctuary of María Liona in Yaracuy had always been a sacred place. According to a legend, María Lionza, or rather the prototype of the spiritual entity, who was the daughter of an Indian chief, was raped by the guardian of a lagoon, an Anaconda snake. While God punished the snake with death, the maiden herself became the guardian of the lagoon and later became the protectress of nature in this area of Yaracuy. In recent years, María Lionza has slightly lost her central position in the cult in favor of Afro-Cuban divinities, such as Ogun or Chango, whom the faithful consider to be very powerful spirits. Other spiritual entities invoked are: the guardians of mountains, rivers, and forests, the so-called *Don Juanes*; the Indian chiefs who fought against the Spaniards during the Conquest (Guaicaipuro, Tamanaco etc.); Simón Bolívar, the liberator of Venezuela; the Afro-Cuban divinities known under the generic name *Las Siete Potencias Africanas*, and the aforementioned Dr. José Gregorio Hernandez, who is not only a folk saint but also the spiritual helper of curers.

The cult is mainly an urban phenomenon with spiritual centers located in the poorer sections of the large cities. In recent years, some of the more sophisticated and better-educated leaders opened centers in more affluent *urbanizaciones*, catering to the middle and upper classes. Only in the course of the past ten years was the cult carried into the countryside by returning migrants and there it has influenced the practices of local *curanderos* (both herbalists and spiritual healers). It also spread to the Dominican Republic, the Dutch islands of the Caribbean and Colombia.

The cult leaders may be men or women and usually belong to the lower classes. They are self-styled and usually maintain that they received a vocation from the spiritual world after they had been afflicted by an illness, of which they were miraculously cured by a cultist. Some have outside jobs while others are full-time leaders or mediums. To each center are attached a number of mediums who have been trained by the *banco* (as the leader is called). They also assist the *banco* in performing *trabajos* (magic work). Often the mediums are recruited from former patients who were advised to develop their spiritual faculties to get well and serve the community. Eventually they may become cult leaders and open their own centers. A group of faithful is permanently attached to the center, but the majority only come when they have to cope with problems they can not solve on their own.

Although sessions take place twice or three times a week, the leader may be consulted at any time. When a client wants to get in touch with a spiritual entity in a private session, a medium is called and the *banco* interprets her words. Mediums have to undergo special training in order to "establish the spirit in their head" (in order to learn the appropriate behaviour of the spiritual entity and the role played in the ritual drama). Most mediums are women although some are male homosexuals. The *bancos* are usually men, though there are also some female leaders. The faithful in search of help may be men or women, old or young. The core members contribute regularly to the upkeep of the cult center, but pay extra for *trabajos* and *consultas*. Outsiders have to supply the material used in the rituals and often pay high fees for exorcisms and consultations. Cult centers are usually found in the private home of the *banco* or attached to his house. There is a large altar, decorated with the statues of the most important spirits, flowers, jars with water and rum, candles, incense, food offerings, and the symbols of the African divinities of the Santería – a double-axe for Chango, for example, or some iron for Ogun. While the faithful sit in the back of the room, the rites are performed in front of the altar.

Occasionally the cult leader may decide to organize a pilgrimage to the sanctuary in the mountain range of Sorte, situated in the state of Yaracuy. The *banco* calls the core members together to decide on the trip whenever there is a serious problem to be solved. Most centers organize a pilgrimage at least once a year to give thanks for the successful *trabajos* performed or to summon the spirits to cooperate with the group. The mountain is about 1,400 meters high, overlooking the fertile valley of the Rio Yaracuy, where large sugar-cane plantations are found. The town of Chivacoa is about ten kilometers away. The sanctuary can be reached by car since many dirt roads cross the cane fields. Pilgrimages usually take place on weekends or during holiday seasons, such as Christmas, Carnival, and Holy Week.

About fifteen years ago the area was declared a national park and a few guards are stationed there to keep an eye on the pilgrims. Permanent structures are forbidden and pilgrims are expected to clean up when leaving their campsites. The guards also try to keep forest fires under control. Actually there is no great danger that the pilgrims would destroy the vegetation, since the mountain range is considered to be sacred to María Lionza, who strictly prohibits the destruction of forests. The Rio Yaracuy flows parallel to the mountain range with sacred campsites located on both sides of the river or along small streams that flow down from the mountain. A few parking lots were constructed nearby and there are also a number of small stalls where food, drinks, and ritual materials are sold. A number of *perfumerias* (shops where ritual paraphernalia such as soap, perfumes, candles, statues, and lithographs are sold) do a good business in the town of Chivacoa. Also a few hotels cater to the more affluent pilgrims and *botequines* sell food and drinks. Taxis and jeeps run from the town to Sorte at regular intervals. The owner of the largest *perfumería* has several factories in the town that manufacture candles, perfumes, and ritual objects. He is in contact with cult leaders and drivers who stop at his place so that the pilgrims buy his merchandise before moving on to the sanctuary.

There is no one single sacred spot on Sorte, but the whole area is considered to be sacred. The pilgrims usually remain on the bottom of the mountain either in the area called Sorte or in Quivallo, about two kilometers upstream. Only for very special *trabajos* will they climb up the steep path to the *Escalera*, a steep rock where it is said that sometimes María Lionza appears to the faithful. There are a few small caves nearby where water comes out of the rocks. All these sites are considered to be sacred. Candles are burned at the entrance of these rock shelters and sometimes food offerings are placed in the caves. From there one may climb even further up to the summit of the mountain, where the sacred lagoon of María Lionza is located. Here the faithful perform "very special work."

A PILGRIMAGE TO SORTE

Pilgrimages are organized by the urban cult leaders in order to perform special *trabajos* on the mountain or to pay for a miracle. Sometimes a cult center is visited by an itinerant *banco* who promises to obtain special graces for the faithful if they join him on a pilgrimage to Sorte. Those who go on a pilgrimage are usually the core members of the center, the mediums, and those adherents who have to "pay for" a vow or hope that their problems will be solved in a satisfactory way when they perform *trabajos importantes* in the scared place. Preparations are made well in advance. A *caravana* usually consists of about 25 to 30 men, women, and children. A bus is rented or those among the faithful who have cars agree to take others along for a small fee. Pilgrimages are more frequently organized just after the first or 15th of each month, when people have just received their salaries. During the rainy season, large-scale pilgrimages rarely take place, as the dirt roads to the mountain become impassable and camping is impossible. During Holy Week, more than 50,000 faithful may gather in Sorte. The pilgrims may remain at the mountain for four or more days. Columbus Day is another important holiday and many faithful may go to Sorte. Individual pilgrimages are rare, people usually come in groups with their own *banco* and mediums and stay together. They do not interfere in the rituals taking place on the right and left of their campsite and other pilgrims are not supposed to enter their precinct. Generally speaking, those who belong to a *caravana* are friends or have known each other for some time in the cult center. Ordinarily a pilgrimage starts on a Saturday morning. About five hours are required to drive from Caracas to Sorte, which means that the pilgrims arrive around noontime. It takes some time to set up camp. People carry drinks, food, camping equipment, clothing, and ritual objects along. Usually they sleep on mats or in hammocks which they hang up between the trees. About 80 kilometers before reaching Chivacoa, there is a sacred spot on the highway where pilgrims always stop in order to burn a candle in front of the image of the Virgin Mary and drink water from the sacred spring. The buses usually stop in Chivacoa too, where the last purchases are made.

After arriving at one or another spot along the Rio Yarcuy at the foot of the mountain range of Sorte, pilgrims carry their heavy equipment across the river to the spot they select for camping. *Bancos*, who are frequent visitors to Sorte, have their sites marked with a small altar that is set up on a cement base. These cement bases were made before the area was declared a national park. Here statues are put up, candles are lit, and food and rum are placed in jars. These offerings supposedly allure the spirits to the site. Then a "fence" is often made around the camp site with ropes slung around the trees. These "fences" are intended to keep curious strangers out, as each *caravana* wants to remain on its own. While the leader prepares the altar, the faithful put up their hammocks, tables, chairs, and tents. A fire is lit and soon the women begin preparing food for the group. The afternoon is usually spent with these preparations. Some children and adults may sleep, a "siesta," or just sit around and talk. Camping in the mountains is a pleasant change from daily routines in the city, where people often live in overcrowded houses. Informal visiting provides another important aspect of the pilgrimage.

The rituals usually start when the sun goes down, after 6:00 P.M. The pilgrims come to Sorte for a special purpose and the rites that will be performed here during the night were prescribed by the mediums in trance, that is by the spiritual entities during previous sessions in the urban cult center. The faithful come to Sorte to receive special magical treatments or to perform rites of thanksgiving after their prayers have been answered.

The rites usually start in an informal way with a bath taken in the Rio Yaracuy or in one of the small streams. The cult leader and his assistants wash the faithful with magic soap and may pour perfumes or rum over them. Then they have to submerge themselves in the water. It is said that the bath in the river gives spiritual strength and keeps bad influences away. After this cleansing ceremony, those in need of further exorcisms have to undergo a *velación*. These rites were completely unknown around fifteen years ago, but are now the most popular practices, both on the sacred mountain of Sorte and in urban cult centers. The earth is cleared and the believer has to lie down on the ground with arms outstretched. Then candles are placed around him, and sometimes knives are driven into the earth above his head. A white line is drawn with baby powder around his body and then the candles are lit. The color of the candles indicates the spirit or spirits that are summoned. The cult leader now recites a magical formula to invoke the spirits, who are supposed to descend. Then rum, brandy, wine, water, perfumes, baby powder, dirt, sometimes flowers, and even the blood of a sacrificed animal are poured over the adept, while the *banco* and his helpers mumble prayers. Bloody sacrifices became popular after the Santería was introduced to Venezuela. The blood gives strength and it may contain the power of the spiritual entity. The chicken or goat that is about to be sacrificed is first consecrated to the spirit. It is important to cut its head with one single stroke. The blood is sprinkled directly from the neck of the chicken on the person undergoing the *velación*. All the objects poured over the individual should strengthen his body and mind. He has to remain quiet until the candles burn down completely and sometimes may fall into a state of trance or semitrance. He is finally aroused by the *banco*. Sometimes it is necessary to help him to get to his feet again. When he stands up, a white line is drawn around him, on which gunpowder is sprinkled and then burned. The explosion is supposed to carry away all evil influences. Then the adept has to take a bath in the river and usually returns immediately to his hammock to rest. *Velaciones* are prescribed when a person is ill and believes that envy or witchcraft caused his ailments; when he feels weak; when he is a student and has failed his examinations; when he has "bad luck" (*pava*) or when his lover has deserted him; when he needs a job; or when he wants to get rid of a neighbor. The materials used in the *velación* have to be supplied by the cult members. Moreover, the fees for this "special work" are high, depending on the length of the treatment and whether or not animal sacrifices are involved. While the *velaciones* are performed, other rites may take place at the same time. The leader or an assistant may try to exorcise an evil spirit from the body of a client by blowing tobacco smoke over him or he may flagellate him with branches cut in the woods. He may also wash him again with magic soap or other substances. Sometimes people are "washed" with crushed fruits (papaya, melons, watermelons) that are put on their heads. Later in the evening, the participants in the *caravana* are called together and some communal rites may take place in front of the altar. The *banco*, wearing no shoes and no shirt, but a large cross on a multicolored ribbon around his neck, stands in front of the altar with a cigar in his mouth, invoking the spirits, who are supposed to descend on the mediums. One medium after another approaches the altar, also barefoot and with a cross around her neck. The *banco* prays over the woman, blows tobacco smoke over her body and face, and pours rum on her head. She may now fall in trance or start to act out her habitual spirit role. Some mediums really fall in trance, others only pretend. While "in trance," the mediums often drink great quantities of rum and smoke one cigar after another, without feeling ill or getting drunk. The mediums now perform special rites, usually exorcisms. A medium may make cuts on her arm with a knife and then smear the blood over the face of a client. She may also blow cigar smoke over another person to cleanse him from all evil. She may violently shake her clients head in order to rid him from an evil spirit. Some mediums also offer advice to their followers; however, diagnostic rites are not performed in the mountains but have already taken place in the city.

Later in the evening, some mediums in true trance may begin to dance in the glowing ashes of the camp-fire while the *banco* beats a drum. Sometimes bottles are broken and the mediums dance in the shreds, supposedly not hurting themselves. The rites may go on until midnight. In order to awaken a medium, the *banco* washes her face with fresh water, blows into her ears, and mumbles a magic formula over her head. Sometimes she has to be beaten violently before she becomes conscious again. Afterwards, the mediums usually take a refreshing bath in the river. Sometimes the sessions go on, but the mood changes. Mediums may receive happy-go-lucky spirits that entertain the audience with "dirty" jokes. The pilgrims start drinking rum and *aguardiente* (liquor) and the ceremony turns into a party, where food and drinks are shared.

While all these activities take place around the water holes and along the Rio Yaracuy, some pilgrims, usually in small groups, venture to the *Escalera* for very special work. Before they cross the river, they recite a prayer, and when entering the stream they sip some water or wash their faces. The narrow path to the sanctuary on top of the mountain is lined with small shrines where the pilgrims, climbing up to the *Escalera* place candles and flowers and may rest for a few moments to utter a prayer. When they finally reach the *Escalera*, they prepare a small altar beneath the large rock. Then they settle down.

Later in the evening a *trabajo especial* may take place. A *baptism* is a rite that supposedly "opens up" a medium so that he or she can receive the spirit to whom he or she is dedicated in the ceremony. The medium is dressed all in white, while the cult-leader blows tobacco smoke over her and cleanses her with rum. Then he pours water over her head, while everybody prays an Ave Maria and a Holy Father. The *Coronation* rite, which is the second step toward perfection, is similar. A more experienced medium is permanently dedicated to a certain spirit in a ritual which is almost the same, only after the usual cleansing rites have taken place, she is solemnly crowned. The pilgrims say that the invisible forces of nature are especially powerful at the *Escalera* and therefore work done here is of great importance. Other rites may cleanse a car from "bad luck," mainly after being involved in an accident. The car is "washed" with rum, tobacco smoke is blown over it, and then gun powder is burned around the vehicle.

Sunday morning, most pilgrims sleep. Then breakfast is prepared and around noon more *velaciones* may take place and some people take baths in the river. After lunch most *caravanas* begin to get ready for their trip home. The people feel good. In the bus they may sing and chat and often plans are made for the next pilgrimage. They feel clean and are no longer afraid of evil influences that may disturb their lives. Psychologically they are better prepared to cope with their problems. In addition, the *velaciones* and other rites may help those who suffer from psychosomatic diseases. As a result of their faith in the efficacy of the *bancos*, they may be cured. All rituals are utilitarian and are considered to be more "powerful" when performed in the natural setting of Sorte.

CONCLUSIONS

Since pilgrimages to Sorte serve utilitarian purposes, religious fervour is not stimulated. They are performed because the adherents of the cult of María Lionza wish to "repay" a vow they made to a spirit who granted them a special favor or because they are convinced that rituals taking place at the sacred mountain are more effective. Thus the curative and charismatic aspects of the pilgrimages come to light. The pilgrims are more eagerly involved in group rituals when they are performed at Sorte, as they are not distracted. Since most people have to cope with the same or similar problems, the rites may be considered as a kind of group therapy. Most adherents to the cult believe in the efficacy of magical rites and therefore may actually be cured by faith, as most of the illnesses that come to the attention of the *bancos* are psychosomatic in nature. Once the ultimate causes are apparently removed through cleansing rites, cult members are protected against further attacks of evildoers by submitting to a *velación* or by obtaining a charm. The direct contacts with the spiritual entities that supposedly speak through the mouths of the mediums or act through them, are an important aspect of the curing rituals. They may be closer to the people when they visit the sacred mountain, as it is believed that many spirits actually dwell in the forests. The supernatural beings truly take a personal interest in the well-being of humble folks on earth. In addition, it is possible that the water of the Rio Yaracuy and its tributaries contains minerals that also have curative powers.

Pilgrimages are important for many of the faithful as an escape from the daily routine in cramped homes and unpleasant surroundings in factories or workshops. When spending the weekend in a pleasant environment, one easily forgets problems or looks upon them from a different point of view. Many of the pilgrims were born and raised in the countryside and a trip to the mountains means a return to this accustomed environment.

Pilgrimages also offer entertainment and fun, especially when the official rituals come to an end and the members of the *caravana* socialize informally. Community bonds and ties of friendship are strengthened. Pilgrims who belong to the same *caravana* feel like "family" and call each other *hermano* (brother) and *hermana* (sister). When they return to the city they may continue to help each other. Thus most of the aspects of pilgrimages described by Turner and Turner (1978) exist in the Venezuelan setting.

REFERENCES

Margolies-Suarez 1976   Turner & Turner 1978
Pollak-Eltz 1972, 1987

12

The Ethnography and Archaeology of Two Andean Pilgrimage Centers

HELAINE SILVERMAN

Archaeology reconstructs past societies through their material remains. Since not all cultural behavior leaves behind permanent residues in the ground or over the landscape, the archaeological record is incomplete. During the past decade the use of ethnographic analogy, or ethnoarchaeology, has emerged as an important supplement to archaeological data (see Gould 1978; Kramer 1979). Kramer states the basic assumption of ethnoarchaeology as, "Observations of contemporary behavior can facilitate the development and refinement of insights into past behaviors, particularly when strong similarities can be shown to exist between the environments and technologies of the past and contemporary sociocultural systems being compared" (1979:1). In this chapter I provide an example of the great utility of ethnographic data for the archaeologist by describing the ethnographic observations made at a contemporary Catholic pilgrimage center on the south coast of Peru and their parallels with material remains recovered through excavation at an archaeological site in the same area.[1]

CAHUACHI

The archaeological ruins of Cahuachi, on the south bank of the Nazca River (Figure 12.1), have long been recognized as the major site of Nasca

Figure 12.1 Archaeological Ruins of Cahuachi, Nazca River

culture, which flourished on the south coast during the first seven centuries of our era (see Strong 1957:32). Excavations have been conducted at the site by various investigators since the 1920s, but all of these projects (Farabee in 1922: see Mason 1926; Kroeber in 1926: see Kroeber n.d., 1956; Tello in 1927: see Tello and Mejía 1967; Doering in 1932: see Doering 1958) save one (Strong in 1952: see Strong 1957) involved Cahuachi's cemeteries, from which fabulous Nasca pottery and textiles could be recovered, rather than the reconstruction of Nasca lifeways. Only Strong expressed an interest in both the dating and nature of Nasca culture and excavated in several of the site's semi-artificial mounds rather than in graveyards. The results of Strong's excavations have been widely interpreted as indicating the existence of a dense residential population at Cahuachi (Rowe 1963:11-12; Lumbreras 1974:123-24; Matos 1980:488 inter alia).

In 1984-85 I conducted new excavations at Cahuachi in order to gather more data on the site's occupational history, nature, and function within Nasca society (Figure 12.2). I was especially interested in the growth of Cahuachi as an urban center. The most notable fact which emerged from my new excavations at Cahuachi, however, is that little supporting evidence exists for the contention that the site was a great pre-Columbian city. Twenty-three test pits and broad areal excavations revealed no houses or refuse of a domestic nature in the extensive open areas between Cahuachi's

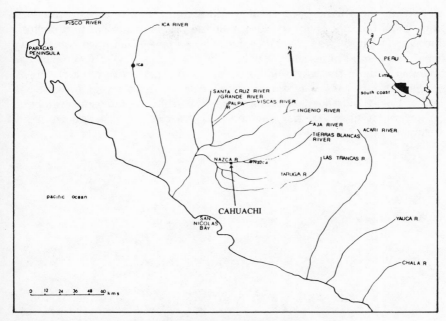

Figure 12.2 Map of the South Coast of Peru

mounds. Furthermore, reanalysis of Strong's so-called habitation mounds
indicated that these were composed of construction fill rather than
stratified domestic remains, as Strong and others believed.[2] In addition,
the surface of most of these mounds is littered with abundant remains of
ritual paraphernalia: fancy pottery, panpipes, elaborate textile fragments,
and other miscellanea. Clearly these represent temple mounds. Thus,
Cahuachi appears to have been a ceremonial rather than an urban center.
The ethnographic study of a modern-day Catholic pilgrimage center, which
provides a congruent model for the cultural behavior represented in
Cahuachi's material remains and spatial patterns, suggests how Cahuachi
functioned as a ceremonial center.

YAUCA

In late July 1984, while excavating at Cahuachi, I attended a party at
one of the local farms. As I was helping the women cook I heard them
inquire of each other if they had made a *promesa* ("promise," a vow to a
patron saint). When I inquired "promise for what?" they told me about the
miraculous Virgin whose cult was celebrated the first Sunday in October
every year at Yauca. It was not, however, until my colleague, Miguel Pazos,
and I visited his aunt and uncle in Ica in September that the possible value

of visiting the shrine became clear. That night at dinner, Dr. and Mrs. Rejas began to talk about the Yauca shrine whose fiesta was approaching and what a pity it was that the sanctuary was used just once a year save for an occasional Mass. Since two months of excavation at Cahuachi had revealed little in the way of a dense residential population and Cahuachi seemed to be a vacant ceremonial center rather than a populated urban center, Pazos and I visited Yauca in the hope that the modern ceremonial center might give us some insight into the ancient one. We were not disappointed.

Figure 12.3 Dessication in the Region

Located some 190 kilometers north of Nazca and about 30 kilometers east of the city of Ica, the sanctuary of the Virgen del Rosario de Yauca stands in the middle of a desolate, sandy plain in a side-branch of the Ica Valley that is undergoing drastic desiccation (Figure 12.3). This Yauca valley sidebranch provides the natural communication route to the adjacent highlands of Huancavelica. Williams (1980) and Pazos (Williams and Pazos 1974) mention several pre-Hispanic sites in this valley, such as Chokoltaja, a Nasca 3-4 habitation site similar in layout and geographical setting to another early Nasca settlement along the middle reaches of the Aja River in Nazca (Silverman 1983; Silverman and Pazos n.d.). Also, local informants speak of the Yauca area's *huacas* or natural shrines. Like Cahuachi, where one crosses the Pampa de San José from the north and the Pampa de Atarco from the south to arrive at the site, a pampa also must be traversed to reach Yauca. At both shrines the wind frequently blows fiercely.

The cult of the Virgin of Yauca could be classified as a fourth-order shrine. It is not international like the Virgin of Guadalupe, or national like

Señor de los Milagros, whose church is in Lima, nor is it a local shrine (see Sallnow 1982). Rather it is a regional one, but not on a par with Señor de Luren, also in Ica. The Virgin miraculously appeared on October 3, 1701, which conforms to the shepherds' cycle tradition as defined by Turner and Turner (1978:41-42). This cycle itself suggests pre-Hispanic origins or a connection with the earth or striking natural features that in Peru would be called *huacas*. There was probably a pre-Hispanic shrine in the Yauca area. Landowner Don Nicolas Ortega witnessed the appearance of the Virgin precisely where his Indian peons were working in the field because he may have seen them performing some pre-Hispanic or syncretic rite associated with the place and thus associated the location with sacred power. After years of trying to move the image of the Virgin to the city of Ica and the Virgin physically refusing to budge, the locals finally acceded to the Virgin's wishes and built her chapel on the Yauca plain.

Figure 12.4 The Shrine of Yauca, Ica

Visited weeks before its festival, the Yauca shrine is a lonely spot indeed (Figure 12.4). Its austere, white, neocolonial church is closed because there is no priest in residence. The buildings around the large (approximately 10,000 square meters) plaza are abandoned and in varying degrees of disrepair. The plaza itself is empty except for the presence of two posts which visibly serve to tie up the burros of the muleteers who travel between the Huancavelica highlands and Ica. In fact, abundant burro excrement surrounds these hitching posts. The muleteers stop here because there is a well where they can obtain water. The plaza surface is a broken *apisonado* with little evidence of the activities that take place yearly.[3] Only some corn husks, a bit of broken glass, broken china, a fragment of rope, bits of textile, and some loose canes were observed on the *apisonado* of the plaza at this time. Behind the abandoned houses surrounding the plaza there was a greater concentration of refuse. It was noted during this visit that the shrine has a strong echo when the wind does not blow. Interestingly, the same aural feature was observed at Cahuachi down the length of its main plaza during a similar, quiet day.

We revisited the Yauca sanctuary ten days before the festival to observe the ritual *barrido* or "sweeping of the plaza." When we returned to Yauca for the sweeping, we asked what would be swept since we had noted weeks earlier that the plaza was basically clean. Informants at the shrine and in Ica contradicted us, saying "no, it's really dirty." This seems to be a shared perception. The faithful thus came with their new brooms, carrying shawls and plastic sacks, and enthusiastically swept the plaza, removing the loose dirt and burro excrement and the few other surface remains we had already noted. This dirt was thrown out behind the plaza in the plain through which the dry Yauca River runs. The wind blows the refuse up against the backs of the plaza houses, catching it there while the rest of the dirt is carried away by the wind in other directions or washed away by the river when it occasionally floods. Following the brief sweeping, the shrine was again deserted.

What a change had taken place the next week when we returned to the sanctuary for the celebration of the festival of the Virgin. By late Friday afternoon the sanctuary was filling up with pilgrims. Many of the faithful, who had made a promise to the Virgin, had crossed the dry Yauca plain

Figure 12.5   The Plaza in Yauca during the Festival

on foot on a six- to eight-hour trek from Ica under the hot spring sun. As is the case with Christian pilgrimage in general, the pilgrims pass a series of smaller religious waystations en route to the shrine (Turner and Turner 1978:23). In Yauca these are natural and man-made stops: a special *huarango* tree, a little dry river that flows during the summer when it rains in the highlands, and several crosses. Most pilgrims, however, arrived by public transportation (a service provided by the municipality), in private cars, or by truck (both privately owned business trucks which earn extra money carrying pilgrims and trucks from the various agrarian cooperatives, which transport their members to the shrine).

By Saturday there were thousands of people camping outside the plaza area, on the terrace of the church itself, sleeping in cars and trucks, or lodged in the otherwise abandoned houses lining the plaza which, during the festival, service the pilgrims of the distinct *cofradías*, with each *cofradía* having a house on the plaza. Certain families have houses on the plaza as well. The plaza itself was transformed into a great market, closely packed with kiosks selling food, alcoholic beverages (beer and moonshine), and soft drinks (Figure 12.5). Among these ephemeral reed structures that served as restaurants circulated the pedestrian hawkers of cold drinks, ice pops, and sweet bean paste from Chincha in its enticing, white gum-sealed gourd containers. On the main staircase of the church and on the terrace on which the church rests, many vendors of religious paraphernalia such as candles, images, orations, and amulets were observed. The candle makers told me that they are a guild and travel from shrine to shrine all over Peru selling their wares during the particular saints' days.

Figure 12.6 The Plaza in Yauca after the Festival

It was only on Sunday, at the moment of removing the Virgin and her four little assistant Virgins (altar Virgins for the four altars in the four corners of the plaza) from the church, that a partial cessation in secular activity could be noted when many (but by no means all or even the majority) of the people lined up behind the priest and litters to form the procession. After the procession, the throng of pilgrims quickly abandoned the site.

We returned the next day, Monday, to watch the process of abandonment of the ceremonial center, and especially to note the material condition of the site, once abandoned. The shrine was filthy. We saw the refuse, left by the thousands of pilgrims, littering the site surface: food remains, toppled hearths, broken glasses and plates, and lots of plastic bags and paper blowing about. Once the kiosk owners had taken down and rolled up the mat walls of their stands, there was virtually no trace of the Brigadoon city that had existed the day before (Figure 12.6). The "city" had been dismembered almost as quickly as it had been installed. We asked various vendors if they were going to clean up the mess or leave the shrine in this littered condition. All answered that they would not clean it now nor did they ever clean up "because the wind carries away all of the filth in a short while. Here the air blows hard." Indeed, three months later when I returned to the site, it was almost as devoid of surface refuse as it had been several weeks before the sweeping.

ETHNOGRAPHIC ANALOGY FOR A PILGRIMAGE FUNCTION, CAHUACHI

The patterns of behavior and material remains observed at the Yauca pilgrimage center correspond quite closely to the situation encountered in my excavations at Cahuachi. I would argue that, like Yauca, Cahuachi functioned as a pilgrimage center. Pilgrimage activity explains the abundance of cultural remains at Cahuachi, particularly materials of a ritualistic rather than domestic quality, in the absence of a large, permanent, domestic residential population.

Nevertheless, there are obvious and expected differences in the pilgrimage activity of the two Andean ceremonial centers. The most salient is intensity of use. Yauca, as a relatively low-order shrine in the Catholic hierarchy, is used just once a year. Cahuachi was manifestly the most important early Nasca site and was surely used more continually throughout the year, presumably in accordance with a ritual calendar. The more frequent use of Cahuachi is indicated by the abundance of cultural materials in the construction fills of its mounds as well as on certain areas of the site surface. Furthermore, at Yauca there is just one shrine, the church, in which the image of the Virgin is housed. Cahuachi, on the other hand, is characterized by more than 40 mounds of varying shape and form.

I have argued (Silverman 1986) that Cahuachi's multiple mounds (Figure 12.1) are the distinct shrines of the various Nasca social groups comprising the Nasca macroethnic group and polity. The differences in the physical characteristics of Cahuachi's mounds are due both to the nature of the underlying topography upon which the mounds were constructed and the heterogeneous and specialized activities which occurred on them.

As centers of pilgrimage, both Yauca and Cahuachi have open areas for the congregation of masses of people. At Cahuachi, these areas between mounds are delimited as four- and three-sided spaces by low adobe walls or by the arms of the mounds themselves. Their surfaces are virtually devoid of cultural materials and excavation revealed a similar subsurface situation except for pockets of trapped garbage. These open spaces are not the loci of quotidian dwellings nor are they cemeteries, but rather should be interpreted as plazas.

The ritual sweeping of sacred space is well-known in the ethnographic and archaeological record, for example, Pedro Pizarro's (1978:37) eyewitness account of the sweeping of the Cajamarca plaza by Atahualpa's retainers prior to his fateful entry. I would argue that, like Yauca, Cahuachi's plazas were maintained by means of ritual sweeping. The refuse that accumulated at Yauca through pilgrimage activity either blew away or was swept off the plaza premises to be disposed of elsewhere. At Cahuachi the lack of stratified kitchen middens has been noted by various researchers and I would suggest that Cahuachi was likewise kept clean by wind and humans. The refuse that accumulated during the cyclical use of Cahuachi both blew away and was either deliberately removed by dumping it nearby or in the Nazca River valley bottom, to be carried away by periodic, intense floods or recycled in the construction fill with which Cahuachi's monumental architecture was built. At Yauca the infrequent use of the site permitted the wind to maintain a clean plaza and sweeping was more a perfunctory ritual gesture than hygienic act. In contrast, at Cahuachi, where the use of the shrine(s) was frequent and intense, wind alone was not a sufficient cleaning agency and sweeping may have been necessary to maintain both the ritual purity of the zone (see Douglas 1966: Chapters 1, 2) and a certain level of sanitation. Indeed, sweeping may very well explain the scarcity of artifactual material within the plazas of Cahuachi.

Excavating into the surface of the main plaza at Cahuachi, I encountered round depressions containing small amounts of refuse, utilitarian sherds, and ash (Figure 12.7). Based on analogy with the temporary cooking facilities at the Yauca shrine (Figures 12.8), I would now interpret these depressions as temporary hearths into which refuse later blew. Also cut into the surface of the main plaza at Cahuachi were postholes. As I found no habitation or activity floors in association with these postholes I suggest that they correspond to temporary structures which were erected in the plaza and subsequently removed. These postholes correspond perfectly to the construction technique still used today to build simple, cane walled

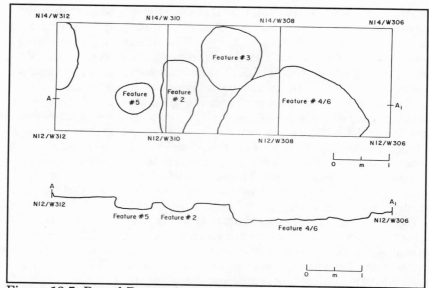

Figure 12.7 Round Depressions in the main plaza, Cahuachi

structures such as those observed not only at Yauca but all over the south coast (Figure 12.9).

Pottery constitutes the most interesting of the parallels in material remains found at Yauca and Cahuachi. At Yauca various broken plates (Figure 12.10) and glasses were left behind in the sand following the festival. Although the plaza surface at Cahuachi was essentially clean, we

Figure 12.8 Cooking in Temporary Facilities at Yauca

Figure 12.9 The Construction of a Simple Cane Wall

did nevertheless recover the remains of a fine polychrome goblet (Figure 12.11) and some broken utilitarian ware.

These shared patterns of material remains and space have led me to identify Cahuachi's open areas as plazas for the congregation of nonresidential pilgrims and to attribute a pilgrimage function to the site.

Figure 12.10 Broken Plates Remain at Yauca after the Festival

Figure 12.11 Reconstructed from Remains of a Fine Goblet, Cahuachi

CONCLUSIONS: INTERDIGITATION OF PILGRIMAGE AND SOCIOPO-LITICAL COMPLEXITY

For a brief period of time on the south coast of Peru, ca. 200-400 A.D., Cahuachi was the primary or capital site of a short-lived regional polity known as Nasca. The patterns of behavior which we have been able to reconstruct for Cahuachi tell us a great deal about the nature of the early Nasca polity. Clearly, at Cahuachi the Nasca elite was emphasizing ceremonialism over mere displays of political administration of its territory. Indeed, the elite of Nasca society appear to have been a decidedly theocratic caste. In such a situation we can well appreciate the role played by pilgrimage to Cahuachi. Writing about modern-day Andean pilgrimage in this volume (chapter 17), Poole observes that pilgrimage functions to affirm the internal, ultimately vertical or hierarchical structuring of the social groups travelling to a pilgrimage shrine. Contemporary Andean pilgrimage enables individuals to attain prestige cargos within their community. Furthermore, these pilgrims, as ritual representatives of their community, identify throughout their journey with their local and hierarchized group and not—as in some models of Christian pilgrimage—with a large, "undifferentiated" mass of pilgrims at a shrine.

Similarly, Sallnow (1981) has shown that modern Andean pilgrimage centers are characterized by manifestations of competition and conflict.

Following Turner (1974c), I contend that the pilgrimage center becomes an arena for the enactment of social drama.

Nowhere is the hierarchical nature of Andean pilgrimage or, in generic terms, Andean religious practice, more evident than in the ceque system of Inca Cuzco. Zuidema (1964, 1983a, 1986) has demonstrated that this system of imaginary lines radiating out from the Temple of the Sun was, in actuality, a spatial, social, religious, calendrical, and political map of the hierarchical organization of the Inca Empire. I would argue, following Zuidema (1964, 1983a, 1986), Shimada (1981a:420-21), and Anders (1986), that the ceque system did not originate with the Incas but rather reached its maximum elaboration with them when it came to be manipulated for imperial purposes. Similarly to the ceque system, the hierarchical relationships among the different Nasca social groups were probably played out in the context of pilgrimage as they came to worship and pay homage at Cahuachi. Local social identities were enhanced at the ceremonial center. During the performance of sacred rites and within the liminality of such a context, structural changes in the hierarchical social organization could occur. The testing and reaffirmation of Nasca social and political organization could, in fact, only occur at Cahuachi, since removed from this context the component members of the larger social groups were in less frequent contact with each other and dispersed over the region. The enactment of religious celebrations at Cahuachi thus constituted political acts and social dramas.

These social dramas and rites may have been actualized in a manner similar to dance in modern-day Andean pilgrimage. Certainly the archaeological record for Nasca abounds with the remains of panpipes, drums, flutes, and the images of elaborately masked and costumed ritual performers. The great Nasca lines marking the pampas to the north and south of Cahuachi were integrally related to the ceremonial center as pilgrimage routes and loci of ritual congregation and dance. The relationship between dance and religious and political acts in the context of pilgrimage is also applicable to the role of many of the Nazca lines:

> Here the religious and social transformation, which was closely related to shifts in political ranking and prestige and was achieved through pilgrimage, was specifically related to this juxtaposition of both movement along a straight line into a sacred precinct and also a spiral or circular movement around that center. (Zuidema 1978)

Through pilgrimage and ritual, early Nasca society was cyclically, periodically, and ephemerally reordered. Each celebration at Cahuachi provided the opportunity for the previous hierarchy to change. The crucial point was the preservation of the hierarchy even if those occupying positions at the top of that hierarchy did not maintain their roles permanently. Personnel may have changed or deliberately rotated but a permanent hierarchy structure surely must have existed. Morinis and Crumrine in this volume (chapter 1) also emphasize that the artistic presentation in pilgrimage performance acts to impress upon the pilgrims the meanings of the activities which are taking place (see also Maquet 1979:30-31).

The public performances at Cahuachi were not just religious acts but also political ones clothed in ritual and embodying Nasca polity's ideology. This represents a major divergence in our ethnographic analogy with a modern-day Catholic pilgrimage center at which communitas and equality are the overt themes.

NOTES

1. The author wishes to thank the National Science Foundation, Social Science Research Council, Fulbright-Hays Act, and the University of Texas at Austin, who funded this research. Field work in Peru was carried out under Resolución Suprema 165-84-ED. The cooperation of the Instituto Nacional de Cultura of Peru and the Museo Nacional de Antropología y Arqueología are gratefully acknowledged. I also wish to give many thanks to my friend and colleague, Miguel Pazos, for his participation in this project.

2. These mounds are natural hills which have been modified through terracing and the addition of adobe walls to become truncated pyramids of varying form. The irregularities of the underlying hills were evened out through the containment of vegetal fiber, dirt, and adobe rubble fills within adobe wall chambers.

3. An *apisonado* is a dirt floor compacted by foot traffic. These are usually made of sand which is smoothed and wet. They become hardened by use and yet break with traffic. *Apisonados* contrast with carefully prepared clay floors which are laid down in layers and become cement hard.

REFERENCES

Anders 1986
Doering 1958
Douglas 1966
Gould 1978
Kramer 1979
Kroeber 1956, n.d.
Lumbreras 1974
Maquet 1979
Mason 1926
Matos Mendieta 1980
Pizarro 1978
Rowe 1963

Sallnow 1981, 1982
Shimada 1981a
Silverman 1983, 1986
Silverman-Pazos n.d.
Strong 1957
Tello-Xesspe 1967
Turner 1974
Turner-Turner 1978
Williams 1980
Williams-Pazos 1974
Zuidema 1964, 1978, 1983a,
    1983b, 1983c, 1986

13

Pilgrim's Progress:
The Emergence of Secular Authority
in a Traditional Andean Pilgrimage

JAMES M. VREELAND, JR.

La religiosidad tradicional es una religiosidad itinernante.
Manuel Marzal

Transhumance, literally movement across the earth, is characteristic of all forms of pilgrimage, and as a process articulates one of the principal themes in the study of Andean societies.[1] By noting the essentially peregrine nature of traditional Andean religiosity, Manuel Marzal (1971:225) implies that pilgrimage has both social and cognitive dimensions, as well as physical parameters. The pilgrim moves through and between places charged with specific cultural attributes, meanings, and shared values. Although the actual sites or points of reference in the transhumant "round" linking *huacas* (sacred places) may shift through time, the fundamental importance of specific geographical regions and ecological zones to a social or ethnic group appears to endure.[2] I believe that it is this commonality in the timing and direction of pilgrimages to *huacas* that demonstrates a basic continuity between past Andean belief systems with contemporary worldviews of members of traditional peasant communities.

The persistence of indigenous cognitive structures was no doubt facilitated to a large degree by the parallel nature of several major concepts of both Hispano-Catholic and native Andean religiosity. I would like to draw attention to two similarities, the symbol of the cross and the cycles of religious festivals tied to a calendar closely related to astronomical, ecological, and telluric phenomena.[3] Several major celebrations of the official state religion of the Inca empire were transformed into Catholic festivals corresponding to a similar ritual performed at about the same time of year. For example, November was, and is, the month of the dead in the indigenous Andean religious calendar, celebrated in the Catholic Church as the Feasts of All Saints and All Souls.[4]

Similarly, the cross, represented in ancient Peru by the constellation of the Southern Cross (see Pachacuti Yamqui 1950:226), survives today as a dominant symbol, having a multiplicity of referents which reappear as the principal images in many traditional rituals throughout the Andes and Central America.[5] Symbol of death and of powerful mountain spirits occupying *huacas*, the cross embodies the indigenous concepts of fertility and abundance, and represents the sympathetic union of male and female deities (Isbell 1978:138; Palomino 1968).

This duality is particularly apparent during the traditional, biannual festivals celebrated in August and February, a time in the Andean world when mountain spirits must be propitiated, sacrifices made to the *huacas* of the common people, and great offerings of gold and silver given to the sun and moon (Huaman Poma 1936:238-39, 250-51). In short, the earth is perceived as being "open" and therefore dangerous; consequently it must be appeased through offerings (Isbell 1978:154-55). I suggest that it is for these reasons that the two major biannual Andean pilgrimages to rural shrines occur in February and August, one to Copacabana on the shores of Lake Titicaca high in the southern Andes, and the other to Motupe, in the coastal desert of northern Peru. Both regions are associated with major traditions of pre-Hispanic pilgrimages which have left abundant evidence in the archaeological records compiled in those areas.[6]

Figure 13.1 Motupe with central road connecting to Cerro Chalpón

THE CROSS OF CHALPON AT MOTUPE

August fifth is the most important day of the year for the residents of the town of Motupe (Figure 13.1), located about 90 kilometers north of Chiclayo, in of the department of Lambayeque, Peru. Hundreds of thousands of pilgrims from all over the Andes journey to a small cave high in a rocky canyon to visit and pay spiritual homage to a gold- and silver-clad wooden cross (Figure 13.2). Once a year, this cross becomes the focus of one of the largest religious festivals in the Americas. But unlike other, much older Catholic pilgrimage shrines, such as those of the Virgin of Guadalupe in Mexico, Lourdes in France, Santiago de Compostella in Spain, and Copacabana in Bolivia, that of the Cross of Chalpón (Cruz de Chalpón) is only 122 years old as of 1990. Yet, second only to the festival of Señor de los Milagros in Lima, the pilgrimage to Motupe is one of the most heavily attended in South America, due in large measure to the long-standing religious importance of the

Figure 13.2 Santísima Cruz del Cerro Chalpón in processional embroidered raiments festooned with silver adornments and filigree arc

region to peoples of the north highlands and coast of Peru. Attributed with miraculous healing, protective, and procreative powers, the Cross of Chalpón also attracts pilgrims seeking cures, advice, miracles, and festival distractions from countries as distant as Japan, the United States, Great Britain, and continental Europe.

As part of a six-year study of the socioeconomic and religious history of the Cross of Chalpón and its biannual celebration, I began visiting Motupe in 1978 to investigate the pilgrimage process that has transformed this once isolated village into a city with several outlying settlements, most of whose inhabitants are engaged, part or full time, in providing essential services to the throngs of pilgrims each year.[7] The following pages are offered as a guide for future research, which will more fully explore the complex relationships between the social, political, historical, and economic aspects of this process. Here I will focus on documenting the demographic and urban growth of the present pilgrimage sites in the district of Motupe, and on tracing the recent history of the festival itself. This ceremonial has culminated with the emergence of a secular, anticlerical festival organization which replaced the ecclesiastical authority that had itself earlier displaced the traditional *mayordomía* or brotherhood association of celebrants organized by the founder of the Cross of Chalpón in 1868.

This pattern of coopting growing cult centers for economic, political, religious, or other reasons is not limited to contemporary cases of conflict between Catholic and secular power groups. Rather, it may also have characterized the Inca domination of the sacred islands of Lake Titicaca, as well as several late prehistoric cases in Central America as described by Adams in chapter 6. The concentration of wealth derived from pilgrims' offerings or tribute to shrine centers may also have provided a mechanism for expanding controls over neighboring polities, much as the great wealth that accrued to medieval pilgrimages enabled their administrators to fortify the shrine center or town in which they lay, to retain knights and servants, and to acquire seignorial rights over adjacent towns and villages (Sumption 1975). In other cases this centralization may have stimulated the initial transformation of the ceremonial center into an administrative capital with a more urban format (see Turner and Turner 1978:25, 234; Wheatley 1971; Fox 1977:39-57). The recent chain of sociopolitical events at Motupe may also provide a useful ethnographic analogy in the study of the processes of evolution that led to the emergence of a secular basis of authority through the manipulation of antecedent belief systems associated with the rural segments of prehistoric stratified societies.

BRIEF HISTORY OF THE CROSS OF CHALPON

As with many religious festivals, the precise origin of the pilgrimage to the Cross of Chalpón is still widely disputed by devotees as well as local historians and cognoscenti. Most sources, however, are more or less in agreement on several important points. The cross was apparently made by a mendicant friar or anchorite sometime during the mid-nineteenth century. Although several apocryphal biographies of the enigmatic friar have been proposed by Church and secular authorities alike, there is no clear evidence of his name or origin.[8] It is said that this recluse descended from solitary meditation in the rocky Chalpón mountain promontory, where he lived, to obtain a few necessities in the neighboring village of Olmos and in Motupe on alternating Saturdays, earning the deepest respect and admiration of residents of both towns. They believed, as tradition has it, that he was endowed with special healing powers, and indeed, with a touch of saintliness.

Then, as mysteriously as he had appeared, the mendicant friar disapeared sometime between 1855 and 1865. Some say that he contracted *uta* (American leishmaniasis), forcing him to return to Lima, where he died in about 1866. Before leaving Motupe he is said to have left a monk's surplice[9] and several notes or verbal messages to the effect that he had made and deposited three crosses on mountain peaks surrounding Motupe, one each on the promontories of Chalpón, Rajada, and Penachí. Tradition also has it that the crosses were to be sought out in times of need or danger, and carried into town for adoration, but always returned again to the places of their original discovery.

Such an event appears to have occurred in 1868, but here accounts diverge. Some hold that it was the German clairvoyant Adolph Falb's prediction of the end of the world in that year that stimulated a search for the cross supposedly left on the side of the Chalpón promontory as a means of avoiding the impending catastrophe.[10] Others, including the account of the only surviving daughter of the cross's eventual discoverer, maintain that it was sought out of devotion to the recluse and to the symbol itself. A third version has it that the cross turned up serendipitously when a handful of draft dodgers hiding in Chalpón's rocky flanks, possibly during José Balta's revolt in Chiclayo that year against the caudillo Prado, stumbled upon it.

But all sources do agree on one point: the cross was found by José Mercedes Anteparra on the fifth of August, 1868, when he was about 26 years old. With some difficulty he retrieved the cross from a small natural rock cave several meters high, located at the top of a steep ravine. Apparently, evidence of a rude bed and stone pillow at the side of the narrow grotto suggested that the hermit monk once inhabited the cave. By tying tree roots together to form a cord, the exuberant Anteparra, assisted by one Rudecindo Ramírez, managed to extract the stout, two-meter-long cross of native *guayacán* (*Tecoma* Sp.) wood, which he carried triumphantly into Motupe, ten kilometers away, through several outlying villages. Twice a year pilgrims carry the cross in a procession from the cave to the plaza of Motupe by way of these same settlements, Guayaquil, Zapote, and Salitral. During the three-day procession, the cross is set up overnight in the villages of Zapote and Salitral, Motupe, in chapels crammed with pilgrims holding candles in memory of those not able to make the pilgrimage that year.[11]

Whether or not most devotees believe that the finding of the cross stayed Falb's predicted cataclysm, my recent investigations show that relatively little attention seems to have been paid either to the cross or its annual procession for many years following its discovery. Anteparra's octogenarian daughter, still of sound mind, recounted the difficulties her father had in finding celebrants and funds for the cross's yearly procession and celebration. He went from house to house soliciting alms and, periodically, other *mayordomos* or principal devotees whose duty it was to help underwrite the main costs of the festival. The earliest surviving photograph of the Cross of Chalpón, taken by E. Brüning in 1907 (see Figure 13.9, Schaedel 1988:174-75 and Vreeland 1989:foto 41),[26] shows relatively few people accompanying the cross back to its grotto following a four-day period of veneration in the church or plaza of Motupe. But by the beginning of the 1920s the cult of the cross seems to have begun a spectacular ascent, for reasons which are not completely known. Today the annual fiesta highlighted by the procession of the cross attracts about one-third of the estimated half million pilgrims who visit the shrine each year (Vreeland 1981b).

DEMOGRAPHIC AND URBAN GROWTH OF A SHRINE CENTER

Motupe and its outlying shrine centers of Salitral, Zapote, and Guayaquil, which lie along the procession route of the Cross of Chalpón from its cave shrine (Figure 13.3) to the town plaza chapel, have experienced a

marked growth, making Motupe (Table 13.1) the largest rural pilgrimage site in South America. Since 1960 an entire village, Zapote, has sprung up at the base of Cerro Chalpón, and another settlement, Guayaquil, is emerging at the foot of the cave shrine. Both of these young settlements are inhabited almost exclusively by families who specialize in providing food, beverages, and a wide variety of *ex votos*, candles, incense, religious medallions, and other paraphernalia, much of which is made locally by artisans, to the streams of pilgrims who climb to the cave shrine.

I suspect that the initial success of the cult of the Cross of Chalpón in the late nineteenth and early 20th centuries is directly linked to the precontact importance of the northern portion of the present-day department of Lambayeque as a major interregional and interethnic pilgrimage center (Shimada 1979, 1981b; Vreeland 1981a). Chalpón, derived from the root *pon*, means "hill" in the indigenous coastal language called Mochica or

Figure 13.3 Grotto shrine clings to the rocky flanks of Cerro Chalpón

Table 13.1 Population series for Motupe district and principal settlements which mark the route of the Cruz de Chalpón in its ceremonial procession from Guayaquil to Zapote, Salitral, and finally to Motupe accompanied by thousands of pilgrims each year.

Census locale	Total	Population		by	Census	Date
	1862	1876[1]	1940	1960	1972	1981
Motupe District	5,715	6,050	8,119	11,831	14,010	16,050
Motupe Town			4,396	5,864	6,702	7,770
Salitral Village			180	140		397
Zapote Village				85		93
Guayaquil Village						26

Sources: Perú, Dirección de Estadística (1878:686 and 1944:85), Perú, Oficina Nacional de Estadística y Censos (1974:60-61). See Castillo (1968:59-60).
[1] Census distributes total population among four races: "Indio" (31%), "Mestizo" (54%), "Blanco" (11.5%), and "Asiático" (0.5%)

Yunga (R. P. Schaedel, personal communication, 1981). It is still associated with an important oral tradition related to the forces of "good" and "evil" (León Barandiarán n.d.:84-85,87-89; Brüning 1922:31, 35).[12]

Scant census data available suggest that the district of Motupe largely grew during the period following World War I through the early 1970s, a period which coincides with the probable major expansion of the cult itself. Not only were numerous miracles recorded during this time, but the opening of the Pan-American highway in the 1930s facilitated travel to the shrine, linked now to the department capitals of Piura and Lambayeque.[13] Automobile travel also shortened the amount of time merchants needed to travel between major traditional pilgrimage sites, which they presently visit according to a precise calendar of annual religious celebrations (Table 13.2). Professional festival *tolderos*, peregrine vendors who sell sweets, crafts, *ex votos*, food, beverages, and other products from portable tents, routinely hire trucks to move from site to site. Table 13.3 gives the number of tents erected in August 1980, a figure which has fluctuated during the past five years. Receipts collected by the municipal authority in the form of rents charged to *tolderos* for setting up their tents, and to itinerant vendors without tents, *ambulantes*, has tripled during the same period.

The greatest range of artisan products and religious paraphernalia assembled anywhere on the north coast of Peru is probably found at the settlement of Guayaquil, located at the edge of a small spring at the foot of the cave shrine. Vendors here are some of the wealthiest in the district and specialize in the sale of *ex votos* in the form of Peru's most popular saints, images of recent Marian or other apparitions, and replicas of other celebrated crosses attributed with miraculous healing powers. One of the

Table 13.2 Preliminary calendar of Hispano-Catholic traditonal north coast festivals

Date	Place	Festival
August 5	Motupe	Cruz de Chalpón
August 25	Olmos	Cruz de Olmos
September 14	Monsefú	Señor Cautivo
September 14	Jaén	Señor de Humantanga
September 24	Paita and Mórrope	Virgin de las Mercedes
October 12	Ayabaca	Señor Cautivo de Ayabaca
October 25	Ferreñafe	Señor de la Justicia, ½ year festival
November 1	Catacaos and Mórrope	Todos los Santos
November 18	Pátapo	San Martin de Porres
November 28	Chongoyape	Santa Catalina
December 8	Guadalupe	Virgin Purísima Concepción
December 25	Cayaltí	Navidad
January 6	Illimo and Mórrope	Los Reyes
January 6	Salas and Monsefú	Los Reyes
January 6	Sullana	Los Reyes
January 22	Eten, Villa	Divino Niño del Milagro, ½ year festival
January 20	Chepen	San Sebastian
February 5	Motupe	Cruz de Chalpón, ½ year festival
February 11	Túcume	La Purísima Concepción
March 14	Monsefú	Señor Cautive, ½ year festival
March 19	San José	San José

April 25	Ferreñafe	Señor de la Justicia
May 15	Various Cooperatives*	Cruz de Mayo and Fatima
June 29-30	Pácora	San Pedro and San Pablo (patrones)
July 22	Eten, Villa	Divino Niño del Milagro
July 28	Monsefú	Fexticum (festival of traditional culture)

Note: These festivals are attended by many professional *tolderos* and *ambulantes* who sell religious paraphernalia, artisan products, food, and beverages at the fair. Many vendors will attend a large number of these festivals each year, when the dates de not overlapp.
* Various Cooperatives; Batan Grande, Calupe, Tuman, etc.

most important items provided are the figures cast or cut into the shapes of over 130 different objects, ranging from body parts to mechanical objects, animals, agricultural plants, homes, farms, and people carrying out a variety of activities. Processed and naturally pigmented cotton is also sold, used by pilgrims who rub the fiber over the cross and carry the cotton along with bundles of *palo santo* (incense sticks), water from the spring, and candles back to home altars (Vreeland 1981b:27).

Table 13.3 Official receipts recorded by concejo for six-year period, during annual and semi-annual festivals, indicating number of lots leased to *tolderos*, receipts from the lots, and receipts from itinerant merchants (*ambulantes*)

	Annual	Festival		Half-Year	Festival	
	Num. lots	*Receipts (lots)*	*Receipts (ambul.)*	*Num. lots*	*Receipts (lots)*	*Total*
1975	241	175,000	8,500	44	21,375	204,875
1976	292	242,327	5,490	54	31,562	279,379
1977	259	232,789	3,230	52	25,300	261,319
1978	184	207,125	10,670	48	52,825	270,620
1979	239	317,896	19,670	40	71,850	409,416
1980	252	466,631	49,740	75	125,900	642,271

Source: Concejo Municipal de Motupe.
Note: Variation in numbers of lots leased partially explained by varying degree of municipal control in registering and collecting rents.

PROFESSIONAL *TOLDEROS* AND PILGRIMS: ESTIMATING THE SCALE OF THE FESTIVAL

During the annual festival celebrated officially from July 25 through August 14, and for a two-week period during the semiannual festival in February, permits are sold to *tolderos* and *ambulantes*, who pay the town council for the space occupied by their tents or for the right to sell their merchandise and services to pilgrims and visitors. Vendors with insufficient funds to install tents will purchase the licenses daily to sell from tabletops, tricycles, or from the street. Their increased mobility allows them to move from settlement to settlement, following the procession of the cross from Chalpón to Motupe's central plaza. *Ambulantes* provide a wide variety of services, such as shoe shining, hair cutting and advice on the use of herbal medicines they sell (Figure 13.4). Similarly, *tolderos* make (Figure 13.5) or sell a large selection of artisan products from places as distant as Puno and Arequipa, in the southern Andes of Peru.

Figure 13.4 Vendors of traditional medicines to sell in Motupe

On the basis of interviews with about 150 *tolderos* and *ambulantes*, town officials, and local historians, I believe that festival sales were relatively less successful in 1980 than in 1979. Overall sales generated by these two types of sellers alone, not counting the permanent residents and merchants of Motupe, I estimate very conservatively to have ranged between 25 and 50 million soles, about U.S.$ 250-500 thousand in 1979, and about 30 percent less in 1980. When adjusted for the rate of inflation, about 80 percent annually, the 1980 figure thus represents a significant decrease in real sales. Shop and restaurant owners who live in Motupe probably grossed at least that much during the three-week festival period alone, and perhaps that much again during the nonfestival weeks of the year.

Estimating the number of pilgrims attending the annual festival is just as difficult a problem as trying to calculate the gross cash receipts. At several intervals during the annual festival in August 1980 and 1981, I counted the number of pilgrims who filed past the cross as it was on display in the chapels of Zapote, Salitral, and in the district church at Motupe (Table 13.4). For a total of four hours, timed in 20-minute inter-

Figure 13.5 Hundreds of thousands of miniature replicas of the Cruz de Chalpón are made by local artisans and sold

vals, groups ranging in size from 46 to 493 persons, including pilgrims carrying infants, were tabulated. Most deposited cash offerings in sealed alms boxes at the foot of the cross, hung *ex votos* from it, and kissed the richly embroidered garments made for the cross by its devotees. Others rubbed wads of cotton over the cross to absorb some of the miracle-working powers for those back home who could not join the pilgrimage that year.

In a sample of 3,096 pilgrims counted at regular intervals during the six-day sample survey, 39 percent were women, 27 percent men, and 34 percent children under about twelve years of age. About 37 percent of a smaller sample of 256 pilgrims hailed from the departments of Piura and Tumbes to the north of the department of Lambayeque, from which latter department 24 percent of the pilgrims came. Eight percent arrived from the adjacent highlands of Cajamarca, seven percent from the department of La Libertad to the south, 15 percent from Lima and Callao, and eight percent from Chimbote, with the remaining one percent from the tropical lowlands to the east and other places (Table 13.5).[14] During the central days of the annual festival, from the second to the sixth of August, some 70 buses, 100 *colectivos*, and 30 microbuses arrived daily from the city of Chiclayo alone, and the normal ten-man police force is augmented to 40.

ALMS AND THE RISE OF SECULAR FESTIVAL AUTHORITY

Figure 13.6 On the steps of the church, members of the secular Comision Multisectorial count pilgrims' offerings, which amounted to over 11,000,000 Peruvian soles in 1980

As in most large Hispano-Catholic pilgrimages, devotees of the Cross of Chalpón deposit offerings of cash and precious metals in alms boxes at the several chapels and shrine site. In Motupe, this practice has led to a bitter struggle between rival ecclesiastical and secular authorities for control over the substantial resources and revenues collected during the year. Cash offerings received during the 1980 annual pilgrimage amounted to approximately seven million soles (Figure 13.6), about U.S.$ 25,000, and another hundred thousand to one million soles were collected each month throughout the rest of that year (Table 13.6). This figure represents a substantial increase over the receipts for 1979, though the Peruvian sol has been devalued heavily on the international money market (Table 13.7). Moreover, these figures indicate an enormous increase over the poorly documented amounts received during the early part of the 20th century, before the church became actively involved in the administration of the festival and cult of the Cross of Chalpón.

My interviews indicate that for the first 53 years following the discovery of the cross by José Mercedes Anteparra in 1868, the local curate of Motupe played a minor role in the cult that slowly grew at the shrine at Cerro Chalpón and the annual pilgrimage of the cross to the town. Apparently, during much of this first phase of the cult the cross was worshipped in its cave and annually in the plaza of Motupe, but was not taken inside the church, at least initially. During these early years Anteparra, as *mayordomo*, had some difficulties in finding devotees and contributors for the yearly celebration marking his finding of the cross.[15] Several sources agree that at one point he fashioned a small replica of the cross from a piece of wood cut from its base that was carried to district settlements and later to adjacent provinces, where devotees contributed offerings to the cult to maintain the festival celebration.[16]

Table 13.4 Rate of flow of pilgrims past the Cross of Chalpón during its adoration in chapels listed by place, date, and time of day

Place	Date	Time (P.M.)	Female	Male	Children	Total	Pilgrims / minute
Zapote	2/8/81	6:05-6:25	32	19	31	82	4.1
		6:25-6:45	23	5	18	46	2.3
Salitral	3/8/81	6:10-6:30	54	39	51	144	7.2
		6:30-6:50	48	39	43	130	6.5
Motupe	4/8/80	10:00-10:20	89	71	67	227	11.4
		10:20-10:40	72	72	74	218	10.9
Motupe	5/8/81	5:55-6:15	179	151	134	464	23.2
		6:15-6:35	193	111	155	459	23.0
Motupe	5/8/80	5:30-5:50	182	115	140	437	21.9
		5:50-6:10	218	110	165	493	24.7
Motupe	7/8/80	6:50-7:10	58	54	100	212	10.6
		7:10-7:30	59	53	72	184	9.2
Totals			1207	839	1050	3096	12.9
Percent			39	27	34	100	

Note: Number of pilgrims recorded in units of 20 minutes, and differentiated by sex and age. "Children" are identified only by approximate age of twelve years or younger. The sample covers the first four "central days" of the crosses procession from the cave to Motupe. The times chosen were arbitrary, but more or less consistently selected in afternoon and evening.

By the end of the third decade of this century, sufficient income had been established on a regular basis to enable the Anteparra family to obtain a crown, two chasubles, a set of candelabras, and *contoneras* or cross arm end festoons, all made of solid silver (Figure 13.2). These decorations were placed on the cross during its traditional processions to Motupe, and kept at other times with the treasurer of the *mayordomía* controlled by the Anteparra family. A few years after Anteparra's death, his son, who continued the cult of the cross, had it covered with flat bands of silver and gold to protect the wood from pilgrims' candles, which had twice burned the base of the venerated icon.

Much of the precious metal used to decorate the cross derived from silver and gold *ex votos* bestowed on it by pilgrims during the August celebration and procession, which clearly had expanded in scale during the 1920-30s. By 1934, the "grand festival in honor of the most miraculous and saintly

Table 13.5 Number of pilgrims from different towns, listed by departments

Piura & Tumbes	37%	Lambayeque	24%	Cajamarca	8%
Catacaos	2	Cayaltí	2	Bambamarca	1
Chulucanas	19	Chiclayo	29	Cajamarca	9
La Matanza	5	Colaya	1	Combayo	4
La Unión	2	Ferreñafe	3	Cutervo	2
Máncora	1	Jayanca	3	Huambos	1
Morropón	8	Lambayeque	1	Lives	1
Paita	10	Motupe	3	Jaén	2
Piura	12	Niepos	2		
Sechura	17	Pátapo	1		
Sullana	7	Pimentel	3		
Talara	6	Pomalca	1		
Tumbes	4	Pucala	1		
Vicús	2	Reque	2		
		San José	1		
		San Pedro de Lloc	3		
		Tumán	2		
		Udima	3		
Total	95		61		20

La Libertad	7%	Other	24%
Chepen	4	Lima	38
Pacasmayo	8	Callao	1
Trujillo	6	Chimbote	20
		Bagua	1
		Huacho	1
		Arequipa	1
Total	18		62

Note: The sample survey of 256 pilgrims was recorded as they were leaving the chapel at Salitral, about 2:00 P.M. August 4, 1980, when the cross was temporarily on display there.

Table 13.6 Official records of receipts and expenditures for year 1980 of Comisión Multi-sectorial. Receipts include cash offerings plus sale of spent wax and *ex votos* in months marked with *. Offerings comprise those made in the cave shrine, various chapels, and town church

Month	Receipts	Expenses	Balance
January	24,300	959,850	
February	657,400	1,407,085	
March	256,590	145,936	
April	—	59,974	
May	109,500	128,462	
June	173,000	141,253	
July	980,280	650,781	
August	*6,997,150	4,052,881	
September	*1,245,000	372,497	
October	544,500	654,527	
November	290,000	292,681	
December	183,250	234,449	
Total (in Soles)	11,460,970	9,100,376	2,360,594

Source: Comisión Multisectorial "Cruz de Chalpón"
Note: Amounts given in Peruvian *soles*, when about 350 *soles* equalled U.S. $1.00

Cross of Cerro Chalpón of Motupe," as publicity of that year advertised, had become one of the largest on the north coast.[17]

Interestingly, Anteparra himself rose only briefly to a position of prestige in the local civil hierarchy, achieving the title of governor about 1907 or 1908 for one term. He probably never held significant political influence or wealth in the district. In this light it is also interesting that, although he was reported to have been trained as a surgeon in the army, his real notoriety was as a curer using traditional medicine. Today, replicas of the Cross of Chalpón figure prominently in the *mesas* or arrangements of ritual objects used by north coast *curanderos* (Rodríguez 1975:183), one of whom made a sizable contribution of cash to the 1980 annual festival.

Although Anteparra reportedly did keep records of receipts and expenditures, I was unable to locate them, except for one note that in 1920, 80 Peruvian pounds (Lp 80.0.00) were spent and some 50 pounds of silver and two pounds of gold ex votos were collected at the termination of the annual pilgrimage festival (Bachmann 1921:357). Control over the collection and distribution of the revenues and the precious metals seems to have resided exclusively in the hands of the founder and his family. The only palpable

Table 13.7 Annual balance sheet listing major sources of receipts and expenditures, the official records, Comisión Multisectorial "Cruz de Chalpón", since its formation in November 1972

YEAR	RECEIPTS				
	Alms	Wax	Ex Votos	Other	Total
1972[1]					
1973[2]	2,764,915.01	32,817.00	59,880.00		2,857,612.01
1974[3]	287,560.00	6,930.00	6,900.00		301,390.00
1974					
1975	3,399,469.20	32,400.00	58,715.00	466,268.10	3,956,852.30
1976	3,649,030.00	81,120.00	92,160.50	54,439.00	3,876,749.50
1977					5,777,550.00
1978[7]				2,146,000.00	
1979[8]	6,305,405.00	105,700.00	95,700.00	305,000.00	6,811,805.00
1980	10,668,970.00	720,000.00	72,000.00		11,460,970.00

YEAR	EXPENDITURES			BALANCE
	Festival	Other	Total	Balance
1972				140,786.14
1973	206,897.00	590,196.00	797,093.16	2,060,518.85
1974	122,924.00[4]	1,577,168.12	1,700,092.12	(1,398,702.12)[5]
1974[6]				(114,345.00)
1975			3,207,588.70	749,263.60
1976	754,725.20	3,304,728.00	4,059,453.20	(182,703.70)
1977	1,010,400.00	663,500.00	1,673,900.00	4,133,650.00
1978				
1979	1,627,272.50	1,326,377.00	2,953,649.50	3,858,155.50
1980	1,751,400.00	7,348,976.00	9,100,376.00	2,360,594.00

Source: Comisión Multisectorial "Cruz de Chalpón", and José Toscanelli Falla.
Notes: Amounts given in Peruvian *soles* whose value against the U.S. dollar decreased markedly over period recorded. Approximately 43 *soles* equalled U.S. $1.00 in 1972, and 350 *soles* in 1980. "Alms" includes only recorded cash offerings made by pilgrims annually; "wax" represents the receipts from sale of spent candles sold in bulk to candle makers; "ex votos" represents sale of *milagros* and other nonprecious metalic religious paraphernalia given by pilgrims to the Cross, and later sold by the kilogram to vendors of ex votos; "other" indicates sources of diverse nature, including sale of precious metals. Note that data are uneven and incomplete in many cases.

[1] recorded for 22 November to 30 December, 1972.
[2] recorded from May through December, 1973.
[3] recorded from January through May, 1974.
[4] half-year festival expenditures.
[5] figures in parentheses indicate deficits.
[6] figure recorded as balance at end of year, as deficit.
[7] receipts from sale of gold and silver ex votos.
[8] recorded for 14 July through 31 October, 1979.

role played by the parish priest during this phase of the cult seems to have been to perform daily masses while the cross was on display in Motupe, and to use the occasion to preach to the assembled pilgrims, who, according to one eyewitness, hardly listened to or understood the sermons of the curate (Bachmann 1921:354). No doubt the priest was paid for saying masses during the celebrations, but it seems unlikely that he received a percentage of the offerings collected.

Following Anteparra's death in 1921, his son and widow continued to control the traditional *mayordomía* structure with some rotation of the principal celebrant, or *mayordomo*, who apparently was picked by the Anteparra family. The traditional features of the pilgrimage and festival procession also continued, and additional luxurious, embroidered garments, often embellished with threads of precious metals, and a finely carved wooden litter were made for the cross. Money derived from the sale of *ex votos* and spent wax collected in the shrine helped pay for these items. But more important, the revenues also subsidized the following year's annual and later, half-year festivals. Bands of musicians, traditional dancers (including *diablicos*), *globos aerostáticos*, horse races, cock fights, fireworks displays by none other than the famous pyrotechnic Juan Sin Miedo, food and drink for many pilgrims, temporary lodging in the nave of the church and other places, program printing, publicity, incense and candles, prayers for the masses said by the curate, and institutional reciprocity owed by any *mayordomo* of a traditional Andean festival, all had to be arranged and financed. Indeed, the reveling, commercial hubbub, and carnival-like atmosphere in this rural setting very much resembled descriptions of medieval pilgrimages in Catholic Europe and the Islamic world (Sumption 1975:211; Turner and Turner 1978:36). By the mid-1930s, the entry of the cross in procession at the outskirts of the town of Motupe was greeted by civil authorities, regiments of school children, and the parish priest himself, whose influence over the festival was beginning to take a sharper focus about this time.

The district church was described as filled to capacity when the cross was installed there for adoration on the eve of the principal festival day, the fifth of August (León Barandiarán and Paredes 1934:341-45). The role of the Church was brought directly into question in 1937 when an aristocratic woman from Lambayeque, herself a pilgrim, initiated a local power struggle between the curate and the *mayordomía*, still largely controlled by the Anteparra family. She obtained the backing of the bishop of Trujillo as Motupe then pertained to the diocese of Trujillo. Her goal was to wrest control of the cross from the family in favor of an administrative committee made up of influential Motupe families and the priest, with herself appointed as president. That she was able to effect this administrative transformation only briefly was mainly due to what was considered by the community to be inappropriately aggressive behavior on the part of a woman. In any case, her influence was not strong enough to change the ritual format of the festival, which she had desired to reduce drastically in scale.

Probably sensing the weakness of this new committee, the bishop sent a new priest to Motupe later in 1937 to assume charge of the matter, forcing the all-female committee members to resign before they could actually conduct one of the festivals. A new, all-male *mayordomía* consisting of eight persons was then installed under more direct control of the curate, who began to exercise a central role in the administration and organization of the cult of the Cross of Chalpón. During this period the cave shrine was substantially expanded and "Christianized," with the addition of an atrium, a side chapel of concrete and permanent steps leading to this ample space, which would accommodate the throngs of pilgrims wishing to adore the cross in its shrine and where the priest could now properly say Mass (Figure 13.3). The church in Motupe was also refurbished, and a special chapel was constructed adjacent to it where the cross could be displayed

Figure 13.7 Adoration of the Cross in an open chapel-like tent set up outside the church on Motupe's central plaza, filled with pilgrims and vendors' stalls. Church policy presently prohibits giving mass here

during the annual and half-year festivals (Figure 13.7). By the 1960s, "election" to fill one of the positions of the *mayordomía* meant considerable benefits for secular community members. The term of office generally was about four years and all members were in fact selected by the curate, who presided as permanent president; the oath of office was administered by a vicar sent to Motupe by the bishop for this purpose (Figure 13.8).[18]

Figure 13.8 Bishop and curate of Motupe surrounded by Catholic clergy invited to celebrate the annual festival of the Cross in the mid 1960s

The first serious threat to the ecclesiastical authority over the cult of the Cross of Chalpón did not occur until the national revolution of 1968 drastically altered political consciousness and organization at the grass-roots level throughout much of the north coast of Peru. In 1969, a group of university students from Motupe, supported by its mayor, began to influence public opinion in favor of investing revenues from the cult of the cross in public works projects instead of traditional festival activities, considered to be frivolous and outdated. They also called for a public accounting by the priest of the offerings made by pilgrims. In 1971, town leaders consolidated various dissident groups into a civic association called the Frente Cívico dedicated to the general progress and modernization of Motupe as a political and economic center commensurate with its official urban status in the province of Lambayeque. On November 22, 1972, the president of the Frente Cívico and also the town's mayor, in the name of Motupe's citizens, confronted the vicar who had come with an ecclesiastical delegation sent by the bishop to swear in a new *mayordomía* committee that had just been formed by the local parish priest. Then, most of the members of the committee were from conservative Motupe families or were friends of the priest, but it did not include any of the local civil authorities.

A postponement of the oath-taking ceremony of the *mayordomía* was obtained from the bishop, who agreed to permit a local alternative body, the Comisión Reorganizadora, or reorganizing committee, headed by the town's mayor, to administer the festival for a trial period of six months.[19] With the begrudging collaboration of the priest, the popular Comisión Reorganizadora organized and celebrated the half-year festival in February 1973, after which revenues amounting to about 150,000 Peruvian soles remained after all expenditures were liquidated. Despite the bishop's explicit orders to deposit the excess funds in a bank account established for this purpose previously in Chiclayo, which had just become the seat of the new diocese including Lambayeque, the Comisión voted to use the money to finish a potable and waste water project in Motupe. This conflict between Church and civil authorities rapidly came to a head when the bishop rejected this proposal outright and ordered the local priest to withdraw permanently from his parish on May 9, 1973. It was subsequently left vacant for two years and then all classes of religious services requiring a Catholic priest were suspended.[20]

Following the collapse of ecclesiastical authority over the cross, the mayor and president of the Comisión invited representatives of all district institutions to name members to a new public association for the administration of the festival. The Comisión Multisectorial "Cruz de Chalpón" was thus constituted on May 14, 1973, with the mayor again named as president, and some 200 townspeople participating as voting members.[21] Several members of the directorate formed to head the new Comisión Multisectorial included individuals with strongly leftist political ideology. Some of these members, including the vice-president, began to take an increasingly active role in the Comisión Multisectorial, which led to the gradual resignation of the more conservative committee members. At the end of 1974 the mayor himself resigned and the vice-president assumed the role of president. Since then the Comisión has identified with the Marxist FOCEP party, but in practice appears to operate with a mix of populism and opportunism. Although in theory anyone is eligible to join the Comisión, a small group of leaders essentially limits enrollment and makes all decisions privately for the allocation of revenues, without an explicit budget open to public scrutiny. Irregularly issued official statements provide general figures regarding receipts and expenditures, but appear to many townspeople and others not to reflect accurately the actual cash flow and operating costs or how the public disbursements are actually made (Tables 13.6, 13.7, and Figure 13.6).

In protest against the clearly anticlerical position of the Comisión Multisectorial, a group of conservative family heads, with the advisory help and support of the bishop later in 1974 formed the Comunidad Cristiana de Base, a Christian community association whose members favored a return to the previous ecclesiastical structure for administering the cult activities. At the same time, members inveighed against the Comisión for having brought about the suspension of religious services in the parish. Two years later, when the bishop reinstalled a priest at Motupe, the Comunidad Cristiana de Base lost its popular base, causing many of the critics of the Comisión Multisectorial to fall temporarily silent. Still ardently opposed to the Comisión's control of the cult and its revenues, the bishop of Chiclayo continues to recall the local priest during the entire three-week festival at Motupe so that ecclesiastical sanction of the procession and the cross's manipulation by the Comisión is forcefully denied.[22] The fact that most Motupanos and pilgrims alike have tolerated not having an officiating curate and religious services for nine years is probably due to the fact that the priest was never an indispensible component of the Chalpón Cross cult itself, centered largely in the cave shrine outside the city limits of Motupe.

By the mid-1970s, the Comisión Multisectorial had consolidated its control over the celebration of the annual and half-year festivals and had begun dispensing revenues to underwrite a modest program of public works projects, generally centered around the district capital itself. Some of the projects included expensive street paving, a school house, and later church roof replacements, medical and funeral subsidies for the poor, and subsidies for the purchase of school supplies. By 1980 the leaders of the Comisión had emerged as the most powerful civil authorities in the city of Motupe, threatening the autonomy of the town council and calling stridently for the resignation of its mayor in a series of newspaper articles published in the major department daily during the 1980 annual pilgrimage.[23] Effective journalists and orators, some of the leaders have managed to win, or purchase, legal and political support for the reform program outside Motupe (see Gastulo n.d.; Falla n.d.; Motupe 1979-80; and Multivoz 1980-81). Using radio, a public address system, and locally produced pamphlets, leaders have attacked social problems as well as their political adversaries and have mounted a public campaign aimed at reducing speculation in basic food stuffs, lessening fares on public transportation, and demanding that the town council disinfect the city streets after each festival.

By 1981, following the sudden death of its president (an event thought by conservative townspeople to reflect some sort of divine castigation of its principal antagonist), a palpable challenge to the nearly total authority of the Comisión Multisectorial in administering the pilgrimage activities and distributing their revenues for progressive public works began to take shape from scattered but sizable segments of the community. The Comisión has recently been roundly accused of mismanaging the revenues and outright theft of them by some critics. Official statements and records prepared by the Comisión do little at present to counter the rising tide of popular criticism aimed at the principle members of that body. The present mayor, elected in 1981 by popular vote, has begun an investigation of the Comisión and has brought suit against it in civil court in Chiclayo, charging that it does not represent the town as a corporate body because elected public officials had withdrawn from it in 1974.

SECULAR AUTHORITY VERSUS TRADITIONAL BELIEF

Perhaps the most serious accusation levelled at the Comisión concerns the obvious lack of sincerity and devotion with which its leaders celebrate the festivals of the cross twice yearly. Many of my informants voiced serious complaints that the Comisión, with its obvious political affiliation, paid too little or no attention to the maintenance of the cult of the cross as it had traditionally been celebrated. Specifically, these people, many of them part-time vendors of *ex votos* and services to pilgrims, but all also devotees of the cult, are less interested in hearing rhetoric about progress and social consciousness than in ensuring a proper procession, punctuated with the cadence of first-class regional festival bands, fireworks displays, and traditional dancers during the pilgrimage celebrations. They are less concerned with paving Motupe's streets and shoring up its school roofs than with maintaining the road from Motupe to Zapote and the steep path and stairway to the atrium and side chapel of the cave shrine.[24] Furthermore, these and other pilgrims aware of the political turmoil in Motupe feel that the prestige of the Cross of Chalpón will continue to suffer if cuts in expenditures for traditional festival activities are systematically sought in order to divert the offerings made to the cross to secular ends, most of which are of no benefit to the hundreds of thousands of pilgrims who flock to the shrine each year.[25]

In conclusion, I hardly need to emphasize the paradoxical situation one finds today in Motupe. Here one of the largest rural pilgrimage festivals in South America is administered by a purportedly Marxist body that was not popularly elected nor representative of any religious belief system, and is publicly committed to a radical community program of social and material improvements that are of little or no direct interest to the "real owners" of the cult of the Cross of Chalpón—the pilgrims themselves. Nevertheless, I feel that devout believers in the curative, miracle-working, apotropaic, even salvationist powers of the Cross of Chalpón will continue to visit the shrine despite the current policy of redistributing the cross's revenues for nontraditional purposes. Through the mechanism of an internationally renowned religious pilgrimage and popular festival to an historically important center on the north coast of Peru, many ethnic, political, and economic boundaries have been crossed, uniting literally hundreds of thousands of pilgrims in a shared belief system.

Disregard for the traditional values surrounding the maintenance of this pilgrimage center has not seemed to have appreciably alienated many regular pilgrims from visiting Motupe. Resisting the intensifying secular stratification pattern, some pilgrims, however, have now begun to gravitate toward neighboring pilgrimage shrines such as the relatively young site centered on the Cross of Olmos, located on the opposite side of Cerro Chalpón and celebrated in the latter part of August. The prestige and attraction of the cult focused currently at Motupe will not, I think, suffer for this reason alone, but failure on the part of the present Comisión Multisectorial's leaders to recognize the nature of coastal pilgrimages will lead to the erosion of the economic base which supports the public works programs, that is, the offerings of the pilgrims. Nor has the absence of a parish priest during the celebrations since 1973 significantly dampened the enthusiasm of the devotees of the cross. They will continue to come to this and other major shrines to seek cures and miracles and to make collective offerings to ensure the continuity of their shared belief system.

Associated with a pre-Hispanic sacred place, the cross's location in an unorthodox setting by usual Catholic standards, in a cave, further highlights the paradigmatic nature of the cult of the Cross of Chalpón, which is firmly rooted in a traditional, precontact Andean matrix. Despite secular and clerical efforts over the years to coopt and reorient the cult and its economic benefits, the tradition of the multiethnic, interregional pilgrimage will probably continue as it has for centuries. This pattern involves one traditional pilgrimage site rising only to be eclipsed later by another in a pattern long established on the north coast of Peru.

POSTSCRIPT

Following the democratic elections in 1981, a confrontation between ranking members of the Comisión Multisectorial and regionally appointed officials of the ruling Acción Popular political party resulted in the alliance between the *concejo* (town council), largely composed of opposition Aprista party members, and Comisión leaders. The Comisión felt its interests would be better served sharing control over the cross rather than facing its possible loss in a direct struggle with the dominant party's departmental and ecclesiastical authorities. As a result, the *alcalde* (mayor) and three councilmen took the four most important positions in the hierarchy of the Comisión, which presently functions largely as a dependency of the municipal government. Moderately progressive and determined to win back the support of the Church in celebrating the annual and semiannual festivals, the new Comisión's major project at the time of this writing is the construction of a public fairground at the edge of the city. Here future festivals are to be held, much to the distress of the *tolderos* and *ambulantes*, who perceive the move as highly detrimental to their traditional businesses providing food, beverages, artisan products, and religious paraphernalia to the hundreds of thousands of north coast pilgrims coming to Cerro Chalpón.

Figure 13.9 Adoration of The Cruz de Chalpon on the steps of the Motupe church altar, August 1907

NOTES

1. The concept of transhumance has been explored to great advantage by Professor Long from both anthropological and historical perspectives. Turner and Turner (1978:1-39) also emphasize the process of movement, but from the point of view of the individual as a kind of liminoid phenomenon in which the pilgrimage constitutes a rite of passage.

2. Regular movement of people through closely spaced ecological zones is central to the principal of "vertical control" of multiple resource niches by a single ethnic group. This distinctly Andean social innovation may have evolved from an antecedent and more universal pattern of hunter-gatherer transhumance linking the coast with the highlands in post-Pleistocene times. See Lynch (1971), Murra (1972) and Bonnier et Rosenberg (n.d.)

3. See recent ethnographic studies by Isbell (1978), Bastien (1978), Fonseca (1974) and Guillet (1978:92-93). Crumrine (this volume, 1977) contrasts slightly different ritual patterns which characterize northwest Mexican and north coast Peruvian traditional pilgrimage festivals in terms of ecological and historical factors. See also Marzal (1971) and Sallnow (1974). Reina (1969:130-31) presents a similar interdigitation between Indian and Catholic feast days for the eastern highlands of Guatemala.

4. In his treatment of death and the dead in the pilgrimage process, Turner (1975:112-22) argues that the Christian cult of the dead united Galician and Asturian beliefs of this type with the Aztec precontact ritual Day of the Dead. Similarly, in both Catholic and Andean theological thought, at the folk and formal levels, the dead can spiritually influence the living in matters regarding health, fertility, and well-being.

5. See Albó (1974), Bastien (1978:69), Bowman (1924:fig.7), Gillin (1947:111), Isbell (1978:60, 138, 207), Linares Málaga (1978:375, fig. 1), Mariscotti de Görlitz (1978:419 ff.), Sivirichi (1930:248, fig. 81), Sabogal Dieguez (1956:31-35), Laughlin (1969:177), Aveni, Hartung, & Buckingham (1978), Urton (1981, 1982), Zuidema & Urton (1976), Straub Ch.9.

6. The Inca pilgrimage to the islands of the Sun and Koati on Lake Titicaca adjacent to the colonial and contemporary pilgrimage center at Copacabana, is described by Bandelier (1910), who excavated several sites there. He also interpreted the architectural and burial remains based on his reading of several chroniclers. See Cieza de Leon, 1553, chap. 103 (1947:445), Ramos Gavilán, 1621 (1976), and Cobo, 1653, book 13, chap. xcii (1964:192-93), and the sketch maps of Rivero and Tschudi, 1854 (1971), Squire (1877) and Wiener (1880), which I have summarized and reinterpreted briefly (Vreeland 1980a) with a new map of one of the principal structures. See also Urteaga (1914:135) and Portugal and Ibarra Grasso (1957). MacCormack (1984) presents a masterful synthesis and analysis of the events surrounding the emergence of the early postconquest cult at Copacabana itself.

The massive pyramid complexes in the Batán Grande-La Leche area immediately to the south of Motupe served as a major New World pilgrimage center from perhaps as early as 1300 BC. The Batán Grande sites achieved their most intensive occupation during the classic Lambayeque times, ca. 900-1250, when the shrines served principally as the foci for rituals associated with the burials of high-status individuals, accompanied by staggering quantities of precious metals and other mortuary offerings (see Shimada 1979, 1981b; Vreeland 1981a). The contemporary importance of pilgrimage to adjacent highland lakes by traditional coastal *curanderos* is pointed out by Sharon (1978).

The best-described archaeological pilgrimage site in ancient Peru is Pachacamac, a pre-Hispanic city near modern Lima, thought to have contained architectural and other features for pilgrims who came there to consult a famous oracle. Ethnohistoric references include those of Pizarro, 1571 (1938), Jérez, 1534 (1938), Estete (in Jérez 1938:339), and Cobo, 1653 (1964). Much of the ethnohistoric evidence suggesting pilgrimage is summarized by Uhle (1903:97-98); see also Hrdlicka (1911:6), Lorente (1860:209), Mariscotti de Görlitz (1978:81), Tello (1943), and Urteaga (1914:13-14).

7. Support for this study has been provided by the Inter-American Foundation of Rosslyn, Virginia, and the University of Texas at Austin. My special thanks are extended to the Cervecería del Norte and Gerd Arens, Gerente General, and to the *familia* Aimoto, Motupe, for their generous hospitality. I would also like to thank past mayor Hernán García Laines, current mayor José Cristiansen Chu, the municipal office staff, and the many members of the Comisión Multisectorial "Cruz de Chalpón" for their assistance. My principal informants and friends deserve more than a note of thanks for their help: Walter Alva, Alicia Anteparra, Víctor Raul Gastulo Calvay, Angélica León Adrianzén, José Mirenghi, Raul Morante, Sebastian Morante, Nancy Kaufman, Gregorio Saavedra, José Toscanelli Falla, and especially Dr. Richard P. Schaedel, as well as the many *tolderos* and pilgrims with whom I journeyed to Motupe.

8. Although several elaborate biographies of this enigmatic individual have been proposed by Church and secular historians alike, there is no clear evidence of his name or origin. Popular wisdom has it that he was known as "Padre Guatemala," after the region from whence he is supposed to have emigrated. Others refer to him as Friar Juan Agustín de Abad or Juan Ramón Rojas. Still others, whom I am inclined to believe, insist that no one ever surely knew the name of the cross maker during his years as a pilgrim-recluse, when he was referred to simply as "El Hermitaño."

Popular historical accounts of the cross and its maker include one by a native son of Motupe, Castillo (1967). One can also consult the shorter contributions by Bachmann (1921), Brüning (1922), Castillo (1968), Falla Failoc (n.d.), Gastulo Calvay (n.d.), León Barandiarán and Paredes (1934), Vreeland (1981b), and Anonymous (1940). The recent articles in *La Voz de Motupe* and *Multivoz* (1980-81), and several short pamphlets and booklets sold during the festivals in Motupe (Anonymous n.d.a, n.d.b, n.d.c) reflect the constantly changing "official" history of the cult.

9. Don Angélica León Adrianzén of Motupe showed me this garment, a simple brown plain-weave linen fabric which was obtained by her aunt from a resident of Olmos years ago, and appears to belong to the religious Order of San Diego.

10. The circumstances of this event, if true, indicate that the genesis of the shrine site and development of the ensuing pilgrimage parallel Kubler's (1985:313) description of pre-Columbian Mesoamerican pilgrimages as "collective endeavors for guaranteeing the continuity of the creation of the universe against catastrophic dissolution in an unstable world."

11. The "brother" or twin cross of Penachí was found sometime later, while that of Rajada Peak is said to have been spotted at the bottom of a deep ravine where it had supposedly come to rest after slipping from the hands of its maker, presumably the same mysterious friar, over a century ago.

12. An Inca captain remained at Motupe to greet Pizarro as he and a small advance band worked their way south toward Cajamarca (Jérez [1534] 1938 T. II:213; Castillo 1968:158). See also the references to pilgrimages in the region given in note 6.

13. *Libelli miraculorum*, or collections of miracle stories appear in Anonymous (1940), Anonymous (n.d.b, n.d.c), Castillo (1967), and León Barandiarán and Paredes (1934:431-37). A similar spurt in the growth of the pilgrimage to Limoges, center of the cult of Saint Leonard, who "began to corruscate in miracles around 1017" (Sumption 1975:116), not only stemmed from the spread of news of these miracles, but also because Limoges lay on one of the principal roads leading to the great Galician sanctuary of Santiago. The Maya pilgrimage site of Cozumel rose in part due to trade (Kubler 1985:314-15).

14. Percentages of pilgrims and the places of their origin will vary according to the day a sample is taken and the time of day selected for measurement. The later census, of 256 persons, was taken in Salitral at about 2:00 P.M., 4 August 1980, while the cross was temporarily on display there during its procession to Motupe.

15. Whether Anteparra was designated or, more likely, simply assumed the role of *mayordomo* or chief steward of the cross, it does seem that he performed this role nearly without interruption and without significant challenge until his death in 1921.

16. Despite periodic attempts to carry the Cross of Chalpón to neighboring cities for worship, it has never left its traditional setting in the cave except for the biannual processions to Motupe, and when heavy rains threatened to flood the town in 1972 and 1983 (Falla Failoc n.d.:8). The replica was, however, carried as far south as Lambayeque, although no information regarding its travel to the north, toward Olmos and Piura, is available. Nevertheless, all sources agree that Anteparra died a poor man. In traditional fashion, it appears that he did not personally enrich himself by the revenues collected, but used them instead to redistribute to the faithful through what Wolf designated the "ceremonial fund."

17. The pilgrimage surpassed in scale the traditional festival of Santa Cruz in Motupe itself, and also those of the larger festivals of La Purísima in Chiclayo, El Cautivo in Monsefú, San Pedro and San Pablo in Pacora, and of the *capilla* (chapel) of the Divino Niño del Milagro in Eten (Bachmann 1921:347-59; León Barandiarán and Paredes 1934:341-45). The rise in popularity of the festival under an essentially traditional *mayordomía* system thus occurred before ecclesiastical authorities assumed control over the biannual cult.

18. Members of the *mayordomía* included the *presidente* (priest), *vice presidente*, *secretario*, *pro-secretario*, *tesorero*, *fiscal*, and two *vocales*.

19. Serving also were the *gobernador*, *juez de paz*, and head of the district school.

20. Motupe had to solicit or participate in religious services provided in the neighboring districts of Olmos and Jayanca.

21. The organization of the Comisión Multisectorial consists of the *presidente*, *vice presidente*, *secretario*, *tesorero*, *pro-tesorero*, *fiscal*, *adjunto fiscal*, and some 200 *vocales*. The public institutions represented at the open town meeting were those of provincial government, justice of the peace, public welfare, ministry of agriculture, Banco de la Nación, sports institutions, and associations of household heads.

22. Similar community-initiated attempts to gain control of receipts from other traditional religious pilgrimage festivals at Monsefú and at Eten collapsed about six months after Church authorities suspended religious services there. Civil authorities, acting under popular pressure, were forced to solicit the bishop for reinstatement of the parish priests.

23. The president of the Comisión Multisectorial in 1980 was also the president of the Comunidad Campesino "San Julián de Motupe," a peasant corporation with political and territorial autonomy.

24. When torrential rains threatened to flood Motupe in 1972, not only was the cross brought down to the district church to protect the town and its citizens, but community members also joined together to repair the path and stairway to the cave shrine, both heavily damaged by the flooding. Perhaps it is more than coincidental that later that same year administration of the cult passed into the hands of the community, headed by its mayor.

25. The difficulty in accounting for the balance of offerings is compounded by the nature of the alms given today. During the earlier phases of the cult, most offerings consisted of *ex votos* and other religious objects, many of precious metal. Few such offerings occur today, while the great majority of offerings consists of cash deposited in alms boxes placed at the foot of the Cross.

26. This photograph, Figure 13.9, take by the German ethnologist and historian Heinrich Brüning, was found in the Museo für Völkerkunde, Hamburg, and made available to me by Richard P Schaedel (see Schaedel 1988:174-75 and Vreeland 1989:foto 41).

REFERENCES

Albo 1974
Anonymous 1940, n.d.a,
  n.d.b, n.d.c
Aveni-Buckingham 1978
Bachmann 1921
Bandalier 1910
Bastien 1978
Bonnier and Rosenberg, n.d.
Bowman 1924
Brüning 1922
Castillo Nino 1967, 1968
Cieza De Leon 1947
Cobo 1964
Crumrine 1977b
Direccion De Estadistica 1878
Direccion Nacional De
  Estadistica 1944
Empresa Nacional De
  Turismo 1970
Estete 1938
Falla Failoc 1980/n.d.
Fonseca Martel 1974
Fox 1977
Gastulo Calvay n.d.
Gillin 1947
Guaman Poma de Ayala 1936
Guillet 1978
Hrdlic'ka 1911
Isbell 1978
Jérez 1938
Kubler 1985
Laughlin 1969
León Barandiaran n.d.
León Barandiaran-Paredes 1934

Linares Málaga 1978
Lorente 1860
Lynch 1971
MacCormack 1984
Mariscotti de Gorlitz 1978
Marzal 1971
Motupe 1979
Multivoz 1980
Murra 1972
Onec 1974
Osvaldo 1974
Pachacuti Yamqui 1950
Palomino Flores 1968
Pizarro 1938
Portugal-Grasso 1957
Ramos Gavilan 1976
Reina 1969
Rivero-Tschudi 1971
Rodriguez Suy Suy 1975
Sabogal Dieguez 1956
Sallnow 1974
Schaedel 1988
Sharon 1978
Shimada 1979, 1981b
Sivirichi 1930
Squire 1877
Sumption 1975
Tello 1943
Turner 1975
Turner-Turner 1978
Uhle 1903
Urteaga 1914
Urton 1981, 1982

Vreeland 1980a, 1980b,
   1981a, 1981b, 1989
Wheatly 1971

Wiener 1880
Zuidema-Urton 1976

14

Locational Symbolism:
The Fiesta de los Reyes
o del Niño in Northern Peru

RICHARD P. SCHAEDEL

> Este es el milagro primicias desta terra santa de promision i si despues de
> nacido Cristo, entran a reconocerle en los bracos de su madre tres Reyes,
> cada uno de diferente nacion, color y tierra... aqui en este indiano Belen
> adoran al ijo i madre los primeros a quen llamo con el milagro esta estrella
> de Jacob, un blanco, un Indio i una negra.
>
> Calancha[1]

The Fiesta de los Reyes Magos (Royal Magi) is a type of pageant cum
religious rite, similar to the Diablos Fiesta in Bolivia and Southern Peru
(Delgado and Schaeffer 1978). It was probably introduced into Andean
religious practices at the end of the seventeenth century. Having sufficient
symbolic correspondence to indigenous cosmological beliefs, it found fertile
ground for inviting elaboration of indigenous symbolic pageantry, more or
less incrementally until the early part of this century. The celebration of
the Fiesta de los Reyes Magos at the village of Narigualá on the far north
coast of Peru attracts pilgrims from a wide radius within the department
of Piura, and for this reason is an important event deserving attention.
Also, the ceremony celebrated at Narigualá is important to the study of
pilgrimage because the central motif of its dramatic pageant is the sacred
journey of the magi, which is a paradigm for all Catholic pilgrimage. In this
fiesta we encounter an embedded theatrical pageant displaying fundamental themes of the Catholic pilgrimage tradition, which in its New World
presentation incorporates significant elements of indigenous cosmological
symbolism.[2]

Unlike the Diablos Fiesta which has continued to grow, the Fiesta de
los Reyes Magos has been undergoing a period of decline probably since
the turn of the century, although because of its regional importance, it

retains its significance as a major fiesta for the Piura indigenous peasantry. Three villages celebrate this ceremony in the broad area from Lambayeque to Piura: Morrope, Ferreñafe, and Narigualá. Only Narigualá, however, utilized the pre-Hispanic shrine as the transformational locus for receiving God or moving from the profane to the sacred.[3] Here, the locational symbolism is particularly clear, and is the theme that I want to emphasize.

Within the modern department of Piura, within which the Narigualá fiesta is largely circumscribed, the community structure of Narigualá is that of an agricultural *caserío* (hamlet) of which Catacaos is the district capital, the lowest echelon in the formal national urban hierarchy. Catacaos is the most "indigenous" district capital of the province and includes within its jurisidiction another famed *caserío* of potters, Simbilá. While other *caseríos* celebrate their Patron Saint's Day fiesta, there is relatively little pilgrimage from other than immediately adjoining villages; and all the other major and minor fiestas involving large pilgrimage contingents from the *caseríos* are celebrated at Catacaos, except for los Reyes at Narigualá. The other major fiesta, in terms of size and radius of attendance, is Semana Santa, celebrated in Catacaos. In terms of its uniqueness, the *caserío* of Narigualá lies at the foot of the only major *huaca* (adobe pyramid) in the region Figure 14.1). The inference is inescapable that this is the feature that marked it as the appropriate village for this ceremony, although the empirical validation of this inference must await research in the archives.

The organization of the fiesta is not unlike that described for one of the other major pageantry fiestas (those involving more than a procession and accompanying dancing and musical groups) at Otuzco dedicated to La Virgen de la Puerta (see Robert Smith 1975), other than that the demo-

Figure 14.1 The chapel (*huaca*), also called "cathedral" by Narigualeños

graphic and economic base of the supporting *mayordomos* is much smaller. The basic difference in this type of fiesta organization and that of the more common procession fiesta is that it requires one or more specialists, who do not rotate annually and are responsible for preserving the libretto script and the choreography and training of new actors and dancers. Not enough data were obtained to elaborate further on the administrative organization (see Marzal 1977:234-86). Suffice it to say that the staging of the fiesta is one of the most complex of any Andean fiesta in terms of its involvement with the district capital, Catacaos, which as we shall see plays a crucial role in the locational symbolism.

NARRATIVE OF THE FIESTA

Morning of the sixth of January: Activities at the shrine of El Niño prior to ascending to the Huaca de Nariguală. The shrine of el Niño is the center of activity. It is a chapel or small church with a large cross at the street axis. Both chapel and cross reveal recent repainting and refurbishing.

Ceremonies begin with a kind of serenade by the five-piece band at the home of the *mayordomos* who are custodians of the silver standards which are then marched to the shrine; and then the incense bearers are recruited in similar form.

The procession to ascend the hill is formed and the Niño is held on very little cushioning in the hands of the major sponsor Figures 14.2, 14.3). This

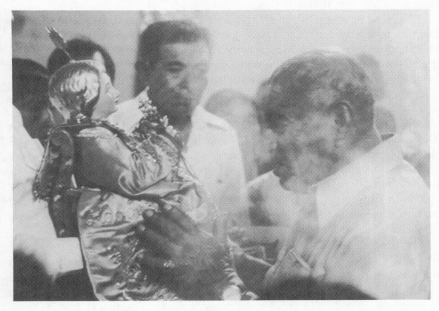

Figure 14.2 Positioning of el Niño before the ascent to the chapel

Figure 14.3 The Mayordomos bring el Niño from the shrine (residence) up to the chapel (Huaca)

procession ascends the hill to the Capilla Catedral de Narihualá (chapel-cathedral). Accompanying the procession are the standard and incense bearers who precede the Niño, who is flanked by adult peasants of both sexes, attired in the traditional Mochica "Sundays best." The procession enters the church through the southern side door.

The Niño is taken to the altar where it is installed with the standards and made ready for the ornate exit from the chapel after the Mass. Meantime, the *pastorcitas* representing shepherds arrive, a group of ten slightly preadolescent girls in white dresses wearing straw hats with red bands and a red ribbon at the waist. They are apparently accompanied by their mothers or other adult female sponsors, and take their places in the pews at the front of the altar.

Mass (Revelation), 9:57 A.M.: *Mayordomos* of the Sociedad Niño Dios (Child-God Society) light four large candles at the main altar. The band plays appropriate music inside the small church or "temple" while fireworks are shot off outside. Forty matrons, barefooted and wearing somber but elegant black dresses of the Catacaos style with black shawls, enter silently and with dignity. A singing Mass ensues, in which, after each chanted portion, the band sounds a refrain. The Gospel of the Epiphany is read, followed by a sermon on the Epiphany.

The procession, 10:30 A.M.: The *pastorcitas* take communion to the sound of music by the band. Then the procession leaves the church by the north side, where the cemetery is located, to descend the *huaca* and enter the village from the side where there are only fields (Figures 14.4, 14.5). The *pastorcitas* precede the canopy, carrying incense. The priest carries the

Figure 14.4 Procession of *pastorcitas* descending from the chapel after "baptism" with el Niño in canopy, going through the community graveyard

image of El Niño on a velvet pedestal under a canopy supported by four bearers. One of the *mayordomos* carries a basket with leaves and flowers that seem to represent the myrrh of the biblical account. The flowers are strewn along the path before the image by the *pastorcitas* as more fireworks are lit. A paper globe is heated and launched from the back of the church, and floats out over the fields of cotton.

The procession proceeds a short distance through the cemetery in a northerly direction and then turns abruptly to the left to descend (Figure 14.4) to the village (Figure 14.5). By 10:44 A.M., the procession goes through the village along the main north-south street, accompanied always by appropriate ceremonial music to mark the slow cadence. When the procession comes to the throne of Herod, which is not yet completely furbished, it turns to the right to encircle the block between the throne and the shrine, and finally approaches the shrine chapel.

First adoration: the Niño is enshrined in its own altar, which has been prepared with maize seedlings, banana plants, moss rose, and several images — one apparently of Joseph, two horses, and a llama. On the base of the altar the three Reyes Magos have been painted, three on each side. The shepherds, *mayordomos*, and others of the procession adore by kissing the Niño and then other village people come in to do the same and leave cash offerings. Outside, the crowd begins to grow, some outsiders come in, and the vendors of ice, fruit, lollipops, etc., circulate among them.

Figure 14.5 *Mayordomos* with standards lead the *pastorcitas*, accompanying el Niño toward his shrine (residence), where he will receive adoration

Intermission, 11:15 A.M.-2:15 P.M.: During this time, in Narihualá the horses of the three kings and ambassador are made ready and the personages are assisted in assembling their costumes to take to Catacaos. They leave and later the *pastorcitas* go by truck to Catacaos. There the entourage of the three kings assembles at the house of the representative in Catacaos (district capital of Narigualá). They are fed and the entourage is dressed.

The procession of the Three Kings from Catacaos, 2:15 P.M.: The procession is initiated from a corner of the Plaza de Armas de Catacaos in the center of town. The ambassador, with a three-cornered hat, precedes the procession, followed by two *negritos* (ritual jesters dressed as blacks), a transvestite woman (later the wife of the hacendado), an *ingeniero* (engineer) with pith helmet (later the hacendado), and another helmeted figure. Then there is the Vaca Loca (man dressed as a crazy cow) with its attendant. Then come the Reyes, an archangel, and the *pastorcitas*. They are accompanied by a new band, playing in somewhat different style. A dance group of *negritos* dances along with the *pastorcitas*. The procession circles the plaza and disbands after entering the street leading to Narigualá. The *pastorcitas* get into a pickup truck and go to Narigualá while the four horsemen proceed on horseback. By 3:45 P.M., the three kings and ambassador, trailed by the band, arrive in Narigualá and, after brief refreshments, proceed to the *huaca* through which they pass rapidly and descend to approach the court of Herod. The jesters (hacendado, his wife, and *negritos*) join the court of Herod, composed of Herod, and the talking chief, a priest

Figure 14.6 The three kings and ambassador arriving in Narigualá from Catacaos with the Vaca Loca between two of the kings

or shaman of Herod, all on the platform (Figures 14.6, 14.7). The ambassador and the three kings, flanked by the *pastorcitas* and *negritos,* await in front. The audience crowds around on all sides where they can view the interface, including appropriate perches on the *huaca.*

From 4-5:00 P.M. (Act III in the following analysis), the formal presentation proceeds with considerable seriousness. A complex series of exchanges

Figure 14.7 The three kings just before they ascend the *huaca,* prior to being received by Herod

takes place between the ambassador and Herod's representative prior to the seating of the three kings and their dialogue with Herod. Simultaneously the jesters carry out a series of comic acts that stimulate and provoke intervention from the public. Much of the horseplay involves imitation of black stereotypes, and mockery of the hacendado and his lifestyle.

The adoration of the Magi: The three kings remount their horses and proceed, led by the shepherds, around the block separating the throne of Herod (Jerusalem) from the shrine (church) of El Niño (Bethlehem) and down to the shrine, where they proceed to bestow gifts and adore the Niño.

The court of Herod proceeds to argue about what to do to find the Niño and reflects a general environment of consternation and frustration. Finally Herod orders the slaughter of the innocents. Both the adoration of the Magi and the condemnation scene at Herod's court are the denouement, and the audience begins to become distracted in procuring refreshment, seeking friends, or joining in the dance which has been a diversionary attraction going on in the background since before the arrival of the three kings.

ANALYSIS: CHRISTIAN PAGEANT LEITMOTIF

Act I
Setting: Bethlehem
Scene 1: Manger
  Dramatis Personae: El Niño Jesus, shepherds
Scene 2: Church. Revelation to Child Jesus (baptism) Mass
  Dramatis Personae: Child Jesus, shepherds, priest

Act II
Setting: Foreign Kingdoms
  Dramatis Personae: Balthasar, shepherds, Gaspar, Melchior,
            ambassador, jesters, archangel

Act III
Setting: Jerusalem, Court of Herod
  Dramatis Personae: three kings, ambassador, jesters, shepherds,
            angel, herald, King Herod, functionary/astrologer

Act IV
Setting: Bethlehem   Double focus: Jerusalem
  Dramatis Personae: three kings, ambassador, jesters, Herod's court,
            shepherds, Niño Jesus, angel

Commentary: Comparing this reconstruction of what is considered to be the format of the Spanish sixteenth-century miracle plays or pageant of the Epiphany with the version reported for Morrope in 1978 by James Vreeland (personal communication), it would appear that Act I is clearly separated from Act II, but that in Morrope, and presumably in the Spanish prototype, Acts II and III are consolidated, in inverse order. All action takes place within the plaza, and the inauguration of activities involves the installation of Herod's court, followed by the appearance of the Magi from the far corner of the plaza. Act IV is essentially the same in both Morrope and Narigualá, except that Joseph and Mary are introduced to mediate between the three kings and El Niño in the adoration.

The southern Mediterranean interpretation of the Epiphany as the Feast of Revelation to the Gentiles is clearly captured in the miracle play — for example, the baptismal notion is recognized in the first act. Also, the importance of the three kings as good Gentiles from foreign lands is opposed to the nefarious image of Herod, the dissolute regional or national authority figure.

ANALYSIS: TRANSFORMATIONAL UR-MOTIF

Act I Setting:
Scene 1: Sidestreet of Rural Hamlet
  Dramatis Personae: El Niño, who will be sacrificed, sponsors,
    pastores (campesinos)

Scene 2: Sacred World (*Huaca*-Chapel), Campo Santo
  Dramatis Personae: Niño, shepherds, *padrinos* (godparents)
  Entre-acte (Intermission)-(Procession-Catacaos)

Act II Setting:
Scene 1: Foreign Lands (Catacaos)
  Dramatis Personae: foreign lords or priests of ancient religions,
    ambassador, interpreter, tricksters (buffoons, angel)
  Entre-acte (Intermission)
Scene 2: Rural Hamlet — Arrival of Magi
  Entre-acte (Procession, Ascension, Sanctification,
    Descent from the *Huaca*-Chapel)

Act III Setting:
Rural Hamlet — Town Square
  Dramatis Personae: King Herod, "talking chief" herald, ambassador:
    foreign lords, tricksters, *pastores* (campesinos)

Act IV Setting:
Sidestreet of Rural Hamlet — Shrine of Niño
  Dramatis Personae: All save Herod/herald, act their roles in the plaza

Commentary: The core symbol in the fiesta is manifest in El Niño. The coincidence of the name El Niño to describe the equatorial current that arrives about this time of year to heat the coast of Piura relates the Christian Niño Jesus to a cosmological phenomenon personified with the current, qua extraterrestrial force. The other attributes of the Niño, in terms of the indigenous cognition, predestine him as a person to be sacrificed. This concept is known in Quechua as Capac Hucha (Zuidema 1973:28-29), wherein the act of bloodless sacrifice confers a high status on the preadolescent victim. Underlying the adoration of the Child as originating from the rural hamlet, the sidestreet of Narigualá represents Bethlehem where the Christ Child might well have been born. The shrine of the Niño incorporates the Christ Child into the community. His divine mission is made known to Him in the ceremony, Mass as officiated by a contracted priest. After the *pastores-campesinos* with their *padrinos* share in the revelation in the holy place, *Huaca*-Chapel, the Niño is carried back to his shrine to await the adoration.

The authoritarian world of Israel is represented by the hamlet of Narigualá where the throne of Herod is erected, a scaffolding arrangement, the underpinnings of which remain in situ throughout the year. The plaza is Jerusalem. The foreign lands where the Magi originate are exemplified by Catacaos, the district capital, some five kilometers away. The Magi and their retinue are recruited from Narigualá, but proceed on horseback to Catacaos, where they go to the house of the Narigualá representative in Catacaos and put on the royal regalia. They then form a procession, which assembles in front of the church, and proceeds around the plaza and down the street leading toward Narigualá. The three separate homelands of the monarchs are symbolically encapsulated in the procession out of Catacaos. After their arrival in Israel, which is awaited with much anxiety, and a preliminary reception, the Magi are then sanctified by a procession around the holy place, where the divine revelation is made known to them. They then descend to the environs of Jerusalem and seek an audience with King Herod through their collective ambassador. After officialdom is satirized in the elaborate interface between envoy and "talking chief," the audience with Herod is finally granted.

A long scene with much dialogue, speech-making, by the delegation and Herod's court, and horseplay by the jesters ensues. At last the Magi depart to Bethlehem by the long route to adore El Niño and bestow gifts. Herod remains disconsolate on his throne. With the adoration, the pageant breaks up and merriment ensues. At the same time, in the plaza there is some attempt to represent Herod's ordering of the slaughter of all newly born infants, but this does not attract much attention from the public since by then, 5:30 P.M., many had strayed to the sources of *chicha* (alcoholic corn drink) for refreshment and camaraderie.

MEANING OF THE SYMBOLISM

The identification of the Niño Jesus with the hamlet, with the indigenous peasantry (campesinado de Baja Piura), as champion of the powerless who is destined to be sacrificed, is the main theme. Then, the importance of the Niño as champion is validated, first from within the community by the *pastores*, and later from outside by the Magi confronting the opposition, represented by the authority figure of Herod. The major two-hour long dialogue of the authority figure with the ambassador and kings (Magi) has a clearcut alternative motive, burlesqued by the "Big landowner and his wife" (a man dressed as a woman), which takes place while Herod is pontificating with the Magi. Until recently, the threat of encroachment on Narigualá lands by the Criollo non-Indian landowners, was very real, so the role of these characters as basically part of Herod's court is clearly a symbolic identification of them with the authority figure and opposition to the Christ Child. The authority figure's court includes a black contingent, one *negrito* who best fulfills the role of court jester, and another who fulfills the role of bailiff. To a certain degree this symbolism, which represents the blacks as lackeys of the authority figure, embodies a general interethnic bias. This view was shared by the coastal peasantry against the slaves and ex-slaves who were used by the Colonial and later Criollo hacienda owners to buffer labor relations with the indigenous peasantry.

The symbolism of the pageant as a counter-authority popular drama is similar to that of the Muerte de Atahualpa described by R. Smith (1975) and Schaedel (1952), with different actual symbols, protagonists, and antagonists. However, Smith neglects to comment upon the relationship of the pageant-drama to the audience and the duration of the pageantry. In both the Otuzco representation of the death of Atahualpa and the Narigualá main act, at least two hours of relatively undivided attention is focused on the drama. This focusing of attention in the case of Otuzco is achieved through the choreography, while in Narigualá, it is born by the chanting and pantomime. The persons in the audience are under no constraint to pay attention to the drama, and in both instances there are abundant refreshment purveyors to distract them. Nonetheless, their concentration is riveted on the performers. These are two clear instances of folk or vernacular drama that form the high points of longer fiesta programs based upon Christian symbols that have been reinterpreted to become meaningful to Andean cognition. It appears that the tradition of the pageant is derived from the miracle play of Europe and is accommodated to what seems to be a north coast prehispanic prototype as reconstructed in Donnan's (1976) interpretation of the presentation scenes.

In the case of Otuzco, the locational symbolism is present, but relatively simple; and incorporation of the *Huaca*-Chapel is absent. I suspect that Narigualá is one of very few places where the *Huaca*-Chapel transformation occurs, although there is some indigenous-Christian symbol juxtaposition in Oruro, Bolivia. Although rare, the Narigualá ritual is confirmation of the continuity of the temple mound as sacred in Andean cognition. A second emphasized aspect develops the concept of levels or scale of society embedded in the locational symbolism. The hinterland-city relationship is reflected in the Bethlehem-Jerusalem or adoratorio-plaza juxtaposition. The kingdom of Israel within the world of surrounding kingdoms is reflected in the Catacaos-Narigualá connection, and may well reflect the concept of either regional areas, departments, or the Peruvian authority structure. The transcendental world is, of course, symbolized in the *Huaca*-Chapel.

The importance of the locational symbolism lies in the regional opposition between the powerless peasantry fighting for survival against an oppressive power structure and authority. The peasantry has allies outside the region and through the transcendental powers of El Niño these powerful allies are brought in to censure the status quo authority. The innuendos in the horseplay that runs as a dramatic counterpoint to Herod's reception of the three kings in Act III seems to touch upon the Hispano-Catholic meaning of the Epiphany, conceived as a feast, not only as revelation to the Gentiles, but to represent Christianity encompassing all races equally. This concept is expressed in Calancha who doubtless played a major role in interpreting the miracle play to the indigenous north coast people in the seventeenth century.[4] Does this comedy aspect, in which the blacks and whites are satirized, represent the contemporary Piura peasantry's protest against the interpretation of the Church fathers?

NOTES

1. Cited by Sabina MacCormack (1982), Cronica 564, and translated as follows by the editors: "This is the primary miracle of this promised holy land and then after the birth of Christ, three kings enter to acknowledge Him in the arms of his Mother, each one from a different nation, color, and land...it is here in this Indian Bethlehem where they adore the Son and the Mother, the first ones whom this star of Jacob leads to the miracle, a white, an Indian, and a black person."

2. The description of the fiesta is taken from the joint observations of José Sabogal Weisse, Noemi and Herbert Eling, and the author. It was compared to the fiesta witnessed in the previous year by V. Antonio Rodriguez Suy Suy.

3. Editor's note: in January 1985, N. Ross Crumrine observed this ceremonial and at that time, due to the El Niño torrential rains of 1983, the old church on the *huaca* had been seriously damaged and could not be used unless repaired. Thus the morning Mass on 6 January was held in the small church in the village and the procession did not ascend or descend the *huaca* (see Crumrine n.d.).

4. See note 1.

REFERENCES

Crumrine n.d.

Delgado-Schaeffer 1978

Donnan 1976

MacCormack 1982

Martinez de Companon 1936

Marzal 1977

Schaedel 1952

Smith, Robert 1975

Zuidema 1973

15

A Pilgrimage Fiesta:
Easter Week Ritual
at Catacaos, Piura, Peru

N. ROSS CRUMRINE

During each Holy Week an elaborate ceremonial takes place in Catacaos, Piura, in northern coastal Peru.[1] Many pilgrims as well as local participants and visitors crowd the main plaza beside the church of Saint John, taking part in the processions and events described in this chapter. Numerous booths presenting foods, clothes, religious artifacts, and crafts have been set up in order to attract pilgrims and visitors and encourage them to make purchases. This ceremonial, a kind of folk and ritual drama, portrays the passion of Christ through the use of images, events, processions, and specific rituals. Numerous Peruvian fiestas attract many pilgrims who have made promises to attend and take part in the ritual events. This chapter focuses upon an understanding of the structure and organization of the ritual drama in which the pilgrims and visitors participate. Thus it examines the typical local organization necessary to maintain pilgrimage fiestas.

Yet this type of pilgrimage fiesta is not unusual along the Peruvian coast. James Vreeland (chapter 13) discusses the pilgrimage fiesta for the Cross of Chalpon in the town of Motupe just to the south of the department of Piura, where Catacaos is located. Further south on the north central coast at Otuzco in the department of La Libertad, Robert Smith described and analyzed the fiesta for the La Virgen de la Puerta (the Virgin of the

Door). In 1966, the year of his study, the band of Santa Cecilia of Catacaos made a devotional trip to attend and perform at the fiesta in Otuzco (R. Smith 1975:58). Considerably further south in the coastal department of Ica, both Helaine Silverman (chapter 12) and I (Crumrine 1977b, 1978) have described three major pilgrimage centers: the sanctuary at Yauca for the Virgin of the Rosary in the Ica valley (Silverman) the House of Melchorita in the Chincha valley, and the village of Humay, the center of the cult of the Beatita de Humay in the Pisco valley. The latter two, like the pilgrimage center of Sarita Colonia in the cemetery of Callao just outside of Lima, are dedicated to recent historical individuals and are ritually considerably less complex than the pilgrimage fiestas of the far north coast. These pilgrimage centers and fiestas only cover several of the numerous coastal departments of Peru. I would expect other such centers in additional departments as well. Thus the Peruvian coastal pilgrimage fiesta complex is extremely popular and still very dynamic.

Within the department of Piura itself, in addition to Holy Week in Catacaos, there are numerous pilgrimage fiestas spread throughout the yearly cycle. Richard Schaedel (chapter 14) discusses and analyzes the fiesta of los Reyes o del Niño of the village of Nariguala, which lies just beyond the outskirts of Catacaos. Several other pilgrimage fiestas are also celebrated within this department, that of El Señor Cautivo in Ayabaca, of El Señor de Chocan in the province of Sullana, and of El Señor de la Piedad de Yapatera near Chulucanas in the province of Morropon. Manuel Marzal (1977:225-26) also mentions the following sacred images located in "regional" sanctuaries: el Señor Cautivo de Ayabaca, Nuestra Señora de la Merced de Paita, Nuestra Señora de Perpetuo Socorro de Piura, and the Santa Cruz de Motupe.

Ayabaca, with only some 10,000 permanent inhabitants (Cortázar 1975:7), is located high in the Andes above the Piura desert region. Receiving considerable rainfall, this very mountainous region is heavily forested. Leaving extremely early in the morning from Piura, local pilgrims can drive up to Ayabaca for a brief visit to Señor Cautivo and his sanctuary and return the same day, arriving in Piura very late that night. However, the road is very difficult and most serious pilgrims plan to stay several days, sleeping in buses or trucks as there are no hotels in Ayabaca. Many, of course, walk rather than ride and remain for the entire week of festivities, which reach a climax on October 12, the feast day of Señor Cautivo. The walk requires some four days in each direction. The pilgrims pray to Señor Cautivo, either thanking him for a cure, or requesting a favor or personal miracle, participate in processions and other rituals, and take part in the large diverse market which is associated with the fiesta. Woven cloth, candies, famous Ayabaca hams, and numerous other foods and articles are sold. Numerous tradesmen, pilgrims, and returning native sons and daughters arrive from all regions of the department of Piura, from neighboring Ecuador, and from as far as Lima and other regions of Peru.

Established more than 200 years ago, this pilgrimage fiesta is one of the most ancient and humble in Piura. In addition to this pilgrimage fiesta, a new church has been constructed in Querecotillo as the shrine of el Señor de Chocan, whose feast day is celebrated in February. And a recently discovered image, el Señor de la Piedad de Yapatera, has become the focus of a pilgrimage fiesta in Chulucanas which takes place in the middle of September. The image, which is kept in a little chapel in Yapatera, is carried to nearby Chulucanas for the festival and is reputed to be very powerful as a curer. Thus a similar general north coastal Peruvian pilgrimage fiesta pattern emerges. However, in this chapter I shall concentrate upon a description of the Easter week festival of Catacaos.

Catacaos is located near the city of Piura, the capital of the department of Piura. Acting as a ceremonial and economic capital of the Bajo Piura region, which extends west of Catacaos down the Piura River valley to the Pacific Ocean, Catacaos and its other ten related districts include some 100,000 persons according to the 1972 census, with 20,000 in Catacaos and 40,000 in Catacaos district (Cortázar 1975:7). The area consists of hot, dry coastal plains broken by green irrigated river valleys such as the region of the Bajo Piura. In contrast with the rainless coastal deserts to the south, some rain usually falls during the "rain season" from around January to May and the weather is warm the entire year, however, it is never unpleasantly cold or extremely hot. The area represents a prime agricultural region with cotton ranking as the major crop and food crops grown in smaller garden areas (Orlove 1978). Most people work as small-scale farmers, wage labor, craftsmen, or fishermen. The town of Catacaos also acts as a craft center, with numerous small craft stores located just off the central plaza. In terms of the general ecology, the region is densely populated and has a high percentage of under- or unemployment.

Since the time of the Spanish conquest, the area has experienced intense contact resulting in the loss of the indigenous languages and the disappearance of the two local indigenous groups. During early colonial times, the Catacaos area fell under the *encomienda* system and la Comunidad de Indigenas was created on January 10, 1533, and given the name San Juan de Catacaos. Growing, Catacaos became a Parroquia and on January 11, 1828, was made a Distrito. Catacaos cemetery dates to 1843; the telegraph, mail service, and telephone to 1890; the paved Piura-Catacaos highway to 1924; the railroad service which was opened in 1887 in Piura also had an extension to Catacaos; and public lighting to 1934. However, the major church of Catacaos does not date to the colonial epoch as does the one of Sechura near the mouth of the Piura River. The colonial temple of Catacaos was damaged by flooding and finally destroyed by the earthquake of 1912, after which the present church was constructed. Although the area is recognized as an "Indian" one in the guide books, the present cultural tradition reflects years of fusion or syncretism between indigenous and foreign elements. Chicha, the very popular fermented corn drink and staff of life, the use of a three-log balsa raft for ocean fishing, pottery making, and cotton agriculture, to name only a few, are aboriginal features and contrast with electricity, running water, and television, which exist in many homes in Catacaos. Concerning the Easter pilgrimage ceremonial itself, I shall point out several suggestive implications of fusion in specific rituals and ritual symbols as we examine the events of Semana Santa in Catacaos. What is unique and special is a certain type of syncretism which has produced a ritual complex unique in its fusion of ritual fervor and intense labor with a ritual massiveness and a ritual complexity. This complexity that the pilgrim experiences is a phenomenon, not of finicky details, although details are of some importance, but one of massing ritual upon ritual. For example, the main church in Catacaos houses some 45 images, many of which are statues, life-sized or even larger, that take part in the Easter week ritual. Holy Week simply compacts a pattern of saints' day rituals within one week. Many of these rituals reveal the same forms and symbols as the north coastal pilgrimage fiestas mentioned earlier. Usually the ritual for each saint is not extremely complex, but with such a large number being worshipped, decorated, and carried in procession during Holy Week, the overall picture is impressive. It is especially impressive when one considers that the church in Catacaos is only one of the numerous churches in the Bajo Piura, all with their own special set of saints and ceremonies, although the Catacaos Easter week is the one attended by the major number of pilgrims. I was also told numerous times that "Catacaos is a very religious pueblo, probably the most religious in the world." This general belief and attitude, coupled with the massiveness of the images, length of processions, numbers of pilgrims and locals attending, and this specific massing type of complexity represents a general ritual orientation and ritual symbol which is extremely characteristic of and may be unique to this "Indian" region of the Bajo Piura. During Easter week, I have observed individuals wearing narrow banners across their chests from as far away as Talara, north of Catacaos, walking toward the Catacaos church, although most individuals attending Holy Week rituals in Catacaos do not wear such symbols of their pilgrim status. Even though these pilgrims purchase and carry photographs of the Catacaos image of Christ in His coffin, yet they are soon lost in the huge amorphous crowds that participate especially in the Good Friday and Easter Sunday rituals.

In order to present what the pilgrim experiences and to examine the ritual orientation of Catacaos, I turn now to a description of Semana Santa. After discussion with Richard Schaedel, who suggested that very little research had been done in the area and that the ritual system was complex and still well integrated, I visited the area that summer (1977), for several weeks during Holy Week (1978-81), and for the latter weeks of June in 1979 and 1985. Besides several tourist guides such as the *Documental del Peru, Departamento de Piura* (Cortázar 1975) and the printed program for Semana Santa, the published material has been very scanty. The only exception is the study by Manuel M. Marzal (1977:215-302), published as a very long chapter "El Sistema Religioso del Campesino Bajopiurano," in his book, *Estudios sobre Religion Campesina*. In his excellent survey of the religious life in the Bajo Piura, Marzal discusses the belief, ritual, and ceremonial systems and their social organization. Although his data are excellent, Marzal does not include much specific information concerning and describing individual ceremonies or specific ritual symbols and devotes essentially no space to the Holy Week of Catacaos. Thus the following main section of this chapter provides a description of the Semana Santa ritual and symbolism of Catacaos. The final concluding section will discuss the social and symbolic organization of Semana Santa in Catacaos, develop a broader understanding of the *cofradías* and societies which produce the Easter ceremonial, and provide the more general ritual context experienced by the pilgrims.

SEMANA SANTA IN CATACAOS

After the Fridays of Lent, Semana Santa in Catacaos begins with Palm Sunday and its morning Mass and blessing of the palms in the Catacaos church. Under the direction of the Society del Señor de Ramos, a small white donkey, the image of Señor Triunfante, the Catacaos priest (Vicario Cooperador), certain members of the *cofradías*, the Depositario, and the Doliente gather in the afternoon in the church of Carmen located in the Monte Sullon section of greater Catacaos, a number of blocks down Calle Comercio from the main Catacaos church. The *cofradías* of la Virgen de Dolores and San Juan Bautista bring the images of Dolores and of San Juan Evangelista down Calle Comercio to the plaza in front of the church of Carmen. Late in the afternoon the procession takes place with Señor Triunfante mounted on the white donkey and the officials moving past Dolores and San Juan, who bow and then join the procession, with San Juan following the little donkey and Dolores at the end. They proceed up Calle Comercio with residents throwing flowers from second-story windows and roof tops and triumphantly enter the front door of the Catacaos church. This early in Holy Week rather few pilgrims or visitors would yet have arrived. Thus this procession is attended chiefly by local people.

Monday, Tuesday, and Wednesday, *cofradía* and *sociedad* members gather in the church to mount their images on the *andas* (carrying frames), decorate them with lights, gold, silver ornaments, and flowers, and carry them in the processions which last around six hours. To power its lights, each image has its own rented generator, which follows behind on a three-wheeled bicycle, and many also have their own bands which play in their honor, following behind the image or behind the members of the *cofradía* or *sociedad* when they go on official errands. Late Monday afternoon the image of Señor Cautivo is highlighted in the procession and followed by

San Juan Evangelista and Dolores. This image, a replica of the Ayabaca one, is owned by a local society and represents the Ayabaca center. On Tuesday the image of el Señor del Prehendimiento appears, followed by the others. Wednesday the Gran Despedimiento takes place with the image of el Señor Jesus Nazareno making its appearance. In the procession the images of Jesus leave the front door of the church whereas the images of San Juan Evangelista, Veronica, and Dolores leave the side door, the one thorough which images usually return to the church. The latter images circle the Plaza de Armas in a clockwise direction and meet the image of Jesus on the far side of the plaza. When they meet, each approaching image is brought up in turn and bowed to the image of el Señor Jesus Nazareno. Then the procession with all the images, the others following those of Jesus, leaves the plaza, moves around the town, and returns to the church later that night.

The Cofradía Jurada del Santisimo Sacramento takes charge of the preparation and ritual symbols on Thursday. With wooden figures, a table, and real fruit and bread they construct a replica of the Last Supper in the

Figure 15.1 The "Last Supper", Catacaos

center of the altar area (Figure 15.1). To the far right of the major altar area they erect a diorama of Abraham preparing to sacrifice Isaac when the angel stops him, on the far left a monument of angels, and on top la Custodia, an image enclosed in a glass-faced elaborate wooden box (Figure 15.2). In the morning the officials of the *cofradía* gather and visit both the home of the Depositario, who hosts the Thursday banquet, and also the office building of the town concejo (council), collecting the Depositario and the town, department, and military officials and proceeding to the church.

In front of the main altar, the priest places the gold Llaves Sagradas de la Custodia del Santisimo Monumento (the keys to the Custodia) over the head of the Depositario. Then all the officials retire to the home of the Depositario for the Gran Almuerzo (lunch), el banquete de "los siete potajes" (the banquet of seven traditional dishes). It is said that over 1,000 persons are served at this banquet. On Good Friday, the Cofradía Jurada del Santo Cristo takes over the ritual, constructs three huge crosses at the front of the church, and places the images of Nuestro Señor Jesucristo del Calvario on the center cross and, on the worshiper's left- and right-hand crosses, San Dimas and Alejandro (Figure 15.3). The photographs

Figure 15.2 The "Last Supper" with The Monument of Angels

of the center image, Jesucristo del Calvario, are the ones often carried by the pilgrims. On Good Friday the Doliente replaces the Depositario. In front of all the officials, the priest places la Insignia de Duelo por la Muerte de Nuestro Señor Jesucristo (the insignia of the mourning for the death of Jesus) around the neck of the Doliente and he in turn is responsible for the Gran Almuerzo (a banquet completely of fish and shellfish dishes). After the banquet the sermon of three hours takes place and los Santos Varones, men dressed in white gowns, remove Christ from the cross and place Him in the Santo Sepulcro (sacred coffin). As many in the huge crowd of worshipers try to throw perfume on the body of Christ as it is moved toward and lifted into the Sepulcro, one of the emotional peaks of the ceremonial is attained. His Sepulcro is decorated and carried in a huge procession which lasts all night and only returns to the church early Saturday morning. It is estimated that 4,000 worshipers take part in this Good Friday and Saturday of Gloria ritual.

The Cofradía Jurada del Santo Cristo also organizes the preparations and ritual symbols utilized on Easter Sunday. After the return of the procession Saturday morning, the Santo Sepulcro is taken apart and the

Figure 15.3 The Crucifixion, Good Friday, Catacaos

image of Christ is returned to the cross standing in the case on the left-hand front wall of the church. His gold adornments are stored by the *procurador* (head) of the *cofradía*. The former Sepulcro is made to symbolize the resurrection by placing the image of the Señor de la Resurrección on top of the decorated *anda*. After the Misa de Resurrección at 4:00 A.M. Sunday, the last Semana Santa procession and the Gran Despedimiento take place. The images of la Santisima Cruz and el Señor de la Resurrección leave the front door of the church and proceed around the Plaza de Armas in a counterclockwise direction, moving quickly. The images of San Juan Bautista, la Veronica, la Virgen del Transito, and la Virgen de La Luz emerge from the side door of the church and move around the plaza in a clockwise direction. Halfway around the plaza the image of el Señor de la Resurrección stops and the ones of the approaching procession, San Juan, Veronica, and the Virgin of Transito, are carried up one by one and bowed in front of Christ. When, at last, the Virgin of La Luz is carried up, both the Virgin and the huge *anda* with the image of Christ are bowed. At this same instant, while the first rays of the rising sun are striking the figure of Christ standing high above the former Sepulcro, numerous white doves are released from beneath the image, the church bells are rung, and the *castillo* (fireworks) is lit. Then several hours pass as the Holy Cross and Christ lead the procession on around the plaza in a counterclockwise direction and the other images, San Juan, Veronica, the Virgin of Transito, and the Virgin of La Luz, follow behind (Figure 15.4). Returning through the side doors, the images are left on display for the remainder of the morning and early afternoon. However the members of the *cofradías* and *sociedades* are first busy removing the gold and silver adornments from the images and returning some of them to the glass cases which line the walls of the church, and are then occupied in feasting next year's new members, visitors, and pilgrim relatives. Semana Santa in Catacaos is over for another year and many pilgrims and visitors are on their way home, yet many of the *cofradías* and *sociedades* remain active, especially during certain times of the coming year when they will celebrate their patron saint's day.

THE ORGANIZATION OF SEMANA SANTA

In addition to the above events, experienced by pilgrims and participants in general, which present the meaning of the Easter Week, the organization of the *cofradías* and *sociedades* provides the human cooperative basis for the action observed by the pilgrims. The societies

Figure 15.4 Virigin of Transito, Returning to the Church, Easter Sunday, Catacaos

maintain their own *locales*, which often are chapels housing their patron saint. They maintain much the same membership through the years and possess a proper charter which provides for officers such as president, vice-president, secretary, and treasurer. Society members pay dues and ideally the *sociedad* will aid members who are sick, in trouble, or have died and require funeral ritual. On the other hand, the *cofradías juradas* are organized through the Church and change in membership each year. Ideally, each *cofradía* consists of fourteen members; the *procurador* and the *secretario*, who are the heads of the first and second *fila* (file), a first and second *mayor* (a *mayor* for each *fila*) and ten *mayordomos* (five in each *fila*). The *procurador* keeps the adornments of the saint, a small image of the saint, two angels, and similar objects in his home, which is open to the public for worship. The home of San Dimas, that of the *procurador* of the *cofradía* of Santo Cristo, is very popular throughout the year, with worshipers dropping in all day long to burn candles and make donations to Christ or San Dimas. Many of these individuals arrive from some distance and thus are pilgrims to the shrine of San Dimas. In fact, each *mayordomo* of this *cofradía* must spend a week in turn at the home of the *procurador* making sure that the worshipers have candles and taking care of the images. The home of the *procurador* of the *cofradía* of the Santisimo Sacramento houses three images of the Custodia (one of which is used during Easter week, another during Corpus Cristi, and another for the Octavo processions) and also an image of Cristo Niño which is worshipped at Christmas time. The third and fourth most important *cofradías* are Animas Benditas and San Juan Bautista. The former is active during funeral services and plays little, if any, role in the Easter ritual, while the latter carries two images in Easter week processions, San Juan Evangelista and San Juan Bautista, and celebrates the fiesta of San Juan Bautista. Several days after the celebration of the *cofradía* fiesta, the outgoing members and the incoming members meet with the priest in the church. The old secretary presents the books and accounts of the *cofradía* and the gold and silver adornments of the saint are examined, weighed, and passed on to the incoming *procurador* and his *secretario*, *mayores*, and *mayordomos*. In summary, in addition to the pilgrims and participants in general, the Semana Santa ritual is supported by these two sets of organizations, the *sociedades* and the *cofradías*, who work together to produce a most complex and extremely powerful ceremonial.

THE STRUCTURE AND MEANING OF SEMANA SANTA

Similar in structure to other north coast pilgrimage fiestas yet different in specific meanings, the Easter ritual in Catacaos develops toward two major events or dramatic climaxes; the crucifixion and funeral procession of Jesus and the Resurrection and farewell of Christ on Easter Sunday. Beyond a doubt, the Sunday ritual is timed to take place just as the sun rises and is located at the only position in the Plaza de Armas where the first rays of the rising sun shine on the face of the risen Christ. This image of Christ dressed in a gold kilt with a gold sunburst behind him and gold rays around his head, looks more like a young Greek athlete than Jesus Christ. It is as if Good Friday's ritual represents the death of the sun god, perhaps the Inca or a pre-Inca deity, and the Easter Sunday ritual the return of the sun as a young deity. Clearly the Good Friday afternoon ritual enacts the descent of the Deity as Christ is removed from the cross, lifted and carried to his coffin, and borne throughout the town during the hours of darkness.

Structurally this Good Friday descent-crucifixion parallels the descent of El Niño in Narigualá (chapter 14), the descent of the Cross of Chalpón from its sacred hillside shrine and pilgrimage-procession to Motupe (chapter 13), La Bajada of the Virgin of the Door in Otuzco, and the dual removal from the mountains to the chapel in Yapatera which is now a legend, and procession-pilgrimage to Chulucanas of el Señor de la Piedad for his fiesta. The second climax, the return and Despedimiento (farewell) of Christ in the Easter Sunday procession and feasting also is structurally identical with the second climax of the other pilgrimage fiestas of the north coast — for example, la Salida of the Virgin of the Door as described by R. Smith (1975). Thus the pilgrims and participants experience two major climax events before returning to their homes.

The meaning and symbolism of these dual sets of events suggest that the pilgrimage on the north coast of Peru is on another level a dual process: as the individual moves to greet, honor, worship, and absorb health and power from the supernatural, the saint or Christ also move in the opposite direction, descending so that an encounter, a mediation, can take place. At the place of mediation, communication, and encounter, pilgrims give gifts to the deity and the supernatural reciprocates. Feasting, processions, and ritual leave-taking provide the second climax event and symbolize both the return of human and supernatural personages to their permanent homes and the rupture of the encounter, reduced communications, and the lack of mediation. Thus the ritual pattern is one of reciprocity with both humans and supernatural power moving to an encounter which mediates the life versus death and this world versus other world opposition. The place of encounter and mediation, the shrine or church center, therefore becomes crucial in this power exchange and transformation of individuals and supernaturals. The pilgrimage fiesta also takes place not only at a specific location in space but also at the point in time in the ceremonial cycle when the supernatural power descends, the images are "alive," and thus the transformational mediation becomes possible.

NOTES

1. The field work upon which this chapter is based was financed in part by grants from the Canada Council, the Social Sciences and Humanities Research Council of Canada, and the University of Victoria. I wish to thank these institutions for their kind financial help. Professors Richard Schaedel, Juan Ossio, Antonio Rodrigues Suy Suy, and Manuel Marzal and Mr. Edward Franco Temple were most kind in their encouragement and assistance and in their open exchange of ideas and information. I wish to thank them all for their most considerate interest and aid. I especially wish to thank the people of Catacaos and the Bajo Piura for their warm hospitality and generosity. Besides being the "most religious pueblo in the world," the people of the Bajo Piura are some of the most hospitable peoples in the world.

REFERENCES

Cortazar 1975
Crumrine 1977b, 1978
Marzal 1977

Orlove 1978
Smith, Robert 1975

16

Dual Cosmology and Ethnic Division in an Andean Pilgrimage Cult

MICHAEL J. SALLNOW

Clinging to a scree in a desolate, uninhabited Andean valley 4,750 meters above sea level, overhung by a semicircle of glaciers and snow-capped peaks, is a gaunt stone building roofed with galvanized iron and surmounted by a belltower. At one end of its cavernous interior is a large glass panel behind which is a painting of the crucified Christ on an outcrop of black rock. This is the miraculous shrine of El Señor de Qoyllur Rit'i, Lord of the Snow Star, which every year in the run-up to the feast of Corpus Christi in June is the focus of an extensive pilgrimage attracting some 25,000 devotees, mainly peasants but also some townspeople, from the southern Peruvian highlands.

It would be impossible within the confines of this chapter to give anything like a comprehensive picture of this extraordinary event, on which there is in any case, a fairly extensive literature.[1] The focus here is on two specific and related aspects of the Qoyllur Rit'i cult. Ritual activities at and around the shrine, it will be shown, unfold according to a central dualist logic, giving expression thereby to an endemic Andean cultural theme. Somewhat paradoxically, this ephemeral assembly offers an especially vivid manifestation of Andean dual cosmology, dramatically enacted over an extended period across a large tract of the landscape. At the same time, this ostensibly traditional event is pervaded by ecclesiastical hierarchy and ethnic cleavages. Not only is the cult controlled by a zealous Roman

Catholic brotherhood and frequently presided over by the archbishop of Cuzco, but the cardinal ethnic polarity between Indian and mestizo is woven into its liturgy and organization at every level. It will be argued that these two aspects of the cult are inextricably linked, that it is in the nature of the Qoyllur Rit'i shrine to host a peculiarly theatrical conjunction between the categories of power and domination in Andean society and vernacular conceptions of the cosmos.

THE SHRINE

El Señor de Qoyllur Rit'i is situated in the department of Cuzco, some 90 kilometers east of Cuzco city, in the northern reaches of the Ausankati mountain range.[2] It is a composite shrine, comprising a number of sites linked by a series of ritual movements and transfers during the three weeks between the movable feasts of the Ascension and Corpus Christi (Figure 16.1 and Table 16.1). At the head of the Sinakara valley, in addition to the

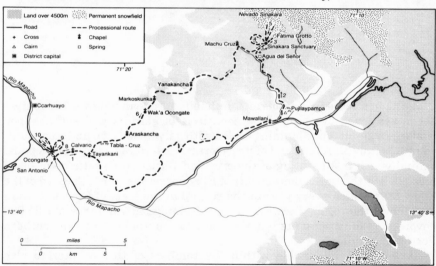

Figure 16.1 Map of the Qoyllur Rit'i Shrine Complex

main sanctuary housing the principal image, there is a grotto of the Virgin of Fátima. Access to Sinakara is by footpath from the hamlet of Mawallani, eight kilometers distant. Here, a small chapel houses a three-dimensional representation of the main image, which is moved to the sanctuary on the Ascension in preparation for the titular fiesta. Yet another crucifix, known as Señor de Tayankani and intimately associated with the rock-painting at Sinakara, is kept for most of the year in the parish church in the village of Ocongate, and moved to the chapel of the eponymous hamlet Tayankani,

Table-16.1 Principal Processions of Titular Fiesta of Señor de Qoyllur Rit'i

Phase	Map reference & date	Icon	Route
I	1. Ascension Thursday	Señor de Tayankani	Ocongate to Tayankani
	2. Ascension Thursday	Señor de Qoyllur Rit'i	Mawallani to Sinakara Sanctuary
	3. Wednesday after Pentecost	Virgen de Fátima	Sinakara Sanctuary to Fátima Grotto
II	4. Monday after Trinity	Señor de Qoyllur Rit'i	Sinakara to Sanctuary precints
III	5. Tuesday after Trinity	Glacier crosses	Sinakara glacier to Sinakara Sanctuary
IV	6. Tuesday after Trinity	Señor de Qoyllur Rit'i and Virgen Dolorosa	Sinakara Sanctuary to Tayankani
	7. Wednesday after Trinity	Señor de Qoyllur Rit'i	Tayankani to Mawallani
	8. Wednesday after Trinity	Señor de Tayankani and Virgen Dolorosa	Tayankani to Ocongate
V	9. Friday after Corpus	Señor de Tayankani	Ocongate plaza
	10. Saturday after Corpus	Señor de Tayankani and Virgen Dolorosa	Ocongate plaza to village boundary and return

35 kilometers from the main sanctuary, on the same day. In addition, the area is littered with numerous crosses, wayside oratories, and *apachitas* (cairns) marking the routes between these various holy sites.

The official version of the Qoyllur Rit'i legend, compiled from the church records in Ocongate by the priest who served in nearby Ccatca from 1928 to 1946, tells of an Indian boy named Mariano Mayta, younger son of a herd-owner living near Mawallani around the year 1780, who together with his elder brother tended his father's flocks of llamas and alpacas. One day, to escape his brother's bullying, Mariano fled toward the Sinakara snowfields. There he encountered a mestizo boy, fair and very handsome, with whom he struck up a friendship. They would meet day after day to chat and play, with the mestizo boy sharing his food with Mariano so that the shepherd had no need to return home for provisions. When his father heard what was happening and went to investigate, he found that his flock had miraculously increased, and promised his son a new suit of clothes as a reward.

Next day, at his father's prompting, Mariano asked his friend his name. The boy replied that he was called Manuel and he was from Tayankani.

Mariano, seeing that his friend's clothing was tattered, took a sample of the material to Cuzco to obtain a new suit for him. The fragment turned out to be of fine canonical cloth. The matter came to the attention of the bishop of Cuzco, who instructed the curate of Ocongate to inquire into the suspected sacrilege.

Accordingly, on 23 June 1783, the priest organized an expedition to Sinakara with the local political authorities. They saw the silhouette of the child, standing next to Mariano near a rock, and radiating a blinding light. The priest reached out to grab the child, but instead caught hold of a *tayanka* tree (*Baccharis odorata*). Looking up, he saw Christ's body hanging from the tree in dying agony. The party fell to their knees. When they had recovered their senses they saw only the *tayanka* tree in the shape of a cross and the body of Mariano, who, believing his friend to have been tortured, had collapsed of a fit and died. He was buried beneath the rock.

The miraculous events at Sinakara came to the notice of the king of Spain, who asked that the *tayanka* cross be sent to him. When he did not return it the Indians of the locality became restless, and to calm them the priest commissioned a replica. This image, known as Señor de Tayankani, is now kept in Ocongate. Nevertheless, it was Mariano's sepulchre at Sinakara which commanded the devotion of the Indians, and in order to avoid superstition the religious authorities had an image of Christ crucified painted on the rock itself (Ramírez 1969:61-68).

In this official mythohistory, the original seer was a humble Indian boy. The devotion was initiated, however, by the priest and the local, predominantly Spanish elite.[3] Furthermore, almost from the outset the shrine was split, as it were, between two icons, which were likewise ethnically contrasted: Señor de Tayankani, whose original first manifested itself to the higher- status, mainly Hispanic visionaries, and which was later retained by the monarch himself, and the rock-painting at Sinakara, the object of Indian devotion in particular. Now, of course, there is a third image, the portable representation of the Sinakara painting. As will be seen presently, the ritual passages of the two portable images in the course of the titular fiesta map out two contiguous spatial domains, in a manner consistent with the roles of their respective prototypes in the official mythohistory.

Oral tradition corroborates most of the elements of the written myth, though there are many local variations.[4] All the oral, peasant versions, however, share two features which distinguish them from the official one. The first is their stress on the rock as opposed to the *tayanka* branch. It is claimed that the figure of Christ crucified, the *taytacha* (little father), appeared on, or rather, entered within, the rock miraculously, in the instant that Manuel was apprehended by the priest. Second, oral tradition links the Sinakara shrine to Mount Ausankati 26 kilometers to the south, at 6,384 meters the tallest mountain in southern Peru and site of the most powerful *apu* (hill spirit) in the region. A pilgrimage to Sinakara is deemed

to be a pilgrimage to Apu Ausankati as well. Both Qoyllur Rit'i and
Ausankati are believed to bestow health, fertility, and abundance on their
devotees, and Apu Ausankati sometimes appears to the people in the guise
of a fair-skinned mestizo child. Yet the association stops short of identification and indeed, the powers of the mountain spirit are waning in proportion
to the increasing popularity of the Christian shrine and the number and
size of chapels erected on its slopes (Gow 1980:288).

Given the importance of Mount Ausankati in native cosmology from pre-
Hispanic times down to the present, it is perhaps surprising that the pagan
site was colonized by a Christian divinity as late as 250 years after the
Spanish conquest.[5] Most of the other major miraculous shrines in the region
were founded early in the colonial period, tended to lie on or near principal
transport routes, and became the venues for annual regional fairs. If poor
communications explain the late arrival of Ausankati's Christian counterpart, political factors help to explain why it arrived when it did.

In 1780, the Cuzco region was torn apart by the most severe rebellion
of the colonial epoch, the Tupac Amaru uprising. The revolt was not finally
crushed until 1783, when on July 19 the last of the rebel leaders were
executed in Cuzco. The revolt was in large measure a conflict between
Indians, mobilized for either the rebel or the royalist cause by their *kurakas*
(native chiefs). Broadly speaking, the predominantly pastoral provinces to
the southeast of Cuzco city sided with the rebels, the predominantly
agricultural ones to the north and northeast with the loyalists (Mörner
1978:109-29). The Ccatca-Ocongate area, transitional between these two
sociogeographic zones, thus saw some of the most extreme polarization of
the Indian populace of any locality in the region.

And on 23, June 1783, if for the moment the official legend is accepted
as testimonially true, just as the last embers of this internecine revolt were
being stamped out, a party of Ocongate notables led by the priest descends
from Sinakara and announces a miracle. The suffering Christ has appeared
before them on the mountain all Indians consider the most sacred. Instantly
there is created a shrine capable of transcending the divided loyalties of
a distressed people and extending its grace to all comers. Conscious strategy
on the part of the priest, seeking a spiritual unguent for his troubled flock,
perhaps played its part in this scenario, much as Kurtz (1982) has argued
for the miracle of the Virgin of Guadalupe in Mexico. At the very least, the
miracle appears to have been based almost entirely on the priest's testimo-
ny, backed up by the local worthies.

Be that as it may, the cult's fortunes seem to have ebbed and flowed over
the years with, the latest surge in its popularity dating from the retouching
of the rock image, 1935, and the bestowal of archdiocesan blessing in 1944.
An additional factor must have been the improvement in communications
at this time, as the road from Cuzco to Ocongate was completed in 1938.

As the number of pilgrims increased, an organizational hierarchy took
shape. In 1948 a group of devotees formed an association to keep order at

the fiesta and to improve facilities. The group was later reorganized as an *hermandad* (lay brotherhood), and with the increased revenue from the pilgrims the present sanctuary was built and an electric generator installed. The brotherhood is based in Urcos, capital of Quispicanchis province in which the shrine lies. Its 20 or so members, known as *celadores* (wardens), ardently devoted to the shrine, are seen as the mestizo guardians of a traditional Indian cult. Several times in recent years they have been honored by the presence of the archbishop himself at the fiesta.

THE CULT

In the contemporary cult, two levels of ritual activity may be distinguished. There is, first, the pilgrimage process itself—the convergence of human traffic on the miraculous rock at Sinakara. The majority of pilgrims attend during the novena of Corpus, arriving in small, community-based groups known as *naciones*, each contingent having its own troupe of ceremonial dancers and musicians as well as "lay" pilgrims. A *nación*—the word is a Spanish archaism meaning "race" or "tribe"—effectively serves as an escort for a small portable icon, the *lámina* or *demanda*, which is borne from the community to the shrine to lodge in the sanctuary for a period during the fiesta before being returned to its home chapel. At the same time, individual members of the contingent might make requests to the *taytacha* for personal favors or offer thanks for requests already granted, often in fulfillment of a vow. This type of pilgrimage is the predominant devotional style at other miraculous shrines in the region, and in its essentials varies but little from instance to instance.[6]

What gives the Qoyllur Rit'i fiesta its uniqueness is the second level of ritual activity, a complex sequence of processions and rites embracing the various component shrines. This level is superimposed on the first, though by no means all the visiting pilgrims participate in it in its entirety. It is here that dual organization of the event becomes manifest. The entire congeries of pilgrims is conceived in terms of two great moieties, labelled "Paucartambo" and "Quispicanchis" respectively. These are the names of the adjacent provinces whose mutual boundary passes through the Sinakara mountain range. In fact, the labels are synecdochic. "Paucartambo" in this context also includes the provinces of Cuzco, Calca, Urubamba, and beyond—that is, the predominantly agricultural zone to the northwest of the shrine, the zone stretching toward the tropical forest. "Quispicanchis" includes the provinces of Acomayo, Canas, Canchis, and beyond—that is, the mainly pastoral zone to the southeast of the shrine, the zone stretching toward the tundra. This sociogeographic division is amplified still further to connote the ecological contrasts of valley versus mountain, *kishwa* versus *puna*, and, polarized to the extreme, jungle versus highland, *montaña* versus *sierra*.[7] Ethnically, it comes to stand for the linguistic and cultural divide between Quechua and Qolla (Aymara), which in turn is transformed into the critical cleavage of Indian (native) versus mestizo (Spanish).

But in certain of the ritual contexts, the extensive, categorical division is condensed into a polarity between just two villages: Paucartambo, capital of the province of the same name, and Ocongate, in the province of Quispicanchis.[8] Indeed, I shall argue that a ritual fixture technically extraneous to the Qoyllur Rit'i liturgy takes this process of condensation a stage further, compressing the opposition into an internal polarity within a single village, that of Paucartambo itself.

The ethnic-ecological opposition and complementarity between *puna*-dwellers and *kishwa*-dwellers, pastoralists and agriculturalists respectively, is general throughout the Andes (see Duviols 1973). The specific Quechua-Qolla opposition receives frequent elaboration in the mythology both of the Cuzco region and of the *altiplano* (see Flores Ochoa 1973:306-09,322-23; Valderrama and Gutiérrez 1975:178-80). The stories typically involve competitive confrontations and affinal alliances between representatives of the two sociogeographic categories. The commonest site for these mythic encounters is La Raya, the pass across the Pacific-Atlantic watershed that has always constituted an elemental divide in Andean cosmography. The moiety division in the Qoyllur Rit'i cult between Paucartambo and Quispicanchis recapitulates this macrocosmic, ethnic-ecological dualism, variously expanding and reducing it in the course of the ritual performance. The ceremonial activities effect a seamless transition, by means of binary logic, through a succession of geographical levels: from the interregional to the intraregional, to the interlocal, to the intralocal. At the same time they transform the relation between the elements from an emergent opposition to a dialectical duality.

It is primarily through the medium of dance and dance styles that this transcendent bipartition and its multiple connotations are signalled. The fiesta permits the plethora of Andean ceremonial dance styles to be seen as an open set, making manifest the way in which the intrinsic characteristics and associations of each come to acquire relational meanings when juxtaposed with one another. Here, only the four dance styles centrally involved are described.[9]

First, the style of *ukuku* (bear). This role, seen as demanding energy and strength, should properly be danced by a young, unmarried man. Each *nación* generally has one or two *ukukus* in addition to its principal dance style. The *ukuku* dancer wears a woollen mask and a long black or brown shaggy smock, and carries a rope whip, whistle, gourd, or some other improvised wind instrument, and a small doll on whose behalf he begs money from strangers. While in costume he speaks in a high falsetto voice, and keeps up a constant patter of jokes and sexual innuendo to bystanders. Yet *ukukus* are powerful. They discharge a peacekeeping role during the fiesta, and in many ways are impervious to the jurisdiction of the *celadores*.

The *ukuku* is an ambivalent, trickster-like figure, who both preserves order through his constabulary role and is at liberty to subvert it through his jokes and burlesque.[10]

The *ukuku* figure is intimately related to that of the *condenado* (condemned one or ghoul). This is the feared spirit of a person who has committed a grievous sin, paradigmatically the sin of incest, and is therefore barred from *hanaqpacha* (the afterworld) and doomed to roam this world terrorizing the living. It is widely believed that the glaciers in the vicinity of Mount Ausankati are infested with *condenados*, for by climbing the mountain, naked and in chains, they can obtain forgiveness from the *apu* and release from their tortured state of living death. But they invariably fail to reach their goal, slipping backward on the snow and ice. Some also seek forgiveness from the *taytacha* at Sinakara, but he forbids them to enter the sanctuary and they are obliged to worship him from the glacier (see Casaverde Rojas 1970:206). The *ukukus* at Qoyllur Rit'i are in one sense the protectors of their fellow pilgrims against the dangerous *condenados*, but they also enact the penance of the ghouls and are sometimes said to be *condenados* themselves.

Until 1978, the Qoyllur Rit'i *ukukus* were organized into the two moiety groupings of Paucartambo and Quispicanchis. These were not merely ad hoc coalitions but were formally constituted bodies, having their own hierarchies of presidents, secretaries, and treasurers based on the provincial capitals of Paucartambo and Urcos, respectively. In 1979 a splinter group from Acomayo province broke away from the Quispicanchis grouping (Randall 1982a:38), but seems not to have survived as an independent entity. There has since been another secession from the Quispicanchis moiety, by *ukukus* from the province of Canchis. The latter faction has been institutionalized, with its center in Sicuani, the capital of Canchis. There are therefore now three *ukuku* bodies: Paucartambo, Quispicanchis, and Canchis.

Second, there are the *qhapaq qollas* (noble Qollas). Aymara traders from the altiplano to the southeast were frequent visitors to the villages of the Cuzco region, and the *qhapaq qolla* dancers are a mimetic portrayal of these. Their costume includes a white woollen mask, a flat embroidered hat decorated with beads, spangles, and gold coins and having short trailing ribbons on either side, a woollen *llijlla* (shawl), a *vicuña* or alpaca skin slung across the shoulders, and a rope sling. *Qolla* music is generally played on a *kina* (notched flute), harp or violin, accordion, and drum; the choreography is energetic, but nevertheless has a graceful, courtly air. Many villages from both moieties send *qhapaq qolla* dancers, but it is the troupe from Ocongate village, the moiety capital, who are the principal representatives of the Quispicanchis moiety, and who discharge an important ritual role in the fiesta.

Finally, two styles of *ch'uncho* dancers are on display at Qoyllur Rit'i. *Ch'uncho* is a derogatory term in both Quechua and Aymara for the tribal, "uncivilized" inhabitants of the lowland jungle to the north. It was to the jungle that the first race of beings in the Andes, the *ñaupa machus* (ancients from long ago), fled to escape the heat of the sun when the Creator raised it in the sky. Consequently *ch'uncho* dancers are associated with the ancestral forebears of present-day highlanders, especially of the agriculturalists of the eastern Andean slopes. There are now several distinct *ch'uncho* dance styles, some of them explicitly associated with particular highland villages or areas, though they have been adopted by *naciones* elsewhere. The two that concern us here are *ch'uncho extranjero* and *wayri ch'uncho*.

The style of *ch'uncho extranjero* (literally, foreign savage) is associated with the village of Paucartambo. Its costume includes a headdress of pink heron feathers with a long decorated plait, a gauze mask, a brightly colored skirt with matching shoulder sashes, and a staff of *chonta* wood (*Bactris ciliata*). The leader of a troupe, the *rey* (Spanish, king), is distinguished by a crown and a long cape.

The costume of the *wayri ch'unchos* is subtly contrasted. They wear a headdress and plait of orange and red macaw feathers, a brightly colored waistcoat, and black trousers with rayon scarves trailing from the waistband, and they also carry *chonta* staves. They are not masked, though they may choose to wear dark glasses. Their leader is known as the *arariwa*, the Quechua word for field guardian or work organizer. *Wayri* is not in fact a Quechua word at all, but means "chief" in the language of the tribal Machiguenga to the northwest (Camino 1978:92). Thus, while both *ch'uncho* styles are mimetic portrayals of jungle Indians, they are contrasted to each other as "native chiefs" to "aliens," as indigenous savages to foreign savages.

The two *ch'uncho* styles share a "traditional" instrumentation of two *pitos* (transverse flutes), tambour, and bass drum. *Ch'uncho extranjero* troupes, however, frequently display the more Hispanic instrumentation of violin, harp and accordion, or—a mark of real modernity—a brass band. The choreographies of both are gymnastic and warlike, with pairs of dancers clashing their staves against each other. Many of the formations exhibit the basic Andean designs of diametric and concentric dualism, to be discussed presently. *Ch'unchos extranjeros* have a fairly wide musical and choreographic repertoire (see Roel Pineda 1950). The *wayri ch'unchos*, however, use just one tune, in the pentatonic scale, and unlike most of the other dance music at the fiesta, in compound time. Played with a pounding drumbeat, it is this distinctive rhythm that sets the music apart from the rest. Indeed, the *wayri ch'uncho* tune is in many ways the leitmotif of the entire pilgrimage. When dance troupes of whatever style dance from point to point, rather than perform in an arena, their musicians frequently adopt this piece while the dancers imitate the basic *wayri ch'uncho* step.

Ch'uncho dancers feature in some oral, peasant versions of the Qoyllur Rit'i legend. The crucified Christ who appeared miraculously at Sinakara is said to have been carried down to Ocongate by the mestizo witnesses, but he escaped and returned to the scene of the miracle. He was recovered, but escaped again. After his third escape, he appeared in a dream to the Ocongate priest, saying he would remain in the village only if the *wayri ch'uncho* dancers of Paucartambo came to perform for him. This they did, and he stayed, in the form of Señor de Tayankani (Gow 1976:217-18, 227). Not only is ritual dancing the typical Indian devotional style, but *wayri ch'uncho* dancers in particular are identified with the poor and underprivileged. By making these rituals—of the Indians rendering cult service to it—a condition of the Ocongate mestizos' custody of the Tayankani image, this myth attempts to resolve the ethnic conflict that surrounds the miraculous *taytacha*.

Ch'unchos also feature in the legend of the patron saint of Paucartambo village, the Virgen de Carmen, whose fiesta, 16 July in one sense constitutes a finale to the Corpus sequence of Qoyllur Rit'i. The Paucartambo Virgin also prefers *ch'uncho* dancers to all others, though in this case their exalted status is at first sight paradoxical. One version of the legend has it that the Virgin was being brought to Paucartambo by Qollas from the *altiplano* when they were attacked by *ch'unchos* and she was cast into the river. She was carried downstream and beached near the village, undamaged except for the marks of the *ch'unchos'* arrows on her breast. Yet she prefers *ch'uncho* dancers above all and if they did not attend her fiesta, her face would turn pale, signifying imminent disaster (Barrionuevo 1969:276).

As far as ritual duties are concerned, the principal dance troupe of the Paucartambo moiety is the team of *wayri ch'unchos* from Paucartambo village, though there are usually *ch'unchos extranjeros* and *qhapaq qollas* from the village as well. Ocongate, too, has a troupe of *wayri ch'unchos*, who also have a particular role to play in the ritual performance alongside the village's principal dance troupe of *qhapaq qollas*.

Superimposed upon this geographic coding of dance styles is an ethnic one. The *qhapaq qolla* style is regarded as having a distinctly mestizo connotation, one that it shares with certain other styles on view at Qoyllur Rit'i—the *auqa chilenos* (wild Chileans), for instance, who represent the invading Chilean soldiers in the nineteenth-century War of the Pacific, and the *tontunas* from Juliaca in the department of Puno to the southeast, a thoroughly criollo formation that has recently made its appearance at the fiesta. Against these "mestizo" dance styles, the *ch'uncho* forms are associated with Indian ethnic status. There is a dimension here of newcomers or outsiders versus natives or autochthons. Mestizo styles commonly represent either foreigners who have trespassed into the Cuzco region for one reason or another—Qolla traders, Chilean soldiers—or are clearly Hispanic in inspiration, as are the Juliaca *tontunas*. Ch'uncho dancers, on the other hand, though also representing outsiders in a literal sense, tend to be identified with native Quechua highlanders.[11]

Yet *ch'uncho* styles, in their turn, are differentiated among themselves along ethnic lines. That of *ch'uncho extranjero* connotes mestizo status when counterposed to that of *wayri ch'uncho*, which is associated with an unqualified Indian ethnic identity. This contrast, too, fits the newcomer-native dichotomy. I should stress here that I am talking of associations with ethnic categories rather than monopolization by ethnic groups, however the latter might be defined. It is relevant to note that the *ukuku* style to a large extent stands outside this pattern of ethnic discrimination, apparently immune to either Indian or mestizo stereotyping.

I return now to the fiesta (see Figure 16.1 and Table 16.1). The following account, much abridged, is based on observations made in 1984. By Trinity Sunday, numbers at Sinakara had swelled to perhaps 25,000 or more. Ritual activities at this stage of the proceedings were principally directed toward sanctifying and circumscribing the Christian sanctuary and its immediate precincts. In the evening there was a procession of the Blessed Sacrament through the sanctuary precincts, while the following morning an open-air Mass was celebrated from the sanctuary balcony. The *ukukus*, however, now segregated themselves from the rest of the congregation and gathered on the hillside opposite the sanctuary. They divided into assemblies based on their three groupings, Paucartambo, Quispicanchis, and Canchis, and each laid its own plans for the visit to the glaciers that night.

Later that day, after a detailed recitation of the official foundation myth over the public address system, a dignified procession departed from the sanctuary and made its way slowly to the Virgin's grotto, whence it descended in a wide arc to the cairn cross marking the entrance to the shrine precincts before returning to the sanctuary. It consisted of two parallel lines of walking dancers, with all the *ukukus* grouped toward the front, followed by a random mix of other styles, each dancer holding the whip, staff, or scarf of the one behind. Toward the end of the procession, between the two lines, was the leader of the Ocongate *qhapaq qollas*, two *celadores*, and the archbishop of Cuzco, flanked by his auxiliary and the local officiating priest. Behind him came the statue of Señor de Qoyllur Rit'i, enclosed in a glass-fronted wooden cruciform case surmounted by three sprays of *wayri ch'uncho* headdress feathers, a clear sign that this was an Indian Christ, a Christ of the peasants.

The special function discharged in this procession by the *qolla* leader of Ocongate stems from the status of the village as the "capital" of the Quispicanchis moiety. Ocongate in fact regularly sent three dance troupes to the fiesta: *qhapaq qollas*, *contradanzas* (countrydance), and *wayri ch'unchos*. The *qollas* were the village's chief dancer delegates. The *qolla* and *contradanza* troupes were composed mostly of habitual Spanish speakers in wage employment, who as individuals projected an obviously mestizo status. It was noticeable, however, that during the fiesta they frequently chose to speak Quechua to one another, especially in their joking and banter, and in various other ways collectively affected an Indian identity. The *wayri ch'uncho* troupe, on the other hand, were Quechua-speaking peasants from the village and its environs. While the *qollas* and *contradanzas* traveled together as the *nación* of Ocongate, and by 1984 had built adjacent *celdas* (cells) for themselves at Sinakara—one of the few *naciones* to enjoy such facilities—the tiny band of *wayri ch'unchos* kept themselves apart from their fellow villagers throughout the fiesta. There was practically no interaction between the two contingents.[12]

That night, the fiesta reached its climax. The sanctuary was filled to capacity with pilgrims. One dance troupe after another came to take leave of the *taytacha*, dancing before the altar as best they could in the crush, while the *celadores* and some *ukukus* endeavored to maintain order.

Now, however, the ritual focus was shifting from the Sinakara sanctuary to the encircling mountains. Early in the morning, *ukukus* started to call to one another by blowing on their whistles and gourds. Gathering in their groups, they began to ascend the steep hogbacks to the glaciers. Four separate snowfields overhang the Sinakara valley. Formerly, only the two central ones were occupied by *ukukus*, the one on the left by those from the Paucartambo moiety and the one on the right by those from Quispicanchis. Since 1980, the Canchis group has claimed a vacant glacier.

Each group followed a separate route to its snowfield. As they stepped off the moraine onto the glacier, the *ukukus* linked themselves into long chains with their whips to prevent their slipping backward on the treacherous, icy slopes. By dawn there were about a thousand of them, possibly more, dotted across the three great tongues of snow that swept down from the mountain peaks. Some were kneeling singly or in groups of two or three, facing the summit, lighted candles planted before them in the snow, their lips moving in silent prayer. Others indulged in horseplay, throwing snowballs at one another and sliding down snow chutes with yells and shouts. Where a single *nación* included several *ukukus*, they tended to gather in *nación* groups with other, uncostumed companions who had come up with them, displaying the banner of their community or village. Among such groups an *ukuku* visiting the glacier for the first time was obliged to receive a *bautismo* (baptism) in the form of three strokes of the whip on the rump administered by the *ukuku* leader of his *nación*. An *ukuku* who had "sinned," that is, committed a ritual infraction, received similar treatment. After such a whipping, the victim kissed the whip and embraced the whipper.

Originally, the ostensible purpose of the *ukukus'* ascent to the glacier was to reclaim a cross that had been planted there a few days before. For this, the two *ukuku* armies of Paucartambo and Quispicanchis would engage in a battle, pelting each other with snowballs in the darkness. The victors would then bear the cross in triumph back to the sanctuary (Ramírez 1969:86).

Although deaths were not actively sought in this encounter, it was nevertheless apparently not uncommon for *ukukus* to be killed by falling into crevasses as they chased each other across the glacier. Nowadays there is no battle. Instead, each group, including, since 1980, that from Canchis, has its own cross erected beforehand on its particular section of the glacier, which it merely retrieves and returns to the sanctuary.

In preparation for the descent, *ukukus* set about carving out chunks of ice from the glacier, sawing away laboriously with their rope whips. The blocks of ice were then tied to their backs and carried down to the sanctuary as a penance. Many were simply dumped, but some people collected their meltwater in bottles and conserved it for medicinal use.

After the *ukukus* had returned to the sanctuary precincts and dispersed to their *nación* groups, a final open-air Mass was celebrated. As soon as it was over, there was an exodus. The majority of pilgrims began to stream down the path toward Mawallani, whence they would board trucks for home. A substantial contingent, however—more than a thousand—set off up the trail on the opposite side of the valley. This was the beginning of the minipilgrimage to Tayankani and thence to Ocongate, a 25-kilometer trek across the hills retracing the steps of Mariano and Manuel in the legend of the founding of the shrine.

On this pilgrimage within a pilgrimage, besides the *láminas* and *demandas* of the various *naciones* taking part, there were two images to which the entire company served as a collective escort. One was the portable statue of Señor de Qoyllur Rit'i, enclosed within its wooden case decorated with the macaw feathers of the *wayri ch'unchos*. The other was the Virgen Dolorosa (Virgin of Sorrows) which had been donated some years earlier by a pious devotee from Ocongate. The Virgin would be taken all the way to Ocongate. The crucifix, though, would be exchanged at Tayankani for another, that of Señor de Tayankani, which would proceed to Ocongate, while Señor de Qoyllur Rit'i would be escorted back across the hills to Mawallani. This stage of the ceremonial cycle was transitional in both time and space, intermediate between two centers: Sinakara, the regional mountain center of the rock shrine and the *apus*, where the main rites of the fiesta have been enacted, and Ocongate, the local valley center of the district and parish, which was to host the feast of Corpus Christi. The hamlet of Tayankani, the provenance of the divine child in the myth, is the boundary between these two spheres of influence.

For this central, collective pilgrimage of the shrine statues themselves across their sacred territory, the ritual escort at once coalesced and divided along moiety lines into two great regional *naciones*. It is a convention strictly observed on this march that the task of carrying the images alternates between the Paucartambo and Quispicanchis groups for successive sections of the journey, and within each group between its constituent *naciones*. Just as local *nación* groups on a pilgrimage relate to one another according to a rigid ritual symmetry, so also do the moieties, as regional *naciones*, observe a strictly symmetrical complementarity throughout the overnight march.[13]

Where the trail reached the rim of the valley there was a small shrine-shelter. The Qoyllur Rit'i crucifix and the Virgin were placed inside, along with the *láminas* and *demandas* of the various local *naciones*. The ragged column of pilgrims now grouped themselves into their local *naciones* and, apart from two brief episodes, were to remain thus for the entire pilgrimage.

The president of the brotherhood then addressed the assembly, in a manner that set the tone for these ritual stops for the rest of the journey. After introducing himself, he immediately launched into an ill-tempered harangue, castigating first of all the Paucartambo group, who had been responsible for carrying the images on this initial leg of the journey, for their late arrival at the spot. The person who bore the brunt of this rebuke was the *arariwa* of the *wayri ch'uncho* dancers from Paucartambo village, for it was his duty to lead the principal images and to arrange the succession of their bearers on the Paucartambo sections of the procession. He was dragged forward and stood in silence with his head bowed while the president delivered his tirade. A few of the onlookers demanded that the *arariwa* be whipped there and then for his dereliction, but the president demurred, saying he did not want to commit an abuse. He then turned his attention to the musicians, or rather to those of them who had arrived inebriated, and chided them for their disrespect.

This outburst was delivered in Spanish. When he had finished, the president, who was bilingual, asked his audience disdainfully whether they had understood, for the Quechua monolinguals among them obviously had not. The intention seems to have been deliberately to humiliate the monolingual members of the congregation. Two of his colleagues then repeated the general message concerning discipline and sobriety in Quechua, in more moderate tones.

For the next section of the journey, it was the turn of the Quispicanchis group to carry the principal images. Now that the moiety and its constituent *naciones* had been consolidated, matters proceeded in a better organized fashion. The aim was to allow everyone in each *nación* to carry one of the images for a short distance, men the crucifix and women the Virgin. Men far outnumbered women, so the crucifix changed hands more often, every dozen paces or so. In order to facilitate smooth transfers from one bearer to the next, the members of the different *naciones* went ahead and spaced themselves along the path; when the crucifix arrived each would carry it on his back, holding it in place by means of a rope, until he came to the next volunteer.

It was for the supervision of the intermittent passage of the crucifix that the Ocongate *wayri ch'unchos*, or at least the *arariwa*, took charge. He walked immediately before the image and directed its loading and unloading in a confident, almost imperious manner, frequently issuing peremptory orders to the volunteers at the side of the path to position themselves still farther ahead. He wore his dance costume, minus the headdress; all the other dancers except for the *ukukus* were in mufti. Immediately behind the crucifix the musicians were playing the *wayri ch'uncho* tune continuously, and those pilgrims waiting to assume the holy burden did not stand still but performed a vestigial dance on the spot, executing rhythmic *ch'uncho* foot movements in time to the music. The entire journey, like the *nación* pilgrimage on which it was modelled, was in effect not walked but danced.[14]

This dance-like character of the march became explicit on two occasions. The first was the descent into the broad valley of Yanakancha, the site of the next ritual halt, where the company customarily rests for several hours until the moon rises at about 1:00 A.M. Here, dancers donned their costumes and formed into three groups. On the left were the *ukukus* and other dancers from the Paucartambo moiety, on the right those from the Quispicanchis moiety, and in the center, women crossbearers from both. The three groups ran down the slope in parallel lines with Christ and the Virgin following, and the two images were installed in the chapel of the little hamlet.

For the next section of the journey it was the turn of the Paucartambo moiety to transport the images. At the next stopping place, as the images were being installed in the shrine-shelter, there was another vigorous remonstrance. This time, the president accused the *arariwa* of another troupe of *wayri ch'unchos* of not showing proper respect for the group's *lámina* during its formal placing in the shelter. On this occasion, though, the president's strictures met with defiant rejoinders not just from the *arariwa* but from other members of his *nación*. All to no avail: the president insisted he must be whipped. The punishment was administered, not by the president, but by one of his colleagues from the brotherhood. The victim received the usual three strokes and afterward kissed the whip and embraced his scourger. The incident was greeted with *Schadenfreude* as members of other *naciones* evidently relished the fact that someone had been arraigned and punished.

So it went on through the night, each moiety having custody of the images for a few hours before handing them over to the other at an appointed spot. As the sky was beginning to lighten with the gathering dawn, the company arrived at a narrow plateau. One ridge commanded an extensive view of the eastern horizon. From the other, the ground swept down toward the hamlet of Tayankani. Here, *inti alabado*, the hymn of praise to the sun, was to take place.

The dancers changed into costume and formed a single line strung out across the eastern ridge, Paucartambo to the left and Quispicanchis to the right. Seconds before the sun appeared, the musicians fell silent and everyone knelt. As it came up they all scrambled to their feet and gave an exultant cry of *Alabado!* (hail!)

There followed a series of *bautismos*, whippings administered by the leader of a dance troupe whose dancers were serving for the first time. This was treated as good sport, and an excited crowd pressed close to watch. At one point, the president intervened and drew aside the *rey* of a troupe of *ch'uncho extranjero* dancers who had just finished enthusiastically initiating his neophytes. After the two had conferred briefly, the president announced that the *rey* had committed a delict—he did not specify what—and would have to be disciplined. Begging the crowd to excuse him, he then proceeded to administer the flogging himself. While all this was going on, the officiating priest, who was accompanying the procession, looked on inscrutably.

Everyone now ran across to the opposite ridge, where they reformed into moiety lines. First, they faced the sun, kneeling in silence for a few seconds. Then they stood, turned around, and knelt facing the escarpment. Suddenly they arose as a single body and proceeded to filter down the hillside at a trot in two columns, led respectively by the *ukukus* of each moiety with Peruvian flags streaming in the wind. All the musicians were playing the same tune, the *alabado*, with an obvious attempt at synchronization. The two lines of dancers wheeled, wove, and zigzagged across the landscape, successively converging, crossing, and separating in a serpentine choreography that was entirely symmetrical across a vertical axis. This was the climax of the procession. For the participants, it must have been a brief experience of submersion in a vast, coordinated moving design, one that transcended the boundaries of *naciones* and linked the two moieties together in perfectly symmetrical complementarity. For the observer, it was a stunning, unforgettable spectacle.

The two principal images joined the ends of the lines and wound up in a small whitewashed chapel on a hillock overlooking Tayankani. Within minutes, the fleeting, Terpsichorean unity had given way to exclusiveness and localism, as *naciones* reformed into separate groups dotted about the hillside, to take breakfast.

The actual entry into Tayankani later in the morning was less dramatic——a conventional procession of two lines of dancers, with the principal images in their midst. At the chapel the image of Señor de Qoyllur Rit'i was relinquished, later to be carried by a different escort to the chapel at Mawallani, and replaced by that of Señor de Tayankani for the final stage of the main pilgrimage to Ocongate. As the president took formal possession of the Tayankani image, he delivered yet another harangue, directed this time at the *arariwa* of the *wayri ch'unchos* of Paucartambo, who was alleged to have committed another ritual solecism.

On the walk to Ocongate the images of Christ and the Virgin again passed from bearer to bearer, though there seemed to be no rigid demarcation now between the moieties. Just outside Ocongate the procession was met by the village *alcalde* (mayor), who took Señor de Tayankani onto his shoulders and carried it the last few hundred meters to the chapel on the edge of the village.

The images were given new clothes before being carried to the parish church. Señor de Tayankani having been once more appropriated by the village, the regional setting now gave way to a local one. Activities in Ocongate took on a recreational, civic aspect, with processions and dance displays in the bustling plaza amid the market stalls and *cantinas* (café-tents) erected for the occasion.

One event in particular commands our attention. The following day, Corpus Christi, there is supposed to take place a mock battle between the *qhapaq qollas* of Ocongate and the *wayri ch'unchos* of Paucartambo, a piece of comic theater eagerly anticipated by the spectators. Unfortunately, in 1984, because of a dispute among the dance groups, it was not staged. I therefore summarize Ramírez' account from the 1960s.

The *qollas*, grouped into one corner of the plaza, come under attack from the *ch'unchos*. They consult coca leaves to divine who will win the fight, and invoke Ausankati and the other *apus* to turn back the *ch'unchos'* arrows. But eventually one of the *ch'unchos* breaks through and slaughters the bodyguard of the *imilla*, the *qolla* woman. When the *ch'unchos* have left with their prize, the *qollas* return to collect their dead. The bodyguard is carried in the cortège by a group of *ukukus*. Suddenly, from one corner of the plaza emerges a group of *k'achampa* dancers from the village, driving mules laden with gifts for the festive farewells; at the same time the *qollas* enter from the opposite side, with loaded llamas.[15] The two groups then invite the village authorities to celebrate the conclusion of the fight. The result of the battle is the same every year: the *qollas* are always defeated (Ramírez 1969:80-82; see also Gow 1976:232-33). In this confrontation the two great moieties are at once metonymically condensed into their head villages and symbolically contrasted in the juxtaposition of the two dance styles. Two days later, the *ch'unchos* formally take their leave of the Ocongate *qollas*, and return to Paucartambo.

So ends the fiesta of Qoyllur Rit'i. But there is another festivity that takes place in Paucartambo village a month or so later that begs to be included in the overall ceremonial cycle, for here the metonymic condensation is taken a stage further. This is the festival of the village's patron saint, the Virgen de Carmen, on 16 July, whose foundation myth was recounted earlier. The central feature of this fiesta is another ritual battle between troupes of *qhapaq qollas* and *ch'unchos*, on this occasion *ch'unchos extranjeros*. Both troupes are drawn from the village itself. The battle follows the same pattern as that enacted at Ocongate and the *ch'unchos* again emerge victorious (Roel Pineda 1950:63-64; Barrionuevo 1969:276). In both cases, the symmetrical relation between the moieties in the transitional stage of the pilgrimage procession has been superseded by a dialectical one: *qollas*, senior as ritual officiants, are defeated by *ch'unchos*, favorites of the *taytacha* and the Virgin.

THE RITUAL TOPOGRAPHY

It is clear from this account that the cultural design of the Qoyllur Rit'i festival is spatialized across the landscape. The shrine territory is ritually demarcated into two mutually exclusive spheres. One is centered on Sinakara, the regional pilgrimage site in the mountains, situated on the territorial boundary between the two moieties of Paucartambo and Quispicanchis. The other is focused on the village of Ocongate, the seat of local political and parochial control. The latter sphere has its own internal polarity of local centers, between Ocongate, capital of Quispicanchis moiety and straddling the ecological divide between the *puna* and *kishwa* zones, and Paucartambo village, capital of the eponymous moiety and straddling the divide between *kishwa* and *montaña*.

The heart of this extensive sacred geography, the Sinakara center, is itself partitioned into two sectors: the valley with its miraculous, Christianized crag, and the encircling glaciated peaks, northern outposts of the Ausankati range. The snow-covered slopes of Mount Ausankati, as noted, are peopled with *condenados* vainly attempting to scale the peak and attain salvation. The *taytacha*, too, ascends the glacier in the shape of a cross, or, nowadays, crosses, but he is reclaimed and returned to the sanctuary by the *ukukus*, themselves *condenados* and hence the only beings capable of performing such a feat. Imprisoned in his rock abode just beneath the peaks, permanently denied the possibility of release from his condition, his living corpse, a kind of enshrined *condenado*, radiates a power that can be tapped by human beings to alter their personal or collective destinies.

Señor de Qoyllur Rit'i, then, is a petrified Christ situated in the very heartlands of his kindred spirits, the *condenados*. It is this unique concatenation that has caused the cult, of all the miraculous shrine devotions in Cuzco, to assume such a distinctive character. While its current mass popularity stems from its relaunching and promotion by Church authorities, assisted by the improvement in communications in the area, the particular and intricate liturgy of its titular fiesta is a consequence of the direct, material insertion of the miraculous shrine into the regional cosmography of the living dead.

Why, though, should this liturgy be pervaded by dualism? To answer this question it is necessary to consider for a moment the theme of agonistic confrontation in Andean culture.

FIGHTING FOR ORDER

Annual intergroup duels between men, and occasionally between women, are commonplace throughout the Andes. Their generic Quechua name is *tinkuy*, meaning an encounter between two like entities or a combination of two substances. They vary in their ferocity, but in many of them deaths are not unusual. Some also involve the capture and rape of women. The span of the participating groups varies from case to case. They may be two sections of a single village or town, or of an ethnic group, or they may be coalitions of communities in a locality or region. Some *tinkuys*, in other words, seem to express a "within" relation, others a "between" relation. This apparently relative distinction can be given substance by reference to the physical location of the encounter. Some—let us call them "internal" *tinkuys*—take place squarely within human settlements, generally in the center, in the village plaza. Others, the "external" *tinkuys*, are just as obviously staged far away from human habitation, in the high *punas* and cordilleras. Internal *tinkuys* take place between groups standing in a fixed relation to each other, a relation on which the outcome of the *tinkuy* has a redundant effect. External *tinkuys*, on the other hand, take place between populations which stand to each other in no such predetermined relation—the *tinkuy becomes* their relationship.

Qamawara, the community in which I was based during fieldwork in the 1970s, used to join in one of these external *tinkuys* until a death some 40 years ago came to the notice of the police and the event was prohibited. The encounter was held every Comadres Thursday at an isolated spot in the high *puna* roughly equidistant from the participating groups. These were all upland agropastoral communities and haciendas situated in adjacent administrative districts. But the two coalitions that formed for combat were fluid, and allegiances shifted from year to year. The principal weapon was the sling, but once felled with slingshot a fighter risked death by dismemberment or decapitation. Women attended to animate the men and to rouse them to feats of bravery, but risked abduction, being regarded as potential brides of their captors. The *tinkuy* was explicitly portrayed as a sacrifice, or at least a bloodletting, to the local *apus* in return for the fertility of the soil and the welfare of people and animals. After 40 years members of the various communities still gather at the spot for a *parabién* (felicitation). Despite the irenic nature of the event, the young men talk about how they would attack the enemy if only given the chance, and the cross-band pairing for dancing takes place in an atmosphere of latent hostility. Sexual competition and veiled antagonism remain.

The same features are found in external *tinkuys* still fought today.[16] They are generally staged on politico-territorial boundaries in the high mountains, the realm of the *apus*. They involve two groupings conceptualized initially as equivalent, though victory, an incipient relation of superiority-inferiority, may be claimed through the idiom of bride-capture. There are, however, no permanent winners or losers, and in any case the coalitions themselves may be in a constant state of flux.

An extreme example of such conflict, a kind of super-*tinkuy*, is afforded by the annual pilgrimage to Copisa, in the *puna* zone in the department of Apurímac (Skar 1985). Copisa does not have a Christian shrine and derives its focal significance solely from the importance of a nearby mountain *apu*. The fiesta enjoys wide renown and attracts people from throughout the department. The community contingents that attend comport themselves en route in a similar fashion to the *nación* pilgrim groups in Cuzco, stressing egalitarianism and brotherhood. At the ritual center, however, the mood changes dramatically. The entire gathering assumes the form of a violent melee, with men kicking and punching one another and lashing out viciously with studded whips. At one level the fighting appears indiscriminate, but an informant's account does suggest that the major lines of cleavage are between communities, or between coalitions of communities. The bloodletting appears to proceed unchecked, there being no visible organizational hierarchy to maintain order as at Christian shrines.

Here, dualism has all but broken down, or rather, has not been generated. There is little evidence of any transcendent bipartition: the pattern of conflict and coalition at any one moment is practically random. This, then, is a limiting case: something approaching total intergroup flux, embracing communities from throughout the region, centered on an apical mountain shrine, which, it is worth noting, is unashamedly pagan. As a modality of dualism it represents nondualism, the chaotic extreme.

Internal *tinkuys* signify the opposite pole, that of institutionalized, diametric dualism.[17] This is the domain of human habitation, of social order, of political control, subordination, and reaction, and it is here that moieties, as constituent parts of communities, towns, or ethnic groups, take on more or less fixed relational attributes in each case. Some of the more common ones can be summarized.

The moieties as such are typically referred to as *hanan* (upper) and *hurin* (lower), although they may or may not correspond to the upper and lower halves of the village or territory in geographical terms. Where they do not, another, spatial dualism founded on ecological complementarity is frequently encountered. The *hanan-hurin* distinction can be further colored by reference to "foreigners," newcomers from without (upper moiety), versus "natives," original inhabitants of the territory (lower moiety); or, more strongly, "conquerors" and "conquered" respectively. All these distinctions signal potential or actual asymmetry and hierarchy.

There is frequently, however, a simultaneous parallelism and equivalence between the moieties which, though residentially interspersed, may be conceived as spatially symmetrical, right versus left, and mutually self-contained. Thus each may control, at least ideally, territory in all ecological floors, and wherever a strict rule of marriage applies, it is always one of moiety endogamy. This equivalence may be further expressed in patterns of ritual complementarity. In this domain, then, dualism has become stable and institutional and the two components distinguished and differentiated to create a closed, bounded world in which relations of equivalence, symmetry, and reciprocity between the moieties coexist with difference, asymmetry, and potential hierarchy.

Where they occur, *tinkuys* between such groups—internal *tinkuys*—are an echo of their external counterparts. They bring to the surface the essential mutability and constructed, cultural quality of the directed relation between the moieties, throwing up the possibility of dialectical inversion in their mutual standing. Their relation is thus placed in temporary abeyance, and the endogamic boundary may be breached in the seizure and violation of women. But in the end, the internal *tinkuy* has a redundant effect on the institutional relations between the moieties; on the contrary, it sustains them.

This cultural portrayal of the passage from entropy to order is variously mapped onto the vertical landscapes of different localities according to a consistent pattern. The descent from the high *punas* to the intermontane valleys is a movement from the unbounded field of wild, uncontrolled fertility to the bounded domain of society and controlled reproduction. The natural environment is continuous, a variegated landscape whose multiple centers - sacralized mountains, lakes and crags - contour space but do not themselves enclose it. Human populations use these same centers to establish discontinuities, defining themselves by the sacred features of the landscape around them. Different populations perhaps placate the same spirits of nature in order to guarantee their continued reproduction, but in the act of such appeasement generate an incipient opposition between themselves. The unbounded field of the nature spirits is thus fragmented into a mosaic of numerous bounded communities and groups, each typically recapitulating the original, formative opposition now condensed into a rigid, diametric duality that at once encloses, balances, and ranks its component parts.

This portrayal of the transition from disordered chaos to bisected cosmos is, however, incomplete. There is a further stage beyond that of dialectical dualism, the stage of pure concentrism (see Lévi-Strauss 1968). Once moieties are not merely distinguished but differentiated, the structure can transform into one of center and periphery, the moiety of higher rank constituting the dominant center, that of lower rank the dominant periphery. Power is now crystallized and focused, anchored to a point but diffusing outward in an unbounded field. It reproduces itself in new centers elsewhere, in a kind of cultural imaging of the multicentric natural environment. In a concentric system as opposed to a diametric one, hierarchy is no longer dual but linear, no longer attenuated by any countervailing equivalencies but celebrated as an attribute of the comsos itself.

Seen in this light, dialectical dualism, charged diametricality, appears as a mixed modality. It is a compromise between pure or neutral diametricality on the one hand and pure concentrism on the other, an attempt to reconcile symmetry with asymmetry, equality with hierarchy, fixity with change. As such, it is a system in tension, containing within itself the structural possibilities both of an enduring, perfectly balanced reciprocity and of the rise of hegemonic, centralized states.[18]

The fiesta of Qoyllur Rit'i, focused upon the syncretized powers of Sinakara, annually reiterates this cultural achievement. Inscribed within the cult is a ritual cycle that reveals itself as a paradigm of Andean dualism, an inventory of its successively more highly organized forms, displaying the passage from entropy to society. The cycle reads as an extended dramatization on a regional scale, deploying the landscape itself as its mise-en-scène, of the process whereby the harnessing of extrasocial powers ipso facto organizes human society into a dual system. First there is the battle on the glacier, an external *tinkuy* between the massed *ukukus* of the respective moieties. Here the goal involves the capture of the *taytacha* himself and his sacrifice once more to the *apus* so that his power may continue to flow. Here, there is competition, fission, and fusion; hierarchy between the moieties, indeed the boundary between them, is indeterminate. Next comes the intermediate stage of the pilgrimage procession, as the portable image of the miraculous *taytacha* is borne on its extended passage to the domain of civilization. Intermoiety relations now take on the form of neutral diametricality, with rigid equivalence and mirrored symmetry between them. Identical escorts of *wayri ch'unchos*, whose style is regarded as the most autochthonous, are here deployed by both moieties in imitation of the typical regional style of *nación* pilgrimage, the dancers now signalling the capitals of the respective moieties.

Finally, in the valley, the moieties crystallize and differentiate into contrasting groups of *qollas* and *ch'unchos* who engage in ritual battles in village plazas. First, with the miraculous *taytacha* from the mountains now transformed into a domesticated one from the parish church, Ocongate hosts a confrontation between its own *qhapaq qollas* and Paucartambo's *wayri ch'unchos*. Later, Paucartambo's patronal Virgin presides over the concluding stage of the internal *tinkuy*. A ritual battle takes place between the village's *qhapaq qollas* and *ch'unchos extranjeros*, the latter representing the foreign, "civilized" variant of the savage autochthons. Dualism is finally realized in the local setting in dialectical opposition and inversion.

ETHNICITY AND HIERARCHY

But there is another dimension to this native Andean cosmology revealed through the Qoyllur Rit'i ceremonies. Cosmic dualism is conjoined in the cult with a dualism of another kind. The dialectic of the ritual practices enters directly into the endemic tensions and contradictions of a society riven by a double cultural identity.

The official mythohistory inscribes the Indian-mestizo polarity into the cult at the outset. The polarity is permanently enshrined in the two icons of the crucified Christ, Qoyllur Rit'i and Tayankani, the one tainted by its proximity to the *apus*, the other protected from pagan contagion. It is topographically encoded in the contrast between the two mutually exclusive domains of Sinakara and Ocongate, wild mountains and parish seat. It suffuses the moiety division between Paucartambo and Quispicanchis, whose polysemy captures the opposition between natives and foreigners, conquered and conqueror. Finally it infects the symbolism of dance styles, which have acquired Indian and mestizo connotations, tradition and modernity, respectively.

Over and above these internal ethnic oppositions and relativities, the entire cult is encased within a rigid, Church-sanctioned lay brotherhood which sustains a categorical divide between staff and devotees. The projection of mestizo status enables the members of the brotherhood to mark themselves apart from and superior to the cult clientele. Through a contrived superciliousness, through their ostentatious use of Spanish, through their ultimate sanction of the use of physical violence, they are able to define their position in relation to the broad mass of devotees as an ineluctable ethnic superiority. Lest this be seen as a mere carryover of an intrinsic ethnic status from outside the cult, it is worth mentioning that ethnic superordination in a weak form is similarly deployed by the peasant staffs of some minor miraculous shrines, people who in other relations are scarcely distinguishable from the devotees over whom they preside (Sallnow 1981:168).

The devotees of Qoyllur Rit'i, meanwhile, defy any simplistic characterization as Indian. At the titular fiesta, the traditional devotional style of *nación* pilgrimage predominates. But this masks a wide span of meanings and motives, of Indianness unambiguously proclaimed, resentfully acquiesced in, purposely recovered, or even temporarily affected by people who would otherwise consider themselves to be thoroughly mestizo. Furthermore, there is a growing number of private, individual pilgrims, many of them from urban areas, some of whom have begun to schedule their visits to take place just before the main influx of *nación* groups.

The diacritical rites described and analyzed in this paper, which have earned Qoyllur Rit'i the reputation of principal Indian shrine of the Cuzco region, are eschewed by most of these individual devotees. For them it is sufficient that such rites are performed, thus guaranteeing in their eyes the authenticity of the shrine as a source of indigenous sacred power. But they are not the only abstainers. The ceremonies are also shunned by not a few of the *nación* groups of peasant pilgrims, who merely stay overnight, their *láminas* sojourning briefly in the holy presence of the *taytacha*, and depart to celebrate Corpus in their own communities.

Why this should be so now becomes clear. The central ceremonial sequence of the fiesta, in particular the main pilgrimage procession from Sinakara to Ocongate, makes blatant the cultural and social contradictions that pervade the cult. It transports the pilgrim from the loose congeries of devotees in the mountain fastness of Señor de Qoyllur Rit'i to the hierarchical, mestizo-controlled world of Señor de Tayankani. Latent oppositions between the ethnic dance styles and between the groups performing them suddenly become all too explicit. To participate in the cult in any capacity, moreover, is inevitably to submit directly to an overweening mestizo officialdom. The choice of many *naciones*, particularly those from upland peasant communities, is to segregate themselves as much as possible from these activities, to pay their respects to the shrine and leave, with their self-esteem intact.

CONCLUSION

Ritual practice both reflects and reconstructs the categories within which social practice unfolds. In the Qoyllur Rit'i cult, Andean cosmic dualism interpenetrates with a historically configured ethnic dualism, both of them transforming together as the ceremony unfolds. The cultural antagonism between Indian and mestizo that lies at the heart of Andean society is here transmuted into the vernacular religious idiom. Just as, in the cosmological design, order and fertility repose upon division and differentiation, so the ethnic hierarchy becomes almost a necessary condition for the reproduction of society.

Pilgrimage in other religious traditions has a similar categorizing and polarizing effect on ethnic and caste differences (see Messerschmidt and Sharma 1981; Pfaffenberger 1979). In the central Andes, there is evidence that in pre-Hispanic times, especially in the politically fluid pre-Inca epoch, important religious shrines were the foci of interaction between different local and regional groups, serving not only to structure political and economic dealings between them but also as operators in the very process of ethnogenesis—the emergence and definition of ethnic boundaries themselves (see Poole 1982). Today, religious shrines—miraculous Christian ones—are potent, transcendent symbols around which a complex and changing society represents itself reflexively via a simple, enduring, ineluctable, hierarchic, ethnic polarity.

NOTES

This chapter is based on fieldwork conducted in the course of three visits to Peru over the period 1972-84, for which acknowledgement is due to several funding bodies: the Foreign Area Fellowship Program of the U.S. Social Science Research Council, the U.K. Social Science Research Council, the Radcliffe-Brown Fund of the Association of Social Anthropologists, the London School of Economics Staff Research Fund, and the Nuffield Foundation. I am also grateful to members of the Anthropology Seminars at the London School of Economics and the University of St. Andrews for their helpful comments on earlier drafts.

1. The best general account of both the mythohistory and the fiesta of Qoyllur Rit'i is still that by Juan Ramírez (1969), who served as priest in nearby Ccatca for six years and who had charge of the shrine sanctuary. David Gow (1974) aims to depict the cult within the setting of colonial Christianity in general, and offers good treatments of the ceremonial dancers, with interpretations based on his fieldwork in Pinchimuro, not far from the shrine. David Gow (1976) also provides a fuller discussion of the cult with reference to this community, while Rosalind Gow and Bernabé Condori (1976) present detailed myths relating to the shrine. David Gow (1980) explores the relation between Qoyllur Rit'i and Mount

Ausankati. Robert Randall (1982a) attempts to locate the cult within a general Andean cosmological framework. Accounts of pilgrimage to Qoyllur Rit'i include those of Thomas Müller (1980) (from Q'eros, Paucartambo province), Michael J. Sallnow (1974:110-17) (from Qamawara, Calca province), and Catherine J. Allen (1978:52-67) (from Sonqo, Paucartambo province). José María García (1983:52-67) gives an account by a Jesuit priest working in communities in Quispicanchis province of visits to the shrine during the late 1970s, on one of which the author served as a ritual dancer. *Sur* (1982:51-53) sets out a local legend (from Ccatca, Quispicanchis province) of the origin of the shrine. Manuel Marzal (1971:231-43) gives a general description of the cult, together with the results of a questionnaire submitted to people in the Urcos area concerning the visits to the shrine and motives for going. Rodrigo Sánchez-Arjona Halcón (1981:151-56) offers a similar account, together with a Jesuit's theological reflections on the cult, while Ana Gisbert-Sauch (1979) interprets the fiesta as part of a "cult for the poor." Popular illustrated reports include those of Alfonsina Barrionuevo (1969:201), Robert Randall (1982b), Peter Cloudsley (1985) and Louis-Marie Blanchard (1987). The fiesta is also the subject of several recent documentary films, among them those by Carlos Pasini and Michael J. Sallnow (1974), Peter Getzels and Harriet Gordon (1985), and Alain Dumas (1986). Since the present paper was written, the author has published a detailed historical and ethnographic account of cults of miraculous shrines in Cuzco (Sallnow 1987) which incorporates much of the data and analysis set out here.

2. Peru comprises 23 departments, each divided into provinces, which are in turn divided into local districts.

3. A similar pattern of successive visions, the first to an Indian and the second, decisive one to a Spaniard, is found in the official mythohistories of other apparitional shrines in the region, for example Señor de Wank'a (Sallnow 1982).

4. See, for example, David Gow (1976:217-18,227), Sallnow (1987), and *Sur* (1982:52-53).

5. In 1620 the chronicler Guaman Poma de Ayala placed Ausankati first in a list of the most important *wak'as* (holy sites) in the Inca quarter of Qollasuyu, and notes that the emperor used to offer it much gold and silver (1966:I,196).

6. See Sallnow (1981) for a sociological treatment of this form of pilgrimage.

7. *Kishwa* (temperate intermontane valley zone); *puna* (cold high plateau zone); *montaña* (subtropical forested hill zone); *sierra* (mountain range).

8. At the time of the founding of the shrine, Ocongate was in the anomalous position of lying within the political jurisdiction of Quispicanchis province while it was an ecclesiastical annex of the parish of Ccatca, which was then in the province of Paucartambo (Mörner 1978:plates 10 and 11). Ocongate is now a parish in its own right. Ccatca was transferred to the province of Quispicanchis in 1920, but it still pertains to the Paucartambo moiety as far as the fiesta alignments are concerned (D. Gow 1974:89).

9. See chapter 17 for a discussion of religious dance in the Andean tradition.

10. See Allen (1983) for a perceptive analysis of this aspect of the *ukuku* figure.

11. See chapter 17 for further discussion of this point.

12. For the opportunity to gather the information in this paragraph I am indebted to Penny Harvey, then a doctoral student at the London School of Economics, who carried out research on bilingualism and social differentiation in Ocongate between 1983 and 1985.

13. See Sallnow (1981) for an account of the social relations and ritual transactions between *naciones* in Cuzco pilgrimage.

14. See Sallnow (1987) for a discussion of pilgrimage as dance, and chapter 17.

15. *K'achampa* is a dance style supposed to have originated in Inca war dances. Ocongate does not now have a *k'achampa* troupe.

16. *Tinkuys* are described in Alencastre and Dumézil (1953), Barrionuevo (1969), Gilt Contreras (1955), Gorbak, Lischetti, and Muñoz (1962), Hartmann (1972), and Platt (1978). For an attempt at synthesis, see Mariscotti de Görlitz (1978:159-63).

17. Instances of dual organization of local groups are described in Arguedas (1956), Barette (1972), Brush (1977), Harris (1978), Isbell (1978), Mitchell (1976), Platt (1986), Skar (1982), and Stein (1961). Theoretical syntheses include Fuenzalida (1970) and Skar (1982:93-102;

1985).

18. This essential ambivalence of charged diametricality is recapitulated, finally, within the dual group itself, in the elemental dyad of the conjugal couple. The perception of the conjugal relationship in Andean culture epitomizes the dialectical ambiguity. As Platt has demonstrated, the word for couple, *yanantin*, "may indicate a pair of perfect symmetry and equality; but it may also serve as an ideological disguise for a relationship that is in fact unequal, such as that between man and woman" (1986:256). The concept thus merges into a single semantic field the idea of perfect mirror symmetry, right-left or male-male, and the idea of asymmetrical complementarity, high-low or male-female. It is here, in the cultural nucleus of the conjugal pair, that charged diametric dualism is imaged in miniature, and it is here that the potential fertility of nature is finally and completely realized.

REFERENCES

Alencastre-Dumézil 1953
Allen 1978, 1983
Arguedas 1956
Barrette 1972
Barrionuevo 1969
Blanchard 1987
Bourricaud 1970
Brush 1977
Camino 1978
Casaverde Rojas 1970
Cloudsley 1985
Cotler 1968
Dumas, Alain 1986
Fernándes-Gutiérrez 1975
Flores Ochoa 1973
Fuenzalida 1970
García 1983
Getzels and Gordon 1985
Gilt Contreras 1955
Gisbert Sauch 1979
Gorbak, et al. 1962
Gow 1974, 1980
Gow-Condori 1976
Gross 1979
Guaman Poma de Ayala 1966
Halcón 1981
Hartmann 1972

Harris 1978
Isbell 1978
Kurtz 1982
Lévi-Strauss 1968
Mörner 1978
Marzal 1971
M. de Gorlitz 1978
Messerschmidt-Sharma 1981
Mitchell 1976
MÜller 1980
Oricaín 1790
Pasini and Sallnow 1974
Pfaffenberger 1979
Pittivers 1973
Platt 1978, 1986
Poole 1982
Ramírez E. 1969
Randall 1982a, 1982b
Roel Pineda 1950
Sallnow 1974, 1981,
   1982, 1987
Skar 1982, 1985
Stein 1961
SUR 1982
van den Berghe 1974
van den Berghe-Primov 1977

17

Rituals of Movement, Rites of Transformation: Pilgrimage and Dance in the Highlands of Cuzco, Peru

DEBORAH A. POOLE

Pilgrimage has enjoyed a prominent status in Andean religion for many centuries. As part of a vast sacred geography, institutionalized cults to such pan-Andean sanctuaries as Pachacamac and Copacabana, as well as those addressed to numerous regional shrines (huacas), formed an integral part of the vast political and economic network linking ethnic chiefdoms and conquered provinces to the Inca capital of Cuzco, itself a religious center of great import (Poole 1982; Rostworowski 1977; Sallnow 1987:19-40; Zuidema 1964, 1982a). With the arrival of Spanish hegemony and its attendant Catholic ideology, many of these sanctuaries were transformed, at least in name, into Christian pilgrimage centers housing miraculous images of saints, Virgin Marys, and an assortment of Christ figures.

The rituals and beliefs of today's Quechua- and Aymara-speaking campesinos portray an image of pilgrimage which combines the heritage of these pre-Hispanic, or "Andean," and postconquest, or "Catholic," traditions. Mixing precise knowledge of nature and ecology with beliefs in the powers of sacred mountains (apus), rivers, and an omnipresent Earthmother (Pachamama), contemporary Andean pilgrims revere their local and regional pilgrimage images as representatives not only of a Catholic pantheon, but also of the natural forces which govern their agricultural and pastoral society. Studies of pilgrimage in the Andes have traditionally focused on these syncretic aspects of religious belief, ritual, and sacred space, and on the historical continuity of selected pilgrimage sanctuaries, in an attempt to define the "Andean" quality of such regional devotions (Allen 1989; Gow 1974; Poole 1982; Ramírez 1969; Randall 1982; Sallnow 1974, 1981, 1982, 1987; Urbano, this volume).

Here, I will address similar issues by analyzing one particular component of pilgrimage ritual, the dance groups or *comparsas* which perform at regional shrines. Rather than analyze the specific symbolism, costuming, and meaning of individual dances, emphasis will be placed upon the generalized relation of dance to pilgrimage. Insofar as these dances are orchestrated around specifically Andean concepts of space, hierarchy, and transformation, an exploration of their integration with Christian pilgrimage cults will aid in defining what the institution of pilgrimage means in its Andean setting.[1]

PILGRIMAGE AND DANCE

Masked, costumed, and elaborately choreographed ritual dance is a tradition of great antiquity throughout the Andean area. Early Spanish chroniclers of Indian life in Peru such as Cristóbal de Molina (1575), Francisco de Avila (1608), and Inca Garcilaso de la Vega (1609) encountered ornately adorned dancers performing at provincial shrines or huacas, as well as in the seasonal state feasts of Inca Cuzco. The descriptions they have left us portray a multitudinous array of specialized dance forms and costume types, whose uses were also multiform.[2] With the arrival of Spanish political institutions and religion, these preconquest dance forms were rapidly adapted and perpetuated as forms of Christian devotion. Like the annual feast days on which they were performed, indigenous choreographic interpretations of nature, society, and the gods were overlaid and eventually fused with those of their new Spanish lords. Although Spanish priests observed with some dismay the prominent role of dance in promulgating indigenous beliefs under the auspices of "Catholic" festivals (Acosta [1590] 1954:174-75; Arriaga [1621] 1920), their initial doubts about the propriety of dance were tempered by their familiarity with dance as an accepted form of Christian worship in peninsular Spain (Backman 1952:77-85; Cotarelo y Mori 1911; Ivanova 1970; Rosa y López 1904). Dance was thus legitimized as either a harmless form of religious "recreation" (Acosta [1590] 1954:206-09) or a profoundly devout and peculiarly "Christian" form of worship (Guaman Poma de Ayala [1614] 1936:f.784). Following the example of Spanish choirboys or *seises* (Ivanova 1970:90-91; Rosa y López 1904), Indian groups from early on were dancing before the sacrosanct altars of cathedrals in Cuzco and other Spanish cities (Garcilaso de la Vega [1609] 1960:V,3, 152; Guaman Poma de Ayala [1614] 1936:f.783).

This is not to say, however, that indigenous or Andean dance was entirely coopted by the Catholic traditions it in some ways adopted. On the contrary, precisely because of this official sanction and institutional tutelage provided by the Church, certain Andean dance forms were able to flourish unrecognized and unpunished. Dances performed at Catholic feasts became a means of perpetuating traditional symbolic forms of expression, and perhaps more importantly, of improvising upon these symbolic codes to devise satirical, often deeply political statements about the Spanish society which watched and tolerated indigenous dance, but failed to grasp its social meaning as a form of cultural resurgence and political satire (see Poole 1989; Tord and Lazo 1980:217-42; Wachtel 1971:66-75).

Within this new colonial and nominally Christian context for dance, one of the most vital roles which dance fulfilled was that of representation. Much as pre-Spanish dances had served to legitimize the presence of different political lords or curacas in Inca Cuzco, or the diverse ethnic groups in attendance at a huaca's feast, colonial-period dances were a means of formalizing attendance at a Catholic procession like Corpus or regional pilgrimages such as those of Copacabana, Cocharcas, and other early sanctuary sites. More importantly, the distinctly Andean dance forms, costumes, and music became a means of asserting indigenous participation in and control over their most powerful sacred sites. Like so many other aspects of Christian religion, pilgrimage dances were exploited as a means of expressing indigenous identity and nonsubmission to the foreign culture which pilgrimage and Christianity ostensibly represented. Dance conveyed not the weakness, but the power of Andean cultural forms (cf. Fine 1982; Salomon 1981; Wachtel 1971:66-75).

Today, dance is still the primary means through which campesinos participate in and control pilgrimage cults. In one of Cuzco's oldest and most important pilgrimage sanctuaries, Huanca (San Salvador, Calca), dances have been forbidden since the 1920s by the priests and mestizo brotherhood (hermandad) who now control the shrine. Undaunted by such restrictions, indigenous dance groups and pilgrims have simply shifted locale, going instead on the same date, September 14, to a new shrine directly across the valley from Huanca (Sallnow 1982:739-41). Although for the Cuzco campesinado the Christ of Huanca has retained his status as an exceptionally powerful benefactor and protector of crops, their participation in his pilgrimage was effectively stripped of its meaning and efficacy when dancing was prohibited.

In yet another important Cuzqueño shrine, Qoyllur Rit'i (Ocongate, Quispicanchis), the presence of literally hundreds of separate dance groups is effectively employed to counteract mestizo incursions at this powerful sacred site which is believed to control human and animal fertility and health. Dances are performed during Mass and, as if deliberately taunting the exhortations of the priests and cantors to stop dancing, *comparsas* and their bands perform at increasing pitch whenever the church loudspeaker commences its pleas for quiet. Many pilgrims to Qoyllur Rit'i—which is probably the largest pilgrimage center in southern Peru—never enter the church, and few indeed attend Masses, although confessions remain for some an important focus of the pilgrimage. Most pilgrims' attention is instead directed toward caring for and assisting the dancers, whose duties call for almost constant nocturnal dancing, and accompanying the image of the Christ of Qoyllur Rit'i in his outdoor procession. As in many other sanctuaries around Cuzco, the bear dancers or *ukukus* at Qoyllur Rit'i are solely responsible for maintaining order, preventing excessive drinking, and allaying theft at the sanctuary.

In these and many other smaller pilgrimage sanctuaries of Cuzco, I have frequently seen dancers confront the authority of mestizo officials and priests either by playing and dancing during Mass or by directly harassing, in comic fashion, the hapless, always complaining priest. To be sure, masks and costumes lend anonymity and thus courage. But more importantly the status of "dancer" insures an audience for such antics, as well as the approval of those who view, and understand, their dance and misbehavings. Though many more examples could be cited, these few suffice to conclude that dance is indeed a central and very vital medium for the maintenance of Quechua cultural identity and control at present-day Andean pilgrimage sanctuaries. It remains to question, however, why dance is particularly suited to pilgrimage, and why dance is the means for formalizing and communicating devotion toward a powerful outside (i.e., regional) sacred image.

The motivation for dancing at pilgrimage shrines can be traced to three basic functions which dance groups are felt to fulfill. The first of these is transportation of their community's icon or *lámina* to the sanctuary and back. This lámina is felt to represent the community as a whole at the sanctuary, and to receive blessings on the community's behalf. The second duty of the dancers is to appease, and in a sense entertain, the saint, virgin, or Christ figure housed in a particular sanctuary. Each image is said to have his or her own favorite dance groups whose performances are repaid through the bestowal of spiritual or material rewards, for example, plentiful harvests or abundant herds. These "rewards," moreover, are believed to benefit all the members of the community the *comparsa* represents.

Finally, dance fulfills a more localized function of "passing" *cargo* or fiesta sponsorship. Each man in the community is expected to undertake certain responsibilities in the organization and financing of town feasts and pilgrimage expeditions. These "responsibilities" or cargos (meaning quite literally, "burdens") collectively form a prestige hierarchy within which an individual's social status is determined by the number and ranking of the fiestas he (or she) has sponsored. Within the traditional Andean political system, these religious cargos were further integrated into the hierarchy of secular community offices called *varayuq*, or those who "have the staff (*vara*) of office" (see Isbell 1978). In many communities around Cuzco, sponsorship for a comparsa's trip to a pilgrimage sanctuary is considered among the highest-ranked prestige cargos of the local social hierarchy. Similarly, participation in a *comparsa* is itself often a cargo of lesser rank within the total system, and one therefore carried out by younger men just entering the social hierarchy. This integration of dance into the religious-political network is further reflected in the ranking of the dances themselves into those appropriate for very young, inexperienced men (e.g., the *ukuku* or "bear" dancer), and those for more mature men who have held more community offices and sponsored more cargos.

On the one hand, then, the journeys of dance groups to pilgrimage sanctuaries are an important component of the sociopolitical and religious hierarchies of local village life; not only do dancers themselves hold cargos, but, as a vehicle for acquiring the sacred blessings or power concentrated in regional centers, dance benefits the community and its hierarchy as a whole. On the other hand, however, and coupled with its role in these local community systems, dance is also a central part of the regional devotion uniting people from numerous communities in their affection and respect for a particular pilgrimage shrine. In order to better understand how this local idiom of hierarchical status, the dance cargos, is related to the emotions and power invested in a regional pilgrimage image, I will analyze in the next section the formal choreographic structure of three contemporary pilgrimage dances. These modern-day dances will be seen to reflect interests in the representation and hierarchical classification of social groups with respect to a central sacred image, i.e., a pilgrimage sanctuary. The choreographic forms will themselves be related to specifically Andean principles of social hierarchy, spatial organization, and ritual transformation. Following this choreographic analysis, I will expand upon these principles of hierarchy, space, and transformation to elaborate a definition for a uniquely Andean pilgrimage tradition. As a part of pilgrimage ritual, I suggest that dance choreography is at once a formal transformation or analogue of pilgrimage and a devotional, entertaining, or emotive means for integrating spectators and dancers alike into the larger pilgrimage ceremony of which dance forms a crucial part. On both these "formal" and "emotive" levels, moreover, dance will be seen to elaborate particularly on the hierarchical systems underlying an individual's perceptions of and participation in the larger social order in which pilgrimage occurs, and which, as ritual-symbolic practice, it validates and reproduces.

CHOREOGRAPHIC STRUCTURES

In the following I present a description and brief analysis of three Cuzqueño pilgrimage dances. Each *comparsa* will be discussed in its own right, and then compared to the other two in terms of five unifying themes. These themes are linear formation, spatial orientation, zigzag movement, concentric hierarchy, and regeneration. Together they reflect the relationship between pilgrimage and dance as complementary expressions of hierarchy, space, and ritual transformation. For each dance, I will also discuss the principles of social hierarchy and ethnic classification through which dance is interpreted and made meaningful at both a local and regional level of participation.

Kanchis

The *kanchis* dancers, though infrequently danced by people from the region they portray, are said to represent maize agriculturalists from the province of Canchis in the southeastern department of Cuzco (see Figure 17.1). Though varying somewhat from region to region, typical *kanchis*

Figure 17.1 *Kanchis Comparsa* with *Ukukus* Kneeling in Front Row and the *Capitán Kanchis* Standing to the Left Rear Holding up the *Vara*

costume consists of a *montera* (round flat hat), a pair of brightly colored woolen whips, a *ch'ullu* (woolen knit cap with ear-flaps), *llijlla* (woolen shawl), and an optional *kanchis*-style poncho. In addition to his costume, each dancer carries a *vara* (staff of political office). Dancers are internally ranked by seniority and age, with the eldest or *capitán* ("captain") carrying a *vara* of *chonta* wood (a hard black palm wood from the jungle used only for manufacture of varas and other ritual objects). The *capitán's vara* is also decorated with silver engraved bands, while the younger dancers (called simply, *kanchis*) carry undecorated *varas* of common unfinished wood or cane. Masks are not worn, though the capitán will frequently wear dark glasses.

A typical *comparsa* of *kanchis* dancers consists of one capitán who directs the dancing, one very young dancer called *chanaku* ("youngest son"), four to six *kanchis*, and two to four *ukukus* or bear-dancers. The clownish disorderly dancing of these *ukukus* stands in marked contrast to the orderly formations of the *kanchis* themselves. *Ukukus* also carry leather whips. The flexibility of these long whips is visually opposed to the rigidity of the *varas* displayed in several of the formations (see especially A-2, A-4, and A-6 in the following section), while their leather material differentiates them as well from the woolen dance whips of the *kanchis*.

The age ranking of the *kanchis*, from older *capitán*, symbol of authority and responsibility, through to the young chanaku six to eight years of age, resembles the traditional hierarchy of the *varayuq*, in which community political-religious offices were held consecutively by men of different ages. Older men, having begun their career as lower-ranked authorities, thus assumed the highest office of *alcalde* (mayor) *vara* only after several years of experience with this governing hierarchy of village life. The symbol of this high office was the largest *chonta vara* with its silver bands like that which the *capitán kanchis* carries. The *chanaku*, by comparison, represents the new initiate to this secular/religious authority hierarchy, a role which surfaces clearly in the choreography to be discussed below.

Variations in costuming and in number of dancers depend largely upon the wealth of the community or individual sponsoring the dance in a given year. Choreography likewise varies somewhat from community to community, although in each case a diagnostic core repertoire of steps and figures, as outlined in Figures 17.2 to 17.6, is retained. The dance is accompanied by a *huayno* played on harp, *quena* (flute), and drum.[3] Unlike most Cuzqueño *huaynos*, whose binary structure (Roel Pineda 1959:133) consists of a *paseo* (slower dance) followed by a *zapateo* (foot-stomping fast section), the *kanchis* dance is organized in three parts. The basic progression of these three parts is based on the *kanchis'* use of varas as opposed to dance whips, and on the increasing centrality and eventual incorporation of the *chanaku* into the *kanchis* dancers' hierarchy. In contrast, the *ukukus* use the same leather whip throughout all their movements. These parts have been designated with the letters A through C in the description which follows (see also Figures 17.2-17.6).[4]

A. The figures are based on double parallel columns of dancers who hold their varas either upright or place them horizontally in different figures on the ground. The *capitán* and *chanaku* remain at the head of the double column formation throughout and never place their *varas* on the ground (actual *varas* of community office are likewise never placed on the ground or in any horizontal position).

B. *Varas* are replaced by woolen dance whips and figures are constructed by linking these whips. The double column formation progresses through a "weaving" structure to a concentric formation centered on the *chanaku*. The *capitán* remains outside the formation directing the choreography and does not relinquish his *vara* at any time.

C. *Varas* are returned to the dancers, who resume the double column formation. *Varas* are joined in a spoke formation and used to elevate the *chanaku*.

Break-down of individual movements.

A-1. (see Figure 17.2) Opening salutation formation: each opposing pair of *kanchis* dancers give individual turns in place and then advance together to bow to or *saludar* ("greet") the *capitán* and *chanaku*, who stand stiffly to the left and right of the two lines of dancers. The *kanchis* are followed in the same movement by the *ukukus*. After "greeting" the *capitán* and *chanaku*, each pair returns to the end of their respective columns. In this way

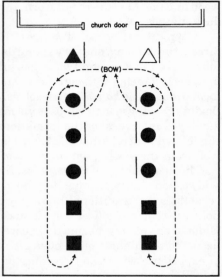

Figure 17.2 *Kanchis* Movement, A-1, Salutation formation. Key: ●=*kanchis*, ■=*ukukus*, ▲=*capitán*, △=*chanaku*, ǀ=*vara*

the lines rotate until each pair has greeted the head figures and the formation is in its original position.

A-2. (see Figure 17.3) Parallel *vara* formation: Each pair of *kanchis* places their *varas* on the ground between them in horizontally arrayed parallel lines. *Ukukus* do the same with their leather whips. Throughout this movement, dancing is maintained in a hopping or skipping step. *Chanaku* and *capitán* dance in place at the head of the two columns holding their *varas* upright.

A-3. Repeat salutation formation (A-1 above).

A-4. Crossed *vara* formation: same as formation A-2 above only with *varas* and whips placed in "X's."

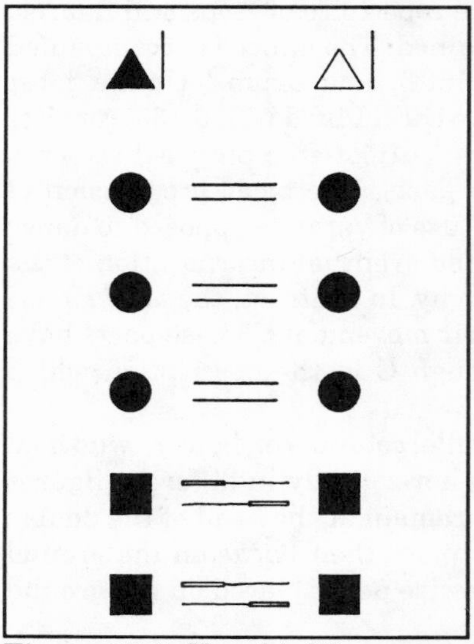

Figure 17.3 *Kanchis* Movement, A-2, Parallel *Vara* Formation with *varas* and leather whips

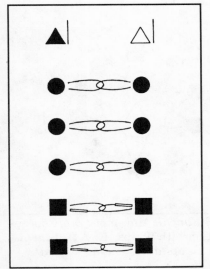

Figure 17.4 *Kanchis* Movement, B-1, Linked Whip Formation

A-5. Repeat salutation formation (A-1 and A-3 above).

A-6. Diamond *vara* formation: same as formations A-2 and A-4 above, only with *varas* and whips arranged in diamond shapes. (Variations in the sequence may exclude either the X's or the diamonds, as well as the salutation formation (A-5) between them.)

A-7. Presentation of *varas* (transition from part A to part B): each *kanchis* advances with his pair (from opposing column) and hands over his *vara* to the *chanaku* who stands at the head of the two columns. The *capitán*, however, does not relinquish his *vara*.

B-1. (see Figure 17.4) Opposing pairs link their woolen dance whips which they have removed from across their chests. *Ukukus* link their leather whips in a similar fashion. Each pair thus dances in place in a skipping step, after which they unlink their whips and dance separately with hands crossed behind their backs. In this latter step, dancing is no longer stationary but rather advances along the two lines and rotates as in A-1 above. *Capitán* and *chanaku* do not rotate but dance in place at the head of the two columns.

B-2. (see Figure 17.5) Weaving or braiding formation (*simp'a*, "braid"): dancers in each column link whips with dancers to their immediate front and back in the same column. Thus linked, the right-hand column advances and turns to weave in and out, or braid through, the linked whips of the left-hand column's stationary formation. The right-hand column returns to the original position, and the movement is repeated with the left-hand column weaving through the stationary right-hand line. *Capitán* and *chanaku* dance in place at the head of the two columns.

B-3. (see Figure 17.6) Dancers form a circle with whips woven into a concentric pattern, so that each dancer

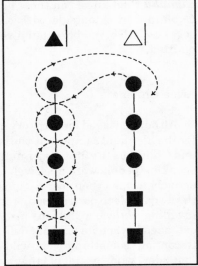

Figure 17.5 *Kanchis* Movement, B-2, Weaving Formation

holds both ends of his own whip. The *chanaku* moves to the center space of this formation, while the *capitán* dances in place outside the circle directing the movements of the dancers. Ducking in and out, the *kanchis* then unweave their whips without letting go of either end of the whip each is holding.

C-1. *Varas* are returned to the *kanchis* and woolen whips tied back across their chests. *Kanchis* dance in a tight circle holding *varas* upward in a

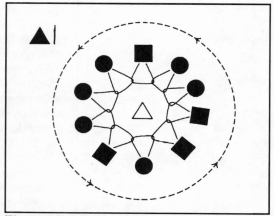

Figure 17.6 *Kanchis* Movement B-3, Concentric Formation with Whips. Key: ●=*kanchis*, ■=*ukukus*, ▲=*capitán*, △=*chanaku*, ∤=*vara*

conical formation with tips held loosely together by *ukukus'* leather whips. *Chanaku* stands under these linked *varas* while dancers circle him first clockwise, then counterclockwise. *Capitán* dances in place outside the circle.

C-2. All again in double column formation. Each dancer skips in place with hands crossed behind his back. This time, however, the columns are very close together so as to be almost touching shoulders as they dance. *Capitán* and *chanaku* resume their positions at the head.

C-3. *Varas* of *kanchis* are placed on the ground in a spoke pattern. The *chanaku* then kneels on these *varas* and is lifted up into the air clapping. *Capitán* dances outside with own *vara*. (Order of C-2 and C-3 may be reversed. Also, in abbreviated versions of the dance, B-2 through C-1 are omitted.)

Awqa Chileno

Although waged for territory and economic interests of little real import for the highland campesino, the late nineteenth-century war between Peru and Chile was the first major nationalist confrontation for which Quechua-speaking people were massively recruited, and for which they themselves actively formed their own regional militias (Manrique 1981). The dance of the awqa chileno portrays a thoroughly Quechuaized representation of these invading *chileno* (Chilean) *awqa* (soldiers). In Quechua, *awqa* can be extended beyond its primary definition(s) of "soldier," "warrior," or "enemy," to connote something semi-wild or untamed, in this case a new class of "outsider" who, by dint of language, strange mannerisms, and exaggerated national differences, presented a novel variety of social being. In short a new type of "wild outsider" previously unknown to the indigenous population.

In the dance of the awqa chileno, this historically "new" outsider is assigned a festive, gay, and raucous personality. Chileno dancers dress in high leather boots and spurs which jingle loudly in the heavy *zapateos* of their huayno-based choreography. In addition to this heavy footwear, each "soldier" wears long pants (or jodphurs if available), a white shirt, two *warak'as* (woven slings) crossed over his chest, one or more brightly colored synthetic *pañuelos* (scarves) on his back, a woven belt with colorful designs, a straw hat, and a wire mesh mask. In lieu of the *vara* and woolen Carnival whip carried by the *kanchis* dancers, each chileno dances first with his *pañuelo*, and later with his *warak'a*. This *pañuelo* and the exaggerated *zapateos* distinguish his "Chilean" *huayno* as a traditionally more mestizo dance form, different from the *campesino huayno* danced with lighter foot and less flamboyant handkerchief waving (Roel Pineda 1959:138-39). These *zapateos*, as well as the spurs and riding attire, which in addition call to mind the classic image of the southern Peruvian *gamonal* or large landholder, also resemble the Chilean *cueca* dance, of which the awqa chilenos may

be a Quechuaized takeoff (Frank Salomon, personal communication).

The awqa chileno, a very popular dance throughout the department of Cuzco, is regularly performed at the pilgrimage sanctuaries of Qoyllur Rit'i and Pampak'ucho. The description which follows is based on performances of the awqa chileno *comparsa* from Lucre (Quispicanchis, Cuzco) at both of these shrines in 1977, 1978, and 1980. This rather large *comparsa* is formed of twelve "chilenos," four *ukukus*, four *maqt'achas* ("young or adolescent boys"), one *sanitario* or *médico* (government health worker or "medic"), one *imilla* (shepardess who is actually a man dressed as a *chola* or market woman with white top hat and a wire mesh mask), one *doctor* (lawyer) dressed in black tails, top hat, and papier mâché mask, and

Figure 17.7 *Awqa Chilenos; Ukuku* and *Sanitario*, Pampak'ucho, 1981

one *diablo* or "devil" (see Figures 17.7, 17.8). Of these 24 dancers, only the twelve "chilenos" play a serious role, maintaining consistent formations and well-orchestrated choreographic movements. The other twelve act as buffoons and dance for the most part on the peripheries of the chilenos' precise formations.

Awqa chileno choreography is structured around the same basic elements as that of the *kanchis* dance described above. The dancers begin in double column formation and the dances themselves consist of a series of weaving or zigzag movements, followed by a rotational cycling of the columns. In both dances, couples are formed by linking the scarves, *varas*, or *warak'as* belonging to dancers from the two opposing columns. Like the *kanchis*, the dance commences with a salutation movement in which pairs advance and "greet" the church door in front of which they perform, since there is no principal authority figure like the *kanchis capitán*. Instead, when necessary, dancers are directed by the first pair of dancers, who are also the oldest and most experienced. Dancing is accompanied by a band of accordion, harp, and drum and, like that of the *kanchis*, has no lyrics (cf. Villasante Ortíz n.d.:107).

Figure 17.8 *Awqa Chileno; Diablo* and *Maqt'acha*, Pampak'ucho, 1981

Awqa Chileno Choreography (see Figures 17.9-17.11).

1. *Pasacallemesa* ("street pass"). This is the basic approach to the temple atrium, where the main performance takes place. Chilenos advance in two orderly columns dancing a *zapateo* (*huayno* with heavy foot-stomping). The others follow, theoretically in two columns as well, although they frequently break rank.

2. *Primera Parada* ("first stand"). This is the salutation formation like that of the *kanchis* outlined above. All dancers do this *paso* (step) with the exception of the *sanitario* and *diablo*.

3. *Chinkana* ("labyrinth"). Similar to figure B-2 of the *kanchis'* choreography. Opposing columns weave through and under each other's linked scarves in zigzag formation. The right-hand column goes first, then resumes position, and is "passed through" by the left-hand column. Again, only the *sanitario* and *diablo* do not participate.

4. *Pasapuentes* ("pass bridges"; see Figure 17.12). Opposing pairs link scarves to form a "bridge" of scarves. The pair nearest the church door leads, passing under the "bridge," and is followed by each consecutive pair. The *doctor* and *imilla* pass through last as a couple. They are severely hampered in their pass however by the other dancers' feet and scarves over which they are made to trip and fall in a deliberately comic fashion. The *sanitario* and *diablo* remain outside, dancing in wandering circles.

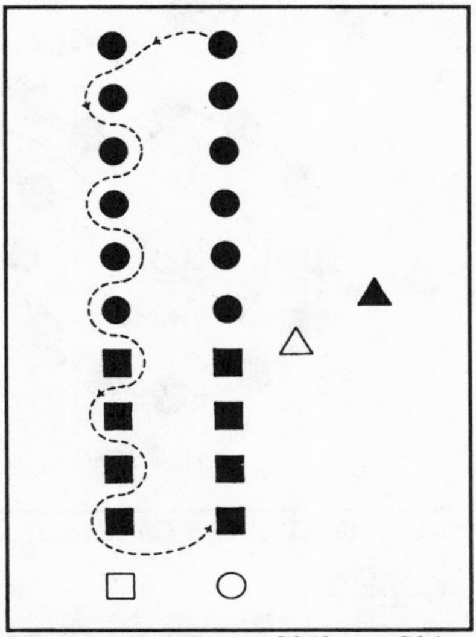

5. *Rueda* ("wheel"). The twelve chilenos link scarves to form a circle, inside of which dances the *imilla*. She holds one end of a scarf, the other end of which is held precariously by the *doctor* who is outside the circle. He attempts to get into the inside, but repeatedly fails. The *ukukus* and *maqt'achas* hit, whip, trip, and otherwise harass the *doctor* as he dances. They also molest the *sanitario*. Finally, the *diablo*, as always, remains alone.

6. Repeats #3 above.

7. Repeats #4 above.

8. Repeats #5 above. These repetitions are optional and done only where time permits, for example, in Qoyllur Rit'i, where many *comparsas* compete for time in the atrium, they are frequently omitted.

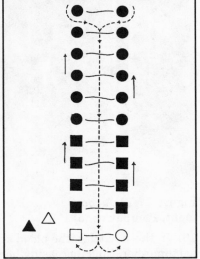

Figure 17.9 *Awqa Chileno, Chingana* Movement. Key: ●=*chilenos*, ■=*ukukus* & *maq'tachas*, ▲=*diablo*, △=*sanitario*, □=*doctor*, ○=imilla

Figure 17.10   *Awqa Chileno, Pasapuentes* Movement

9. *Yawar Mayu* ("river of blood"). This is a whipping dance in which opposing dancers pair off and, after first saluting the church door three times, whip each other about the legs. Chilenos perform first, in the order

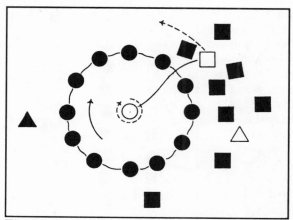

Figure 17.11 *Awqa Chileno, Rueda* Movement

Figure 17.12, *Awqa Chileno, Pasapuentes* Movement, Pampak'ucho, 1981

dictated by their column formation. They are followed by the *ukukus* and *maqt'achas* who whip harder with leather whips, whereas the chilenos use braided woolen *warak'as*. At the same time they are also funnier and a bit more chaotic about it. Next the *doctor* enters the *ukukus'* melee demonstrating no ability whatsoever to whip well. He immediately drops his whip and/or has it seized from him by an *ukuku*. He is then attacked from all sides by the *ukukus* and *maqt'achas*. The *imilla, sanitario,* and *diablo* do not participate in the whipping.

This *yawar mayu* dance carries marked connotations of fertility, initiation, and renewal. The *yawar mayu* song which accompanies this *paso*, in contrast to all other *pasos* which are without lyrics, is the same as that sung for ritual battles (Poole n.d.:17-18). In these battles, the blood shed on the battlefield is said to "feed" the earthmother, thus increasing her fertility and generosity (Alencastre and Dumézil 1953; Gilt C. 1966). Whipping too has long been an important part of initiation ceremonies in the Andes, where it symbolizes regeneration and renewal (Cobo [1653] 1956:T.II,210-11; Molina [1575] 1943:100-01).

10. *Kacharpari* ("sending off"). Dancers return to their two-column formation and, in repeating the salutation formation (#2 above), take leave

of the church. They then return to their encampment in the *pasacalle* formation (#1 above).

Analysis: Whereas the *kanchis* dance, representing an indigenous ethnic classification, was based on the choreographic "initiation" or incorporation of a *chanaku* differentiated from the other dancers by age, in these *awqa chileno* formations the oppositions set up are by social category instead of age. Representing in the first place an "outsider" who is also (historically) an enemy, the dance further differentiates three other social groups. First, the world of *mestizo* or "Spanish" professionals is represented by the bumbling, incompetent *doctor* and *sanitario*. Of these, the *sanitario* remains passive and hence ineffectual, while the *doctor*—representing not a medical doctor, but a lawyer or politician—is aggressive yet impotent in his attempts to dance and to get at the *imilla*. This figure of the *doctor* or *abogado* is common in dance traditions throughout the Andes and Central America, where they frequently form their own separate *comparsa* (Paredes Candia 1966:-93-100; Moreno 1972:-206-08; Villasante Ortíz n.d.:107-09). In all cases they represent comic versions of the power of the law and a society which controls, yet can still be satirized and resisted by the Andean dancer (see Figure 17.13).

A second group present in the chileno dance is that of the indigenous Andean clowns: the half-man, half-bear *ukuku* (Allen 1983) and the half-boy, half-man *maqt'acha*. These dancers fulfill the dual mediating role of entertainer, mediating between dancers and spectators, and go-between, buffering and protecting the insider chilenos from the *doc-*

Figure 17.13   Wall Mural in Popular Cuzco Picanteria Depicting *Doctor* Dancer as Repressor of Indigenous Culture and Language as He Reads a Law Condeming the Quechua Language and Those Who Speak It to Death

tor, *sanitario*, and *diablo* who dance outside. They torment both audience and dancer, trip each other, harass the *doctor* and *imilla*, and generally create chaos. Although on the surface raucous and unruly, they nonetheless manipulate with great success the difficult formations of the dance, above all the competitive whipping symbolic of fertility and regeneration (*yawar mayu*). It will be recalled that the *doctor*, although representing a powerful figure in the real world, fails repeatedly in both these dance maneuvers. The third group portrayed in this dance are the *imilla* and the *diablo*. Both represent equivocal figures in the system of social classification: the *imilla* as a *chola* (half-urban, half-rural) transvestite, the *diablo* as a half-human, non-Christian being. While the *diablo*, through his completely random wanderings outside the others' dance formations, stands opposed to the group of "Christian" dancers as a whole, the *imilla*, as a man dressed as a *chola* (mestiza), mediates the inside circle of the male chilenos and the outside group of nonchilean dancers.

Despite their differences in representational or classificatory intent, the two dances of *kanchis* and awqa chileno nonetheless contain similar choreographic themes. Awqa chilenos, though foreign outsiders, are ranked like the *kanchis* in hierarchized double column formations. One could even propose that the social classifications in their dance, (1) Chileans, (2) *ukukus* and *maqt'achas*, and (3) "outside" characters, represent a similar age classification as exists in the *kanchis* hierarchy: (1) adult *capitán* and *kanchis*, (2) adolescent *ukukus*, and (3) immature outsider, *chanaku*. Both dances, moreover, are based on similar choreographic formations in which linear hierarchies are formed into zigzags and circles with an outside figure incorporated into it, the *chanaku* or *imilla*, respectively. Finally, both dances terminate in the "renewal" or "regeneration" symbolized respectively by the initiation of the *chanaku* and the fertility of the *yawar mayu* whipping ceremony.

In the last dance to be discussed, the alzados, these standardized choreographic movements are treated as an object of jest and as a disruptive instead of orderly element of the religious pilgrimage in which they occur. The dancers themselves dispense with the classifications of "nsider" and "outsider" found in these other two *comparsas* to become the permanent Outsiders—asocial, wild, obscene, and disorderly.

Los Alzados

The alzados (Spanish: "rebel; mutineer; insolent; or fraudulent person") are one of a number of dance groups in Cuzco which represent clowns, ruffians, or "wildmen." Like other dancing trickster figures, the alzados have a highly improvisatory choreographic style, based for the most part on mocking and satirizing through chaotic or obscene gestures the formations of the other, more serious dances theirs is intended to deride. Alzados not only chide the sobriety of other dancers, but also flaunt in the most extravagant and lewd manner possible the established order of the entire fiesta. As such, they represent a chaotic element of disorder constantly present at the fringes of the pilgrimage and procession they attend.

For example, at the sanctuary of Sankha in the province of Paruro where a minor regional pilgrimage is celebrated each year on August 30 for Santa Rosa de Lima, the alzados shirk the other dancers and devotees who accompany the procession of the saint, and instead leave the plaza so as to climb to the top of a nearby hill. Accompanied by their "band," which consists of a single drum, the alzados make as much noise as possible while dancing on the hill. Finally, as the solemn procession stands about halfway through its route around the plaza, they come literally rolling down the hill into the plaza, screaming, laughing, and telling loud obscene jokes. As they tumble and wrestle their way down the hill, they strip their costumes of any distinctive element of ritual "dancer's" dress so as to arrive in the plaza in not only a disorderly fashion, but also, at least conceptually, naked. As the procession makes its final entrance into the church, the alzados reassemble and redress noisily on the fringes of the group, which, for their part, attempt to ignore the dancers' disturbances. When the priest emerges from the church, the alzados converge upon him forming a tight circle around him and "shade" him with their monteras placed on the tips of their varas in parody of the parasol used to shade religious images in processions. In a final gesture of irreverence, they then accompany the complaining priest back to his house and return to dance in the church atrium. Throughout this display, the alzados are a source of much amusement for the assembled pilgrims, except during the procession, when their mischievous doings remain for the most part at least outwardly unacknowledged.

Like the kanchis and other comparsas which the alzados mock, the alzados carry carved wooden "varas," which are used liberally through the performances both as choreographic props and as aggressive phalluses. The rest of their costume consists of black bayeta pants and vests, boots, white shirts, ch'ullus, monteras, pallay ch'umbis (wide woven belts), and chalinas (woolen mufflers), as well as white felt embroidered masks with long noses (see Figure 17.14). As with other dance groups, the number of alzados in a comparsa varies. The group I saw at Sankha was formed of six dancers. All were identically dressed and differentiated only by the size of their varas and by their titles: sargento (sergeant), capitán, and alcalde . The sargentos carried thick, carved wooden varas (not of chonta) with silver adornments like an alcalde vara or capitán vara of the kanchis. These two varas, which stood about four feet high and eight inches in diameter, were crudely worked and unfinished. The other four dancers carried even longer varas of very thin, flexible wood or cane which, as such, stood opposed to the thicker, stiffer varas of the two leaders.

Alzado choreography, which is danced to a drum alone, incorporates the intricate pasapuentes (or pasamanos) and chinkanas (zigzags) of the awqa

Figure 17.14 *Alzados*, Sankha, 1981

chilenos and *kanchis*, and like these two dances, is premised upon a double-line formation. The alzados, however, perform all these steps and formations in an extremely confused, disorderly fashion, fusing them with obscene phallic gestures and threatening assaults in which the *vara* is held up at a 45 degree angle from the dancer's crotch. Although done in this joking, improvisatory style, the choreography of the alzados nonetheless breaks down into three basic movements, performed in random order, and followed by a theatrical burlesque of a death and resurrection in which two of the dancers "kill" each other. These movements are shown in Figure 17.10 and described below.

Alzado Choreography.

1. (see Figure 17.15-A) The two leaders with their *varas* held in a phallic position charge from opposite ends through the double line of dancers. The other dancers hold their *varas* upright in a vertical position. They also use their *varas* aggressively to prevent the two leaders from passing through the line. This is then repeated by each successive pair of dancers.

2. (see Figure 17.15-B) The two leaders with *varas* again in a phallic position attempt to dash through the lines, only this time the other six dancers hold their *varas* in a horizontal position and use them to trip the leaders. This is repeated with each pair of dancers.

3. (see Figure 17.15-C) Each of the three pairs of dancers run under the upraised *varas* or "phalluses" of the other two pairs, which are raised so as to touch tips. This time, leaders do not run through the columns but rather around the outside, chasing one another.

4. Two of the alzados engage in a humorous mock battle in which one or both of them "die." The "dead" dancer is unceremoniously mourned by his fellow dancers, who hit him with their *varas* and carry him about the plaza. In the case of two "dead" dancers, a rather humorous competition ensues in which each attempts to determine who will stand up or "come alive" first. This dying scene should be compared with the final movements of the *kanchis* and *awqa chileno* dances, which likewise portray types of rites of passage, symbolic of regeneration and fertility.

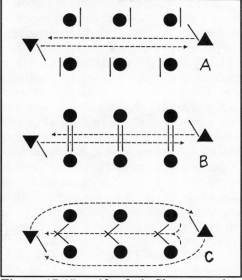

Figure 17.15   *Alzados'* Choreography. Key: A=First *Alizado* Movement, B=Second *Alizado* Movement, C=Third *Alizado* Movement, ●=*alzados*, ▲=leaders

Interpretation: The Structure of Dance

Comparing these three representative dance forms, a basic repertoire of five choreographic features emerges:

1. Linear formation of dancers in two parallel hierarchies with sequential or imitative patterning of dance movements
2. Shifting divisions of the space between these two columns (*kanchis* #A-6; awqa chilenos #4; alzados #2 and #3)
3. Braiding or zigzag movement (*kanchis* #B-2; awqa chilenos #3)
4. Concentric or circular formations (*kanchis* #B-3 and C-1; awqa chilenos #5)
5. Reformation of linear hierarchies within a context of renewal or regeneration (*kanchis*——initiation; awqa chilenos—*yawar mayu*; alzados—death and resurrection)

These five formations, movements, or figures are also used by the majority of other dance groups I have seen performing at Cuzco pilgrimage shrines, as well as in the dances of the Bolivian and northern Chilean traditions (Oblitas P. 1963:327-45; Paredes C. 1966; van Kessel 1982). Insofar as these same five figures are repeated and improvised upon in such a wide range of Andean dances, it is possible to speculate generally upon their meaning in terms of what role is played by "dance" itself. More particularly, I will examine how dance as a ritual form expresses or reflects certain cultural concepts about hierarchy, space, and social/spatial/hierarchical transformation.

This presumed "meaning" of dance, however, is by no means restricted to its dance context, for such choreographic formations are interpreted by spectators and dancers alike in terms of the social experiences and cultural-symbolic codes which they share as Quechua-speaking *campesinos* (peasants). Such an interpretation in turn includes both intellectual and emotive recognition of the formal similarities and analogies of choreographic structures as transformations of other aspects of Quechua social practice and community organization. In particular I will suggest that the hierarchical mode of determining social prestige and status provides a basic metaphor for the ways in which an individual, whose own life is intimately inscribed in such local hierarchies, would interpret both the hierarchies of dance and those of the dance's associated pilgrimage. These *campesinos* would perceive the rituals as means through which to attain some transformation in personal or community hierarchical standing (e.g., religious, material, or prestige rewards). Other metaphors would include the use and appropriation of social space and its differing divisions and boundaries as a practical referent for deciphering the qualities of space in both pilgrimage and dance. Here I discuss each of the five choreographic features in terms of the sociosymbolic configurations and metaphors to which they refer.

Although presented here as separate movements, these five formations are all integral, inseparable components of one dance performance or sequence of movements. As a sequential, or quasi-narrative structure, the ordering of these five features in dance is therefore of equal importance as their individual interpretations. Specifically, I will suggest that their ordering resembles the sequential structure of pilgrimage itself: linear hierarchical movement into a sacred center; movement around the sacred precinct; and the renewal or regeneration of individuals as a result of this combined linear and circular movement.

1. Sequential or Imitative Parallel Hierarchies.

All dance formations are initially structured around two parallel columns of dancers, with individual steps or *pasos* performed by pairs of opposing dancers, one from each column. The "head" or top of the two columns is always that which stands nearest the church door or, lacking a church door, the columns may also be directionally oriented (van Kessel 1982:274). The presentation of consecutive dance steps is also hierarchically arrayed from the head, *capitán*, or senior pair, to the ends of each line where *ukukus* or *maqt'achas* dance. The choreography is likewise directed by *capitánes* who stand at the head of the two lines or by the first or senior pair. This performance hierarchy reflects in all cases the age and experience of the different members of the *comparsa*. Since younger, less experienced performers follow the steps of the senior dancers who precede them, dancing can be considered "imitative" (cf. van Kessel 1982:269). Much of the humour of the alzado dance is derived from the distortions and deliberate mocking of this dual hierarchical formation, and by the dancers' systematic refusal to obey their two frantic *capitánes*. Alzados likewise play games with the general rule of imitation and attempt to out-trick each other into imitating consecutive faux pas. Principles of hierarchical ordering are similarly mocked in all three movements of the alzado pairs who, instead of passing together from head to tail of the two columns, split up and charge at each other with upraised staff or "phallus" from opposite directions.

This double column formation of Andean dance is premised upon a symmetrical or mirror-image structuring of dual hierarchies which, as pointed out in the *kanchis* description, is similar to those underlying traditional modes of Andean political and ritual organization (cf. Platt 1978). Parallel hierarchies of dancers evoke the dual organization of moiety-divided communities in which each moiety maintains its own hierarchy of political-religious authorities (Palomino 1970; Urton 1984). A similar dual structure provided the foundation for the elaborate Inca imperial system of parallel dynasties and "brother" kings (Zuidema 1964, 1982a), and also appears in models of Inca and Quechua kinship systems (Isbell 1978; Zuidema 1973).

The rotational or sequential mode of dance movement can also be best understood in relation to these dual hierarchies of political-religious offices. Whereas the structuring of local authority at any one time was likened to a dual, symmetrical, or parallel set of hierarchies, when seen over time these political systems come to resemble the rotational ranking of dance. Thus, through the imitative sequence of a dance, individuals and their hierarchically static symbols of costuming, *vara* size, and age are seen to advance through a temporal sequence. This sequence is characterized by the delegation of authority which is acquired, as in real life, through age, experience, and the imitation of successively higher ranks. In this way too, hierarchy is itself renewed as dancers proceed through fixed hierarchical positions and eventually "pass out of" the structure itself. Like the *varayuq* hierarchies, or the ancestral mummy hierarchies of the Incas (Zuidema 1973, 1978), an overall structure with fixed number of ranks is thus maintained, while individuals move out of position or office and into an undifferentiated and unranked high social status. In modern-day political and cargo hierarchies, one who has attained this status is called *pasado* (passed) or *tukusqa* (finished, or transformed).

However, while dance movement formally mirrors the progression and hierarchies of secular-religious offices, it also differs radically from these real-life structures in that dance movement is not only sequential but rotational. In other words, the progression of a fixed hierarchy over time is represented in dance by a limited number of performers. As each dancer advances through and out of the structured ranks, he passes back to the beginning and not, as in social hierarchies, to a position outside or beyond the hierarchy itself. In such rotation, structure is regenerated through loss of individual hierarchical identity, a loss which is further symbolized in the masked, costumed, socially anonymous identity of dancers. Their ritual role acquires sacred status precisely through the transformation of the social individual into a representative dancer. In this sense, the uniquely ritual character of dance movement can be seen to lie in the transformation of the dancer into a component of structural hierarchical regeneration. This process is realized in social life only over several generations with the constant "feeding-in" and "passing-out" of new participants.

2. *Definition of Internal Space: The Kancha.*

There is also an obvious concern in these and other Andean dances with the definition of an internal space or area between the two columns of dancers (cf. Salomon 1981). *Varas* or whips are used for this purpose in the *kanchis* dance. Chilenos approximate the same effect with their linked scarves since, as foreigners, they do not carry the indigenous staffs of authority. And finally, the alzados, though wielding *varas*, neither define nor retain any consistent spatial divisions in the course of their disorderly performances. Although temporarily displaying structures similar to those of the *kanchis* and chilenos, these forms are immediately abstracted by the alzados into menacing, obscene weapons in a mock battle pitting dancer against dancer.

The space between dancers' columns defined and divided in these movements is referred to as the *kancha*. *Kancha* in Quechua is used to refer to a walled field or patio area, or to any other bounded or "defined" unit of space, and is iconographically represented by a square or rectangle (Isbell and Fairchild 1980 :11-13). In dance, however, the *kancha* is not only "walled" or "defined" by two columns, but repeatedly sub-divided through sequential dance formations. Chilenos, for example, pass under and through their "bridge" of upraised scarves (a move which is thoroughly garbled in the third formation of the alzados). And *kanchis* pass under, over, and through their horizontally displayed *varas* and dance whips. In each case, moreover, the hierarchy of the twin columns is visually maintained in the internal structure of the *kancha* through the opposition of stiff *varas* to flexible whips (*kanchis* versus *ukukus*) or of scarves to leather whips (chilenos versus *ukukus* and *maqt'achas*).

These temporary rotational divisions of the dance *kancha* can be compared with the Quechua concept of *chuta*—a division of horizontal space which is periodically and ritually defined by the activity, movement, or work of social groups (Urton 1984). The forms chosen for representing these "*chutas*" of the dancers' *kancha*, moreover, are constructed around pan-Andean themes. Parallel *varas*, for example, reflect symmetrical pairing of opposing moieties and hierarchies, while the spaces or *chutas* between them recall the iconographic convention for cultivated land (Girault 1969:40; Oblitas P. 1963:204). In both cases, moreover, the movement of work, cultivation, or dance is the means for defining spatial structure. The diamond form is likewise a leitmotif in Andean iconography, representing the regeneration of spatial form through processes of movement, circulation, and flow (Allen 1982:26; cf. van Kessel 1982:261-62). Finally, the crossed *varas* of the *kanchis* dance—resembling the ceques of Inca Cuzco (Zuidema

1964)—dissolve these binary oppositions into a centrifugal radial pattern of expanding social order.

3. *Weaving, Braiding, or Zigzag Forms.*

Each dance includes a *simp'a* (weaving or braiding movement) in which opposing columns snake in and out through each others' stationary linked positions. In other dances of Cuzco such as the *qapac qolla* and *waqcha qolla*, dancers sing repeatedly *"chinka, chinka, chinka"* while weaving in and out. (From the Quechua verb *chinkay*, meaning "to lose"; the entire movement may also be called *chinkana*, or labyrinth.) Since this is in all cases a transitional movement between linear columns and circular formations, *chinka* possibly refers to the temporary loss of hierarchical position or identity in the ensuing circle pattern, where dancers are not internally ranked (recall the first choreographic feature above, concerning the "transformation" of dancer as hierarchical icon). This movement also reveals the ranking of the two columns with respect to each other since one must necessarily pass first through the others' line. By comparison, in all other column formations ranking is internal to each line and relations between the two columns remain symmetrical.

Similar zigzag formations are found throughout Andean art and iconography, where they symbolically convey concepts of transformation, circulation, the synthesis of opposites, and regeneration of difference (Allen 1982). It is thus appropriate that this same form should appear in dance as a mode of annulling order and hierarchy in favor of a new order of internally undifferentiated concentricity. Isbell and Fairchild identify this zigzag transformational concept or movement in Andean art with the step pattern called *pata* (slope or side of a hill) as a physical region or line where "definition takes place" (1980:13).[5]

4. *Concentric Hierarchies of Exclusion, Inclusion, and Transition.*

Dance formations are not only linearly but also concentrically structured. Once the double columns are broken and the circle formed via a zigzag movement, certain dancers may remain excluded, for example, the *ukukus*, *maqt'achas*, *doctor*, *diablo* and *médico* in the chileno dance. Or they may occupy secondary positions, as the *ukukus* in the *kanchis* circles, where their leather whips hold together *varas* but do not function to lift up the *chanaku*. Where present, Spanish, mestizo, or devil figures always dance outside the main circle of dancers as in the chileno example (cf. Cáceres M. 1970:54-67; van Kessel 1982:283). As an intermediary formation, moreover, this circle may represent not only exclusion, but also the inclusion of a new member in the double columns, as in the *chanaku's* "initiation" or "transformation" in the *kanchis* dance. Finally, this concentric structure is always displayed as a transitional formation in a longer sequence of dance figures beginning and ending with the parallel linear hierarchies (cf. Cáceres M. 1970:79-80; Paredes C. 1966:166-67; van Kessel 1982).[6]

Studies of Andean social organization have frequently pointed out the predominance of similar concentric hierarchies in the spatial and productive organization of Quechua and Aymara communities (Isbell 1978:57-63; Palomino 1970; Urton 1984; Zuidema 1964, 1982a). A typical Andean settlement pattern, for example, opposes a central village to the fields which lie around it, while these lands are subsequently opposed to the less populated, uncultivated, and hence symbolically "wild" *punas* (grasslands) outside of them. Hierarchies of political authority may incorporate such territorial criteria in the opposition of moiety, or *ayllu varayuq*, to a parallel system of outside authorities called *campo* (country) or *sallqa* (wild) *varayuq* (Isbell 1978:85-93; Palomino 1970). As with the "social" and "asocial" dancers discussed above, concentricity is further replicated in the expressions of social exclusivity used to define such basic categories as kin and non-kin, "us" and "them," and Quechua- and Spanish-speaking populations (Isbell 1978:99-136).

In these social examples, concentric form adopts a transitional or transformational mode similar to that which it displays in dance. This is because "inside" social hierarchies, like dance columns, are always defined by means of the dialectical opposition of their ordered, bounded space or *kancha* with the more primary, though less stable division between inside and outside (cf. Lévi-Strauss 1972:132-66). Someone from the outside, a *chanaku* or *doctor* for example, attains access to the inside only through transgression of the circular moving boundary between member or social dancer and outside or asocial dancer. In the chileno dance it is particularly interesting that this potential entrance into the inner ranks—an entrance whose outcome is the comically disastrous performance of the *doctor* in the bravado of the *yawar mayu*—is attained through an inside female figure (the *imilla*).

As part of their disorderly mode of being, alzados never utilize this circular form in their choreography. Their nonhierarchical, inverted columns are seemingly incapable of evolving into a concentric structure, while their permanently asocial behavior precludes the necessity of a boundary which might differentiate inside and social from outside and asocial. Instead, at least in Sankha, concentricity is evoked by leaving the plaza and procession, and by then reentering it in a disorderly, chaotic, thoroughly "outside" manner which stands in defiant opposition to the entire fiesta of which they are nonetheless part.

5. *Transformation and Renewal.*

The final movement of each dance is premised upon a regrouping of dancers into their original parallel columns in a context of ritual renewal, regeneration, or transformation. Thus, in the case of the *kanchis*, the *chanaku* is initiated into the group; in the chileno dance the columns reform so as to perform the *yawar mayu* dance evocative of fertility and renewal; and the *alzados* enact a parody of death and revitalization. Seen as part of the overall sequence of the dance, each of these transformational scenes evolves out of the zigzag and circular structures which immediately precede it. Linear hierarchy is first rendered fluid through the weaving or zigzag, then annulled in the circle, and finally redefined as a result of these consecutive movements.

It is here perhaps that dance can be most closely compared to the pilgrimage ritual in which it transpires, for both are ritual formulas for attaining a transformation through movement. Dancers representative of the linear hierarchies of community authority advance in pilgrimage to a ritual center. There dancers deconstruct and redefine the hierarchies they represent through a series of complex, fluid, formulaic movements at the sanctuary center. Likewise, it is the dancers who bear the image of a saint, virgin, or Christ figure in its procession around the sacred precinct. In one Cuzqueño sanctuary (Qoyllur Rit'i), the transformational zigzag of choreography is explicitly evoked in the weaving dance through which pilgrims enter the sanctuary.[7] Finally, as in dance, at the end of the procession and fiesta, pilgrims and *comparsas* will regroup and return home in "linear" fashion, bearing with them the rewards of pilgrimage: increased fertility, abundance, new cargo status, assured health, and general good fortune.

A similar conjunction of linear, zigzag, and circular or spiral movements underlay Inca pilgrimage and dance. In these pilgrimages, priests or sacrificial victims, depending on the type of pilgrimage, would travel in a straight line to a sacred center, circumambulate the plaza, temple, or the sacred person of the Inca, and subsequently return to their place of origin (Zuidema 1973, 1982a). Here the religious and social transformation—a transformation itself closely related to shifts in political ranking and prestige—was specifically related to this juxtaposition of movement along a straight line into a sacred precinct and a spiral or circular movement around that center (Zuidema 1978). Similar principles of movement were reiterated in dance. For example, an elaborate dance performed in January after the Incaic solstitial ceremonies and initiation rites of December, began with a random movement of dancers through the outer streets of Cuzco but directed toward the central plaza. Upon converging in this central plaza, dancers picked up a *muyurqo* (multicolored woolen rope), with which they danced in a spiral form around the Inca himself (Molina [1575] 1943:121-23). The transformational powers of dances such as this spiral rope dance later became a focus for one of the early indigenous rebellions against Spanish and Catholic domination, the *taqui onqoy*, or "dancing sickness." In this rebellion, or "plague of dancing," dance was perceived as a means to effect an idealized *pachacuti* ("turning of the world") or transformation of the world order (Zuidema 1964:235).[8]

HIERARCHY, SPACE, AND TRANSFORMATION IN ANDEAN PILGRIM-
AGE AND DANCE

The choreography of Andean dance thus appears to be firmly grounded
in the forms of spatial and hierarchical organization which underlie all
aspects of Quechua social life, while the characters portrayed reflect an
interest in the representation or classification of different social strata and
ethnic or class groups. Like the different contextual layers of kinship
classifications, territory, and local authority which they reflect, the general
ordering of these dance movements reveals a marked interest in defining,
transforming, inverting, and redefining the relationship between (horizontal) spatial structure and the shifting (vertical) social hierarchies of
Quechua society. Moreover, in both pilgrimage and dance, this conjunction
of vertical linear hierarchies with horizontal, circular, and zigzag spatial
patterns is interpreted as a form of social transformation affecting the
individual in his or her relationship to local social organization as well as
to the regional religious image for whom dance is performed.

The specificity of these concepts found in dance to Quechua society and
to Andean modes of symbolic thought becomes more apparent if we briefly
compare them with other types of choreographic expression. In the first
place, when compared with other culturally defined dance traditions in
which dancers dance alone, emphasizing individual body gestures and aerial
movements (Royce 1977), these Quechua dances reflect a clear interest in
delineating concise spatial configurations through cooperative group
movement. This movement, moreover, is focused almost exclusively on the
earth or kancha as evidenced by the patterning of varas or whips laid on
the ground and by the emphatic zapateos which accompany most such
dance movements.

Secondly, even when compared with other traditions of group-choreo-
graphed ritual dance, these Quechua dances display certain unique
configurations. These center primarily on the use of linear, imitative
hierarchy, the transformational zigzag and circle, and the connotative or
formal properties of each figure. Thus, for example, comparing the dances
just described with the choreography of the Spanish seises of Seville
(Backman 1952:76-85; Rosa y López 1904:263-78), we find the following
differences:

1. As in the Andean dances, the Spanish seises begin each figure with
parallel double columns of dancers. The number of dancers (ten) is always
fixed, however, for the nonlinear, hierarchical form they use is less flexible
insofar as it does not allow for additions as in the Andean comparsas. Thus,
each line of five dancers pivots around the center or tranca. The oldest or
tallest of the five boys stand at both ends of the two lines, while the

smallest run the *trancas*. Hierarchy is thus neither linear nor imitative, as in the Andean examples.

2. Though possessing a fixed repertoire of figures, the *seises* perform these movements in no fixed order. Therefore, although circular forms are generated from the two columns, the concentric formation is not consistently "transformational" or transitional as in the Andean fixed-order choreography. Moreover, in no case is a zigzag movement utilized to form the circle. Instead, the two lines pivoting around their *trancas* converge at opposite ends to form a circle. Finally, in many of the *seises'* circular formations, the four ends (*puntas*) remain outside, forming a square frame for the inner circle of dancers.

3. Not only do the movements and hierarchical forms themselves differ, but their mode of interpretation is much more denotative and literal. The circle, for example, is taken by some authors as symbolic of the round host of the Catholic communion, while the various "S"-shaped figures are popularly interpreted as the "S.S." of the words *Santísimo Sacramento* or Holy Sacrament. All other figures of the *seises* dance are likewise interpreted as semi-mystic, hieroglyphic, literary emblems relating to the Catholic Mass.

These three properties—linear imitative hierarchy, transformation through zigzag or circular forms, and interest in the formal, connotative properties of choreographic space—through which Andean dance differs from the Spanish tradition are all intimately related, as we have seen, to the use of dance as part of pilgrimage ritual. Although the Spanish *seises* are part of a Catholic liturgical service from which they derive their meaning, Andean dances—as part of regional pilgrimage cults—are likewise meaningful religious activities precisely because of the type of ritual context in which they occur. It remains to see, however, what these classificatory and choreographic properties of Andean dance can tell us about the meaning and practice of this "context," that is pilgrimage, in Andean society.

By way of conclusion, therefore, I will briefly compare each of these properties of Andean dance to the act of pilgrimage itself. It will be suggested that both the use and display of these hierarchical, spatial, and transformational principles in dance parallel and recursively reinform the importance of these same abstract principles in the pilgrimage rituals which present the context for dance performance. In this respect, the ritualized movement of Andean pilgrimage will itself be seen to derive much of its coherence and meaning as a religious, devotional act from these dances in which the formal characteristics of pilgrimage are presented in the entertaining, emotive, anonymous (masked), and artistic form of dance. In each case I will also point out possible ways in which Andean pilgrimage, as a product of its own unique historical and cultural association with dance, may differ from other Christian pilgrimage traditions.

Vertical Hierarchy

Pilgrimage in the Andes functions, as we have seen, to affirm the internal, ultimately vertical (i.e., hierarchical) structuring of the social groups traveling to a pilgrimage shrine. Pilgrimage is an important means by which individuals attain prestige *cargos* within their community. As ritual representatives of their community, moreover, pilgrims identify throughout their journey with this local hierarchized group and not, as in some models of Christian pilgrimage (see Turner and Turner 1978), with a larger, theoretically "undifferentiated" mass of pilgrims at a sanctuary (cf. Sallnow 1981). At all Andean pilgrimages I have attended, local groups remain aloof from each other, and *comparsas*, as the principal representatives of local hierarchy and as bearers of their community's sacred icon or *lámina*, dance separately.

Like the pilgrimage in which it occurs, dance couples the representation of local hierarchy with a concept of outward movement both through its choreography and through the types of personages represented in dance, for in all such dances local (inside) hierarchy is portrayed by some type of outsider. *Kanchis*, for example, are danced by non-*kanchis*; *awqa chilenos* are foreigners from a remote historical period; *alzados* are nonsocial buffoons; and *ukukus* are presocial adolescent half-humans. All other Cuzco dance groups can likewise be said to portray ethnic, cultural, historical, ancestral, or normative ("wild") outsiders.[9] Images of mythic, historic, or social outsiders are thus used in Andean pilgrimage dances to represent the presence of a local, inside group at a regional, outside, shrine. Yet, as in the awqa chileno *comparsa*, these "outsiders" are themselves differentiated by their relative ability to manipulate the "insiders'" cultural, religious idiom of dance as the means for reproducing and strengthening inside hierarchies of authority, prestige, and power. It is these hierarchies, and the dance forms which validate them, to which a real "outsider" like the *doctor*, or an asocial agent such as the *alzado* would have no access.

Horizontal Space

Pilgrimage is most easily defined as the ritual movement of people outside their local territory to a mutually revered regional shrine. In the literature, such movement of individual pilgrims or, as is the case in the Andes, of community contingents, is usually said to "integrate" local territory with respect to a larger regional system and to induce the pilgrim to cross a variety of territorial, ecological, and social boundaries (Deffontaines 1948; Dupront 1973; Turner and Turner 1978). In the Andes this ritual integration of social space through pilgrimage functions on two related levels: (1) through the actual movement of people, both pilgrims and dancers, and (2) through the symbolic cognitive structures of the dances performed at shrines and along pilgrimage routes. In the mountainous Andes, the journey of pilgrimage articulates a horizontal social space across the predominantly vertical physical space over which the pilgrim travels. In pre-Columbian pilgrimage this emphasis on connecting the disparate social centers separated by high peaks and deep valleys was formalized in ritual journeys following straight lines as opposed to the rise and fall of winding mountain roads. Today as well, the journey to a pilgrimage shrine follows carefully demarcated routes with ritual stopping points at those places where a shrine or sacred mountain first comes into view. As in the Inca pilgrimage following straight sightlines, this ritualized visual recognition of spatial relationships involves the sighting of the horizontal planes connecting social or sacred centers in an otherwise vertical terrain.[10]

At these stopping points, pilgrims pause to rest and pray to the newly visible mountain or shrine while dancers perform their choreographic routines, whose formal concern with defining horizontal spatial structure resembles that of the horizontal religious space addressed in the pilgrims' invocations. Thus, as in the movement of the hierarchical (cargo-bearing) pilgrimage contingent across horizontal social space, a vertical hierarchy of dancers is first used to define the space of the dance *kancha* into a sequence of parallel, bounded (diamond shaped), and finally radial *chutas*. These three modes of *kancha* division correspond respectively to three forms of territorial structure integrated through pilgrimage itself: the vertical or ecological, the boundedness of local territory, and the unbounded radial or centric form used since Inca times to define the political and religious centrality of place and the expansion of territory out from that central place (Zuidema 1964, 1982a). Finally, the concentric forms evoked in dance as transformational structure reflect the opposition of all these forms to the primary division of "inside" versus "outside" as the basic conceptual opposition underlying all pilgrimage ritual. Whereas the Inca concern with precise definition of social space through *ceques* or straight-line pilgrimages may no longer pertain to the actual journeys of modern-day "Christian" pilgrims, these forms are nonetheless manifestly reproduced in pilgrimage dances. Similarly, as in the Inca or Andean interest in straight movement to a sacred place and then circular or spiral-zigzag movement around it, pilgrimage today retains the ideal of travel to a shrine, dancing "around" it, and then returning out again.

Transformation through Movement

All pilgrimage must offer its participants and devotees some tangible reward. This reward is frequently envisioned as a type of personal spiritual transformation or, as is more often the case in the Andes, as the bestowal of a material reward or insurance which benefits not only the participant, but the entire community he or she represents. The sacramental medium through which this reward or transformation is attained is that of "movement," or the act of traveling to a distant sanctuary. Such physical movement, which in European Christian pilgrimage is seen as a penitential act of suffering, involves the crossing of the social, territorial, and conceptual boundaries which otherwise segregate locality and person from the larger networks focused on the religious shrine.

Like pilgrimage, Andean dance explicitly equates physical movement with the personal and social transformation communicated through choreographic forms. Unlike the Christian, or European, tradition, however, movement in Andean pilgrimage and associated dance is no longer a means of acquiring personal transformation through suffering or penitence, but a means of achieving a classificatory transformation through the formal properties of the dance or the pilgrimage. Hierarchical columns are subverted and redefined through the zigzag patterns and concentric oppositions of the dancers' movements. Dancers themselves are shuffled through these forms as icons of hierarchical order whose masks, costumes, and repeated, conventionalized movements transform the social individual into anonymous ritual representative. In this way too the dancer is temporarily transformed into another class of being. He acquires the ritualized, temporary face of an "outsider," while his everyday social status is also permanently transformed through having carried out the "burden" or cargo of dancing or sponsoring the dance for his community.

On this level too, then, dance can be related to the formal qualities and conceptual characteristics of pilgrimage. Like pilgrimage it relies upon physical movement as a sacrament for expressing devotion and for achieving a "transformation." It is also here, however, that dance differs qualitatively from pilgrimage, for the transformational or sacramental movements of dance are performed for and presented to an audience which includes not only the religious image housed at a shrine, but also the assembled group of pilgrims. Just as dancers and pilgrims represent their villages, the dances they perform represent and condense the more diffuse principles of the pilgrimage as a whole. This representation, moreover, is presented as entertainment, as musical performance, and as a spectacle which emotionally, aesthetically, and personally unites the individual to the collective devotion of the pilgrimage shrine. As a formal intellectual analogue of pilgrimage, it is nonetheless to its creative, emotive, and participatory qualities that dance owes its remarkable longevity and vitality as a form of regional pilgrimage devotion.

NOTES

1. Research on pilgrimage in Cuzco, Peru, was conducted from 1976 to 1981 under the auspices of grants from the Department of Anthropology, University of Illinois, Urbana; the Henry and Grace Doherty Foundation, Princeton, New Jersey; and the Fulbright-Hayes

Doctoral Dissertation Program. I would also like to thank the Charlotte W. Newcombe Program (Woodrow Wilson National Fellowships), Princeton, New Jersey, for financial support while writing this field material.

2. Dance was a means of paying tribute (Santillán [1553] 1950:68), of entertaining as "clowns" (González Holguín [1608] 1952:80; Guaman Poma de Ayala [1614] 1936:f.327), of reciting history (Betanzos [1551] 1924; Morúa [1590] 1922:130-1; Schecter 1979), of mimicking the power of wild animals (Duviols 1967:20), and, finally, of simply celebrating or legitimizing a group's own ethnic or occupational identity (Acosta [1590] 1954:195,206; Cobo [1653] 1956:II,133,270-1; Garcilaso [1609] 1960:I,156; Guaman Poma de Ayala [1614] 1936:ff.315-27).

3. The *huayno* is the most widespread and popular form of Andean dance music, characterized by its unique rhythmic structure and pentatonic scale. The *huayno* has been most fully discussed in both its historical and modern-day contexts by Josefat Roel Pineda (1959).

4. I have observed *kanchis'* dances at the pilgrimage sanctuaries of Qoyllur Rit'i (Quispicanchis, Cuzco) and Pampak'ucho (Paruro, Cuzco), as well as in several village patronal feasts around Cuzco. The description given here is therefore based on a compilation of these diverse performances, with significant variations noted parenthetically. When dancers have more time to perform their dance, they will simply repeat figures or sequences of figures. On the other hand, in situations where other comparsas are waiting to dance or when a procession or Mass is imminent, figures may be omitted in the interests of finishing quickly.

5. These zigzag movements also, of course, suggest the art of weaving (see van Kessel 1982:294-96) and the various symbolic interpretations of this form of material expression in the Andes. Here again, the movement of threads through a linear pattern is seen to momentarily break down the order of separate parallel warp colors so as to eventually produce a new, transformed design or *pallay*. In one dance of northern Bolivia, reminiscent of the European maypole dance, a weaving movement is used to produce woven figures on a pole from which hang colored ribbons carried by the dancers as they weave through each others' lines (Oblitas P. 1963:332-34).

6. Circular dances called *qashwas* are frequently performed during Carnival and harvest festivals from May to June. These circular dances, however, are not performed by masked dancers but rather by all community members. They are specifically associated with fertility rituals and the ritual battles that are believed to lead to increased fertility for both competing sides (Alencastre and Dumézil 1953; cf. Cobo [1653] 1956:II, 85, 271). Wherever or whenever they occur, however, *qashwas*, like the transitional circular forms of *comparsa* choreography, are based on the concentric opposition of community members (insiders) to outsiders, or those excluded from the *qashwa*. In pre-Spanish dance traditions, circular forms were specifically associated with war dances (Cobo [1653] 1956:II, 271) or with recitation of imperial historical narrative (Betanzos [1551] 1924:158; Morúa [1590] 1922:130-31). Both these functions might equally well be interpreted as means of distinguishing insider "us" from outsider "them," as enemies or those not included in a legitimating historical discourse.

7. *Comparsas* approaching the sanctuary of Qoyllur Rit'i stop some distance outside the precinct to dress and prepare their dance. They enter the sanctuary itself in skipping, vaguely zigzag lines. This zigzag mode of entry is, however, more explicit at another associated temple center, Tayankani. Just above this latter site they await the sunrise, which they salute on bended knee, and then descend en masse in two long interweaving, zigzag lines of skipping dancers and pilgrims to the town of Tayankani, where the Christ figure will be honored with a Mass.

8. The *taqui onqoy* differed from the dances discussed here in that it apparently did not include group dances or formal choreography. Instead dance was more individualized-—reflective perhaps of the newly commodified Spanish economy and individualized religion to which the movement was a response—and took the form of "trance-dances" (Molina [1575] 1916:96-101).

9. For example, the *ch'uncho* and *qolla* dances which represent lowland and highland peoples respectively; the *majeños*, which portray nineteenth- and early twentieth-century

vendors of cane alcohol from the Arequipa valley of Majes; or the *saqsa* dance in the province of Paruro said to represent ancestral beings from a time before the sun first appeared (Poole 1990. Perhaps the best-known example of these outsider dancers, however, are the devil (*saqra* or *diablo*) dancers of Paucartambo (Cuzco), Puno, and Bolivia, who represent the presence of symbolically non-Christian elements in Christian religious feasts (Cáceres M. 1970; van Kessel 1982:283-84; Villasante O. n.d.:102-05).

10. Similar stops may also be made at important territorial or ecological boundaries. Or dancers themselves may represent the social and ecological boundaries crossed in pilgrimage. For example, many dances portray peoples from different productive zones. Valley peoples dance as *altiplano* traders or *puna* herders. *Puna* dwellers, for their part, are more interested in dancing as Indians from the jungle (*ch'unchos*). The presence of these various dance groups at a given shrine may reflect the geographic correspondence of a sanctuary with trade routes or the historical boundary location of the shrine itself (Poole 1982; Randall 1982).

REFERENCES

Acosta 1954
Alencastre G. 1953
Allen 1982, 1983, 1989
Arriaga 1920
Avila 1975
Backman 1952
Betanzos 1924
Cáceres Monroy 1970
Cobo 1956
Cotarelo y Mori 1911
Deffontaines 1948
Dupront 1973
Duviols 1967, 1971
Fine 1982
Garcilaso de la Vega 1960
Gilt Contreras 1966
Girault 1969
González Holguin 1952
Gow 1974
Guaman Poma de Ayala 1936
Isbell 1978
Isbell-Fairchild 1980
Ivanova 1970
Lévi Strauss 1972
Manrique 1981
Molina "El Cusqueño" 1943

Morúa 1922
Moreno 1972
Oblitas Poblete 1963
Palomino 1984
Paredes Candia 1966
Platt 1978
Poole 1982, 1989, 1990, n.d.
Ramírez E. 1969
Randall 1982
Roel Pineda 1959
Rosa y Lopez 1904
Rostworowski de Diez
  Canseco 1977
Royce 1977
Sallnow 1974, 1981,
  1982, 1987
Salomon 1981
Santillán 1950
Schecter 1979
Tord 1980
Turner-Turner 1978
Urton 1984
van Kessel 1982
Villasante Ortiz n.d.
Wachtel 1971
Zuidema 1964, 1973, 1978, 1982a

18

Mythic Andean Discourse and Pilgrimages

HENRIQUE URBANO

Ceremonial centers have existed in the Andes since very remote periods. According to the Spanish chroniclers, Andean peoples or nations gathered around these sacred sites in search of an answer to their collective preoccupations, or as Durkheim would say, in celebration of their own sociopolitical existence (Durkheim 1968:609-12). Twentieth-century archaeologists also speak of these places, suppressing such lucubrations to a vision generally too Western in orientation. In comparison to modern archaeologists, however, the earliest sixteenth-century sources do mention some of these pilgrimage centers by name and classify them according to religious categories of the period.[1] A study of these accounts reveals pilgrimages and pilgrimage shrines to be the issue which perhaps most clearly reveals the problem of an encounter between the two religious and liturgical traditions in Andean history, the pre-Hispanic and the Judeo-Christian.

Who, for example, has not noted how the first conquistadors were impressed by the ceremonial center at Pachacamac, south of the future city of Lima, Peru? A few months after the conquest the chronicler, Francisco de Jérez (1574), wrote that "they hold this one [Pachacamac] as a god and they made many sacrifices to him... they came to this devil in a pilgrimage of 300 leagues... all the people of this coast served in this temple..." (Jérez [1574] 1947:II, 339). Another text, which Porras Barrenechea attributes to Mena, describes this sanctuary and town as being "larger than Rome" (Anónimo Sevillano [1534] 1967:94). Cuzco evoked no less admiration in many Spaniards, and other sanctuaries also attracted the attention of the conquistadors.

The pre-Hispanic Andean definition of urban and ritual space is closely related to this problem of ceremonial or pilgrimage centers. However, because of the practical difficulties involved in studying the pre-Hispanic point of view we have to develop our definition through two related channels. On the one hand, we consider an Andean pre-Columbian mythic discourse which recounts the *space* of pilgrimage, and on the other, we examine some related themes collected from contemporary mythic cycles. First I shall examine Andean discourse about the sacred journeys of pre-Hispanic heroes. Next I shall analyze some of the images which appear in these accounts. Finally, with the aid of some brief examples, I shall question to what extent contemporary mythic discourse has maintained the ancient model of pilgrimage and how it places mythic heroes in the Andean context of Christian pilgrimage.

PREHISTORIC PILGRIM HEROES: THE WIRACOCHA

Our knowledge of the epic origins of Andean peoples is constructed on the basis of an oral tradition collected for the most part in Cuzco and the southern regions of Peru. In spite of this fact, the narratives recounting the mythic cycle of the Wiracocha and the set of functions within pre-Hispanic Andean society which these pilgrimaging heroes define, appear to ignore the importance of this Inca capital as a center of socio-religious pilgrimages and politico-administrative space.[2]

Instead, the majority of these mythic cycles place the Wiracocha heroes' first heroic acts on the banks of Lake Titicaca. These narratives transform the sites which the Wiracochas visited, or established, into the first ceremonial centers of the lake region. Some of these sites, which are on islands situated in the middle of Lake Titicaca, bear the marks of the works carried out by the heroes. The pre-Inca center of Tiawanaku is also close by and it is clear from the narratives that the Wiracochas knew that place as well.

The projects and activities of the mythic pilgrim-heroes are not restricted to this zone. The narratives which tell us about one or the other of the hero-brothers often take the Wiracochas along routes with the explicit purpose of arranging things according to a predefined sociopolitical and religious model. Each hero follows his own route, which departs initially from the banks of Lake Titicaca. Advancing toward the northwest, they mark places, "create" peoples or "nations", and designate population centers which are transformed into places of profound and extensive ritual influence. According to the great majority of the chroniclers of the sixteenth and seventeenth centuries, the end of the heroes' earthly routes through Antinsuyu, Chinchaysuyu, and Continsuyu was the north coast of Peru near Puerto Viejo. The trip extended toward the ocean and, according to some written sources, the final objective of the pilgrimaging Wiracocha heroes was heaven.

Although the sites marked by the presence of the heroes are still known today, the Spanish chroniclers are not unanimous about either the number or names of the locations. Molina, "El Cusqueño" (1575), maintains that the principal hero, Tecsi Wiracocha Pachayachachic, had two sons, Imaymana and Tocapo, who, following the will of their father, traveled through the Andes and along the Pacific coast, proclaiming the order which all peoples and things should have and follow. They were not always well-received, however, in their pilgrimages. Rebellious people were punished, while those who received the message favorably were rewarded. This same chronicler adds that there remain vestiges of their pilgrimages in Tiawana-ku, Pukará, Jauja, Pachacamac, Cajamarca, and in many other pre-Hispanic settlements where the petrified ancestors of the peoples or nations who inhabited the cited places were worshipped (Molina [1575] 1943:8-15; Urbano 1981).

The traditions collected by Molina, however, do not make reference to a fourth Wiracocha hero, whom other versions of the mythic cycle mention as Taguapica or Taguapaca. Both Las Casas (1550) and Sarmiento (1572) describe him as a rebellious person in complete opposition to his father or "Lord". Therefore, writes Las Casas, an angry and hostile Tecsi Wiracocha threw Taguapaca into the sea "in order that he would die a bad death, but he [nonetheless] never died" (1958:III, 433). Sarmiento gathered similar information. He maintains that Taguapaca's hands and feet were tied and that he was then thrown on a raft in Lake Titicaca, disappearing at that side of the lake which is called Desaguadero. In order to record the site of this and other events, the principal Wiracocha ordered the construction of a *solemne huaca* or celebrated tomb (Sarmiento [1572] 1960:208-09).

Following the movements of the mythical Wiracocha heroes we encounter some other places whose strategic importance is without a doubt related to pre-Columbian liturgical ceremonies or rituals. Located on the central route which the principal hero traveled, Cacha is one of these places which caught the attention of the chroniclers of the sixteenth and seventeenth centuries. It is located "eighteen leagues from the city of Cusco," in territory occupied by the *nation* of Canas. When the Wiracocha hero Pachayachachic approached these Canas, nobody recognized him. Humiliated, the hero made a rain of fire fall from the heavens. Realizing the offence which they had committed, the Canas asked pardon and decided to construct a *suntuosa huaca* (luxurious huaca) in the form of a massive stone figure honoring the pilgrim-hero (Betanzos [1551] 1968:10-11; Sarmiento [1572] 1960:209-10; Ballesteros Graibois 1979; Urbano 1981).

Abandoning Cacha, Pachayachachic then followed the road on toward Urcos, where this time he was well-received. In order to mark the place of his encounter with the Urcos *nation*, the inhabitants constructed "a rich and luxurious memorial, where because this Viracocha had sat in that place, those who built the *huaca* placed a seat or throne of fine gold, and the image which they put in the place of this Viracocha was seated upon that throne" (Betanzos [1551] 1968:10-11; Sarmiento [1572] 1960:210). Betanzos adds that immediately after this the hero left for Cuzco and, having arrived there, named as head of the community a certain Alcaviza, who gave the place itself the name of Cuzco.

The Wiracocha's epic narrative thus remains associated with those locations or ceremonial centers around which liturgical rites are developed or settlements or nations founded. Although the radius of religious, economic, and political influence varies according to the circumstances, each one of those pilgrimage places which were visited or established by the Wiracocha pilgrims emphasizes one of the characteristics of pre-Columbian pilgrimage distinguishing it from other religious experiences or ritual events: the celebration of the origins of a nation. The Wiracocha heroes organize the world and the things in it according to a pre-established pattern, and they bring peoples or nations into existence in conformity with this model. From this act of ordering, the sanctuaries or places of pilgrimage remain as part of a common, collective registry reminding each people of the sociopolitical, religious, and economic commandments through which they were constituted as their own individual nation.

But the mythic cycle of the Wiracocha pilgrim heroes also suggests something else about the pre-Hispanic idea of pilgrimage. As we have seen, two codes are employed in the hierarchical distribution of the pilgrims, one of kinship, and the other of space. The first is defined by the relations between a father and his sons, and the second by the routes the heroes themselves travel. The relations of complementarity and opposition which exist between these two codes are the foundation for a general theory of pre-Hispanic Andean society based on a trifunctional distribution of the pilgrim heroes. Of course, Tecsi or Pachayachachic, as father or *Lord* of the other heroes, embodies the functions of political or religious authority and assesses the organization of the world and of the events in which the other personages will themselves participate. Judging by what the accounts say about him, Imaymana appears above all as the ritual and symbolic expression of an agricultural function, and is associated as well with some of the overlapping aspects of agriculture's magico-ritual concerns. Finally, Tocapo is the hero under whose protection fall all those who make or use textiles. His functions too are ritual or liturgical (Molina [1575] 1943:8-15; Avila 1966:21; Urbano 1981:IX-LXIII).

The mythic cycle of the Wiracocha is very sketchy concerning the activities of the principal hero's sons and the places which they visit. Nevertheless, we know that the routes which are entrusted separately to them correspond in some way to the totality represented in the person of their father or *Lord*. Through his sons or servants, the principal Wiracocha assumes those three functions which, when taken together, globally express pre-Columbian society in its different aspects—political, religious, and agricultural. According to the conventions of each one of the peoples or nations, the heroes embody the characteristics which best express the concerns of that nation. Their ceremonial centers are also adjusted to these symbolic deliberations, without however, affecting the functions which other personages assign them. One of the roles of the pilgrim heroes or sons and servants of the principal hero is to precisely and explicitly define the multiple implicit functions embodied by the principal hero. Therefore, to ritually celebrate one of the functions or one of the heroes is in a certain sense to celebrate them all, even though each one of them has, in addition, his own people or nation.

With regard to this aspect of complementary and oppositional logics, the figure of Tawapaca, however mysterious it may be, nonetheless fulfills an important role in the mythic cycle. This rebellious hero appears as the opposing face with regard to the type of behavior demanded by the principal hero and his nonrebellious sons or servants. Thus, it would not be inappropriate to assume that the ceremonial centers or memorial places on the shores of Lake Titicaca, as well as those which lie to the south of the lake, were established in pre-Hispanic times, so as to carry in some way the imprint or marks of that hero and pilgrim. Las Casas (1550), who provides us with the earliest information about this hero, writes that according to established tradition this fourth hero never died. Some decades later, the Catholic missionary tradition transforms Tawapaca into a personage with the characteristics of the Christian apostle, Saint Thomas or Saint Bartholomew, who traveled across the south of the Andes preaching the Gospel and died a martyr on the shores of Lake Titicaca (Urbano 1981, 1982a; Gisbert 1980).

This tripartite division of the heroic functions as outlined by the mythic cycle of the Wiracocha affirms then, a basis not only for a symbolic reading of pre-Hispanic Andean pilgrimage, but also for that representation which was later reformulated by Spanish designs for the evangelization of the Andean world. I refer here principally to the functional qualities of the pilgrim-heroes insofar as they are expressions of the models of the daily symbolic gestures performed by the peoples, nations, or social groups involved. It is important to note, for example, that Tocapo, because of the logical characteristics which the mythic cycle attributes to him, may very well be the pilgrim-hero of a group or nation which is specifically interested in the ritual production of textiles, or of the priestly, religious functions which these presuppose. In the same way one believes that Imaymana is the protector hero of the roads of Antinsuyu and of the symbolic images which this route expressed. The agricultural functions also have something to do with Imaymana. Concerning the principal hero, Tecsi or Pachayachachic, I have argued that his condition as father or *Lord* places him in political command, complete with the sapient qualities which so many times enshroud such positions of power. Obviously this is also a global expression of societal functions considered in their totality.[3]

EARTHLY PILGRIMAGES AND HEAVENLY ABODES

The majority of the chroniclers commonly agreed that the disappearence of the Wiracocha pilgrim-heroes was on the north coast of Peru at a place called Puerto Viejo. There, the pilgrims reunited after traveling through the Andes, each one following his own respective route. Arriving from whence they came, they entered the water, walking on it "as on land without sinking" (Sarmiento 1960:210; Betanzos 1968:11). Molina (1575) affirms that "the heroes went down into the sea at the deepest part and from there they rose to heaven" (1943:14). Gutierrez de Santa Clara (s. XVI, finales) adds that the fishermen of the north coast of Peru believe that one of the Wiracocha taught them the arts of seamanship (Gutierrez de Santa Clara 1963:III, 244-45).

The expression employed by Molina (1575) that the pilgrim heroes "rose up to heaven," may serve as a pretext to suggest that the Wiracocha, as personages of a mythical group, express some of the astronomical preoccupations of pre-Hispanic Andean peoples. In the same way, one should keep in mind the tradition recognized by Gutierrez de Santa Clara in the late sixteenth century (1963:III, 244-45). In interpreting the mythical accounts of the cycle of the Wiracocha, one may hypothesize that the northern fishermen of the coast oriented their activities by means of some celestial figure of the pilgrim heroes, or that the fishermen followed maritime fishing routes by observing an orientation outlined by the heavenly figure of the heroes.

According to the logic of the Wiracochas' mythic cycle and the religious and sociopolitical structure it suggests, there would be no reason to suppose that both the number of the heroes and their spatial orientations had anything to do with these superficial indications of heavenly abodes mentioned by the chronicler Molina (1575). In fact, the routes followed by the heroes lead approximately from the southeast to the northwest, that is from the shores of Lake Titicaca to Puerto Viejo. If my hypothesis is correct, it can then be assumed that the direction indicated by the hero Tawapaca likewise expresses, in part, the astronomical preoccupations of pre-Columbian peoples. Although it is more difficult to verify the route followed by this rebel hero, it may not be without grounds to suggest that in some way the regions of the north of Chile or of the southeast of Lake Titicaca relate to the actions of this Wiracocha (Urbano 1981:XXVIII; Cuneo Vidal 1977:t. V).

One somewhat obvious conclusion which might be drawn from this representation is that the limits outlined by the end points of the heroes' pilgrimages coincide with the frontiers, more or less accurately defined, of Inca territory. In this sense, the celestial expression of these mythical pilgrims' routes translates as the geographical horizons of that which one might suppose to be the religious, economic, and political tradition of pre-Hispanic Andean expansion. The celestial abodes of the heroes would thus correspond to the symbolic and logical orientations which lay at the foundations of the Inca occupation of Andean space. The celestial horizon of the heroes, expressed in terrestrial terms, would have as its limits the geographical horizontal extremes of their pilgrimages.

Based exclusively on the route followed by the principal hero, Urton affirms that there is an analogy between Wiracocha and the course of the Vilcanota River, which flows in the southeast-northeast direction (Urton 1981:202-04). In his reading, however, Urton overlooks that there are various other personages associated with the generic name of Wiracocha and that the limits of the mythical pilgrimages of the heroes mark a larger space than that which is suggested by the course of this river. There are, of course, references in the myths to Cacha, which lies close to the sources of the Vilcanota. However, although the mythic cycle of the Wiracocha does not mention any specific analogy between the routes of the heroes and the origins of the actual river, it should be stated that the Milky Way is called *Mayu* (river) in Quechua and that in this general but limited sense the suggestion of Urton is correct. Yet a focus upon the set of personages allows us to extend the analogy beyond the Wiracocha heroes to encompass other ritual activities as described in pre-Hispanic liturgical calendars.

Having dismissed this specific riverine scheme of Urton's, it remains to verify which might have been the celestial figures corresponding more closely with the routes and acts of the Wiracocha pilgrims. Based on Zuidema's identification of the Pleiades in Inca astronomy as the constellation of Catachillay, Randall has suggested that the annual pilgrimage to Qoyllur Rit'i (Cuzco) is in celebration of these stars and of the Wiracocha with whom they are associated (Randall 1982; Zuidema 1982b). But, like Urton, both of these authors reduce the Wiracocha heroes to a single personage, thus following faithfully sixteenth- and seventeenth-century Spanish orientations regarding the existence of a pre-Hispanic creator who was one god (Duviols 1977; Urbano 1982a).

Having discarded these reductions of the heroes to a single personage, there remains to be considered the hypothetical relation between Andean agrarian cycles and astronomical observations. Treating this theme, Urton speaks of "religious syncretism." According to him, the activities of fishermen and coastal farmers "are timed by the helical rise and set of the Pleiades" (Urton 1982:237). But the large majority of dates used by Urton are approximate and cannot therefore be evaluated without danger of arbitrary reasoning. The liturgical celebrations of coastal and Andean peoples coincide with the appearance of some stars or constellations, as well as with reference to the periods of their movement through the heavens. Nevertheless, none of these celestial events corresponds exactly to the astronomical dates suggested by the specialists in that field.

As an alternative to these explanations, I consider it more valuable to seek other grounds for affirming that the Wiracocha pilgrim-heroes have their celestial abodes and that their figures corresponded to some of the constellations or groups of stars which interested pre-Columbian people. Although none of the previously mentioned authors states the problem in these terms, Molina (1575) does mention that the liturgical fiestas celebrated between August and September were particularly dedicated to the Wiracochas, which he, as well as the other chroniclers, interpreted as the creator and only god (Molina 1943:29-46). What possibilities do the liturgical celebrations of this period of the year offer us as a foundation for an astronomical reading of the pilgrimages of the Wiracocha?

The references which we can use are clear. We know, for example, that the celebrations of September, also called the Coya, (Inca Queen), were very solemn. "The reason why they made it this month, was because then it began to rain, and with the first rains there were always some illnesses..." (Cobo 1964:II, 217; Molina 1943:29). The liturgical acts, then, developed from a date near the time of the September equinox, when planting was taking place. According to some authors, the rainy season as well as the amount of rains were predicted some months or weeks before September by observations of the Pleiades or other stars and constellations (Urton 1981, 1982; Zuidema 1982b). But at the moment of celebrating the Situa or the Coya these were not the astronomical orientations for that time of the year, as is indicated in the texts of Cobo (1653) and Molina (1575) to which I referred above.

There is no doubt that some symbolic relations exist between the Pleiades and the rainy period, which was suggested previously by Lévi-Strauss (1964:246-60) in his survey of the ethnographic data of the southern hemisphere. He pointed out that in association with the Pleiades there also appeared the stars of Orion, which the Spanish called Three Marys and the Quechuas *Chacana* (Urton 1981). In the same way, many Amazon peoples utilize these stars to ascertain dates for the arrival of the rainy season and the relative abundance or scarcity of water. But they do not perform the same logical function as the Pleiades, at least not in many cases, although they refer to the same kind of astronomical observations.

Nevertheless, neither the Pleiades nor Orion can be directly related to the pilgrimages of the Wiracocha heroes. There are no data or references in the ancient texts which could support a reading of that kind. What we know in the mythic cycle of the Wiracocha, among the episodes which mark the beginning of the pilgrimages of the heroes, is the punishment of Tawapaca. The principal Wiracochas, Tecsi or Pachayachachic, Imaymana or Tocapo, advance toward the north coast and Tawapaca travels toward the territories of the Andean southeast, passing by Desaguadero. These mythic circumstances express a rupture by the Desaguadero River as well as in the heroic group which serves to demarcate space. Globally considered, the first rupture would be defined by the north-south axis and the other by the pilgrims' routes through the Andes and along the coast. This confirms the hypothesis of Urton (1981:139): "Chacana, as the belt of Orion, marks the eastern and western points at which the sun makes its transition (crossing) between the northern and southern hemispheres."

Another aspect mentioned in the accounts of the mythic cycle of the Wiracocha refers to the presence of water in the acts of the heroes, both waters of Lake Titicaca and of the ocean. Tawapaca is punished in water, being tied hand and foot and thrown into the lake, and the three other heroes arrive on the north coast and disappear into the sea. There is no doubt that the heroes and their acts have something to do with the symbolism of water and presuppose a pre-Hispanic logic separating two types of waters, earthly and heavenly. The first is defined by Tawapaca and the lake, while the second is associated with the other three heroes, who rise to heaven and order the waters of the heavens. This same logic also postulates the alternating pattern of the cycles of the rains and drought.

The mythic cycle of the Wiracocha suggests a third aspect drawn from two characteristics of Chacana or Orion, referred to by Urton as a bridge and as represented by a cruciform figure. These two dimensions of Chacana indicate a symbolic link between terrestrial waters and heavenly waters, the two being separated by a bridge. In the same way, this figure could establish the division between the seasonal cycles, that of the rains and that of the dry period. On the other hand, the cruciform image differentiates the two waters, those of Lake Titicaca and those of the ocean, or possibly even those of the mountains and those of the coast (Urton 1981:193).

I will mention a final and fourth aspect which permits the formulation of an hypothesis concerning a symbolic relation between the acts of the Wiracocha pilgrim-heroes and the constellation of Orion. This is the ethnographic tradition which associates Chacana with the human body or some of its parts. Lévi-Strauss (1964:230-31) points out some of these figures studied by investigators in the Amazon area. Also Urton (1981:138) describes one in which the stars that compose it represent the image of a man with legs and arms. Nevertheless, this figure is not contradictory to that which could be the celestial representation of Tawapaca, his acts, and his punishment, because the hero appears, as we have seen, bound hand and foot. And the three heroes, brothers or companions, express the number of units in the figure of Orion or Chacana.

For all these reasons and taking into consideration its hypothetical character, the symbolic relations between the constellation of Orion or Chacana and the pilgrimages of the Wiracocha pilgrim heroes may not be discarded. The notes of Molina (1575) make reference to them, or at least suggest the idea of a differentiated pre-Hispanic Andean space and of a division of meteorological cycles according to two seasons, to the dualism of heavenly and earthly waters, and to the economic dual division indicated by the opposition of abundance to agricultural scarcity.

These logical divisions occurring throughout the mythic cycle of the Wiracocha heroes are one of the keys which best express that which should be understood by pre-Hispanic Andean pilgrimage. The ceremonial sites are places around which populations, peoples, or nations develop and in which they celebrate the origins of the economic, religious, and sociopolitical models which govern and differentiate them from other nations or peoples near and far. The celestial figures are the symbolic mark of the terrestrial pilgrimages and the mythic cycle employs them to give form to the divisions suggested by the mythic routes of the heroes. These figures remind each people or nation of that which they could otherwise forget in celebrating their origins or particular characteristics. That is to say, they reproduce the image and logical distribution of heroic personages which may be utilized on different occasions and on different horizons. In this sense, to make a pilgrimage is not only to establish peoples or nations or give to each one of them the body of a nation and its proper personality, but also to make known symbols by means of which these nations celebrate not only their differences, but also their common characteristics.

Into this mythic and ritual context the Spanish introduced their liturgical categories, the ritual systems of Judeo-Christian origin, their concept of pilgrimage, and their historical experiences of the sanctuary. The sixteenth century assured a long tradition of continental and peninsular pilgrimages, among which figured most prominently Los Caminos de Santiago, a route all the conquistadors and missionaries of that time revered. The Iberian peninsula was the home for many images and myriad ceremonial centers in which conversions, prayers, and miracles multiplied. Encountering the Andes, the missionary or instructor could not react otherwise, because for him the figure of the demon dominated all Andean symbolic expressions and inhabited all the ceremonial sites. A new ritual order was indispensible and the ceremonial centers had to respond to the necessities generated by other religious principles.

ANDEAN CATHOLIC PILGRIMAGES AND PRE-COLUMBIAN APPARITIONS

To inquire concerning the fate of the ceremonial centers founded in the epic narratives of the Wiracocha or who appropriated the mythic discourse which legitimized them, is tantamount to raising, at a global level, the problem of spiritual conquest in the Andes and of the consequences of evangelization throughout the conquered territory. In order to respond with utmost clarity to these questions one would have to take into account both the existence of pre-Columbian sanctuaries and the religious perspectives of the first evangelists in the Andes. An encounter of two opposed religious conceptions, in which that of the conqueror is imposed by force more than by reason, does not leave a wide margin for the harmonious development of a network of sanctuaries which would in some sense retain at least a few of the ritual principles presiding over the diffusion of pilgrimage centers in preconquest times. Under these circumstances, then, we have to realize that the legacy of the mythical Wiracocha heroes, just like that of the other mythic cycles which served as foundations for pre-Columbian ceremonial centers, was rapidly forgotten and dismantled. And above all, pre-Hispanic ritual principles were never again called to preside in the development of Andean pilgrimage centers.

If we examine the ceremonial centers known in the pre-Hispanic Andes through the eyes of the chroniclers of the sixteenth and seventeenth centuries, we will easily conclude that very few warrant consideration as appropriate sites for the ceremonial spaces of Catholic pilgrimages. The exceptions are so few that the rule can be seen as a firmly established one concerning all Catholic practices, both conscious and unconscious. Huana-cauri in the urban space of prehispanic Cuzco was the principal *huaca* (*waca*, shrine) of the Incas and Pachacamac was, according to tradition and archaeological investigations, the most famous and impressive coastal center at the moment of the conquest. However, neither of these shrines served as a pretext for a conversion of pre-Columbian Andean space. Likewise, the sites correlated with the Wiracochas' pilgrimage, such as Cacha, Urcos, and those near Lake Titicaca, did not merit the attention of the sixteenth-century evangelists. Those shrines which exist today do not therefore correspond to any pre-Hispanic mythic discourse, at least in respect to the southern Andes, particularly those of the Cuzco region.

The questions previously formulated remain, nevertheless, without adequate response. It is convenient to distinguish two fields which provide for us some means of investigation capable of explaining the oblivion into which the ritual spaces of the pre-Hispanic pilgrimage have fallen. The first field is that of a contemporary Andean mythic discourse, which, although not complete, has been sufficiently established for the southern Andes. The second refers to places situated near Cuzco which are today considered to be important ceremonial or pilgrimage centers.

Among the contemporary mythic cycles which circulate in the southern Andes, those which refer to heroes with pilgrim characteristics are, in the first place, those which relate the deeds of Inkarrí (Inca king). Not all, however, are related to the pilgrimages of this hero. But, among those which oral literature has conserved until now, there do exist some which explicitly mention routes or roads on which privileged places are marked and on which signs are left to record symbolically important acts. Among such examples, the most well-known insofar as it is also one of the first, is undoubtedly the account of Inkarrí and Qollarrí collected some 30 years ago in the community of Q'eros in the department of Cuzco, Peru. Two somewhat different versions circulate, though both share common elements (Nuñez del Prado 1973:276-79; Morote Best 1958:39-58). According to these accounts, after having been created, the pilgrim heroes (Inkarrí and Qollarí) begin their pilgrimages in search of lands on which to establish villages with sufficient resources to survive. The ritual act which the mythic cycle generally employs is the casting of a staff of gold which should fall vertically and remain in that position as a sign allowing the heroes to identify the fertility of the land.[4]

This ritual act performed by the heroes Inkarrí and Qollarrí is tradition-al because the mythic cycle of the Ayar, the founding ancestors of the Inca city of Cuzco, also uses the casting of a staff to discern the fertility of the land. In doing so, Inkarrí and Quollarrí realize that the valley of Huatanay is the one sought for their purpose, which was agricultural, politico-military, and religious (Urbano 1981). In the cycle of Inkarrí, there is a preoccupation with the establishment of settlements capable of subsisting by working the land. By comparison, there is no reference whatsoever to the designation of a place for ritual or liturgical purposes. Nevertheless, the record of the mythic cycle of the Wiracocha is in some way contained in the intent which guided the search of Inkarrí and Qollarí for lands to populate and select for future generations. Whereas the Wiracocha heroes did the same, the peoples or nations they founded constructed chapels and later ceremonial centers for pilgrimage.

In other accounts of the mythic cycle of Inkarrí the same image appears (Ossio 1973). Ritual acts, which are different from that of the casting, also exist, although with identical purpose, that is to say, the selection of lands to populate and work. For example, in one cycle of accounts concerning Inkarrí and Qollarí, the two heroes place bets in order to realize a series of trials and see who, as the hero, has the right to the most productive lands, in this case the valley. The cycle to which we refer most often places the action in the region of La Raya, more or less at the midpoint between Cuzco and Puno and at the end of the plains of the altiplano where the waters of the Vilcanota River originate. The place of the wagers has great symbolic importance, both in these accounts and in the ancient pre-Hispanic liturgical ritual acts, although the presently known versions do not make the slightest reference to this aspect (Urbano 1981:77-104; Ossio 1973). The outcome of this wager means that the victorious Inkarrí gains the lands of the valley and earns the right to the daughter of Qollarí. She is subse-quently violated on the same site, as is evidenced by the color of the water which today springs from that place. In and of itself, however, this act does not confer the space of La Raya status as a ceremonial pilgrimage center. Nevertheless the Andean symbolism is reminiscent of the ritual acts of *tinkuy* in which groups from two opposed regions meet and fight in order to germinate the land by means of blood spilled in ceremonial battles.

The traditions, which explain the existence of present-day regional pilgrimage centers, instead use other more Christian types of heroes, who are therefore more in conformance with both ancient and modern Catholic models of the sanctuary. Among the better-known accounts we will briefly mention those concerning the founding of the Christ of Qoyllur Rit'i (Cuzco, Peru). The published versions tell that a local shepherd boy encountered a mysterious white-skinned youth. The latter invited him to eat his bread and gave him a little cloth instructing him that he should seek in the city of Cuzco a sufficient quantity of this material to dress himself decently. The shepherd went to the city and verified where one would be able to buy that type of cloth. After searching he learned that only priests used this cloth for their ecclesiastical habits.

Amazed by these events, some officials of the city of Cuzco decided to accompany the shepherd to Tayancani, in the vicinity of Ocongate, Cuzco, Peru. They went with the intention of verifying what the herder had told them. When they arrived at the place indicated by him, the shepherd saw the white child, although the others could not see him. This scene was repeated several more times, until they arrived at the place where one now finds the pilgrimage temples. The shepherd pointed out the white child jumping among the rocks of the cliff, and suddenly all his companions could see the mysterious child, who "removing his robe, he disappeared into a rock... and from that time our miraculous Father was formed there on the rock..." (Urbano and Salazar Segovia 1982b:51-53).

There exist several versions of the legend of the cycle of Qoyllur Rit'i (Gow 1974; Sallnow 1974; Randall 1982). In the account which I have cited, the ritual act of the foundation for the pilgrimage center is clearly indicated. The rock will remain as a sign of the physical presence of the mysterious child, his associated ritual acts, and the intentions which he had when he appeared to the shepherd. The theme and the discursive expression are very traditional in the Andes even for pre-Hispanic times. Nevertheless, it is also one of the discursive forms best known in the Catholic mythic cycles of apparitions and in the ceremonial pilgrimage centers which these apparitions usually generated.

Without presenting details of the fiesta of Qoyllur Rit'i, which is celebrated the Sunday before Corpus Christi, it is important to keep in mind one of the characteristics which we mentioned earlier of the Catholic sanctuary—its remoteness or spatial distance in relation to population centers. The example of the sanctuary of Qoyllur Rit'i adheres to this principle. The location of images or churches on mountains or hills or rocky or precipitous sites and the explanation of these sites by mysterious acts or mythic cycles of the last centuries, also conforms to the modern Catholic pattern. The Iberian peninsula conserves some of these legendary events in which the figure of a shepherd or herder plays a role of primary importance due to the characteristics of his work, such as spatial isolation from population centers and the consequent peculiarities in their manner-isms.

The example of the legend which originated with the sanctuary of the Christ of Huanca, Cuzco, calls attention to yet another type of pilgrim. Located a few hours from Cuzco, in the province of Calca, Huanca achieved fame for its miraculous attributes and the presence in the mythic cycle of a Bolivian personage, who was represented in different versions as either a rich miner from Potosí or a resident of Cochabamba, Bolivia. The foundation story relates that an Indian of Chincheros, Cuzco, who used to work in the mines of Marques of Valle Humbroso, in Quispicanchis, a village to the south of the city of Cuzco, was fired for reasons which we do not know. He then sought refuge in the zone of Huanca where the sanctu-ary is now located, near the village of San Salvador. Among the rocks of the cave where he hid, there appeared the image of Jesus, in the form of a whipped figure. He went to Chincheros to inform the priest about what had happened and to comply with the ritual recommendations which the figure of the Lord had presented to him. Years later in Cochabamba, Bolivia, a mine owner became ill without any hope for a cure. One day an unknown doctor passed through the city and cured him. The sick man was so grateful that he asked him how he might repay him for the service. The mysterious doctor referred him to Huanca. He came on a pilgrimage to Cuzco and, after various unforeseen accidents, found the previously unmarked sanctuary.[5]

The mythic cycle which governs the foundation of this sanctuary is very well-known in all of the southern Andes, including Bolivia. In it, the characteristics of the ceremonial center or Catholic pilgrimage site remain fixed. The estrangement of the Indian miner, Diego Quispe, is highlighted by the fact that upon leaving his village and his work he hides himself in a cave, close to the rocks of Huanca. It is also interesting to notice that these same lands were the property of the Mercedarian Order, which has always been in charge of the liturgical services and which was not opposed to the visit of the rich miner of Potosí, a resident of Cochabamba, Bolivia. Once more, the account affirms the importance of cliffs and solitary places for the construction of pilgrimage centers. This pattern is also verified in the final example which I will present, the Christ of Pampacucho.

The Christ of Pampacucho took the name of the place in which the figure of an old man gathering wood appeared in the province of Paruro, Cuzco. One of the narratives says that the Lord came out of Cuzco carrying a cross and went through deserted places seeking the region which his heavenly father had designated for him. After eight months of pilgrimage and agony he arrived near K'apa, a short distance from Pillpinto on the edge of Aqoha, Paruro. In front of him there were steep hills which, in his state of agony, made him afraid. The figure of the devil then appeared to tempt him and convince him to desist. But the Lord prevailed over him. He advanced toward the summits passing close to some cliffs from which he drew water to drink. Upon leaning over, however, he fell, and left at this place the marks of his hands and knees. In this place the earth is white from the saliva which the *Lord* spat, and red with the blood which he shed. They say that the white land is therefore very productive. And finally, on the route which took him to the designated site, the *Lord* was seen by an old man who was casually gathering wood. He advised the settlers of his vision, and they constructed a chapel and later a large temple.

The mythic discourse of Pampacucho thus supports what has been said so far about the Andean Catholic pilgrimage sanctuary. There is, nevertheless, a theme which other narratives about this Christ include and which calls to mind characteristics not previously mentioned. For example, one legend reports that the "celestial God" called his sons together in Cuzco so that they might travel through the world preaching. He ordered the older brother, who was the *Lord* of Pampacucho, to go to the most distant places, revealing himself to the people in dreams in the form of a high-ranking military officer. To the middle son, he then said: "You, my son, will have to bleed even more and suffer more as you travel toward the hills and mountains, a much greater distance. But you will be lucky because the people will take pity on you because of your wounds and you will gain more followers than your older brother. You will reveal yourself by the name of Lord of Huanca." Finally, he ordered the youngest son to go even further toward the south across the mountain ranges. He gave him the name of Lord of Pampamarca. Before each one left on his journey he instructed the oldest son, Lord of Pampacucho, not to stop watching over his youngest brother since the latter would pass through barren lands in order to bless them and so that the animals could reproduce.

The mythic distribution of the functions of the three brothers, the sons of the "celestial God," is analogous with that of the three sons or servants of the principal Wiracocha, Tecsi or Pachayachachic, in the heroic pilgrimage cycle. In the first place, the code utilized is again that of kinship. And also in both cases it is the routes that determine some of the characteristics of the heroes. The Lord of Pampacucho, the Lord of Huanca, and the Lord of Pampamarca traverse spaces which long ago formed the divisions of the *suyu*. The sanctuary of Huanca is in the direction of Antisuyu, Pampamarca in that of Collasuyu, and Pampacucho in that of Contisuyu. Nevertheless these routes are simply approximations and the functions are not those of the Wiracocha heroes. Thus, each one of the *Lords* fulfills his duties, which in their respective fields are differentiated and complementary.

We must also emphasize one of the most interesting aspects of this Andean Catholic mythic cycle. The functions are distributed among pilgrims following a trifunctional model which we had deduced from other pre-Hispanic mythic cycles. Although the dates do not have the clarity of a logical demonstration, the attributes of the different *Lords* are sufficiently characteristic to interpret them as possible directions. The Lord of Pampacucho is described as a military officer of high rank. The youngest son, the

Lord of Pampamarca, under the protection of Pampacucho, travels through barren lands in order to bless them and make them produce and take care of the animals so that they will reproduce. Thus the youngest son, Pampamarca, reveals one of the characteristics often associated with that category of hero, that of expressing the female roles, of reproduction and fertility.

The middle son, the Lord of Huanca, through the links which he holds with the Indian miner of Chincheros, Cuzco, Peru, and with the owner of the mines of Potosí, Bolivia, represents, although indirectly, the disobedient personage of the cycle of the Wiracocha, Tawapaca. On the one hand, the "middle position he occupies in the age hierarchy translates temporarily" into that which the Wiracocha heroes express spatially, a center which lies in the direction contrary to that of the father or *Lord*. And on the other hand, Tawapaca, by his name and defiance, is destined to inhabit the subterranean spaces which are transformed in the contemporary oral tradition into mining places. According to other Andean Catholic mythic cycles, it is known that the Devil is present in such places.

Although the conclusions drawn from these examples are certainly hypothetical, they are not without foundation, because the images which the pilgrim heroes define approach the model of real or ideal society as defined in the Andean contemporary mythic cycles. The destiny of the personages favored by the appearances of the *Lords* is different. In Pampacucho it is an old man who gathers wood in a distant location. In some of the narratives the Lord of Pampacucho is described as an officer of high rank and each time he performs a miracle his followers grant him the right to rise one rank higher in the military hierarchy. In Huanca, the personages are clearly related to work and the production of mines and in Pampamarca, the people who receive the celestial favors are shepherds or farmers. Be it through the characteristics of the Christs or through the roles of the people who receive their visitations or witness their apparitions, the great lines which structured the Wiracocha mythic cycles are present in the contemporary Catholic mythical narratives in the form of a common logic and in the same symbolic expression of the three functions which form the great axis of the social order. According to the contemporary model, the "celestial God," as the narrative of Pampacucho calls him, gives the commands to his sons and distributes them through space. The image could not be any closer to that of the principal Wiracocha in the mythic cycle of the Wiracocha. But the eldest son does not have the characteristics attributed to Imaymana or Tocapo. This is nevertheless not without interest, because the Lord of Pampacucho refers to a role with military characteristics and is therefore symbolically related to a military or warlike force. The third and youngest son, the Lord of Pampamarca, is linked to agriculture and herding. In this way, the trifunctional model is complete with the "celestial God" as the hero in whose supernatural powers the priestly and religious functions perform a role of utmost importance. With regard to the other two, the heroes portray warlike physical force and agricultural and pastoral aspects of the contemporary Andean societies.

CONCLUSION

The importance of both the prehistoric and contemporary Andean mythic cycles for the definition of pilgrimage in the Andes is demonstrated in the mythic cycles of the Wiracocha and in narratives concerning contemporary Andean Catholic sanctuaries. It is certain that pilgrimage is a social and religious phenomenon which mobilizes under certain circumstances and at specific times of the year a great number of other aspects of social life. In this respect the examples chosen reveal that the pre-Hispanic pilgrimage tradition was above all a means of ritually celebrating the origins of a people or a nation. Around those places of origin, pre-Hispanic Andean societies were established and many of the settlements served to affirm their identity and their particular way of life.

With the conquest, the Spanish experience of the sixteenth and seventeenth centuries introduced another model of pilgrimage throughout the Andes. In this model the space of the fiesta or ritual celebration was isolated from the inhabited places and fulfilled other purposes. In the contemporary Catholic narratives or in the myths of present-day pilgrim heroes, the theme of the origin of the settlements does not appear, or, if it is mentioned, no explanation is given in the majority of the cases, for the founding of the pilgrimage sanctuary. Nevertheless, it is worthwhile to note the logical distribution of the heroes who in some manner conform to the model of the three pre-Hispanic functions. The fact is that, according to the contemporary Catholic mythical narratives, the personages express symbolic preoccupations ordained and structured according to the pre-Hispanic model of the Wiracocha.

NOTES

1. A rich literature exists concerning the Spanish pilgrimages of the sixteenth and seventeenth centuries. In the last few years the pilgrimage to Santiago de Compostela, Spain, has been the object of excellent studies (see Caro Baroja 1978; Christian 1981a; Layton 1976). Of these, the monumental work of Vazquez de Parga, Lacarra, and Uria Riu (1948-49) is unquestionably the most complete. Other complementary studies are: Baby (1980), Bottineau (1983), Dupront (1971, 1973), Leclercq (1964), Oursel (1963), Raphael (1973), Roussel (1955), Vicaire (1980), and Vielliard (1963).

2. The explanation of the Andean pre-Hispanic mythic cycles based on the trifunctional scheme is not only applicable to the cycle of the Wiracocha. It can easily be applied to the majority of texts and Andean mythic traditions. For the mythic cycle of the Ayar and the Chanca see my previous studies (Urbano 1981, 1982a).

3. It is not completely out of place to mention that in the trifunctional divisions of the cycles of the Wiracocha and Ayar, the role played by the youngest son may hide a feminine personage. In the case of the Ayar this does not happen through the presence of feminine

personages in the tripartite divisions. But it may be considered that it could be the role played by Tocapo Wiracocha in the cycle of those heroes (for this discussion see Urbano 1981).

4. The mythic cycle of Inkarrí is frequently used as an example of the continuity between mythic pre-Hispanic cycles and modern Catholic cycles. (Urbano 1974, 1980, 1982a).

5. Few monographs have been published about Andean sanctuaries. However, el Señor de Huanca is well represented in the works of Eyzaguirre (1936).

REFERENCES

Anonimo Sevillano 1967
Avila 1966
Baby 1980
Ballesteros Graibois 1979
Betanzos 1968
Bottineau 1983
Caro Baroja 1978
Christian 1981a
Cobo 1964
Cuneo Vidal 1977
Dupront 1971, 1973
Durkheim 1968
Duviols 1977
Eyzaguirre 1936
Gisbert 1980
Gow 1974
Gutierrez de Santa Clara 1963
Jerez 1947
Lévi-Strauss 1964

Las Casas 1958
Layton 1976
Leclercq 1964
Molina "El Cusqueño" 1943
Morote Best 1958
Nuñez del Prado 1973
Ossio 1973
Oursel 1963
Randall 1982
Raphael 1973
Roussel 1955
Sallnow 1974
Sarmiento de Gamboa 1960
Urbano 1974, 1980, 1981, 1982a, 1982b
Urton 1981, 1982
Vazquez de Parga-Riu 1948
Vicaire 1980
Vielliard 1963
Zuidema 1982b

IV
CONCLUSION

19

Discussion and Conclusions:
Agrarian Conflict and Pilgrimage

FRANS J. SCHRYER

In the introduction to this volume, Alan Morinis and N. Ross Crumrine present a tentative framework for studying Latin American pilgrimages. They suggest that researchers should not only examine the beliefs and rituals associated with pilgrimages in terms of their symbolic structure but also analyze pilgrimages as rites of passage. They add that these researchers should even discuss the manner in which politics impinges upon this religious institution. To carry out such a holistic analysis would require the collaboration of scholars from various disciplines, each focusing on some specific aspect of the pilgrimage using different methods and theoretical perspectives. The seventeen chapters following the introduction to this volume certainly illustrate the broad range of approaches already used by scholars interested in pilgrimage shrines and their associated oral literature, dances, and rituals. The individual contributions also vary considerably in terms of the mix of either historical or ethnographic descriptive narrative and theoretical analysis and the extent to which they generalize about pilgrimages in Latin America as a whole. These different approaches, ranging from sociological and political analysis to the examination of historical origins and symbolism, are indicative of the contrasting styles of research and diverse theoretical orientations found not only between the humanities and the social sciences but often within a single discipline. This interdisciplinary and multiparadigm treatment of the pilgrimage is inevitable given the fact that the institution not only has a long history but even today draws together a great variety of pilgrims from so many different walks of life.

DISCUSSION

Despite the great diversity in the way various authors deal with the subject of the pilgrimage, there are a few common themes, as set out in the introductory chapter, which run throughout the book. All of the authors show how the beliefs and practices associated with pilgrimage shrines in Latin America represent a blend of European-Catholic, pre-Hispanic-indigenous, or African elements. Most of them also focus on the continuity of the pre-Hispanic elements, although most pilgrimages are predominantly Catholic in both form and content. Only Mary Lee Nolan emphasizes the medieval European roots of the Latin American pilgrimage and examines how it has been continually influenced by changes in subsequent pilgrimage traditions in Western European Catholicism. This emphasis on the overwhelming influence of Catholicism does not appear again until the last chapter, written by Henrique Urbano. However, Urbano does point out that while pre-Hispanic and postconquest pilgrimage concepts are radically different, contemporary Catholic pilgrimages in Peru do express symbolic preoccupations "ordained and structured" according to a pre-Hispanic model. Helaine Silverman likewise draws our attention to continuities in patterns of actual behavior and the use of physical space. Most of the scholars represented in this volume also relate, to some extent, the pilgrimages they examine to a broader political, economic, and cultural context.

In terms of theoretical orientations, the predominant paradigm, which is especially evident in the three chapters written or co-authored by N. Ross Crumrine, is that of modern formalism as represented by Claude Lévi-Strauss. His brand of anthropology, primarily used in the study of myth and kinship, consists of "transformation models" which are used to ascertain the "deep structures" which correspond to the working of the human mind itself. Other theoretical perspectives, especially a political economy approach, are less well represented. Several chapters do, however, relate the pilgrimages to the broader socioeconomic or political structures of specific geographical regions. Because these chapters more closely correspond to my own area of research interest, I will discuss them in somewhat greater detail.

Candace Slater's brief analysis of padre Cicero's shrine in Juazeiro in northeast Brazil can be used to illustrate how well-known pilgrimage sites can be better understood by analyzing them in the broader context of the socioeconomic conditions which gave rise to such shrines. Although most of this chapter analyzes the miracle stories associated with pilgrimages to this shrine, the section dealing with the historical background to such pilgrimage tales indicates a close interlinking between religious and secular institutions as well as the political dimensions of this pilgrimage as an expression of widespread lower-class dissent. The analysis of the miracle stories themselves, especially the comparison between orallytransmitted stories and their literary counterparts, also suggests a political dimension at another level, since poets in this region who write popular *folhetos* are not likely to develop stories that may offend powerful individuals.

Although Slater only refers to the class structure and the political situation of northeastern Brazil in passing, any scholar dealing with pilgrimages which take place in the part of Latin America known as highland Indo-America cannot help but include, in his or her analysis, the system of ethnic stratification involving the domination of Indians by Spanish-speaking mestizos or Ladinos. For example, Mike Sallnow, in his analysis of pilgrimages in the highlands of Peru, shows how the use of ethnic dichotomies reflects the differences in class and status between Indians and mestizos as well as class differences among Indians, which is related to their degree of assimilation into the national culture. Likewise, Walter Adams shows how pilgrimages in southern Mexico, involving both Tzeltal and Tojolabales Indians, express social and economic inequalities among different Indian groups themselves. In the case of southern Mexico, such ethnic hierarchies date back to precolonial times. The opposition of different political strata and ethnic groups are reflected not only in the use of symbolic ritual language but even in the choreography associated with pilgrimages as shown by Deborah Poole. Her case study also illustrates how pilgrimages can simultaneously reflect the structure of inequality and exploitation and be an expression of rebellion and discontent. This dual secular function of pilgrimages as potentially subversive while at the same time mystifying or legitimizing a class structure, becomes more apparent in the chapters written by James Vreeland and Carl Kendall. These two authors analyze cases where pilgrimages actually became politicized because political groups either on the right or the left tried to utilize well-known pilgrimage sites for political ends. They also show to what extent specific pilgrimages are modified in this process. Apart from situating this religious institution in a broader socioeconomic context, these studies indicate that symbolic anthropology is not incompatible with the study of political conflict and social change. Kendall's chapter, which most explicitly combines a political economy framework—in order to analyze the relationship between a popular pilgrimage and the military regime of Guatemala —with a structural analysis of meaning, comes the closest to this ideal synthesis.

AGRARIAN CONFLICT AND THE PILGRIMAGE IN HUEJUTLA

While some scholars who have written about pilgrimages have either ignored or not paid enough attention to economic and political variables, researchers who focus on the latter can likewise be criticized for not examining, in sufficient depth, pilgrimages and similar cultural institutions. This was certainly the case for the research on land invasions and ethnic conflict in a region of Mexico undertaken by myself. Most of this research was completed prior to reading the studies presented in this volume. However, an additional field trip, some data already collected on religious institutions, and a general knowledge of the area made it possible to comment, at least, on the relationship between agrarian conflict and religion. The tentative analysis which follows will also provide some original data on a minor but certainly well-established pilgrimage involving an image of Nuestro Padre Jesus in the area of Huejutla.

The region of Huejutla, which belongs to the Mexican state of Hidalgo, is inhabited by both mestizos and Nahuatl-speaking Indians. Here, violent conflicts over land, perceived by many as an "Indian revolt," erupted in the mid-1970s. These conflicts can be understood as a reaction by poor peasants to the negative impact of the expansion of modern cattle production. The reverberations of these economic changes, emanating from the wider society, and the subsequent political turmoil, had a profound effect on religious institutions and other cultural patterns which had remained virtually unchanged for a hundred years. This was particularly the case for former communal villages which, unlike the villages located within the boundaries of local haciendas, had a well-developed civil-religious hierarchy and other institutions usually associated with Mesoamerican communities. The numerous religious feasts associated with this traditional hierarchy had already dwindled to less than half their former size as a result of the rapid inflation, high level of unemployment, and other economic pressures that hit the area in the early 1970s. With the initiation of land invasions and political chaos in the region, additional feasts were lost and in some cases, rival groups of peasants, agrarians versus conservatives, set up their own chapels and held their own separate feasts in honour of different patron saints. However, despite the decline of many local customs, including religious practices and traditional Indian weddings, one religious institution held its own and even expanded right up until my last visit in 1985. This religious institution involves the enacting of pilgrimages, using the statue of Nuestro Padre Jesus.

Nuestro Padre Jesus is an image normally kept in the cathedral of Huejutla. This predominantly Spanish-speaking city of Huejutla is a small city surrounded by and partly located within the boundaries of several large Indian villages, including the artisan center of Chililico and the village of

Panacaxtlan. It is also the principal market town and gathering place for thousands of Nahuatl-speaking Indians throughout the entire region. According to local oral history, the head of the statue of Nuestro Padre Jesus was originally unearthed by Indian peasants in the nearby village of La Candelaria, which belonged to a hacienda owned by a mestizo family. The landowner had the rest of the statue reconstructed and built a small chapel on his own property sometime around the turn of the century. A large celebration to commemorate the original discovery of Nuestro Padre Jesus was held every February on Candlemas day, from which this village derives its name. The celebrations, which were attended by the inhabitants of other villages, ceased during the revolutionary period as a result of numerous armed attacks on this hacienda. It was particularly vulnerable because the owners' son was one of the leading participants on the side of the revolutionary faction led by Carranza during the prolonged civil war that lasted until 1917. In the early 1920s, when the hacienda had already gone downhill economically, the statue was transferred to the nearby town of Huejutla on the orders of a bishop recently appointed to a new diocese created in 1923.

For several years the native inhabitants of the village of La Candelaria disputed this removal of "their statue" and, according to local legends, the statue mysteriously reappeared in its original chapel on various occasions until the owner of the chapel turned it into a granary and had it filled with corn. According to local folklore, the subsequent illness of the hacienda owner was caused by the role he played in this affair. Nevertheless, the transfer of the statue of Nuestro Padre Jesus to the city of Huejutla initiated yearly pilgrimages to the cathedral by the inhabitants of numerous Nahuatl villages in the region. It also became a practice for the authorities of these Indian villages to "borrow" this statue for their own religious celebrations.

Apart from attracting a number of individual pilgrims who come to worship in the cathedral, the majority of pilgrimages today are organized by the inhabitants of Indian villages who come to escort the image back to their home communities for one or more nights of adoration and then return to Huejutla again. The villages which participate in these rotating pilgrimages all belong to the very large *municipio* of Huejutla as well as the *municipio* of Jaltocan, which also was part of Huejutla prior to 1936. The necessary preparations for such pilgrimages, including the formal petition submitted to and received from the bishop of Huejutla and the collection of funds to cover the costs of candles, incense, musicians, and dancers (either their food and drink or an actual monetary payment for services rendered if they come from other villages), is the responsibility of a religious official called a *mayordomo* or a *gobernador*. Such religious officials collaborate closely with a *juez* (judge), who is the official representative of the municipal government. The processions to and from Huejutla, with musical accompaniment and dances in traditional Indian costumes, are usually done on foot. More remote villages have also instituted the custom of hiring a taxi or bus to first transport both statue and a smaller number of organizers from Huejutla to a location reasonably close to their home village, from whence the processions can proceed on foot. There is no fixed date of worship and various villages petition to "borrow" Nuestro Padre Jesus on any one of several days usually between March and June. This period corresponds to the preparation of the most important corn crop, the (xopamili) rainy season crop, which is planted whenever it starts to rain. In years of drought, the number of processions increases.

The statue of Nuestro Padre Jesus and its processions and vigils could be analyzed from various points of view. For example, it is certainly no coincidence that these celebrations at the start of the agricultural cycle coincide with a series of pre-Hispanic festivals dedicated to a rain god in the Aztec pantheon. Archaeological research might well come up with other links between this 20th-century pilgrimage and earlier celebrations carried out by the Huasteco-speaking people who originally inhabited this part of the Huasteca (see Ochoa 1979). While this pilgrimage could be looked at from this and other perspectives as exemplified by the other studies in this volume, I decided to examine the cult of Nuestro Padre Jesus primarily from a political economy perspective.

The history of the pilgrimage of Nuestro Padre Jesus reflects the changing spheres of both economic and political influence from another town, called Yahualica, to the city of Huejutla. Yahualica was an administrative center of a once much more densely populated neighbouring district during three centuries of colonial rule. However, Yahualica was amalgamated with Huejutla and lost its status as an administrative center during the second half of the nineteenth century, although Yahualica continued to be an important ceremonial center up until the time of the Mexican revolution. Yahualica's importance as a religious center also declined when its Holy Week celebrations, which used to attract larger numbers of visitors, were overshadowed by the new cult of La Candelaria. The designation of Huejutla as the official shrine of Nuestro Padre Jesus as well as capital of a newly created diocese, which now included Yahualica, marked the end of any social importance for the town of Yahualica and the municipio of the same name. Today Yahualica is an almost forgotten village located three hours by truck from Huejutla.

Processions with another saint, the Virgen del Rosario, are still sporadically held in a few Indian villages in the municipios of Yahualica and Atlapexco, which belonged to Yahualica prior to 1936. However, every year fewer villages contribute funds to the upkeep of this statue, housed in an ancient church located in the town of Yahualica. Processions with this statue, undertaken by the inhabitants of several hamlets in this municipio, are but a poor shadow of what was once a famous regional pilgrimage. For the villages that still participate in this celebration, the actual procession is carried out in the close proximity of the village itself, usually to a nearby mountain peak. Only a *mayordomo* and a few of his assistants, not practically the entire village, goes to Yahualica to "borrow" this statue. The transfer of the statue of Nuestro Padre Jesus from a hamlet which belonged to a hacienda to Huejutla coincided with a change in the local class structure. This transfer took place at a time when the power of the hacienda owners had already been greatly eroded by the emergence of a class of smaller entrepreneurial landowners called rancheros, who took the leading role in the Mexican revolution in the state of Hidalgo (see Schryer 1979). These rancheros, mostly mestizos, had earlier infiltrated the southern portion of the district of Huejutla formerly set aside as separate "Indian republics" with their own communal lands. The rancheros were not only able to buy such land as a result of the breakdown of communal land tenure, but they also allied themselves to rich Nahuatl peasants who usually represented the large Nahuatl villages. Together these two groups manipulated the civil-religious hierarchy and other institutions of such villages to enhance their own economic interests. For example, the leaders of Indian villages recruited "voluntary" labour for public works projects in mestizo towns and even for mestizo landowners who were politically influential. The mestizo rancheros, in turn, gave a free hand to a small Indian elite to run their own internal affairs, including religious festivals, which had previously been controlled by secular priests. The religious affairs of Nahuatl communities located within the boundaries of local haciendas, however, continued to be controlled by large landowners. The transfer of a new pilgrimage site from a hacienda village to Huejutla was the first sign of the decline of the religious influence of these hacienda owners, who had already lost their political power during the revolution.

The land reform of Lázaro Cárdenas, implemented in 1940, destroyed the economic power of the few remaining hacienda owners in the region when all villages located within private estates were given their own land in the form of *ejidos* (landholding societies). After this change in legal status, a number of Nahuatl villages in the northern zone of Huejutla, which were formerly subject to local haciendas, built their own chapels and started to participate in the pilgrimage of Nuestro Padre Jesus. Such villagers had previously not been allowed to hold their own religious celebrations or participate in the pilgrimage of Nuestro Padre Jesus. Their participation in this pilgrimage thus expressed their independence from local landlords after Cárdenas' government gave them the same rights and administrative independence in religious affairs as Indian villages in the southern, "communal" zone. Although the religiosity of such Indian villages contrasted with the more secular attitudes of the most influential ranchero politicians, the folk Catholicism of the former was not incompatible with the anticlericalism of the latter. Moreover, many mestizo rancheros were themselves very religious and held their own religious celebrations and sometimes even served as *mayordomos* in Indian villages. A combination of improved Church-state relations and economic growth after 1945 even facilitated an expansion of ceremonial life, including pilgrimages, with or without the participation of Catholic clergy. This situation changed with the economic crises starting in the early 1970s as well as with the impact of the further expansion of modern cattle production on local peasant communities.

A series of land invasions primarily undertaken by poor Indian peasants in the 1970s led to a situation of political turmoil. Such land invasions were directed against both the rancheros and wealthy Nahuatl peasants, who had so far manipulated local religious institutions. Although the amount of time and money expended in pilgrimages involving Nuestro Padre Jesus was initially reduced due to the declining standards of living of the majority of local peasants, success in gaining access to more land for subsistence cultivation made it possible for local peasants to again participate in this religious institution. However, this pilgrimage, like other religious celebrations, now became associated with different political factions, agrarian versus conservative, in various Indian communities. Which faction continued to participate in the pilgrimages varied from village to village.

In some southern villages in the *municipio* of Huejutla, radical agrarian peasants affiliated with several peasant organizations withdrew from this pilgrimage and from other religious celebrations which continued to be led by better-off Indian peasants who still controlled the main administrative posts in their home towns. However, in some of the already existing Indian *ejidos*, such as Chalahuiapan, which had once belonged to haciendas, members of radical peasant organizations actually increased their participation in pilgrimages involving Nuestro Padre Jesus.

The way in which Catholicism has become identified with left-wing as opposed to conservative politics in different parts of the region of Huejutla largely depends on the role of local priests, not all of whom openly support the agrarian movement. If local priests support radical agrarian peasants and simultaneously promote the preservation of traditional values, it is more likely that wealthy landowning Nahuatl peasants, allied to mestizo power holders, will abandon religious activities associated with the Catholic Church, including pilgrimages. In some cases, conservative peasants have even been converted to one of several protestant sects in reaction to what they perceive as the increasing political involvement of the Catholic clergy. On the other hand, if a traditional village elite, consisting of wealthy Nahuatl peasants, receives the support of more conservative elements in the Catholic Church, such rich peasants are more likely to continue to organize and participate in pilgrimages, together with other traditional institutions. In such cases, it is the militant peasants who are more likely to become protestants as a way of declaring their opposition to rich peasants who have blocked their own economic mobility by forcing them to make ritual expenditures.

However, pilgrimages and other religious institutions in Huejutla have an internal dynamic of their own and serve many emotional and intellectual functions that cannot be reduced to economic and political factors. For example, some peasants who participated in land invasions and who also support a Marxist political party, are members of a fundamentalist evangelical sect recently introduced by American missionaries. For these peasants, their new religious beliefs and values shape their worldview to a much greater extent than the Marxist ideology of the party with whom they are affiliated for more pragmatic reasons. Another example of the lack of correspondence between religious and secular phenomena is the fact that, among Catholic peasants, radical agrarians who have been influenced by radical priests and their theology of liberation, preserve the same folk beliefs and customs as their more conservative counterparts. This separate, or at least partly independent, nature of religious sentiments and values, as well as their emotional importance, can be illustrated by an incident that occurred in the Nahuatl hamlet of Olma in the *municipio* of Yahualica several years ago.

The peasants of Olma, a hamlet which also took part in land invasions, still participate in the religious ceremonies of the town of Yahualica and several of them have, in the past, served as *mayordomos* in the *cabecera*, located only a half hour away on foot. However, Olma is politically autonomous, with its own *juez* and a separate *ejido*. In 1984 I was invited to attend a banquet held in this village on the occasion of the inauguration of a new village school building. The activities organized during this event were also designed to celebrate Mother's day. In the course of the early afternoon, village representatives and various political dignitaries gave speeches and watched the village schoolchildren perform group dances and present gifts to their mothers. However, while the banquet was still underway a group of villagers, who had gone to Yahualica an hour before, entered the small plaza of Olma in a procession, carrying the statue of the Virgen del Rosario on their shoulders. They were accompanied by a brass band from another village, hired for the occasion, and several members of the procession threw firecrackers into the air.

Their entry into the center of Olma, with music and fanfare, was carried out in the middle of a speech by a local politician who continued his public duties, oblivious to what was going on around him. The statue was then placed inside the new school building, which was also to serve as a chapel from time to time. A group of village women then initiated a period of adoration that was to continue, in shifts, for the rest of that afternoon and throughout the night and following day, when the image was brought back to Yahualica. Both the secular and religious events were organized by the same group of villagers, who select their officials from a population of only twelve families in Olma. However, the religious ceremonies obviously had much greater symbolic importance and evoked a stronger emotional response from the villagers than the secular ceremonies, which were also carried out exclusively in Spanish. Both villagers and outsiders accepted the apparent conflict between two simultaneous rituals by either ignoring the religious or the secular ceremonies or, in the case of most of the inhabitants of Olma, participating in or observing first one and then the other. For example, while the statue was being placed in the two-room school, the village teacher, a bilingual man born in a Nahuatl village and married to a woman who is very religious, continued to eat his meal at the table of honor set up in the village square. When I asked him what he thought about what was going on, he said that he did not mind the school building being used for religious purposes, although this is technically forbidden under Mexican law.

Although these examples, together with a brief overview of a little-known Mexican pilgrimage, give some insights into the religious life of Huejutla, many questions remain unanswered. For example, I did not investigate whether or not pilgrimages involving Indian villages in the *municipio* of Huejutla corresponded to earlier exchanges of saints or religious visits. Both the written and oral history of the origins of the pilgrimage of Nuestro Padre Jesus is very scanty. Another lacuna is information on how the pilgrimage was administered during the period of religious persecution that started soon after Huejutla became a diocese. I know that the Indian inhabitants of the region of Huejutla were not dramatically affected by the anticlerical campaign of president Calles that led to the well-known Cristero rebellion in other parts of Mexico. Although the new bishop of Huejutla, Jose Manriques y Zarate, was an outspoken opponent of the new revolutionary regime and was subsequently arrested and brought to Mexico City (see Meyer 1963), local authorities let the inhabitants of former Indian communes practice their own religious celebrations in much the same way as in the past. In the meantime, the few priests in the area went underground and were not able to operate openly until at least the mid-1940s. However, although religious leaders of Nahuatl communities continued to run local religious feasts by themselves, I did not investigate exactly how such pilgrimages were conducted between 1925 and 1940 without the support of the clergy. A great deal of investigation still needs to be done; the little-known pilgrimage of Huejutla is still a rich area of research waiting for anyone willing to take up the challenge!

CONCLUSIONS

Reading the various chapters of this volume provided me with a greater awareness and appreciation of the pilgrimages in the region of Huejutla. The case studies in this book also left me eager for further information on pilgrimages in other parts of Latin America. For example, in his study of the Tzeltales as Lords and Servants, Adams wonders how the pilgrimages he observed a number of years ago might appear today as a result of the influx of large numbers of Central American refugees and the agrarian conflicts presently raging in the state of Chiapas which have involved both Tojolabales and Tzeltales (see Marion Singer 1984). The analysis of the operation of contemporary pilgrimages in politically volatile areas both in Mexico and other parts of Mesoamerica would be a fascinating, though challenging and risky undertaking.

Another topic for future research is the use and meaning of indigenous terms relating to pilgrimages undertaken by people whose first language is not Spanish. For example, in the Huejutla region where I did my field work, the Nahuatl word for a religious procession, *tlayahualohua*, can be literally translated as "to go around." The use of this term is consistent with Konrad's emphasis on the cyclical nature of pilgrimages in the worldview of another Indigenous group of Mexico. Also, the fact that the contemporary Nahuatl word *tlaixpiya* refers to both religious vigils and festivities involving dancing and drinking indicate an Indian worldview that does not make the same distinctions between the sacred and profane as does European Christianity. I suspect that studies of Indian pilgrimage prayers by linguists specializing in contemporary Nahuatl, Quechua, or other native languages would re-inforce the findings already reported in this volume concerning the endurance of pre-Hispanic cultural patterns. It might possibly lead to the discovery of additional non-Christian motifs in the syncretic traditions of Latin American pilgrimages. Other specialists in the humanities might well want to investigate the sculptures and paintings associated with pilgrimages which were at various time referred to in passing, for example, the stars in the image of the Virgen of Guadalupe in Mexico mentioned by Konrad.

A number of inconsistencies between various authors in this volume also indicate the need for further research. For example, Konrad, in his chapter on the Quintana Roo Mayans, refers to the importance of the continued use of jungle paths in pilgrimages despite the introduction of paved highways. Yet several other authors make a special point of showing that the introduction of roads and other modern means of communication in no way detracted from the viability or continued symbolic significance of traditional pilgrimages. This and other apparent discrepancies can be used to illustrate the necessity for further research on the almost endless facets of the Latin American pilgrimage. However, the most rewarding results are bound to come by examining the interrelationships between these different facets, as illustrated in many of the chapters in this book. This volume is certainly a step in the right direction for reaching the goal of the analysis of the pilgrimage as a structured whole, as set out by Morinis and Crumrine in the introduction of the book. Such a task can be accomplished only through the collaboration of scholars from different disciplines.

REFERENCES

Marion Singer 1984
Meyer 1963

Ochoa 1979
Schryer 1979, 1990

References

Aban May, Benito

1982 *Yum Santísima Cruz Tun: Historia de la Santísima Cruz Tun "Centro del Mundo."* Mérida: SEP.

Acosta, P. José de la

1954 *Historia Natural y Moral de las Indias* (1590). Madrid: Biblioteca de Autores Españoles, T. LXIII.

Adair, J.

1978 *The Pilgrim's Way: Shrines and Saints in Britain and Ireland.* Over Wallop, Hampshire: Thames and Hudson.

Adams, Richard N.

1957 *Cultural Surveys of Panama, Nicaragua, Guatemala, El Salvador, Honduras.* Washington: Pan American Sanitary Bureau, World Health Organization; reprint ed. Detroit: Blaine Ethridge Books, 1976.

1966 Changing Patterns of Territorial Organizations in the Central Highlands of Chiapas, Mexico. *American Antiquity* 26:341-360.

Adams, Walter Randolph

---

[1] These *References* include a few additional items recently added but not listed in the *References* at the end of any of the chapters.

1981a Political and Economic Correlates of Pilgrimage: The Tzeltal Example of Southeastern Chiapas, Mexico. Paper presented at the conference "Pilgrimage: The Human Quest." Pittsburgh.

1981b An Ethnohistorical Approach to Sacred and Secular Interpretations of Pilgrimages: The Tzeltal Example of Chiapas. Paper presented at the Annual Meeting of the American Folklore Society. San Antonio.

1983 Political and Economic Correlates of Pilgrimage Behavior. *Anales de Antropologia* 20(2):147-172.

1988 Tzeltal-Tojolabal Religious Interaction: The Pilgrimages. In Lyle Campbell, ed., *The Linguistics of Southeastern Chiapas*, Papers of the New World Archaeological Foundation 50:299-354. Provo, Utah: Brigham Young University.

n.d.   Some Religious Practices of Southeastern Chiapas, Mexico. Manuscript on file with the American Philosophical Society, Philadelphia.

Aigrain, René
1953 *L'Hagiographie*. Poitiers: Bloud et Gay.

Albo, Xavier
1974 Santa Vera Cruz Taita. *Allpanchis* 7:163-216. Cuzco: Instituto de Pastoral Andina.

Alencastre G., Andres, and Georges Dumézil
1953 Fêtes et usages des indiens de Langui. *Journal de la Société des Américanistes* n.s., T.XLII:1-118.

Allen, Catherine J.
1978 "Coca, Chicha and Trago: Private and Communal Rituals in a Quechua Community." Ph.D. dissertation, Department of Anthropology, University of Illinois, Urbana-Champaign.

1982   Passages and Body Processes: The Symbolism of Andean Drinking Vessels. Manuscript, Dept. of Anthropology, George Washington University, Washington, D.C.

1983   Of Bear-Men and He-Men: Bear Metaphors and Male Self-Perception in a Peruvian Community. *Latin American Indian Literatures* VII(1):38-51.

1988 *The Hold Life Has: Coca & Cultural Identity in an Andean Community*. Washington, D.C.: Smithsonian Institution Press.

Almeida, Atila de, and José Alves Sobrinho
1978 Dicionário Bio-bibliográfico de Repentistas e Poetas de Bancada. 2 vols. João Pessoa/Campina Grande: Universidade Federal da Paraíba Centro de Ciências e Tecnologia.

Alonso, Isidoro, Gines Garrido, José Dammert Bellido, and Julio Tumiri
1962 *La Iglesia en Peru y Bolivia*. Madrid: OCSH, Estudios Socio-Religiosos Latino-Americanos 3(II).

Altman, Charles F.
1975 Two Types of Opposition in the Structure of Latin Saints' Lives.

In Paul Maurice Clogan, ed., *Medieval Hagiography and Romance* (Medievalia and Humanistica, n.s. 6). Cambridge: Cambridge University Press.

Amato, Enrique
1965 *La Iglesia en Argentina*. Buenos Aires: CISOR, America Latina, Estudios Socio-Religiosos 5(II).

Anders, Martha
1986 Dual Organization and Calendars Inferred from the Planned Site of Azangaro—Wari Administrative Strategies. Diss. in Anthropology at Cornell University.

Andrade, Mário de
1963 O Romanceiro de Lampeão. In Marío de Andrade, ed., *O Baile das Quatro Artes*. São Paulo: Martins/MEC.

Anonimo Sevillano
1967 *Las relaciones primitivas de la conquista del Perú* (1534). Lima: Ed. Porras Barrenechea.

Anonymous
1940 *Novena y Milagros de la Santisima Cruz del Cerro Chalpon de Motupe*. Chiclayo: Imprenta Guererro.
n.d.a *Gran Festividad Religiosa y Comercial "Santisima Cruz de Chalpon" Motupe*. Chiclayo: Editorial Kimoy /1980/.
n.d.b Novena de la Venerada Imagen de la Santisima Cruz del "Cerro Chalpon". Motupe.
n.d.c *Relacion Minuciosa y Veridica de la Vida y Milagros del Padre Fray Juan, Autor de la Existencia de la Exitencia de la Santisima Cruz de Chalpon en el Distrito de Motupe*. Chiclayo: Imprenta Guererro.

Anselmo, Otacílio
1908 *Mito e Realidade*. Rio de Janeiro: Civilização Brasileira.

Antier, J. J.
1979 *Le pèlerinage retrouvé*. Paris: Centurion.

Apostolic Brazilian Catholic Church
1980 Volta por Cima: A Igreja já Respeita a Fe no Padre Cícero. *Veja* November 12, 1980:71,73.

Argentina.
n.d. *Guia de Santuarios*. Argentina: Pan y trabajo.

Arguedas, José Maria
1956 Puquio, una cultura en proceso de cambio. *Revista del Museo Nacional de Lima* 25:184-232.

Arriaga, P. José de
1920 *Extirpación de la idolatría del Perú* (1621). Lima: Colección de libros y documentos referentes a la Historia del Perú, Series 2, Vol. I.

Aveni, Anthony F, Horst Hartung, and Beth Buckingham
1978 The pecked cross symbol in ancient Mesoamerica. *Science*

372　References

102:267-279.

Avila, Francisco de

1966 *Dioses y hombres de huarochirí* (1560). Lima: Arguedas y Duviols.

1975 *Dioses y hombres de Huarochirí* (1608). Mexico: Siglo XXI. Trans. J. M. Arguedas.

Azzi, Rolando

1978 *O Catolicismo Popular no Brasil: Aspectos Históricos.* Petrópolis: Vozes.

Baby, François

1980 Toponomastique du pèlerinage en Languedoc. In Privat, ed., *Le pèlerinage*, pp.57-78. Toulouse.

Bachmann, Carlos D.

1921 *Monografia Historico Geografico, Departamento de Lambayeque.* Lima: Torres Aguirre.

Backman, E. Louis

1952 *Religious Dances in the Christian Church and in Popular Medicine.* London: Allen and Unwin.

Ballesteros Graibois, M.

1979 Mito, leyenda, tergiversacion en torno a Cacha y el "templo de Racchí." *Historia y cultura*, 12:7-26.

Bancroft, Hubert Howe

1962 *History of Arizona and New Mexico 1530-1888.* San Francisco: History Co., 1889; Alburquerque: Horn & Wallace.

Bandalier, Adolph F.

1910 *The Islands of Titicaca and Koati.* New York: Hispanic Society of America.

Barabas, Alicia M.

1974 Profestismo, milenarismo y mesianismo en las insurrecciones Mayas de Yucatán. México: SEP/INAH.

Barragan, C. F.

1985 *Novena a la Virgen de Acahuato Patrona de la diocesis de Apatzingan, Michoacan.* Apatzingan, México.

Barrette, Christian

1972 Aspects de l'ethno-écologie d' un village andin. *Canadian Review of Sociology and Anthropology* 9:255-67.

Barrionuevo, Alfonsina

1969 *Cuzco, Magic City.* Lima: Editorial Universo.

Barrera Vásquez, Alfredo

1980 *Diccionario Maya Cordemex.* A. Barrera Vásquez, ed. Mérida: Ediciones Cordemex.

Bartholomé, Miguel A.

1974 *La iglesia Maya de Quintana Roo.* México: SEP/INAH.

Bartholomé, Miguel A., and Alicia M. Barabas

1977 *La resistencia Maya: relaciones interétnicas en el oriente de la Península de Yucatán.* México: SEP/INAH.

Bartlett, John R.

1854 *Personal Narrative of Explorations and Incidents in Texas, New Mexico, California, Sonora, and Chihuahua, Connected with the United States and Mexican Boundary Commission during the Years 1850, '51, '52 and '53.* New York: D. Appleton & Co.

Bastien, Joseph W.

1978 *Mountain of the Condor.* The American Ethnological Society, Monograph N.64. St. Paul, Minnesota: West.

Batista, Sebastião Nunes

1977 *Antologia da Literatura de Cordel.* Natal: Fundação José Augusto.

Bean, Lowell John, and William M. Mason

1962 *Diaries & Accounts of the Romero Expeditions in Arizona and California 1823-1826.* Palm Springs: Palm Springs Desert Museum.

Benevides, Aldenor

1969 *Padre Cícero and Juazeiro.* Brasília: Artes Gráficas Regina.

Benuzzi, Silvia

1980 The Pilgrimage to Chalma: The Analysis of Religious Change. M.A. thesis, University of Texas at Austin.

Besen, J. A.

1977 *Azambuja 100 Años.* Brusque, Brazil: Grafica Mercurio.

Betanzos, Juan de

1924 *Suma y narración de los Incas* (1551). H. H. Urteaga, ed. Lima: Colección de libros y documentos referentes a la Historia del Perú, Serie 2, Vol. VIII.

1968 *Suma y narración de los Incas....*(1551). Madrid: Biblioteca de Autores Espanoles.

Bhardwaj, S. M., and G. Rinschede

1988 Pilgrimage—A World Wide Phenomenon. In S. M. Bhardwaj and G. Rinschede, eds., *Pilgrimage in World Religions.* Geographia Religionum 4:11-19. Berlin: Dietrich Reimer.

Billet, B., et al

1976 *Vraies et fausses apparitions dans l'Église.* Paris: Editions P. Lethielleux.

Blacker, Carmen, and Michael Loewe

1975 *Ancient Cosmologies.* London: Allen and Unwin.

Blanchard, Louis-Marie

1987 Vers les dieux de la cordillére. *Geo* 98:168-81.

Bliss, Wesley L.

1952 In the Wake of the Wheel. In Edward H. Spicer, ed., *Human Problems in Technological Change.* New York: Russell Sage Foundation.

Boissevain, Jeremy

1968 The Place of Non-Groups in the Social Sciences. *Man* n.s., 3:542-556.

374   References

Bolton, Herbert E.
    1917 The Mission as a Frontier Institution in the Spanish-American
    Colonies. *American Historical Review* 23.
Bonnier, Elisabeth and Catherine Rosenberg
    1988 "Du sanctuaire au hameau. A propos de la néolithisation dans la
    Cordillère des Andes Centrales." *L'Anthropologie* 92(3):983-96. Paris.
Borhegyi, Stephen F. de
    1953 The Miraculous Shrine of our Lord of Esquipulas in Guatemala
    and Chimayo, New Mexico. *El Palacio* 60:83-111.
    1954 The Cult of Our Lord of Esquipulas in Middle America and New
    Mexico. *El Palacio* 61:387-401.
    1958 Aqualung Archeology. *Natural History* 67, 3:120-125.
    1959 Underwater Archeology in the Maya Highlands. *Scientific
    American* 100, 3:100-103.
Bottineau, Yves
    1983 *Les chemins de Saint-Jacques*. Paris.
Bourricaud, François
    1970 *Power and Society in Contemporary Peru*. New York: Praeger.
Bowman, Isaiah
    1924 *Desert Trails of Atacama*. American Geographical Society, Special
    Publication no.5. Greenwich, Conn: Condé Nast.
Boyd, E.
    1946 *Saints and Saint Makers of New Mexico*. Santa Fe: Laboratory of
    Anthropology.
Bricker, Victoria Reifler
    1981 *The Indian Christ, the Indian King: The Historical Substrate of
    Maya Myth and Ritual*. Austin: University of Texas Press.
Brooks, John
    1980 *The South American Handbook*. Bath: Trade and Travel
    Publications.
Browe, Peter
    1938 *Die Eucharistischen Wunder des Mittelalters*. Breslauer Studien
    zur historischen Theologie, NF 4. Breslau: Müller & Seiffert.
Brown, P.
    1981 *The Cult of the Saints: Its Rise and Function in Latin
    Christianity*. Chicago: University of Chicago Press.
Brüning, Heinrich
    1922 *Estudios Monograficos del Departamento de Lambayeque*.
    Fasciculo II: Olmos. Chiclayo: Dionisio Mendoza.
Brush, Stephen B.
    1977 *Mountain, Field and Family: The Ecology and Human Economy
    of an Andean Valley*. Philadelphia: Univ. of Pennsylvania Press.
Brustoloni, J.
    1982 *A Senhora da Conceicao Aparedida Historia da imagem da capela
    das romarios*. Aparedida: Editora Santuario.

Caboclo e Silva, Manoel
1978 *Jesus, São Pedro e o Ferreiro: Rei dos Jogadores.* Juazeiro do Norte: Casa dos Horóscopos.

Cáceres Monroy, Jorge Mariano
1970 *Los Sikho Morenos de Llavini (Puno).* Cuzco: Universidad Nacional de San Antonio Abad, Anthropology Thesis No. 1198.

Cámara Barbachano, Fernando, and Teófilo Reyes Couturier
1975 Los Santuarios y las peregrinaciones. In: *Anales* (Instituto Nacional de Antropologia e Historia) Epoca 7a, IV.

Cámara Cascudo, Luís da
1939 *Vaqueiros e Cantadores.* Porto Alegre: Editorial Globo.

Camilo dos Santos, Manuel
n.d. *Um Grande Milagre de São Francisco do Canindé.* Campina Grande: A Estrella da Poesia.

Camino, Alejandro
1978 Trueque, correrias e intercambios entre los quechuas andinos y los piro y machiguenga de la montaña peruana. In *Etnohistoria y Antropologie Andina* 1:70-100. Lima: Museo Nacional Historia.

Campbell, Lyle
1988 *The Linguistics of Southeastern Chiapas.* L. Campbell, ed., Papers of the New World Archaeological Foundation, No. 50. Provo: Brigham Young University.

Campos, Eduardo
1951 Romanceiro do Padre Cicero. *Boletim da Comissão Catarinense de Folclore* 2:30-33.

Cancian, Frank
1965 *Economics and Prestige in a Maya Community: A Study of the Religious Cargo System in Zinacantan, Chiapas, Mexico.* Stanford: Stanford University Press.

Cantel, Raymond
1972 *Temas da Atualidade na Literatura de Cordel.* Alice Mitika Koshiyama et al., transl. São Paulo: Universidade de São Paulo, Escola de Comunicações e Artes.

Carmack, Robert M.
1981 *The Quiche Mayas of Utatlán. The Evolution of a Highland Guatemalan Community.* Norman: University of Oklahoma Press.

Caro Baroja, Julio
1978 *Las formas complejas de la vida religiosa.* Madrid.

Carrasco Pizana, Pedro
1950 *Los Otomíes: Cultura e historia prehispánica de los pueblos mesoamericanos de habla otomiana.* Mexico: Instituto de Historia, UNAM.

Carrillo Dueñas, M.
1975 La Imagen de Ntra. Sra. del Rosario de Talpa. *Boletin Elesiastico.* Tepic: Iglesia diocesana de Tepic.

Carroll, Michael
  1986 *The Cult of the Virgin Mary: Psychological Origins*. Princeton: Princeton University Press.
Casaverde Rojas, Juvenal
  1970 El mundo sobrenatural de una comunidad. *Allpanchis* 2:121-243.
Casillas, S.
  1974 Breve Resena Historica de la Parroquia de Compostela. *Boletin Eclesiastico*. Tepic: Iglesia diocesana de Tepic.
Cassidy, J. L.
  1958 *Mexico: Land of Mary's Wonders*. Paterson, N.J.: St. Anthony Guild Press.
Castillo Nino, Carlos del
  1967 *La Cruz del Chalpon: Leyenda, Tradicion, Relato*. (2d Ed.). Lima: Escuela Nacional de Artes Graficas.
  1968 *Motupe en la Historia; Estudio Historico Geografico*. Lima: Escuela Nacional de Artes Graficas.
Cava, Ralph Della
  1970 *Miracle at Joaseiro*. New York: Columbia University Press.
Chavez, Angélico
  1954 The Penitentes of New Mexico. *New Mexico Historical Review* XXIX:2.
Chefdubois, Couturier de
  1953 *Pèlerinages de Notre-Dame*. 3 vols. Paris: Editions Spes.
Chinchilla Aguilar, Ernesto
  1961 *Historia y Tradiciones de la Ciudad de Amatitlán*. Guatemala: Biblioteca Guatemalteca de Cultura Popular. Ministerio de Educación Pública.
  1965 *Historia del Arte en Guatemala. Arquitectura, Pintura y Escultura*. 2d ed. Guatemala: Departamento Editorial—José de Pineda Ibarra. Ministerio de Educación Pública.
Christian, William A., Jr.
  1972 *Person and God in a Spanish Valley*. New York: Seminar Press.
  1976 De los santos a María: panorama de las devociónes a santuarios españoles desde el principio de Edad Media hasta nuestros días. In C. L. Tolosana, ed., *Temas de Antropolgia Española*, pp. 49-106. Madrid: Akal.
  1981a *Local Religion in Sixteenth-Century Spain*. Princeton: Princeton University Press.Christian, William A., Jr.
  1981b *Apparitions in Late Medieval and Renaissance Spain*. Princeton: Princeton University Press.
  1985 Devotion to Dark Images in Catalonia: The Case of the Virgin of Montserrat. Paper at the conference on the Dark Madonna. Los Angeles, November.
Cieza De Leon, Pedro de
  1947 *La Cronica del Peru* (1553). In Biblioteca de Autores Espanoles,

T. 26:349-458. Madrid: Ediciones Atlas.

Cloudsley, Peter
1985 Peru's living Inca heritage. *The Geographical Magazine* 57(2):84-89.

Cobo, Bernabé
1956 *Historia del Nuevo Mundo* (1653). In Biblioteca de Autores Españoles, Tomo I. Madrid.
1964 (1963) *Historia del Nuevo Mundo* (1653). In Biblioteca de Autores Españoles, Tomo I. Madrid.

Cohen, Abner
1974 *Two-Dimensional Man: An Essay on the anthropology of Power and Symbolism in Complex Society*. London: Routledge and Kegan Paul.

Colangeli, Mario
1977 *Le feste dell'anno*. Rome: Sugar Edizioni.

Colby, B. N., and P. L. van den Berghe
1969 *Ixil Country: A Plural Society in Highland Guatemala*. Berkeley: University of California Press.

Comblin, Joseph
1977 *Teologia da Enxada: Uma Experiência da Igreja no Nordeste*. Petrópolis: Vozes.

Comision National Coordinadora de Santuarios de Chile
1977-79 *Informativo Santuarios* (various issues). Bellavista, La Florida, Chile: Instituto Secular de Schonstatt.

Consejo Superior de Investigaciones Científicas
1978 Santuarios. In *Diccionario de historia eclesiástica de españa*, Vol. IV, pp. 2207-2381. Madrid: Instituto Enrique Florez.

Considine, John J.
1946 *Call for Forty Thousand*. Toronto: Longmans, Green & Co.

Coordenação Diocesana de Pastoral de Turismo
1979 *Nossa Senhora do Monte Serrat: historico, culto, devocionario*. São Paulo: Editora Verbo Divino.

Corbett, Jack and Scott Whiteford
1983 State Penetration and Development in Mesoamerica 1950-1980. In C. Kendall, J. Hawkins, and L. Bossen, eds., *Heritage of Conquest: Thirty Years Later*. Alburquerque: University of New Mexico Press.

Cortázar, Pedro Felipe
1975 *Informe del Peru, Departamento de Piura*. Vol. IV. Lima: Promotora Editorial Latinoamericana Newton-Cortázar, S.R.L.

Costa Clavell, Xavier, ed.
1980 Romerías Callegas. In *Bandolerismo, romerías y jergas gallegas*. La Coruna: Biblioteca Gallega.

Cosulich, Bernice
1939 Ancient Tryst Beckons Thousands of Faithful. *Arizona Daily Star*

(Tucson), October 1, 1939:1, 7.

Cotarelo y Mori, Emilio

1911   *Colección de Entremeses, Loas, Bailes, Jacaras y Mojigangas desde fines del Siglo XVI a mediados del XVIII.* Madrid: Nueva Biblioteca de Autores Españoles, T.17.

Cotler, Julio

1968   La mecánica de la dominación interna y del cambio social en el Perú. In José Matos Mar, ed., *Perú Problema: 5 Ensayos.* Lima: Instituto de Estudios Peruanos.

Cousin, Bernard.

1981   *Ex-voto de Provence: Images de las religion populaire et de la vie d'autrefois.* Paris: Besclee de Brouwer.

Couts, Cave J.

1961   *Hepah, California! The Journal of Cave Johnson Couts from Monterey, Nuevo Leon, Mexico, to Los Angeles, California, During the Years 1848-1849.* Ed. H. F. Dobyns. Tucson: Arizona Pioneers' Historical Society.

Crane, Thomas Frederick

1967   *The Exempla or Illustrative Stories of Jacques de Vitry.* Publications of the Folklore Society XXVI, 1890. Nedelin, Lichtenstein: Kraus Reprint.

Cristo Rei, João de

n.d.   *O Nascimento Misterioso de Padrinho Cícero.* Juazeiro do Norte. n.p.

Crumrine, Lynne S.

1969   Ceremonial Exchange as a Mechanism in Tribal Integration among the Mayos of Northwest Mexico. *Anthropological Papers of the University of Arizona,* Number 14. Tucson: University of Arizona Press.

Crumrine, N. Ross

1964   The House Cross of the Mayo Indians of Sonora Mexico: A Symbol of Ethnic Identity. *Anthropological Papers of the University of Arizona,* Number 8. Tucson: University of Arizona Press.

1975   A New Mayo Indian Religious Movement in Northwest Mexico. *Journal of Latin American Lore* 1(2):127-145.

1977a   *The Mayo Indians of Sonora, Mexico: A People Who Refuse to Die.* Tucson: University of Arizona Press. (Reissued by Waveland Press, Inc. 1988)

1977b   Three Coastal Peruvian Pilgrimages. *El Dorado* 2 (1):76-86.

1978   Romerías en el Campo Peruano. *Américas* 30(8):28-34. (Published in the English edition as The Peruvian Pilgrimage).

1981   The Ritual of the Cultural Enclavement Process: The Dramatization of Oppositions among the Mayo Indians of Northwest Mexico. In George P. Castile and Gilbert Kushner, eds., *Persistent Peoples,* pp. 109-131. Tucson: University of Arizona Press.

1983 Mayo. In William C. Sturevant, ed., *Handbook of North American Indians*. Alfonso Ortiz, volume editor, volume 10, Southwest pp. 264-275. Washington: Smithsonian Institution.

1986 Drama Folklórico en Latino América: Estructura y significado del ritual y simbolismo de Cuaresma y de la Semana Santa. *Folklore Americano* 41/42:5-31.

1987 Mechanisms of Enclavement Maintenance and Sociocultural Blocking of Modernization among the Mayo of Southern Sonora. In N. Ross Crumrine and Phil C.Weigand, eds., *Ejidos and Regions of Refuge in Northwestern Mexico*. Anthropological Paper of the University of Arizona Number 46, pp. 21-30. Tucson: University of Arizona Press.

1988a Ritual Mediation of the Life-Death Opposition: The Meaning of Mayo Parisero Lenten Masks. In Janet Brody Esser, ed., *Behind the Mask in Mexico*, pp. 77-105. Santa Fe, New Mexico: Museum of New Mexico Press.

1988b Los Ritos Funebres y Las Fiestas Sagradas de La Costa del Norte del Peru en la Integración de los Pueblos, con Enfoque Especial en los Ceremoniales de La Semana Santa y Del Santisimo Sacramento de Catacaos, Piura. In, *Rituales y Fiestas de las Américas*, Elizabeth Reichel, ed., pp. 113-121. Bogotá, Colombia: Editorial Presencia Ltda.

Cuneo Vidal, R.

1977 *Obras completas*, V. Lima, Peru.

Cunniff, Roger Lee

1971 The Great Drought: Northeastern Brazil, 1877-1880. Diss. University of Texas, Austin.

Curran, Mark J.

1973 *Literatura de cordel*. Recife: Universidade Federal de Pernambuco.

Daus, Ronald

1969 *Der episch Zyklus der Cangaceiros in der Volkspoesie Nordostbrasiliens*. Berlin: Colloquium.

Deffontaines, Pierre

1948 *Géographie et religions*. Paris: Gallimard (Chpt. III, pp.205-338: Geographie des pèlerinages)

De Lambertie, Charles

1955 *Le Drame de la Sonora*. Paris: Chez Ledoyen.

Delehaye, Hippolyte

1921 *Les Passions des martyrs et les genres littéraires*. Brussels: Bureau de la Societe des Bollandistes.

De León Meléndez, Ofelia Columba

1980 La Fiesta de la Santa Cruz en el Municipio de Amatitlán. *Boletín del Centro de Estudios Folklóricos, Universidad de San Carlos de Guatemala*. Número 28. Guatemala: Centro de Estudios Folklóricos.

Delgado, Guillermo, and Nancy Schaeffer
   1978 A Critical Review of Documentary Films on the Andes. *Andean Perspective*. Institute of Latin American Studies, University of Texas at Austin, pp. 44-45.
Demarest, D., and C. Taylor
   1956 *The Dark Virgin: The Book of Our Lady of Guadalupe*. New York: Coley Taylor.
Demonte de Torres, M. C.
   1980 *Paraná y su parroquia sentesis historica*. Paraná.
De Ribas, Andres Perez
   1944 *Triunfos de Nuestra Santa Fe Entre Gentes las Mas Barbaras y Fieras del Nuevo Orbe*. Madrid: Alonso de Pardes (Mexico: Editorial "Layac").
Diccionario Geográfico de Guatemala
   1961-62 *Diccionario Geográfico de Guatemala*. 2 vols. Guatemala: Dirección General de Cartografía.
Diccionario Maya Cordemex
   1980 Alfredo Barrera Vásques, ed. Mérida: Ediciones Cordemex.
Dirección de Estadistica
   1878 *Censo General de la Republica del Peru Formado en 1876*, T.V. Departamento de Lambayeque Lima: Imprenta del Teatro.
Dirección Nacional de Estadistica
   1944 *Censo Nacional de Poblacion y Ocupacion 1940*. Ministerio de Hacienda y Comercio. Lima: Torres Aguirre.
Dobyns, Henry F.
   1950 Papago Pilgrims on the Town. *Kiva* 16 (October-November):1-2.
   1951a Blunders with Bolsas. *Human Organization* 10:3.
   1951b *Papagos in the Cotton Fields, 1950*. Tucson: Author, for the Arizona State Museum.
   1960 The Religious Festival. Diss. Cornell University.
   1976 *Spanish Colonial Tucson: A Demographic History*. Tucson: University of Arizona Press.
   1981 *From Fire to Flood: Historic Human Destruction of Sonoran Desert Riverine Oases*. Socorro: Ballena Press, Anthropological Papers No. 20.
   1986 The Military Power of the Gila River Pima-Maricopa Confederation 1848-1886. Manuscript.
Dobyns, Henry F., and Paul L. Doughty
   1976 *Perú, A Cultural History*. New York: Oxford University Press.
Doering, Heinrich Ubbelohde
   1958 Bericht über archäologische Feldarbeiten in Perú. *Ethnos* 23(2-4):67-99.
Donnan, Christopher
   1976 Moche Art and Iconography. *UCLA Latin American Center Publications*. Los Angeles.

Dorn, L.
1975 *Die Wallfahrten des Bistums Augsburg*. Augsburg: Eos.
Doughty, Paul L.
1976 Social Policy and Urban Growth in Lima. In David Chaplin, ed., *Peruvian Nationalism: A Corporatist Revolution*. New Brunswick: Transaction Books.
Douglas, Mary
1966 *Purity and Danger*. Baltimore: Penguin.
Dumas, Alain
1986 *Quoyllur Rit'i*. Paris: Films du Mangrove. Film.
Dupront, Alphonse
1971 Formes de la culture des masses: de la doléance politique au pèlerinage panique. In *Niveaux de culture et groupes sociaux*, Paris.
1973 Pèlerinage de lieux sacrés. In *Mélagnes en l'honneur de Fernand Braudel. Méthodologie de l'Histoire et des sciences humaines* pp. 189-206. Paris: Privat Editeur.
1987 *Du Sacré: Croisades et pèlerinages, images et languages*. Paris: Gallimard.
Durand-Lefebvre, Marie
1937 *Etude sur l'origine des Vierges Noires*. Paris: G. Durassie.
Durkheim, E.
1968 *Les formes élémentaires de la vie religieuse*. Paris.
Duviols, Pierre
1967 Un Inédit de Cristóbal de Albornoz, "Instrucción para descubrir todas las guacas del Pirú y sus camayos y haziendas." *Journal de la Société des Américanistes* n.s., LVI(1):7-39.
1971 *La Lutte contra les réligions autochtones dans le Peroú colonial. L'extirpacion des Idolatries entre 1532-1660*. Lima: Institute Français des Etudes Andines.
1977 Los nombres quechuas de Viracocha supuesto "Dios creador" de los evangelizadores. *Allpanchis* X:53-64.
Earls, John C.
1973 Andean Continuum Cosmology. Diss. University of Illinois, Urbana-Champaign.
Edmonson, Munro et al
1960 *Nativism and Syncretism*. New Orleans: Middle American Research Institute, Pub. 19.
Edwards, Frank S.
1966 *A Campaign in New Mexico with Colonel Doniphan*. Philadelphia: Carey and Hart, 1847; New York: Readex Microprint Corp.
Eggan, Fred
1954 Social Anthropology and the Method of Controlled Comparison. *American Anthropologist* 56:5.
Eliade, Mircea

1959 *Cosmos and History: The Myth of the Eternal Return.* New York: Harper and Row.

1959a *The Sacred and the Profane: The Nature of Religion.* New York: Harcourt Brace Jovanovich.

Elias, Julio Maria

1981 *Copacauana—Copacabana.* Tarija, Bolivia: Editorial Offset Franciscana.

Emory, William H.

1857 *Report on the United States and Mexican Boundary Survey, Made under the Direction of the Secretary of the Interior.* Washington: Cornelius Wendell, Printer (34th Congress, 1st Session, House of Representatives Exec. Doc. N. 135).

Empresa Nacional de Turismo

1970 *Lambayeque.* Lima: Entur Peru.

Enriquez, M.

1984 *Historias del templo de San Lorenzo y misiones aldeanas.* Chihuahua: Talleres de Editorial Camino.

Erasmus, Charles J.

1967 Culture Change in Northwest Mexico. In Julian H. Steward, ed., *Contemporary Change in Traditional Societies, Mexican and Peruvian Communities,* vol. 3, pp. 3-131. Urbana: University of Illinois Press.

Estete, Miguel de

1938 *Noticia del Perú* (ca.1540). In Horacio H. Urteaga, ed., *Los Cronistas de la Conquista.* Paris: Desclée de Brouwer.

Eyzaguirre, Luis G. M.

1936 *Huanka Rumi. Historia de las apariciones del Señor de Huanca y de su célebre sanctuario.* T.1. Cuzco.

Ezell, Paul H.

1968 The Maricopa Mail. In Ray Brandes ed., *Brand Book N. 1.* San Diego: San Diego Corrall of the Westerners.

Falla Failoc, Ruly

n.d. La santisima Cruz de Chalpon. *Antarqui* (1980) (no number). Lima.

Faulk, Odie B.

1968 Projected Mexican Military Colonies for the Borderlands, 1848. *Journal of Arizona History* 9:1.

Fernández, Justino

1945 *Catálogo de construcciones religiosas del Estado de Yucatán.* 2 vol. J. Fernández, ed. Mexico: Talleres Gráficos de la Nación.

Fine, Kathleen

1982 The Molecaña and the Yumbo: Masked Dance Performance and Protest in Urban Ecuador. Paper presented at the annual meeting of the American Ethnological Society, Baton Rouge, December 1982.

Finley, M. I.

1975 *The Use and Abuse of History*. New York: Viking Penguin.

Fischer, R., and A. Stoll
1977-79 *Kleines Handbuch Österreichischer MarienWallfahrtskirch*. 3 vol. Vienna: Bergland.

Florentino Duarte, Manuel et al.
1976 *Literatura de Cordel: Antologia*. 2 vol. São Paulo: Global Editora.

Flores Ochoa, Jorge
1973 Indariy y Qollariy en una comunidad del altiplano. In Juan M. Ossio, ed., *Ideoloqia Mesiánica del Mundo Andino*. Lima: Ignacio Prado Pastor.

Fonseca Martel, Cesar
1974 Modalidades de la minka. In G. Alberti and E. Mayer, eds., *Reciprocidad e Intercambio en los Andes Peruanos*, pp:86-109. Lima: Instituto de Estudios Peruanos.

Fontana, Bernard L.
1983 History of the Papago. In Alfonso Ortiz, ed., *Southwest Volume 10*. Handbook of North American Indians. Ed. W. H. Sturtevant. Washington: Smithsonian Institution.
1987 Santa Ana de Cuiquiburitac: Pimeria Alta's Northernmost Mission. *Journal of the Southwest* 29:2.

Fontenelle, E.
1970 *O Aleijadinho na Serra de Piedade*. Minas Gerais: Universidade Federal de Minas Gerais.

Forman, Shepard
1972 *The Brazilian Peasantry*. New York: Columbia University Press.

Forsyth, I. H.
1972 *The Throne of Wisdom: Wood Sculptures of the Madonna in Romanesque France*. Princeton: Princeton University Press.

Fortes, Meyer
1945 *The Dynamics of Clanship among the Tallensi*. London: Oxford University Press.
1949 *The Web of Kinship among the Tallensi*. London: Oxford University Press.
1969 *Kinship and the Social Order*. Chicago: Aldine.
1971 Some Aspects of Migration and Mobility in Ghana. *Journal of Asian and African Studies*, 6:1-12.

Fought, John G.
1972 *Chortí (Mayan) Texts*. Philadelphia: University of Pennsylvania Press.

Fox, Richard G.
1977 *Urban Anthropology. Cities in Their Cultural Settings*. Englewood Cliffs: Prentice-Hall.

Fox, R. L.
1987 *Pagans and Christians*. New York: Alfred A. Knopf.

Fuente, Julian

1929 *Los heraldos de la civilización centro-americana, reseña histórica de la provincia dominicana de San Vicente de Chiapa y Guatemala* (Vergara: Tip. de "El Santísimo Rosario").

Fuentes y Guzmán, Francisco Antonio de
1969 *Obras históricas de Don Francisco Antonio de Fuentes y Guzmán. I. Edición y Estudio Preliminar de Carmelo Saenz de Santa María (de la Recordación Florida)*. Madrid: Atlas.

Fuentes Aguirre, J. A.
1978 Resena Historica. In *Novenario al Santo Cristo de la Capilla*. Saltillo, Mexico.

Fuenzalida, Fernando
1970 Poder, raza y etnía en el Perú contemporáneo. In José Matos Mar, ed., *El Indio y el Poder en el Perú*. Lima: Instituto de Estudios Peruanos.

Gabrielli, A. K.
1949 *Saints and Shrines of Italy*. Rome: Holy Year 1950 Publishing Company.

Gage, Thomas
1958 *Thomas Gage's Travels in the New World*. Introduction by J. E. S. Thompson. Norman: University of Oklahoma Press.

García Huidobro, P. F.
1978 *Santuarios Marianos del Ecuador*. Guayaquil: Colaboración al Año Nacional del Movimiento Apostólico de Schonstatt.

García, José Maria
1983 *Con las Comunidades Andinas del Ausangate*. Lima: Centro de Proyección Cristiana.

Garcilaso de la Vega, Inca
1960 Comentarios Reales de los Incas (1609). In *Obras Completas*. Madrid: Biblioteca de Autores Españoles, T.CXXXII-CXXXV.

Garibay K., Angel Ma.
1957 *Supervivencias de cultura intelectual precolumbina entre los Otomíes de Huixquilucan*. Instituto Indigenista Interamericano, 33. Mexico: Ediciones especiales.

Gastulo Calvay, Victor Raul
n.d. *La Verdad Sobre el Problema de Motupe*, Primera Parte. Motupe: Imprenta Sanches Cerro.

Getzels, Peter, and Harriet Gordon
1985 *In the Footsteps of Taytacha*. Watertonn, Massachusetts: Documentary Educational Resources. Film.

Gibson, Charles
1964 *The Aztecs Under Spanish Rule: A History of the Indians of the Valley of Mexico, 1519-1810*. Stanford: Stanford University Press.

Gillet, H. M.
1949 *Famous Shrines of Our Lady*. London: Samuel Walker.

Gillin, John

1947 *Moche, A Peruvian Coastal Community*. Publication no.3. Washington: Smithsonian Institution

Gilt Contreras, Mario Alberto
1955 Las Guerrilas indigenas de Chiyaraqe y Toqto. *Archivos Peruanos de Folklore*, 1(1):110-19.
1966 Las Guerrilas indígenas de Chiyaraqe y Toqto. Cuzco: mimeo.

Giménez, Gilberto
1978 *Cultura Popular y Religión en el Anahuac*. Mexico: Centro de Estudios Ecuménicos, A.C.

Girard, Rafael
1966 *Los Maya. Su Civilización—Su Historia, Sus Vinculaciones Continentales*. Mexico: Libro Mex. Editores.

Girault, Louis
1969 Textiles Boliviens; Région de Charazani. *Catalogues de Musée de l'Homme*. Série H. Amérique IV (Paris).

Gisbert-Saunch, Ana
1979 La fiesta del Señor de Qoyllur Rit'i. *Páginas* (Lima) 4(24).

Gisbert, T.
1980 *Iconografía y mitos indígenas en el arte*. La Paz.

Gomme, G. L.
1892 *Ethnology in Folklore*. London: Kegan Paul, Trench Trubner and Co.

Gonçalves, Severino
n.d. "A Moça que Virou Cobra." n.p.

Gonzalez, José Luis, and Teresa Maria van Ronzelen
1983 *Religiosidad popular en el Peru: Bibliografia: antropología historia sociología y pastoral*. Lima: Centro de Estudios y Publicaciones.

Gonzalez Holguín, Diego
1952 *Vocabulario de la Lengua . . . Qquichua o del Inca* (1608). Lima: Univ. Nacl. Mayor de San Marcos.

Gorbak, Celina, Mirtha Lischetti, and Carmen Paula Muñoz
1962 Batallas rituales del Chiaraqe y del Toqto de la provincia de Kanas (Cuzco-Perú). *Revista del Museo nacional de Lima* 31:245-304.

Gossen, G.
1974 *Chamulas in the World of the Sun*. Cambridge: Harvard University Press.

Gould, Richard A.
1978 *Explorations in Ethnoarchaeology*. Albuquerque: University of New Mexico Press.

Gow, David
1974 El Taytacha Qoyllur Rit'i. *Allpanchis* VII:44-100. Cuzco.
1976 The Gods and Social Change in the High Andes. Diss. Madison: University of Wisconsin.

1980   The roles of Christ and Inkarri in Andean religion. *Journal of Latin American Lore* 6:279-96.

Gow, Rosalind, and Bernabé Condori
1976   Kay Pacha. *Biblioteca de la Tradición Oral Andina* no. 1. Cusco: Centro de Estudios Rurales Andinos "Bartolomé de las Casas."

Grimes, Ronald L.
1976   *Symbol and Conquest: Public Ritual and Drama in Santa Fe, New Mexico.* Ithaca: Cornell University Press.

Gross, Daniel R.
1971   Ritual and Conformity: A Religious Pilgrimage to North-eastern Brazil. *Ethnology* 10:132-139.
1979   Review of van den Berghe and Primov 1977. *American Ethnologist* 6:401-403.

Guaman Poma de Ayala, Felipe
1936   *El Primer Nueva Cronica y Buen Gobierno* (1584-1614). Paris: Institut d'Ethnologie, Travaux et Mémoires T.XXIII.
1966   *Nueva Crónica y Buen Gobierno* (1620). Ed. Luis F. Bustios Gálvez. 3 vol. Lima: Editorial Cultura.

Guardian, The
1982   Mexico Backs Central America Left. June 9:16.

Gugitz, G.
1956-58   *Österreichs Gnadenstätten in Kult und Brauch.* 5 vols. Vienna: Bruder Hollinek.

Guillet, David
1978   The Supra-Household Sphere of Production in the Andean Peasant Economy. *Actes du XLIIe congrés International des Américanistes* IV:89-105. Paris: Musée de l'Homme.

Gutierrez de Santa Clara, Pedro
1963   *Quinquenario o Historia de las guerras civiles del Perú* (s. XVI), III. Madrid: Biblioteca de Autores Espanoles.

Hammond, N.
1972   Obsidian Trade Routes in the Mayan Area. *Science* 178, (4065):1092-1094.

Harris, Benjamin Butler
1960   *The Gila Trail: The Texas Argonauts and the California Gold Rush.* Ed. Richard H. Dillon. Norman: University of Oklahoma Press.

Harris, Olivia
1978   Kinship and the vertical economy of the Laymi ayllu, Norte de Potosi. *Actes du Congres XLIIe International des Américanistes 1976,* vol.4. Paris: Foundation Singer Polignac.

Hartinger, W.
1984a   Mariahilf ob Passau. In L. Kriss-Rettenbeck and G. Mohler, eds., *Wallfahrt kennt keine Grenzen*, pp. 248-299. Munich: Schnell & Steiner.

1984b Neukirchen bei Heilig Blut. In L. Kriss-Rettenbeck and G. Mohler, eds., *Wallfahrt kennt keine Grenzen*, pp. 407-417. Munich: Schnell & Steiner.

Hartman, Roswith
1972 Otros datos sobre las llamadas "batallas rituales." *Folklore Americano* (Lima) 17:125-35.

Harvey, H. R.
1980 Religious Networks of Central Mexico. *Geoscience and Man* XXI:135-140.
n.d. *El Códice Hemenway, Títulos de Tierra de San Antonio Huixquilucan*. Mexico: Biblioteca Enciclopédica del Estado de México. (In press).

Harvey, H. R., and Barbara J. Williams
1975 *Huixquilucan Project: 1973-1975, Final Report*. Madison: University of Wisconsin International Studies and Programs, Center for International Population Research.

Henggeler, P. R.
1968 *Helvetia sancta: Heilige Stätten des Schweizerlandes*. Einsiedel: Franz Kalin.

Henning, Pablo
1911 Apuntes etnográficos sobre los Otomíes del Distrito de Lerma. *Anales*. Museo Nacional de Arqueología, Historia y Etnología, Tercera epoca, III:1, 57-85 (Mexico).

Hobgood, John
1970a *A Pilgrimage to Chalma*. Huixquilucan Project Working Papers, 12. Madison: University of Wisconsin, Department of Anthropology.

Hobgood, John
1970b *Chalma: A Study in Directed Cultural Change*. Huixquilucan Project Working Papers, 14. Madison: University of Wisconsin, Department of Anthropology.

Hodgen, Margaret
1952 *Change and History*. Viking Fund Publications in Anthropology No. 18. New York: Viking Fund.

Hole, C.
1954 *English Shrines and Sanctuaries*. London: Batsford.

Horcasitas, Fernando
1979 *The Aztecs Then and Now*. Mexico: Editorial Minutiae Mexicana, S.A.

Hoyt, E.
1963 *The Silver Madonna: Legends of Shrines Mexico-Guatemala*. Mexico: Editorial Letras S.A.

Hrdlic'ka, Ales'
1911 Some Results of Recent Anthropological Exploration in Peru. *Smithsonian Misc. Collection* 56(16). Also in *Proceedings*, 2d Session, International Congress of Americanists, Mexico City (1910)

1912:72-88.

Hulet, Claude L.
1980 Padre Cícero: Algumas repercussões na literatura de Cordel. *Encruzilhadas/Crossroads* 1:17-29.

Hutchinson, C. Alan
1973 General José Figueroa's Career in Mexico, 1792-1832. *New Mexico Historical Review* 48:4.

Isbell, Billie Jean
1978 *To Defend Ourselves. Ecology and Ritual in an Andean Village.* Latin American Monographs, No. 47. Institute of Latin American Studies. Austin: University of Texas Press.

Isbell, Billie Jean, and Ann Fairchild
1980 Moiety Systems and the Integration of Socio-Economic Space in the Andes. Manuscript. Dept. of Anthropology, Cornell University (paper presented at the annual meeting of the American Anthro. Assn., Washington, December 1980).

Ivanova, Anna
1970 *The Dance in Spain.* New York: Praeger.

Jérez, Francisco de
1938 *Verdadera Relación de la Conquista...*(1534). In Horacio H. Ureata, ed., *Los Cronistas de la Conquista.* Paris: Desclée de Brouwer.

Jérez, Francisco de
1947 *Historiadores primitivos de Indias* (1534), II. Madrid: Biblioteca de Autores Espanoles.

Johnson, Allen
1972 *Sharecroppers of the Sertao.* Stanford, California: Stanford University Press.

Johnson, Harry P.
1945 Diego Martinez de Hurdaide, Defender of Spain's Pacific Coast Frontier. In *Greater America: Essays in Honor of Herbert Eugene Bolton.* Berkeley: University of California Press.

Joseph, Alice, Rosamund Spicer, and Jane Chesky
1949 *The Desert People.* Chicago: University of Chicago Press.

Juarros, Domingo
1823 A Statistical and Commercial History of the Kingdom of Guatemala in Spanish America. Transl. J. Baily. London: J. F. Dove.

Kay, M. A.
1977 Health and Illness in a Mexican American Barrio. In E. H. Spicer, ed., *Ethnic Medicine in the Southwest*, pp. 99-166. Tucson: University of Arizona Press.

Kelsey, Vera, and Lilly de Jongh Osborne
1978 *Four Keys to Guatemala.* 2d Rev. Ed. Revised by Larry Handel. New York: Funk and Wagnalls.

Kessell, John L.

1976 *Friars, Soldiers, and Reformers: Hispanic Arizona and the Sonora Mission Frontier, 1767-1856*. Tucson: University of Arizona Press.

Kino, Eusebio Francisco
1919 *Kino's Historical Memoir of Pimeria Alta, A Contemporary Account of the Beginnings of California, Sonora, and Arizona*. Transl. Herbert E. Bolton. Cleveland: Arthur H. Clark Co.

Klein, H. S.
1966 Peasant Communities in Revolt: The Tzeltal Republic of 1712. *Pacific Historical Review* 35:247-263.

Kocik, L.
1982 *Lapa o Santuario do Bom Jesus*. Bom Jesus da Lapa, Brazil: Grafica Bom Jesus.

Kolb, K.
1976 *Marien-Gnadenbilder, Marienverehrung heute*. Würzburg: Echter.
1980 *Vom heiligen Blut: Eine Bilddokumentation der Wallfahrt und Verehrung*. Würzburg: Echter.

Konrad, Herman W.
1983 Barren Bulls and Charging Cows: Cowboy Rituals in Copal and Calgary. In Frank Manning, ed., *Perspectives on Contemporary Cultural Performance*, pp. 145-164. London, Ontario: University of Western Ontario; Bowling Green, Ohio: Bowling Green University Press.
1987 Capitalismo y trabajo en los bosques de las tierras bajas tropicales mexicanas, *Historia Mexicana* 36(3):465-505.

Kramer, Carol A.
1979 *Ethnoarchaeology: Implications of Ethnography for Archaeology*. New York: Columbia University Press.

Kroeber, A. L.
1956 Toward Definition of the Nazca Style. *University of California Publications in American Archaeology and Ethnology* 43(4):327-432.
n.d. Untitled manuscript in the A. L. Kroeber collections, Field Museum of Natural History, Chicago.

Kselman, Thomas A.
1978 Miracles and Prophecies: Popular Religion and the Church in Nineteenth Century France. Diss. University of Michigan.

Kubler, George
1985 Pre-Columbian Pilgrimages in Mesoamerica. In Merle Greene Robertson, ed., *Fourth Palenque Round Table, 1980*, pp. 313-16. San Francisco: The Pre-Columbian Art Research Institute.

Kunkel, John H.
1961 Economic Autonomy and Social Change in Mexican Villages. *Economic Development and Cultural Change* 10.

Kurtz, Donald V.
1982 The Virgin of Guadalupe and the Politics of Becoming Human. *Journal of Anthropological Research* 38:194-210.

Ladame, J.
1980 *Notre-Dame de toute la France.* Paris: Éditions France-Empire.
La Farge, Oliver
1947 *Santa Eulalia. The Religion of a Cuchumatan Indian Town.* Chicago: University of Chicago Press.
La Farge, Oliver, and Douglas Byers
1931 *The Year Bearer's People.* New Orleans: Middle American Research Institute, Pub. 3.
Lafaye, Jacques
1976 *Quezalcoatl and Guadalupe: The Formation of Mexican National Consciousness, 1531-1813.* Chicago: University of Chicago Press.
Lange, Yvonne
1978 Santo Nino de Atocha: A Mexican Cult is Transplanted to Spain. *Palacio* 84(4):2-7.
Las Casas, Bartolomé de
1958 *Apologética historia* (1550), III. Madrid: Biblioteca de Autores Espanoles.
Laughlin, Robert M.
1969 The Huastec. In *Handbook of Middle American Indians*, Vol. 7, pp. 298-311. Austin: University of Texas Press.
Laurentin, Rene and Rupcic, Ljudevit
1984 *Is the Virgin Mary Appearing at Medjugorje?* Transl. Francis Martin. Washington: The World Among Us Press.
Layton, Th. A.
1976 *The Way of Saint James or the Pilgrim's Road to Santiago.* London.
Lazzarini, P.
1980 *Il Volto Santo di Lucca: origine, memorie e culto del taumaturgo crociffisso.* Lucca: Eurograf Viale C. Castracani.
Leclercq, J.
1964 Monachisme et pérégrination. *Aux sources de la spiritualité occidentale,* Paris, pp. 35-90.
Lefeuvre, A.
1980 Religious Tourism and Pilgrimage. On the Move. *Pontifical Commission on Migration and Tourism,* 10, pp. 80-81.
León Barandiarán, Augusto D.
n.d. *Mitos, Leyendas y Tradiciones Lambayecanos. Contribucion al Folklore Peruano.* Lima: Club de Autores y Lectores de Lima.
León Barandiarán, Augusto D., and Romulo Paredes
1934 *A Golpe de Arpa.* Lima.
Leroy, J.
1984 *La tradition vivante Notre-Dame des Miracles la Vierge Noire d'Orléans.* Sainte-Maxime: Éditions C.I.F.
Lessa, Orígenes
1973 *Getúlio Vargas na Literatura de Cordel.* Rio de Janeiro:

Documentário.

Lessa, W. A.
1966 Discoverer-of-the-Sun: Mythology as a Reflection of Culture. In
      M. Jacobs, comp., J. Greenway, ed., *The Anthropologist Looks at
      Myth*, pp. 3-51. Austin: University of Texas Press.

Lévi-Strauss, Claude
1963 The Structural Study of Myth. In Claude Lévi-Strauss, ed.,
      Structural Anthropology, pp. 206-231. New York: Basic Books.
1964 *Mythologiques, I: Le cru et le cruit*. Paris.
1966 The Culinary Triangle. *New Society*, December 22:937-940.
1968 Do dual organizations exist? *Structural Anthropology*. Transl.
      Claire Jacobson and Brooke Grundfest Schoepf. Harmondsworth,
      England: Penguin.
1972 *Structural Anthropology*. Harmondsworth, England: Penguin.

Lewin, Linda
1988 Oral Tradition and Elite Myth: The Legend of the "Good" Thief
      Antônio Silvino in Brazilian Popular Culture. *Journal of Latin
      American Lore* 5:157-204.

Linares Málaga, E.
1978 Prehistory and Petroglyphs in Southern Peru. In David L.
      Browman, ed., *Advances in Andean Archaeology* pp. 371-91. Mouton.

Literatura Popular em Verso: Antologia, vol I
1964 Rio de Janeiro: Fundaçao Casa de Rui Barbosa/MEC.

Literatura Popular em Verso: Antologia, vol. II
1976 Rio de Janeiro: Fundaçao Casa de Rui Barbosa/Fundaçao
      Universidade Regional do Nordeste.

Literatura Popular em Verso: Antologia, vol. Ill
1977 Rio de Janeiro and Joao Pessoa: MEC/Fundacao Casa de Rui
      Barbosa/Universidade Federal da Paraiba.

Literatura Popular em Verso: Antologia, vol. IV
1977 Rio de Janeiro: MEC/Fundaçao Casa de Rui Barbosa.

Literatura Popular em Verso: Catálogo
1962 Rio de Janeiro: Fundaçao Casa de Rui Barbosa/MEC.

Literatura Popular em Verso: Estudos
1973 Rio de Janeiro: Fundaçao Casa de Rui Barbosa/MEC.

Lorente, Sebastian
1860 *Historia Antigua del Peru*. Lima: Imprenta Arbieu.

Lumbreras, Luis G.
1974 *The Peoples and Cultures of Ancient Peru*. Washington:
      Smithsonian Institution Press.

Lustenberger, P. O.
1978 *Wallfahrtsorte in der Schweiz*. Einsiedeln: Benediktiner-kloster.

Lynch, Thomas F.
1971 Preceramic Transhumance in the Callejon de Huaylas, Peru.
      American Antiquity 36(2):139-148.

MacCormack, Sabina
　1982　Un agostino del siglo XVII en el nuevo mundo. *Buletin Hispanique* 84:60-94.
　1984　From the Sun of the Incas to the Virgin of Copacabana. *Representations* 8:30-60.
Machado, B.
　1981　*Senhor Bom Jesus de Iquape*. São Paulo: Editora Boa Viagen.
Macklin, B. June, and N. Ross Crumrine
　1973　Three North Mexican Folk Saint Movements. *Comparative Studies in Society and History* 15(1):89-105.
MacLeod, M. J.
　1973　*Spanish Central America: A Socioeconomic History, 1520-1720.* Berkeley: University of California Press.
Madsen, William
　1960　*The Virgin's Children: Life in an Aztec Village Today*. Austin: University of Texas Press.
　1967　Religious Syncretism. In *Handbook of Middle American Indians*, 6. Austin: University of Texas Press.
Magoffin, Susan S.
　1926　*Down the Santa Fé Trail and into Mexico*. Ed. Stella M. Drumm. New Haven: Yale University Press.
Mâle, E.
　1978　*Religious Art in France. The Twelfth Century. A Study of the Origins of Medieval Iconography*. Bollingen series XC 1. Princeton: Princeton University Press.
Malinowski, Bronislaw
　1922　*Argonauts of the Western Pacific*. New York: E. P. Dutton.
　1944　*A Scientific Theory of Culture and Other Essays*. Chapel Hill: University of North Carolina Press.
Manfredi, D.
　1954　*Santuarios de la Virgen en España y America*. Madrid: Editorial Edisa.
Manrique, Nelson
　1981　*Las Guerrillas Indígenas en la Guerra con Chile*. Lima: Centro de Investigaciones y Capacitación, Editora Ital Perú.
Maquet, Jacques
　1979　*Introduction to Aesthetic Anthropology*. 2d rev. ed. Malibu, Calif.: Undena.
Maranhão de Souza, Liêdo
　1976　*Classificaçao Popular da Literatura de Cordel*. Petrópolis: Vozes.
Margolies, Luisa, and Maria Matilde Suarez
　1976　Promises and Pilgrimages: Religious Devotion to José Gregorio Hernandez in Venezuela. *Actas y Memorias del XLI Congreso Internacional de Americanistas* Vol. 6, pp. 100-110. Mexico.
Marion Singer, M.

1984 *El Movimiento Campesino en Chiapas. 1983.* Mexico: Centro de Estudios del Agrarismo en Mexico.

Mariscotti de Görlitz, Ana Maria

1978 *Pachamam Santa Tierra. Contribucion al Estudio de la Religion Autoctona en los Andes centro-Meridionales.* Indiana, Beiheft 8. Ibero-Amerikanisches Institut, Preussischer Kulturbesitz. Berlin: Gebr. Mann.

Martinez de Compañon, Baltasar J.

1936 *El Trujillo del Peru* (1797). Ed. J. Dominguez Bordona. Madrid: Biblioteca de Palacio.

Martínez Marín, Carlos

1972 Santuarios y peregrinaciones en el México prehispánico. In *Religión en Mesoamerica*, XII Mesa Redonda, pp. 161-179. Mexico: Sociedad Mexicana de Antropología.

Marzal, Manuel M.

1971 *El Mundo Religioso de Urcos.* Cuzco: Instituto de Pastoral Andina.

1977 El Sistema Religioso del Campesino Bajopiurano. In *Estudios sobre Religion Campesina*, pp. 215-302. Lima: Pontificia Universidad Catolica del Peru.

1983 *La transformación religiosa Peruana.* Lima: Pontificia Universidad Catolica del Perú.

Mason, J. Alden

1926 Dr. Farabee's Last Journey. *Museum Journal* 17(2):128-165.

Mata Amado, Guillermo

1964 Apuntes arqueologicos sobre el lago de Amatitlán. *Antropología e Historia de Guatemala* 16(1):63-77.

Matos Mendieta, Ramiro

1980 Las culturas regionales tempranas. In Juan Mejía Baca, ed., *Historia del Perú* 1:353-524. Lima: Editorial Juan Mejía Baca.

Maudsley, A. C., and A. P. Maudsley

1899 *A Glimpse at Guatemala.* London.

McNeill, William H.

1986 *Mythhistory and Other Essays.* Chicago: University of Chicago Press.

Mecham, J. Lloyd

1934 *Church and State in Latin America: A History of Politico-Ecclesiastical Relations.* Chapel Hill: University of North Carolina Press.

Medina Villegas, H.

1971 *Monografía de Ntra. Sra. de la Soledad y Album del Cincuentenario de su coronación, Oaxaca.* México: Editorial Progreso, S.A.

Méndez-Domínguez, Alfredo

1975 Big and Little Traditions in Guatemalan Anthropology. *Current*

Anthropology 16:541-546.

Mendizabal, Miguel Othon de
1925 El Sanctuario de Chalma. In *Anales*, Epoca LV, III, pp. 93-103. Mexico: Museo Nacional de Arqueología, Historia y Etnografía.

Messerschmidt, Donald A., and Jyoti Sharma
1982 Hindu pilgrimage in the Nepal Himalayas. *Current Anthropology* 22:571-72.

Mexican Government Tourism Department
1968 *Fiestas in Mexico*. Mexico.

Meyer, Jean
1963 *La Cristiada*. Vol. 1. Mexico: Siglo Ventiuno.

Meza, Saul Peredo
1973 *La Merced basilica y convento*. Lima: Juan Barea.

Miles, Carlota
1962 *Almada of Alamos: The Diary of Don Bartolome*. Tucson: Arizona Silhouettes.

Miles, Susan W.
1957 The Sixteenth-Century Pokom-Maya: A Documentary Analysis of Social Structure and Archeological Setting. *Transactions of the American Philosophical Society* 47:731-781.

Mintz, Jerome R.
1982 *The Anarchists of Casas Viejas*. Chicago: University of Chicago Press.

Mitchell, William P.
1976 Irrigation and community in the central Peruvian highlands. *American Anthropologist* 78:25-44.

Molina "El Cusqueño", Cristóbal de
1943 *Fábulas y Ritos de los Incas* (1575). Buenos Aires: Editorial Futuro. Also reprinted in 1916.

Moorhead, Max L.
1968 *The Apache Frontier: Jacobo Ugarte and Spanish-Indian Relations in Northern New Spain, 1769-1791*. Norman: University of Oklahoma Press.

Morely, Sylvanus G., and George W. Brainerd
1956 *The Ancient Maya*. 3d. Ed. Stanford: Stanford University Press.

Moreno, Segundo Luís
1972 *Historia de la Música en El Ecuador*. Quito: Editorial Casa de la Cultura Ecuatoriana.

Morinis, E. Alan
1984 *Pilgrimage in the Hindu Tradition*. New Delhi: Oxford University Press.

Mörner, Magnus
1978 Perfil de la sociedad Rural del Cuzco a fines de la Colonia. Lima: Universidad del Pacífico.

Morote Best, E.

1958 Un nuevo mito de fundación del Imperio. *Revista del Instituto Americano del Arte* VIII:38-58.

Morúa, Martín de

1922 Orígen de los Reyes del Gran Reino del Perú (1590). Ed. H. H. Urteaga. Lima: Colección de Libros y documentos referentes a la Historia del Peru, T.IV (2a série).

Moss, L. W., and S. Cappannari

1982 In Quest of the Black Virgin: She is Black Because She is Black. In J. J. Preston, ed., *Mother worship: Theme and Variations*, pp. 53-74. Chapel Hill: University of North Carolina Press.

Motupe

1979-88 *La Voz de Motupe Hacia Una Nueva Provincia*. Motupe.

Mould, D. D. C.

1955 *Irish Pilgrimage*. Dublin: H. M. Gill and Son.

Müller, Thomas

1980 El Taytacha de Qoyllur Rit'i. *Pastoral Andina* 32:51-66.

Multivoz

1980-81 *Multivoz*: Organo de la Comision Multisectorial "Cruz de Chalpon." Nos. 25, 26, Años V and VII. Motupe.

Murra, John Victor

1972 El "Control Vertical" de un maximo de pisos ecologicos en la economia de la sociedades andinas. In *Visita de la Provincia de Leon de Huanuco en 1562*. Inigo Ortiz de Zuniga, visitador, Vol. II, pp. 427-476. Huanuco, Peru: Universidad Nacional Hermilio Valdizan.

Nash, June

1970 The Change of Officials in Tzóontahal, Chiapas, Mexico. *Middle American Research Institute Publication* No.24, pp. 207-248. New Orleans: Tulane University.

Nava Rodriguez, L.

1975 *Historia de Nuestra Señora de Ocotlan su aparición milagrosa y su culto a traves de los tiempos*. México: La Prensa.

Needham, Rodney

1975 Polythetic Classification: Convergence and Consequences. *Man* n.s., 10:349-369.

Neumann, E.

1972 *The Great Mother*. Princeton: Princeton University Press.

Nicholson, Henry B.

1971 Religion in Pre-Hispanic Central Mexico. In *Handbook of Middle American Indians*, 10, pp. 395-446. Austin: University of Texas Press.

Nolan, Mary L.

1967 Aspects of Middle Class Family Organization in Monterrey, Mexico. M.A. thesis. University of Texas at Austin.

1972 The Towns of the Volcano: A Study of the Human Consequences of the Eruption of Paricutin Volcano. Diss. Texas A&M University.

1973   The Mexican Pilgrimage Tradition. *Pioneer America* 5(2):13-27.

1978 Pilgrimage Traditions and Perception of Hazard in Europe. Paper presented at the 74th annual meeting of the Association of American Geographers. New Orleans, April 9-12.

1979 A Time to Make Pilgrimage: Seasonality of Religious Travel in Europe. Paper presented at the 75th annual meeting of the Association of American Geographers. Philadelphia, April 23-26.

1983   Irish Pilgrimage: The Different Tradition. *Annals of the Association of American Geographers* 73(3):421-438.

1984 *Communities: The Northern Shore of the Mediterranean*, pp. 239-266. New York: Mouton Publishers.

1985   Apparitions in Western Europe. *Geography of Religions and Belief Systems* 7(1):2, 7-8.

1986   Pilgrimage Traditions and the Nature Mystique in Western European Culture. *Journal of Cultural Geography* , 7(1):5-20.

1987a A Profile of Christian Pilgrimage Shrines in Western Europe. *National Geographic Journal of India* , 33(3):229-238.

1987b Christian Pilgrimage Shrines in Western Europe and India: A Preliminary Comparison. *National Geographic Journal of India*, 33(4):370-378.

1987c Roman Catholic Pilgrimage in the New World. In Mircea Eliade, ed., *The Encyclopedia of Religion*, vol. 11, pp. 332-335. New York: Macmillan.

1987d Tapping and Defining New Power: The First Month of Visions at Ezquioga. *American Ethnologist* 14:140-166.

1988 Pilgrimage and Perception of Hazard in Western Europe. In S. M. Bhardwaj and G. Rinschede, eds., *Pilgrimage in World Religions*. Geographia Religionum 4:41-64. Berlin: Dietrich Reimer.

Nolan, Mary L., and Sidney Nolan

1988 The Evolution of Tourism in Modern Mexico. *Journal of the West*, 27(4):14-25.

1989 *Christian Pilgrimage in Modern Western Europe*. Chapel Hill: University of North Carolina Press.

Nunes Batista, Sebastião

1977   *Antologia da Literatura de Cordel*. Natal: Fundação José Augusto.

Nuñez del Prado, O.

1973   Versión del mito del Inkarrí en Q'eros. In Juan Ossio, ed., *Ideología mesiánica del mundo andino*, pp. 275-80. Lima: Edicion de Ignacio Prado Pastor.

Oakes, Maud

1951 *The Two Crosses of Todos Santos: Survivals of Mayan Religious Rituals*. New York: Bollingen Foundation.

Oblitas Poblete, Enrique

1963 *Cultura Calawaya*. La Paz: Talleres Gráficos Bolivianos.

Ochoa, L.
1979 Historia Prehispánica de la Huaxteca. Mexico: Universidad Nacional Autonoma de Mexico.
Ochoa, V. A.
1961 *Breve historia de Nuestra Señora de Zapopan.* Zapopan, México.
Ojeda Sanchez, José de Jesus
1973 *Tabor Mexicano: historia minimal del monumento votivo nacional a Cristo Rey.* Leon, México.
Oliveira, Pedro A. Ribeiro.
1980 *Expressõs Religiosas Populares e Liturgia.* Rio de Janeiro: Centro de Estatística Religiosa e Investigações Sociais.
Oliveira, Severino Gonçalves de
n.d. A Moça que Virou Cobra. n.p.
ONEC
1974 *Censos Nacionales.* Lima: Oficina Nacional de Estadistica y Censos (ONEC).
Ong, Walter J.
1975 The Writer's Audience Is Always a Fiction. *PMLA* 90.
Oricaín, Pablo José
1790/1906 Compendio breve de discursos varios sobre diferentes materias y noticias geográficas comprehensivas a este Obispado del Cuzco que claman remedios espirituales. In Víctor Maurtua, ed., *Juicio de Límites entre el Perú y Bolivia*, Vol. XI. Barcelona.
Orlove, Benjamin S.
1978 Some Interactions of Production Scale, Natural Environments, and Socio-economic Impacts on Food Production Strategies in Latin America. Paper presented at the Annual Meeting of the American Association for the Advancement of Science. Washington, D.C., February 1978.
Osborne, Lilly de Jongh
1959 Folk-lore Guatemalteco. Actas del XXXIII Congreso Internacional de Americanistas. San José, Costa Rica. July 20-27, 1958.
Ossio, Juan
1973 *Ideología mesiánica del mundo andino.* Lima: Edicion de Ignacio Prado Pastor.
Osvaldo, Urbano H.
1974 La representacion andina del tiempo y del espacio en la fiesta. *Allpanchis* 7:9-48. Cuzco: Instituto de Pastoral Andina.
Oursel, Raymond
1963 *Les pèlerins du Moyen Age.* Paris.
Pachacuti Yamqui, Joan de Santa Cruz
1950 Relación de Antigüedades deste Reyno del Piru (1613). In Marco Jiménez de la Espada, ed., *Tres Relaciones*, pp. 207-281. Asunción: Editorial Guaraní.
Palacios, H.

1980   *Nuestra Señora de Lujan.* Buenos Aires: Talleres Graficos San Francisco.

Palomino Flores, Salvador

1968   La cruz en los andes. *Amaru* 8:63-66. Lima.

Palomino, Salvador

1984   *El Sistema de oposiciones en la comunidad de Sarhua: La complementaridad de los opuestos en la cultura andina.* Lima: Pueblo Indio.

Paredes Candia, Antonio

1966   *La Danza Folklórica en Bolivia.* La Paz: Ediciones Isla.

Paredes Candia, Antonio

1974   *Antología de tradiciones y leyendas Bolivianas.* La Paz: Editorial Los Amigos del Libro.

Pasini, Carlos, and Michael J. Sallnow

1974   *The Quechua.* Manchester, UK: Granada Television. Film.

Paz, Octavio

1961   *The Labyrinth of Solitude: Life and Thought in Mexico.* New York: Grove Press.

Paz Soldan, E.

1985   *Historia del Santuario de Chapi en Arequipa.* Arequipa, Perú.

Pedro Pontual, José

n.d.a O Crente que Profanou do Frei Damião. n.p.

n.d.b *O Crente que Profanou do Padre Cícero.* Recife: Edson Pinto.

Pélach y Feliu, E.

1972   *Nuestra Señora de Cocharcas.* Abancay, Perú.

Pereira dos Santos, Sebastião

n.d.   O Monstro que Raptava Moças e os Milagres do Padre Cícero. n.p.

Pérez, Gustavo, and Alfonso Gregory, and Francois Lepargneur

1965   *O Problema Sacerdotal No Brasil.* Estudios Socio-Religiosos Latino-Americanos 17. Rio de Janeiro: CERIS.

Pérez Martin del Campo, R.

1969   *Camino de San Juan Nuevo: un reportaje de las peregrinaciones al santuario de Señor de los Milagros.* México.

Pérez Ramírez, Gustavo, and Yvan Laballa

1964   *El Problema Sacerdotal en America Latina.* Estudios Socio-Religiosos Latino-Americanos 16. Bogotá: Central de Investigaciones.

Pfaffenberger, Bryan

1979   The Kataragama Pilgrimage: Hindu-Buddhist Interaction and Its Significance in Sri Lanka's Polyethnic Social System. *Journal of Asian Studies* 38(2):253-270.

Pitt-Rivers, Julian

1967   Words and Deeds: The Ladinos of Chiapas. *Man* n.s., 2:71-86.

1973   Race in Latin America: The Concept of "Raza." *Archives Europe'enes de Sociologie* 14:3-31.

Pizarro, Pedro

1938 Relación del descubrimiento y conquista de los reinos del Perú (1571). In H. Urteaga, ed., *Los Cronistas de la Conquista*, pp. 265-305. Biblioteca de Cultura Peruana Primera Serie, No. 2. Paris.

1978 *Relación del Descubrimiento y Conquista de los Reinos del Perú*. Lima: Pontificia Universidad Católica del Perú.

Platt, Tristan

1978 Symetries en miroir. Le concept de yanatin chez les Macha de Bolivie. *Annales E.S.C.* V-VI (September-December):1081-1197.

1986 Mirrors and Maize: The Concept of *Yanantin* among Macha of Bolivia. In John V. Murra, Nathan Wachtel, and Jacques Revel, eds., *Anthropological History of Andean Polities*. Cambridge: Cambridge University Press.

Polaco Brito, H. E.

1979 *María de Altagracia y Juan Pablo II*. Santo Domingo.

1984 *Exvotos y "milagros" del Santuario de Hiquey*. Santo Domingo: Ediciones Banco Central.

Pollak-Eltz, Angelina

1972 *Maria Lionza, mito y culto venezolano*. Caracas: U.C.A.B.

1987 Las Animas Milagrosas. *Montalban* 19.

Poole, Deborah A.

1982 Los Santuarios religiosos en la economía regional andina. *Allpanchis* 19:79-116. Cuzco.

1988 Entre el milagro y la mercancía: Qoyllur Rit'i, 1987. *Margenes* 2(4):101-50.

1990a Time and Devotion in Andean Ritual Dance. In R. Thiercelin, ed., *Mélanges offerts a Pierre Duviols*, in press. Aix-en-Provence: Department d'Etudes Latino-Américaines, Université de Provence.

1990b Accommodation and Resistance in Andean Ritual Dance. *TDR* 34(2,T126):98-126 (The Drama Review).

n.d. Intercambio económico y la frontera con lo foráneo: Generación de la riqieza y de la pobreza en la religion del campesinado sur-andino. Paper presented in the colloquium, Méxique-Péou: Identité et idéologies. Quebec: Université Laval, April 8-10, 1982.

Portugal, Maks, and Dick Edgar Ibarra Grasso

1957 *Copacabana. El Santuario y la Arqueologia de la Peninsula e Islas del Sol y la Luna*. Cochabamba: Editorial "Atlantic."

Pötzl, W.

1984 Santa-Casa-Kult in Loreto und in Bayern. In L. Kriss-Rettenbeck and G. Mohler, eds., *Wallfahrt kennt keine Grenzen*, pp. 368-382. Munich: Schnell & Steiner.

Presas, J. A.

1961 *Nuestra Señora del Buen Viaje: resena historica*. Moran, Argentina.

Queiroz, Maria Isaura Pereira de

1965 *O Messianismo no Brasil e no Mundo*. São Paulo: Dominus

Editora.

Radcliffe-Brown, A. R.

1933 *The Andaman Islanders*. New York: Free Press.

Ramirez, A.

1968 *Apuntes historicos sobre el Sr. de la Misericordia y su culto*. Guadalajara: Talleres Vera.

Ramírez E., Juan Andrés

1969 La Novena al Señor de Qoyllur Rit'i. *Allpanchis* I:61-88 (Cuzco).

Ramos, Rutilio, Isidoro Alonso, and Domingo Garre

1962 *La Iglesia en Mexico*. Estudios Socio-Religiosos Latino-Americanos 7. Madrid: OCSH.

Ramos Gavilan, Alonso

1976 *Historia de Nuestra Senora de Copacabana* (1621). Academia Boliviana de la Historia. La Paz: Empresa Editora Universo.

Randall, Robert

1982a Qoyllur Rit'i', An Inca Fiesta of the Pleiades; Reflections on Time and Space in the Andean World. *Bulletin de l'Institut Français des Etudes Andines* 11(1-2):37-81. Lima.

1982b Peru's pilgrimage in the sky. *National Geographic* 162(1):60-69.

Raphael, Freddy

1973 Le pèlerinage. Approche sociologique. In *Les pèlerinages de l'antiquité biblique et classique à l'Occident medieval*, pp. 11-30. Paris.

Rappaport, R. A.

1979 *Ecology, Meaning, and Religion*. Richmond: North Atlantic Books.

Reed, Nelson

1964 *The Caste War of Yucatan*. Stanford: Stanford University Press.

Reina, Ruben E.

1966 *The Law of the Saints*. Indianapolis: Bobbs-Merrill.

1969 Eastern Guatemalan Highlands: the Pokomames and Chortí. In *Handbook of Middle American Indians*, Vol. 7, pp. 101-132. Austin: University of Texas Press.

Remesal, Fr. A. de

1964 *Historia General de las Indias Occidentales y Particular de la Gobernacion de Chiapa y Guatemala*. Biblioteca de Autores Espanoles, Vol.175. Madrid: Ediciones Atlas.

Ribeiro Filho, A.

1977 *Historia de Nossa Senhora do Rocio*. Curitiba, Brazil: Grafica Vincentina.

Ricoeur, Paul

1971 What Is a Text? Explanation and Interpretation. In David M. Rasmussen, ed., *Mythic-Symbolic Language and Philosophical Anthropology: A Constructive Interpretation of the thought of Paul Ricoeur*. The Hague: Martinus Nijoff.

Rivero, Mariano Edward, and John James von Tschudi

1971 *Peruvian Antiquities* (1854). New York: A. S. Barnes & Company. Reprinted by Kraus Reprint Co., New York.

Roca, Paul M.
1967 *Paths of the Padres through Sonora.* Tucson: Arizona Pioneers' Historical Society.

Rodriguez Suy Suy, Victor Antonio
1975 La medicina traditional en la costa norte del Peru actual. In *Chimor. Una Antologia Sobre El Valle de Chicama.* Instituto Indigenista Inter-Americano, Ediciones Especiales, No. 73, pp. 161-186. Mexico: Edimex.

Roel Pineda, Josefat
1950 La danza de los 'c'uncos' de Paucartambo. *Tradición* (Cuzco) 1:59-70.

Roel Pineda, Josefat
1959 El Wayno del Cuzco. *Folklore Américano*, Año VI(6)/Año 7(7):130-246.

Romero Quiroz, Javier
1957 *Tezcatlipoca es el Oztoteotl de Chalma.* Toluca: Gobierno del Estado de Mexico, Dirección de Turismo.

Rosa y López, Simón de la
1904 *Los Seises de la Catedral de Sevilla.* Seville.

Rosaldo, Renato
1968 Metaphors of Hierarchy in Mayan Ritual. *American Anthropologist* 70:524-536.

Rossenegger, J., and E. Bartl
1980 *Wallfahrten in und um München.* Munich: Pannonia.

Rostworowski de Diez Canseco, María
1977 Etnia y Sociedad. Lima: Institute de Estudios Peruanos.

Rothkrug, L.
1979 Popular Religion and Holy Shrines. In J. Obelkevich, ed., *Religion and the People, 800-1700*, pp. 20-86. Chapel Hill: University of North Carolina Press.
1980 Religious Practices and Collective Perceptions: Hidden Homologies in the Renaissance and Reformation. *Historical Reflections*, pp. 1-254.

Roussel, Romain
1955 *Les pèlerinages.* Paris.

Rowe, John H.
1963 Urban Settlements in Ancient Peru. *Nawpa Pacha* 1:1-27.

Royce, Anya Peterson
1977 *The Anthropology of Dance.* Bloomington: Indiana University Press.

Roys, Ralph. L.
1957 *The Political Geography of the Yucatan Maya.* Carnegie Institution of Washington, Publication No. 613. Washington, D.C.

1967 *The Book of the Chilam Balam of Chumayel*. Norman: University of Oklahoma Press.

Ruxton, George F.
1847 *Adventures in Mexico and the Rocky Mountains*. London: John Murray.

Ruz Lhuillier, A.
1964 Aristocracia o democracia entre los antiguos Mayas? *Anales de Antropologia* 1:63-75.

Sabogal Dieguez, José
1956 *El Desven de la Imagineria Peruana* Lima, Peru: Juan Mejia Baca and P. L. Villanueva.

Sallnow, Michael J.
1974 La pergrinación andina. *Allpanchis* 7:101-142. Cuzco: Instituto de Pastoral Andina.
1981 Communitas Reconsidered: The Sociology of Andean Pilgrimage. *Man* n.s., 16:163-82.
1982 A Trinity of Christs: Cultic Processes in Andean Catholicism. *American Ethnologist* 9(4):730-749.
1987 *Pilgrims of the Andes*. Washington, D.C.: Smithsonian Institute Press.
1990 *Contesting the Sacred: The Anthropology of Christian Pilgrimage*. London: Routledge.

Salomon, Frank L.
1981 Killing the Yumbo: A Ritual Drama of Northern Quito. In N. Whitten, ed., *Cultural Transformations and Ethnicity in Modern Ecuador*, pp.162-208. Urbana: University of Illinois Press.

Sánchez-Arjona Halcón, Rodrigo
1981 *La Riliqiosidad Popular Católica en el Perú*. Lima: Seminario Conciliar de Santo Toribio.

Sánchez Pérez, José Augusto
1943 *El Culto Mariano en España*. Madrid: Sucs. de S. Ocana y Cía.

Santillán, Ledo. Fernando de
1950 Relación del orígen, descendencia política y gobierno de los Incas (1553). In Marcos Jimenez de la Espada, ed., *Tres Relaciones Peruanas*, pp. 33-131. Asunción, Paraguay: Editora Guarania.

Sapia Martino, Raul
1963 *Guatemala. Mayaland of Eternal Spring*. 3d illus.-ed., Spanish-English. Guatemala: Tipografía America-Editorial José de Pineda Ibarra.

Sarmiento de Gamboa, Pedro
1960 *Historia de los Incas* (1572). Madrid: Biblioteca de Autores Espanoles.

Schaedel, Richard P.
1952 La representación de la muerte del Inca Atahualpa en la fiesta de la Virgen de la Puerta en Otuzco. *Cultura Peruanua* II(53).

1988 La Etnografía Muchik en las Fotografías de H. Brüning, 1886-1925. Lima, Peru: COFIDE.

Schaffer, G., and G. Peda
1978 *Wallfahrten im Passauerland*. Munich: Pannonia.

Schecter, John M.
1979 The Inca Cantar Histórico: A Lexico-Historical Elaboration on Two Culture Themes. *Ethnomusicology* XXII(2):191-204.

Schmalenbach, Herman
1965 The Sociological Category of Communion. In Parsons, Talcott et al., eds., *Theories of Society*, pp. 331-347. New York: Free Press.

Schryer, Frans J.
1979 The Role of the Rancheros of Central Mexico in the Mexican Revolution. *Canadian Review of Latin American Studies* 4(7):21-41.
1990 *Ethnicity and Class Conflict in Rural Mexico*. Princeton: Princeton University Press.

Serracino Calamata, G.
n.d. *Ayquina historia y festividad de Santuario de Nuestra Señora Guadalupe de Ayquina*. Calama: Impreso en Siel.

Shadow, Robert, and María J. Rodríguez V.
1990 Símbolos que amarran, símbolos que dividen: hegemonía e impugnación en una peregrinación campesina a Chalma. *Mesoamérica* 19:33-72.

Sharbrough, S.
1977 The Cult of the Mother in Europe: The Transformation of the Symbolism of Women. Diss. University of California, Los Angeles.

Sharon, Douglas
1978 The Return to Origins in North Peruvian and Huichol Pilgrimages. In *Actes du XLIIᵉ Congrés International des Américanistes*, V. IV, pp. 397-403. Paris: Musée de 'Homme.

Shimada, Izumi
1979 Behind the Golden Mask: The Research Problems and Preliminary Results of the Batan Grande-La Leche Valley Archaeological Project. Manuscript. Department of Anthropology, Princeton University.
1981a The Batan Grande-La Leche Archaeological Project: The First Two Seasons. *Journal of Field Archaeology* 8(4):405-446.
1981b Batan Grande and Ideological Unity in the Central Andes. Paper presented at the 4th Andean Archaeology Colloquium. Austin, Texas.

Silva, José Bernardo da
n.d. *O Nascimento Misterioso de Padrinho Cícero*. Juazeiro do Norte: Tipografia São Francisco.

Silveira, Ildefonso
1976 Estado Atual da Pesquisa sobre o Padre Cícero. *Revista Eclesiástica Brasileira* 36.

Silverman, Helaine

1983   Informe Final del Estudio de Factibilidad Realizado en la Zona de Nazca, Costa Sur del Perú. Lima, Peru: Instituto Nacional de Cultura.

1986   Cahuachi: An Andean Ceremonial Center. Diss. Department of Anthropolgy, University of Texas at Austin.

Silverman, Helaine, and Miguel Pazos
n.d.   Asiento: un asentamiento nasca en la frontera del territorio nasca. Manuscript.

Sivirichi, Atilo
1930   *Pre-Historia Peruana*. Lima, Peru: Editorial La Revista.

Skar, Harald
1982   *The Warm Valley People: Duality and Land Reform among the Quechua Indians of Peru*. Oslo Studies in Social Anthropology, no. 2. Oslo: Universitetsforlaget.

1985   Communitas and Schismogenesis: The Andean Pilgrimage Reconsidered. *Ethnos* 50:88-102.

1982   *Stories on a String: The Brazilian Literatura de Cordel*. Berkeley: University of California Press.

1983   Oral and Written Pilgrims' Tales from Northeast Brazil. *Journal of Folklore Research* 9(2):191-230.

1984a   Representations of Power in Northeast Brazilian Pilgrims' Tales. *Latin American Research Review* 19(2):71-91.

1984b   Afirmações Pessoais. A Presença individual nas Histórias de Padre Cícero. *Religião e Sociedade* 11(2):20-35.

1990   *City Steeple, City Streets. Saints' Tales from Granada and a Changing Spain*. Berkeley and Los Angeles: University of California Press.

Smith, M. C.
1979   Esquipulas. *Americas* 31:26-31.

Smith, Robert J.
1975   *The Art of the Festival*. University of Kansas Publications in Anthropology 6. Lawrence: University of Kansas Publications.

Smith, Waldemar
1975   Beyond the Plural Society: Economics and Ethnicity in Middle American Towns. *Ethnology* 14:225-243.

Solorzano, F. V.
1970   *Evolución Economica de Guatemala*. Seminario de Integración Social, Publicación Numero 28. Guatemala: Editorial José de Pineda Ibarra.

Sopher, David E.
1980   The Message of Place: Addendum to a Geography of Indian Pilgrimage. Seminar on Pilgrimage as Communication. Southern Asia Institute, Columbia University, April.

Soustelle, Jacques
1937   *La famille Otomi-Pame de Mexique central*. Travaux et Mémoires,

no. 26. Paris: Institut d'Etnologie.

1961   *Daily Life of the Aztecs on the Eve of the Spanish Conquest.* Stanford: Stanford University Press.

Souto Maior, Mário

1970   Antônio Silvino no Romanceiro do Cordel. *Revista Brasileira de Folclore* 10:35-42.

Souza, Antonio Caetano

n.d.   *A Moça de Cajazeiras.* Juazeiro do Norte: Tipografia São Francisco.

Souza, Liêdo Maranhão de

1976   *Classificação Popular de Literatura de Cordel.* Petrópolis: Vozes.

Spicer, Edward H.

1952   Reluctant Cotton Pickers. In E. H. Spicer, ed., *Human Problems in Technological Change.* New York: Russell Sage Foundation.

1954   *Potam: A Yaqui Village in Sonora.* Menasha: American Anthropological Association, Memoir 77.

1961   The Yaqui. In E. H. Spicer, ed., *Perspectives in American Indian Culture Change.* Chicago: University of Chicago Press.

1962   *Cycles of Conquest: The Impact of Spain, Mexico and the United States on the Indians of the Southwest, 1533-1960.* Tucson: University of Arizona Press.

1980   *The Yaquis: A Culture History.* Tucson: University of Arizona Press.

Spitzer, Allen

1958   Notes on a Merida Parish. *Anthropological Quarterly* 31:1.

Spores, R.

1967   *The Mixtec Kings and Their People.* Norman: University of Oklahoma Press.

1973   The Zapotecs and Mixtec at Spanish Conquest. In Robert Wauchope, ed., *Handbook of Middle American Indians*, Vol. 3, pp. 962-987. Austin: University of Texas Press.

Squire, George E.

1877   *Incidents of Travel and Exploration in the Land of the Incas.* London.

Staehlin, Carlos Maria

1954   Apariciones: Ensayo Critico. Madrid: Editorial "Razon y Fe."

Staercke, A. E. de

1954   *Notre-Dame des Belges: traditions et folklore du culte Marial en Belgique.* Brussels.

Stagg, Albert

1976   *The First Bishop of Sonora: Antonio de los Reyes, O. F. M.* Tucson: University of Arizona Press.

Stanner, W. E. H.

1967   Reflections on Durkheim and Aboriginal Religion. In Maurice Freedman, ed., *Social Organization*, pp. 217-240. London: Frank

Cass and Co.

Stein, William W.

1961 *Hualcan: Life in the Highlands of Peru.* Cornell University Press.

Stephens, John L.

1969 *Incidents of Travel in Central America, Chiapas and Yucatán.* New York, N.,Y.: Dover Publications, Inc. (Originally published in 1841 by Harper & Brothers in two volumes.)

Stoddard, Robert

1988 Spatial and Environmental Relationships Associated with Major Pilgrimage Places of the World. Paper presented at the Interdisciplinary Symposium on Religion and Environment, Eichstatt, West Germany, May.

Straub, Leslie Ellen

1985 La romería como modelo de la peregrinación en las tradiciones centroamericanas. *Mesoamérica* 6:104-132.

1989 "La Patrona, su santuario nacional y la ciudad de Cartago." In Carlos Alvarez Santaló, María Jesús Buxó i Rei, and Salvador Rodríguez Becerra, *La Religiosidad popular. Hermandades, romerías y santuarios* 3:253-268. Autores, Textos y Temas. Antropología. Barcelona and Seville: Editorial Anthropología in association with Fundación Machado.

n.d. The Prism of Pilgrimage in Costa Rica. Manuscript in progress.

Strickton, Arnold, and Sidney Greenfield

1972 *Structure and Process in Latin America: Patronage, Clientage and Power Systems.* Albuquerque: University of New Mexico Press.

Strong, William Duncan

1957 Paracas, Nazca, and Tiahuanacoid Cultural Relationships in South Coastal Peru. *American Antiquity* 22(4):part 2. Memoir 13 of the Society for American Archaeology.

Suassuna, Ariano

1974 Notas sobre o Romanceiro Popular do Nordeste. In *Seleta em Prosa e Verso de Ariano Suassuna*, pp.162-190. Rio de Janeiro: José Olympio INL/MEC.

Sumption, Jonathan

1975 *Pilgrimage. An Image of Mediaeval Religion.* Totowa, N.J.: Rowman and Littlefield.

Sur (Boletin informativo agrario)

n.d. (1982) Cuzco: Centro de Estudios Rurales Andinos "Bartolomé de las Casa."

Tambiah, S. J.

1978 *Buddhism and the Spirit Cults in Northeastern Thailand.* Cambridge: Cambridge University Press.

Tanaka, Hiroshi

1988 On the Geographic Study of Pilgrimage Places. In S. M. Bhardwaj and G. Rindschede, eds., *Pilgrimage in World Religions.*

Geographia Religionum 4:21-40. Berlin: Dietrich Reimer.

Tax, Sol
1953 World View and Social Relations in Guatemala. In Olen, Leonard E. and Charles P. Loomis, eds., *Readings in Latin American Social Organization and Institutions*. East Lansing: Michigan State University Press.

Tax, Sol, and Robert Hinshaw
1970 Panajachel a Generation Later. In W. Goldschmidt and Harry Hoijer, eds., *The Social Anthropology of Latin America*. Los Angeles: University of California Latin American Center.

Taylor, J. W.
1979 Tree Worship. *Mankind Quarterly* 20:79-141.

Tello, Julio Cesar
1943 Arreglo y presentacion de las ruinas de Pachacamac. In *Memoria de la Junta Departamental de Lima pro-Desocupados, 1939, 1949 y 1941*. Empresa Grafica Grafica, T. Scheuch S.A.

Tello, Julio Cesar, and Toribio Mejía Xesspe
1967 Historia de los Museos Nacionales del Perú, 1822-1946. *Arqueológicas* 10. Lima.

Thompson, Donald E.
1954 Maya Paganism and Christianity: A History of the Fusion of Two Religions. *Middle American Research Institute*, Nativism and Syncretism Pub. 19, pp. 1-36. New Orleans: Tulane University. Issued 1954, Pub. 19 published in 1960.

Thompson, J. Eric S.
1934 Sky Bearers, Colors and Directions in Maya and Mexican Religion. Washington: Carnegie Institution of Washington Pub. 436.
1939 The Moon Goddess in Middle America, with Notes on Related Dieties. Washington: Carnegie Institution of Washington Pub. 509.
1964 Trade Relations between the Maya Highlands and Lowlands. *Estudios de Cultura Maya* 4:13-48.
1970 *Maya History and Religion*. Norman: University of Oklahoma Press.

Tonna, H.
1983 *Virgen de los Treinta y Tres*. Florida, Uruguay: Gadi.

Toor, F.
1947 *A Treasury of Mexican Folkways*. New York: Crown.

Tord, Javier, and Carlos Lazo
1980 Economía y Sociedad en el Perú Colonial. In *Historia del Perú*, T.5, pp.9-330. Lima: Mejia Baca.

Tubach, Fredric C.
1969 *Index Exemplorum*. Folklore Society Communications, No. 9, 204. Helsinki: Suomalainen Tiedakatemia.

Turner, Victor
1974a *Pilgrimage to Santiago*. London: Secker and Warburg.

1974b *Dramas, Fields and Metaphors: Symbolic Action in Human Society*. Ithaca: Cornell University Press.

1974c *Process, Performance and Pilgrimage: A Study on Comparative Symbology*. New Delhi: Concept Publishing Co.

1975 Death and the Dead in the Pilgrimage Process. In Michael G. Whisson and Martin West, eds., *Religion and Social Change in Southern Africa. Anthropological Essays in Honour of Monica Wilson*. Cape Town: David Philip; London: Rex Collins.

Turner, Victor, and Edith Turner

1978 *Image and Pilgrimage in Christian Culture: Anthropological Perspectives*. New York: Columbia University Press.

Uhle, Max

1903 *Pachacamac*. Philadelphia: University of Pennsylvania Press.

Urbano, Henrique O.

1974 Le temps et l'espace chez les paysans des Andes péruviennes. In *Bulletin de l'Institut français des études andines*, III, pp. 31-50. Lima.

1980 Dios Yaya, Dios Churi, Dios Espíritu. Modelos trinitarios y arqueología mental en los Andes. In *Journal of Latin American Lore* 6(I):111-127.

1981 *Wiracocha y Ayar. Héroes y funciones en las sociedades andinas*. Cuzco, Peru.

1982a Representaciones colectivas y arqueologia mental en los Andes. In *Allpanchis* XX: 33-84.

Urbano, Henrique O., and S. Salazar Segovia

1982b Notas etnográficas de Maras, Catca y Toqto Waylla (1972-1974). *SUR* July, pp. 51-53. Cuzco, Peru.

Urteaga, Horacio H.

1914 *Bocetos Históricos. Estudios Arqueológicos, tradicionales é Histórico-Críticos*. Lima: E. Rosay.

Urton, Gary

1981 *At the Crossroads of the Earth and Sky. An Andean Cosmology*. Austin: University of Texas Press.

1982 Astronomy and Calendrics on the Coast of Peru. In Anthony F. Aveni and Gary Urton, eds., *Ethnoastronomy and Archaeoastronomy in the American Tropics*, pp. 231-248. New York: New York Academy of Sciences. Annals of the New York Academy of Sciences, v. 385.

1984 Chuta: El Espacio de la práctica social en Paqariqtambo. *Revista Andina* II(1):7-44 (Cuzco).

Valderrama Fernández, Ricardo, and Carmen Escalante Gutiérrez

1975 El Apu Ausangate en la narrativa popular. *Allpanchis* 8:175-84.

Van den Berghe, Pierre L.

1974 The Use of Ethnic Terms in the Peruvian Social Science Literature. *International Journal of Comparative Sociology* 15:134-142.

Van den Berghe, Pierre L., and George P. Primov
   1977 *Inequality in the Andes: Class and Ethnicity in Cuzco*. Columbia: University of Missouri Press.
Van Gennep, Arnold
   1960 *The Rites of Passage*. Chicago: University of Chicago Press. Translated from the French edition, 1908.
Van Kessel, Jan
   1982 Danzas y estructuras sociales de los Andes. Cuzco: Centro de Estudios   Bartolomé de las Casas'.
Vargas, F.
   1976 *La santisima Virgen de San Juan de los Lagos*. San Juan de los Lagos, México.
Vargas Ugarte, R.
   1956 *Historia del culto de María en Iberoamerica y de sus imagenes y santuarios mas celebrados*. Madrid: Talleres Gradicos Jura.
Vazquez de Parga, L., J. M. Lacarra, and J. Uria Riu
   1948-49 *Las peregrinaciones a Santiago de Compostela*. 3 vol. Madrid.
Vicaire, M. H.
   1980 Les trois itinérances du pèlerinage aux XIIIe et XIVe siècles. In *Le pèlerinage*, Privat, ed., pp. 7-10, 17-41. Toulouse.
Vielliard, Jeanne
   1963 *Le guide du pèlerin de Saint-Jacques de Compostelle*. Mâcon.
Villa Rojas, Alfonso
   1945 *The Maya of East Central Quintana Roo*. Washington: Carnegie Institution of Washington Pub. 559.
   1978 *Los Elegidos de Dios: Ethnografía de los Mayas de Quintana Roo*. México: Instituto Nacional Indigenista.
Villasante Ortiz, Segundo
   n.d. *Paucartambo: Provincia Folklórica: Mamacha Carmen (T.I.)*. Cuzco: Editorial Leon.
Vinciotti, A.
   1960 *Imille santuari mariani d'Italia illustrati*. Rome: Associazione Santuari Mariani.
Vogt, Evon Z.
   1969a *Zinacantan: A Maya Community in the Highlands of Chiapas*. Cambridge: Belknap Press.
   1969b The Maya: An Introduction. In *Handbook of Middle American Indians*, vol.7, pp. 21-29. Austin: University of Texas Press.
   1976 *Tortillas for the Gods*. Cambridge: Harvard University Press.
Vreeland, James M., Jr.
   1980a An Examination of the Acllawasi as a Diagnostic Feature of Inca Town Planning. Manuscript. Department of Anthropology, University of Texas, Austin.
Vreeland, James M., Jr.
   1980b *El Algodon y el Arte de Tejer: Un Estudio de la Produccion*

Artesanal del Distrito de Morrope, Departemento de Lambayeque.
Lima: Oficina Tecnica de Formacion Profesional, Ministerio de
Trabajo, and Direccion General de Artesanias, Ministerio de
Industria, Turismo e Integracion.

1981a Gold for the Gods' Graves or Scholars? An Examination of the
Burial and Looting Patterns and the Emergence of Complex Society
at Batan Grande, Peru. Paper presented at the 4th Andean
Archaeology Colloquium. Austin, Texas.

1981b La Cruz de Chalpon: centro de un peregrinaje no usual. *Boletin
de Lima* 10:21-29. Lima: Editorial Los Pinos.

1989 Lambayeque: Estudios Monográficos de Enrigue Brüning, (1922-
1923). Facsimile edition. Monsefú, Peru: Sociedad de Investicación
de la Ciencia, Cultura y Arte Norteño (SICAN), El Horizonte.

Wachtel, Nathan
1971 *La Visión des vainçus: Les Indiens du Pérou devant la Conquête
espagnole.* Paris: Gallimard.

Wagley, Charles
1953 *Amazon Town.* New York: MacMillan.
1968 *The Latin American Tradition*, pp. 155-174. New York: Columbia
University Press.

Wallace, A. F. C.
1966 *Religion: An Anthropological View.* New York: Random House.

Weaver, Muriel P.
1972 *The Aztecs, Maya and Their Predecessors: The Archeology of
Mesoamerica.* New York: Seminar Press.

Weber, David J.
1981 Failure of a Frontier Institution: The Secular Church in the
Borderlands under Independent Mexico, 1821-1846. *Western
Historical Quarterly* XII:2.

Webster, D. L.
1976 On Theocracies. *American Anthropologist* 78:812-823.

Wheatly, Paul
1971 *Pivot of the Four Quarters: A Preliminary Enquiry into the
Origins and Character of the Ancient Chinese City.* Chicago: Aldine.

Wiener, Charles
1880 *Pérou et Bolivie. Récit de Voyage.* Paris: Librairie Hachette et Cie.

Williams, Carlos
1980 Arquitectura y Urbanismo en el Antiguo Perú. In Juan Mejía
Baca, ed., *Historia del Perú*, vol. 8, pp. 369-585. Lima: Editorial
Juan Mejía Baca.

Williams, Carlos, and Miguel Pazos
1974 *Inventario, Catastro, y Delimitación del Patrimonio Arqueológico
del Valle de Ica.* Lima: Instituto Nacional de Cultura.

Wisdom, Charles
1940 *The Chortí Indians of Guatemala.* Chicago: University of Chicago

Press.

Wolf, Eric

1966 Kinship, Friendship, and Patron-Client Relations in Complex Socities. In M. Banton, ed., *The Social Anthropology of Complex Socities*, pp. 1-22. London: Tavistock.

Wolf, Eric, and E. D. Hansen

1972 *The Human Condition in Latin America*. Oxford: Oxford University Press.

Woodward, Ralph Lee, Jr.

1972 Social Revolution in Guatemala: The Carrera Revolt. In Margaret A. L. Harrison and Robert Wauchope, eds., *Applied Enlightenment: 19th Century Liberalism*. Middle American Research Institute Publication 23, pp 45-70. New Orleans: Tulane University.

1976 *Central America: A Nation Divided*. New York: Oxford University Press.

Xavier de Oliveira, Amália

1969 *O Padre Cicero que Eu Conheci: Verdadeira História de Juazeiro do Norte*. Rio de Janeiro.

Zambrano Palacios, A.

1978 *La plegeria del rosario y el Santuario del Cisne*. Loja, Ecuador.

Zantwijk, Rudolf A. M. van

1969 *La Estructura Gubernamental del Estado de Tlacupan (1430-1520)*, pp. 123-155. Estudios de Cultura Náhuatl, VIII. Mexico.

Zavala Alfaro, D.

1972 *Agonía y Estasis de un Pueblo*. Morelia, México: Fimax.

Zavala Paz, J.

1965 *El Señor de los Milagros*. Morelia, México: Fimax.

Zimmerman, Charlotte

1963 The Cult of the Holy Cross: An Analysis of Cosmology and Catholicism in Quintana Roo. *History of Religions* 3(1):50-71.

Zuidema, R. T.

1964 *The Ceque System of Cuzco*. Leiden: E. J. Brill.

1973 La Parenté et le culte des ancêtres dans trois communautés péruviennes; un compte-réndu de 1622 par Hernández Príncipe. *Signes et Langages des Amériques. Récherches amérindiennes au Québec* II(1-2):129-145 (Montreal).

1978 Shaft-tombs in the Inca Empire. *Journal of the Stewart Anthropological Society* IX(1-2):133-177 (Urbana).

1982a Bureacracy and Systematic Knowledge in Andean Civilization. In *Inca and Aztec States 1400-1800*. G. Collier, R. Rosaldo, and J. Wirth, eds., pp.419-458. New York: Academic.

1982b Catachillay. The Role of the Pleyades and of the Southern Cross and Centauri in the Calendar of the Incas. In Anthony F. Aveni and Gary Urton, eds., *Ethnoastronomy and Archaeoastronomy in the American Tropics*, pp. 203-229. New York: New York Academy of

Sciences. Annals of the New York Academy of Sciences, v. 385.

1983a Hierarchy and Space in Incaic Social Organization. *Ethnohistory* 30(2):49-75.

1983b Masks in the Incaic Solstice and Equinoctial Rituals. In N. Ross Crumrine and Marjorie Halpin, eds., *The Power of Symbols: Masks and Masquerade in the Americas*, pp. 149-156. Vancouver: University of British Columbia Press.

1983c Towards a General Andean Star Calendar in Ancient Peru. Manuscript. Department of Anthropology, University of Illinois, Urbana-Champaign.

1986 *La Civilisation Inca au Cuzco.* Presses Universitaires de France, Collège de France. Paris.

Zuidema, R. T. and Gary Urton

1976 La constelación de la llama en los Andes peruanos. *Allpanchis Phuturinga 9:59-119.*

Index

aboriginal 56, 74, 272
Abraham 274
adaptation 87
adornments 231, 276-278, 323
agrarian 221, 345, 357, 360, 364, 366
agrarians 360, 365
agriculture 72, 201, 254, 272, 342, 354
ahuehuete tree 101
ahuehuetes 35
alliance 103, 179, 251
alliances 74, 287
altar 40, 57, 59, 73, 76-80, 82-85, 96, 121,
　131, 132, 134, 152, 162, 176, 180, 206,
　209, 211-213, 222, 252, 260, 261, 274,
　275, 292
altars 5, 57, 77, 78, 105, 144, 145, 222,
　237, 308
amate 158
amerindian 35, 207
amerindians 43
ancestors 124, 162, 341, 350
Andes 7, 206, 230, 231, 238, 270, 287,
　289, 298, 304, 307, 320, 321, 334, 335,
　337, 339, 341, 343, 344, 347-349, 351,

352, 355
angel 264, 265, 274
animas 158, 166, 206, 278
Annals of the Cakchiquel 161
anti-church 87
anticlerical 54, 55, 155, 232, 248, 366
antistructure 140
Apache 58, 62, 63
apparition 10, 23, 36, 37, 40, 91, 106
apparitions 5, 23-25, 28, 35-38, 43, 201,
　235, 348, 351, 354
archaeology 2, 215
archangel 262, 264
archdiocese 67
Arequipa 28, 238, 242, 338
Argentina 22, 25, 28-30, 33, 46, 48, 66
Arizona 59
artisan 235, 237, 238, 251, 360
artisans 234, 240
assimilation 73, 74, 359
astrologer 264
astronomy 136, 345
Atahualpa 223, 267
Austria 22, 25, 39-42

authority 53, 114, 130, 144, 161, 171,
    177, 179, 193, 229, 232, 235, 240, 247,
    248-250, 265-268, 310, 313, 318, 327,
    328, 330-332, 334, 342
Avignon 125
Ayar 350, 355
Aztec 126, 252, 362

Balthasar 264
Banco 208-213, 254
bancos 209, 211, 213, 214
Bancroft, Herbert Howe 63, 67
band 79, 81, 82, 254, 259, 260, 262, 270,
    289, 292, 299, 318, 323, 365
bands 63, 241, 245, 250, 260, 273, 309,
    312, 313
banquet 274, 275, 365
Baroque 30, 46, 141
basilica 106, 141, 143-146, 154, 155, 163
Bautista 57, 59, 273, 276, 278
Belgium 25, 37
Bethlehem 26, 159-161, 264, 266-268
bicycle 273
bishops 20, 53-55, 201
blessing 14, 106, 118, 273, 285
body 16, 24, 33, 41, 44, 46, 79, 116, 117,
    140, 148, 163, 178, 211, 212, 237, 248,
    249, 250, 275, 284, 296, 332, 347, 348
Bolivia 20, 22, 231, 257, 267, 337, 338,
    352, 354
Bolton, Herbert E. 61
books 20, 21, 271, 278
borderlands 54
boundaries 2, 6, 7, 12, 66, 71, 72, 144,
    147, 154, 162, 250, 296, 299, 304, 326,
    334, 336, 338, 360, 363
boundary 61, 63, 67, 89, 283, 286, 293,
    298, 301, 302, 330, 338
bow 273, 314
bowed 5, 82, 85, 274, 276, 294
Brazil 3, 22, 26, 46, 66, 67, 150, 175, 179,
    181, 184, 186-189, 201, 358, 359
bread 76, 82-84, 86, 145, 274, 351
British 46, 140
bullfight 133
bus 100, 106, 114, 145, 150, 152, 182,
    201, 210, 213, 362
buses 65, 145, 149, 150, 211, 239, 270
byzantine 26, 46

Cajamarca 223, 239, 242, 254, 341
calpul 116-118
calvario 275
campesina 273

campesino 148, 255, 273, 316, 317
Canada 131, 279
candies 270
candle 131, 132, 134, 210, 221, 244
candles 41, 77-79, 85, 96, 105, 111-113,
    115, 132, 134, 145, 150, 160, 166, 209,
    210-213, 221, 233, 234, 237, 241, 244,
    245, 260, 277, 278, 292, 361
candy 164
capilla 254, 260
capital 56, 65, 67, 151, 153, 158, 179,
    226, 232, 249, 258, 259, 262, 266, 271,
    286-288, 291, 298, 307, 340, 362
Capuchin 29, 43
caravana 210-212, 214
caravanas 213
cargo 76, 111, 115, 117-120, 310, 311,
    327, 331, 335, 336
Caribbean 31, 207, 208
carnival 86, 152, 177, 209, 245, 317, 337
Carranza, Venustiano 99, 110, 114, 361
castillo 77, 155, 156, 164, 235, 253, 254,
    276
cataclysm 233
catastrophe 37, 233
catedral 260
catholic 1, 4, 7, 19, 24, 25, 30, 31, 45, 46,
    53-57, 60-62, 64, 65, 67, 93, 95, 106,
    111, 113, 115, 117, 124, 125, 128, 129,
    131, 134, 167, 168, 179, 180, 201, 205,
    207, 215, 217, 222, 228-232, 236, 240,
    245, 247, 248, 251, 252, 257, 268, 282,
    307-309, 331, 333, 343, 348, 349, 351,
    352, 353-356, 358, 364, 365
catholicism 4, 9, 16, 30, 53, 55-59, 64-66,
    92, 106, 115, 124, 161, 169, 205, 206,
    358, 363, 364
caudillo 155, 233
caves 34, 35, 91, 94, 100, 102, 105, 112,
    210
celebrate 27, 28, 56, 64, 89, 98, 102, 177,
    184, 247, 250, 258, 277, 297, 303, 343,
    348, 365
celebrated 96, 105, 153, 159, 160, 162,
    169, 217, 230, 236, 238, 248, 250, 251,
    257, 258, 270, 271, 291, 293, 301, 323,
    341, 346, 351
celebrates 278
celebration 1, 7, 9, 85, 88, 129, 164, 166,
    170, 220, 227, 231, 233, 240, 241, 249,
    257, 278, 339, 342, 345, 355, 361, 362
celebrations 24, 131, 152, 153, 227, 229,
    235, 245, 250, 251, 345, 346, 361, 362,
    363, 364, 366

cemeteries 98, 216, 223
cemetery 260, 261, 270, 271
census 145, 235, 254, 271
center 3-5, 7, 8, 14, 27, 28, 30, 45, 71, 74,
    76, 77, 80, 82, 83, 87-89, 95, 112, 113-
    115, 127, 130, 132, 135, 143, 158, 164,
    170, 206, 208-210, 211, 215-218, 222,
    227, 228, 232, 234, 247, 250, 253, 254,
    259, 262, 270, 271, 274, 275, 279, 288,
    293, 295, 298-301, 307, 310, 316, 326,
    331, 332, 337, 339, 340, 349-352, 354,
    360, 362, 365
centers 2, 5, 7, 8, 16, 20, 21, 24-29, 31,
    38, 44, 71, 75, 81, 82, 88, 120, 130, 135,
    136, 140, 151, 171, 179, 208, 209, 211,
    215, 222, 223, 227, 232, 234, 270, 293,
    298, 301, 307, 311, 335, 339, 340, 342,
    343, 348, 349-352
ceque 227
ceremonial 64, 74-76, 87, 88, 93, 104,
    105, 120, 128, 150, 168, 217, 218, 222,
    227, 232, 235, 254, 261, 268, 269, 271-
    273, 275, 278, 279, 286, 287, 293, 297,
    303, 304, 339, 340, 342, 343, 348-352,
    362, 364
ceremonialism 72, 74, 87, 88, 226
ceremonies 8, 67, 87, 94, 105, 119, 131,
    146, 149, 152, 153, 169, 259, 272, 273,
    302, 303, 320, 331, 341, 365, 366
ceremony 75, 89, 95, 99, 118, 127, 164,
    167-169, 211, 213, 248, 257, 258, 266,
    304, 311, 322
chaacs 127
Chalma 31, 91, 93, 100-102, 101-103,
    102-104
change 9, 11, 15, 16, 21, 27, 53, 54, 65-
    67, 116, 119, 120, 140, 155, 159, 166,
    169, 170, 186, 190, 205, 211, 220, 227,
    246, 277, 301, 359, 363
changes 9, 15, 20, 22, 23, 40, 56, 59, 66,
    87, 116, 121, 140, 188, 213, 227, 300,
    358, 360
chants 78
chapel 33, 34, 36, 40, 48, 59, 88, 96-98,
    160, 161, 164, 166, 170, 194, 219, 234,
    242, 246, 250, 254, 258-261, 265-267,
    271, 278, 282, 286, 295, 296, 353, 361,
    365
chapels 57, 87, 95, 132, 134, 233, 239-2-
    41, 243, 277, 285, 350, 360, 363
charter 3, 175, 277
Chiapas 6, 109, 117, 119-121, 148, 367
chicha 266, 271
chicken 211, 212

chickens 73, 112, 134, 182, 184
Chihuahua 63, 67
Chile 22, 26, 28, 29, 46, 48, 316, 344
chinkana 319, 329
chinkanas 323
choreography 259, 267, 288, 296, 311,
    313, 314, 317-319, 323-325, 324, 326,
    330-334, 337, 359
Christ 23, 26, 27, 30-32, 43-45, 66, 75,
    91, 96, 99, 102, 125, 139, 141, 156, 161,
    163, 164, 178, 180, 266-269, 272, 275-
    279, 281, 284, 285, 289, 291, 295, 296,
    298, 302, 307, 309, 310, 331, 337, 351-
    -353
christendom 19, 25, 29, 33, 55, 57
Christianity 20, 24, 25, 35, 43, 45, 55-57,
    65, 93, 123-125, 128, 136, 268, 304, 309,
    367
Christmas 100, 160, 162, 209, 278
chroniclers 253, 308, 339-341, 344, 346,
    349
church 4, 5, 9, 14, 19, 21, 30, 33, 36, 40,
    41, 53-62, 64-66, 71, 74-89, 93, 96,
    97-99, 101, 104, 106, 112-114, 116, 117,
    126, 129-134, 142-144, 145, 150, 153,
    155, 158-167, 169, 171, 176-181, 183,
    186, 187, 197, 201, 205, 206, 219, 221,
    222, 230, 232, 234, 239, 240, 243, 245,
    246, 248, 249, 251-255, 259-261, 264,
    266, 268, 269, 271-273, 274-279, 282,
    283, 296, 298, 302, 303, 309, 310, 318-
    320, 323, 326, 362-364
churches 26, 29, 38, 40, 42, 44, 63, 67,
    87, 88, 98, 131, 143, 160, 168, 272, 351
Cieza de Leon, Pedro de 253
cities 35, 55, 61, 151, 182, 183, 207, 208,
    254, 308
city 27, 55, 56, 61, 63, 65, 67, 93, 104,
    106, 116, 142, 146, 150-153, 155, 158,
    175, 177, 179-184, 186, 188, 189, 199,
    202, 211, 212, 214, 216, 218, 219, 222,
    231, 239, 249, 251, 253, 267, 271, 282,
    285, 339, 341, 350-352, 360-362, 366
clairvoyant 233
cleansing 211, 213, 214
climax 15, 167, 270, 278, 279, 292, 296
climaxes 278
clockwise 77, 84, 113, 274, 276, 316
cloth 9, 33, 65, 78, 83, 96, 101, 131, 270,
    284, 351
clothes 104, 144, 147, 148, 269, 283, 296
coast 8, 86, 215-217, 224, 226, 231, 235,
    236, 243, 247, 250-252, 257, 265, 267,
    268-270, 278, 279, 339, 341, 344-47

coffin 178, 272, 275, 278
cofradía 221, 273-278
cofradias 74, 87
cognitive 229, 335
colonia 270
colonial 23, 25, 26, 29, 34, 35, 43, 46, 47,
  55, 57, 59, 60, 63, 64, 67, 91, 93, 97, 98,
  99, 104, 118, 126, 168, 169, 205, 208,
  253, 267, 271, 285, 304, 309, 362
colonists 87, 187, 201
colonization 87
Columbus 27, 210
commercial 61, 72, 86, 130, 132, 245
communion 15, 80, 134, 147, 151, 154,
  179, 260, 333
communitas 139, 156, 184, 228
communities 7, 40, 92, 93, 97, 100, 104,
  105, 111, 117, 129, 131, 132, 135, 144,
  145, 149, 152, 154, 155, 170, 229, 299-
  301, 303-305, 310, 311, 327, 329, 360,
  361, 363, 364, 366
community 3, 6, 8, 15, 16, 35, 40, 81, 88,
  104, 116-118, 128, 131-133, 135, 143,
  144, 147, 148, 152-154, 162, 163, 168,
  199, 200, 208, 214, 226, 246, 247, 249,
  250, 254, 255, 258, 261, 266, 286, 292,
  299, 304, 310, 311, 313, 326, 331, 334,
  336, 337, 342, 350
compensation 81
Compostella 231
comunidad 248, 249, 255, 271
concejo 237, 251, 274
confederation 58, 63, 67
confessions 83, 84, 180, 310
conquest 9, 86, 92, 93, 95, 97, 102, 104,
  115, 116, 118, 125, 126, 128, 129, 136,
  141, 155, 159, 208, 271, 285, 339, 348,
  349, 355
contact 43, 75, 89, 116, 143, 144, 206,
  209, 227, 271
continuity 6, 9, 44, 45, 126, 129, 141,
  158, 166, 167, 170, 229, 251, 254, 267,
  308, 356, 358
contribution 20, 61, 132, 145, 163, 243
contributions 45, 80, 111, 153, 176, 253,
  357
conversion 35, 44, 57, 61, 65, 66, 86, 91,
  125, 349
cooperative 74, 76, 277, 332
Copacabana 32, 230, 231, 253, 307, 309
cordel 175, 176, 187-190, 192-200, 202
corn 105, 220, 266, 271, 361, 362
corpus 5, 198, 278, 281-283, 286, 290,
  293, 297, 303, 309, 351

cosmological 5, 6, 124, 125, 127-130, 132,
  136, 257, 265, 304, 305
cosmology 5, 127, 133, 136, 281, 285, 302
Costa Rica 22
cotton 59, 187, 237, 239, 261, 271, 272
Cozumel 254
craft 271
crafts 2, 235, 269
craftsmen 271
create 2, 45, 115, 144, 199, 300, 321, 340
created 2, 27, 37, 38, 44, 47, 126, 129,
  143, 149, 271, 285, 350, 361, 362
creator pair 94
creole 60, 61
Cristo 139, 143, 188, 191, 202, 203, 257,
  275, 277, 278
crop 57, 73, 94, 104, 105, 110, 271, 362
crops 104, 271, 309
cross 6, 16, 27, 30, 60, 73-75, 77, 78, 82,
  85, 86, 91, 94-99, 101, 102, 117, 123,
  124, 127-136, 146, 161, 162, 164-170,
  181, 209, 212, 213, 229, 230, 231-234,
  237-251, 253-255, 259, 269, 275, 276,
  278, 284, 291, 292, 293, 298, 299, 334,
  352
crosses 42, 87, 97, 99, 101, 112, 128-130,
  132, 134-136, 162, 168, 200, 218, 221,
  233, 236, 241, 275, 283, 298
crucifix 32, 33, 73, 101, 129, 141, 156,
  282, 293, 294
crucifixes 24, 32, 76
crucifixion 43, 277, 276, 278
Cuba 22
cult 20, 21, 23-25, 27-34, 36, 37, 39, 40,
  43-47, 59, 87, 88, 100, 126, 129, 147,
  150, 168, 205-214, 217, 218, 232, 234,
  235, 240, 241, 245-247, 249-255, 270,
  281, 282, 285-287, 290, 298, 302-305,
  362
cults 4, 9, 20, 21, 25-29, 31, 32, 35, 43,
  44, 46, 47, 121, 305, 307-309, 333
culture 3-6, 11, 12, 14, 17, 56, 57, 72-74,
  140, 148, 160, 161, 167, 184, 216, 237,
  298, 306, 309, 321, 359
curanderos 208, 243, 253
cure 14, 42, 75, 81, 96, 176, 178, 183,
  185, 202, 206, 207, 270, 352
cured 16, 208, 213, 214, 352
curer 94, 243, 271
curing 111, 214
Cusco 341
Cuzco 227, 282, 284-288, 290, 291, 298,
  300, 303, 305, 307-310, 312, 317, 321,
  322, 325, 328, 329, 331, 334, 336-338,

340, 342, 345, 349-351, 352-354
cycle 47, 74, 110, 117, 119, 120, 124, 128, 153, 167, 168, 219, 270, 279, 293, 297, 302, 340-348, 350-356, 362

dance 6, 8, 15, 44, 62, 64, 65, 75, 81, 88, 101, 104, 105, 212, 227, 262, 264, 287, 289-292, 294-297, 303, 305, 307-318, 320-323, 325-338
dancers 65, 75, 77, 78, 81, 104, 105, 112, 245, 250, 259, 286, 288-291, 294, 295, 296, 297, 302, 304, 308, 310-333, 335-338, 361
dancing 77-79, 81-85, 104, 258, 290, 292, 299, 308-310, 313-315, 318, 319, 322, 323, 326, 331, 335, 336, 338, 367
darkness 32, 127, 278, 292
daughters 67, 130, 179, 270
death 11, 13, 29, 74, 75, 123, 125, 127, 128, 133, 155, 159, 178, 180, 181, 184, 187, 194, 195, 198, 199, 201, 206, 208, 230, 241, 245, 249, 252, 254, 267, 275, 278, 279, 288, 299, 321, 324, 325, 330, 341
debts 76, 186
decorate 241, 273
decorated 84, 87, 105, 134, 144, 164, 166, 209, 272, 275, 276, 288, 289, 293, 312
dedicated 1, 28-31, 43, 60, 76, 87, 95, 213, 247, 258, 270, 346, 362
deer 40, 64, 65, 75
deity 5, 76, 89, 99, 100, 104, 105, 119, 128, 141, 159, 168, 186, 278, 279
department 48, 158, 171, 231, 234, 235, 239, 249, 257, 258, 269-271, 274, 282, 290, 299, 312, 317, 336, 350
departments 163, 239, 242, 267, 270, 305
descending 142, 261, 279
descends 279, 285
descent 76-78, 140, 265, 278, 293, 295, 301
desert 57-59, 61, 62, 64, 66, 73, 230, 270
deserts 271
devil 100, 177, 178, 184, 199, 208, 318, 329, 338, 339, 352, 354
devotional 31, 37, 38, 41, 42, 46, 64, 95, 270, 286, 290, 303, 311, 333
died 29, 43, 57, 88, 175, 176, 178, 179, 186, 206, 233, 254, 277, 284, 341, 343
dinner 105, 218
diorama 274
dios 81, 111, 160, 168, 169, 260
dishes 61, 134, 275
displays 15, 77, 86, 226, 245, 250, 297,

330
divine 5, 8-10, 14, 15, 23, 96, 97, 99, 107, 128, 167, 169, 180, 186, 198, 201, 249, 266, 293, 297
doctrina 134, 171
doliente 273, 275
dolores 273, 274
Dominican 22, 27, 159, 162, 163, 171, 208
Dominican Republic 22, 27, 208
Dominicans 160
donation 14, 76
donations 65, 80, 111, 277
donkey 201, 273
doves 80, 276
drama 6, 136, 139, 154, 209, 227, 267, 269
dramas 5, 124, 227
drink 16, 183, 206, 210, 212, 245, 266, 271, 353, 361
drinking 83, 84, 132, 144, 145, 213, 310, 367
drinks 209, 210, 213, 221
drummers 121
dual 11, 12, 278, 279, 281, 286, 301, 302, 305, 306, 321, 326, 327, 348, 359
duelo 275
dues 277
Durkheim, E. 10, 339

earthquake 163, 271
easter 8, 75, 87, 98, 147, 180, 269, 271-2-73, 275, 277-279
ecology 72, 88, 271, 307
economic 16, 17, 43, 61, 63, 73, 74, 87, 107, 112, 113, 115, 119, 120, 140, 146, 147-150, 152, 154, 155, 181, 185, 232, 247, 250, 251, 259, 271, 304, 307, 316, 342, 345, 348, 358-360, 362-365
Ecuador 20, 22, 28, 30, 31, 270
El Salvador 22, 146, 151, 152, 156, 159
electricity 182, 272
elements 3, 9, 20, 115, 129, 136, 139, 140, 144, 149, 158, 161, 166, 167, 169, 186, 190, 193, 257, 271, 284, 287, 318, 338, 350, 358, 364
Eliade, Mircea 123-125, 130, 133
enacts 126, 278
encargado 111, 112, 114-116
encargados 112, 115-117
encomienda 271
England 22, 66
entertainers 77
entertainment 75, 83, 100, 133, 187, 214,

336
epidemics 131
epoch 168, 271, 285, 304
Esquipulas 4, 31, 139, 141-144, 146-156, 171
ethnographic 21, 120, 142, 147, 152, 154, 158, 167, 169, 215, 217, 222, 223, 228, 232, 252, 305, 346, 347, 357
ethnohistoric 109, 158, 253
Europe 19-30, 32-47, 57, 125, 201, 231, 245, 267
evangelical 365
evangelista 273, 274, 278
event 15, 33, 98, 105, 111, 114, 118, 128, 133, 146, 164, 180, 183, 187, 233, 249, 254, 257, 279, 281, 286, 297, 299, 365
events 7, 20, 21, 25, 33, 37, 38, 40, 42, 47, 53, 54, 56, 59, 65, 74, 86, 87, 92, 96, 109, 110, 113, 124, 128, 129, 132-135, 139, 143, 152, 153, 156, 171, 178, 180, 181, 184, 186, 188, 189, 191, 232, 253, 269, 272, 277-279, 284, 341, 342, 346, 351, 365
exchange 14, 30, 71, 75, 76, 82, 86, 88, 89, 176, 279
exorcise 206, 212

face 33, 96, 97, 99, 124, 146, 169, 180, 185, 192, 200, 212, 213, 278, 290, 336, 343
falls 54, 59, 176, 177, 190, 271
farewell 278
farmers 59, 73, 74, 86, 182, 187, 271, 345, 354
farming 72, 73, 188
father 25, 60, 71, 76, 94, 98, 99, 114, 119, 130, 134, 178, 187, 192, 202, 207, 213, 233, 283, 284, 341-344, 351, 352, 354
Fatima 43, 237
feast 89, 134, 147, 153, 158, 160-162, 164-170, 180, 252, 265, 268, 270, 271, 281, 293, 308, 309
feasting 15, 78, 276, 279
festival 8, 58, 61, 62, 141, 153, 159, 168, 219-221, 224, 225, 231, 232, 234, 235, 236-241, 243-250, 254, 271, 297
festivals 1, 40, 56, 139, 229-232, 236, 237, 245-247, 249-254, 308, 337, 362, 363
fiesta 6, 76, 80, 95, 97, 98, 101, 102, 104, 106, 162, 164, 218, 234, 257-259, 265, 267-271, 278, 279, 282-284, 286-293, 297-299, 301, 303-305, 310, 322, 330, 331, 351, 355

fiestas 15, 71, 93, 153, 258, 269, 270, 272, 278, 279, 310, 346
fiesteros 75, 78
fila 277
financed 59, 60, 245, 279
fireworks 75, 77, 78, 83, 86, 111, 146, 152, 245, 250, 260, 261, 276
fish 189, 275
fishermen 86, 162, 271, 344, 345
fishing 272, 344
five 28, 30, 34, 60, 75, 88, 116, 127, 131, 132, 158, 186, 190, 198, 210, 235, 259, 266, 277, 311, 325, 326, 332
flag 78, 82, 88, 112, 114
flags 77-80, 82, 83, 85, 86, 88, 112-114, 117, 296
flooding 255, 271
flower 77, 111
flowers 41, 61, 76, 94, 95, 97, 101, 105, 112, 114, 115, 134, 159, 163, 164, 209, 211, 213, 261, 273
folk 5, 6, 8, 26, 27, 39, 46, 53, 56-60, 64-66, 74, 105, 148, 169, 175, 176, 186, 189, 200, 205, 206, 208, 252, 267, 269, 363, 365
food 15, 44, 61, 63, 65, 75, 76, 84, 99, 104, 112, 132-134, 146, 150, 154, 164, 177, 183, 191, 209-211, 213, 221, 222, 234, 235, 237, 245, 249, 251, 271, 283, 361
foods 134, 269, 270
forest 40, 73, 96, 118, 123, 128, 131, 133, 209, 286
forested 96, 270, 305
forests 118, 129, 208, 209, 214
France 22, 24-28, 30, 33, 37, 39, 40, 42, 44, 231
Franciscan 29, 57, 59, 60, 126, 129, 131
Franciscans 57, 59, 60
friday 86, 104, 109-112, 179, 180, 220, 272, 275, 276, 278, 283
frontier 9, 35, 53-57, 61-63, 65, 67
fruit 73, 159, 160, 163, 177, 261, 274
funeral 74, 249, 277, 278
funerals 75
fusion 74, 193, 271, 272, 302

garden 182, 271
genesis 130, 254
gentiles 265, 268
geysers 158
gift 134, 167
gifts 33, 60, 84, 88, 160, 161, 170, 264, 266, 279, 297, 365

glass 143, 165, 166, 179, 220, 274, 276,
    281, 291
Gloria 131, 132, 134, 275
gobernador 254, 361
god 2, 5, 10, 14-17, 74, 88, 89, 91, 94, 95,
    99, 101, 102, 106, 111, 116, 121, 129,
    130, 156, 161, 164, 168, 169, 178, 185,
    207, 208, 258, 260, 278, 339, 345, 346,
    353, 354, 362
goddess 26, 32, 94, 100, 105, 126, 161,
    208
godparents 74, 265
gods 95, 100, 107, 116, 118, 124, 125,
    127, 130, 133, 159, 169, 170, 308
gold 62, 163, 177, 230, 231, 241, 243,
    245, 273, 275, 276, 278, 288, 305, 342,
    350
governors 62, 75
gowns 41, 275
Great Britain 231
green 94, 97, 105, 127, 128, 163, 168, 271
Guadalupe 3, 4, 27, 28, 32, 36, 46, 48, 65,
    75, 80, 91, 93, 101, 104, 106, 125, 126,
    218, 231, 236, 285, 367
Guatemala 7, 9, 22, 31, 67, 109, 111, 115,
    120, 139, 141, 142, 145, 148, 149, 150-
    153, 155, 156, 158-160, 162, 165, 166,
    169, 171, 252, 253, 359
Guatemalan 121, 126, 144, 146, 170, 171

hacendado 262, 264
hacienda 267, 361, 363
haciendas 299, 360, 363, 364
hams 270
healer 178, 186
healers 39, 208
healing 29, 141, 207, 231, 233, 236
heaven 10, 14, 15, 23, 41, 127, 130, 176,
    177, 184, 199, 341, 344, 347
herald 264, 265
hermit 41, 233
hermits 34, 36
hero 128, 161, 181, 199, 340-345, 347,
    349, 350, 354
heroes 5-7, 124, 128, 194, 340-351, 353-
    -356
hierarchy 115, 116, 119, 121, 156, 222,
    227, 228, 243, 251, 258, 281, 285, 300,
    301, 302, 304, 308, 310-313, 322, 325-
    330, 332-335, 354, 360, 363
highway 79, 80, 84, 106, 142-144, 158,
    210, 235, 271
hills 34, 44, 101, 228, 293, 351-353
holy 4, 10, 19, 23, 26, 27, 29, 30, 32-34,
    36, 39-45, 60, 71, 74-76, 82, 84, 85, 98,
    101, 123-125, 127-136, 141, 142, 144-
    146, 153, 159, 161, 162, 164-170, 175,
    183, 205, 206, 209, 210, 213, 266, 268-
    270, 272, 273, 276, 283, 295, 303, 305,
    333, 362
home 4, 5, 8, 10-12, 15, 16, 58, 62, 78,
    81, 86, 88, 99, 103, 106, 121, 143, 145,
    146, 147, 151, 152, 177, 178, 181-183,
    188, 209, 213, 237, 239, 259, 274, 275,
    277, 278, 283, 286, 293, 331, 348, 361,
    362, 364
homes 2, 5, 10, 56, 113, 182, 206, 214,
    237, 272, 279
Honduras 22, 141, 151, 156
honor 27, 74, 76, 79, 86, 88, 104, 125,
    129, 162, 171, 179, 241, 273, 279, 366
hospitable 279
host 16, 76, 81, 83, 178-180, 201, 282,
    293, 333
hosted 76, 88
hosting 89, 112
hosts 76, 86, 180, 201, 274, 302
hotel 145, 150, 152
hotels 143, 145, 150, 209, 270
house 62, 105, 112, 134, 143, 150, 161,
    168, 171, 176, 178, 187, 191, 192, 209,
    221, 233, 249, 262, 266, 270, 323
houses 97, 132, 134, 141, 142, 145, 168,
    179, 181, 182, 211, 216, 220, 221, 272,
    278, 282
housing 88, 160, 277, 282, 307
huaca 258-260, 262, 263, 265-268, 309,
    341, 342, 349
huacas 218, 219, 229, 230, 307, 308
huayno 313, 317, 318, 337
Huitzilopochtli 95, 102, 126
human 1-6, 9, 11, 15-17, 33, 37, 42, 44,
    66, 76, 89, 125, 126, 133, 134, 136, 144,
    158, 159, 162, 178, 185, 195, 199, 206,
    277, 279, 286, 298-300, 301, 302, 309,
    322, 347, 358
humans 127, 128, 136, 207, 223, 279, 334
humble 14, 17, 145, 214, 271, 284

icon 33, 140, 141, 146, 154, 155, 241,
    283, 286, 310, 329, 334
iconoclasm 26, 33
icons 5, 26, 112, 113, 115, 140, 284, 302,
    336
ideology 71, 86, 156, 228, 248, 307, 365
idol 91, 104, 164
idols 45
image 5, 7, 16, 23, 26-28, 30, 32, 33,

35-37, 40-42, 44, 45, 48, 58, 60, 65, 71,
78-80, 82, 85, 86, 88, 96, 97, 99, 101,
104, 106, 125, 126, 141, 144, 145, 153-
155, 158-160, 162-166, 168-171, 178,
210, 219, 222, 261, 265, 271-278, 282,
284, 285, 290, 294, 296, 302, 307, 310,
311, 317, 327, 331, 332, 336, 342, 347,
348, 350, 352, 354, 360, 361, 365, 367
images 4, 5, 7, 24, 26, 29-33, 35, 36,
38-40, 43, 44, 73, 77, 78, 80-87, 136,
140, 144, 158, 160-163, 166, 170, 186,
221, 227, 230, 235, 261, 269, 270, 272-
276, 278, 279, 284, 293-296, 307, 323,
334, 340, 343, 348, 351, 354
Inca 9, 227, 230, 232, 253, 254, 278, 304,
305, 307-309, 327, 328, 331, 335, 340,
345, 346, 349, 350
incense 97, 209, 234, 237, 245, 259, 260,
361
indian 28, 30-32, 58, 62, 66, 67, 74, 91,
93, 94, 97, 99, 105, 106, 126, 144, 145,
147-150, 152, 153, 155, 158, 167-169,
171, 208, 219, 252, 267, 268, 271, 272,
282-287, 290, 291, 302-305, 308, 352,
354, 359-361, 362-364, 366, 367
indians 27, 71, 94, 105, 129, 130, 142,
145, 146, 148-150, 155, 159-161, 162,
163, 167-170, 208, 284, 285, 289, 290,
338, 359-361
indigenas 271
indigenous 1, 4, 20, 31, 35, 44-46, 58, 91,
92, 95, 104, 117, 125, 126, 136, 153,
169, 229, 230, 234, 257, 258, 265-268,
271, 289, 303, 308, 309, 317, 320, 321,
328, 331, 358, 367
initiate 17, 74, 76, 156, 313
initiated 6, 57, 86, 109, 120, 121, 154,
245, 254, 262, 284, 330, 361, 365
Inquisition 37
insignia 275
Ireland 22, 30, 32, 37, 39, 41, 42, 46
Islamic 26, 245
Israel 266, 267
Italy 22-26, 28-30, 32, 35, 39, 41, 42, 44

January 98, 106, 141, 142, 144, 146,
151-153, 163, 165, 236, 243, 245, 259,
268, 271, 331
Jerusalem 4, 142, 182, 183, 264, 266, 267
jesters 262, 264, 266
Jesucristo 275
Jesuit 25, 57, 64, 74, 86, 305
Jesus 3, 5, 10, 30, 101, 164, 178, 179,
182, 202, 203, 264-266, 274, 275, 278,

352, 360-364, 366
Juazeiro 175-184, 186-190, 192, 194,
196-203, 358

key 6, 10, 12, 59, 66, 88, 314, 316, 319,
325
keys 275, 348
kilt 278
Kino, Eusebio F. 25, 57-59, 65
koati 253
Kubler, George 102, 254

labor 64, 73, 183, 267, 271, 272
labyrinth 319, 329
ladino 144, 147-149, 155, 158, 171
ladinos 110, 145, 146, 148-152, 159, 163,
167, 169, 170, 359
landlords 363
landowner 219, 267, 361
landowners 179, 182, 267, 363
language 57, 74, 86, 93, 104, 115, 116,
121, 126, 234, 289, 317, 321, 359, 367
languages 45, 115, 271, 367
Latin America 1, 2, 4, 8, 9, 14, 16, 17,
19-23, 25-29, 32, 34-39, 43, 45, 47, 54,
124, 126, 132, 136, 357-359, 366
legend 99, 105, 164, 208, 278, 283, 285,
289, 290, 293, 305, 351-353
Lévi-Strauss, Claude 11-13, 133, 301,
330, 346, 347, 358
life 3, 5, 10, 11, 13-15, 29, 37, 38, 42-45,
67, 72-75, 88, 92, 100, 115, 125, 127,
128, 130, 131, 149, 159, 170, 175, 177,
179, 180, 183, 185, 186, 188, 194, 195,
197-200, 206, 272, 273, 279, 308, 311,
313, 326, 327, 332, 355, 358, 364, 366
lighting 182, 271
Lima 29, 30, 67, 201, 219, 231, 233, 239,
242, 253, 270, 323, 339
liminality 206, 227
lord 91, 94, 97, 100-102, 104, 118, 119,
142, 145, 281, 341-344, 352-354
lords 109, 120, 161, 265, 308, 309, 353,
354, 366
Lourdes 28, 44, 231
Lutheran 19

madonna 28
magic 207, 208, 211-213
maize 110, 134, 168, 169, 261, 312
manger 264
margaritas 110, 113, 114, 116
market 63, 113, 120, 141, 160, 188, 221,
240, 270, 297, 318, 361

marriage 11, 93, 300
Mary 5, 10, 14, 19, 23, 26-28, 31, 33, 35,
    36, 43, 60, 125, 126, 157, 158, 161, 163,
    166, 171, 176, 205, 208, 210, 265, 358
Maryknoll 66
mass 16, 56, 64, 80, 83-86, 98, 99, 104,
    111, 112, 115, 150, 164, 179, 218, 226,
    246, 260, 264, 266, 268, 273, 291, 293,
    298, 303, 309, 310, 333, 334, 337
Maya 5, 66, 106, 116-118, 123-133, 135,
    136, 141, 159, 161, 163, 167-169, 170,
    254
Mayo 5, 7, 48, 62, 71-76, 79-81, 83, 85-
    89, 237
mayor 62, 102, 116, 118, 181, 247-249,
    251, 253, 255, 277, 296, 313
mayordomo 105, 116-118, 240, 245, 254,
    277, 361, 363
mayordomos 104, 115-118, 234, 259-261,
    277, 278, 363, 365
mayores 118, 278
Mediterranean 26, 265
medium 208, 212, 213, 287, 310, 336
mediums 207-214
Medjugorje 28
member 117, 118, 121, 134, 329, 330
members 53, 64, 65, 73, 76, 113, 116,
    117, 132, 134, 145, 147, 149, 162, 184,
    186, 187, 200, 209, 210, 212, 214, 221,
    227, 229, 240, 246-248, 249, 251, 253-
    255, 273, 276-278, 286, 294, 295, 299,
    303, 304, 310, 326, 337, 364, 365
membership 71, 116, 148, 149, 277
Mesoamerica 44, 92, 147, 367
Mesoamerican 102, 116, 125, 126, 154,
    254, 360
messianic 89, 180, 201
Mestizo 60, 72-74, 87, 88, 147, 235, 282,
    283, 285-287, 289-291, 302-304, 309,
    310, 317, 321, 329, 361, 363, 364
Mexican 9, 28, 32, 48, 53-56, 60-64, 66,
    67, 72-74, 87, 91, 105, 109, 113, 117,
    128-131, 133, 135, 140, 146, 252, 360,
    362, 363, 366
Mexico 3, 6, 7, 9, 20, 22, 26-29, 31, 35,
    36, 44, 46, 53-58, 60, 63-67, 71, 74, 87,
    88, 91-93, 99, 104, 106, 107, 110, 120,
    123, 132, 140, 142, 163, 164, 231, 285,
    359, 360, 366, 367
milagro 112, 236, 237, 254, 257
milagroso 139, 153, 154, 203
military 60-63, 67, 87, 128-130, 135, 144,
    180, 274, 350, 353, 354, 359
miracle 37, 43, 154, 175-178, 180, 181,
    183-187, 189, 190, 193, 194, 197, 198,
    202, 205, 210, 239, 250, 254, 264, 265,
    267, 268, 270, 285, 290, 354, 358, 359
miracles 5, 37, 38, 95, 96, 180, 183, 186,
    189, 201, 206, 231, 235, 251, 254, 348
miraculous 26, 30-33, 35-37, 42, 43, 45,
    86, 91, 96, 99, 104-106, 131, 159, 178,
    180, 181, 183, 185, 186, 201, 202, 217,
    231, 236, 241, 281, 284, 285, 286, 290,
    298, 302-305, 307, 351, 352
misa 276
mission 35, 46, 57, 59-61, 65, 67, 71, 86,
    87, 180, 266
missionaries 20, 24, 25, 35, 36, 44, 56,
    57, 59, 60, 63-65, 86, 348, 365
missionary 21, 25, 57, 61, 65, 74, 91, 93,
    343, 348
missions 53, 57, 59, 60
Mochica 234, 260
moieties 286, 288, 293, 296-298, 300-302,
    328
moiety 287, 288, 290-296, 298, 300-302,
    305, 327, 330
Montserrat 125
monument 274, 275
monumento 275
Moors 164
mounds 158, 159, 216, 217, 222, 223, 228
mountain 42, 94, 96, 100, 102, 105, 182,
    206, 208-211, 213, 214, 230, 232, 233,
    282, 284-286, 288, 292, 293, 299, 300,
    303, 305, 335, 353, 363
mountains 39, 44, 86, 91, 141-143, 146,
    155, 208, 211, 212, 214, 278, 292, 298,
    299, 301, 302, 307, 347, 351, 353
mourning 275
muerte 267, 275
music 15, 41, 104, 134, 162, 164, 260,
    261, 288, 289, 295, 309, 337, 365
myth 4, 66, 100, 117, 124, 128, 133, 146,
    284, 290, 291, 293, 297, 358
mythology 87, 287
myths 3, 304, 345, 355

Nahuatl 93, 124, 159, 360, 361, 363-367
Nicaragua 28, 151

oasis 57, 59
obsidian 141
offer 17, 47, 99, 101, 117, 132, 133, 140,
    145, 150, 160, 170, 183, 212, 214, 286,
    305, 335, 346
offering 14, 37, 38, 42, 44, 101, 142, 163
officer 62, 353, 354

officers 62, 277
oracle 207, 253
oral 6, 26, 92, 96, 98, 100, 104, 117, 128,
  145, 176, 179, 186, 189-195, 198, 199,
  200, 201, 235, 284, 289, 340, 349, 354,
  357, 361, 366
organization 74, 75, 88, 93, 117, 119,
  121, 129, 140, 148, 155, 227, 232, 246,
  247, 254, 258, 259, 269, 273, 277, 282,
  286, 305, 310, 311, 326, 327, 329, 332,
  342
organizations 64, 117, 278, 364
ornaments 126, 164, 273
Otomi 9, 94

Pachacamac 253, 307, 339, 341, 349
Pacific 54, 58, 142, 271, 287, 290, 341
padre 29, 30, 43, 175-192, 195-203, 253,
  358, 360-364, 366
padrinos 265, 266
pagan 9, 21, 26, 33, 44, 45, 91, 93, 95,
  104, 105, 164, 186, 285, 300, 302
pagans 34, 56, 99, 107
palm 273, 312
palms 177, 273
Panama 22, 31
Paraguay 22
paraphernalia 84, 209, 217, 221, 234,
  235, 237, 244, 251
parent 104
parents 59, 74, 142, 143, 177, 184, 198,
  201
patron 71, 76, 80, 87, 89, 97, 98, 101,
  119, 125, 133-135, 144, 150, 153, 159,
  162, 168, 217, 258, 277, 290, 297, 360
peasant 72, 73, 91, 129, 229, 255, 284,
  289, 303, 304, 364
peasantry 258, 266-268
peasants 73, 129, 260, 281, 291, 325, 360,
  361, 363-365
penitente 56, 64
people 2, 6-10, 14, 17, 24, 28, 35, 40, 46,
  53, 57-62, 64-67, 71, 72, 76, 78, 79,
  80-83, 85, 86, 89, 93-96, 98-101, 104,
  106, 111, 117, 142, 148, 158, 159, 161-
  164, 166, 167, 170, 175, 178, 179, 181-
  187, 190, 193, 195, 198, 200, 201, 205,
  206, 210-214, 221-223, 230, 234, 237,
  250, 252, 261, 268, 271, 273, 279, 285,
  293, 299, 303, 305, 311, 312, 316, 334,
  339, 341-343, 346, 348, 353-355, 362,
  367
peregrinación 1, 170
perfume 275

person 14, 26, 27, 41, 42, 83, 94, 107,
  111, 149, 162, 169, 170, 184, 185, 188,
  195, 199, 206, 212, 265, 268, 288, 294,
  322, 331, 336, 341, 343
personage 94, 95, 107, 343, 345, 352,
  354, 355
personages 94, 125, 161, 199, 262, 279,
  334, 342-345, 348, 354-356
persons 23, 26, 27, 29, 30, 38, 41, 43, 54,
  60, 66, 76, 86, 106, 131, 135, 164, 175,
  179, 180, 182-185, 188, 194, 198-200,
  206, 207, 239, 246, 254, 267, 271, 275
Peru 7, 8, 20, 22, 26, 28-31, 54, 55, 66,
  67, 142, 215, 217, 219, 221, 226, 228,
  230, 231, 235, 238, 247, 250, 251, 253,
  257, 269, 270, 272, 279, 284, 304, 305,
  307, 308, 310, 316, 336, 339-341, 344,
  350, 351, 354, 358, 359
pilgrim 7, 13-16, 23, 26, 27, 30, 36, 42,
  44, 97, 101, 114, 123, 124, 126, 129,
  143, 145, 147, 158, 163, 164, 175, 177,
  182-185, 190, 199, 202, 207, 229, 245,
  253, 272, 277, 300, 303, 334, 335, 340-
  344, 346, 347, 349, 350, 352, 354, 355
pilgrimage 1-17, 19-21, 24-34, 37-40,
  42-47, 58-61, 63-66, 76, 81, 91-93, 95,
  98-100, 102-107, 109-115, 117-121,
  123-129, 131, 132, 135, 136, 139, 140-
  147, 149-154, 156, 158-160, 163, 164,
  167, 169-171, 175, 176, 180, 182, 184,
  189, 190, 209-211, 213, 215, 217, 221-
  223, 225, 226, 227-229, 231-235, 239,
  240, 243, 245, 249-254, 257, 258, 269,
  270, 271, 272, 278, 279, 281, 284-286,
  289, 293-299, 302-305, 307, 308, 309-
  312, 317, 322, 323, 325, 326, 330-340,
  342, 343, 345, 348, 349, 350-353, 355,
  357-360, 362-364, 366, 367
pilgrimages 1-5, 7-9, 11, 15-17, 19, 20,
  24, 28-30, 35, 38, 39, 43-47, 64, 66, 71,
  74, 93-95, 98, 100, 102, 104, 106, 109-
  115, 117, 119-121, 124, 134, 145, 151,
  153, 158, 159, 162, 167, 201, 205-207,
  209, 210, 214, 229, 230, 232, 240, 245,
  251, 254, 309, 331, 334, 335, 339-341,
  344, 345, 346-350, 355, 357-361, 364,
  366, 367
pilgrims 1, 3, 4, 6, 10, 14-16, 19, 21, 26,
  28-30, 34, 44, 58-62, 64, 65, 67, 95,
  96-101, 104, 106, 111-113, 112-114, 113,
  114, 121, 123, 126, 134, 141-148, 150-
  154, 158, 159, 163, 164, 169, 170, 180-
  184, 189, 200, 201, 205, 206, 209-211,
  213, 214, 221, 222, 225, 226, 228, 229,

231, 232-235, 237-242, 244-247, 249251,
  253, 254, 257, 269, 270, 272, 273, 275,
  277-279, 285, 286, 288, 292-295, 303,
  307, 309, 310, 323, 331, 334-337, 342,
  344, 345, 347, 353, 358, 361
place, sacred 8, 10, 170, 207, 208, 251,
  335
places, sacred 5, 168, 169, 205, 229
plaza 61, 85, 96, 97, 113, 144, 145, 163,
  182, 219-224, 223, 224, 233, 234, 238,
  240, 246, 262, 264-267, 269, 271, 273,
  274, 276, 278, 283, 297, 299, 323, 324,
  330, 331, 365
political 7-9, 16, 24, 47, 64, 87, 88, 111,
  115-117, 119-121, 130, 136, 139, 140,
  141, 148, 149, 152, 154-156, 161, 177,
  181, 226-228, 232, 243, 247, 248-251,
  255, 284, 285, 298, 300, 304, 305, 307-
  313, 327, 330, 331, 335, 342-345, 357-
  360, 362-365
politics 116, 120, 139, 154, 155, 357, 364
pope 29, 45, 178, 181, 185
Portugal 22, 25, 28, 37, 39, 41, 42, 179,
  201, 253
pottery 66, 99, 100, 216, 217, 224, 272
poverty 73
power 4, 5, 7-10, 13-17, 24, 43-45, 54, 55,
  64, 67, 76, 87, 92, 93, 107, 119, 127,
  130, 156, 162, 170, 178, 181, 184, 206,
  211, 219, 232, 245, 268, 273, 279, 282,
  298, 301-303, 309, 311, 321, 334, 337,
  344, 363, 364
pray 77, 78, 81, 82, 86, 98, 176, 270, 335
prayer 6, 14, 15, 76, 79, 109, 117, 118,
  120, 121, 144, 145, 213, 292
prayers 64, 76, 78, 79, 85, 86, 99, 109,
  117, 119, 120, 129, 132, 134, 145, 167,
  206, 211, 245, 348, 367
pre-Columbian 1, 4, 6, 7, 20, 31, 33, 35,
  43-47, 115, 126, 141, 169, 208, 216, 254,
  335, 340-344, 346, 348, 349
pre-Conquest 125
pre-Hispanic 91, 97, 104-106, 116, 118,
  129, 218, 219, 230, 251, 253, 258, 267,
  285, 304, 307, 339-345, 347-351, 353,
  355, 356, 358, 362, 367
pre-historic 7, 232, 340, 355
pre-Inca 278, 304, 340
priest 29, 43, 58, 60, 64, 66, 67, 80, 83,
  85, 98, 111, 112, 115, 116, 120, 121,
  156, 159, 175-181, 183-186, 188, 189,
  198, 199, 201, 202, 219, 222, 245-249,
  251, 254, 260, 262, 264, 266, 273, 275,
  278, 283-285, 290, 291, 296, 304, 305,
  310, 323, 352
priestly 54, 165, 343, 354
priests 25, 53-56, 60, 62, 64-67, 107, 129,
  144, 145, 169, 178, 187, 205, 206, 254,
  265, 308-310, 331, 351, 363-366
procession 78-82, 84-87, 98, 106, 112,
  134, 143-145, 153, 160, 162, 164, 165,
  166-169, 222, 233-235, 238, 241, 245,
  249, 250, 254, 258-260, 261, 262, 265,
  266, 268, 272-276, 278, 279, 291, 294,
  296, 297, 302, 303, 309, 310, 322, 323,
  330, 331, 337, 362, 365, 367
processions 39, 44, 134, 146, 241, 254,
  269, 270, 272, 273, 278, 279, 283, 286,
  296, 323, 361, 362
profecia 202, 203
promesa 131, 143, 217
promesas 131, 133
promise 14, 74-76, 143, 217, 220
prophecy 202
Protestant 22, 24, 30, 39, 46, 57, 153,
  189, 190, 364
Protestants 56, 201, 364
pueblo 64, 71, 75, 77, 79, 81, 82, 84,
  86-89, 159, 162, 167, 272, 279
pueblos 64, 71, 82, 86, 89, 158
Puerto Rico 22

qolla 287, 288, 290, 291, 297, 329, 337
Qoyllur rit'i 281-283, 285-291, 293, 296-
  298, 301-305, 309, 310, 317, 319, 331,
  337, 345, 351
Quechua 124, 265, 287-291, 294, 298,
  307, 310, 316, 321, 325-330, 332, 345,
  367
Quintana Roo 123, 129, 367

raft 272, 341
railroad 58, 162, 271
rain 73, 91, 94, 99, 100, 102, 127, 159,
  162, 167, 168, 177, 185, 186, 196, 271,
  341, 346, 362
rainfall 183, 270
rainless 271
ranchero 363
rancheros 363, 364
rank 161, 165, 171, 301, 311, 318, 353,
  354
ranking 77, 83, 134, 166, 227, 251, 271,
  310, 311, 313, 327, 329, 331, 353
rays 276, 278
reciprocates 279
reciprocity 245, 279, 300, 301
Redemptorist 29

reform 73, 98, 249, 330, 363
religion 4, 24, 38, 45, 53, 93, 95, 105-107,
    115, 116, 120, 129, 140, 161, 164, 169,
    205, 207, 230, 273, 307-309, 337, 360
religious orders 53
replica 240, 254, 274, 284
representation 7, 64, 267, 282, 284, 309,
    311, 316, 332, 334, 336, 343, 345, 347
resurrection 75, 276, 278, 324, 325
revelation 260, 264-266, 268
revitalization 87, 330
revolution 99, 133, 155, 206, 247, 362,
    363
risen 278
rises 158, 278, 295
rising 142, 143, 188, 249, 251, 276, 278
ritual 3, 4, 7-9, 15-17, 39, 40, 56, 57, 64,
    66, 71, 72, 74-78, 81, 83, 85, 87, 89,
    109, 114, 115, 124-130, 133, 134, 136,
    139, 142, 145, 146, 150, 153, 155, 161-
    163, 166-170, 206, 209, 210, 213, 217,
    220, 222, 223, 226, 227, 228, 230, 243,
    246, 252, 262, 267, 269, 272-275, 277-
    279, 281, 282, 284, 286-288, 290-297,
    300, 302, 304, 305, 308, 311, 312, 320,
    323, 325, 327, 330-337, 340, 342, 343,
    345, 348-352, 355, 359, 364
rituals 8, 11, 40, 44, 64, 71, 74-76, 88, 89,
    95, 106, 107, 110, 111, 121, 124, 131,
    133, 139, 168, 170, 206, 207, 209-211,
    213, 214, 230, 253, 269, 270, 272, 290,
    307, 326, 333, 337, 341, 357, 365
river 41, 57-65, 71-75, 79, 85-88, 101,
    209, 211-213, 216, 215, 218, 220, 221,
    223, 271, 290, 320, 345, 347, 350
road 79, 84, 85, 102, 135, 143, 177, 230,
    250, 270, 285, 342
role 6, 10, 13-17, 36, 58, 76, 100, 112,
    115, 117, 125, 131, 133, 134, 136, 154,
    163, 167, 176, 181, 194, 197, 199, 209,
    212, 226, 227, 240, 245, 246, 248, 254,
    259, 267, 268, 278, 287, 288, 290, 308,
    311, 313, 318, 321, 325, 327, 343, 351,
    354-356, 361, 363, 364
Roman Catholic 19, 53, 55, 57, 61, 62,
    64, 65, 179, 201, 282
romería 158, 170
romerias 110
roof 59, 249, 273
rosary 29, 57, 83, 161, 182, 270

sacred 1, 2, 4-13, 15-17, 30, 31, 33-35, 39,
    43, 44, 74, 87, 89, 91, 93-100, 102, 101,
    102, 105-107, 111, 121, 124, 126-128,
    131, 132, 134-136, 145, 159, 162, 168-
    170, 178, 179, 182, 205-211, 214, 219,
    223, 227, 229, 232, 251, 257, 258, 265,
    267, 270, 275, 278, 285, 293, 298, 301,
    303, 307-311, 326, 327, 331, 334, 335,
    339, 340, 367
sacred stones 33, 35
sacrifice 40, 44, 125, 133, 156, 265, 274,
    299, 302
sacrificed 211, 212, 265, 266
saint 10, 27-29, 33, 36, 37, 42, 74-76, 80,
    87, 89, 98, 119, 125, 144, 150, 153,
    156-158, 168, 178, 181, 185, 186, 201,
    206, 208, 217, 254, 258, 269, 272, 277-
    279, 290, 297, 310, 323, 331, 343, 362
saints 1, 5, 14, 26, 27, 29, 31, 32, 38, 39,
    43, 44, 57, 59, 71, 73, 74, 76, 89, 96, 97,
    118, 126, 129, 134, 136, 144, 145, 152,
    160, 170, 175, 184, 186, 188, 205-207,
    221, 230, 235, 272, 307, 360, 366
salt 42, 121
sanctuaries 91-93, 98, 105, 205, 270,
    307-311, 317, 337, 340, 342, 349, 355,
    356
sanctuary 33, 93-103, 102, 104-106, 205,
    207-209, 213, 218, 220, 254, 270, 282,
    283, 286, 288, 291-293, 298, 304, 309-
    311, 323, 331, 334, 336, 337, 338, 340,
    348, 351-353, 355
santo 27, 32, 33, 71, 74-76, 79, 82, 84-86,
    88, 89, 159, 162, 203, 237, 265, 275, 277
santos 160, 182, 202, 203, 236, 275
Scandinavia 22, 25
Scotland 22, 41, 42
season 73, 96, 99, 104, 110, 143, 144,
    151, 153, 167, 182, 189, 190, 210, 271,
    346, 362
seasons 47, 73, 107, 124, 153, 209, 348
sermon 83, 177, 260, 275
service 66, 76, 79, 115, 152, 221, 271,
    290, 333, 352
shellfish 275
shepherds 96, 161, 219, 260, 261, 264,
    265, 354
shrine 2, 4-8, 10, 14, 16, 20-25, 27, 28,
    32, 33, 35-40, 42-45, 47, 91, 93-96,
    98-100, 102, 104-106, 126, 130, 134-136,
    139-141, 149, 158, 159, 160, 163, 166,
    169, 170, 205, 218-223, 226, 232, 234,
    235, 240, 243, 245, 246, 249, 250, 254,
    255, 258-261, 264-266, 271, 277-279,
    281, 282, 284-286, 291, 293, 295, 297-
    300, 303-305, 309, 311, 334, 335, 336,
    338, 349, 358, 359, 362

shrines 1-5, 7, 9, 14, 15, 17, 19-39, 43, 45-47, 58, 91-95, 99, 100, 105, 107, 124, 126, 136, 140, 141, 151, 153, 206, 213, 218, 223, 230, 231, 251, 253, 285, 286, 300, 303-305, 307, 308, 310, 317, 325, 335, 339, 349, 357, 358

silver 42, 63, 96, 163, 230, 231, 241, 243, 245, 259, 273, 276, 278, 305, 312, 313, 323

sky 125, 127, 161, 189, 289, 295

sociedad 260, 273, 277

sociedades 276-278

societies 73, 74, 87, 116, 117, 120, 121, 124, 136, 139, 140, 148, 215, 229, 232, 273, 277, 355, 363

society 3, 7, 9, 10, 38, 72, 74, 75, 88, 91, 107, 118, 120, 124, 129, 133, 134, 139, 140, 148, 171, 216, 226, 227, 260, 267, 273, 274, 277, 282, 301, 302, 304, 307-309, 321, 332, 333, 340, 342, 343, 354, 360

sodalities 56, 64, 71, 74, 87

sodality 74, 75, 154

solar god 168

solstice 164, 168

Spain 22-25, 28, 29, 34, 36, 38, 39, 41, 42, 46, 55, 67, 125, 155, 163, 171, 201, 231, 284, 308, 355

spaniard 86, 305

spaniards 24, 34, 57, 67, 116, 159, 208, 340

spirit 71, 82, 84, 85, 94, 121, 177, 207, 209, 211-214, 284, 285, 288

spirits 207-209, 211-214, 230, 298, 301

spiritual 11, 13-15, 17, 92, 144, 164, 168, 175, 207-209, 211, 214, 231, 285, 310, 335, 348

sponsor 93, 133, 259

sponsors 74, 134, 153, 260, 265

status 3, 9, 11, 61, 76, 88, 93, 112, 115, 151, 154, 184, 195, 206, 247, 253, 265, 268, 272, 284, 290, 291, 303, 307, 309-311, 326, 327, 331, 336, 350, 359, 362, 363

stigmata 43

stranger 35, 41

strangers 35, 143, 152, 183, 211, 287

stratification 161, 169, 251, 359

structure 1, 3, 8-11, 13, 16, 45, 55, 58, 87, 97, 98, 109, 116, 117, 119, 120, 124, 128, 131-133, 140, 163, 171, 187, 202, 228, 245, 249, 258, 267, 268, 269, 278, 301, 304, 311, 313, 314, 325-330, 332, 335, 337, 344, 357, 359, 363

summer 20, 40, 62, 73, 107, 164, 176, 181, 182, 221, 272

sun 43, 62, 95, 102, 124-128, 159, 168, 177, 182, 211, 221, 227, 230, 253, 276, 278, 289, 295, 296, 338, 347

sunburst 278

supernatural 13, 74, 76, 92, 94, 100, 102, 175, 180, 183, 185, 199, 206, 207, 214, 279, 354

supernaturals 279

Sweden 19

sweeping 220, 222, 223

Switzerland 22, 41, 42

symbol 5, 72, 99, 116, 118, 129, 133, 155, 156, 167, 168, 181, 229, 230, 233, 265, 267, 272, 313

symbolic 6, 23, 72, 76, 89, 92, 139, 257, 267, 273, 309, 311, 321, 325, 332, 333, 335, 337, 342, 343, 345-348, 350, 354, 355, 357-359, 365, 367

symbolism 3, 5, 8, 9, 24, 87, 89, 132, 133, 168, 169, 257-259, 266-268, 273, 279, 303, 308, 347, 350, 357

symbolize 45, 89, 148, 276, 279

symbols 3, 7, 17, 72, 88, 99, 118, 125, 126, 128, 136, 170, 209, 267, 272, 273, 274, 275, 304, 327, 348

syncretism 20, 21, 45, 47, 105, 126, 148, 271, 272, 345

syncretistic 169, 207

system 3-7, 44, 46, 61, 72, 74, 87, 94, 109, 111, 115-121, 155, 188, 227, 249, 250, 251, 254, 271, 272, 291, 301, 302, 310, 311, 322, 327, 330, 334, 359

systems 4, 327

talismans 39

temple 60, 126, 141, 144, 150, 217, 227, 260, 267, 271, 279, 318, 331, 337, 339, 353

temples 125, 126, 135, 142, 168, 169, 351

Tepeyac 91, 126

theocratic 116, 120, 121, 226

throne 261, 264, 266, 342

Titicaca 230, 232, 253, 340, 341, 343, 344, 347, 349

tourism 20, 48, 135

tourist 272

tourists 19, 44, 65, 147

tradesmen 270

traditional 6, 27, 31, 33, 45, 66, 74, 87, 88, 93, 100, 105-107, 113-115, 121, 139, 147, 155, 167, 169, 188, 205, 229, 230, 232, 235, 237, 238, 241, 243, 245, 247,

250-254, 260, 275, 281, 286, 289, 303,
    309, 310, 313, 327, 350, 351, 360, 361,
    364, 367
trance 207, 211, 212, 337
transcendental 267, 268
transformation 8, 9, 11, 13, 16, 178, 180,
    186, 201, 227, 232, 246, 267, 279, 307,
    308, 311, 312, 325-327, 329-333, 335,
    336, 358
transformational 13, 258, 265, 279, 329-
    333, 335, 336
transhumance 40, 229, 252
transitional 12, 285, 293, 297, 329, 330,
    333, 337
transvestite 262, 322
treasurer 241, 277
tree 35, 40, 84, 94, 102, 101, 127, 130,
    132, 133, 158, 177, 190, 221, 233, 284
trees 33-35, 39, 41, 42, 158, 177, 200,
    210, 211
tribal 72, 88, 129, 140, 148, 288, 289
tribe 286
tricksters 265
trinity 71, 76, 82, 85, 98, 127, 130, 283,
    291

Ukrainian 46
university 17, 47, 67, 120, 166, 228, 247,
    253, 279, 304, 336
urban 46, 54-56, 61, 66, 67, 91, 106, 135,
    144-152, 155, 156, 207, 208, 210, 211,
    216-218, 232, 234, 247, 258, 303, 322,
    340, 349
Uruguay 22, 26

van Gennep, Arnold 11, 154
Venezuela 22, 28, 29, 205-208, 211
vision 23, 37, 176, 181, 193, 339, 353
visionaries 23, 38, 43, 284
visionary 24, 29, 36, 38
visit 2, 5, 7, 29, 40, 44, 48, 93, 94, 100,
    106, 135, 140, 142, 143, 146, 158, 163,
    165, 175, 184, 192, 214, 220, 231, 234,
    235, 250, 270, 274, 291, 342, 352, 360
visited 20, 21, 28, 29, 42-45, 58, 93, 94,
    98, 147, 161, 162, 170, 206, 210, 217,
    218, 219, 272, 340, 342
visitors 21, 61, 79, 81, 84-86, 158, 182,
    183, 211, 238, 269, 273, 277, 288, 362
volcano 158, 162
votive 24
votives 38

wage 72, 73, 182, 271, 291

wagon 58, 59
wagons 58, 59
Wales 42
walk 16, 80-82, 85, 98, 99, 101, 104, 106,
    153, 178, 270, 296
walking 80, 112, 147, 170, 272, 291, 344
war 30, 54, 56, 58-60, 64, 87, 129, 151,
    155, 177, 186, 187, 189, 196, 235, 290,
    305, 316, 337, 361
water 33, 34, 39, 41, 42, 45, 62, 65, 99,
    101, 102, 112, 144-146, 158, 159, 162,
    163, 164, 166, 168, 182, 206, 209-211,
    213, 214, 219, 237, 248, 272, 344, 346,
    347, 350, 352
West Germany 19, 22
wife 29, 100, 102, 105, 120, 177, 192,
    262, 267
wiracocha 5, 340-350, 353-356
wiracochas 340, 344, 346, 349
wives 118
woman 29, 80, 100, 165, 176-178, 184,
    185, 189, 191, 192, 194, 199, 200, 212,
    245, 246, 262, 267, 297, 306, 318, 366
women 57, 58, 61, 62, 99, 101, 105, 118,
    121, 135, 152, 153, 164, 179, 182, 183,
    185, 190, 197, 199, 208-211, 217, 239,
    294, 295, 298, 299, 301, 365
wood 5, 41, 42, 99, 100, 116, 118, 161,
    168, 182, 233, 240, 241, 289, 312, 313,
    323, 352-354
worship 9, 92, 95, 105-107, 129, 130, 141,
    150, 160, 206, 227, 254, 277, 279, 288,
    308, 361, 362
worshippers 144

Yucatan 125
yucatec 123, 141
Yugoslavia 28

Contributors

Walter Randolph Adams received his doctorate in anthropology from Michigan State University in 1988. He has conducted fieldwork in Chiapas, Mexico; Guatemala, and in the United States. His research interests include cultural ecology, ethnicity, and the physiological bases of behavior. A cultural ecologist by training, he views culture processually, hence develops an understanding of cultural phenomena through diachrony and with reliance upon ecological models. His works include his unpublished doctoral dissertation, "Fission, Maintenance, and Interaction in an Anishinabe Community on Keweenaw Bay, Michigan, 1832-1881". He is currently an Assistant Professor in Anthropology at Kansas State University.

N. Ross Crumrine is a professor of anthropology at the University of Victoria and a student of Mayo culture and traditions. In addition to the research among the Mayos, he has done fieldwork on the far north coast of Peru focusing upon the modern ceremonialism of the lower Piura River valley. Academically, he studied philosophy at Northwestern University and obtained his Ph.D. in anthropology from the University of Arizona.

Henry F. Dobyns received a B.A. and M.A. in anthropology from the University of Arizona and a Ph.D. in anthropology from Cornell University.

He has taught at Cornell, Prescott College, and the Universities of Florida, Kentucky, Oklahoma, and Wisconsin-Parkside. His ethnohistorical research and investigations have taken Dobyns through much of western South America and northwestern Mexico, and among United States Indian peoples, Hispanic mountain villagers and rural Kentuckians. He is the author or coauthor of 36 books and numerous scholarly journal articles and reviews. Dobyns maintains an affiliation with the D'Arcy McNickle Center for the History of the American Indian, Newberry Library, 60 W. Walton Street, Chicago, Illinois 60610.

H.R. Harvey is a Professor of Anthropology, Department of Anthropology, University of Wisconsin at Madison. He received his Ph.D. in anthropology from Harvard University in 1962. Within the field of Anthropology, his specialty is the ethnohistory of Mesoamerica. Within that frame, he is a specialist on the valley of Mexico. The focus of his current work is the decipherment and analysis of native pictorial manuscripts (codices). He has worked for more than a decade in Tepetlaoztoc, State of Mexico and prior to that for a decade in Huixquilucan, State of Mexico, both in or near the Valley of Mexico.

Carl Kendall received his B.A. in Anthropology from Swarthmore College and his M.A. and Ph.D. in Anthropology from the University of Rochester. He is currently an Associate Professor in the Department of International Health at the Johns Hopkins University. Dr. Kendall is also the Director of the Center for International Community-based Health Research at the Johns Hopkins University, School of Hygiene and Public Health and co-editor of *Heritage of Conquest: Thirty Years Later*.

Herman W. Konrad received his B.A. from the University of British Columbia and his M.A. and Ph.D. from the University of Chicago. He is currently Professor of Anthropology and History at the University of Calgary, Alberta, Canada. Although a native of northern Alberta his interests in tropical Mexico began while he was director (1966-69) of an Interuniversity Research Institute in Merida, Yucatan. He previously researched colonial agrarian problems in highland Mexico. This research resulted in the book, *A Jesuit Hacienda in Colonial Mexico: Santa Lucía, 1576-1767* (Stanford, 1980), winner of the Bolton Memorial Prize for 1981. His recent work involves a long-term study of the transformation of Mexico's tropical lowlands. Preliminary results have been published in a variety of academic journals and he is currently writing a three-volume study on ideology and ecological transformation of the Mexican tropical lowlands.

Luis Millones is a professor at the University of San Marcos, Lima, Peru. He is currently developing a comparative study of Andean religiosity—in

Peru, Northern Chile, and Northwestern Argentina—based on the still popular traditional cult of the saints. His recent publications include: *Historia y poder en los Andes centrales*, Alianza Editorial, Madrid: 1987 (History and Power in the Central Andes); *El Inca por la Coya*, Fundacíon Ebert, Lima: 1988 (The Inca through the Coya); *Amor Brujo: Imagen y cultura del amor en los Andes*, Instituto do Estudios Peruanos, Lima, Peru, 1989 (Images and Culture of Love in the Andes); and in press *Taki Onqoy: las informaciones de Cristóbal de Albornoz* (Accounts by Cristóbal de Albornoz).

Alan Morinis is a Canadian who received his doctoral in Social Anthropology from Oxford University in 1980. His doctoral thesis focused on the contemporary practices and beliefs surrounding pilgrimage in the West Bengal state of India. This research was later published by Oxford University Press under the title *"Pilgrimage in the Hindu Tradition"*. Dr. Morinis has published numerous articles on pilgrimage, and was instrumental in convening the seminal conference on the study on pilgrimage held at the University of Pittsburgh in 1981. In addition to co-editing the present volume, he is currently editing a collection entitled *"Sacred Journeys: The Anthropology of Pilgrimage"*. Dr. Morinis resides in Vancouver, Canada, with his wife and two daughters, where he is primarily engaged in making films.

Mary Lee Nolan focused on art history as an undergraduate and holds M.A. degrees in history and in anthropology. She combined her multiple interests into a Ph.D. program in Cultural Geography. After receiving her doctorate from Texas A & M University in 1972, she briefly served as a Texas A & M University archivist and creator of a new oral History program before joining the Oregon State University Geography Department in 1973, where she currently holds the rank of Professor. Her co-investigator, editor, and husband, Dr. Sidney Nolan, has made some important contributions to the development of her interpretations of the relationships between European and Latin American pilgrimages. The Nolan's are currently writing a book about visions, as related to pilgrimage shrines in the Christian traditions.

Angelina Pollak-Eltz Born in Austria, Angelina Pollak-Eltz has been living in Venezuela since 1959. In 1964 she received her Ph.D. in anthropology from the University of Vienna. A cultural anthropologist, her thesis was on the black culture of Venezuela. Since 1970 she has been a professor of anthropology at the Catholic University in Caracas, the editor of the University's yearbook, Montalban, and the director of the research center on religion. Her research areas involve Afroamerica, popular culture, folk catholicism, folk medicine, migration, and family structure and her publications include at least 16 books and 250 papers.

Deborah A. Poole is assistant professor of Anthropology at the Graduate Faculty, New School for Social Research, New York. She received her Ph.D. in anthropology in 1984 from the University of Illinois at Urbana-Champaign. Its title is "Ritual-economic Calendars in Paruro: the Structure of Representation in Andean Ethnography (Religion)". Her publications and research include studies of religion, photography and representation, and violence in the Andes.

Michael J. Sallnow studied Social Anthropology at Trinity College, Cambridge, and carried out Doctoral research in the Peruvian Andes from the University of Manchester, England. From 1975 to 1977 he was Education Officer for the Royal Anthropological Institute. Since 1977 until his death, May 1990, he taught in the Department of Anthropology at the London School of Economics, University of London, where he was Senior Lecturer. His research centered on the Andean region, where he investigated Quechua peasant ritual and political economy. He served as ethnographic consultant for several films, and published various articles and reviews in both scholarly and popular journals. He is the author of *Pilgrims of the Andes: Regional Cults in Cusco* (Smithsonian Institution Press, Washington DC 1987).

Richard P. Schaedel is currently professor of Anthropology at the University of Texas in Austin. He received his Ph.D. in anthropology from Yale University. He has been carrying out field work on Andean cultures since 1948. His main area of concentration is the North Coast of Peru where the Muchik people constitute the present day peasantry. He has just published a turn-of-the-century ethnography pertaining to these people, *La Etnografía Muchik En Las Fotografias De H. Bruning 1886-1925*, Lima, 1989 and has edited *Urbanization in the Americas from Its Beginnings to the Present*, in the World Anthropology Series, Mouton Press, 1978

Frans J. Schryer is professor of anthropology at the University of Guelph, Ontario, Canada. He received his Ph.D. in anthropology from McGill University in 1974. He has done extensive field work in Mexico and among other articles and reviews he has published *The Rancheros of Pisaflores: The History of a Peasant Bourgeoisie in Twentieth-Century Mexico*, University of Toronto Press, 1979, and *Ethnicity and Class Conflict in Rural Mexico*, Princeton University Press, 1990.

*Helaine Silverman.*Archaeologist Helaine Silverman received her doctoral degree at the University of Texas at Austin in 1986. She is currently a visiting assistant professor in the Department of Anthropology at the University of Illinois at Urbana-Champaign. Dr. Silverman has carried out archaeological fieldwork in California, Israel, Ecuador, and Peru. Her long-term research interests are the precolumbian cultures of the Andean countries, the evolution of ancient civilizations, and the role of religion and ideology in these complex societies. Dr. Silverman's current fieldwork is an outgrowth of her excavations at Cahuachi, discussed in this volume. She and her colleagues have discovered more than 800 sites in the northern half of the Nazca drainage, among them great complexes of geoglyphs, major ceremonial centers, large towns, and tiny farming hamlets. Dr. Silverman was featured in a 1987 National Geographic Society television program about the "Nazca lines." She is the author of many scholarly articles (the most recent are: A Nasca 8 Occupation at an Early Nasca Site: the Room of the Posts at Cahuachi in *Andean Past*; Nasca 8: A Reassessment of its Chronological Placement and Cultural Significance in *Michigan Discussions in Anthropology*; and Cahuachi: Non-Urban Cultural Complexity on the South Coast of Peru in *Journal of Field Archaeology*) and is finishing two books about Cahuachi (B.A.R., England) and ancient Nasca culture (Basil Blackwell Publishers, England; with David M. Brown).

Candace Slater is Professor of Spanish and Portuguese at the University of California, Berkeley. She has held Guggenheim, NEH and Fulbright Fellowships. Among her books are two studies of contemporary miracle stories: *Trail of Miracles: Stories from a Pilgrimage in Northeast Brazil* (1986, Elsie Clews Parsons Prize for Folklore), *Stories on a String: The Brazilian **Literatura de Cordel***, and *City Steeple, City Streets, Saints' Tales from Granada and a Changing Spain*, all from the University of California Press.

Leslie Ellen Straub, O.P. received her Ph.D. in Anthropology from the Catholic University of America, Washington, D.C. She is Associate Professor of Anthropology and Director of the Anthropology Program at Providence College, Providence, Rhode Island, U.S.A. Her research interests lie in Latin American traditions of Central America. A recipient of grants from the Organization of American States, the Committee on Aid to Faculty Research (Providence College), the American Philosophical Society, and the Fulbright Scholars Program (Central American Regional Research Award), she has done field work in Columbia, Guatemala, and Costa Rica. Her publications reflecting these interests include: *Cultural Values and Social Reality: Self-Concept Formation in a Columbian Urban Barrio*; "Orientación de valores correspondientes a muchachas de un barrio popular de Cali", in Irving L. Webber and Alfredo Ocampo Zamorano, Editors., *Valores, desarrollo e historia: Popyán, Medellín, Cali y El Valle del Cauca*; "La romería como modelo de la peregrinación en las tradiciones centroamericanas", *Mesoamérica*; and "La Patrona, su santuario y la ciudad de Cartago", *In* C. Alvarez Santaló, María Jesús Buxó, and S. Rodríguez Becerra, Coordinators, *La religiosidad popular*. Vol. 3. *Hermandades, romerías y santuarios (Antropología. Autores, Textos y Temas*, No. 20). She is presently writing a monograph on pilgrimages of Costa Rica.

Henrique Urbano is a University of Laval Professor in the Facultad Ciencias Sociales, Université, Laval, Québec, Canada. He is a founding member of the Centro Las Casas in Cusco, Peru and director of the *Revista Andina* and of *Cuadernos para la Historia de la Evangelización en América Latina*. He also is the founder of the working group "Historia y Antropología Andinas" in the Consejo Latinoamericano de Ciencias Sociales (CLACSO), Buenos Aires, 1987. And he has written the following books: *Wiracocha y Ayar. Héroes y funciones en las Sociedades Andinas*, Cusco, 1981 and *Fabulas y Mitos de los Incas* (Crónicas de América), Madrid, Historia 16, 1989 (in collaboration with P. Duviols).

James M. Vreeland, Jr. is a Ph.D. candidate in anthropology at the University of Texas. Currently residing in northern Peru, he leads the Native Cotton Research and Development Project sponsored by UT Institute of Latin American Studies, Instituto Indigenista Interamericano, and FAO/IBPGR. James M. Vreeland, Jr. is also the cofounder of Sociedad de Investigacion de la Ciencia Cultura y Arte Norteiro, SICAN, a research center dedicated to identifying and evaluating preHispanic technologies that might be used for rural development in northern Peru today. Trained in New World anthropology and archaeology, he has worked on archaeological projects including those at Tikal, Guatemala, Nioche and Batan Grande, Peru, all major centers of precolumbian peregrination, the topic that stimulated research leading to the present chapter.